palgrave macmillan law masters

family law

palgrave macmillan law masters

Series editor: Marise Cremona

Business Law   Stephen Judge
Company Law   Janet Dine and Marios Koutsias
Constitutional and Administrative Law   John Alder
Contract Law   Ewan McKendrick
Criminal Law   Jonathan Herring
Employment Law   Deborah J. Lockton
Evidence   Raymond Emson
Family Law   Kate Standley and Paula Davies
Intellectual Property Law   Tina Hart, Simon Clark and Linda Fazzani
Land Law   Mark Davys
Landlord and Tenant Law   Margaret Wilkie, Peter Luxton and Desmond Kilcoyne
Legal Method   Ian McLeod
Legal Theory   Ian McLeod
Medical Law   Jo Samanta and Ash Samanta
Sports Law   Mark James
Torts   Alastair Mullis and Ken Oliphant
Trusts Law   Charlie Webb and Tim Akkouh

If you would like to comment on this book, or on the series generally, please write to lawfeedback@palgrave.com.

palgrave macmillan law masters

family law

kate standley

Former Senior Lecturer in Law, University of Essex

paula davies

Senior Lecturer in Law, BPP Law School, London

Eighth edition

This edition first published 2013 by PALGRAVE MACMILLAN

Palgrave Macmillan in the UK is an imprint of Macmillan Publishers Limited, registered in England, company number 785998, of Houndmills, Basingstoke, Hampshire RG21 6XS.

Palgrave Macmillan in the US is a division of St Martin's Press LLC, 175 Fifth Avenue, New York, NY 10010.

Palgrave Macmillan is the global academic imprint of the above companies and has companies and representatives throughout the world.

Palgrave® and Macmillan® are registered trademarks in the United States, the United Kingdom, Europe and other countries.

ISBN 978–0–230–39238–0

This book is printed on paper suitable for recycling and made from fully managed and sustained forest sources. Logging, pulping and manufacturing processes are expected to conform to the environmental regulations of the country of origin.

A catalogue record for this book is available from the British Library.

Contents

Preface to the eighth edition

Two decades have passed since the publication of the first edition of *Family Law* in 1993. During that time families and family life have undergone considerable change. For instance, cohabitation has become increasingly common and families now take many different forms.

Family law has also undergone many changes, and continues to change at a pace. Proposals for reform also abound. In fact, since the last edition of *Family Law*, there has been a major review of the family justice system (the 'Family Justice Review') by the Norgrove Committee which has made important and wide-ranging recommendations for reform, most of which have been accepted by the Coalition Government but which may or may not be brought into law. These recommendations include, for example, proposals to reduce delays in care and adoption cases, the creation of a new Family Court and the introduction of a new order (a 'child arrangements order') to replace residence and contact orders. Since the last edition there has also been a major overhaul of the rules of procedure in family law cases, which are now contained in the Family Procedure Rules 2010.

Recent Government discussions of reform have focused on a range of different issues, for instance on whether gay marriage should be permitted, whether a new criminal offence of forcing someone to marry should be introduced, and whether there should be a presumption of shared parenting. The Law Commission, the Government's law reform body, has also been looking at a range of family law issues, including, in particular, the law governing financial relief on divorce and on civil partnership dissolution, with a view to making recommendations for reform.

Family law never seems to stand still. While this makes it a fascinating subject to study, it means that keeping up to date is always a challenge. However, despite the multifarious changes both to family life and family law over the years, the aim of this book remains the same as it was two decades ago, which is to provide a clear and detailed account of family law in England and Wales, including current debates and proposals for reform.

Table of cases

Table of legislation

Part I

Family law – an introduction

Chapter 1

Family law

This chapter provides an introduction to family law in England and Wales by looking at a range of matters, such as legal and social trends and developments, the nature of judicial decision-making, the importance of agreement, and the impact of human rights. It starts, however, by considering the nature of family law as a subject to be studied.

1.1 Studying family law

Family law is a fascinating but demanding area of law as it is in a constant state of flux. Keeping up to date with all the changes is challenging. A wide range of legal materials also have to be absorbed. Thus, in addition to a wealth of statutory provisions and a substantial body of reported case-law, there are rules of court, detailed practice directions, guidances, Government papers and other materials which have to be digested. Furthermore, there continue to be discussions of reform on a wide range of family issues.

Although family law is largely codified in the sense that the law is based on statute, it is also an area of law where, because of the infinite variations in family circumstances, cases are decided on their own particular facts. In other words, decisions are largely fact-specific. To do well as a family law student it is therefore necessary not only to have a sound knowledge of the relevant statutory provisions and case-law principles but also a sense of how to apply them. In other words, a practical common-sense approach and an understanding of the human condition are required. This is what family law judges have to show when exercising their various statutory powers and duties. In other words, they have to apply the statutory provisions to the facts of the case. This often requires competing considerations to be balanced and the discretionary nature of the judicial exercise means that there may be more than one decision which is reasonable in the circumstances of the case.

A distinguishing feature of family law is that there is a considerable emphasis on the parties reaching agreement, whether, for instance, it is about arrangements for children on family breakdown or about property and financial matters. Agreement and settlement are actively promoted, and increasingly so. Thus, instead of taking their case to court, parties are encouraged to use alternative forms of dispute resolution, such as mediation or collaborative law. Arbitration is also beginning to be used for resolving family disputes. There has also been recent recognition by the Supreme Court that premarital agreements about property and finance can, in some circumstances, be binding.

Another distinguishing feature of family law is that it involves both private and public law. Private law is the law which applies to disputes between individuals, such as spouses, civil partners, or parents. A divorce dispute, for instance, is a private law matter, and so are a domestic violence case and a parental dispute about arrangements for children on family breakdown. Public law disputes, on the other hand, involve a public authority such as a local authority child protection team or a housing authority. Child abuse cases and housing cases are therefore public law cases.

It is important when studying family law to understand that a wide range of different personnel work in the family justice system. Thus, in addition to lawyers and judges, other personnel, such as mediators, social workers, housing officers, police officers and Cafcass officers, are often involved. In a domestic violence case, for instance, the police may be involved, and, if a victim needs accommodation, then so may a local housing officer. This may be in addition to a solicitor. In a child protection case, not just lawyers and judges, but the police, social workers and Cafcass officers may also be involved.

Other distinguishing features of family law are that it is an area of law where children are involved and also where the emotions of the parties are sometimes highly charged and where difficult balancing decisions have to be made. Cases therefore require sensitive handling. Also, court decisions, unlike decisions in other areas of the law, tend to be forward-looking rather than backward-looking. They look to the future rather than to the past. The court on divorce, for instance, may have to consider what future arrangements should be made for the children or what financial provision should be made for a party to the marriage.

Before moving on to consider some of the changes and trends in family law, it is useful to consider the functions which family law performs in order to understand the nature of the subject. Family law can be regarded as performing several functions. Thus, it can create a status, such as the status of spouse, civil partner, guardian or special guardian. It can remove a status, for instance by divorce or civil partnership dissolution. It can create and, where necessary, enforce the various rights and obligations arising from a particular status, such as the obligation to provide financial provision to a spouse or a child. It can adjust the property and financial rights of family members, for instance on family breakdown; and it can provide protection for family members, such as for victims of domestic violence, child abuse or forced marriage.

1.2   Family law – changes and trends

Family law is a dynamic area of law which is constantly changing. Although this makes the subject interesting, it also makes it particularly challenging. In fact, over the past 30 to 40 years radical changes have been made which persons living in the 1970s or 1980s would have not thought possible. For instance, before the 1970s, and even for some years afterwards, divorce was regarded as a social stigma, and cohabitation even more so. Divorces, whether or not defended, were heard in court with a full hearing before a judge; and cohabitation was regarded by some as 'living in sin'. Protection against domestic violence was also restricted to a much narrower group of persons than today in that only married couples and heterosexual cohabitants could obtain injunctive protection in the family courts. With respect to arrangements for children on family breakdown, different terminology was used (namely 'custody' and 'access'), and it was much more likely that mothers, rather than fathers, would be granted custody of children. Also, unlike today, all child maintenance disputes were heard in the courts. In family law cases, litigation also tended to be the norm, as mediation and other alternatives to litigation had not been widely developed.

Today family law is therefore in many respects almost unrecognisable from what it was three or four decades ago. This due in part to the fact that a wider range of family forms exist, not just what may be considered to be the stereotypical family, namely a married heterosexual couple with children. Instead, we now have civil partnerships and same-sex couples with children; and many couples choose to cohabit. Although social changes have had, and continue to have, impact on family law, family law may itself be partly responsible for changing social attitudes. For instance, the ease with which a divorce can now be obtained may have had an impact on removing the stigma that once attached to it. Due to increasing cohabitation, cohabitants, whether opposite-sex or same-sex, have been accorded more family law rights than they once had, although some commentators consider that they have not been given enough, particularly on relationship breakdown. There has also been an increasing recognition in family law of the importance of fathers, including unmarried fathers. Furthermore, transsexual persons can now marry in their acquired sex, and the Government is also proposing to introduce same-sex marriage. All these changes in family law would probably not have been imagined possible thirty or forty years or so ago.

(a)   Legislative developments

There have been many important legislative and case-law developments over the last two decades or so. During the 1990s there were many important and radical changes to family law. Of particular importance was the enactment of the Children Act 1989, which came into force in October 1991 and made far-reaching changes to the civil law relating to children. In 1993 the Child Support Act 1991 moved child maintenance from the courts into the Child Support Agency; and in the mid-1990s family law remedies for victims of domestic violence were made available to a wider class of family members by Part IV of the Family Law Act 1996. There was also an attempt during the 1990s to introduce a radically new law of divorce, although this was abandoned as the proposals were found to be unworkable in practice.

In the first few years of the new millennium there were further important legislative developments. Of particular importance was the Human Rights Act 1998, which came into force in the year 2000. In 2003, new provisions were introduced to allow unmarried fathers to acquire parental responsibility by birth registration. Pension sharing on divorce was also introduced. A significant development was the introduction of civil partnerships by the Civil Partnership Act 2004; and transsexual persons were given the right, by the Gender Recognition Act 2004, to enter into a valid marriage in their newly acquired sex. There were also changes to the law to give victims of domestic violence greater protection under new provisions introduced by the Domestic Violence, Crime and Victims Act 2004. New civil law remedies for victims of forced marriage were introduced in 2008 by Part 4A of the Family Law Act 1996. Changes to the law governing parenthood in cases of assisted reproduction were made by the Human Fertilisation and Embryology Act 2008.

Important changes have also been made in the last decade or so to the law relating to children and parents. Radical reforms of adoption were made by the Adoption and Children Act 2002, which also introduced special guardianship and inserted new provisions into the Children Act 1989 to improve the facilitation and enforcement of contact on family breakdown. The Children Act 2004 introduced other family law reforms, such as placing restrictions on the use of corporal punishment by parents, changing the structural framework governing the practice of child protection, and creating the office of the Children's Commissioner. Changes to the child support system were also implemented by the Child Maintenance and Other Payments Act 2008.

(b) Case-law developments

In addition to the many legislative developments, there have been important case-law developments. These have included decisions dealing with the approach the courts must adopt in proceedings for property and financial orders on divorce, including, more recently, the question of whether premarital agreements should be binding. There have been important decisions, for example, on the rights of transsexuals and also on the property rights of cohabitants on relationship breakdown. In addition, there are an increasing number of cases involving matters with an international dimension, such as, for instance, whether the courts in England and Wales have jurisdiction to grant financial relief after a foreign divorce.

Important decisions have also been handed down on the law governing children, for instance on the threshold conditions for making care and supervision orders, on international child abduction, and on the importance of the biological bond between parent and child as a consideration in residence and contact disputes. Important cases on the voice of the child in family proceedings and the right of a child to refuse or consent to medical treatment have also been heard.

Due to their obligations under the Human Rights Act 1998, the family courts in England and Wales are required to exercise their powers in the light of the European Convention for the Protection of Human Rights and Fundamental Freedoms (the ECHR). Human rights arguments play an important part in some cases, particularly those where public authorities are involved, such as in child protection cases and housing cases. Human rights have also, for example, had an impact on the law regarding the right of a person to succeed to a deceased partner's tenancy and on the law governing the rights of transsexuals. In children's cases, in addition to the protection afforded by the Human Rights Act 1998 and the ECHR, the UN Convention on the Rights of the Child gives children another set of human rights.

(c) Family law reform

A wide range of family law issues have been the subject of discussion with regard to reform. Some of these discussions have been taken no further (such as proposals to reform the law governing the property rights of cohabitants on relationship breakdown), whereas other proposals may or may not be passed into law. The Law Commission, for instance, is currently reviewing the law governing finance and property on divorce and on civil partnership dissolution. It has also been looking at the law governing the inheritance rights of cohabitants on the death of a partner. In June 2012 the Government announced that it would be introducing new legislation to make forcing a person into marriage a specific criminal offence; and in the same month it also announced that it was proposing to introduce civil marriage for same-sex partners. The Family Justice Review (see below) has also recommended a wide range of reforms to the family justice system, and most of its proposals have been accepted by the Government.

With respect to children, there has been ongoing discussion about reforming the law to enable them to have a greater voice in private family law proceedings. There has also been discussion about whether legislation should be enacted to create a presumption of shared parenting; and about whether it should be mandatory for an unmarried father to be named on his child's birth certificates. There has been, and continues to be, concern about the problem of delay in the family justice system, in particular in care cases and adoption cases, and the Government has recently made proposals to tackle the problem. The Children and Families Bill 2012–2013 (see further below), if enacted and brought into force, will make important and wide-ranging changes to family law. The Bill is, in part, a response to the recommendations of the Family Justice Review.

The Family Justice Review

In March 2010, the then Labour Government appointed a panel, led by David Norgrove, to carry out a comprehensive independent review of the family justice system in England and Wales. The Coalition Government which took office soon afterwards supported the review. After the publication of an interim report and a consultation period during which evidence was collected, the final report of the Family Justice Review (the 'FJR') was published in November 2011 (see *Family Justice Review: Final Report*, available at www.justice.gov.uk). The recommendations were comprehensive and far-reaching and applied both to private and public family law. The aim of the proposals is to make the family justice system more effective and to reduce the delays inherent in the system. Some of the key recommendations include the introduction of a new single family court; a new 'child arrangements order' to replace residence and contact orders; and increased mediation provision.

In February 2012 the UK Government published its response to the FJR (see *The Government Response to the Family Justice Review: A system with children and families at its heart*, Cm 8273, Ministry of Justice and Department of Education, available at www. justice.gov.uk). In its response in which it accepted most of the FJR's recommendations in full, the Government announced that it would be conducting a major overhaul of the family justice system with the aim, among other things, to help strengthen parenting, reduce the time it takes cases to progress through the courts, and to simplify the system. It proposed radical changes both to private and public family law, some of which were contained in the Children and Families Bill 2012–2013.

The Children and Families Bill 2012–2013

This Bill, which was announced in the Queen's Speech in May 2012 and published in September 2012, is part of the Government's response to the final report of the FJR (see above). Among other things, the Bill aims to reduce delays in care and adoption cases and require parents engaged in disputes to consider mediation as a means of settling the dispute rather than engaging in litigation. It also contains provisions strengthening the powers of the Children's Commissioner. The Bill was introduced into Parliament in early 2013. Although the Government, in line with the recommendations of the FJR, has decided not to introduce a presumption of shared parenting, it intends to strengthen the law to ensure children have a relationship with both parents after family separation where that is safe and in the child's best interests. (The Bill is available at www. education.gov.uk.)

(d)   Demographic and social changes

There have been important demographic and social changes which have impacted on family law. Many people cohabit, fewer people marry and family breakdown is common. There are also increasing numbers of single-parent families and many children are born outside marriage. A particularly important change in family law has been the recognition given by legislators and the courts to different forms of family living. The 'traditional' family (married couple with children) is no longer the only family form. There are cohabiting families and same-sex families, for instance, and also an increasing number of step-families. The recognition of these increasingly complex family forms has resulted in an increasingly complex set of statutory provisions in family law.

The driving forces behind the changes which have taken place in family life are articulated by Mr Justice Munby in the following extract:

▶ **Mr Justice Munby, 'Families old and new – the family and Article 8' [2005]** *Child and Family Law Quarterly* **487**

'There have been very profound changes in family life in recent decades. They have been driven by four major developments. First, there have been enormous changes in the social and religious life of our country. The fact is that we live in a secular and pluralistic society. But we also live in a multi-cultural community of many faiths...

Secondly, there has been an increasing lack of interest in – in some instances a conscious rejection of – marriage as an institution. There is no lack of interest in family life (or at least in intimate relationships) but the figures demonstrate a striking decline in marriage. At the same time, it has never been easier for the married to be divorced. The truth is that, for all practical purposes, we permit divorce on demand.

Thirdly, there has been a sea-change in society's attitudes towards same-sex unions...

Fourthly, there have been enormous advances in medical and in particular reproductive science so that reproduction is no longer confined to "natural" methods.'

The following extract from the Government Green Paper, *Support for All*, lists some of the changes which have had an impact on family life:

▶ *Support For All*, **Department for Children, Schools and Families, Cm 7787, 2010, pp.5–6**

'The very significant economic, social and demographic changes seen in recent decades have had a pronounced effect on family forms, family life and public attitudes. For example:

▶ in 2008 64 per cent of children were living in families with married couples, 13 per cent with co-habiting couples and 23 per cent with a lone parent;
▶ most children still live in a married family and marriage remains the most common form of partnership in Britain today. However, marriage rates show an overall decline since their peak in the 1970s;
▶ divorce rates increased considerably between the 1950s and the mid-1980s but then levelled off. In recent years they have started to fall and in 2007 the divorce rate reached its lowest level since 1981;
▶ the numbers of step-families are growing;
▶ in general, women are having fewer children and doing so later in life;
▶ since the Second World War the proportion of children born outside marriage has increased very significantly, right across Europe;
▶ about ten per cent of the adult population in England and Wales was cohabiting in 2007; cohabitation covers a wide range of relationships, including a precursor to marriage and an alternative to it;
▶ there is greater acceptance and recognition of same-sex relationships and this is reflected in the introduction of civil partnerships; and
▶ people are healthier than ever and living longer which means that many more grandparents now see their grandchildren grow up.'

1.3   Openness and transparency in family proceedings

Changes have been made in the last few years to allow the media, in certain circumstances, to attend some family proceedings. The Government's aim in allowing media attendance is to improve public confidence in the family justice system and to educate the public about the work and decisions of the family courts. In other words, the aim is to promote transparency and eliminate accusations of secrecy and bias. (For the background to these changes, see *Family Justice in View*, Ministry of Justice, 2008, Cm 7502.)

In April 2009 the family courts were opened to accredited members of the media. Thus, media representatives can attend certain proceedings held in private subject to the court's power to exclude them from all or part of the proceedings where it is in the interests of a child, or where it is necessary to do so for the protection of a party to the proceedings or where justice will be impeded or prejudiced (see r 27.11(3) Family Procedure Rules 2010). However, the media are not permitted to attend hearings which are conducted for the purpose of, among other things, judicially assisted conciliation or negotiation (see r 27.11(1)(a)). There are also restrictions on media access to court documents. Courts also have powers to restrict what can be reported to protect the welfare of children and families, or to relax reporting rules in individual cases.

Special restrictions apply to media attendance in children's cases. Cases in family courts involving children are heard in private and there are restrictions on publishing information about the proceedings (see s 12 Administration of Justice Act 1960) and about protecting their anonymity (see s 97 Children Act 1989). The court may also exclude the media from a case involving adults if such attendance may adversely affect any children involved (see, for example, *Re Child X (Residence and Contact; Rights of Media Attendance; FPR Rule 10.28(4))* [2009] EWHC 1728 (Fam) where the media were excluded from residence and contact proceedings involving a father who was a celebrity because of concerns about the child's welfare if the media were admitted).

As the Family Procedure Rules 2010 (above) did not alter the statutory basis for media reporting, Part 2 of the Children, Schools and Families Act 2010 was enacted to give the media even greater access to family proceedings, including access to documents filed for such proceedings, and to lift some of the restrictions on publication. However, after strong opposition to this new legislation and following the recommendations of the House of Commons Justice Committee in July 2011 and the outcome of the Family Justice Review in November 2011 (see p. 7 above), the Government announced that Part 2 would not be implemented. Concerns about the legislation included concerns about the protection afforded to children, including their right to privacy under Article 8 ECHR; and the fact that they might be less willing to talk to experts or give evidence if they knew the media had access to what they said. (For discussion of these concerns, see, for example, Wall LJ [2010] Fam Law 40; Macdonald [2010] Fam Law 190; Mole [2010] Fam Law 75; and Bessant [2011] Fam Law 987.) There was also a risk that cases might be misreported and sensationalised by the media.

1.4   The exercise of judicial discretion

A distinguishing feature of family law is that discretion plays a significant part in judicial decision-making. The outcome of cases depends to a large degree on their particular facts. Judicial discretion is essential in family matters because family life is infinitely variable

– no two families are the same. The main advantage of discretion is its flexibility, in that an outcome can be decided on for each individual case and set of circumstances. The disadvantages are that it can create unpredictability and the exercise of discretion can be a time-consuming exercise which can increase the cost of litigation. There is also a risk of arbitrariness in that judges may reach different conclusions in cases which are factually similar. The alleged arbitrariness of court decisions about child maintenance one of the reasons given by the Government for moving most child maintenance cases out of the courts and into the Child Support Agency. In some areas of the law a checklist of factors is provided in the legislation to help guide judges when exercising their discretion and in reaching their decision. There are statutory checklists which must be taken into account, for example, in residence and contact cases, in adoption proceedings, and in finance and property proceedings on divorce and civil partnership dissolution.

The discretionary nature of family law also has an impact on appeals. Thus, as there may be several possible reasonable decisions when deciding a family law dispute, the appeal courts are unwilling to overturn decisions made by the lower courts unless they are wrong in law or plainly wrong on their facts.

1.5   The importance of reaching agreement

Most private law family matters (such as those involving divorce, residence and contact) are settled by the parties themselves. Thus, despite the impression given by the number of reported cases, most cases do not go to court. Furthermore, if family lawyers are consulted, they work within a conciliatory framework.

There is an increasing emphasis on the importance of reaching agreement in family law cases. Agreement between the parties can be facilitated by the use of ADR (alternative dispute resolution) techniques such as mediation, collaborative law and arbitration. In fact there has been an increasing trend to use, and promote the use of, ADR in family disputes. It has, for instance, been actively promoted by Resolution (an organisation of family lawyers), whose Code of Practice requires members to 'conduct matters in a constructive and non-confrontational way' and to 'inform clients of the options e.g. counselling, family therapy, round-table negotiations, mediation, collaborative law and court proceedings' (see Resolution's *Guide to Good Practice*, 2009). The principles of the Code also form part of the Law Society's rules of good practice for family law solicitors (see the *Family Law Protocol*, 3rd edn, 2010, Appendix 2).

(a)   Mediation

Mediation is a form of ADR whereby a mediator helps the parties identify the issues in dispute with the aim of them reaching agreement. The mediator acts as an impartial third party. The agreement is not imposed by the mediator. It is the parties themselves who must endeavour to reach agreement. The mediator's role is merely that of facilitator. In other words, the process is non-coercive. Mediation can take place out of court or in court, and it is available from independent mediation agencies and from some law firms. In financial order proceedings on divorce, the district judge performs a mediatory role by encouraging the parties and their lawyers to reach a settlement.

Part 3 of the Family Procedure Rules 2010 ('Alternative Dispute Resolution: The Court's Powers') and *Practice Direction 3A - Pre-application Protocol for Mediation Information and Assessment* (which supplements Part 3) and its accompanying *Pre-application Protocol* aim to '(a) encourage and facilitate the use of alternative dispute resolution; (b) set out good practice to be followed by any person who is considering making an application to court for an order in relevant family proceedings; and (c) ensure, as far as possible, that all parties have considered mediation as an alternative means of resolving their disputes' (para 2.1). The rationale for promoting mediation is explained in para 3. The *Protocol* lays down important principles including an expectation in certain cases, such as those involving children, property and finance on divorce, that the parties have attended a Mediation Information and Assessment Meeting (MIAM) before going to court, unless there are exemption reasons (such as domestic violence or child protection issues), or where, in prescribed circumstances, there is no mediator available. The courts can insist that mediation is used, or at least attempted, by the parties in cases dealing with financial orders or cases relating to children. A judge must also consider, at every stage of the proceedings, whether it is appropriate to send the parties to mediation (rule 3.2 FPR 2010).

The final report of the Family Justice Review (see p. 7 above) included a number of proposals to increase the use of mediation. These proposals were accepted by the Government, which wishes mediation to become the norm for parents in dispute. The Government has also recommended that the phrase 'alternative dispute resolution' should be rebranded as 'Dispute Resolution Service' to give out the message that it is the primary way of solving family disputes. The Children and Families Bill, which was published in September 2012, contains measures to increase the use of mediation, including a requirement that attendance at a MIAM should be a prerequisite for separating parents who are in dispute.

Mediation has many advantages over going to court. For instance, reaching agreement by way of mediation is more likely to result in the parties making and maintaining cooperative relationships on family breakdown. It reduces conflict and encourages continuing contact between children and parents. It also avoids the cost, trauma, uncertainty and delay of court proceedings, and helps improve communication between the parties thereby reducing conflict and bitterness. By making disputes less hostile, mediation may make things better for the parties' children. It may also empower the parties and make them better able to deal with disputes in the future. Mediation does, however, have certain disadvantages. For instance, it may work against a party's best interests because of a lack of legal knowledge or it may fail to take sufficient account of the welfare needs of a child. For these reasons, collaborative law may provide a better alternative.

(b)   Collaborative family law

Collaborative law, like mediation, is a form of ADR which provides a way of resolving issues about finance and property and/or children on family breakdown. It is a relatively new practice, having been first used in England and Wales in 2003. It is used only by clients who agree to use it after having received legal advice about the other options available. With collaborative law, the parties and their lawyers sign a participation agreement in which they agree to a commitment to make a transparent search for fair solutions and not go to court. The parties and their lawyers then conduct round-table negotiations in order to find the best outcome. The process is transparent and written correspondence is actively discouraged. The parties set both the pace and scope of the negotiations, but with the assistance of their lawyers. The parties can also seek the assistance of mediation and counselling. If a settlement is not reached, and a party decides to go to court, then each party must consult a new lawyer.

Resolution has trained some of its members as collaborative lawyers, who have formed themselves into 'pods' (practice and organisational development groups). These act as support groups to enable lawyers to share experiences and to build trust with fellow lawyers with whom they work collaboratively. Research conducted by Resolution (*Collaborative Law in England and Wales: Early Findings*, 2009) found that collaborative law was increasingly and successfully being used. Disputes were settled more quickly and, in cases involving cohabitants, more generous settlements were reached than would have been possible if the law relating to cohabitants had been strictly applied. (For other research on collaborative law, see Wright [2011] CFLQ 370.)

(c) Arbitration

Arbitration is a form of ADR whereby disputes are resolved outside the court system by an arbitrator by whose decision the parties agree to be bound. It is beginning to be used for resolving family disputes. Thus, in February 2012 the Institute of Family Law Arbitrators (IFLA) launched a scheme to enable certain family disputes to be resolved by arbitration. The aim of the scheme is to enable financial disputes to be resolved more quickly, cheaply and less formally than in court. It has the support of Resolution and the Family Law Bar Association (FLBA). (For information on the scheme, see www.ifla.org.uk.)

1.6 The courts administering family law

There are three tiers of court with jurisdiction to hear family cases: magistrates' family proceedings courts (FPCs); county courts; and the Family Division of the High Court. Some proceedings can be heard in any of these courts, but others must be heard in a particular court. For instance, divorce proceedings must be heard in a divorce county court, and child abduction and other cases with an international dimension must be heard in the High Court.

(i) Family proceedings courts (FPCs) These courts are staffed by lay magistrates who are specially trained in family work and who are assisted by the clerk of the court. Sometimes district judges sit with lay magistrates. Broadly speaking, all family matters, except divorce and cases which are complex (as defined by specified criteria), can be heard in FPCs. They have concurrent powers with the other family courts in private and public law proceedings under the Children Act 1989 and in adoption proceedings under the Adoption and Children Act 2002. Public law cases under the Children Act 1989 must start in the FPC, but may be transferred to the county court to minimise delay, to consolidate with other family proceedings, or where the matter is exceptionally grave, complex or important. Private law proceedings can commence in any FPC or county court, but can be transferred laterally between courts, and vertically to the High Court in some circumstances.

(ii) County courts These courts deal with most family law matters. There are different types of county court. For instance, some county courts are designated as divorce county courts, where all actions for divorce, nullity and judicial separation must start. Some are family hearings centres which hear contested private family matters (such as applications for residence and contact orders, and domestic violence injunctions). Some county courts are adoption centres (specialised centres with jurisdiction to deal with adoptions); and some are care centres (with full jurisdiction in all private and public matters, such as care and supervision orders, divorce, and adoptions).

(iii) The Family Division of the High Court   The Family Division of the High Court hears a wide range of different family law cases, including wardship cases and cases with an international dimension. It also has an inherent parental type of jurisdiction, and it hears cases transferred from county courts or magistrates' family proceedings courts. These are usually complex and difficult cases requiring the expertise of the High Court. The President of the Family Division is the senior family law judge in England and Wales. The current President is The Right Honourable Lord Justice Munby.

A Single Family Court?

The Family Justice Review (FJR) (see p. 7 above) recommended, among other things, that the three-tier court system should be replaced by a single family court with a single point of entry. In its *Report,* the FJR stated that there were wide variations nationally in how different cases are allocated to courts which caused confusion and uncertainty for families about where cases would be heard. This complexity was particularly difficult for litigants in person to navigate. The FJR recommended that all levels of the family judiciary (including magistrates) should sit in the family court and work should be allocated according to case complexity. However, it recommended that the Family Division of the High Court should remain, and have exclusive jurisdiction over cases involving the inherent jurisdiction and international issues. All other matters should be heard in the single family court, with High Court judges sitting in that court to hear the most complex cases and issues. Provisions for the creation of the new single family court are contained in clause 17 of Part 2 of the Crime and Courts Bill 2012–2013, which had its second reading debate in the House of Commons in January 2013.

1.7   Cafcass

Cafcass (the Children and Family Court Advisory and Support Service), which was established under section 11 of the Criminal Justice and Court Services Act 2000, is responsible for looking after the best interests of children involved in family proceedings. The principal functions of Cafcass officers (who are called 'family proceedings officers' in Wales) are: to safeguard and promote the welfare of children in family proceedings; to make provision for children to be represented; and to provide information, advice and other support for children and their families (s 12(1)).

One of Cafcass' main functions is to advise courts on issues such as residence and contact and on placing children in local authority care. It also performs an important reporting function in family proceedings, for instance in residence and contact disputes. Cafcass performs other important tasks, including facilitating contact on family breakdown and conducting risk assessments to establish whether children are at risk of abuse or domestic violence.

Cafcass provides the following officers for the family courts:

▶ *Children and Family Reporters* When parents cannot agree about arrangements for their children on family breakdown, the court will usually appoint a Children and Family Reporter who will meet and talk with the family and help and encourage parents to agree about arrangements for their children. The Children and Family Reporter may be asked to prepare a welfare report explaining what enquiries have been made and making recommendations about arrangements for the children. The Children and Family Reporter is also responsible for conveying the child's wishes and feelings to the court.

▶ *Children's Guardians* are responsible for investigating the case and safeguarding and promoting the child's welfare before the court in public law proceedings for care and supervision orders and emergency protection and child assessment orders under the Children Act 1989. They work in tandem with the lawyer who is representing the child. In some private law proceedings a Children's Guardian may also be appointed.

▶ *Reporting Officers* are responsible for ensuring that the required consents to adoption and to placements for adoption have been given.

1.8 Family law and the Human Rights Act 1998

The Human Rights Act (HRA) 1998 is relevant to family law, as the family courts and public authorities must abide by its provisions. The effect of the Act is to weave the European Convention for the Protection of Human Rights and Fundamental Freedoms (the ECHR) into the fabric of UK law. The Act makes Convention rights directly enforceable in the UK. Thus, the HRA 1998 gives persons the right to rely on the Convention in proceedings before the domestic courts. However, persons who have exhausted all their remedies before the UK courts can take their case to the European Court of Human Rights in Strasbourg.

(a) The family courts and the Human Rights Act 1998

When deciding any question which has arisen in connection with a Convention right the family courts, like other courts in the UK, must 'take into account' the judgments, decisions and opinions of the European Court of Human Rights (s 2). The courts, so far as it is possible to do so, must also read and give effect to primary and secondary legislation in a way which is compatible with Convention rights (s 3). If the High Court, Court of Appeal or the Supreme Court determines that a UK legislative provision is not compatible with the Convention, and cannot be read to make it compatible, then it may make a 'declaration of incompatibility' to that effect (s 4).

As courts are public authorities for the purposes of the HRA 1998 they must not act in a way which is incompatible with a Convention right (s 6). Thus in family cases, the court must ensure that it considers and upholds Convention rights, otherwise it may be in breach of the Convention.

(b) Public authorities and the Human Rights Act 1998

It is unlawful for a public authority to act in a way which is incompatible with a Convention right, subject to some exceptions (s 6). There is no definition of 'public authority' in the HRA 1998, but the term includes Government departments, local authorities, the National Health Service, the police and any other body or person exercising a public function. Because of the obligations imposed on public authorities by the Act, the Convention is particularly important in public family law, for instance in child protection and adoption cases.

(c) Asserting a Convention right

A victim of an unlawful act or proposed act of a public authority (because it is a breach of a Convention right) may bring free-standing court proceedings against the public authority under the HRA 1998 or rely on a Convention right in any other legal proceedings (s 7). In practice, claims in family law are usually brought as supporting arguments in family proceedings, although human rights challenges against local authorities in child protection cases are usually brought in judicial review proceedings (see pp. 405–407). If an applicant proves that a public authority has acted in breach of a Convention right, the court may grant such relief or remedy or make such order within its powers as it considers just and appropriate, including awards of damages (s 8). When assessing awards of damages the courts take into account the levels of damages set by the ECtHR, which tend to be lower than those awarded under domestic law.

(d) Convention rights

The following Convention rights are those most likely to impact on family law: the right to a fair trial (Art 6); the right to a private and family life (Art 8); the right to marry and found a family (Art 12); the right to an effective remedy (Art 13); and the right to enjoy Convention rights without discrimination (Art 14).

The ECHR and the decisions of the ECtHR have been raised in a wide variety of different situations before the family courts in England and Wales. Thus, for instance:

- Transsexuals have argued that the UK's failure to allow them to change their birth certificates and to marry in their newly acquired sex is a breach of their right to family life under Article 8 and the right to marry under Article 12.
- Children and parents have argued that corporal punishment of children by parents and teachers is inhuman and degrading treatment under Article 3.
- Unmarried fathers have argued that their lack of automatic parental responsibility is a breach of the right to family life under Article 8 and is thereby discriminatory under Article 14.
- Parents in contact cases and in relocation applications have argued that there has been a breach of their right to family life under Article 8.
- Parents have argued in child protection cases that local authorities have breached their right to family life under Article 8 and that the procedures have breached their right to a fair hearing under Article 6.

   (For a useful and informative account of the impact of the HRA 1998 on the family justice system in England and Wales by Moylan J, see [2010] Fam Law 810.)

(e) The right to family life (Article 8)

The right to family life in Article 8 ECHR is particularly relevant to family law:

Article 8 of the European Convention for the Protection of Human Rights

'1. Everyone has the right to respect for his private and family life, his home and his correspondence.

2. There shall be no interference by a public authority with the exercise of this right except such as is in accordance with the law and is necessary in a democratic society in the interests of national security, public safety or the economic well-being of the country, for the prevention of disorder or crime, for the protection of heath or morals, or for the protection of the rights and freedoms of others.'

The aim of Article 8 is to protect the individual against arbitrary interference by public authorities. In addition, national authorities have positive obligations to promote family life under Article 8. However, the right to family life is not an absolute right (because of the exceptions laid down in Article 8(2)). Thus, interference with the right is permitted, provided it is lawful, necessary and proportionate. The right to family life is also subject to the rights and freedoms of others. For instance, the rights of a child might prevail over the rights of parents where that is in the child's best interests. With respect to the right to life, States Parties enjoy a 'margin of appreciation' (see over).

What is 'family life' for the purposes of Article 8?   There is no definition of 'family life' in the ECHR. Whether or not there is a family life depends on the facts and circumstances of the case. However, the ECtHR has made the following statements about 'family life' for the purposes of Article 8:

▶ The existence or non-existence of family life is a question of fact depending on the real existence of close personal ties (*Lebbink v The Netherlands (Application No. 45582/99)* [2004] 2 FLR 463; and *K and T v Finland* (2000) 31 EHRR 18, [2000] 2 FLR 79).

▶ The bond between natural parents and children is a strong indicator of the existence of family life, and that bond amounting to family life cannot be broken by subsequent events, save in exceptional circumstances (*Ahmut v The Netherlands* (1997) 24 EHRR 62).

▶ Family life is not just limited to relationships based on marriage or blood. The following can also have a have a right to family life: cohabitants (*Abdulaziz, Cabales and Balkandali v UK* (1995) 7 EHRR 471), even if they do not live together (*Kroon v The Netherlands* (1995) 19 EHRR 263); same-sex partners (*Schalk and Kopf v Austria* [2010] ECHR 995); and relatives, such as grandparent and grandchild (*Marckx v Belgium* (1979) 2 EHRR 330) and nephew and uncle (*Boyle v UK* (1995) 19 EHRR 179). Foster-parents and foster-children can also come within the ambit of family life (*Gaskin v UK* (1990) 12 EHRR 36).

▶ When deciding whether a cohabitation relationship amounts to family life, the following factors are relevant: whether the couple live together; the length of their relationship; and whether they have demonstrated their commitment to each other by having children together or by any other means. A family life was found to exist, for instance, in *X, Y and Z v UK* (1997) 24 EHRR 143, [1997] 2 FLR 892 where X, a female-to-male transsexual, and his female partner, Y, had a child by artificial insemination by donor. X was involved throughout the process and had acted as the child's father in every respect.

▶ As the ECtHR considers the Convention to be a 'living instrument' which must be interpreted in the light of societal changes (*Selmouni v France* (2000) 29 EHRR 403), courts must adapt to changing social conditions when interpreting family life (for example, the decline in marriage, the increase in cohabitation, the acceptance of same-sex relationships and developments in reproductive science).

▶ Family life can include the potential for family life, for instance the potential relationship which might have developed between an unmarried father and his child; or where the child is in the process of being adopted.

▶ For the purpose of Article 8, family life must be viewed in the context of the relevant social, religious and cultural setting.

When deciding whether family life exists, the ECtHR takes into account relevant principles of international law. It interprets Article 8 to be so far as possible in harmony with those principles, including those in the UN Convention on the Rights of the Child 1989.

The European Court of Human Rights' approach to Article 8

The European Court of Human Rights (ECtHR) has laid down the following propositions in respect of Article 8:

- Although the main aim of Article 8 is to protect the individual against arbitrary action by public authorities (*Kroon v The Netherlands* (1995) 19 EHRR 263), there are also positive obligations inherent in an effective 'respect' for family life.
- As well as a substantive right to respect for family life, there is also a procedural right inherent within Article 8.
- In respect of the substantive and procedural rights under Article 8, regard must be had to the fair balance that has to be struck between the competing interests of the individual and of the community as a whole; and the State enjoys a certain margin of appreciation (see *Keegan v Ireland* (1994) 18 EHRR 342).
- The right to family life is not an absolute right, but a qualified right. Under Article 8(2) State interference into family life is justifiable if: it is in accordance with the law; it is in pursuit of a legitimate aim; and it is necessary in a democratic society. Any intervention must be relevant and sufficient, meet a pressing social need and be proportionate to that need (*Olsson v Sweden (No. 1)* (1988) 11 EHRR 259).
- Under the principle of proportionality, the more serious the intervention into family life, the more compelling must be the justification (*Johansen v Norway* (1997) 23 EHRR 33).
- In respect of a State's obligation to take positive measures, Article 8 includes an obligation on national authorities to take measures to reunite parents with their children (*Ignaccola-Zenide v Romania* (2001) 31 EHRR 7; and *Nuutinen v Finland (Application No. 32842/96)* (2000) 34 EHRR 358, [2005] 2 FLR 596), unless it is contrary to the interests of those concerned, particularly the best interests of the child.
- When carrying out the balancing exercise under Article 8(2) between the interests of children and parents and/or the wider public, the court takes into account the paramountcy of the best interests of the child.

(f)   The margin of appreciation

Claims under the ECHR have sometimes failed because the ECtHR has recognised a 'margin of appreciation' in the State's decision-making process. In other words, States Parties are accorded a reasonable amount of discretion when exercising their powers in compliance with the Convention. For instance, the margin of appreciation possessed by the UK meant that for many years transsexuals failed in their claims before the ECtHR. Member States also enjoy a margin of appreciation with respect to whether or not they permit or recognise same-sex marriage.

(g)   The principle of proportionality

The principle of proportionality is an important principle in the jurisprudence of the ECtHR which must be applied by courts and public authorities in the UK. This principle requires any interference with a Convention right to be proportionate to the legitimate aim pursued. The principle of proportionality would be breached, for example, if a care order was made to protect a child from significant harm when an alternative remedy (such as a supervision order) would be adequate and appropriate.

Summary

▶ Family law is a fascinating but challenging subject which requires a wide range of materials to be digested. A sound knowledge of, and an ability to apply, statutory provisions is vital, as is an understanding that judges have to exercise a considerable degree of discretion when deciding cases. Distinguishing features of family law are that: there is a considerable emphasis on promoting agreement and settlement; both public and private law are involved; emotions are sometimes highly charged; court decisions are often forward-looking; and a wide range of personnel are involved. The functions of family law include: conferring a status; removing a status; enforcing and adjusting rights arising from a particular status; and providing protection for family members.

▶ Family law is radically different today from what it was three or four decades ago. There have been many legislative and case-law developments. There has also been, and continues to be, considerable discussion of reform, such as with respect to giving cohabitants rights on family breakdown, giving children a voice in private family law proceedings, increasing the use of alternative dispute resolution, and reforming the law governing property and finance on divorce. Current proposals for reform include the introduction of same-sex civil marriage and the criminalisation of forced marriage. In 2011 and 2012 there was an important review of the family justice system (the Family Justice Review). Most of its recommendations were taken up by the Government which proposes to make changes to family law, most of which are included in the Children and Families Bill 2012–2013. Demographic and social changes have had an impact on family law, which has changed dramatically in recent years to give 'non-traditional' family members rights, in particular same-sex partners and transsexual persons.

▶ New legal provisions have been introduced to allow the media into court in certain circumstances, in order to make the family justice system more open and transparent and to improve public confidence in the system. However, proposals to give the media even greater access to family proceedings, including those involving children, have met with resistance.

▶ Judges have considerable discretion in family law cases. The outcome of a case depends on its own particular facts, as no two family situations are the same. The discretionary nature of family justice also has an impact on appeals.

▶ The settlement of family law cases outside the court is actively encouraged. Alternative dispute resolution (ADR) is being increasingly used, such as mediation, collaborative law and, more recently, arbitration. The Family Procedure Rules 2010 contain rules which promote mediation, and the Government is proposing to promote it even more.

▶ Family cases are heard in magistrates' family proceedings courts, county courts and the Family Division of the High Court, but there are proposals to introduce a new single family court.

▶ The Children and Family Court Advisory and Support Service (Cafcass) provides officers to assist the court in family cases involving children. In addition to its duty to provide reports (such as welfare reports) for the courts, it also has other functions, such as facilitating and enforcing contact and conducting risk assessments to establish whether children are at risk of harm.

▶ The Human Rights Act 1998 is relevant to family law as it requires family courts and public authorities to take account of the European Convention for the Protection of Human Rights and the jurisprudence of the European Court of Human Rights. Of particular importance in family law cases is the right to family life (Article 8). However, it is not an absolute right. States Parties have a margin of appreciation (a margin of discretion), but any interference with the right to family life must be lawful, necessary and proportionate to the legitimate aim pursued.

Further reading and references

Bessant, 'Children, openness and the family courts' [2011] Fam Law 987.

Booth and Kennedy, 'The "traditional family" and the law' [2005] Fam Law 482.

Choudhry and Herring, *European Human Rights and Family Law*, 2010, Hart Publishing.

Cretney, 'The family and the law – status or contract?' [2003] CFLQ 403.

Cretney, *Family Law in the Twentieth Century: A History*, 2003, Oxford University Press.

Douglas and Lowe (eds), *The Continuing Evolution of Family Law*, 2009, Family Law.

Gilmore, Herring and Probert (eds), *Landmark Cases in Family Law*, 2011, Hart Publishing.

Harris-Short, 'Family law and the Human Rights Act 1998: judicial restraint or revolution?' [2005] CFLQ 329.

Macdonald, 'Bringing rights home for children: transparency and the child's right to family life' [2010] Fam Law 190.

Maclean (ed), *Family Law and Family Values*, 2005, Hart Publishing.

Mole, 'Media access to family courts and article 8' [2010] Fam Law 75.

Moylan J, 'What have human rights done for family justice?' [2010] Fam Law 810.

Munby J, 'Families old and new – the family and Article 8' [2005] CFLQ 487.

Munby J, 'The family justice system' [2004] Fam Law 574.

Munby LJ, 'Lost opportunities: law reform and transparency in the family courts' [2010] CFLQ 273.

Probert, ' "Family law" – a modern concept?' [2004] Fam Law 901.

Roberts, *Mediation in Family Disputes*, 2008, Ashgate.

Ryder J, 'The family courts of the future' [2008] Fam Law 854.

Wall LJ, 'Justice for children: welfare or farewell?' [2010] Fam Law 40.

Wall P, 'The President's Resolution address 2012' [2012] Fam Law 817.

Wallbank, Choudhry and Herring (eds), *Rights, Gender and Family Law*, 2009, Routledge-Cavendish.

Wright, 'The evolving role of the family lawyer: the impact of collaborative law on family law practice' [2011] CFLQ 370.

Websites

Government services

Department for Education: www.education.gov.uk (formerly the Department for Children, Schools and Families)

Department for Work and Pensions: www.dwp.gov.uk

Law Commission: www.lawcom.gov.uk

Ministry of Justice: www.justice.gov.uk

Office for National Statistics: www.ons.gov.uk

United Kingdom Parliament: www.parliament.uk

Courts, law reports and legislation

British and Irish Legal Information Institute: www.bailii.org

European Court of Human Rights: www.echr.coe.int

Her Majesty's Courts Service: www.hmcourts-service.gov.uk

Supreme Court: www.supremecourt.gov.uk

UK Legislation: www.legislation.gov.uk

Websites cont'd

Other websites

Alternative Dispute Resolution Group (ADRg): www.adrgroup.co.uk
Cafcass (England): www.cafcass.gov.uk
Cafcass (Wales): www.wales.gov.uk/cafcasscymru
College of Mediators: www.collegeofmediators.co.uk
Family Mediation Council: www.familymediationcouncil.org.uk
Family Mediation Helpline: www.familymediationhelpline.co.uk
Family Mediators' Association (FMA): www.fmassoc.co.uk
The Law Society: www.lawsociety.org.uk
National Family Mediation (NFM): www.nfm.org.uk
Resolution: www.resolution.org.uk

Links to relevant websites can also be found at: www.palgrave.com/law/familylaw8e

Part II

Marriage, civil partnership and cohabitation

Chapter 2

Marriage and civil partnership

This chapter deals with marriage and civil partnership, and the legal consequences which attach to these relationships. In addition to considering the law of nullity, it also considers the following issues: the problem of forced marriage; the changes to the law to allow transsexual persons to marry in their newly acquired sex; and the recognition of an overseas marriage. It also considers civil partnership and concludes by looking at the question of same-sex marriage. Cohabitation and its legal consequences are considered in Chapter 3.

2.1 Marriage

Over the last decade or so there has been a decline in the number of marriages in England and Wales. In fact, in 2008, the number of marriages (228,204) was the lowest number since 1895. The average age of marriage for both men and women has increased significantly and a smaller percentage of marriages are now first marriages. The following are provisional figures for marriages in England and Wales in 2010:

Marriage statistics (provisional) for England and Wales for 2010, Office for National Statistics (www.ons.gov.uk), February 2012

▶ The number of marriages increased by 3.7 per cent from 2009 to 241,100.
▶ 158,980 of marriages were first marriage for both parties (66 per cent of all marriages).
▶ The average age at marriage was 36.2 years (for men) and 33.6 years (for women).
▶ The number of religious ceremonies increased by 0.4 per cent from 2009 to 76,770.
▶ Civil ceremonies accounted for 68 per cent of all marriages.
▶ 124,570 marriage ceremonies took place in approved premises (such as hotels, stately homes and historic buildings) and accounted for 52 per cent of all marriages and 76 per cent of all civil marriages.

Although marriage is a contract, it cannot be created and terminated at the will of the parties. It is an arrangement in which the State has an interest. Marriage is also a status from which various legal consequences flow. Thus, as Baroness Hale in *Radmacher (Formerly Granatino) v Granatino* [2010] UKSC 42, [2011] 1 FLR 1851 (see further at p. 179) stated:

> 'Marriage is, of course, a contract, in the sense that each party must agree to enter into it and once entered both are bound by its legal consequences. But it is also a status. This means two things. First, the parties are not entirely free to determine all its legal consequences for themselves. They contract into the package which the law of the land lays down. Secondly, their marriage also has legal consequences for other people and for the State. Nowadays there is considerable freedom and flexibility within the marital package but there is an irreducible minimum. This includes a couple's mutual duty to support one another and their children. We have now arrived at a position where the differing roles which either may adopt within the relationship are entitled to equal esteem.'

There are legal rules governing the creation of a valid marriage (see 2.1–2.5) and also its dissolution (see Chapter 6). The legal effect of marriage is to give the parties various rights, obligations and privileges (see 2.9). Similar provisions apply in respect of the creation and dissolution of a civil partnership; and the rights and obligations of civil partners are similar to those of married couples (see 2.10).

A recent development in relation to marriage was the establishment (in May 2012) of The Marriage Foundation, which aims to champion marriage and to reduce the number of children caught up in the family justice system and the misery which they experience (see www.marriagefoundation.org.uk). There are also Government proposals to introduce same-sex marriage (see 2.11).

(a)   Marriage as a human right

Article 12 of the European Convention for the Protection of Human Rights

'Men and women of marriageable age have the right to marry and to found a family according to the national laws governing the exercise of this right.'

The right to marry in Article 12 of the European Convention for the Protection of Human Rights (ECHR) is not an absolute right, but it is a strong right. There is no second paragraph in Article 12, as there is in Article 8 (the right to family life), permitting interferences with or limitations to the right to marry. Both the House of Lords and the European Court of Human Rights (ECtHR) have emphasised the strength and fundamental nature of the right to marry conferred by Article 12 as the following two cases show:

▶ *R (Baiai and Others) v Secretary of State for the Home Department* **[2008] UKHL 53; [2008] 2 FLR 1462**

Challenges were made to a provision in the Asylum and Immigration (Treatment of Claimants, etc.) Act 2004 requiring persons subject to immigration control to obtain the written permission of the Home Secretary in order to marry in the UK unless they intended to marry in the Church of England. The scheme was introduced to prevent persons entering into marriages of convenience in the UK.

The House of Lords held that this provision breached both Article 12 (the right to marry) and Article 14 (discrimination in respect of an ECHR right). It held that, although the right to marry under Article 12 is not an absolute right, it is a strong right; and whilst it can be regulated by national laws both as to procedure and to substance, national laws cannot deprive a person (or a category of persons) of full legal capacity of the right to marry or substantially interfere with their exercise of that right.

Note: After the *Baiai* judgment modifications were made to the scheme for certification of approval of marriage outside the Church of England; and, more recently, the scheme has been abolished.

The approach in *Baiai* was upheld by the European Court of Human Rights in the following case:

> ▶ *O'Donoghue v UK (Application No 34848/07)*
>
> The case involved an application for a certificate of approval of marriage in respect of a Roman Catholic marriage. The applicants claimed that the certification of approval scheme violated their rights under Articles 12, 14, 9 and 8 of the ECHR. The applicants were successful and the ECtHR found violations of Articles 12 and 14 read together with Articles 12 and 9; the applicants were awarded damages and costs.
>
> The ECtHR held, *inter alia*, that Article 12 secured the fundamental right of a man and woman to marry and found a family. Article 12 was subject to the national laws of Contracting States but such laws should not restrict or reduce the right in such a way as to impair its very essence. States were entitled to prevent marriages of convenience entered solely for the purpose of securing an immigration advantage, but such laws could not otherwise deprive persons of full capacity of the right to marry. Since the wording of Article 12 did not contain the restrictions found, for example in Article 8 (the right to family life), the Court had to determine only whether, having regard to the State's margin of appreciation, the impugned interference had been arbitrary or disproportionate.

Successful challenges to the ECtHR based on Article 12 brought by transsexual persons led to changes being made in UK law (see 2.7); but the lack of availability of marriage for same-sex partners (see 2.11) and a failure to recognise a same-sex marriage contracted overseas (see 2.8) have been held not to constitute breaches of Article 12.

2.2   Capacity to marry

To contract a valid marriage the parties must have the capacity to marry and must comply with the legal formalities governing the creation of a marriage, otherwise the marriage may be void. The parties have the capacity to marry (see s 11 Matrimonial Causes Act (MCA) 1973) if:

▶ they are not within the prohibited degrees of relationship (s 11(a)(i));
▶ they are both over the age of 16 (s 11(a)(ii)) ;
▶ at the time of the marriage neither party is already lawfully married or a civil partner (s 11(b)); and
▶ the parties are respectively male and female (s 11(c)).

A party to a polygamous marriage also lacks capacity to marry if he or she was domiciled in England and Wales at the time of the marriage (s 11(d)).

(a)   Not within the prohibited degrees of relationship

A marriage is void if the parties are within the 'prohibited degrees of relationship' (s 11(a)(i) MCA 1973). Marriages between certain relatives related by blood or by marriage are prohibited by the Marriage Act 1949, as amended by the Marriage (Prohibited Degrees of Relationship) Act 1986.

A person is prohibited from marrying the following blood relatives: parent; grandparent; child; grandchild; brother or sister; uncle or aunt; and nephew or niece. There are fewer restrictions on marrying a relative where that relationship was created by marriage. Thus, a person can marry: a step-child; a step-parent; a step-grandparent; or a parent-in-law. However, a person cannot marry a step-child unless both parties are aged 21 or over and the step-child was not at any time before the age of 18 brought up by that person as a step-child. An adopted child is in the same prohibited degrees of relationship in respect of his or her birth family, but fewer restrictions apply to relationships that have been created by adoption. A person can, for example, marry an adopted brother or sister.

'*In-law' marriages* Restrictions on certain 'in-law' marriages were removed in 2007 as a result of the following decision of the European Court of Human Rights:

> ▶ *B and L v UK (Application No. 36536/02)* [2006] 1 FLR 35
>
> A daughter-in-law (L) and her father-in-law (B) wished to marry. They claimed that the bar on 'in-law' marriages was a breach of their fundamental right to marry under Article 12 ECHR. L had been married to B's son, but their marriage had broken down and she had gone on to develop a relationship with his father. The Superintendent Registrar refused to give L and B permission to marry, because B's son was still alive. L and B took their case to the ECtHR, which found the UK to be in breach of Article 12. The prohibition was neither rational nor logical and served no useful purpose of public policy.

After the decision in *B and L*, Schedule 1 to the Marriage Act 1949 was amended in order to remove the restriction on a person marrying a parent of their former spouse or a former spouse of their child.

(b)   Not under the age of 16

A marriage is void if either party is under the age of 16 (s 11(a)(ii) MCA 1973). The consent of the following persons is needed if a party to the marriage is aged 16 or 17 (s 3 Marriage Act 1949): each parent with parental responsibility for the child and each guardian (if any) of the child; a special guardian; any person with whom the child lives (or is to live) under a residence order if not the parent or guardian; a local authority if the child is in care (in addition to parental and guardian consent); and, if a residence order is no longer in force but was in force immediately before the child attained the age of 16, the consent of the person(s) with whom the child lived under that order. If the child is a ward of court, the court's consent is required. Consent can be dispensed with if a person whose consent is needed is absent, inaccessible or suffers from a disability. If a person refuses to give consent, the court can give consent on his or her behalf, but such applications are rare.

(c)   Not already married

A party to a marriage must not already be married, otherwise the marriage is void (s 11(b) MCA 1973). A spouse who remarries without an earlier marriage being terminated may commit the crime of bigamy. Where a spouse has disappeared and/or is thought to be dead, the other spouse can apply for a decree of presumption of death and dissolution of marriage (see 6.10). If this is granted, it prevents the second marriage being bigamous, even if the first spouse subsequently reappears.

(d)   Respectively male and female

The parties to a marriage must be respectively male and female, otherwise the marriage is void (s 11(c) MCA 1973). Although same-sex marriage is not currently possible in the UK, but at the beginning of 2013 the Government voted in favour of introducing it (see 2.11).

2.3   Preliminary formalities

In addition to having the capacity to marry, the parties must satisfy certain preliminary formalities before the marriage can take place. The purpose of these rules is to establish that the required consents have been given and that there are no lawful impediments to the marriage taking place. The marriage ceremony must also comply with certain formalities and the marriage must be registered. Two systems of preliminary formalities exist depending on whether or not the marriage is a Church of England marriage.

(a)   Preliminaries for non-Church of England marriages

All non-Church of England marriages must be preceded by certain prescribed preliminary formalities. Thus, the marriage can be solemnised in a register office or in any venue that has been approved for the purpose of such a marriage, but only after the grant of (i) a superintendent registrar's certificate; or (ii) a Registrar-General's licence.

(i) A superintendent registrar's certificate   Both parties must give notice of the marriage in the prescribed form to the superintendent registrar in the district (or districts) in which each of them has resided for at least the previous seven days (s 27(1) Marriage Act (MA) 1949) and the register office where the ceremony is to take place (if this is different). Both parties must attend in person to give notice. A fee is payable. Notice must be accompanied by a declaration that there are no lawful impediments to the marriage, that the residence requirements have been satisfied and that the required consents have been given. Notice of the marriage is entered in the marriage notice book, which is publicly displayed in the register officer. At the end of a 15-day period after giving notice, and provided there have been no objections to the marriage, the superintendent registrar issues a certificate. The marriage must then be solemnised within three months from the date of entry in the marriage notice book (s 31 MA 1949). The Registrar-General has the power, in exceptional circumstances, to reduce the 15-day period (s 31(5A) MA 1949). Under the Marriage Act 1983, persons who are housebound due to an illness or disability which is likely to last for at least three months or who are detained in prison or who suffer from mental ill-health can marry on the authority of a superintendent registrar's certificate in the place in which they are residing or detained.

(ii) Registrar-General's licence   This procedure is available only in exceptional circumstances, such as when a person is seriously ill and is not expected to recover and cannot be moved to a place where the marriage can be solemnised. It authorises the solemnisation of marriage in a place other than a register office, an Anglican church or a place registered for worship (Marriage (Registrar-General's Licence) Act 1970).

(b)   Preliminaries for Church of England marriages

A Church of England marriage can be solemnised after the publication of banns (the more usual procedure) or after the grant of a superintendent registrar's certificate or Registrar-General's licence (see above).

2.4 The marriage ceremony

(a) Formalities

The marriage ceremony itself must comply with certain formalities, which differ depending on whether the marriage is civil or religious.

(i) Civil marriages Once the civil preliminary formalities above have been satisfied, the marriage can be solemnised in a register office or in 'approved premises' or, in special cases, in the place where a person is housebound or detained. Under the Marriage Act 1994, 'approved premises' are premises which have been approved for civil marriage by local authorities in accordance with regulations laid down by the Secretary of State. Many hotels, stately homes, castles and other places are 'approved premises'. A civil marriage is public and secular, but it may be followed by a religious ceremony in a church or chapel (s 46 MA 1949). However, it is the civil, not the religious, ceremony which is legally binding. At the civil ceremony the parties must declare that there are no lawful impediments to the marriage and they must exchange vows. The ceremony must be witnessed by at least two witnesses. Some registrars remind the parties of the solemn nature of the vows they are making.

(ii) Church of England marriages After complying with the preliminary formalities, the marriage is solemnised by a clergyman according to the rites of the Church of England in the presence of at least two witnesses.

(iii) Quaker and Jewish marriages A Quaker or Jewish marriage cannot be solemnised until the civil preliminary formalities (see above) have been satisfied. Quakers (members of the 'Society of Friends') must make special declarations when giving notice (s 47 MA 1949) and both parties to a Jewish marriage must profess to belong to the Jewish faith (s 26(1)(d) MA 1949). Quaker and Jewish marriages are celebrated according to their own religious requirements and do not need to be conducted in a registered building, or in public, or before an authorised person. There are special rules regarding the registration of Quaker and Jewish marriages.

(iv) Other religious marriages Other religious marriages can be solemnised after the parties have complied with the civil preliminary formalities (see above). The certificate will state where the ceremony is to be held, which will usually be in a 'registered building' in the district in which one of the parties resides. A 'registered building' is a building registered by the Registrar-General as 'a place of meeting for religious worship' (s 41 MA 1949). Some Sikh and Hindu temples and Muslim mosques are registered. If a marriage takes place in a building which is not registered for the purpose of marriage, the marriage may be void or there may be no marriage at all (see over). A non-Anglican religious marriage must be attended either by a registrar or an 'authorised person' and must take place in the presence of at least two witnesses and be open to the public. The ceremony can take any form, provided that during the ceremony the required declarations are made.

(b) Breach of the formality requirements

Breach of the formality requirements for marriage can attract criminal sanctions. For example, a false declaration that there are no lawful impediments to a marriage is perjury. A failure to comply with the required formalities may render a marriage void or the court may decide that there was no marriage at all (see (i) below). In certain circumstances, however, the court may hold that the marriage is valid under the common law presumption of marriage arising as a result of long cohabitation (see (ii) below).

(i) A Void Marriage or a 'Non-Marriage'?   A failure to comply with the formality requirements may result in the court holding that the marriage is void or it may decide that there was no marriage at all (in other words there was a 'non-marriage'). The distinction between a void marriage and a 'non-marriage' is important because, if the court decides there is a 'non-marriage', then there is no entitlement to a decree of nullity (see 2.5) and consequently no right to apply for property and finance orders under Part II of the Matrimonial Causes Act 1973 (see Chapter 7).

In order to assists courts in determining whether or not there is a void marriage or a non-marriage, Bodey J in *Hudson v Leigh (Status of Non-Marriage)* (see below) provided some guidance in the form of a list of factors to be taken into account. As an application for permission to appeal to the Court of Appeal was refused on the basis that 'Bodey J was plainly right to rule as he did, for the reasons that he gave' (*per* Thorpe LJ in, *Leigh v Hudson* [2009] EWCA Civ 1442), then, as Gaffney-Rhys points out in her case-note ([2010] CFLQ 351), the Court of Appeal has given its approval to the decision.

▶ *Hudson v Leigh (Status of Non-Marriage* {2009] EWHC 1306 (Fam); [2009] 2 FLR 1129

The parties went through a religious ceremony in South Africa with the intention of having a formal civil marriage on their return to England, but, as the relationship broke up, the civil marriage did not take place. Bodey J held that the ceremony was void under South African law due to a failure to comply with the required formalities (they had exchanged rings, but they had failed to provide identity documents and to declare whether or not there were any impediments to the marriage; and they had not signed the marriage register). Bodey J then had to consider whether, under English law, the marriage was a void marriage or a non-marriage. Mr Leigh argued that there was a non-marriage. Miss Hudson, on the other hand, contended that it was a void marriage and she applied for a divorce decree (on the ground of unreasonable behaviour) and, in the alternative, a nullity decree (on the ground of lack of appropriate formalities). Bodey J, holding that each case depended on its own facts, laid down the following non-exhaustive list of factors as indications or guidance for courts when deciding whether a marriage is a void marriage or a non-marriage:

(a) whether the ceremony or event set out or purported to be a lawful marriage;
(b) whether it bore all or enough of the hallmarks of marriage;
(c) whether the three key participants (especially the officiating official) believed, intended and understood the ceremony as giving rise to the status of lawful marriage; and
(d) the reasonable perceptions, understandings and beliefs of those in attendance.

Bodey J held that it was not a case involving a lack of consent (for the purposes of s 12(c) MCA 1973), but that it was one where the parties and the officiating minister never intended the ceremony to effect a lawful marriage. Bodey J therefore concluded that the religious ceremony in South Africa was a 'non-marriage' as, at the time it took place, neither the parties nor the minister who had conducted the ceremony had intended or believed it to be legally binding. He therefore dismissed Miss Hudson's petition and made a declaration that there never was a marriage. As a result, she had no right to apply for financial relief

---

Bodey J's factors in *Hudson v Leigh* were applied in *Galloway v Goldstein* [2012] EWHC 60 (Fam), where Mostyn J held that an alleged ceremony of marriage attended by family and friends in an hotel in England was a non-marriage and therefore of no legal effect whatsoever.

Whether a marriage is a void marriage or a non-marriage will depend on the facts of the case. The following cases provide examples:

▶ *Gereis v Yagoub* [1997] 1 FLR 854

A marriage ceremony which took place in a Coptic Orthodox Church not licensed for marriages and which was conducted by a priest not licensed to conduct marriages was held to be a void marriage, not a non-marriage. The ceremony was held to have all hallmarks of an ordinary Christian marriage and the marriage had been treated as a subsisting marriage by all those who had attended. As it was a void marriage, the application for a decree of nullity was granted under s 11(a)(iii) MCA 1973 (breach of the formality requirements).

▶ *Ghandi v Patel* [2002] 1 FLR 603

A Hindu marriage ceremony conducted by a Brahmin priest in a London restaurant was held to be a non-marriage, not a void marriage.

▶ *Alfonso-Brown v Milwood* [2006] 2 FLR 265

A marriage which had taken place in Ghana was held to be a non-marriage as both parties lacked the necessary intent at the time of the ceremony and neither party had believed it was anything other than an engagement ceremony.

▶ *B v B* [2008] 1 FLR 813

A marriage in a hot air balloon in California was held, in the circumstances of the case (fulfilment of the local requirements as to capacity but a failure to observe a technical preliminary formal requirement), to be nowhere near the category of a non-marriage. As a result, the woman was entitled to petition for a decree of nullity.

▶ *El Gamal v Al Maktoum* [2011] EWHC B27 (Fam)

An Islamic wedding ceremony held in a flat in London, which had been conducted in secret and with no written contract, had not complied in any way with the formal requirements of the Marriage Acts 1949 to 1986. It was therefore a non-marriage, not a void marriage, and so the nullity petition was dismissed.

▶ *Dukali v Lamrani (Attorney-General Intervening)* [2012] EWHC 1748 (Fam)

A Moroccan ceremony of marriage conducted in the Moroccan Consulate in London was held not to be a non-marriage as there had been a wholesale failure to comply with the formal requirements of English law. Neither could the wife establish that there was a valid marriage under the presumption of marriage arising from long cohabitation as the parties had only cohabited for 7 or 8 years.

(ii) The common law presumption of marriage from long cohabitation A marriage which fails to comply with the required formalities may be upheld under the common law presumption of marriage from long cohabitation. The following cases provide examples:

▶ *Chief Adjudication Officer v Bath* [2000] 1 FLR 8

A marriage which had taken place in a Sikh temple that was not registered for marriages was held to be invalid as it had failed to comply with the required formalities. As a result, Mrs Bath was not entitled to a widow's pension. However, the Court of Appeal upheld the marriage under the common law presumption of marriage from long cohabitation.

> ▶ *Pazpena de Vire v Pazpena de Vire* **[2001] 1 FLR 460**
>
> The parties had married by proxy in Uruguay. Neither party was present at the ceremony. The couple came to live in England where they lived as husband and wife for 35 years. The wife applied for a divorce, or alternatively for a decree of nullity on the ground that the marriage had been defective. The High Court held that there was a valid marriage by reason of the presumption of long cohabitation.

In the following cases, the period of cohabitation was held not to be long enough: *A v H (Registrar-General for England and Wales and another intervening)* [2010] 1 FLR 1; *Al-Saedy v Musawi (Presumption of Marriage)* [2010] EWHC 3293, [2011] FLR 287; and *Galloway v Goldstein* [2012] EWHC 60 (Fam) (see above).

2.5 Void and voidable marriages – the law of nullity

The law of nullity is laid down in Part I of the Matrimonial Causes Act (MCA) 1973. This is the same Act of Parliament which governs divorce and judicial separation (see Chapter 6). Petitions for nullity are rare: only 298 nullity petitions were filed in the courts in 2010 (*Judicial and Court Statistics 2010*, Ministry of Justice, 2011). The advantage of nullity, however, is that, unlike divorce, it can be applied for in the first year of marriage. Also, an annulment may be a useful alternative for persons who have a religious or moral objection to divorce. It has proved to be particularly useful for victims of forced marriage (see 2.6).

Procedure for an annulment

Under the Family Procedure Rules (FPR) 2010, the procedure for an undefended annulment is the same as that for an undefended divorce (see 6.6). There is no longer any need for either party to attend court. If the annulment is defended, on the other hand, both parties will have to attend court and will usually have to give evidence on oath. To apply for an annulment, the petitioner must complete and submit to the court a nullity petition (Form D8N), which includes the same essential information as a petition for divorce. It will also be necessary to pay a fee (currently £340). If there are children, it will also be necessary to fill in Form D8A (a 'statement of arrangements for children', see 11.3). Like divorce, the process involves two stages: decree nisi (conditional order) followed by decree absolute (final order). It is the decree absolute, not the decree nisi, which finally annuls the marriage. On or after the grant of a decree of nullity, the court has jurisdiction under Part II of the Matrimonial Causes Act 1973 to make orders relating to property and finance in the same way as it has on divorce (see Chapter 7). (For the relevant forms and guidance on seeking an annulment, see www.directgov.uk.)

One difference from divorce, however, is that, where a nullity petition is sought on either of the non-consummation grounds, the court must decide whether it is necessary to appoint medical examiners to examine the parties or either of them (r 7.26, FPR 2010), but if the petition is based on incapacity to consummate then, according to *Practice Direction 7A – Procedure for Applications in Matrimonial and Civil Partnership Proceedings*, it will not usually be necessary to appoint a medical examiner if the petition is undefended, and, where it is defended, the court should not appoint a medical examiner unless it appears necessary to do so for the proper disposal of the case.

A marriage can be annulled on the ground that it is (a) a void marriage; or (b) a voidable marriage.

(a) A void marriage

A void marriage, unlike a voidable marriage, is void *ab initio* (right from the beginning). Although a nullity decree is not technically necessary, it is useful because it creates certainty and also gives the court jurisdiction to make finance and property orders under Part II of the Matrimonial Causes Act 1973 (see Chapter 7). A third party may bring proceedings in respect of a void marriage, for instance in order to gain inheritance rights. A void marriage is different from a 'non-marriage' (see 2.4 above).

A marriage is void on the following grounds:

Section 11 of the Matrimonial Causes Act 1973

'A marriage celebrated after 31st July 1971 shall be void on the following grounds only, that is to say –

(a) that it is not a valid marriage under the provisions of the Marriage Acts 1949 to 1986, that is to say where –
  (i) the parties are within the prohibited degrees of relationship;
  (ii) either party is under the age of sixteen; or
  (iii) the parties have intermarried in disregard of certain requirements as to the formation of marriage;
(b) that at the time of the marriage either party was already lawfully married;
(c) that the parties are not respectively male and female;
(d) in the case of a polygamous marriage entered into outside England and Wales, that either party was at the time of the marriage domiciled in England and Wales.'

These grounds were considered in 2.2 above. For the purposes of s 11(a)(iii), not every breach of the formality requirements will necessarily invalidate a marriage. There are no 'bars' (statutory defences) for void marriages as there are for marriages that are voidable (see p. 35 below).

(b) Grounds on which a marriage may be voidable

A voidable marriage is a marriage which is valid and subsisting until it is annulled by the grant of a nullity decree (s 16 MCA 1973). A marriage is voidable on the following grounds:

Section 12 of the Matrimonial Causes Act 1973

'A marriage celebrated after 31st July 1971 shall be voidable on the following grounds only, that is to say –

(a) that the marriage has not been consummated owing to the incapacity of either party to consummate it;
(b) that the marriage has not been consummated owing to the wilful refusal of the respondent to consummate it;
(c) that either party to the marriage did not validly consent to it, whether in consequence of duress, mistake, unsoundness of mind or otherwise;
(d) that at the time of the marriage either party, though capable of giving a valid consent, was suffering (whether continuously or intermittently) from mental disorder within

the meaning of the Mental Health Act 1983, of such a kind or to such an extent as to be unfitted for marriage;

(e) that at the time of the marriage the respondent was suffering from venereal disease in a communicable form;

(f) that at the time of the marriage the respondent was pregnant by some person other than the petitioner;

(g) that an interim gender recognition certificate under the Gender Recognition Act 2004 has, after the time of marriage, been issued to either party to the marriage;

(h) that the respondent is a person whose gender at the time of the marriage had become the acquired gender under the Gender Recognition Act 2004.'

(i) Non-consummation (ss 12(a) and (b))

Consummation is the first act of intercourse after marriage. It must be 'ordinary and complete, not partial and imperfect' (Dr Lushington in *D-E v A-G* (1845) 1 Rob Eccl 279 at 298). It takes place whether or not a condom is used (*Baxter v Baxter* [1948] AC 274), and whether or not ejaculation takes place (*R v R* [1952] 1 All ER 1194). There are two grounds for non-consummation: incapacity; and wilful refusal.

Incapacity to consummate (s 12(a))   The petition can be based on the petitioner's or the respondent's incapacity to consummate. The incapacity must be permanent and incurable. It can include not just physical incapacity, but 'an invincible repugnance to the respondent due to a psychiatric or sexual aversion' (*Singh v Singh* [1971] 2 WLR 963).

Wilful refusal to consummate (s 12(b))   To establish wilful refusal there must be 'a settled and definite decision come to without just excuse' and the whole history of the marriage must be looked at (Lord Jowitt LC in *Horton v Horton* [1947] 2 All ER 871). Refusal can be express or inferred (for example, by a party refusing to go through a religious ceremony). Wilful refusal has sometimes arisen in the context of certain religious marriages where a civil ceremony must be followed by a religious ceremony before the parties are deemed to be married in the eyes of their religion. In some cases a nullity petition has been sought because the religious ceremony has not taken place and the marriage has not been consummated. Thus, for instance, in *Kaur v Singh* [1972] 1 All ER 292 a marriage was arranged between two Sikhs. The civil ceremony took place, but the husband refused to arrange the religious ceremony. The wife was granted a nullity decree on the ground of her husband's wilful refusal to consummate the marriage (see also *A v J (Nullity)* [1989] 1 FLR 110).

Unlike incapacity to consummate, a petition cannot be brought on the basis of a *petitioner's* refusal to consummate the marriage (see s 12(b)). This means that a woman who has been forced into marriage and refuses to consummate it must instead prove incapacity to consummate or duress.

Probert (see [2005] Fam Law 382) has argued that non-consummation as a ground for avoiding a marriage is a legacy of ecclesiastical law and that it should be abolished in order to 'define marriage in a way that is relevant for the twenty-first century'.

(ii) Lack of consent (s 12(c))

A marriage is voidable if a party did not validly consent to the marriage, whether in consequence of duress, mistake, unsoundness of mind or otherwise.

Duress The test for establishing duress is subjective. In other words, it depends on whether the particular petitioner was under duress, not on whether a reasonable person would objectively believe so. This rule was laid down in the following case in which the Court of Appeal relaxed the earlier rule (laid down in *Szechter (orse Karsov) v Szechter* [1971] 2 WLR 170), which required a petitioner to prove that his or her will was objectively overborne by an immediate threat of danger to 'life, limb or liberty'.

▶ *Hirani v Hirani* **(1983) 4 FLR 232**

The petitioner, aged 19, had entered into a marriage with a man whom she had never met. She had done so because her parents had threatened to throw her out of the house if she did not go ahead with the ceremony. The Court of Appeal held that there was no requirement that a threat to life, limb or liberty had to be proved. The test for duress was a subjective test. The question to be asked was whether the particular petitioner, taking account of his or her personal qualities, had submitted to the duress. On the facts, it was held that the petitioner's will had been overborne, with the result that her consent to the marriage had been vitiated, and so she was entitled to a nullity decree.

The test for duress laid down in *Hirani v Hirani* is particularly relevant for protecting victims of forced marriage (see 2.6); and, in order to protect them, very little pressure may be required (see, for example, *NS v MI* [2006] EWHC 1646 (Fam), [2007] 1 FLR 444).

Mistake The mistake must be in respect of the identity of the other party, not in respect of his or her qualities. Neither must it be in respect of the nature of the ceremony (such as where a party mistakenly believes that the ceremony was an engagement ceremony; see *Valier v Valier* (1925) 133 LT 830).

Lack of capacity to consent Lack of capacity to consent usually arises as a result of mental disorder or mental illness. However, it may also arise because of coercion in the context of a forced marriage. The test for capacity is whether a person can understand the nature of the marriage contract. In other words, he or she must be mentally capable of understanding the duties and responsibilities that normally attach to marriage (*per* Singleton LJ in *Re Estate of Park, Deceased, Park v Park* [1954] P 112, endorsed by Munby J in *Re E (An Alleged Patient); Sheffield City Council v E and S* [2004] EWHC 2808 (Fam), [2005] 1 FLR 965).

The inherent jurisdiction of the High Court (see 8.7) can be invoked to protect a vulnerable adult who lacks the capacity to marry, as the following two cases show:

▶ *M v B, A and S (By the Official Solicitor)* **[2006] 1 FLR 117**

A local authority was concerned that the parents of a young woman (aged 23 and who suffered from a severe learning disability) were organising an arranged marriage for her in Pakistan. The local authority applied for declarations that the daughter lacked the capacity to marry and that it was not in her best interests to leave the UK. Sumner J made the declarations sought and held that in appropriate circumstances the court has jurisdiction to grant an injunction restraining those persons responsible for an adult who lacks capacity from entering into a contract of marriage, if such an order is required to protect the adult's best interests.

> ▶ *X City Council v MB, NB and Mab (By His Litigation Friend The Official Solicitor)* [2006] 2 FLR 968
>
> A 25-year-old man who, as a result of autism, lacked the capacity to marry was given protection by Munby J under the inherent jurisdiction of the High Court on the application of the local authority. The application was made in order to prevent him being taken abroad by his parents to be married in Pakistan.

(c) Voidable marriages – statutory bars

Section 13 of the Matrimonial Causes Act 1973 lays down the following statutory bars to a petition for nullity in the case of a voidable marriage:

Approbation by the petitioner The court cannot grant a nullity decree on any ground in section 12 MCA 1973 if the respondent proves: (i) that the petitioner knew that he/she could have avoided the marriage but the petitioner's conduct led the respondent reasonably to believe that the petitioner would not do so; (ii) *and* the court considers that it would be unjust to the respondent to grant the decree (s 13(1)).

Three-year bar The court cannot grant a nullity decree on ground (c), (d), (e), (f) or (h) of section 12 MCA 1973 unless proceedings are instituted within three years of the marriage (s 13(2)). However, the court has jurisdiction to grant leave to apply after that period if the petitioner has suffered from a mental disorder (within the meaning of the Mental Health Act 1983) during that three-year period; and it would in all the circumstances be just to grant leave (ss 13(4), (5)). The three-year bar may be waived by the High Court in the exercise of its inherent jurisdiction (for instance, in a forced marriage case).

Six-months bar A nullity decree cannot be granted on ground (g) of section 12 MCA 1973 unless proceedings were instituted within six months of the issue of an interim gender recognition certificate (s 13(2A)).

Ignorance A nullity decree cannot be granted on ground (e), (f) or (h) of section 12 MCA 1973 unless the court is satisfied that the petitioner was ignorant of those facts at the time of the marriage (s 13(3)).

2.6 Forced marriages

(a) Introduction: the problem of forced marriage

A forced marriage is one which is conducted without the valid consent of one or both of the parties and where duress is a factor. It is not the same as an arranged marriage, which is a marriage where the families of both spouses take a leading role in choosing a marriage partner, but where the choice of whether or not to accept the arrangement remains with the parties. Forced marriages are sometimes used for immigration purposes because, by marriage, a person can acquire British citizenship and can gain entry into the UK. Forcing someone to marry involves a wide range of behaviour, such as emotional threats, imprisonment, violence, abduction and blackmail.

Whereas the courts are not opposed to arranged marriages, they do not tolerate forced marriages. In *NS v MI* [2006] EWHC 1646 (Fam), [2007] 1 FLR 444, Munby J said that, while arranged marriages were to be respected and supported, forced marriages were utterly unacceptable, and that 'the court must not hesitate to use every weapon in its protective arsenal if faced with what is, or appears to be, a case of forced marriage'. In *Re K; A Local Authority v N and Others* [2005] EWHC 2956 (Fam), [2007] 1 FLR 399 Munby J described forced marriage as 'a gross abuse of human rights' and as 'a form of domestic violence that dehumanises people by denying them their right to choose how to live their lives'. It was, he said, 'an appalling practice'.

The problem of forced marriages has come to the fore in recent years. To help deal with the problem the Forced Marriage Unit (FMU) (a joint initiative of the Foreign & Commonwealth Office and the Home Office) provides trained professionals who can offer confidential advice and assistance to actual and potential victims and to other persons, such as friends or relatives and also professionals working with actual or potential victims. The FMU is also responsible for developing Government policy on forced marriages. The Unit dealt with 1,468 potential cases of forced marriage in 2011 and nearly 600 cases between January and May 2012. The true number of forced marriage cases is, however, likely to be far higher. Most cases involve young women. Some cases involve very young children. Figures published by the FMU in 2012 showed an increase in the numbers of people willing to come forward to seek protection. They also showed that many cases involved families of Pakistani origin (46 per cent). In 87 per cent of cases the victims were female. 31 per cent of all cases involved victims aged 16–17, whilst 14 per cent involved victims aged 15 and below.

Protection for actual and potential victims of forced marriage is available in: family law; the law of tort; and under the criminal law.

(b) Protection in family law

The following family law 'remedies' are available for victims of forced marriage: (i) annulment; (ii) protection under the inherent jurisdiction of the High Court; (iii) protection in wardship. In addition, since November 2008, it is now possible to apply for a forced marriage protection order to protect an actual or potential victim of forced marriage (see para (c) below).

(i) Annulment

A person who enters into a forced marriage can have the marriage annulled on the ground of lack of consent to the marriage due to duress (see 2.5 above). The following case provides an example of the use of annulment in the case of a forced marriage:

▶ *P v R (Forced Marriage: Annulment)* **[2003] 1 FLR 661**

The petitioner, a 20-year-old girl, had been forced to enter into a marriage in Pakistan. Her brother threatened her with violence and she believed that, if she did not go ahead with the marriage, she would be unable to return to England. Her parents told her that it would bring shame and disgrace on the family if she did not go ahead with the marriage, and during the ceremony her mother forced her to nod by pushing her head forward three times. She signed the marriage certificate out of fear. On her return to England, she petitioned for a decree of nullity. Coleridge J held that she had not validly consented to the marriage as her consent had been vitiated by force, both physical and emotional.

Where an applicant for nullity is reluctant to give oral evidence (if needed) because her family is present, the court will do whatever it can to afford the petitioner protection (*per* Munby J in *NS v MI* [2006] EWHC 1646 (Fam), [2007] 1 FLR 444). A Muslim applicant will be required to remove her veil when giving evidence, but appropriate arrangements can be made (such as screens and a woman judge, if possible) to enable her to do so without breaching her religious principles (*per* Macur J in *Re S (Practice: Muslim Women Giving Evidence)* [2007] 2 FLR 461 where a young Muslim woman was granted a nullity petition because she had entered into a forced marriage following a two-year campaign of family pressure).

(ii) The inherent jurisdiction

The High Court's inherent jurisdiction (see 8.7) can be invoked to protect a victim of a forced marriage. The flexibility of the inherent jurisdiction is shown in the following case where it was exercised in respect of forced marriages which had taken place overseas but where a statutory 'remedy' was not available in England and Wales:

> ▶ *B v I (Forced Marriage)* [2010] 1 FLR 1721
>
> B, a 16 year old girl of Bangladeshi origin, travelled from England to Bangladesh on what she thought was a family holiday but where she entered into a forced marriage with her 18-year-old Bangladeshi cousin. She believed the ceremony to be merely a betrothal, but on her return to England she discovered it had been one of marriage. She issued an originating summons under the inherent jurisdiction of the High Court as the three-year period within which she could petition for a decree of nullity on the basis of lack of consent had passed (see s 13(2) MCA 1973). Baron J held that, although section 58 of the Family Law Act 1986 prohibited the making of a declaration that a marriage was void at its inception, the court could make a declaration under its inherent jurisdiction that the ceremony in Bangladesh had not given rise to a marriage capable of recognition in England and Wales. Baron J held that it was eminently fair to provide such a declaration in a case of forced marriage, and that the inherent jurisdiction was a flexible tool that enabled the court to provided justice for parties where statute had failed to do so.

The inherent jurisdiction of the High Court can also be invoked to protect a potential victim of a forced marriage, as the following case shows:

> ▶ *Re SA (Vulnerable Adult With Capacity: Marriage)* [2006] 1 FLR 867
>
> The local authority feared that a 17-year-old girl (who was profoundly deaf, unable to speak, and had the intellect of a 13- or 14-year-old) might be taken by her family to Pakistan for the purposes of an arranged marriage. Munby J made an order under the inherent jurisdiction of the High Court requiring the girl to be properly informed, in a manner she would understand, about any specific marriage prior to entering into it.

(iii) The wardship jurisdiction

This jurisdiction (which is part of the High Court's inherent jurisdiction, see 8.7) can be invoked in the case of a victim aged under 18. In exceptional circumstances, it can be invoked even where the victim is not living in the UK as the following two cases show:

> ▶ *Re B; RB v FB* [2008] EWHC 938 (Fam), [2008] 2 FLR 1624
>
> A 15-year-old Pakistani girl who was a British national living in Pakistan was made a ward of court on the basis that she was a British national who was in desperate need of help. She had approached the British High Commission in Islamabad for help after learning that it had been arranged for her to marry an older man. Hogg J held that, in the very dire and exceptional circumstances of the case, the tentacles of the court should stretch towards Pakistan to rescue the girl from the situation she found herself in, even though she had no connection with the UK other than the fact that her late father was British.
>
> ▶ *SB v RB* [2008] EWHC 938 (Fam), [2008] 2 FLR 1588
>
> An 11-year-old girl, who had been forced to marry a 20-year-old man in Bangladesh, was made a ward of court. With the assistance of the Forced Marriage Unit she was subsequently returned to the UK and placed with an uncle and aunt. The marriage was subsequently declared void.

(c) Protection in family law: forced marriage protection orders

Under Part 4A of the Family Law Act 1996 the High Court and certain designated county courts have jurisdiction to make forced marriage protection orders (FMPOs). These provisions (which came into force on 25 November 2008) were introduced with the aim of providing greater protection for actual and potential victims of forced marriage, and to send out a strong message that forced marriages were unacceptable and would not be tolerated. The provisions are modelled on the remedies available to victims of domestic violence in Part IV of the Family Law Act 1996 (see Chapter 5). The procedural rules governing applications are laid down in Part 11 of the Family Procedure Rules 2010. *The Right to Choose: Multi-Agency Statutory Guidance for Dealing With Forced Marriage* (available at www.fco.gov.uk) sets out the responsibilities of the various agencies in England and Wales which deal with forced marriage cases. Part 2 of the *Guidance* was issued as statutory guidance under section 63Q(1) of Part 4A of the Family Law Act 1996.

According to *Judicial and Court Statistics 2011* (Ministry of Justice, June 2012), a total of 340 applications for a FMPO were made between their introduction in November 2008 and the end of 2011.

A forced marriage protection order (FMPO) under Part 4A of the Family Law (FLA) Act 1996 is an order which provides legal protection to an actual or potential victim of a forced marriage or an attempted forced marriage (s 63A(1)). A forced marriage is a marriage where a person has not given full and free consent (s 63A(4)). 'Force' is defined to include not only physical coercion but also 'threats or other psychological means' (s 63A(6)) (see *Re P (Forced Marriage)* [2010] EWHC 3467 (Fam), [2011] 1 FLR 2060).

The court has wide powers to include in a FMPO such prohibitions, restrictions or requirements or other such terms as are considered appropriate; and the terms of the order can relate to conduct outside and/or within England and Wales (ss 63B(1), (2)). For example, a FMPO could prohibit a parent from taking an unwilling child outside England and Wales for the purpose of marriage; or prohibit a family from contacting or molesting a victim who has taken refuge away from the family. To prevent a forced marriage occurring the court could, for example, require a passport to be handed over or order someone to reveal the whereabouts of an actual or potential victim.

Orders without notice (section 63D)   The court can make a FMPO without notice. In other words, it can make an order where it is just and convenient to do so even though the respondent has not been given notice of proceedings.

Undertakings (section 63E)   In an appropriate case, the court can accept an undertaking from a respondent instead of making a FMPO; but it cannot do so if it would have attached a power of arrest (see below) to an order. In other words, the court cannot accept an undertaking instead of making a FMPO where the respondent has used or threatened violence.

Applicants   An application for a FMPO can be made by: a person who needs protection; a relevant third party (as specified by order of the Lord Chancellor); or any other person who has leave (permission) of the court (s 63C(2)). Local authorities have been designated as a 'specified' third party, and can therefore apply without needing the court's permission. The court also has jurisdiction to make a FMPO of its own motion (in other words where no application has been made for one) (s 63C(1)).

Factors governing the exercise of discretion to make the order   When deciding whether to exercise its powers to make a FMPO and, if so, in what manner, the court must consider all the circumstances of the case including the need to secure the health, safety and well-being of the victim (s 63A(2)). In ascertaining the victim's well-being the court must, in particular, have such regard to the victim's wishes and feelings (so far as they are readily ascertainable) as the court considers appropriate in the light of the victim's age and understanding (s 63A(3)). In *A Chief Constable v A* [2010] EWHC 3282 (Fam) Wall P drew attention to the pressures which may be placed upon victims, and recommended that they be seen by an appropriate expert so that a realistic assessment can to be made pursuant to section 63A(2). His Lordship also considered it desirable that victims should be separately and independently represented.

Power of arrest (section 63H)   The court can attach a power of arrest to a FMPO (but not a FMPO made without notice), but it can only do so if it considers that the respondent has used or threatened violence. The effect of a power of arrest is to give a police constable the power to arrest without warrant a person whom he has reasonable cause for suspecting to be in breach of an order.

Duration, discharge and variation   The duration of a FMPO can be for a specified period or until varied or discharged (s 63F). The court can vary or discharge an order (s 63G).

Breach   If a respondent breaches a FMPO, it is not a criminal offence (although there are proposals to make it so – see below). A constable may arrest a person whom he has reasonable cause to suspect is in breach or otherwise in contempt of a FMPO. A respondent in breach can be brought back to the original court for it to consider the alleged breach. Failure to comply with a FMPO, or an undertaking, is contempt of court and can result in a fine or imprisonment.

Human rights and applications for a FMPO   The issue of human rights and applications for a FMPO was considered in *A Chief Constable and Another v YK and Others* [2010] EWHC 2438 (Fam); [2011] 1 FLR 1493 which raised the issue of how far it is possible to achieve a fair hearing where some of the evidence cannot be safely revealed as any disclosure is likely to identify and place at risk an informant. Wall P said that he was 'tempted to the view' that Article 6 of the ECHR (the right to a fair trial) was not engaged at all in an application for a FMPO, but his Lordship stated that Article 6 is likely to be relevant to an application to set aside a FMPO.

(d) Protection under the law of tort

Forcing someone to marry may constitute the tort of trespass to the person, false imprisonment or harassment. This gives a victim a right to obtain damages and/or injunctive relief.

(e) Protection under the criminal law

The police take forced marriages very seriously and have policy guidelines for dealing with them. Under the criminal law, parents and other persons who force a person into marriage can be prosecuted for various offences (for example, kidnapping, false imprisonment, assault, harassment, child abduction, rape). Although there is currently no specific criminal offence of forcing someone to marry, the Government has announced plans to introduce such an offence (see below).

A criminal offence of forcing someone to marry For several years there has been discussion about whether a specific criminal offence of forcing someone to marry should be introduced. In September 2005 the Home Office published a consultation paper (*Forced Marriage: A Wrong Not a Right*) to see whether there was any support for such an offence, but the idea was shelved by the Government, as the police, the Crown Prosecution Service and the Probation Service offered little support for the proposal. Although it was accepted that a specific offence would have certain advantages (for example, it might create a change of culture, have a deterrent effect, make the law clear, and empower young people), these were considered to be outweighed by the disadvantages (for example, it might drive forced marriages underground, isolate victims and cause segregation at a time of heightened racial tension). Instead, protection under the civil law was the preferred option, and this resulted in the introduction of forced marriage protection orders (see above).

However, due to public concern that the law was failing to tackle the problem of forced marriages, there was renewed discussion in 2011 and 2012 about introducing a new criminal offence of forcing someone to marry. In May 2011, the Home Affairs Select Committee (in its *Eighth Report of Session 2010–2012*) criticised the lack of progress made by successive governments in addressing the issue of forced marriage and recommended it be criminalised. In December 2011, the Government consulted on the matter seeking views about the criminalisation of forced marriage (see *Forced Marriage Consultation*, Home Office). Following a 12-week period of consultation, the responses were published in June 2012 (see *Forced Marriage – A Consultation. A summary of responses*, Home Office), which showed that 54 per cent of respondents were in favour of a new offence, 37 per cent were against it, and 9 per cent were undecided. However, 80 per cent of those who responded were of the view that the current remedies and criminal sanctions were not being used effectively. Many of those in support were of the view that criminalisation would act as a deterrent and send out a strong message that the practice of forced marriage would not be tolerated and perpetrators would be prosecuted. It would also empower victims to come forward and report incidents of forced marriage. However, those against criminalisation felt that it could drive the issue further underground, as victims would be less inclined to come forward if it would ultimately lead to members of their family being imprisoned. There were also concerns regarding the issues of intent and the burden of proof, and that criminalisation could result in victims being taken overseas for the purpose of marriage at a much earlier age.

Despite the arguments against reform, in June 2012 the Government announced that it intended to create a specific offence of forced marriage, and that the new legislation would be accompanied by a range of measures to increase protection and support for victims with a continuing focus on prevention.

Some commentators, however, have argued against criminalisation. For example, Pearce and Gill [2012] Fam Law 534 have argued that criminalisation will require an enormous amount of extra resources which could be better spent. They concluded that:

> '[Criminalisation would be likely to] leave victims destitute and socially and emotionally isolated, compounding the abuse they already have suffered and further infringing their human rights. It is not clear that criminalisation will deter perpetrators, but there is significant evidence that it will deter victims from seeking help. Thus, instead of advancing efforts to tackle [forced marriage] it may destroy what has been achieved and betray the good work that has been done.'

2.7 Transsexuals and marriage

Transsexualism is a medically recognised gender identity disorder (gender dysphoria). Persons with the disorder may opt to have gender reassignment, which involves hormonal treatment and, in some cases, surgery. These treatments are available on the National Health Service. With the recognition of transsexualism as a genuine medical problem and with advances in medical science, the law has had to grapple with the issue of what the legal effects should be of acquiring a reassigned sex. One question which arose before changes were eventually made to the law was whether a transsexual person who had undergone a gender reassignment could enter into a valid marriage with a person of the transsexual's pre-assignment sex. The starting point in the development of the law was the case of *Corbett v Corbett*.

▶ *Corbett v Corbett (Otherwise Ashley)* **[1970] 2 WLR 1306**

The petitioner, a man, petitioned for a decree of nullity on the ground that the marriage was void as the respondent was male. The respondent had been born male but had undergone gender reassignment surgery and hormone treatment and had lived as a woman. Ormrod J, granting the decree, held that the marriage was void because both parties were male. His Lordship held that a person's biological sex was fixed at birth and could not be altered by a sex-change operation. The respondent was male by chromosomal, gonadal and genital criteria, and it was irrelevant that the respondent considered himself philosophically, psychologically and socially to be a woman.

The biological test laid down in *Corbett* was applied in subsequent cases and, as a result, transsexuals began to take their cases to the European Court of Human Rights (ECtHR). They claimed that they were being discriminated against because the restricted biological approach to gender adopted in *Corbett* was being applied to, and was adversely affecting, other areas of their lives.

(a)   Transsexuals and human rights

▶ *Rees v UK* [1987] 2 FLR 111

The applicant, a female-to-male transsexual, claimed that UK law violated Article 8 ECHR (the right to a private and family life) by failing to provide measures that would legally constitute him a male and allow him full integration into social life. He argued that the discrepancy between his apparent sex and legal sex as stated on his birth certificate caused him embarrassment and humiliation whenever the certificate was required to be produced. He also argued that the UK was in breach of Article 12 (the right to marry and found a family) as he could not marry a woman. The ECtHR held by 12 votes to 3 that there had been no breach of Article 8, and unanimously that there had been no breach of Article 12. Although the ECtHR said that it was conscious of the distress suffered by transsexuals, this was an area of law where States enjoyed a wide margin of appreciation (a wide discretion). The ECtHR stressed the need, however, for appropriate legal measures to be kept under review, having regard to scientific and societal developments.

In *Cossey v UK* [1991] 2 FLR 492 the ECtHR adopted the same reasoning as in *Rees* and dismissed the claim by the male-to-female transsexual, but by a smaller majority. In *B v France* [1992] 2 FLR 249 a French transsexual was successful before the ECtHR as it found that French bureaucracy had made the applicant's daily life unbearable. Despite the requirement in *Rees* that the law should be kept under review, in *Sheffield and Horsham v UK* [1998] 2 FLR 928 the ECtHR took the same approach as it had done in *Rees* and *Cossey* on the basis that there had been no scientific or legal developments which persuaded it that it should depart from those decisions. The UK was still entitled to rely on a margin of appreciation to defend its refusal to recognise a post-operative transsexual's identity. However, the decision was much closer than that in *Rees*, as the ECtHR held by 11 votes to 9 that there had been no violation of Article 8 and by 18 votes to 2 that there had been no violation of Article 12. It nevertheless reiterated the principles in *Rees*, and held that the right to marry guaranteed by Article 12 referred to the traditional marriage between persons of the opposite biological sex. However, in the *Horsham* case the ECtHR forcefully stressed the need for contracting States to keep this area under review, because of increasing social acceptance of transsexualism and growing recognition of the problems which post-operative transsexuals encountered.

In the following case, however, the ECtHR took a different approach and it was this case that led to a change of the law in the UK:

▶ *Goodwin v UK* [2002] 2 FLR 487

The applicant, a male-to-female transsexual, claimed that the UK had violated Articles 8 and 12 ECHR because it failed to recognise the legal status of transsexual persons in respect of employment, social security, State pensions, car insurance and marriage. The ECtHR held, unanimously, that the UK was in breach of Article 8 (the right to family life) and Article 12 (the right to marry). It held as follows:

In respect of Article 8, the unsatisfactory situation whereby post-operative transsexuals lived in an intermediate zone as not quite one gender or the other was no longer sustainable. The UK could no longer claim that the matter fell within their margin of appreciation. As there were no significant factors of public interest to weigh against the interest of the applicant in obtaining legal recognition of gender reassignment, the fair balance inherent in the Convention tilted in her favour. Accordingly, there had been a breach of Article 8.

In respect of Article 12, the term 'man and woman' in relation to the fundamental right to marry in Article 12 could not still be assumed to refer to a determination of gender by purely biological criteria. A test of gender based purely on biological factors (as laid down by Ormrod J in *Corbett*) was not appropriate to the current understanding of transsexualism, and could no longer be decisive in denying legal recognition to the change of gender of a post-operative transsexual. There were other important factors, such as the acceptance of the condition of gender identity disorder by the medical profession, the provision of treatment, including surgery, and the assumption by transsexual people of the social role of the assigned gender. As the applicant had no possibility of marrying a man and yet lived as a woman, was in a relationship with a man and would only wish to marry a man, the very essence of her right to marry had been infringed and there was no justification for barring her from enjoying that right under the circumstances. Accordingly, there had been a breach of Article 12.

In *Goodwin* the ECtHR was referred to *Re Kevin: Validity of Marriage of Transsexual* [2001] Fam CA 1074, a decision of the Australian Family Court where Chisholm J had strongly criticised the reasoning in *Corbett* and had upheld the validity of a marriage between a woman and a female-to-male transsexual. Chisholm J said that sex was to be determined at the date of marriage, having regard to all relevant factors, including life experiences and self-perception.

Changing attitudes to transsexualism As a result of the decision in *Goodwin*, the UK was obliged to comply with its Convention obligations and to consider changing to the law. Consequently, in 2002, the Government announced that it would introduce legislation to reflect the decision in *Goodwin*, which would include not only changes in respect of birth certificates, inheritance provision and pension rights, but which would also give transsexuals the right to marry a person of the opposite sex to their post-operative sex. Measures would also be introduced so that transsexuals would be better protected from constantly and unnecessarily having to reveal their history.

Subsequent to these developments, the House of Lords in the following case had to consider the legal position of transsexuals in the light of the obligations imposed on the courts by the Human Rights Act 1998:

▶ *Bellinger v Bellinger (Lord Chancellor Intervening)* [2003] 1 FLR 1043

Mr Bellinger and Mrs Bellinger (a male-to-female transsexual) had married in 1981. Mrs Bellinger sought a declaration in the High Court under section 55 of the Family Law Act 1986 that the marriage was a valid and subsisting marriage. Johnson J in the High Court, and the Court of Appeal by a majority, refused to grant the declaration, applying the biological test of gender laid down in *Corbett v Corbett*. Mrs Bellinger appealed to the House of Lords, arguing that the Court of Appeal's decision was incompatible with the ECHR and was therefore unlawful under section 6 of the Human Rights Act (HRA) 1998. As the UK courts must take account of the judgments of the ECtHR when determining any question arising in connection with a Convention right (s 2(1) HRA 1998), the *Goodwin* case (see above) became relevant to the appeal before the House of Lords. Under the HRA 1998 a court is a public authority (s 6(3)(a)) and must act in accordance with the ECHR (s 6(1)). Under section 3 of the HRA 1998, the House of Lords had the power to read and give effect to section 11(c) of the Matrimonial Causes Act (MCA) 1973 (which states that the parties to a marriage must be male and female) in a way that was compatible with Convention rights so far as it was possible to do so (s 3(1)). Under section 4 of the HRA 1998, it also had the power to declare section 11(c) of the MCA 1973 incompatible with the ECHR.

The House of Lords held, dismissing the appeal, that to allow the appeal would represent a major change in the law which was better dealt with by Parliament than by the courts, particularly as the Government had already said that it would introduce legislation on the matter. However, it nevertheless made a declaration under section 4 HRA 1998 that section 11(c) MCA 1973 was incompatible with Articles 8 and 12 ECHR.

After the decisions in *Goodwin* and *Bellinger*, the Government was put under pressure to consider reforming the law in order to improve the legal position of transsexuals. As a result, the Gender Recognition Act 2004 was enacted.

(b)   The Gender Recognition Act 2004

The Gender Recognition Act (GRA) 2004 gives legal recognition in their acquired gender to transsexuals who can show that they have taken decisive steps towards living fully and permanently in their acquired gender. The Act came into force on 4 April 2005.

Under the Act, an adult transsexual person can obtain a gender recognition certificate issued by the Gender Recognition Panel (s 1). If a full gender recognition certificate is issued, that person's gender becomes for all purposes the acquired gender (s 9). The practical effect of the certificate is to provide transsexual persons with legal recognition in the acquired gender. Thus, they are entitled to a new birth certificate reflecting the acquired gender; and they can lawfully enter into a valid marriage or civil partnership in their acquired gender.

Before issuing a certificate, the Gender Recognition Panel must be satisfied that the applicant: has, or has had, gender dysphoria; has lived in the acquired gender throughout the preceding two years; and intends to continue to live in the acquired gender until death (s 2). The Gender Recognition Panel can only issue an interim (not full) gender recognition certificate to an applicant who is married or who is a civil partner (s 4). The couple have to end their marriage or civil partnership in order to obtain a full certificate. However, if within six months of the issue of the interim certificate the marriage or civil partnership is ended or the applicant's spouse or civil partner dies, the applicant can seek a full certificate (s 5). The reason why the couple have to end their marriage or civil partnership is because the UK does not allow marriage for same-sex couples or civil partnerships for opposite-sex couples, and so the action of one person legally acquiring a different gender would effectively convert their marriage into an unlawful same-sex marriage or opposite-sex civil partnership. However, as part of its proposals in 2012 to introduce same-sex civil marriage (see 2.11), the Government has proposed changes to allow transsexual persons to change their legal gender without having to legally end their existing marriage.

Parenthood Although a full certificate results in the person's gender becoming for all purposes the acquired gender, that person retains their original status as the father or mother of a child (s 12). This provision ensures the continuity of parental rights and responsibilities.

Annulling a marriage (or civil partnership) to a transsexual party

A party to a marriage can petition for a decree of nullity under the Matrimonial Causes Act 1973 on the ground that it is voidable as one of the parties is seeking a certificate from the Gender Recognition Panel; or on the ground that the petitioner married a transsexual person in ignorance of that fact (s 12(h) MCA 1973 – see 2.5). Proceedings must be instituted within three years of the marriage and the petitioner must have been ignorant of the facts at the time of marriage (ss 13(2) and (3) MCA 1973). The same rules apply to the annulment of a civil partnership under the Civil Partnership Act 2004.

2.8 Recognition of an overseas marriage

(i) Recognition of an overseas marriage A marriage contracted overseas (in other words, outside the jurisdiction of the UK) can be recognised as valid in England and Wales under the Family Law Act 1986 provided that: each of the parties has the capacity to marry according to his or her place of domicile; and the formalities required by the law of the place where the marriage was celebrated were complied with. An overseas marriage celebrated by local custom may be recognised (see, for example, *McCabe v McCabe* [1994] 1 FLR 410 where a marriage which had taken place in Ghana, involving a bottle of whisky and a sum of money, was upheld as valid). Special rules apply in certain cases, for instance where a party is serving in HM Forces.

In the following case, for example, an overseas marriage was not recognised as valid in England and Wales under the Family Law Act 1986:

▶ *City of Westminster v IC (By His Litigation Friend the Official Solicitor) and KC and NNC* **[2008] 2 FLR 267**

A Muslim arranged marriage, which had taken place over the telephone between an autistic man (aged 26, but with a mental age of 3) and a woman in Bangladesh, was held to be invalid, even though it was agreed by all the parties that the marriage was valid under Shariah law and had taken place in Bangladesh. The Court of Appeal refused to recognise the marriage as being valid under English law, as both parties must have capacity to enter into a marriage according to the law of their respective domiciles. The Court of Appeal held that the man, due to his disability, lacked capacity and was therefore unable to give valid consent to the marriage. Wall LJ held that the marriage was not entitled to recognition in English law and that there were powerful public policy grounds to that effect.

(See also *Hudson v Leigh* [2009] 2 FLR 1129 at p. 29 above, where Bodey J made a declaration that a 'marriage' conducted in South Africa did not create a valid marriage because the formal requirements for a valid marriage had not been satisfied.)

(ii) A same-sex overseas marriage is not recognised in the UK A same-sex marriage entered into legally overseas will not be recognised as being a valid marriage by the courts in England and Wales, but it may be recognised as a valid civil partnership. In the following case, a lesbian couple unsuccessfully applied to have their Canadian marriage recognised by the law in England and Wales:

▶ *Wilkinson v Kitzinger and Others (No. 2)* **[2007] 1 FLR 295**

Wilkinson (the applicant) and Kitzinger (the respondent) were a lesbian couple living in England who wished their Canadian marriage to be recognised as a valid marriage in the UK. They therefore applied for a declaration as to marital status under section 55 of the Family Law Act 1986. They argued that sections 212–218 of the Civil Partnership Act 2004 (which treats an overseas marriage as a civil partnership) and section 11(c) of the Matrimonial Causes Act 1973 (parties to a marriage must be respectively male and female) violated their rights under Articles 8 (right to family life), 12 (right to marry) and 14 (discrimination in respect of an ECHR right) of the ECHR. In the alternative, they argued that the common law definition of marriage should be developed so as to recognise same-sex marriages; and they sought a declaration under section 4 of the Human Rights Act 1998 that the statutory provisions above were incompatible with Articles 8, 12 and 14 ECHR.

Sir Mark Potter P dismissed the petition on the ground that there had been no violation of their human rights. There was no consensus, he said, about same-sex marriages in Europe, and the ECtHR had declared itself slow to trespass into this area. Applying the jurisprudence of the ECtHR, his Lordship held that their human rights had not been breached. The difference in treatment of same-sex couples was reasonable, legitimate and proportionate; and the Civil Partnership Act 2004 had accorded to same-sex partners all the advantages of civil marriage, save in name.

(For an interesting discussion of *Wilkinson v Kitzinger*, see Bamforth [2007] CFLQ 133; and for possible reforms on same-sex marriage, see 2.11.)

2.9 The legal consequences of marriage

On marriage, the parties acquire a legal status from which various rights, obligations and privileges flow.

(a) Separate legal personalities

Each spouse has a separate legal personality. This means that a husband and a wife can each own property solely (or jointly) and can bring proceedings in tort and contract separately against each other or against third parties (Law Reform (Married Women and Tortfeasors) Act 1935; s 1 Law Reform (Husband and Wife) Act 1962). They can also enter into contracts with each other. As they have separate legal personalities, they can make unilateral decisions about their own medical treatment. This includes the right of a wife to abort a child born of the marriage. In *Paton v British Pregnancy Advisory Service Trustees* [1979] QB 276 the husband applied for an injunction to prohibit the defendant carrying out an abortion on his wife, but his application failed.

(b) Financial obligations

Parties to a marriage have a mutual duty to maintain each other financially during the subsistence of their marriage (and in some circumstances after it has been dissolved). At one time, the husband had a common law duty to maintain his wife, but this rule is archaic and has not been recognised for many years (and has now been abolished by section 198 of the Equality Act 2010).

During a marriage, a party to a marriage can apply for a financial provision order from the family courts against the other party if that party fails to provide reasonable maintenance. In practice, however, applications are extremely rare today as a divorce is now easier to obtain and there is little social stigma against divorce.

(i) The family proceedings court Under the Domestic Proceedings and Magistrates' Courts Act 1978, the family proceedings court has jurisdiction to make periodical payments

and lump sum orders on the application of a spouse where the other spouse has failed to provide reasonable maintenance or has failed to provide reasonable maintenance for any child of the family; or has behaved in such a way that the applicant spouse cannot reasonably be expected to live with the respondent; or has deserted the applicant (s 1). These powers, however, are rarely invoked for two reasons. One is that it is rare today for a spouse to apply for a court order *during* a marriage; and the other is that most child maintenance cases are now dealt with outside the court system (see Chapter 12). The only situation in which an application might perhaps be made is where the parties to a marriage are unable to divorce, for instance for religious reasons.

(ii) The county court and the High Court   Under section 27 of the Matrimonial Causes Act 1973, the county court and the High Court have jurisdiction, similar to that of the family proceedings court (see above), to make periodical payments and lump sum orders during the subsistence of a marriage. Again, these powers are rarely invoked for the same reasons above.

Agreements about maintenance   Married couples can enter into agreements about maintenance, but an agreement cannot be conclusive as the court has the power to vary or revoke the terms of an agreement and can insert new terms. Private maintenance agreements are not precluded by the child support legislation, but any provision in an agreement restricting the right of a person to apply for child support, or to apply to the court, is void. (For pre-marital and post-marital agreements in the context of divorce, see 7.9.)

(c)   Property rights

As each party to a marriage has a separate legal personality, each party may own property solely or jointly. During a marriage, the rules governing property ownership are the same as those which apply to other persons, but with the exception of some special statutory provisions which apply only to spouses (see 4.2). The position is different, however, on divorce (see Chapter 7). Married persons, unlike cohabitants, also enjoy statutory rights of occupation of the family home under section 30 of Part IV of the Family Law Act 1996 (see 4.2).

Property rights on death   Each spouse is free to make a will leaving his or her property to whomsoever he or she wishes. On intestacy (where there is no will) the surviving spouse succeeds to the estate of the deceased spouse (see 4.12). A surviving spouse can apply under the Inheritance (Provision for Family and Dependants) Act 1975 for reasonable provision from the other party's estate without having to prove dependency or that he or she was being maintained by the deceased party (see 4.13). Marriage automatically revokes an existing will unless it was made in contemplation of marriage (see 4.12).

(d)   Protection against domestic violence and harassment

Spouses (and former spouses) can seek remedies under Part IV of the Family Law Act 1996 and under the Protection from Harassment Act 1997 to protect themselves and their children from violence in the home (see Chapter 5).

(e)   Rights on the breakdown of a marriage

On the breakdown of a marriage, a married person can seek a decree of divorce, nullity or judicial separation under Part I of the Matrimonial Causes Act 1973 (see 2.5 above and Chapter 6). They can also apply to the court under Part II of the 1973 Act for property and financial orders, including orders in respect of the matrimonial home and in respect of pension entitlement (see Chapter 7).

(f)   Children

Parents who are married have 'automatic' parental responsibility for their children (see 9.3) – in other words, they do not need to apply for it. They can apply for residence, contact and other orders under the Children Act 1989 (see Chapters 10 and 11). Married persons have a duty to provide maintenance for any child of the family. A party to a marriage can apply for financial provision for a child under Schedule 1 to the Children Act 1989 and can also seek child support (see Chapter 12).

With respect to adoption, married couples can jointly, and in some circumstances solely, apply to adopt a child. They also have rights in respect of giving consent to, or refusing to give consent to, the adoption of their child (see Chapter 15).

2.10   Civil partnership

(a)   The background

Under the Civil Partnership Act 2004 (CPA 2004), which came into force on 5 December 2005, same-sex partners in the UK can register their partnership and thereby acquire rights and obligations which are virtually identical to those of married couples. Although, same-sex marriage is not currently possible in the UK, in 2012 the Government announced that it was proposing to introduce same-sex civil marriage (see 2.11).

Before the CPA 2004 came into force, various informal registration schemes were available in England and Wales enabling same-sex couples to declare their partnership, but these schemes created no legally recognised status and consequently had no legal effects. Because of the disadvantages and difficulties same-sex couples experienced compared with married couples, there was increasing discussion about implementing new laws to permit civil partnership registration. Discussion was fuelled largely by pressure from members of the gay community, in particular the gay pressure group Stonewall, who argued that they were discriminated against. In fact, the House of Lords, before civil partnerships were introduced, had recognised that same-sex cohabitants were discriminated against in the context of succeeding to a tenancy on their partner's death (see *Fitzpatrick v Sterling Housing Association Ltd* [2001] 1 AC 27, [2000] 1 FLR 271; and *Ghaidan v Godin-Mendoza* [2004] UKHL 30, [2004] 2 FLR 600).

In December 2002 the Government announced that it proposed to introduce a same-sex partnership registration scheme, and in June 2003 it published *Civil Partnership: A Framework for the Legal Recognition of Same-Sex Couples* in which it set out its proposals for reform.

> ### Civil Partnerships: A Framework for the Legal Recognition of Same-Sex Couples (Women & Equality Unit, June 2003), para 1.2
>
> 'Civil partnership registration would be an important equality measure for same-sex couples in England and Wales who are unable to marry each other. It would provide for the legal recognition of same-sex partners and give legitimacy to those in, or wishing to enter into, interdependent same-sex couple relationships which are intended to be permanent. Registration would provide a framework whereby same-sex couples could acknowledge their mutual responsibilities, manage their financial arrangements and achieve recognition as each other's partner. Committed same-sex relationships would be recognised and registered partners would gain rights and responsibilities which would reflect the significance of the roles they play in each other's lives. This in turn would encourage more stable family life.'

The Government was keen to emphasise, however, that civil partnership would not undermine the institution of marriage or offend religious beliefs.

> ### Baroness Scotland QC Introducing the Second Reading of the Civil Partnership Bill:
>
> '[Civil partnership] offers a secular solution to the disadvantages which same-sex couples face in the way they are treated by our laws. ... This Bill does not undermine or weaken the importance of marriage and we do not propose to open civil partnership to opposite-sex couples. Civil partnership is aimed at same-sex couples who cannot marry. However, it is important for us to be clear that we continue to support marriage and recognise that it is the surest foundation for opposite-sex couples raising children.'

(b)   The Civil Partnership Act 2004

> ### Civil Partnerships in the UK, 2011 (Office for National Statistics, July 2012)
>
> **Key findings:**
>
> - The provisional number of civil partnerships in the UK in 2011 was 6,795, an increase of 6.4 per cent since 2010.
> - The mean age of men forming a civil partnership in the UK in 2011 was 40.1 years, while for women the average age was 38.3 years.
> - The provisional number of civil partnership dissolutions granted in the UK in 2011 was 672.

The Civil Partnership Act 2004 enables same-sex partners to register their partnership and by registration to acquire rights, responsibilities and obligations which are virtually identical to those of married couples. If the partnership breaks down, it can be dissolved in a procedure similar to that of divorce. Separation, nullity and presumption of death decrees are also available, and the court has jurisdiction to make finance and property orders on civil partnership breakdown equivalent to those that can be made on divorce. Civil partners have rights and responsibilities in respect of children, and provision is made in respect of residence and contact. They also have rights on death. Thus, the surviving civil partner can register the other partner's death, and can claim a survivor's pension. Civil partners are entitled to bereavement benefits and compensation for fatal accidents or criminal injuries. They have rights in respect to succession of a tenancy on the death of their partner, and rights of inheritance on intestacy like those of married couples. In respect of taxation, civil partners also have the same rights as married couples.

Although the Government has been keen to stress that civil partnership is not 'gay marriage', there are in fact very few differences between civil partnership and marriage. As Sir Mark Potter P said in *Wilkinson v Kitzinger* (see at p. 45 above), the 2004 Act had accorded to same-sex partners all the advantages of civil marriage, save in name. The only differences between civil partnership and marriage are that: civil partnership registration is civil and secular; non-consummation and venereal disease are not grounds for annulling a civil partnership; and there is no adultery ground for dissolution.

(i) Eligibility – who can enter into a civil partnership? Section 3(1) CPA 2004 provides that in order to be able to register a civil partnership: (a) both parties must be of the same sex; (b) either party must not already be a civil partner or lawfully married; (c) each party must be aged at least 16; and (d) the parties must not be within the prohibited degrees of relationship (as determined by section 3(2) and Part I of Schedule 1 to the Act). Where a party is aged under 18, parental (or guardian) consent is required (s 4(1)).

(ii) Formation of a civil partnership Local registration services are responsible for registration, a process which is similar to that for civil marriages. As with civil marriages, preliminary formalities must be satisfied. Thus, under section 8(1), each party must have lived in England and Wales for at least 7 days immediately before giving notice and each party must give the register office notice of their intention to register their partnership. Each party must make a declaration that there is no impediment to the formation of the partnership and that the residence requirements are satisfied (s 8(4)). Notice of the proposed registration must be published (s 10) and, after a 15-day waiting period (ss 11 and 12) and in the absence of any objections (s 13), the registration authority in whose area registration of the partnership is to take place can issue a 'civil partnership schedule' (s 14). The 15-day waiting period can be reduced in special cases (such as where there is military posting or illness) (s 20). Special provision exists for housebound persons (s 18) and hospital patients or prisoners (s 19).

Once the preliminaries above are satisfied, registration can take place. Registration can take place in a register office or (since December 2001) in religious premises which have been approved for the purpose of registration (as a result of an amendment made to section 6 CPA 2004 by section 202 of the Equality Act 2010). However, the registration itself is secular (for instance no hymns or religious readings can form part of the registration). Also, there is no obligation for religious organisations to register civil partnerships if they do not wish to do so.

Registration is completed when each party has signed the civil registration document at the invitation of, and in the presence of, the civil partnership registrar; and in the presence of each other and two witnesses (s 2(1)). The civil partnership document must then be signed, in the presence of the civil partners and each other, by each of the two witnesses and the civil partnership registrar (s 2(4)). There must be no religious service at the registration (s 2(5)).

(iii) Civil partnership agreements   Civil partners can enter into a civil partnership agreement (the equivalent of an engagement to marry). The same rules which apply to engagements also apply to civil partnership agreements (see 4.3), except for the fact that the relevant statutory provisions are found in section 74 of the CPA 2004.

(iv) Legal consequences of civil partnership registration   During the partnership, and on its breakdown, civil partners have the same rights and responsibilities as married couples (see 2.9).

(v) Dissolution of a civil partnership   Under sections 37–64 CPA 2004, county courts and the High Court have jurisdiction to make dissolution and nullity orders (see below) and separation and presumption of death orders. Both the law and procedure are exactly the same as those for divorce (see 6.6), except that there is no adultery ground.

(vi) Nullity   The court has the power under sections 49 and 50 CPA 2004 to make nullity orders in respect of a void or voidable civil partnership. Both the law and procedure are exactly the same as the law for nullity of marriage (see 2.5 above), except that non-consummation and venereal disease are not grounds for nullity in the case of a voidable partnership.

(vii) Applications for a financial order on dissolution, nullity and separation   Under section 72 and Schedule 5 of the CPA 2004 the court has jurisdiction, on or after making a dissolution order (or a nullity or separation order), to make finance and property orders. These powers and the case-law principles which apply are exactly the same as those which apply to financial relief on divorce (see Chapter 7). Thus, for example, in *Lawrence v Gallagher* [2012] EWCA Civ 394, [2012] 2 FLR 643 (the first reported case on the financial outcome of the dissolution of a civil partnership), in addition to the statutory criteria, fairness, needs and sharing were concepts used in the reasoning. The court also has the power to make finance and property orders after the overseas dissolution, annulment or legal separation of a civil partnership (s 72(4) and Sch 7), and the rules are the same as those which apply to overseas divorces (see 6.9).

(viii) Recognition of overseas civil partnerships, dissolutions, annulments and separations   Sections 233–238 of the CPA 2004 make provision for the recognition of overseas civil partnerships, and for the recognition of overseas civil partnership dissolutions, annulments and separations. These are equivalent to the provisions governing the recognition of overseas marriages (see 2.8) and overseas divorces (see 6.9). However, overseas same-sex marriages are not recognised in the UK (see *Wilkinson v Kitzinger* at p. 45 above).

2.11   Proposals to introduce same-sex marriage

Some countries permit same-sex marriage, for instance Argentina, Norway, Belgium, Portugal, Canada, South Africa, Iceland, Spain, The Netherlands, and some states of the USA. Although same-sex marriages are not currently permitted in the UK, same-sex partners can enter into a civil partnership (see 2.10 above). With respect to human rights, the European Court of Human Rights has held that, while same-sex partnerships may fall within Article 8 ECHR (the right to family life), there is no obligation under Article 12 (the right to marry) for States to permit same-sex marriage as states enjoy a margin of appreciation in this matter (see *Schalk and Kopf v Austria* [2010] ECHR 995; *PB and JS v Austria* [2010] ECHR 1146; and also Bamforth at [2011] CFLQ 128 and Barker at [2012] Fam Law 548).

Although civil partnership is virtually the same as marriage in all but name (see 2.10 above), in 2012 the UK Government announced proposals to introduce same-sex marriage in England and Wales. In March 2012, it published a consultation paper (*Equal civil marriage; a consultation,* Home Office Equalities Office) to consult on the matter. This was followed, in December 2012, by the publication of the responses to the consultation, *Equal marriage: the Government's response,* in which the Government stated that it proposed to introduce legislation in England and Wales to enable same-sex couples to have a *civil* marriage ceremony, and to enable religious organisations (except the Church of England or the Church in Wales) to conduct same-sex marriage ceremonies if they wished to do so. However, the Government made it clear that no religious organisation or individual minister would be under any legal obligation to perform a same-sex marriage ceremony. Also, as the legislation would not apply to the Church of England and the Church in Wales, it would not be possible for a same-sex marriage to be lawfully conducted in those churches unless there were further changes to primary legislation.

Under the proposals, civil partnership will be retained for same-sex couples, but existing civil partners will be able to convert their partnership to a marriage if they wish to do so. The legislation will also permit persons to change their legal gender without having to end their marriage (or civil partnership), thereby removing the current requirement that a person who wishes to legally change their gender must end their marriage (or civil partnership) before a full gender recognition certificate can be issued (see 2.7).

The proposals to introduce same-sex marriage have not been welcomed by some individuals and organisations, in particular by faith groups and by those who regard marriage by its very definition as constituting a legal relationship between a man and a woman. However, in February 2013, MPs voted (by a majority of 225) in favour of the introduction of same-sex marriage in England and Wales after a debate in the Commons on the Marriage (Same-Sex Couples) Bill 2012–2013.

Summary

▶ There has been a decline in the number of marriages in England and Wales in recent years. Marriage is a contractual relationship which gives rise to various rights, obligations and privileges. The right to marry is guaranteed under Article 12 ECHR, but, while it is a strong right, it is not an absolute right.

▶ To contract a valid marriage the parties must have the capacity to marry and must comply with certain formalities. Failure to comply with these requirements can render the marriage void (s 11 Matrimonial Causes Act 1973). Parties have the capacity to marry if they: are not within the prohibited degrees of relationship; are aged 16 or over; are not already married; and are respectively male and female (s 11 MCA 1973).

▶ Parties to a civil or religious marriage (other than a Church of England marriage) must obtain a superintendent registrar's certificate or a Registrar-General's licence. Special provisions exist for housebound and detained persons. A Church of England marriage can take place after the publication of banns or after the grant of a superintendent registrar's certificate or a Registrar-General's licence.

Summary cont'd

▶ The marriage ceremony must be celebrated according to certain formalities. A civil ceremony must take place in a register office or approved premises. A religious marriage must take place in a church or other place registered for religious worship.

▶ A nullity decree can be sought under Part I of the Matrimonial Causes Act 1973 (MCA 1973) on the ground that a marriage is void (s 11) or voidable (s 12). There is no prohibition on seeking a nullity decree during the first year of marriage (s 3), as there is for seeking a divorce. A nullity decree gives the court jurisdiction to make financial orders under Part II of the MCA 1973. Breach of the formality requirements needed to create a valid marriage can attract criminal sanctions. Breach may render a marriage void, or the court may decide that the circumstances were such that there was no marriage at all (in other words, a 'non-marriage'). If there is no marriage at all, then a decree of nullity cannot be sought. In some circumstances, the court may decide that, despite a failure to comply with the required formalities, that the marriage is valid under the common law presumption of marriage from long cohabitation.

▶ The law governing annulments (nullity) is laid down in Part I of the Matrimonial Causes Act 1973. The procedure for nullity is the same as that for divorce. The grounds for a void marriage are laid down in section 11 of the MCA 1973, and those for a voidable marriage in section 12. There are certain statutory bars to a nullity petition brought on the basis that it is voidable.

▶ A victim of a forced marriage can have the marriage annulled on the ground that it is voidable (under section 12 MCA 1973) due to duress. There have also been other developments to protect actual or potential victims of forced marriage, including the introduction of forced marriage protection orders which the court can make under Part 4A of the Family Law Act 1996. In June 2012, the Government announced that it intended to make forcing a person to marry a specific criminal offence.

▶ Important developments in the case-law of the European Court of Human Rights and the decision of the House of Lords in *Bellinger v Bellinger (Lord Chancellor Intervening)* (2003) led to the enactment of the Gender Recognition Act 2004 which allows a transsexual person who acquires a full gender recognition certificate to enter into a valid marriage or civil partnership in his or her acquired gender.

▶ An overseas marriage may be recognised as valid in the UK under the Family Law Act 1986 provided each party has the capacity to marry according to his or her domicile and the formalities of the place where the marriage was celebrated have been complied with. An overseas same-sex marriage is not recognised in England and Wales as a valid UK marriage, but it can be recognised as a valid civil partnership. An overseas civil partnership may be recognised as valid in the UK under the Civil Partnership Act 2004.

▶ On marriage, the parties acquire a legal status from which various rights, obligations and privileges flow. Married couples have separate legal personalities. They can own property separately and can bring actions in tort and contract against each other, and separately or jointly against third parties. Husbands and wives have a mutual duty to provide each other with financial support, and either party may apply for financial provision from the courts. Married persons enjoy certain tax advantages. Married parents both have parental responsibility for their children. Married couples have rights and remedies under the criminal and civil law to protect themselves and their children against domestic violence.

▶ The Civil Partnership Act 2004 permits same-sex partners to enter into a registered civil partnership and thereby acquire rights, obligations and privileges which are virtually the same as those of married couples.

▶ The Government is proposing to introduce same-sex civil marriage in England and Wales.

Further reading and references

Auchmuty, 'What's so special about marriage? The impact of *Wilkinson* v *Kitzinger*' [2008] CFLQ 475.

Bamforth, ' "The benefits of marriage in all but name?" Same-sex couples and the Civil Partnership Act 2004' [2007] CFLQ 133.

Bamforth, 'Families but not (yet) marriages? Same-sex partners and the developing European Convention "margin of appreciation" ' [2011] CFLQ 128.

Barker, 'Civil partnership: an alternative to marriage? *Ferguson and Others* v *UK*' [2012] Fam Law 548.

Barlow, Duncan, James and Park, *Cohabitation, Marriage and the Law: Social Change and Legal Reform in the 21st Century*, 2005, Hart Publishing.

Borkowsi, 'The presumption of marriage' [2002] CFLQ 251.

Chokowry and Skinner, 'The Forced Marriage (Civil Protection) Act 2007: two years on' [2011] Fam Law 76.

Cretney, *Same Sex Relationships: From 'Odious Crime' to 'Gay Marriage'*, 2006, Oxford University Press.

Deech, 'Cousin marriage' [2010] Fam Law 619.

Gaffney-Rhys, '*M* v *B, A and S (By the Official Solicitor)* – protecting vulnerable adults from being forced into marriage' [2006] CFLQ 445.

Gaffney-Rhys, '*Hudson* v *Leigh* – the concept of non-marriage' [2010] CFLQ 351.

Gilmore, '*Bellinger* v *Bellinger* – Not quite between the ears and the legs – transsexualism and marriage in the Lords' [2003] CFLQ 295.

Pearce and Gill, 'Criminalising forced marriage through stand-alone legislation: will it work?' [2012] Fam Law 534.

Probert, '*Hyde* v *Hyde*: defining or defending marriage?' [2007] CFLQ 322.

Proudman, 'The criminalisation of forced marriage' [2012] Fam Law 460.

Vallance-Webb, 'Forced marriage: a yielding of the lips not the mind' [2008] Fam Law 565.

Websites

Forced Marriage Unit (Foreign & Commonwealth Office): www.fco.gov.uk
The Marriage Foundation: www.marriagefoundation.org.uk

Links to relevant websites can also be found at: www.palgrave.com/law/familylaw8e

Chapter 3

Cohabitation

3.1 Cohabitation

(a) Introduction

One of the most striking social changes which has taken place in the last few decades is the huge increase in the numbers of couples who choose to cohabit. Thus, according to *Population Trends 145* (Autumn 2011, by Beaujouan and Ni Bhrolcháin), in the early 1960s fewer than one in 100 adults under the age of 50 in Britain were estimated to have been cohabiting at any one time, compared with one in six in 2011. Cohabitation is no longer regarded as being socially deviant. Many people choose to cohabit instead of marrying, but others may cohabit as a precursor to marriage. According to *Population Trends*, above, the vast majority of marriages (80 per cent in recent years) are preceded by a spell of cohabitation. Statistics on cohabitation are more difficult to come by than statistics on marriage and civil partnership as there are no registration and court statistics for cohabitation, but, according to the 2001 Census, there were more than 2 million cohabiting couples in England and Wales (compared to more than 10 million married couples) which was a 67 per cent increase from the 1991 Census. Also, the number of cohabiting couple households with dependent children had doubled from the 1991 Census with more than 1.25 million children being dependent on cohabitant parents. These figures are continuing to increase.

Statistical Bulletin, Families and Households 2001–2011, **published in January 2012** by the Office for National Statistics, www.ons.gov.uk

▶ The number of opposite-sex cohabiting couple families increased significantly, from 2.1 million in 2001 to 2.9 million in 2011.
▶ The number of dependent children living in opposite-sex cohabiting couple families increased significantly, from 1.3 million in 2001 to 1.8 million in 2011.
▶ In 2011, 38 per cent of cohabiting couple families had dependent children, the same percentage as for married couple families.

A study conducted by Barlow, Burgoyne, Clery and Smithson (2008) found that cohabitation was a popular choice of relationship in Britain, but that 53 per cent of the cohabitants surveyed mistakenly believed that 'common law marriage' gave them certain rights and that few cohabitants had taken steps to safeguard their legal position. Only 15 per cent of those who owned their accommodation had a written agreement about their share of the ownership; and only 19 per cent had sought advice about their legal position. The research found that: few cohabitants made legal agreements; there was little support for the law to distinguish between financial remedies for married and cohabiting couples on death; and there was a widespread feeling that children of cohabitants should not be adversely affected by their parents' marital status on separation or death.

Over the past two decades or so there has been increasing pressure for family law to be reformed to remove the injustices which cohabitants may suffer in respect of finance and property, particularly on relationship breakdown (see Chapter 4).

(b) The problem of defining cohabitation for legal purposes

One of the difficulties for the law, whether it be judge-made or statute, is defining the terms 'cohabitation' or 'cohabitant' for the purposes of giving cohabitants legal rights and obligations. Statutory provisions which give cohabitants rights and obligations usually define cohabitation in terms of a quasi-marital relationship, sometimes with a minimal duration and a residence requirement. Thus, in order to apply for reasonable financial provision from a deceased cohabiting partner's estate under the Inheritance (Provision for Family and Dependants) Act 1975, a cohabitant must have lived in the same household as the deceased for at least two years as if he or she were the husband or wife (or civil partner) of the deceased (see 4.13). For the purposes of obtaining protection against domestic violence under Part IV of the Family Law Act 1996, however, the term 'cohabitant' is defined less restrictively, as there is no minimum duration requirement (see Chapter 5). For the purposes of adoption, cohabitants (opposite-sex and same-sex) are defined in the Adoption and Children Act 2002 as persons living as partners in an enduring family relationship (see 15.4). As Wong ([2012] CFLQ 60) has stated, there has been 'an increasing shift from defining cohabitation along the marriage model (and, with it, a sexual nexus) to focusing on the "couple", their commitment and interdependence as the fulcrum for extending protection'. She argues that this trend can also be seen in recent divorce and constructive trust cases where marriage, and even cohabitation, is acknowledged as a form of partnership. She says that this focus on commitment 'is to be welcomed as it moves us away from conjugality as the basis for extending recognition to cohabitants'.

In *Kimber v Kimber* [2000] 1 FLR 383, a social security case, His Honour Judge Tyrer, while accepting that it was impossible to give a completely exhaustive definition of 'cohabitation', especially when personal relationships are so diverse, listed the following facts to be taken into account by courts and tribunals when determining whether couples are cohabitants: membership of the same household; stability; financial support; sexual relationship; children; and public acknowledgement.

How the term cohabitation is defined will be an important policy issue when discussing any future reform of the law.

(c) The vulnerability of cohabitants

Cohabitants are often in a vulnerable position with respect to their legal rights, or lack of them, particularly on relationship breakdown and on the death of their partner. Some cohabitants are under the mistaken belief that there is something called a 'common law marriage' which gives them quasi-marital rights. This is a myth.

Children of cohabiting couples can also be in a more vulnerable position than children whose parents are married, not only because cohabiting relationships are more prone to breakdown, but because the court has no power to oversee the arrangements for children of cohabiting parents as it has when parents are married and divorcing. Children may also be vulnerable if a cohabiting parent loses a right to remain in the family home on relationship breakdown.

3.2 The legal consequences of cohabitation

The position of cohabitants with regard to their legal rights and obligations is, in some respects, similar to that of married couples and civil partners, but in other respects it is significantly different as the following paragraphs show.

(a)   Separate legal personalities

Like married couples, each cohabitant has a separate legal personality. This means they can own property solely (or jointly) and can bring proceedings against each other or against third parties. They can enter into contracts with each other. They can also make unilateral decisions about their own medical treatment.

(b)   Financial obligations

Cohabitants, unlike married couples, have no mutual duty during their relationship or on relationship breakdown to provide each other with financial support. Consequently, they have no right to apply to the court for orders in respect of financial provision. However, cohabiting parents have a duty to maintain their children (see Chapter 12).

(c)   Property rights

The property rights of cohabitants are for the most part determined by the law of property and the law of contract (see Chapter 4), although there is some special family law provision with respect to occupation of the family home in cases of domestic violence (see Chapter 5) and applications for financial provision and transfer of a tenancy on the death of a partner (see 4.14). With respect to property ownership on relationship breakdown, however, the family courts have no jurisdiction like there is on divorce to adjust rights of property ownership. Cohabitants must rely instead on equitable doctrines, such as trusts and proprietary estoppel, to establish interests (see 4.7–4.9). Also, cohabitants, unlike married couples, have no statutory right of occupation of the family home. However, if they have children, property orders can be sought to or for the benefit of a child under Schedule 1 to the Children Act 1989 (see 12.3).

The following case is often cited as the classic example of the injustices which a cohabitant can suffer on relationship breakdown, and it is often referred to in discussions of reform:

> ▶ *Burns v Burns* [1984] Ch 317
>
> The female cohabitant (she had taken her partner's name) cohabited with her partner for nearly 20 years. She brought up the children and looked after the home. On relationship breakdown, she brought a claim against her former partner (the owner of the home) arguing that she had an interest in the home under a trust. Her claim was dismissed by the Court of Appeal because there was no evidence of any intention that she was to have an interest. Looking after the home and bringing up the children were held to be insufficient evidence to enable the court to infer such an intention. While expressing considerable sympathy for her, the Court of Appeal felt that any change in the law was a matter for Parliament, not the courts.

In *Hammond v Mitchell* [1991] 1 WLR 1127, on the other hand, the female cohabitant was successful in obtaining an interest in the home under a trust on facts which were similar to those in *Burns*. This was because the court accepted her evidence that she and her partner had spoken about ownership of the home, even though briefly and many years earlier; and this was held to be sufficient evidence of an inferred intention that she was to have a half-share. The different outcomes in *Burns* and *Hammond v Mitchell* demonstrate the somewhat arbitrary and unsatisfactory nature of the law in this area.

(d)　Property rights on death

On the death of a partner, the surviving cohabitant has no right to inherit from the deceased's estate on intestacy. Instead, any property goes to the deceased's children or parents. It is therefore particularly important for cohabitants to make a will. In the last few years, however, there has been discussion about whether the law should be reformed to give certain surviving cohabitants a right to inherit from a deceased partner's estate on intestacy. Thus, in October 2009, the Law Commission published a consultation paper which looked at a range of issues relating to intestacy, including whether certain surviving cohabitants should have a right to inherit from a deceased partner's estate on intestacy. In December 2011, it published its final report (*Intestacy and Family Provision Claims on Death*, LC 331, 2011), which included a draft Inheritance (Cohabitants) Bill 2012–2013 giving cohabitants the right to inherit from a deceased partner's estate on intestacy if they had lived together for five years or for two years (if they have a child together, and the child was living with them at the time when the deceased died). In March 2012, the Government announced that it was considering the Law Commission's recommendations and aimed to respond (see para 48, *Report on the implementation of Law Commission proposals*, Ministry of Justice, March 2012). In the meantime, in May 2012, the Inheritance (Cohabitants) Bill was introduced into the House of Lords (as a Private Members' Bill by Lord Lester) to make provision about the property of deceased persons who are survived by a cohabitants. It had its second reading in the House of Lords in October 2012 but at the time of writing has not gone any further.

Notwithstanding the above, a surviving cohabitant can apply under the Inheritance (Provision for Family and Dependants) Act 1975 (see 4.13) for reasonable financial provision out of the deceased cohabitant's estate, or claim a beneficial interest in the deceased cohabitant's property under a trust or by way of proprietary estoppel (see 4.7 and 4.8). On the death of a cohabitant partner, the surviving partner can succeed to a tenancy belonging to the deceased (see 4.14).

(e)　Rights on relationship breakdown

On relationship breakdown cohabitants have a duty to maintain their children, but there is no maintenance duty between the partners themselves. Furthermore, the courts have no powers, as they have on divorce, to adjust cohabitants' property entitlements according to their needs and resources. Cohabitants can therefore be in a vulnerable position on relationship breakdown in respect of any property whether it be, for example, the family home, investments or pension provision.

Cohabitation contracts　Cohabitants can enter into a cohabitation contract to regulate their affairs (for example, to make arrangements about the allocation of property and other matters should their relationship break down). In practice, however, few do so. Cohabitation contracts were once considered to be contrary to public policy on the ground that they undermined the sanctity of marriage. This is no longer the case, but cohabitation contracts remain open to challenge in the courts and may not be upheld, for instance if there is no intention to create legal relations, or there is duress, undue influence, misrepresentation or lack of independent legal advice. In *Sutton v Mishcon de Reya and Gawor & Co* [2004] 1 FLR 837 a cohabitation agreement was held not to be valid as it was an agreement about sexual relations rather than about property.

(f) Protection against domestic violence and harassment

Cohabitants and former cohabitants (opposite-sex and same-sex) can apply for non-molestation orders and occupation orders under Part IV of the Family Law Act 1996 to protect themselves and their children against domestic violence (see Chapter 5).

(g) Children

Cohabiting parents have the same maintenance obligations to their children as married couples (see Chapter 12). Only a cohabiting mother has automatic parental responsibility in law for her child, but a cohabiting father may acquire it (see 9.4). A cohabiting parent can apply for section 8 orders under the Children Act 1989, for example, residence and contact orders (see Chapter 10). With respect to adoption, cohabitants can jointly, and in some circumstances solely, apply to adopt a child, provided that their relationship is sufficiently permanent (see Chapter 15). Cohabitant parents with parental responsibility have a right to consent (or to refuse consent) to the adoption of their child.

3.3 Homesharers

Some people who live together are not in fact cohabitants in the sense of being a quasi-married couple, but may be described as 'homesharers'. Such persons do not have the same family law rights as married couples, civil partners and cohabitants, except with respect to protection against domestic violence (see Chapter 5). A 'homesharer' may be particularly vulnerable in respect of property entitlement on the death of the other homesharer and they can suffer tax disadvantages as the following case shows:

▶ *Burden and Burden v UK (Application No 13378/05)* [2008] 2 FLR 787

Joyce and Sybil Burden, two unmarried sisters, aged 90 and 82 respectively, claimed that they were discriminated against in respect of inheritance tax under UK law because they did not have the same inheritance rights as same-sex couples, even though they had lived together for the whole of their adult lives and owned their home in joint names. On the death of one sister, the other would have to sell their house to pay the 40 per cent inheritance tax owed on its value. After their claim failed before the English courts they took their case to the European Court of Human Rights (ECtHR), arguing that UK inheritance tax laws discriminated against them under Article 14 of the European Convention for the Protection of Human Rights (ECHR) taken in conjunction with Article 1 of Protocol 1 ('Every natural or legal person is entitled to the peaceful enjoyment of his possessions'). They also argued that the Civil Partnership Act 2004 was discriminatory under the ECHR as it gave rights to same-sex, but not opposite-sex, couples.

The ECtHR held by 15 votes to 2 that there had been no discrimination against the applicants and no violation of the ECHR. The UK had not exceeded the wide margin of appreciation afforded to it; and the difference of treatment for the purposes of the grant of inheritance tax exceptions was reasonably and objectively justified for the purpose of Article 14. Siblings could not be equated with married couples or civil partners for the purpose of inheritance tax obligations, even though they had lived together all their adult lives. Any workable tax system was bound to create marginal situations and individual cases of apparent hardship or injustice; and it was up to national authorities to decide how to strike the right balance between raising revenue and pursuing social policy objectives.

The Cohabitation Bill 2008–2009 (see p. 64 below) made provision for sibling homesharers and was supported by Joyce and Sybil Burden, but the Bill was not taken forward by the Government.

3.4 Reform of the law

This section should be read in conjunction with Chapter 4 which deals with the law governing property ownership by cohabitants.

(a) Discussion of reform

During the last 30 years or so there has been increasing dissatisfaction with the law governing the property rights of cohabitants on relationship breakdown and on the death of a cohabiting partner. There have been recommendations for reform from, for instance, The Law Society, Resolution, judges, lawyers, academics and the Law Commission. According to the *2008 British Social Attitudes Report*, nearly 9 out of 10 people were of the opinion that a cohabiting partner should have a right to financial provision on separation if the relationship was of long duration and/or included children.

As long ago as 1984 in the case of *Burns v Burns* [1984] Ch 317 (see p. 57 above) the Court of Appeal had drawn attention to the unfairness of the law but had said that any reform of the law was a matter for Parliament. Since 1984, changing social and economic conditions have, arguably, made reform even more pressing.

As the law currently stands, cohabitants, unlike spouses and civil partners, are in a particularly disadvantageous position on relationship breakdown as the courts have no discretionary power to adjust their property interests. Instead, cohabitants must turn to the law of property, in particular the law of trusts. This is not only costly and time-consuming, but the law is sometimes insufficiently flexible to do justice between the parties and is complex and difficult to understand.

Some of the arguments for and against reform are as follows:

Arguments for reform

▶ The law should keep up to date with changing social conditions. Many couples choose to cohabit and many cohabitation relationships break down.

▶ Cohabitants can suffer unfairness and injustice in respect of property ownership, particularly on relationship breakdown.

▶ Children of cohabitants are often in a vulnerable position on relationship breakdown, particularly if the home belongs to one of the cohabiting parents.

▶ Many cohabitants believe, mistakenly, that there is something called a 'common law marriage' whereby cohabitants acquire the same legal rights as married couples or civil partners after a period of cohabitation.

▶ The law has been reformed for same-sex cohabitants by the Civil Partnership Act 2004, and so the law should be reformed for other cohabitants.

▶ The law of trusts is doctrinally unsatisfactory, difficult to understand and not designed to deal with cohabitation breakdown. Property entitlement should therefore be determined by a family law, not a property law, regime.

▶ Many other countries (such as Scotland, Australia, New Zealand and Canada) have introduced reforms, and so England and Wales should do the same.

Arguments against reform

- Cohabitants can choose to marry (or enter into a civil partnership) and thereby acquire the rights that married couples and civil partners have.
- The social reality is that most cohabitants own their home jointly, and so very few cohabitants actually suffer any inequity and unfairness.
- Codification of the law would create its own set of problems.
- Reform of the law would be difficult.
- Reform would undermine the institution of marriage.
- Cohabitants may not wish to have an adjustive quasi-divorce regime forced upon them in respect of their property interests. That may be their very reason for choosing not to marry.
- There is an increasing emphasis on party autonomy and settlement on divorce; and so the same policy should be adopted in the context of cohabitation.

Some commentators have argued in favour of reform because cohabitants and their children can suffer serious injustice. A study by Douglas, Pearce and Woodward found major instances of injustice caused by the current operation of the law of trusts.

▶ **Douglas, Pearce and Woodward, *A Failure of Trust: Resolving Property Issues on Cohabitation Breakdown* (2007), Cardiff University Research Paper, Conclusion**

'Retrospective private ordering in cohabitation breakdown cases, set against a fog of uncertainty and complexity rather than the "shadow of the law", has led to a position where trusts law may now serve to perpetuate rather than redress injustice. Even if the parties reach some sort of rough and ready compromise, ignoring or sidestepping the "true" legal position, this comes at a cost, both actual and figurative. Whatever the fate of the Law Commission's or other similar proposals, the present study has thus indicated that maintenance of the status quo is unarguable. However controversial it may be, reform of the current law to meet the legitimate interests of separating cohabitants is both justified and overdue.'

A former President of the Family Division, Baroness Butler-Sloss, has also drawn attention to the problems which cohabitants may suffer.

▶ **Baroness Butler-Sloss in the House of Lords debate on the Cohabitation Bill 2008 (*Hansard*, 13 March 2009)**

'[There are] very real problems on the ground. Lawyers recognise them and ... as a former family judge for 35 years ... there is a very real problem and I have met it in the cases I have tried. ... I have dealt with similar cases again and again. I should tell you what happens. A couple live together for, say, 17 years ... and the woman subordinates her career to the man. She takes some part-time work, she brings up their children and they live as if they are married but they do not get married. At the end of 17 years the man finds a younger woman ... and tells her to get out. When she says, "But I have a share of the house", he says, "The house is in my name. You have not put any money into it. You are out." ... She becomes a burden on the state.'

Drawbacks of the law of property In addition to the arguments set out above, the law of property is open to criticism, particularly in respect of acquiring an interest in the family home. The law is not only complex and difficult to understand, but even more difficult to apply. As Carnwarth LJ said in the Court of Appeal in *Stack v Dowden* [2006] 1 FLR 254:

> 'To the detached observer, the result may seem like a witch's brew, into which various esoteric ingredients have been stirred over the years, and in which different ideas bubble to the surface at different times. They include implied trust, constructive trust, resulting trust, presumption of advancement, proprietary estoppel, unjust enrichment, and so on. These ideas are likely to mean nothing to laymen, and often little more to the lawyers who use them.'

Cohabitants may have to resort to the law of trusts to establish an interest in property (for instance the family home – see 4.6), but the law of trusts has the following disadvantages:

▶ The principles governing constructive trusts are based on intentions and arrangements which are often vague and which may have arisen many years earlier. For this reason, it may be difficult to establish any evidence of intention; and it is possible that parties may be tempted to perjure themselves. For instance, in *Hammond v Mitchell* [1991] 1 WLR 1127 (where the female cohabitant successfully claimed a half-share in the family home and a share of other property owned by the man) Waite J said that 'both parties were prone to exaggeration' and 'neither side had the monopoly of truth'. Bailey-Harris, commenting on *Rowe v Prance* [1999] 2 FLR 787 (where the female cohabitant successfully claimed a half-share in a yacht owned by the man), said that one is 'commonly left with the impression that the establishment of an interest … turns primarily on whose account of conversations is believed by the judge' ([1999] Fam Law 623, at 624).

▶ A claimant is forced to trawl back through the relationship to find evidence of the intention needed to establish a constructive trust, instead of being encouraged to look at future needs and resources, which is the approach adopted on divorce and on dissolution of a civil partnership.

▶ The requirement of a direct financial contribution to establish an interest under a constructive trust (laid down by Lord Bridge in *Lloyds Bank plc v Rosset* [1991] 1 AC 107, [1990] 2 FLR 155, at p. 78 below) means that some cohabitants are unable to acquire an interest in the home even though they have spent many years contributing to its upkeep and looking after the family. The courts are unwilling to adopt a more flexible approach and accept evidence of an indirect contribution (such as looking after children or paying for household goods).

▶ There is some judicial uncertainty about whether Lord Bridge's interpretation in *Lloyds Bank plc v Rosset* of earlier authorities was correct, or whether it set the hurdle too high.

▶ Because of the vagueness of the relevant legal principles, unsatisfactory and unjust distinctions may be made. In *Hammond v Mitchell* [1991] 1 WLR 1127 the female cohabitant was granted a half-share in the family home on the basis of a short conversation she had had with her partner many years earlier, but the female cohabitant in *Burns v Burns* [1984] Ch 317 (see p. 57 above) failed to establish a beneficial interest in the home, despite her substantial contribution over many years to the household and family.

The drawbacks of the law were recognised by the Law Commission in its 2006 Consultation Paper (see further at p. 64 below):

> ▶ *Cohabitation: The Financial Consequences of Relationship Breakdown* **(Law Com No. 17, 2006)**
>
> 'The rules contained in the general law have proved to be relatively rigid and extremely difficult to apply, and their application can lead to what many would regard as unfairness between the parties. The formulation of a claim based on these rules is time-consuming and expensive, and the nature of the inquiry before the court into the history of the relationship results in a protracted hearing for those disputes that are not compromised. The inherent uncertainty of the underlying principles makes effective bargaining difficult to achieve as parties will find it hard to predict the outcome of contested litigation.'

(b) Reform – questions to be addressed

Any reform of the law governing the financial and property rights of cohabitants will have to address the following difficult questions:

- ▶ *Defining the term 'cohabitant'* This is a difficult issue. Should there be a minimum duration requirement? Should there be evidence of financial dependency? Should there be a list of statutory factors to help define cohabitation? Should the birth of a child automatically result in a couple being deemed to be 'cohabitants'?
- ▶ *Remedies* Should the remedies be the same as those which are available for married couples and civil partners on relationship breakdown? Should financial provision be restricted to lump sum orders, or should cohabitants (like divorcing couples) be entitled to maintenance, and, if so, for how long? Should cohabitants be entitled to property orders and to a share of their cohabiting partner's pension?
- ▶ *The exercise of discretion* When deciding whether to grant a remedy what principles should govern the exercise of the court's discretion? Should there be a statutory list of factors equivalent to those for financial orders on divorce and on civil partnership dissolution?
- ▶ *Opting out* Should cohabitants be given the right to opt out of any new scheme, and, if so, should there be any controls on this? Thus, should certain formalities have to be completed? Should there be a requirement of independent legal advice? Should future changes of circumstances (such as the birth of a child or loss of employment) vitiate the agreement? Should there be a right to have the agreement revoked if is likely to cause manifest injustice?
- ▶ *A limitation period* Should there be a requirement that an application should be brought within so many years of relationship breakdown and/or separation? If so, how long should this be, and should it be extended at the discretion of the court in cases where there may be injustice and/or exceptional circumstances?
- ▶ *Property on death* Should cohabitants on the death of a partner have the same or similar rights to those of married couples and civil partners?

(c) Proposals for reform

Proposals for reform of the law have come from various bodies, including The Law Society, Resolution and the Law Commission (the Government's reform body). Thus, in 2002 The Law Society (see *Cohabitation: The Case for Clear Law; Proposals for Reform*) recommended reform of the law to enable cohabitants (same-sex and opposite-sex) to apply for court orders similar to those available for divorcing couples. Eligibility would depend on whether the parties had lived together for at least two years in a quasi-married relationship or on whether they had children. Applications would be determined having regard to a principle of economic advantage and disadvantage suffered by either party in the interests of the other party or of the family. The proposals also included a wide range of other rights for cohabitants.

In 2000 the Solicitors' Family Law Association (now called Resolution) also published proposals for reform similar to those recommended above by The Law Society (see *Fairness for Families*). In addition, there have been attempts to introduce Bills into Parliament. Thus, at the end of 2008 Lord Lester introduced the Cohabitation Bill 2008–2009 into Parliament, which was also promoted by Resolution. The Bill had its second reading in the House of Lords in March 2009, but met with resistance from some members of the House of Lords and went no further. A Private Member's Bill based on Lord Lester's Cohabitation Bill was presented to Parliament by Mary Creah MP and had its second reading in the House of Commons in July 2009, but it too went no further.

It is the work of the Law Commission, however, which has been particularly important with regard to reform of the law.

(d)   Reform of the law – the work of the Law Commission

The Law Commission has spent many years addressing reform of the law to remove the injustices for cohabitants and other homesharers. As long ago as 1994 it announced that the law was unsatisfactory, arbitrary and unjust, and said that it would make proposals for reform. Its proposals were eagerly awaited, but it was not until 2002 that it published a discussion paper, *Sharing Homes: A Discussion Paper* (Law Com No. 278, 2002) in which it considered reform for homesharers generally, not just cohabitants. The Commission considered a 'contribution-based' model for reform, but concluded that this model would do nothing to improve the law for cohabitants, because it was insufficiently flexible to take account of different types of relationship. The discussion paper was a considerable disappointment, particularly for those who had been in favour of reforming the law. Its downfall was that its ambit was too wide. A relationship-based, rather than a contribution-based, model was thought to offer a better solution.

In 2006 the Law Commission began another project where it focused on the financial hardships which cohabitants and their children suffer on relationship breakdown and on death. In 2006, it published a consultation paper, *Cohabitation: The Financial Consequences of Relationship Breakdown* (Law Com No. 179), which was followed in 2007 by the publication of a report, *Cohabitation: The Financial Consequences of Relationship Breakdown* (Law Com No. 307), in which it made recommendations for the introduction of a new scheme of remedies in England and Wales for cohabitants in respect of property on family breakdown and on death.

Eligibility under the proposed scheme would depend on whether the couple had cohabited for a number of years (2–5 years was suggested); or on whether the parties had a child together. Cohabitants would be able to opt out of the scheme by making binding opt-out agreements, subject to safeguards. The remedies proposed were similar to those available on divorce except that no maintenance for a partner would generally be available. To obtain a remedy under the proposed scheme, a cohabitant would have to prove that the respondent had retained a benefit and the he or she had suffered a continuing economic disadvantage as a result of qualifying contributions made to the relationship. The Law Commission made no recommendations on the law of intestacy, but recommended that the Inheritance (Provision for Family and Dependants) Act 1975 should be amended so that cohabitants would be treated in the same way under that Act as spouses and civil partners.

The Law Commission's proposals, however, were not taken any further by the Government. In March 2008, the Government announced that the proposals were to be shelved in order to see how similar reforms introduced in Scotland by the Family Law (Scotland) Act 2006 would work before any changes were made in England and Wales. In September 2011, however, after having considered the Law Commission's recommendations, together with the outcome of research on the Scottish legislation, the Government announced that there was not a sufficient basis for a change in the law and that it did not intend to take forward the Law Commission's recommendations in that Parliamentary term. In its *Report on the implementation of Law Commission proposals* (Ministry of Justice, March 2012), the Government stated (at para 23) that the Scottish legislation 'did not provide a sufficient basis for a change in the law and the family justice system is currently in a transitional period with major reforms on the horizon'. In a response to the statement, Elizabeth Cooke, the Law Commissioner in charge of family law reform, stated that the Law Commission hoped that implementation would not be delayed beyond the early days of the next Parliament in view of the hardship and injustice caused by the current law.

In outline, the Scottish Act (see above) created new remedies for cohabitants for financial relief on separation and death, regardless of whether they had children and whatever the length of their relationship, provided the applicant had suffered an economic disadvantage. A study of the Scottish provisions by Miles, Wasoff and Mordaunt ([2011] CFLQ 302), which focused on the experiences and perspectives of Scottish family lawyers, found that respondents had given a cautious welcome to the new provisions. The Scottish provisions were considered for the first time by the Supreme Court in *Gow (FC) (Appellant) v Grant (Respondent) (Scotland)* [2012] UKSC 29, an appeal from the Scottish courts, and where the Supreme Court unanimously allowed Mrs Gow's appeal and held that she had suffered economic disadvantage in the interests of the respondent to the extent of £39,500. Baroness Hale, giving judgment, stated that there were lessons to be learned from this case in England and Wales and that there was a need for some such remedy south of the border.

(e) Cohabitation reform: the future

At the time of writing there are no Government proposals to reform the law governing the finance and property rights of cohabitants on relationship breakdown even though there have been reforms in Scotland and in other countries (such as in Australia and New Zealand). Thus, despite the work of the Law Commission and attempts to put Bills before Parliament, there are currently no proposals to change the law. With no reforms on the horizon, then it is vitally important that cohabitants know what rights they have and do not have. In the following extract, Baroness Deech emphasises the importance of building on the autonomy of cohabitants and of informing them of their rights:

► **Baroness Deech, 'Cohabitation' [2010] Fam Law 39**

'What, if anything, should be done to help cohabitants sort out their legal problems? We should build on their autonomy rather than take it away. Their contracts should be recognised; they should be encouraged to make wills leaving their property to each other if that is their wish (needless to say, the proposals of automatic inheritance on intestacy for cohabitants in the recent Law Commission Consultation Paper, *Intestacy and Family Provision*, (LC 191, 2009, Part 4) suffer from the same illogicalities as those already described, albeit rather fewer because at least the relationship lasted until death); they should have explained to them that joint registration of the home in both names will mean an equal split of the equity on separation; they could nominate each other as beneficiaries in insurance and pensions. Above all there should be explained loudly and clearly that living together does not give rise to legal rights.'

Summary

► Many couples choose to cohabit, and the numbers who do so has risen significantly in the last few years. However, few cohabitants make legal agreements and some mistakenly believe that there is something called a 'common law marriage' which gives them rights. There has been increasing pressure for reform to remove the injustices which cohabitants and their children can suffer. One of the problems, particularly for reformers, is the difficulty of defining the term 'cohabitant'.

► Opposite-sex and same-sex cohabitants are given some protection under the law (for example, in respect of remedies against domestic violence). They are, however, particularly vulnerable in respect of property rights on relationship breakdown and on the death of their partner. Cohabitants have no mutual maintenance duty to each other, unlike spouses and civil partners, but they have a maintenance obligation to their children. Cohabitants can enter into cohabitation contracts, but these are open to challenge in the courts.

► Some people who live together are 'homesharers' (persons who are cohabiting but who are not a 'couple'). Homesharers are given some protection under the law (for example, in respect of remedies against domestic violence), but they do not have the same family law rights as married couples, civil partners and cohabitants. They can be vulnerable in particular in respect of property entitlement on the death of the other homesharer and they can suffer tax disadvantages.

► There has been increasing concern about the lack of adequate legal remedies in respect of property and finance on cohabitation breakdown, and about the unfairness and injustice this can cause. As a result, there have been calls for reform to remove the perceived unfairness that exists. Proposals for reform have come from The Law Society, Resolution and from the Law Commission. In July 2007, the Law Commission published a report making proposals for reform, but these were taken no further by the Government, despite the fact that there have been changes to the law in Scotland. Thus, there are currently no Government proposals to change the law in England and Wales, despite the various arguments in favour of reform.

Further reading and references

Barlow, Burgoyne, Clery and Smithson, *Cohabitation and the Law: Myths, Money and the Media*, 2008, in British Social Attitudes 24th Report, Sage Publishing.
Barlow, Duncan, James and Park, *Cohabitation, Marriage and the Law: Social Change and Legal Reform in the 21st Century*, 2005, Hart Publishing.

Further reading and references cont'd

Barlow and Smithson, 'Legal assumptions, cohabitants' talk and the rocky road to reform' [2010] CFLQ 328.

Barton, 'Cohabitants, contracts and commissioners' [2007] Fam Law 407.

Beaujouan and Ni Bhrolchán, 'Cohabitation and marriage in Britain since the 1970s', *Population Trends*, 145, Autumn 2011.

Crawford, Goodman and Joyce, 'Relationship between marital status and child outcomes in the UK using the Millennium Cohort Study' [2012] CFLQ 176.

Deech, Baroness, 'Cohabitation' [2010] Fam Law 39.

Douglas, Pearce and Woodward, *A Failure of Trust: Resolving Property Issues on Cohabitation Breakdown*, Cardiff Research Papers, No. 1 (July 2007) (available at www.law.cf.ac.uk/researchpapers/index).

Douglas, Pearce and Woodward, 'Dealing with property issues on cohabitation breakdown' [2007] Fam Law 36.

Duncan, Barlow and James, 'Why don't they marry? Cohabitation, commitment and DIY marriage' [2005] CFLQ 383.

Fox, 'Reforming family property – comparisons, compromises and common dimensions' [2003] CFLQ 1.

Hess, 'The rights of cohabitants: when and how will the law be reformed?' [2009] Fam Law 405.

McCarthy, 'Cohabitation: lessons from north of the border?' [2011] CFLQ 277.

Miles, 'Property law v family law: resolving the problems of family property' (2003) *Legal Studies* 624.

Miles, Wasoff and Mordaunt, 'Cohabitation: lessons from research north of the border?' [2011] CFLQ 302.

Pawlowski, 'Constructive trusts and improvements to property' [2009] Fam Law 680.

Probert, 'The evolution of the common-law marriage myth' [2011] Fam Law 283.

Probert, 'Sutton v Mishcon De Reya and Gawor & Co – cohabitation contracts and Swedish sex slaves' [2004] CFLQ 453.

Probert, 'Trusts and the modern woman – establishing an interest in the family home' [2001] CFLQ 275.

Probert, 'Why couples still believe In common-law marriage' [2007] Fam Law 403.

Probert and Barlow, 'Displacing marriage – diversification and harmonisation within Europe' [2000] CFLQ 153.

Singer, 'What provision for unmarried couples should the law make when their relationships break down?' [2009] Fam Law 234.

Williams, Potter and Douglas, 'Cohabitation and intestacy: public opinion and law reform' [2008] CFLQ 499.

Wong, 'Shared commitment, interdependency and property relations: a socio-legal project for cohabitation' [2012] CFLQ 60.

Websites

Law Commission: www.lawcom.gov.uk
One Plus One – Married or Not: www.oneplusone.org.uk/marriedornot
The Living Together Campaign: www.advicenow.org.uk/livingtogether.

Links to relevant websites can also be found at: www.palgrave.com/law/familylaw8e

Part III

Family property and finance

Chapter 4
Family property

Introduction

This chapter looks at the law governing the property rights of spouses, civil partners and cohabitants during their relationship, on relationship breakdown and on death. Although the applicable statutory provisions and legal principles are the same for spouses and civil partners, they are radically different for cohabitants. Thus, on the breakdown of a cohabitation relationship, the family courts have no jurisdiction, as they have on divorce or civil partnership dissolution (see Chapter 7), to distribute the property assets of cohabitants according to their needs and resources. Cohabitants must rely instead on the general principles of property law, in particular the law of trusts, to determine a property dispute, such as a dispute about the family home. They may also be in a vulnerable position on the death of a cohabiting partner (see 4.12). Because of the difficulties and unfairness that cohabitants and their children can suffer in respect of property entitlement, there have been many calls for reform but these have not been taken forward (see 3.4).

4.2 The property rights of married couples and civil partners

During the subsistence of a marriage or civil partnership the general principles of property law and contract law apply to property ownership, and also the provisions of various family law statutes (see below).

(a) Ownership of property during marriage and civil partnership

The following principles and statutory provisions govern the ownership of property during marriage and civil partnership:

(i) Separation of property Each spouse or civil partner can own property separately. Thus, subject to a contrary intention, any property brought into the marriage or civil partnership belongs to the party who owns it; and so does any property acquired by either party during the marriage or civil partnership. Ownership depends on the law of contract. For example, if a husband buys shares, then, subject to any contrary intention, it is he who owns them. Similarly, if a wife buys a car, then she owns it. On divorce, however, the divorce court may decide otherwise (see Chapter 7).

(ii) Gifts to married couples and civil partners Each individual spouse or civil partner presumptively owns any gift (such as a birthday present) given to him or her personally. But, if a gift is given to them as a married couple or as civil partners, it is presumed to be a gift to them both. This may include a gift of financial assistance for the purpose of acquiring a home (see, for example, *Abbott v Abbott* [2007] UKPC 53, [2008] 1 FLR 1451). These rules, however, are subject to any contrary intention.

(iii) Improvements to property A spouse or civil partner can acquire a share, or an enlarged share, of property (or the proceeds of sale of such property) if he or she has made a

substantial improvement in money or money's worth to that property, subject to any intention to the contrary (s 37 Matrimonial Proceedings and Property Act 1970; s 65 Civil Partnership Act 2004). These provisions also apply to couples who are engaged to be married (s 2 LawReform (Miscellaneous Provisions) Act 1970). However, they are not often used, and are sometimes overlooked, as they were, for example, in *Dibble v Pfluger* [2010] EWCA Civ 1005, [2011] 1 FLR 659 where the parties were a cohabiting couple who were engaged but who had never married.

(iv) Power of the court to declare property interests   The High Court and the county court have jurisdiction on the application of a spouse or civil partner to make such order as they think fit as to the ownership or possession of any property (s 17 Married Women's Property Act 1882; s 66 Civil Partnership Act 2004). Under these provisions, however, the court can only declare property entitlement; it cannot create or adjust rights (*Pettitt v Pettitt* [1970] AC 777). An application can also be made in respect of money or property which has ceased to be in the other party's possession or under his/ her control (s 7(1) Matrimonial Causes (Property and Maintenance) Act 1958; s 67 CPA 2004). Former spouses or civil partners can also apply under these provisions, provided the application is made within three years of the termination of the relationship (s 39 Matrimonial Proceedings and Property Act 1970; s 68 CPA 2004). Having declared any interest, the court can order the sale of property and order that the proceeds of sale be divided in accordance with the parties' interests (s 7(7) Matrimonial Causes (Property and Maintenance) Act 1958; s 66 CPA 2004).

(v) Property bought by a spouse or civil partner from savings   Any property bought by a wife from housekeeping money given to her by her husband is presumed to belong to them both in equal shares (in other words, subject to any contrary intention) (s 1 Married Women's Property Act 1964). Section 200 of the Equality Act 2010, when it comes into force, will amend this provision so that it refers to housekeeping money given by either spouse to the other, not just husbands to wives; and it will also change the name of the Act to Matrimonial Property Act 1964. Section 201 of the Equality Act 2010 will also insert a similar section (s 70A) into the CPA 2004.

(b)   Occupation of the family home

Spouses and civil partners have a right to occupy the family home if they have right of ownership in the property or a contractual licence to occupy it. Spouses and civil partners who are not so entitled may nevertheless have a statutory right of occupation (a so-called 'home right') under section 30(1) of Part IV of the Family Law Act 1996 (FLA 1996), as amended by Schedule 9 to the Civil Partnership Act 2004. If a spouse or civil partner has a 'home right' and is in occupation of the home, then he or she has a right not to be evicted or excluded from the home by the other spouse or civil partner, except with permission of the court given by an order made under section 33 of Part IV of the FLA 1996 (s 30(2)(a)). If the spouse or civil partner is not in occupation, then he or she has a right, if permission of the court is given, to enter into and occupy the home (s 30(2)(b)). A 'home right' arises only in respect of a dwelling house which is, was or was intended to be the parties' family home (s 30(7)). The right ceases on divorce, dissolution or death of either spouse or civil partner (s 30(8)), unless a court orders otherwise (s 33(5)).

A person with a 'home right' has other rights. Thus, any payment or other thing done by a person with a 'home right' in or towards satisfaction of any liability of the tenant or owner in respect of rent, mortgage payments or other outgoings affecting the home must be treated by the recipient as if it was made or done by the tenant or owner (s 30(3)). For example, if a husband stops paying the rent on a property that was taken in his name, the wife can continue to pay the rent and the landlord will have to accept that payment as if it was made by her husband and will thereby be prevented from evicting her. This does not, however, affect any claim by a person with a 'home right' against the other party to an interest in the property by virtue of that payment (s 30(5)).

A spouse or civil partner's 'home right' is a charge on the other party's estate or interest (s 31). This charge is binding on a third party (for example, a purchaser or a mortgagee) if it has been protected by a notice on the register made under the Land Registration Act 2002 or any enactment replaced by that Act (s 30(10)). (For more on the provisions of Part IV of the Family Law Act 1996 in respect of occupation of the family home in the context of domestic violence, see 5.5.)

4.3 The property rights of engaged couples and parties to a civil partnership agreement

The Law Reform (Miscellaneous Provisions) Act 1970 provides that an engagement to marry is not a contract giving rise to legal rights and consequently no action for breach of promise can be brought against the party who was responsible for terminating the engagement (s 1). On the termination of an engagement, any rule of law relating to the beneficial entitlement of spouses also applies to any property in which either or both parties had a beneficial interest during their engagement (s 2(1)). Also, the fact that one party was responsible for terminating the engagement does not affect any express or implied arrangement in respect of the return of any engagement gift (s 3(1)). Ownership depends on the intention of the donor. In the absence of intention, the court may infer that a gift from a relative belongs to the spouse to whom he/she is related (as it did in *Samson v Samson* [1982] 1 WLR 252). The same rules apply to civil partnership agreements (see ss 73 and 74 Civil Partnership Act 2004).

An engagement ring is presumed to be an absolute gift (s 3(2)), which means that it can be kept on the termination of an engagement unless there is an express or implied condition to the contrary (for instance if it is a family heirloom). There is no equivalent legislative provision for civil partners.

4.4 The property rights of cohabitants

(a) Ownership of property

During their relationship and on relationship breakdown, the property rights of cohabiting couples, whether opposite-sex or same-sex, are governed by the general rules of property law. There are no special family law statutes as there are for married couples, civil partners and engaged couples (see 4.2 above). Cohabitants are in a particularly disadvantageous position on relationship breakdown as there is no discretionary jurisdiction, as there is on divorce or civil partnership dissolution, to adjust their property rights according to their needs and resources. A cohabitant is also in a vulnerable position on death if a deceased partner has made no will. For many years there has been discussion about reforming the law governing the property rights of cohabitants because of the perceived injustices they suffer, but these have been taken no further (see 3.4).

A cohabitant or former cohabitant who wishes to claim a share, or an enlarged share, of property will have to turn to the law of equity (trusts and proprietary estoppel – see 4.7 and 4.8) to bring a claim. Unlike disputes on divorce or on civil partnership dissolution, such claims are heard in the civil or chancery courts and from a property law, not a family law, perspective. Bringing a case is expensive and time-consuming, and the law of trusts is not entirely satisfactory for determining such disputes (see p. 62 above).

(b) Occupation of the family home

Unlike a spouse or civil partner (see 4.2 above), a cohabitant has no statutory right of occupation of the family home. Rights of occupation are instead dependent on a cohabitant having a beneficial estate or interest in, or a contractual licence to occupy, the home. A cohabitant or former cohabitant who is a victim of domestic violence can, however, apply for an occupation order under Part IV of the Family Law Act 1996 which, if granted, will give the applicant a right of occupation of the home for the duration of the order (see 5.5).

4.5 Ownership of personal property

Personal property is property other than land, such as, for example, investments and household goods. Ownership of such property depends on whether there is an interest under a contract or an interest in equity under a trust. As a general rule, title to the property passes to the purchaser, subject to there being a valid contract and no contrary intention. In the case of gifts of personal property, ownership passes to the donee if the donor intended to transfer the gift and it was handed over.

(i) Acquiring a right of ownership A person can claim an equitable interest in personal property under an express, resulting or constructive trust as the following cases show:

▶ *Paul v Constance* **[1977] 1 WLR 527**

The female claimant was held to have an interest by way of express trust in the bank account held in her cohabitant's sole name, as she had been authorised to draw on the account and he had told her on several occasions that the money in the account was as much hers as his.

▶ *Rowe v Prance* **[1999] 2 FLR 787**

The female claimant was held to be entitled to a half-share in a valuable yacht owned by her former partner with whom she had had a close relationship for 14 years. She had not contributed financially to its purchase, but her partner had referred to the yacht as 'our boat', had spoken of 'a share of the boat together' and had said 'your security is your interest in it'. The claimant had given up rented accommodation and put furniture in storage in order to move into the boat, which they intended to sail round the world together. The court accepted this evidence as sufficient to constitute the man as an express trustee of the boat, so that she was entitled to a share.

However, despite the successful outcome in the two cases above, cohabitants should be wary of taking a case to court and should instead attempt to settle any dispute. Taking a case to court is costly, time-consuming and unpredictable. In *Hammond v Mitchell* [1992] 1 FLR 229 Waite J said that cohabitants on relationship breakdown should be encouraged to do their best to settle disputes about personal property on the understanding that the court will usually divide such property equally.

(ii) Bank accounts   If a bank account is held in one person's name then any money in the account belongs to that person, unless there is a contrary intention or another person has made a contribution to the fund. If a bank account is held in joint names the money in the account belongs to both parties as beneficial joint tenants of the whole fund unless there is a contrary intention. With regard to the ownership of the money in a bank account, the court may hold that the money is owned in equal shares even though one of the parties put more money into the account (as it did in *Jones v Maynard* [1951] Ch 572 where the husband had put more money into the account than his wife but where the court held that they had pooled their resources). As a general rule, any property bought with funds from a bank account belongs to the purchaser. But if the parties had a common purpose and pooled their resources, the court may decide that the property belongs to them both.

4.6   Disputes about the family home

Disputes about property are often about the family home as it is not only a valuable asset but it also provides a roof over the family's head. Disputes about the home (and other property) may arise in the following situations:

- ▶ *On relationship breakdown*   Spouses and civil partners who cannot agree about ownership of the family home (and/or other property) can invoke the discretionary powers of the court on divorce or civil partnership dissolution to settle their property disputes on relationship breakdown (see Chapter 7). Cohabitants, on the other hand, must instead use the principles of property law, in particular the law of equity (see 4.7 and 4.8).
- ▶ *On death*   Where there is a will, then that determines the parties' property rights. Where there is no will, a surviving spouse or civil partner has a statutory right to succeed to the deceased's estate (see 4.12). Cohabitants, on the other hand, have no rights of succession (see 3.2) but they can bring a claim under the Inheritance (Provision for Family and Dependants) Act 1975 (see 4.13) or claim an interest in any property in equity under a trust (see 4.7) or on the basis of proprietary estoppel (see 4.8).
- ▶ *Where the interests are not defined*   Where there is no mention of the parties' respective interests on the transfer deed, the court may have to determine the matter (see p. 83 below).
- ▶ *Where a third party seeks possession*   Where a third party (such as a mortgagee or trustee in bankruptcy) seeks possession of the home, a spouse, civil partner, cohabitant (or other family member) may claim an interest in the home under a trust in order to defeat the claim to possession (see, for example, *Lloyds Bank plc v Rosset* [1990] 2 FLR 155, at p. 78 below).

A claim to establish an interest in the home (other than on divorce or dissolution of a civil partnership) is usually brought under section 14 of the Trusts of Land and

Appointment of Trustees Act 1996 (TLATA 1996). This is the mechanism which cohabitants use when bringing a claim to establish an interest in the home (see, for example, *Oxley v Hiscock* [2004] 2 FLR 669, at p. 80 below). The High Court and the county court also have jurisdiction to make declarations in respect of property rights, but the more usual practice is to use section 14 of TLATA 1996.

4.7   Acquiring a right of ownership in the family home under a trust

There are two sorts of ownership: ownership in law; and ownership in equity. A person can own property in law or equity; or in law and equity. Thus, for example, a cohabitant may be the legal owner of the family home but hold it on trust in equity for the other cohabitant as beneficiary. However, many spouses and cohabitants will own their home jointly as co-owners in both law and equity.

A person can claim a right of ownership in the family home under a trust even if there is nothing in writing to that effect. Thus, although writing is required for the creation of interests in land and declarations of trusts of land (see s 53(1) Law of Property Act (LPA) 1925), it is not required for the creation of an implied, resulting or constructive trust in respect of land (see s 53(2) LPA 1925). Similar rules apply in respect of contracts for the sale of land. Thus, while section 2(1) of the Law of Property (Miscellaneous Provisions) Act 1989 requires contracts for the sale of land to be in writing, section 2(5) provides that writing is not required for the creation of an implied, resulting or constructive trust of land. As section 2(5), like section 53(2) of the LPA 1925, was intended to allow a range of equitable remedies, an interest in land can also be claimed under the equitable doctrine of proprietary estoppel (*per* Beldam LJ in *Yaxley v Gotts and Gotts* [1999] 2 FLR 941, and see 4.8).

An interest in land, such as the family home, can be acquired under a resulting or constructive trust. These two types of trust are distinct and each has its own body of case-law.

(a)   Acquiring an interest in the family home under a resulting trust

A resulting trust arises as a presumption of equity where a person makes a financial contribution to the purchase of property (such as the family home or other property). In the absence of a contrary intention (for example, that the contribution was a gift or a loan, or that other shares were intended), a person who contributes money to the purchase of property acquires an interest under a resulting trust proportionate to that contribution. Resulting trusts were claimed in the following cases:

▶ *Sekhon v Alissa* **[1989] 2 FLR 94**

The house had been bought in the name of the defendant daughter. She had contributed to the purchase price, but her mother had paid the balance. The mother claimed a share in the house under a resulting trust, arguing that, although it was bought in her daughter's name, it was purchased as a joint commercial venture and they both intended to own it in proportion to their respective financial contributions. The daughter attempted to rebut the presumption of resulting trust by arguing that her mother's financial contribution was intended as a gift or a loan. The court had to decide what the actual or presumed intention of the parties was at the time of the conveyance. The question was whether the mother's financial contribution was a gift or an unsecured loan, or whether it was intended that she should have a beneficial interest in the property. The Court of Appeal held that the law presumed a resulting trust in the mother's favour, and, on the facts, the presumption was not rebutted by the daughter's allegation that the money was a gift or a loan.

▶ *Springette v Defoe* [1992] 2 FLR 388

The parties, two elderly cohabitants, had bought their council house, but there was nothing in the registered transfer quantifying their respective beneficial interests. Each party had paid half the mortgage instalments, but the claimant had paid most of the balance of the purchase price. When the relationship broke down she issued an originating summons claiming that she was entitled to 75 per cent of the proceeds of sale, as this represented her contribution to the purchase. At first instance, the trial judge granted the parties an equal share of the beneficial interest, on the basis that it was their uncommunicated belief or intention that they were to share the property equally. But the Court of Appeal allowed the applicant's appeal, holding that, as there was no discussion between the parties as to their respective beneficial interests, there was no evidence to rebut the presumption that she was entitled to a 75 per cent share of the beneficial interest under a resulting trust.

Despite the fact that the resulting trust was used in the above cases, most cases are brought on the basis of a constructive trust or proprietary estoppel. The demise of the resulting trust as a mechanism for claiming a share in the family home is due, in part, to the fact that a claimant who establishes a resulting trust obtains only a share proportionate to his or her contribution to the purchase price. Also, only a financial contribution to the initial purchase of property, not a contribution made after its purchase, can give rise to an interest under a resulting trust (see *Curley v Parkes* [2004] EWCA Civ 1515). In fact, both the House of Lords and the Supreme Court have held that the constructive trust is the more appropriate tool of analysis in cases regarding ownership of the family home (see *Stack v Dowden* and *Jones v Kernott*, pp. 83 and 84 below).

The presumption of advancement Under this presumption, a transfer of property from husband to wife and from parent to child is presumed to belong to the wife or child absolutely. It also applies to property purchased by a husband for his wife, or by a parent for a child. In other words, equity presumes that the transfer or purchase is an out-and-out gift. The presumption does not, however, apply to cohabitants (*Chapman v Jaume* [2012] EWCA Civ 476). The presumption can be used to rebut the presumption of resulting trust (for example, by a wife arguing that her husband's contribution to the purchase of the home was an out-and-out gift to her). However, it is regarded as a judicial instrument of last resort and one which can be easily rebutted (see, for example, *Laskar v Laskar* [2008] EWCA Civ 347, [2008] 2 FLR 589). As the presumption is considered to be archaic and discriminatory, and also in breach of Article 5 of Protocol 7 of the ECHR (equality of rights and responsibilities of spouses during marriage), it has little relevance today and is unlikely to be relied on. In fact, section 199 of the Equality Act 2010 will abolish the presumption, with prospective effect, when it comes into force.

(b) Acquiring an interest in the family home under a constructive trust

An interest in the family home can be claimed under a constructive trust or, more specifically, what is known as a 'common intention constructive trust' (to distinguish it from other types of constructive trust used in the commercial sphere). The court cannot find a constructive trust merely to do justice in a particular case. It must consider the evidence and ascertain what the intentions of the parties were. As Dillon LJ said in *Springette v Defoe* [1992] 2 FLR 388, the court cannot exercise a general discretion as to what the man in the street, on the general view of the case, might regard as fair. It cannot ascribe to parties intentions which they never had. Despite *obiter dicta* by Lord Walker and Baroness Hale in *Stack v Dowden* (see further at p. 83 below) that the courts should adopt a broader approach to the question of finding a common intention in constructive trusts cases involving the family home, the courts have not shown themselves willing to do so.

In a claim to a beneficial interest in the home under a constructive trust, the court conducts a two-stage exercise.

(i) The two-stage exercise   First, the court considers the evidence to establish whether or not the claimant has an interest under a constructive trust. Second, if there is such an interest, then the court considers all the evidence in order to decide what share of the beneficial interest the claimant should have. The leading case on constructive trusts is *Lloyds Bank plc v Rosset* in which Lord Bridge in the House of Lords (now the Supreme Court) laid down the approach to be adopted by the courts. This is still the approach adopted in constructive trust cases today.

▶ *Lloyds Bank plc v Rosset* [1990] 2 FLR 155

The home had been purchased in the husband's sole name. His wife had helped to renovate it, but she had made no financial contribution to its purchase or renovation. Mr Rosset charged the house to Lloyds Bank as security for a loan, which Mrs Rosset knew nothing about. When Mr Rosset went into debt, Lloyds Bank claimed possession of the home and an order for sale. Mrs Rosset, by way of defence to the bank's claim, argued that she had a beneficial interest in the house under a constructive trust and that this interest coupled with her actual occupation gave her an overriding interest under section 70(1)(g) of the Land Registration Act 1925 which would defeat the bank's claims. (The 1925 Act has now been repealed and replaced by the Land Registration Act 2002.)

The House of Lords, dismissing her appeal, held that her activities in relation to the renovation of the house were insufficient to justify the inference of a common intention that she was entitled to a beneficial interest under a constructive trust. Lord Bridge summarised and encapsulated the law as laid down in the two earlier House of Lords' decisions of *Pettitt v Pettitt* [1970] AC 777 and *Gissing v Gissing* [1971] AC 886, and referred also to the Court of Appeal decision in *Grant v Edwards* [1986] Ch 638 (the leading case on detriment).

LORD BRIDGE: 'The first and fundamental question which must always be resolved is whether, independently of any inference to be drawn from the conduct of the parties in the course of sharing the house as their home and managing their joint affairs, there has at any time prior to acquisition, or exceptionally at some later date, been any agreement, arrangement or understanding reached between them that the property is to be shared beneficially. The finding of an agreement or arrangement to share in this sense can only, I think, be based on evidence of express discussions between the partners, however imperfectly remembered and however imprecise their terms may have been. Once a finding to this effect is made it will only be necessary for the partner entitled to the legal estate to show that he or she has acted to his or her detriment or significantly altered his or her position in reliance on the agreement in order to give rise to a constructive trust or proprietary estoppel.

In sharp contrast to this situation is the very different one where there is no evidence to support a finding of an agreement or an arrangement to share, however reasonable it might have been for the parties to reach such an agreement if they had applied their minds to the question, and where the court must rely entirely on the conduct of the parties both as the basis from which to infer a common intention to share the property beneficially and as the conduct relied on to give rise to a constructive trust. In this situation direct contributions to the purchase price by the partner who is not the legal owner, whether initially or by payment of mortgage instalments, will readily justify the inference necessary to the creation of a constructive trust. But, as I read the authorities, it is at least extremely doubtful whether anything less will do.'

Lord Bridge's words in *Rosset* have formed the template of analysis in subsequent cases. Thus, in order to establish a constructive trust there must be evidence of a common intention *and* evidence of some act(s) of detrimental reliance undertaken on the basis of that common intention. A common intention can arise where there is an express agreement, arrangement or understanding that the property is to be shared beneficially. However, in a case involving an inference to share it will usually be difficult to establish a claim under a constructive trust where there has been no direct financial contribution to the purchase of the home (see dicta of Lord Bridge above). The outcome is likely to be different, however, in a joint-owner case where a case is brought to court in order to establish whether, and to what extent, one of the parties owns a share of the home under a constructive trust (see p. 83 below).

In *Oxley v Hiscock* [2004] EWCA Civ 546, [2004] 2 FLR 669 Chadwick LJ usefully summarised the correct approach to be adopted in cases where a claim is made to a beneficial interest under a constructive trust:

'[T]he first question is whether there is evidence from which to infer a common intention, communicated by each to the other, that each shall have a beneficial share in the property. In many such cases... there will have been some discussion between the parties at the time of the purchase which provides the answer to that question. Those are cases within the first of Lord Bridge's categories in *Lloyds Bank plc v Rosset*. In other cases – where the evidence is that the matter was not discussed at all – an affirmative answer will readily be inferred from the fact that each has made a financial contribution. These are cases within Lord Bridge's second category. And, if the answer to the first question is that there was a common intention, communicated to each other, that each should have a beneficial share in the property, then the party who does not become the legal owner will be held to have acted to his or her detriment in making a financial contribution to the purchase in reliance on the common intention.'

(ii) Indirect financial contributions   In *Rosset* Lord Bridge said that, on his reading of the authorities, he doubted whether anything less than a direct financial contribution to the purchase price by the partner who is not the legal owner, whether initially or by payment of mortgage instalments, would be sufficient to establish a share in the home where there was no express intention that the claimant should have a beneficial interest. Because of Lord Bridge's dicta, the courts in subsequent cases have been unwilling to accept indirect contributions (such as paying household bills or bringing up children) as evidence to establish an interest under a constructive trust. It has been suggested, however, that judges should be more willing to do so (see further at p. 81 below).

(iii) Detrimental reliance   In addition to proving a common intention, the claimant must also prove that he or she suffered some detriment as a result of relying on the common

intention. Detrimental reliance is usually fairly easily proved. Bringing up a family and running a home, for example, can be used as evidence of detriment. However, the act(s) of detrimental reliance must come *after* the establishment of a common intention (see *Churchill v Roach* [2004] 2 FLR 989, where the cohabitant's claim to property belonging to her deceased cohabitant's estate on the basis of a constructive trust failed, as the acts relied on as constituting detriment had occurred before the common intention was established).

(iv) Establishing the size of the beneficial interest   If the court finds that the claimant is entitled to a beneficial interest under a constructive trust, it must next determine the size of that interest. In *Midland Bank plc v Cooke* [1995] 2 FLR 915 (see below) the Court of Appeal held that a 'broad-brush' approach should be adopted by the court when deciding the size of the share. Thus, the court takes account of all the circumstances of the case, including financial and non-financial circumstances and the intentions of the parties. In *Oxley v Hiscock* [2004] EWCA Civ 546,[2004] 2 FLR 669 Chadwick LJ adopted a broad test based on fairness. This approach was approved by the House of Lords in *Stack v Dowden* and by the Supreme Court in *Jones v Kernott* (see further at pp. 83 and 84 below).

Constructive trusts of the family home: examples from the case-law

▶ *Midland Bank plc v Cooke* **[1995] 2 FLR 915**

The husband purchased the matrimonial home for £8,450, with £6,450 from a mortgage, £1,000 of his own savings and another £1,000 which was a wedding gift from his parents. His wife made no direct contribution to the purchase, except for the £500 which represented her half-share of the wedding gift, but she made considerable financial contributions to the upkeep of the house and to the household. She claimed a beneficial interest in the home. At first instance, the county court judge held that her beneficial interest in the house amounted to a sum equivalent to 6.47 per cent of the value of the property, representing her half-share of the wedding gift of £1,000. The Court of Appeal allowed her appeal, holding that, as she and her husband had agreed to share everything equally, including the house, she was entitled to half the beneficial interest. In respect of establishing the share of the beneficial interest, Waite LJ said that the court was permitted to undertake a survey of the whole course of dealing between the parties in respect of their ownership and occupation of the house and their sharing of its burdens and advantages.

▶ *Oxley v Hiscock* **[2004] EWCA Civ 546, [2004] 2 FLR 669**

The female cohabitant applied under section 14 of the Trusts of Land and Appointment of Trustees Act 1996 for a declaration that the proceeds of sale were held by the man on trust for the parties in equal shares. Chadwick LJ conducted an extensive review of the authorities, and held, in respect of calculating the share of the beneficial interest, that each party 'is entitled to that share which the court considers fair having regard to the whole course of dealing between them in relation to the property'. Applying the broad-brush approach adopted in *Midland Bank v Cooke* (above), the Court of Appeal held that a fair division of the sale of the property was 60 per cent to the man and 40 per cent to the woman, as equal division would have given insufficient weight to the disparity in the parties' financial contributions.

▶ *Cox v Jones* **[2004] 2 FLR 1010**

The claimant had made no direct financial contribution to the purchase price of the property in dispute which was owned by her cohabitant partner. She had made no contribution to the mortgage repayments, but she had spent time renovating it. Mann J found that there was an express arrangement between the parties that she was to have a share of the house, and that she had acted to her detriment by putting her practice as a barrister to one side to spend her time and energy on renovating the property that was to be their home. Mann J granted her a 25 per cent share of the beneficial interest in the property, applying dicta of Chadwick LJ in *Oxley v Hiscock* (above) that her share of the interest in the house must be 'fair having regard to the whole course of dealing between them in relation to the property'.

▶ *Hyett v Stanley* [2003] EWCA Civ 942, [2004] 1 FLR 394

The female cohabitant on the death of the male cohabitant was held to have a beneficial interest in the farm held in his name. The man's statement made in 1992 raised a clear inference that there was an understanding between him and the female applicant of a common intention that she was to have a beneficial interest in the farm. The detriment was assuming the risk of joint liability.

▶ *Walsh v Singh* [2009] EWHC 3219 (Ch), [2010]1 FLR 1658

The female claimant had been instrumental in finding the property that her former partner had purchased in his sole name and from his own resources, and she had carried out works to make the property habitable. She had also given up her career at the Bar at his request to concentrate on their equestrian business. After their relationship broke down, she failed to establish an interest in the home under a constructive trust and (and by way of proprietary estoppel) as there was no evidence of any financial contribution. It was held *inter alia* by the High Court that, although she had made significant contributions to the parties' project, she had not done so pursuant to any common intention or representation that she was to have a 50 per cent interest or any other interest in the property.

▶ *Thomson v Humphrey* [2009] EWHC 3576 (Ch), [2010] 2 FLR 107

The female cohabitant failed in her claim to a beneficial interest under a constructive trust in the former family home held in the sole name of her former cohabitant partner. Although she had given up her part-time job on the basis of assurances that he would look after her, and she had moved into his home with her children, Warren J dismissed her claim on the basis that the male cohabitant's instructions to his solicitor to draft a 'living together' agreement and his attempt to get the woman to sign it made it clear that he did not intend her to have any beneficial interest in the property. Even if there had been a common intention, Warren J held that she would not have established sufficient detriment: she had given up a poorly paid job with no prospects on an assurance that she would be looked after and not on an assurance that she would have a beneficial interest in the property.

All the above claims to a beneficial interest under a constructive trust were brought by cohabitants. Had they been married (or civil partners), then the court might, in the exercise of its discretion, have given them an interest in the home (see 7.7).

(v) Should the courts take a broader approach in constructive trust cases? Should courts in constructive trust cases be more willing to infer or impute a common intention as to the existence of a beneficial interest in the home? Should judges be willing to find evidence of intention not just from direct financial contributions but also from indirect contributions (such as paying household bills, looking after the home and bringing up children)? Although there have been calls for the courts to adopt a broader and more flexible approach than that adopted by Lord Bridge in *Rosset* and to take indirect contributions into account, the courts have been unwilling to do so because of the binding nature of *Rosset*. The Law Commission in its 2002 Report, *Sharing Homes* (see further at p. 64), Lord Walker and Baroness Hale *obiter dicta* in *Stack v Dowden* (2007) (see p. 83 below) and more recently the Supreme Court in *Jones v Kernott* (2011) (see p. 84 below) have recommended such an approach.

Baroness Hale, who gave the leading opinion in *Stack v Dowden*, said that imputed intentions were acceptable. Her Ladyship said that in her view Lord Bridge in *Rosset* might have 'set the hurdle rather too high in certain respects'. Her Ladyship was also of the opinion that the resulting trust was no longer the appropriate tool of analysis in such cases and that 'many more factors than financial contributions may be relevant to divining the parties' true intentions'. These views were subsequently endorsed by the Privy Council in *Abbott v Abbott* [2007] UKPC 53, [2008] 1 FLR 1451 where Lord Walker, commenting on Lord Bridge's words in *Rosset*, said: 'Whether or not Lord Bridge's observation was justified in 1990, in my opinion the law has moved on, and your Lordships should move it a little more in the same direction'. However, the more flexible approach recommended by Baroness Hale and Lord Walker has been held only to apply to the question of the quantification of a beneficial interest, not to the question of whether a beneficial interest exists in the first place.

The following case shows the courts continuing to use the principles laid down in *Rosset*. What was distinctive about the case, however, was that the male cohabitant owned the house *before* the female cohabitant moved in (it was a 'post-acquisition' case). It shows that, although discussions and conduct post-acquisition of the home can be considered by the court, an inferred intention that both parties are beneficial owners is unlikely to be readily drawn from conduct alone in the absence of any evidence of express agreement.

▶ *James v Thomas* [2007] EWCA Civ 1212, [2008] 1 FLR 1598

The male cohabitant was the sole legal and beneficial owner of the property (which prior to him owning it had been owned by his family for about 20 years). Three years after he acquired the house the female claimant moved in and they lived together as cohabitants. She helped him with his business, but all the expenses for the house were paid from his bank account. When she moved in she gave him £5,000 to pay a tax bill, but it was unclear whether this was a gift or a loan. During the relationship various statements were made to the effect that the improvements to the property 'would benefit them both'. When their relationship ended, she claimed an interest in the property on the basis of a constructive trust or proprietary estoppel. After her claim failed at first instance, she appealed to the Court of Appeal.

The Court of Appeal dismissed her appeal. Sir John Chadwick held that a common intention to found a constructive trust can arise post-acquisition and that an intention can be inferred from the whole course of dealing between the parties. However, he held that, in the absence of an express post-acquisition agreement, the court would be slow to infer from conduct alone that the parties intended to vary the beneficial interests established at the time of acquisition. The Court of Appeal held that the evidence was insufficient to establish a constructive trust expressly or by inference; and that, in any event, she had not acted to her detriment in reliance on the assurances by the defendant.

SIR JOHN CHADWICK: 'Miss J's interest in the property (if any) must be determined by applying principles of law and equity which (however inadequate to meet the circumstances in which parties live together in the twenty-first century) must now be taken as well-established.'

The approach in *James v Thomas* was applied in *Morris v Morris* [2008] EWCA Civ 257 (another 'post-acquisition' case) where the Court of Appeal found no express or inferred common intention to share the property in dispute. Gibson LJ, referring to Sir John Chadwick in *James v Thomas*, held that, although a common intention could be inferred from conduct, the court would be slow to infer a subsequent common intention from conduct alone. For a commentary on *James v Thomas* and *Morris v Morris*, see

Piska [2009] CFLQ 104, who states that, while they were correctly decided, the fact that both claimants received nothing seems harsh.

(c)   Joint-owner cases

Cases where the parties are joint owners of the family home are treated differently from cases where the family home is put into the name of one party only. As has been seen above, in sole-owner cases the court has first to decide whether it was intended that the non-owner should have any beneficial interest in the property at all; and then, if so, what that interest is. In joint-owner cases where there is no declaration of the beneficial interests in equity, on the other hand, all the court has to do is to ascertain the share of the beneficial interest. In such cases, *Stack v Dowden* (see further below) establishes that beneficial ownership of the property should follow the legal ownership unless there is a contrary intention. It also establishes that, in determining the parties' intentions, the court may consider a wide range of factors.

Although *Stack v Dowden* was the first case to go to the House of Lords involving a dispute between cohabitants about ownership of the family home, it offers little hope for cohabitants who are non-owners of the family home. Neither does the decision of the Supreme Court in *Jones v Kernott* (see below). This is because sole-owner and joint-owner cases are treated differently. This is despite the fact that Gardner and Davidson, commenting on *Stack v Dowden* ((2011) 127 LQR 12, at 15), expressed the hope that the Supreme Court would 'make clear that constructive trusts of family homes are governed by a single regime, dispelling any impression that different rules apply to 'joint names' and 'single name' cases'.

> ▶ *Stack v Dowden* [2007] UKHL 17, [2007] 1 FLR 1858
>
> The parties had cohabited for 20 years. The family home was registered in their joint names but the transfer deed contained nothing about their interests in equity, as they had failed to draw up a declaration of trust. The purchase price, other than the mortgage advance, had been provided by Ms Dowden. When the relationship broke down, Mr Stack left the house and Ms Dowden remained there with the children. Mr Stack successfully sought an order for sale of the property and was granted a 50:50 division of the proceeds of sale. The Court of Appeal allowed Ms Dowden's appeal and held that she was entitled to 65 per cent of the proceeds of sale (as she had made a greater financial contribution to the purchase of the house), applying the fairness test laid down by Chadwick LJ in *Oxley v Hiscock* (see p. 80 above). Mr Stack appealed to the House of Lords.
>
> The House of Lords unanimously dismissed his appeal (Lord Neuberger dissenting as to the reasoning) and held that, where a house is conveyed into joint names in the domestic consumer context, then *prima facie* joint and equal beneficial interests arise unless and until the contrary is proved. The burden was on the defendant to rebut the presumption by showing that equal beneficial shares were not intended. In the domestic context, factors other than financial contributions could be taken into account. Looking at the facts of the case, there were many factors to which the defendant could point to indicate that the intention of the parties was that the shares were not owned jointly in equity. For instance, when the property was bought, both parties knew that the defendant had paid more than the claimant, and they had kept their financial affairs separate. The defendant had therefore made good her case for a 65 per cent share.
>
> **BARONESS HALE**: 'The search is to ascertain the parties' shared intentions, actual, inferred or imputed, with respect to the property in the light of their whole course of conduct in relation to it.'

Thus the principle recognised in *Stack v Dowden* is that, if parties purchase a family home in joint names, then it is presumed that they also intended to own the property jointly in equity. (For applications of *Stack v Dowden*, see *Fowler v Barron* [2008] EWCA Civ 377, [2008] 2 FLR 831; and *Laskar v Laskar* [2008] EWCA Civ 347, [2008] 2 FLR 589.)

A common intention to share the beneficial interest can change over time

Stack v Dowden was considered by the Supreme Court in the following case, of *Jones v Kernott* which, like *Stack v Dowden*, involved the question of the size of the respective beneficial interests in a house which the cohabitant parties had bought in joint names. At first instance, the trial judge held, on the evidence, that the female cohabitant was entitled to 90 per cent of the beneficial interest in the former family home, following the fairness approach adopted in *Oxley v Hiscock* (see p. 80 above). The question for the Supreme Court was whether such an approach was consistent with *Stack v Dowden*, where the House of Lords had started from the premise that a conveyance into joint names meant that the beneficial interests in the property were joint and equal. The Supreme Court answered that question in the affirmative. In other words, even though a house is bought in joint names and it is presumed that there is a common intention that the beneficial interest is held equally, the court may hold that the intention has changed over time if that is fair in the circumstances of the case. Such an approach is much more like that adopted in property disputes on divorce.

▶ *Jones v Kernott* [2011] UKSC 53, [2012] 1 FLR 45

The parties, Mr Kernott and Ms Jones, were cohabitants. In 1985 they bought a house in joint names for £30,000. Ms Jones contributed £6,000, and the balance was raised by an interest-only mortgage. From this point on they shared payment of the household bills and the mortgage. In 1993, the couple separated, and Mr Kernott left the home where Ms Jones and their two children remained. Mr Kernott stopped paying his share of the bills, and contributed little or nothing towards the maintenance of the children. In 2006, Mr Kernott sought payment of his half-share of the former family home. Ms Jones responded by seeking a declaration under section 14 of the Trusts of Land and Appointment of Trustees Act 1996 that she owned the whole of the beneficial interest in the former family home.

At first instance, the judge in the county court held that Ms Jones and Mr Kernott were entitled to a 90 per cent and 10 per cent share of the beneficial interest in the property respectively for, although they had bought the property in joint names, and a presumption arose that they intended to jointly share the beneficial ownership, the common intention had changed over time. Mr Kernott's appeal to the High Court was dismissed.

Mr Kernott appealed successfully to the Court of Appeal which by a majority (Jacob LJ dissenting) declared that the parties owned the property as tenants in common in equal shares, applying *Stack v Dowden*. There was insufficient evidence to displace the presumption that they had intended to jointly share the beneficially equally. The passage of time was insufficient to do so, even if in the meantime Mr Kernott had acquired alternative accommodation and Ms Jones had paid all the outgoings on the former family home. Mr Kernott's share in the beneficial interest was therefore quantified at 50 per cent of the value of the property.

Ms Jones appealed to the Supreme Court, which unanimously allowed her appeal and reinstated the order of the county court judge. Lord Walker and Baroness Hale, who gave a joint leading opinion, held that the principle recognised in *Stack v Dowden* is that, if parties purchase a family home in joint names, then it is presumed that they also intended to own the property jointly in equity. However, this presumption may be rebutted by evidence that it was not, or it had ceased to be, the common intention of the parties to hold the property jointly. This may more readily be shown where, for example, the parties did not share their financial resources.

Although all the members of the Supreme Court were agreed on the outcome, their reasoning was different. Thus, whereas Lord Walker and Lady Hale were of the view that they were able to *infer* that the parties had intended a 90 per cent: 10 per cent share, Lords Kerr and Wilson, on the other hand, considered that there was insufficient evidence to infer what the parties had intended and that it was therefore necessary to *impute* that intention. It can be argued that such fine linguistic distinctions (between 'inferring' and 'imputing') create unnecessary complexity and make predicting the outcome of cases more difficult and uncertain.

4.8   Acquiring an interest by way of proprietary estoppel

Proprietary estoppel can be used to claim an interest in the family home (and is often used as an alternative to a claim based on a constructive trust).

Although the doctrines of constructive trust and proprietary estoppel are similar in that they are both equitable doctrines providing relief against unconscionable conduct, the doctrines are separate and distinct. An important distinction between the two doctrines is in respect of the remedy available. The existence of a constructive trust results in a right of ownership, whereas, if a proprietary estoppel is established, the court merely has a discretion as to the remedy to be ordered to do justice in the case.

The doctrine of proprietary estoppel was described by Balcombe LJ in *Wayling v Jones* [1995] 2 FLR 1029, at 1031, as follows:

> 'Where one person (A) has acted to his detriment on the faith of a belief, which was known to and encouraged by another person (B), that he either has or is going to be given a right in or over B's property, B cannot insist on his strict legal rights if to do so would be inconsistent with A's belief.'

Thus, to establish a proprietary estoppel the following must be proved: the existence of a promise or assurance that the claimant would acquire a proprietary interest in specified property; reliance by the claimant on that promise or assurance; and some detriment to the claimant caused by such reliance. These are overlapping concepts. Once these elements are proved, then the court has to decide in the exercise of its discretion what is necessary to avoid an unconscionable result. In so doing, it has a wide discretion. Each case, however, depends on its own particular facts.

In *Gillett v Holt and Another* [2000] 2 FLR 266 the Court of Appeal stated that, as proprietary estoppel is a flexible doctrine which is based on preventing unconscionable conduct, the facts must be looked at in the round. It held that detriment is not a narrow or technical concept, but one which must be approached as part of a broad inquiry, and that reliance and detriment should not be treated as being divided into separate watertight compartments.

What constitutes a promise or assurance for the purpose of establishing an estoppel?   In order to found an estoppel there must be a clear and unambiguous promise or assurance given by the defendant and relied on by the claimant. In *Thorner v Majors and Others* [2009] UKHL 18, [2009] 2 FLR 405 the House of Lords considered this requirement and held that the effect of the words or actions must be assessed in their context, and that it would be quite wrong to be unrealistically rigorous when applying the 'clear and unambiguous' test. It held that, if the statement relied on to found an estoppel was ambiguous, that ambiguity should not of itself deprive a person who had reasonably relied on the assurance of all relief, although any relief should be limited to the least beneficial interpretation.

What remedy to grant? Once an estoppel is proved, the court must consider all the circumstances of the case and exercise its discretion to decide what remedy to grant. A claim based on estoppel may not be so advantageous as one based on a trust, as the claimant may not gain a right of ownership, but merely a licence to occupy the property or financial compensation.

The following two cases provide examples where claims were made on the basis of proprietary estoppel:

▶ *Negus v Bahouse and Another* **[2007] EWHC 2628 (Ch). [2008] 1 FLR 381**

A cohabitant claimed that she had an interest by way of proprietary estoppel in a flat where she had lived with her deceased partner. Her claim failed, as the statements made by the deceased had been equivocal and were insufficient to amount to a specific agreement or understanding that she should have an interest. Nevertheless, it was held in the circumstances that the flat (plus a sum of £200,000) should be transferred to her under the Inheritance (Provision for Family and Dependants) Act 1975 (see 4.13).

▶ *Suggitt v Suggitt* **[2011] EWHC 903 (Ch), [2011] 2 FLR 875**

The claimant claimed an interest in his deceased father's estate (a large farming business) on the basis of proprietary estoppel. His claim was successful. The court held that the claimant's father had made some kind of repeated promise or assurance which had led the claimant reasonably to expect that the farmland and somewhere to live would definitely be his after his father's death. With respect to reliance, the claimant had worked from time to time on the farm for no wage in the expectation and reliance that the farmland would one day be his. Thus, he had acted in some way to his detriment or changed his position in reliance on the promises made by the deceased. Looking at matters in the round, it would be unconscionable to deprive the claimant of his expectation based on his deceased father's assurances. The equity would be satisfied by granting him the farmland and a house in which to live.

4.9 A claim based on contract

An interest in property may be acquired under a contract, provided the legal requirements for creating a valid contract are satisfied. If a contract is for the sale or disposition of land it must be in writing (s 2(1) Law of Property (Miscellaneous Provisions) Act 1989), but this requirement does not prevent the creation of a resulting or constructive trust, or the creation of an interest by way of proprietary estoppel. The following cases are examples:

▶ *Tanner v Tanner* **[1975] 1 WLR 1341**

The claimant purchased a house for occupation by the defendant, his female partner, and their children. The claimant moved into the house, but when the relationship broke down the applicant sought possession on the basis that the defendant was only a bare licensee under a licence which he had revoked. The Court of Appeal held that there was an implied contractual licence under the terms of which the defendant was entitled to occupy the house while the children were of school age, or until some other circumstance arose which would make it unreasonable for her to remain in possession.

> ▶ *Layton v Martin* **[1986] 2 FLR 277**
>
> The Court of Appeal held that there was no intention to create a legally enforceable contract, with the result that the claimant mistress failed in her claim against the deceased's estate even though she had accepted the man's offer that, if she were to live with him, he would give her emotional security, and also financial security on his death. Despite living with him for five years after he had made the offer, and for 13 years in total, her claim failed.

4.10   Tenancies

(a)   Transferring a tenancy

Under section 53 and Schedule 7 of Part IV of the Family Law Act 1996, the High Court and the county court have jurisdiction to transfer tenancies on divorce, dissolution of a civil partnership, and on the breakdown of cohabitation.

A tenancy is transferred by the court making a 'Part II order' which it has power to make whether a spouse, civil partner or cohabitant is solely or jointly entitled under a tenancy, provided the house was a matrimonial home in the case of a married couple, a civil partnership home in the case of civil partners, or, in the case of cohabitants, was a home in which the cohabiting couple lived together as husband and wife (paras 2 and 3 of Sch 7 and s 62(1)). Paragraph 1 of Schedule 7 makes it clear that 'cohabitant' includes a former cohabitant. There is no requirement that cohabitants must have lived together for a minimum period, although the court is required to take into account the length of the relationship when deciding whether or not to order a transfer.

In determining whether to make a Part II order, and, if so, in what manner, the court must consider all the circumstances of the case including: the circumstances in which the tenancy was granted, or the circumstances in which either of them became a tenant; the housing needs and housing resources of the parties and of any relevant child; their respective financial resources; the likely effect of any order (or no order) on the health, safety or well-being of the parties and of any relevant child; the conduct of the parties in relation to each other and otherwise; and the suitability of the parties as tenants (see para 5).

Where the parties are cohabitants and only one of them is entitled to occupy the house under the tenancy, the court must also consider (see para 5): the nature of their relationship; the length of time they have lived together as husband and wife; whether there are any children who are children of both parties or for whom both parties have or have had parental responsibility; and the length of time that has elapsed since the parties ceased to live together (see para 5). Where the parties are council tenants, the housing policy of the local housing authority is another factor which the court can take into account.

(b)   Succeeding to a tenancy on the death of a tenant

See 4.14 below.

4.11   Homelessness and the family

Homelessness can arise in many different situations. A victim of domestic violence may be forced to leave the family home. A child leaving care may have no accommodation. A family relationship may break down and one of the parties may have to move out of the home. According to figures published by the Department of Communities and Local Government on 14 June 2012, the number of people in England officially classed as homeless in 2012 increased by 14 per cent on figures for 2011, the largest increase for nine years (see *Statutory Homelessness: October – December Quarter 2011, England*, available at www.communities.gov.uk).

Persons who are homeless can apply to their local housing authority (LHA) for public sector housing. LHAs are responsible for managing, regulating and controlling housing vested in them, and have statutory duties and powers towards homeless persons under Part VII of the Housing Act 1996 (as amended by the Homelessness Act 2002). When exercising their duties and powers, LHAs must comply with the *Homelessness Code of Guidance for Local Authorities* (2006) (ss 169(1) and 182(1) Housing Act 1996). They also have statutory duties to work jointly with LHAs, social services and other statutory, voluntary and private sector partners. Thus, for instance, if homelessness persists, any children in the family could be in need and the family could seek assistance from social services who have powers and duties under the Children Act 1989 in such circumstances (see further in Chapter 14).

The duties and powers of LHAs vary depending on whether an applicant is unintentionally or intentionally homeless (s 191), and on whether or not the applicant has a priority need (s 189(1)) In some cases there is merely a duty to provide advice. In others there is a full housing duty to provide accommodation.

Housing and human rights As LHAs are public authorities under section 6 of the Human Rights Act 1998, they must ensure that they exercise their powers and duties in line with the European Convention for the Protection of Human Rights (ECHR). For example, in *R (Morris) v Westminster City Council* [2004] EWCH 2191 (Admin) it was held that the LHA had breached the applicant mother's rights under Articles 8 and 14 as it had refused to treat her as having a priority need for accommodation. A decision by a LHA which deprives a person of accommodation must be lawful, necessary and proportionate otherwise it may breach the right to family life. Loss of a home is regarded as an extreme form of interference with that right (see *McCann v UK (Application No 19009/04)* [2008] 2 FLR 899, where the ECtHR held that the UK was in breach of Article 8 in respect of the duties owed by LHAs and the courts under the housing legislation).

(a) Local housing authority duties

Under Part VII of the Housing Act 1996 local housing authorities (LHAs) must provide assistance for certain eligible persons who are homeless or threatened with homelessness. LHAs have a range of duties depending on the circumstances of the applicant, which include, for instance: making enquiries to establish whether a housing duty is owed (s 184); providing advice, information and/or assistance (ss 179 and 190); providing interim accommodation (s 188); providing temporary accommodation (s 192); and making sure an applicant's accommodation does not cease to be available (s 195).

(b) When is a person homeless?

Persons are homeless if they have no accommodation available for their occupation in the UK or they have accommodation which is a movable structure and there is no place where the applicant is entitled to place it and reside in it (see s 175).

A person who has accommodation is treated as being homeless if it would not be reasonable for him or her to continue to occupy that accommodation (s 175(3)). Domestic (or other) violence may provide a reason for not continuing to occupy accommodation (s 177).

(c)　The full housing duty

The full housing duty (see ss 193 and 195), which is to secure suitable accommodation or to take reasonable steps to prevent the loss of accommodation, is owed only to eligible persons who have a priority need for accommodation and who are not intentionally homeless.

(i) Priority need (section 189)　The categories of applicants who qualify as having a priority need have been extended over the years. Persons who have a priority need include, for example: pregnant women; persons with dependent children; persons who are vulnerable due to old age, mental illness, handicap, disability; persons under 21 who were formerly in care of the local authority; and persons who are vulnerable due to domestic violence or threats of domestic violence.

(ii) Intentionality (section 191)　A LHA has no duty to provide accommodation to persons who are intentionally homeless, but special rules apply in cases of domestic and other violence (see below).

A LHA can satisfy the full housing duty by providing accommodation from its own stock or by arranging for it to be provided by a housing association or a landlord in the private sector. However, a LHA must provide 'suitable' accommodation. In *R v Ealing London Borough Council ex parte Surdona* [1999] 1 FLR 650, for example, the duty to provide accommodation was not discharged by providing accommodation for a family in separate dwellings, as families should be able to live together as a unit.

(d)　Referral to another local housing authority – the local connection

A LHA has a right to pass the housing duty on to another LHA if the applicant (or any person who might reasonably be expected to reside with the applicant) has no local connection with the LHA to which the application was made but has a local connection with the district of the other LHA, although it cannot do so if there is a risk of domestic or other violence (s 198).

(e)　Domestic violence and other violence

Applicants who are forced to leave their home due to actual or threatened domestic or other violence are not treated as being intentionally homeless (see s 177(1)). Violence is only 'domestic' if the victim and perpetrator are 'associated persons' (s 177(1A)), as defined in section 178. The definition is the same as that used for associated persons in the family law domestic violence legislation (see p. 120). Domestic violence is not defined in the Housing Act 1996 but in the following case the Supreme Court held that it is not restricted to physical violence but can include other forms of abuse, such as psychological and emotional abuse:

> ▶ *Yemshaw v Hounslow London Borough Council* [2011] UKSC 3, [2011] 1 FLR 1614
>
> Mrs Yemshaw claimed that she had been forced to leave the matrimonial home with her two young children and seek accommodation in a women's refuge because of domestic violence on the part of her husband. She applied to the defendant LHA for housing, claiming that, although her husband had not hit her, she was frightened that he might do. She claimed that his controlling behaviour amounted to emotional, psychological and financial abuse and that, as this was domestic violence, she was therefore homeless and eligible for priority assistance from the LHA. The defendant LHA, however, decided that she was not homeless as she had left the home voluntarily in circumstances where she had not been the victim of domestic violence.
>
> Mrs Yemshaw's appeal to the Court of Appeal was dismissed, as it considered itself bound by the decision in *Danesh v Kensington and Chelsea Royal London Borough Council* [2006] EWCA Civ 1404 in which it had been held that 'violence' meant only physical violence.
>
> Mrs Yemshaw appealed to the Supreme Court which unanimously allowed her appeal and held that the meaning of 'domestic violence' in section 177 of the Housing Act 1996 was not restricted to physical contact, but included other forms of abuse, such as psychological and emotional abuse. The Supreme Court also overturned the decision in *Danesh* (see above). Baroness Hale, who gave the leading opinion, stated that 'domestic violence' 'includes physical violence, threatening or intimidating behaviour and any other form of abuse which, directly or indirectly, may give rise to the risk of harm'.
>
> (For a case comment on *Yemshaw*, see Knight [2012] CFLQ 95.)

The *Homelessness Code of Guidance* contains guidance on domestic violence and other forms of violence. In fact, as in *Yemshaw* (above), it adopts a wide and flexible approach to the meaning of these terms (see para 8).

Referral to another LHA is not permitted if there is a risk of violence or domestic violence to the applicant in the area of that other housing authority (s 198). Also, a victim of domestic violence who is living in a refuge is deemed not to be intentionally homeless (see *Birmingham City Council v Ali; Moran v Manchester City Council* [2009] UKHL 36; and the *Homelessness Code of Guidance*, para 16.27).

(f)　Homeless families with children

(i) The duty to dependent children　If there are dependent children an applicant has a priority need and the LHA has a duty to provide accommodation for the family, provided the applicant is eligible for assistance and is not intentionally homeless (above). The *Homelessness Code of Guidance* provides that a child need not be wholly and exclusively dependent on the applicant and/or wholly and exclusively resident with the applicant. Dependent children need not necessarily be the applicant's own children, but there must be a parent–child relationship. The child does not need to have full-time residence with the applicant. Neither does it necessarily matter that the parents are sharing care of the child in different houses (see further below), for, according to the *Guidance*, LHAs should understand that it is usually in the best interests of children to maintain a relationship with both parents.

(ii) Intentional homelessness　There is no duty to provide accommodation for intentionally homeless families with children, but they are entitled to advice and assistance and temporary accommodation. If homelessness continues, the children may be in need for

the purposes of Part III of the Children Act (CA)1989, and help can be sought from a local authority social services department. LHAs must have arrangements in place to ensure that social services are alerted as quickly as possible where the applicant has children aged under 18 and the LHA considers that the applicant may be intentionally homeless (s 213A HA 1996). If social services decide that the child's needs would be best met by helping the family to obtain accommodation, they can ask the LHA for reasonable assistance in this matter and the LHA must respond (s 27 CA 1989).

(iii) Housing applications by children are not permitted   A child cannot apply for local authority housing if the child's parent has made an application and it has failed (see *R v Oldham Metropolitan Borough Council ex parte G and Related Appeals* [1993] AC 509).

(iv) The relationship between the housing legislation and the Children Act 1989   Local housing departments and local authority social services departments are required to work together when dealing with cases of homelessness involving children (s 213A HA 1996). However, there is no guarantee that a social services department will find housing for families where they do not qualify for housing under the housing legislation, as section 17(6) of the Children Act 1989 gives local authorities the power, not the duty, to provide accommodation (see *R (G) v Barnet London Borough Council; R (W) v Lambeth London Borough Council; R (A) v Lambeth London Borough Council* [2004] 1 FLR 454 at p. 175 in Chapter 14).

Under section 13 of the Homelessness Act 2002, LHAs are required to refer homeless persons with dependent children (who are ineligible for homelessness assistance, or who are intentionally homeless) to social services, provided the person consents. If homelessness persists, any child in the family could be in need. In such cases, if social services decide the child's needs would be best met by helping the family to obtain accommodation, they can ask the LHA for reasonable assistance in this, and it must respond.

(vi) Housing homeless teenage children   In *R (G) v Southwark London Borough Council* [2009] UKHL 26, [2009] 2 FLR 380 the House of Lords held that a local authority's children's services unit could not purport to have fulfilled its duties to look after a homeless child under the Children Act 1989 merely by referring the child to a homeless persons' unit under Part VII of the Housing Act 1996. Thus, social services working with children cannot 'pass the buck' by transferring their responsibilities to the LHA if a child or young person is a person to whom an accommodation duty is owed under section 20 of the Children Act 1989.

(vii) Housing and residence orders   The existence of a residence order in favour of an applicant for housing is a highly material consideration for a LHA when exercising its powers and duties under the Housing Act 1996, but it is not the only factor to be taken into account and will not be the determinative factor as to the allocation of housing.

(viii) Housing and shared residence orders   Cases have sometimes arisen with respect to the duties of a LHA when a shared residence order has been made under the Children Act 1989 (see pp. 289–92). Thus, for instance, in *R (Bibi) v Camden London Borough Council* [2005] 1 FLR 413 the parents had a 50/50 shared residence order, but whereas the defendant LHA had given the father a three-bedroom house it had offered the mother only one-bedroom accommodation. In judicial review proceedings brought by the

mother, Davis J quashed the decision of the LHA on the ground that it was flawed, as it had failed to address the question of the position of the children with regard to the mother's own housing needs.

The following case dealt with the question of whether a parent who is the subject of a 50/50 shared residence order has a priority need under the housing legislation. The decision, which dealt with the interface between the housing legislation and family proceedings cases, shows that it is ultimately the decision of the LHA which prevails in cases where a shared residence order is in force. The decision may therefore cast doubt on the decision in *R (Bibi)* (above).

▶ *Holmes-Moorhouse v London Borough of Richmond-upon-Thames* **[2009] UKHL 7, [2009] 1 FLR 904**

Before their separation the appellant father and the mother lived with their four children in council accommodation. By consent the judge in family proceedings made a shared residence order (that the three younger children should spend alternate weeks and half of each school holiday with each parent); and an order that the father should leave the family home. The father's application for housing on the basis that he had a priority need as he had dependent children who might reasonably be expected to reside with him (s 189(1)(b) HA 1996) was rejected by the LHA on the basis that he was not in priority need (as the children would merely be staying, rather than residing, with him). He challenged the decision. He failed at first instance but the Court of Appeal allowed his appeal. The LHA appealed to the House of Lords.

The House of Lords allowed the LHA's appeal and restored the decision of the county court judge, holding *inter alia* that:

▶ A shared residence order did not oblige a LHA to regard a homeless parent as being in priority need on the ground that dependent children might reasonably be expected to reside with that parent. It was for the LHA under Part VII of the Housing Act 1996, not the family courts, to decide whether it was reasonable that a child who already had a home with a parent should also be able to reside with the other parent. The LHA could take into account the wishes of the parents and children and the court's opinion that shared residence would be in the interests of the children, but it was nonetheless entitled to decide that it was not reasonable to expect children who were not in any sense homeless to be able to live with both the mother and father in separate accommodation.
▶ In accordance with the *Homelessness Code of Guidance for Local Authorities* (2002), it would only be in exceptional circumstances that it would be reasonable to expect a child who had a home with one parent to be provided, under Part VII, with another so that he could reside with the other parent as well.
▶ The LHA's reviewing officer had therefore been entitled to conclude that, in the context of the duty of the authority to make provision for the homeless, the children could not reasonably be expected to live with the father as well as the mother.

Baroness Hale was of the opinion that the shared residence order should not have been made in the first place. Her Ladyship said that orders made by the family court were meant to provide practical solutions to the practical problems faced by separating families and were not meant to be aspirational statements of what would be best in some ideal world and which had little prospect of realisation. It was one thing to make a shared residence order when each parent had a home to offer the children, but another thing entirely when the other parent had no accommodation at all. Family courts could not conjure up resources where none existed and could not order or put pressure on public agencies to do so.

Both Lord Hoffman and Baroness Hale emphasised the different roles played by family courts and LHAs, and the fact that decisions made under Part VII of the Housing Act 1996 must have regard to wider considerations than the welfare of the relevant children (for instance the limited availability of public housing stock). Both Lord Hoffman and Baroness Hale were of the opinion that only in exceptional circumstances would it be reasonable to expect that, when a child has a home with one parent, the other parent would also be provided with housing under Part VII of the Housing Act 1996.

4.12   The devolution of property on death

(a)   Making a will

There is complete freedom of testamentary disposition in England and Wales. In other words, adult persons of sound mind may make a will disposing of their property to whomsoever they choose. Thus, there is no legal obligation on spouses, civil partners or cohabitants to leave their property to the other spouse, civil partner or cohabitant. Neither is there any obligation on parents to leave their property to their children. For example, in *Ilott v Mitson & Ors* [2011] EWCA Civ 346 the deceased mother made no provision in her will for her only daughter but left her whole estate to a range of animal and bird charities. This is quite different to the law in some other jurisdictions (such as in countries in Europe) where is not possible to disinherit certain family members, such as a spouse or child. The position with respect to family members in England and Wales, however, is somewhat mitigated in that family members can, in certain circumstances, apply for reasonable financial provision out of a deceased family member's estate under the Inheritance (Provision for Family and Dependants) Act 1975 (see 4.13).

A will is valid if it is made in writing and signed by the person making it in the presence of at least two witnesses, each of whom must attest and sign the will, or acknowledge the signature of the person making it (ss 7 and 9 Wills Act 1837). A will is revoked by the testator's (or testatrix's) marriage or civil partnership, unless it was made in contemplation of marriage or civil partnership to a particular person and the testator (testatrix) did not intend the will to be revoked (ss 18 and 18B Wills Act 1837). In the case of divorce or nullity, or dissolution or annulment of a civil partnership, then, subject to any contrary intention in the will, any legacies and gifts to a former spouse or former civil partner lapse. However, a former spouse or former civil partner may still make a claim for reasonable financial provision from the deceased's estate under the Inheritance (Provision for Family and Dependants) Act 1975 (see 4.13).

According to research, about one-half to two-thirds of adults in England and Wales do not make a will (see para 1.3, *Intestacy and Family Provision Claims on Death*, Law Com No. 331).

(b)   Devolution of property on the intestacy of spouses and civil partners

The law of intestacy determines what happens to property that is not disposed of by will. If a spouse or civil partner dies intestate (without making a will), the inheritance rights of the surviving spouse or civil partner depend on the size of the estate and whether or not the deceased has children or other relatives. In outline, the estate (after the payment of debts and expenses) is distributed or held on trust according to the following rules laid down in the Administration of Estates Act 1925 (as amended):

▶ *If there is a surviving spouse/civil partner, and children* The spouse/civil partner inherits the personal chattels, the first £250,000 and a life interest in half of what is left. The children of the deceased share between them half of what is left straight away (if they are 18 or over), and the other half when the surviving parent dies.

▶ *If there is a surviving spouse/civil partner and relatives, but no children* The spouse/civil partner inherits the personal chattels, the first £450,000 and half of what is left. The parents of the deceased or, if the parents have died, the brothers and sisters or their descendants, share the other half of what is left.

▶ *If there is a surviving spouse/civil partner, but no other relatives* The surviving spouse/civil partner inherits everything.

▶ *If there are children, but no surviving spouse/civil partner* The children share everything equally.

▶ *If there is no spouse/civil partner or children* Everything passes to the next available group of relatives.

▶ *If there are no available relatives* Everything goes to the State.

Rights in the family home Where the family home was owned by the spouses or civil partners as beneficial joint tenants, it devolves to the surviving spouse or civil partner. Where it was owned by them as tenants in common, the deceased's share forms part of the estate and passes according to the will or according to the laws of intestacy. On intestacy, however, the Intestates' Estates Act 1952 allows a surviving spouse or civil partner in certain circumstances to retain the home.

(c) Cohabitants on intestacy

Where a cohabitant dies without making a will there are no provisions equivalent to those above. Thus, a surviving cohabitant has no automatic right to succeed to a deceased partner's estate whatever the length of the relationship. Instead, the estate passes to the children, or otherwise to the parent(s) of the deceased. This is with the exception of any property which was jointly owned by the parties as joint tenants (such as the home or a bank account) where ownership passes to the survivor. As cohabitants are in a vulnerable position on intestacy, it is particularly important for cohabitants to make a will.

A cohabitant can, however, make a claim for reasonable financial provision against the deceased partner's estate under the Inheritance (Provision for Family and Dependants) Act 1975 (see 4.13). An alternative is to make a claim by way of a trust (see 4.7) or on the basis of proprietary estoppel (see 4.8). For example, in *Hyett v Stanley* [2003] EWCA Civ 942, [2004] 1 FLR 394 a cohabitant was held to be entitled to an interest in her deceased partner's estate under a constructive trust arising as a result of a statement he had made during his lifetime. (See also *Negus v Bahouse and Another* [2007] EWHC 2628 (Ch), [2008] 1 FLR 381 at p. 86 in Chapter 3.)

The Law Commission has proposed that certain cohabiting couples should have the same rights on intestacy as spouses and civil partners (see p. 58 in Chapter 3).

4.13 The Inheritance (Provision for Family and Dependants) Act 1975

(a) Introduction

Under the Inheritance (Provision for Family and Dependants) Act 1975 the court can make financial provision orders for certain family members and dependants out of a deceased person's estate where the deceased has failed under his or her will or under the laws of intestacy (or both) to make reasonable financial provision for the applicant. The Act applies if the deceased was domiciled in England and Wales at the time of death (s 1(1)). An application must be brought within six months of the date on which probate or letters of administration were taken out, or otherwise with the permission of the court (s 4).

The Act is concerned with dependency; it is not concerned with deciding how the assets should be fairly divided (*per* Goff LJ in *Re Coventry (Deceased)* [1980] Ch 461). In *Jelley v Iliffe and Others* [1981] Fam 128 Stephenson LJ said that the purpose of the Act is to remedy 'wherever reasonably possible, the injustice of one who has been put by a deceased person in a position of dependency upon him, being deprived of any financial support, either by accident or by design of the deceased, after his death'.

A two-stage exercise When considering an application, the court adopts a two-stage exercise. First (under section 3 of the Act) it has to make an objective assessment of the facts to establish whether or not the deceased made reasonable financial provision for the applicant. If the answer is 'no', then the court must next consider to what extent (if at all) it should exercise its powers to make financial provision under the Act. The first part of the exercise involves a value judgment, the second a question of discretion. When conducting the two-stage exercise the court must take into account a range of factors laid down in sections 2 and 3 of the Act (see p. 104 below). If the court decides to make an order, it has a wide discretion under section 2 as to the nature of the order(s) it can make.

When conducting the two-stage exercise, the court draws a distinction between spouses (and civil partners) and other applicants. Spouses and civil partners are treated much more favourably than other applicants under the Act.

(b) Applicants

(i) Applications by spouses and civil partners (and former spouses and civil partners) The spouse or civil partner of the deceased can apply for reasonable financial provision (s 1(1)(a)), including someone who in good faith entered into a void marriage or void civil partnership (ss 25(4) and 25(4A)). This includes a former spouse or a former civil partner, provided that that person has not entered into a subsequent marriage or civil partnership (s 1(1)(b)). The court must consider the applicant's age, the duration of the marriage or civil partnership, and the applicant's contribution to the welfare of the family, including any contribution made by looking after the home or caring for the family (s 3(2)).

The divorce/dissolution comparison In addition to the above factors, the court must take into account the award the applicant spouse (civil partner) might have expected to receive had the marriage (or civil partnership) been terminated by divorce (or dissolution) not death (s 3(2)) (otherwise known as the 'divorce cross-check'). In *Fielden and Another v Cunliffe* [2006] 1 FLR 745, which is the leading case, the Court of Appeal held that there was no reason why the principles laid down by the House of Lords in *White v White* [2000] UKHL 54, [2000] 2 FLR 981 (see 7.6) should not be applied to a claim by a spouse under the 1975 Act, but that caution was necessary when considering the *White* cross-check of equality. This was because a deceased spouse is free to bequeath his or her estate to whomsoever he or she pleases and the only statutory obligation under the 1975 Act is to make *reasonable* financial provision for the surviving spouse, to which the concept of equality may bear little relation (*per* Wall LJ). Thus, in *Fielden and Another v Cunliffe*, the Court of Appeal allowed the executors' appeal and reduced the amount of financial provision awarded to the surviving spouse from £800,000 to £600,000, as the judge had wrongly applied the principle in *White* (having presumed a starting point of a 50:50 split of the estate).

However, each case depends on its facts; and the Court of Appeal has stated that the 'hypothetical divorce' approach in section 3(2) is only one of the factors for the court to consider, and any decision is subject to the overriding consideration of what is reasonable in all the circumstances (*Re Krubert (Deceased)* [1997] 1 FLR 42). In *Lilleyman v Lilleyman* [2012] EWHC 821 (Ch), a 'big money' short marriage case, Briggs J confirmed that the 'hypothetical divorce' check should be treated as 'neither a floor nor a ceiling in relation to the relief available under the Inheritance Act, nor as something which requires a meticulous quasi-divorce application to be analysed side by side with the application of the separate provisions in section 3 of the Act'. Briggs J stated that the 'divorce cross-check is just that, a cross-check, no more and no less'. Taking into account the assets already held by the widow of the deceased, the claimant was awarded £500,000 out of a total estate of £6 million. (For other cases involving a claim by a spouse see, for example, *Barron v Woodhead* [2008] EWHC 810, and *Baker v Baker* [2008] 2 FLR 1956.)

Awards are not limited to maintenance   Spouses and civil partners are in a better position than cohabitants (see below), as a claim by a spouse or civil partner is not limited to maintenance (s 1(2)(a)).

Provisions relating to divorce, nullity, separation and dissolution of a civil partnership   Where an applicant spouse has applied for ancillary relief under section 23 or section 24 of the Matrimonial Causes Act 1973 (whether or not those proceedings have been determined by the date of death), the court can consider the application under the 1975 Act as if the decree of divorce or nullity had not been made absolute, but only if the decree of divorce or nullity was granted no more than 12 months prior to the application (s 14). Similar provisions apply to judicial separation (ss 14(1), (2)) and to dissolution, nullity and separation in respect of a civil partnership (s 14A).

As part of the 'clean break' policy on divorce (see 7.5), the divorce court on or after the grant of a decree nisi of divorce can, on the application of either spouse, make an order (where it is just to do so) prohibiting the other spouse from making an application under the 1975 Act on the applicant's death (s 15). This power can also be exercised in the case of a decree of nullity, judicial separation or presumption of death. The court has the same powers in respect of a civil partnership order (s 15ZA). This rule also applies to ancillary relief orders made after an overseas divorce or civil partnership dissolution (or after an overseas annulment or separation) (ss 15A and 15B).

If an applicant spouse or civil partner is entitled to secured periodical payments (under Part II of the MCA 1973 or Schedule 5 to the CPA 2004), the court may, on application, vary or discharge the periodical payments order or revive the operation of any provision thereof which has been suspended under section 31 MCA 1973 or Part 2 of Schedule 5 CPA 2004 (s 16).

A maintenance agreement between the applicant and the deceased providing for maintenance on and after death can be varied or revoked (s 17). The court can in certain circumstances set aside a disposition made by the deceased within six years of death with the intention of defeating an application under the 1975 Act (s 10). Where a contract was made by the deceased without full valuable consideration with the intention of defeating an application for financial provision under the 1975 Act, the court can direct the personal representatives not to pass or transfer the whole or part of any money or property involved (s 11).

(ii) Applications by cohabitants The surviving cohabitant (opposite-sex or same-sex) of the deceased can apply (s 1(1)(ba)). An application is sometimes made by a cohabitant who has failed to establish an interest under a trust or by way of proprietary estoppel (see, for example, *Negus v Bahouse* [2007] EWHC 2628 (Ch), [2008] 1 FLR 381 and *Webster v Webster* [2009] 1 FLR 1240 – both claims were successful under the 1975 Act).

A 'cohabitant' is defined in the Act as a person who was living in the same household as the deceased during the whole period of two years ending immediately before the date of the deceased's death, and was living as the husband or wife or civil partner of the deceased (ss 1(1A) and 1(1B)). As this definition does not include a former cohabitant, a former cohabitant will have to apply under section1(1)(e) (see p. 98 below) as a person being maintained by the deceased.

Whether the applicant and the deceased were living together in the same household is a question of fact. In *Re Watson (Deceased)* [1999] 1 FLR 878 Neuberger J held that, when considering the definition of cohabitant, the court should 'ask itself whether, in the opinion of a reasonable person with normal perceptions, it could be said that the two people in question were living together as husband and wife'.

Occasional periods of separation may be permitted (see *Gully v Dix* [2004] EWCA Civ 139, [2004] 1 FLR 918 where the applicant was held to be a cohabitant even though she had separated from the deceased for the last three months of his life, due to his intolerable behaviour). But each case depends on its own facts. In the following two cases the applicants were held not to be cohabitants for the purposes of the Act: *Churchill v Roach* [2004] 2 FLR 989 (the applicant had not lived with the deceased for the full two-year period); and *Baynes v Hedger* [2009] EWCA Civ 374, [2009] 2 FLR 767 (the applicant had not been living in the same household as the deceased as the parties had had two separate houses and two separate economies).

Maintenance provision only Cohabitants are in a disadvantageous position compared with spouses and civil partners as the court is limited to making orders for their maintenance, although 'maintenance' may be interpreted flexibly (as it was in *Webster v Webster* [2009] 1 FLR 1240 where the court ordered the home to be transferred to the applicant whose partner had died suddenly at the age of 54 without making a will).

Bailey-Harris and Wilson (2003) have questioned whether the different treatment of cohabitants breaches Articles 8 and 14 of the European Convention for the Protection of Human Rights.

(iii) Applications by children of the deceased and those treated as children of the deceased   Marital and non-marital children, and adopted children, can apply (s 1(1)(c)) whether born before or after the deceased's death (s 25(1)) and whether or not they are minors or adult children of the deceased.

A person who is not included under section 1(1)(c) but who was, in the case of any marriage or civil partnership to which the deceased was at any time a party, treated by the deceased as a child of the family in relation to that marriage or civil partnership can also apply (s 1(1)(d)). This might include, for instance, a step-child or foster-child, whether or not a minor.

Adult children   Applicants who are adult children of the deceased can apply, but they may find it difficult to succeed in an application, particularly if they are young and able-bodied, are in employment and are capable of maintaining themselves (see, for example, *Re Jennings (Deceased)* [1994] Ch 286). But each case depends on its own facts; and in *Re Abram (Deceased)* [1996] 2 FLR 379 the adult son successfully claimed against his deceased mother's estate as he had worked for her in the family business for many years and for long hours and had received only a minimal wage. In *Garland v Morris* [2007] EWHC 2 (Ch), [2007] 2 FLR 528, on the other hand, an adult daughter's claim against her deceased father's estate was dismissed as she had failed to establish that it was reasonable in all the circumstances for her father to make provision for her (she had neither spoken to nor met her father at any time in the 15 years preceding his death, and had made no real effort to do so; and she had received all of her mother's estate).

At one time the court took the view that an adult child had to prove special circumstances, or that the deceased had a moral obligation to the adult child. However, the courts no longer adopt such a restricted approach. Each case depends on its own facts; and there is no additional hurdle for adult claimants under the Act in terms of establishing special circumstance or a moral obligation. Thus, in *Re Hancock (Deceased)* [1998] 2 FLR 346, for example, the Court of Appeal held that, although the presence of special circumstances or a moral obligation may be relevant factors, particularly where the applicant is in employment or possessed of earning capacity, their absence does not necessarily preclude a successful claim. In *Espinosa v Bourke* [1999] 1 FLR 747 the Court of Appeal allowed the 55-year-old daughter's appeal as the judge had erred in elevating moral obligation to a threshold requirement. However, as each case is fact-specific, the existence of a moral obligation may still be determinative, as it was in *Re Pearce (Deceased)* [1998] 2 FLR 705 where the 29-year-old son succeeded in his claim against his deceased father's estate as his father was held to have a moral obligation to him. The son had done substantial work on his father's farm, and his father had made representations that he would inherit it. (See also *Ilott v Mitson & Ors* [2011] EWCA Civ 346.)

(iv) Persons being maintained by the deceased   Any person who is not included in the categories above, but who was being maintained either wholly or partly by the deceased immediately before his or her death, can apply (s 1(1)(e)). Thus persons such as relatives, friends and carers can apply, and so can cohabitants who do not come within the definition in section 1(1)(ba) (above), provided that the applicant can prove that he or she was being maintained, wholly or partly, by the deceased. For instance, in *Bouette v Rose* [2000] 1 FLR 363 a mother brought a successful claim against the estate of her deceased daughter.

Section 1(3) provides that a claimant is only to be regarded as having been maintained by the deceased if the deceased, otherwise than for full valuable consideration, was making a substantial contribution in money or in money's worth towards the applicant's reasonable needs. An application can therefore be struck out on the ground that there was no dependency. In order to decide whether there was dependency, the court balances what the deceased was contributing against what the applicant was contributing, and, if the applicant made a greater or equal contribution, the claim is struck out (*per* Stephenson LJ in *Jelley v Iliffe and Others* [1981] Fam 128). Although dependency is a question of fact, the court will look at the problem in the round and apply a common-sense sort of approach, avoiding fine balancing distinctions (*per* Butler-Sloss LJ in *Bishop v Plumley* [1991] 1 All ER 236).

When considering a claim under this section the court is required (by s 3(4)) to have regard to the extent to which, and the basis upon which, the deceased had assumed responsibility for the maintenance of the applicant and to the length of time for which the deceased had discharged that responsibility However, the assumption of responsibility does not have to be express.

In *Baynes v Hedger* [2009] EWCA Civ 374, [2009] 2 FLR 767 a goddaughter failed in her claim against her deceased godmother's estate as the Court of Appeal held that she had failed to bring herself within section1(1)(e)) as: there had been no failure to make reasonable financial provision; the godmother had not assumed responsibility for her; and the payment of money by the godmother to enable the applicant goddaughter to pay off her debts did not constitute maintenance.

(c)   'Reasonable financial provision'

All applicants must prove that the deceased's will or the law of intestacy (or both, if there is partial intestacy) failed to make 'reasonable financial provision' for him/her (s 1(1)). The test is not whether reasonable provision has been made, but the more rigorous test of whether the failure to make provision was unreasonable (Judge Roger Cooke in *Re Abram (Deceased)* [1996] 2 FLR 379). However, spouses and civil partners are treated more generously than other applicants, as 'reasonable financial provision' for them means 'such financial provision as it would be reasonable in all the circumstances of the case for a husband or wife or civil partner to receive, whether or not that provision is required for his or her maintenance' (ss 1(2)(a) and (aa)). With other applicants, 'reasonable financial provision' means such financial provision as it would be reasonable in all the circumstances of the case for the applicant to receive for his or her maintenance (s 1(2)(b)).

Maintenance   With applicants other than spouses and civil partners, reasonable financial provision is limited to what it would be reasonable to provide for the applicant's maintenance. 'Maintenance' is not defined in the Act. What constitutes 'maintenance' depends on the facts of the case, but it may be construed broadly (see, for example, *Rees v Newbery and the Institute of Cancer Research* [1998] 1 FLR 1041 where the provision of accommodation by the deceased for 10 years at less than a market rent was held to be 'maintenance'). In *Re Coventry (Deceased)* [1980] Ch 461 Goff LJ said:

> 'What is proper maintenance must in all cases depend upon all the facts and circumstances of the particular case being considered at the time, but I think it is clear on the one hand that one must not put too limited a meaning on it; it does not mean just enough to enable a person

to get by; on the other hand, it does not mean anything which may be regarded as reasonably desirable for his general benefit or welfare.'

(d) Orders that can be made

The court has the power to make a wide range of orders, which include (s 2): periodical payments; a lump sum (which can be paid in instalments); a transfer of property; a settlement of property; acquisition of property and its transfer to the applicant or for the settlement of the applicant; and a variation of an ante-nuptial or post-nuptial settlement. The court can make an interim order if immediate financial assistance is needed (s 5). Periodical payments orders can be varied, discharged, suspended or revived (s 6). A periodical payments order made in favour of a former spouse or former civil partner, or a spouse or civil partner subject to a decree or order of judicial separation (where separation was continuing at death), ceases to be effective on that person's remarriage or civil partnership, except in respect of any arrears due (s 19(1)).

(e) The exercise of discretion – matters to be taken into account

When deciding whether or not the deceased made reasonable financial provision for the applicant, and in what manner to exercise its powers, the court must have regard to the following matters laid down in section 3(1) of the Act:

'(a) the financial resources and financial needs which the applicant has or is likely to have in the foreseeable future;
(b) the financial resources and financial needs which any other applicant…has or is likely to have in the foreseeable future;
(c) the financial resources and financial needs which any beneficiary of the estate of the deceased has or is likely to have in the foreseeable future;
(d) any obligations and responsibilities which the deceased had towards any applicant…or towards any beneficiary of the estate of the deceased;
(e) the size and nature of the net estate of the deceased;
(f) any physical or mental disability of any applicant…or any beneficiary of the estate of the deceased;
(g) any other matter, including the conduct of the applicant or any other person, which in the circumstances of the case the court may consider relevant.'

The weight given to each factor depends on the circumstances of each case. For example, where an application is brought by an adult child against a deceased parent, needs and resources under section 3(1)(a) and obligations and responsibilities under section 3(1)(d) are likely to be crucial (see, for example, *Espinosa v Bourke* [1999] 1 FLR 747).

In addition to the matters in section 3(1) above, the court must take into account other factors as follows:

(i) Applications by cohabitants The court must have regard to the applicant's age, the duration of the cohabitation and the contribution which the applicant made to the welfare of the deceased's family, including any contribution made by looking after the home or caring for the family (s 3(2A)).

(ii) Applications by children or persons treated like children The court must consider the manner in which the applicant was, or might be expected to be, educated or trained (s 3(3)). The court must also consider whether the deceased had assumed any responsibility for the applicant's maintenance (and, if so, its extent, basis and duration, and whether the deceased did so knowing that the applicant was not his own child), as well as the liability of any other person to maintain the applicant (s 3(3)).

(iii) Applications by persons being maintained by the deceased The court must consider the extent, basis and duration of the deceased's responsibility for maintenance (s 3(4)). Thus there must be an assumption of responsibility on the part of the deceased.

(f) Reform of the law

The Law Commission has examined the operation of the Inheritance (Provision for Family and Dependants) Act 1975. In its final report, published in December 2011 (*Intestacy and Family Provision Claims on Death*, Law Com No 331), it recommended, *inter alia*, that a wider range of family members should be entitled to bring a claim under the Act (for example, children who are adopted after the death of a parent; and children treated by the deceased as a child of the family, whether or not the deceased was in a marriage or civil partnership). The Law Commission also recommended the removal of the hurdles that face claims by dependants of the deceased, namely the requirements to show that the deceased assumed responsibility for their maintenance and contributed more to the relationship in terms of financial value. Under the proposed reforms, the courts would still take these matters into account but they would not be sufficient to prevent a deserving applicant from making a successful claim. None of these proposals have, however, been taken forward at the current time.

4.14 Succession to a tenancy on death

Succession to a tenancy on death is governed by Schedule 1 to the Rent Act 1977 (statutory tenancies) and by section 17 of the Housing Act 1988 (assured tenancies). Under these Acts a spouse, civil partner and a surviving cohabitant (opposite-sex or same-sex who had lived in a settled relationship with the deceased) can apply for a transfer of the deceased's tenancy on his or her death.

Under paragraph 2 of Schedule 1 to the Rent Act 1977 a spouse, civil partner or cohabitant (living as a husband or wife, or as a civil partner of the deceased) can succeed to the deceased spouse's or cohabitant's tenancy. Under paragraph 3(1) a family member of the deceased tenant can also succeed to the tenancy. A person who succeeds to a tenancy under paragraph 2 is in a better position than a family member who succeeds under paragraph 3 because he or she succeeds to a statutory tenancy, whereas a family member succeeds only to an assured tenancy. Statutory tenants are in a better position because they enjoy security of tenure and may register a fair rent for the property, whereas assured tenants are subject to a different form of security of tenure and may be charged a market, rather than a fair, rent.

Until amendments were made to the Rent Act 1977 and the Housing Act 1988, only spouses and heterosexual cohabitants could succeed to a deceased partner's tenancy under the Rent Act 1977 and section 17 of the Housing Act 1988. However, the following two cases heard by the House of Lords led to a change in the law, the second decision being influenced by the European Convention for the Protection of Human Rights as a result of the coming into force of the Human Rights Act 1998 (see 1.8):

▶ *Fitzpatrick v Sterling Housing Association Ltd* [2001] 1 AC 27, [2000] 1 FLR 271

The House of Lords held by a majority of 3 to 2 that a surviving same-sex cohabitant could succeed to the tenancy of the deceased tenant, on the basis that he or she could be construed as a member of the deceased tenant's 'family' under paragraph 3(1) of Schedule 1 to the Rent Act 1977. But it was unanimously held that the surviving homosexual partner could not be construed as a 'spouse' of the deceased under paragraph 2(2), because he could not be regarded as 'living with the original tenant as his or her husband or wife'.

▶ *Ghaidan v Godin-Mendoza* [2004] UKHL 30, [2004] 2 FLR 600

Mr Godin-Mendoza had lived in a long, close and loving and monogamous homosexual relationship with his deceased partner, who was the protected tenant of a flat owned by Mr Ghaidan, the landlord. Mr Ghaidan brought possession proceedings, and Mr Godin-Mendoza claimed by way of defence that he was entitled to succeed to the tenancy under Schedule 1 to the Rent Act 1977. At first instance, the judge held that he could only succeed to a tenancy under paragraph 3(1), applying *Fitzpatrick* (above), but the Court of Appeal allowed his appeal, holding that there had been a breach of Article 14 of the ECHR (discrimination) in conjunction with Article 8 (right to family life), and that the court had a duty under section 3 of the Human Rights Act (HRA) 1998 to give effect to the Rent Act in a way which was compliant with the ECHR. The landlord, Mr Ghaidan, appealed.

The House of Lords dismissed the appeal (Lord Millett dissenting), holding that same-sex cohabitants are in the same position as married couples when it comes to security of tenure. It held that paragraph 2(2) of Schedule 1 to the Rent Act 1977, when construed with reference to section 3 of the HRA 1998, violated the surviving partner's right under Article 14 ECHR taken together with Article 8. It held that it was possible under section 3 of the HRA 1998 (which provides that primary and subordinate legislation must be read and given effect in a way which is compatible with the ECHR) to read paragraph 2(2) in a way which was compatible with the ECHR.

Summary

▶ The statutory provisions and legal principles governing property entitlement are virtually the same for spouses and civil partners, but are radically different for cohabitants, particularly on relationship breakdown. Thus, although the family courts have wide discretionary powers to distribute the property of married couples on divorce, and civil partners on dissolution, according to their needs and resources, there is no such provision for cohabiting couples. This can leave cohabitants in a vulnerable position on the breakdown of their relationship. They can also be in a vulnerable position on the death of a cohabiting partner. For these reasons, there have been calls for reform of the law governing the property rights of cohabitants both on relationship breakdown and on the death of a partner.

▶ The property entitlements of spouses, civil partners and cohabitants during the existence of their relationship are governed by the laws of property and contract, but with the addition of some special family law statutory provisions for spouses and civil partners. Spouses and civil partners can own property solely or jointly. Spouses and civil partners with no right of ownership in the family home may have a statutory right of occupation ('home rights') under section 30 of the Family Law Act 1996, which includes the right to remain in occupation of the home and to enter in and occupy it, if the court so orders.

Summary cont'd

▶ Special statutory provisions apply in respect of the property rights of engaged couples and parties to a civil partnership agreement.

▶ Cohabitants have the same property law rights as spouses, civil partners and other persons during their relationship, but there are no special family law statutory provisions for cohabitants. Unlike spouses and civil partners, cohabitants have no statutory right of occupation of the family home ('home rights', see above). Cohabitants have a right of occupation only if they have a right of ownership in the home or a contractual licence to occupy it. However, a cohabitant or former cohabitant who is a victim of domestic violence can apply for an occupation order under Part IV of the Family Law Act 1996 (see 5.5), which, if granted, will give the applicant a right to occupy the family home for the duration of the order.

▶ Ownership of personal property (property other than land, such as investments and household goods) is governed by the law of contract and the law of property. As a general rule, title to personal property passes to the purchaser unless it was a gift. With regard to bank accounts, the money in the account presumptively belongs to the party or parties in whose name(s) the account is held, although the presumption can be rebutted by proof of a contrary intention. A person who has no right to personal property under a contract can claim an equitable interest in it under an express, resulting or constructive trust or on the basis of estoppel.

▶ Disputes about the family home arise in a number of situations, such as: on relationship breakdown; on the death of a party; where there is no mention of the parties' shares on the transfer deeds; and where a third party seeks possession of the home. The courts have wide discretionary powers to adjust a spouse's or civil partner's property rights on divorce or civil partnership dissolution irrespective of who owns what. Cohabitants, on the other hand, have to rely on the law of trusts or on proprietary estoppel.

▶ A person can claim an interest in the family home under a trust even if there is nothing in writing to that effect (s 53(2) Law of Property Act 1925; s 2(5) Law of Property (Miscellaneous Provisions) Act 1989). A resulting trust gives a claimant a share of the beneficial interest in the family home proportionate to his or her financial contribution to its purchase price, subject to any contrary intention. However, the constructive trust is considered to be the more appropriate tool of legal analysis regarding ownership of the family home. A constructive trust arises where there is an express or implied agreement, arrangement or understanding that the claimant has an interest in property and the claimant has acted to his or her detriment on the basis of that agreement, arrangement or understanding. Having established the existence of a beneficial interest under a constructive trust, the court must then decide what the share of that interest is. It does so by considering all the circumstances of the case. In joint-owner cases (where the parties are owners in law of the home, but their interests have not been defined in equity), the usual approach is that equity follows the law and they will be deemed to have equal shares unless there is any evidence of a contrary intention. However, the Supreme Court has held that an initial intention to share the beneficial interest can change over time depending on the circumstances.

▶ A person can claim an interest in the family home on the basis of proprietary estoppel. Applicants must prove that they have acted to their detriment on the basis of a belief encouraged by the other party that they are to have an interest in the property in question and that it would be inequitable for the court to deny the applicant an interest.

▶ An interest in the family home can be acquired under a contract, provided the legal requirements for the creation of a valid contract are satisfied. If a contract is for the sale or disposition of land it must be in writing (s 2 Law of Property (Miscellaneous Provisions) Act 1989), but this requirement does not prevent the creation of a resulting or constructive trust, or the creation of an interest by way of proprietary estoppel.

Summary cont'd

▶ Tenancies can be transferred between married partners, civil partners and cohabitants (including former spouses, civil partners and cohabitants) under section 53 and Schedule 7 of Part IV of the Family Law Act 1996.

▶ Under Part VII of the Housing Act 1996, local housing authorities have duties and powers with respect to persons who are homeless. The nature of these duties and powers depends largely on whether the applicant is intentionally or unintentionally homeless and whether or not he or she has a priority need. Domestic violence is taken seriously by local housing authorities; and victims of violence, or of threatened violence, are not treated as being intentionally homeless if they leave the family home.

▶ There is complete freedom of testamentary disposition in England and Wales. On intestacy (where there is no will), the surviving spouse or civil partner has a statutory right to succeed to the deceased's estate under the rules of intestacy laid down in the Administration of Estates Act 1925. Cohabitants, on the other hand, have no statutory rights of succession. The Law Commission has recently examined the law of intestacy and has made various recommendations, including a recommendation that certain cohabitants should have the same rights on intestacy as spouses and civil partners. But these proposals have not been take forward by the Government at the present time.

▶ Under the Inheritance (Provision for Family and Dependants) Act 1975 certain family members and dependants, including spouses, civil partners, former spouses, former civil partners, cohabitants, and other dependants, can apply for financial relief out of a deceased person's estate where the deceased has failed to make reasonable financial provision either under a will or under the law of intestacy (or both). Under the Act, spouses and civil partners are treated more favourably than other applicants. The Law Commission has recently examined the operation of the Act and has recommended *inter alia* that a wider range of family members should be entitled to bring a claim under the Act and that the hurdles which dependants face when making a claim should be removed.

▶ A deceased's tenancy can be transferred to a surviving spouse, or civil partner, or a surviving opposite-sex or same-sex cohabiting partner under the Rent Act 1977 or under section 17 of the Housing Act 1988.

Further reading and references

Battersby, 'Ownership of the family home: *Stack* v *Dowden* in the House of Lords' [2008] CFLQ 255.

Cooke, 'Wives, widows and wicked step-mothers: a brief examination of spousal entitlement on intestacy' [2009] CFLQ 423.

Fretwell, 'The cautionary tale of *Jones* v *Kernott*' [2012] Fam Law 69.

Gardner and Davidson, 'The future of *Stack* v *Dowden*' (2011) 127 *Law Quarterly Review* 13.

Hayward, 'Family property' and the process of 'familialisation' of property law' [2012] CFLQ 284.

Knight, 'Doing (linguistic) violence to prevent (domestic) violence? *Yemshaw* v *Hounslow LBC* in the Supreme Court' [2012] CFLQ 95.

Piska, 'A common intention or a rare bird?' Proprietary interests, personal claims and services rendered by lovers post-acquisition: *James* v *Thomas*: *Morris* v *Morris*' [2009] CFLQ 104.

(See also the reference list at the end of Chapter 3.)

Links to relevant websites can also be found at: www.palgrave.com/law/familylaw8e

Chapter 5

Domestic violence

5.1 Introduction

This chapter considers the law which is available to protect family members from domestic violence. In furtherance of the Government's aim to improve protection for victims, a range of legislative provisions have been enacted over the years. Also, as part of its drive to fight domestic violence, the Government has increasingly recognised the importance of adopting multi-agency and inter-agency approaches for tackling the problem, involving not just the courts, but the police, housing authorities and other agencies. There are also various organisations which campaign for reform of the law and which provide advice and information for victims (see the references at the end of the chapter).

In terms of the scale of the problem, it is difficult to make accurate assessments of the numbers of people who are victims of domestic violence. This is due in part to a lack of standardised data and also to the fact that only a small proportion of victims come into contact with the statutory authorities dealing with the problem. However, according to the British Crime Survey (BCS) 2010/11, domestic violence comprised 18 per cent of all violent incidents. Between April 2009 and March 2010 the Crown Prosecution Service dealt with 74,113 cases of domestic violence, representing an increase of 7,009 cases on 2008–2009. According to Women's Aid (www.womensaid.org.uk): one in four women will be a victim of domestic violence in their lifetime (many of them on a number of occasions); one incident of domestic violence is reported to the police every minute; and on average two women a week are killed by a current or former male partner.

What is domestic violence? Domestic violence can take many forms. It includes not just physical violence but also psychological and emotional abuse and harassment. It can involve, for instance, pestering, nagging, making nuisance telephone calls and intimidation. The Government has adopted a wide definition of domestic violence to include not just physical violence but other forms of abuse. In fact the definition was extended in 2012 to include controlling and coercive behaviour after the Government had conducted a consultation exercise (see *Cross-Government Definition of Domestic Violence*, Home Office, December 2011) and where the majority of respondents wished to see young persons aged 16–17 included in the definition as well as wording to reflect coercive control. These changes were included in the new definition which was announced in September 2012:

The cross-Government definition of 'domestic violence and abuse', www.homeoffice.gov.uk, September 2012:

'Any incident or pattern of incidents of controlling, coercive or threatening behaviour, violence or abuse between those aged 16 or over who are or have been intimate partners or family members regardless of gender or sexuality. This can encompass but is not limited to the following types of abuse: psychological; physical; sexual; financial; emotional.

Controlling behaviour is: a range of acts designed to make a person subordinate and/or dependent by isolating them from sources of support, exploiting their resources and

---

capacities for personal gain, depriving them of the means needed for independence, resistance and escape and regulating their everyday behaviour.

Coercive behaviour is: an act or a pattern of acts of assault, threats, humiliation and intimidation or other abuse that is used to harm, punish, or frighten their victim.'

According to the Government, this definition, which is not a legal definition, includes so-called 'honour' based violence, female genital mutilation and forced marriage, and it is clear that victims are not confined to one gender or ethnic group.

For the purposes of providing housing assistance for victims of domestic violence, the *Homelessness Code of Guidance for Local Authorities* also adopts a wide definition, as did the Supreme Court in the housing law case of *Yemshaw v Hounslow London Borough Council* (see further at p. 90 above).

Housing problems   Violence can create housing problems. Some victims may have to seek temporary accommodation in a refuge (see www.refuge.org.uk); and/or apply to a local housing authority for public sector housing (see 4.11). Some victims may end up divorcing or dissolving their civil partnership, whereupon the court has jurisdiction to adjudicate on any dispute about ownership and occupation of the home (see Chapter 7). In some cases, the court will provide injunctive protection, and remove the perpetrator from the home and allow the victim back in (see 5.5 below).

Children and domestic violence   Both the civil and criminal law provide protection for children who are witnesses to or victims of domestic violence. Sometimes local authority intervention may be needed under the Children Act 1989 (see Chapter 14). As violence in the home can be damaging to children who witness it, the word 'harm' in the Children Act 1989 includes 'impairment suffered from seeing or hearing the ill-treatment of another'. There is increasing recognition of the problem of domestic violence for children, particularly on family breakdown, and steps have been taken to improve protection for children in residence and contact cases where there is actual or potential violence in the home (see 11.5).

Specialist domestic violence courts   Specialist domestic violence courts (SDVCs) have been established in some parts of England and Wales with the aim of bringing more perpetrators of domestic violence to justice and to ensure that victims and their families are given support. These courts, which are part of the magistrates' family proceedings court, deal with criminal prosecutions and have specially trained magistrates and other staff to deal with domestic violence. Cases are fast-tracked in order to eliminate distress. A multi-agency approach is adopted, bringing together police, prosecutors, court staff, probation officers and specialist support services. Domestic violence advisors are available who are responsible for ensuring that the safety of the victim is co-ordinated across the criminal justice system and for giving expert advice on accessing essential services such as victim and witness agencies, housing, health, counselling and child care.

The legislation   There are various Acts of Parliament which provide protection and support for victims of domestic violence, whether they be adults or children. In family law, the important Acts of Parliament are:

▶ *Part IV of the Family Law Act 1996*   Under these provisions, the family courts have jurisdiction to make orders giving injunctive protection to victims of domestic violence and to make provision in respect of occupation of the family home (see further at p. 109 below).

▶ *The Children Act 1989*   Children who are at risk of significant harm, which includes domestic violence, can be protected by the family courts and by local authorities under the provisions of this Act (see further in Chapters 10 and 14).

In addition to the above two Acts and the various criminal laws which are available to deal with perpetrators of domestic violence, protection is also available under the Protection from Harassment Act 1997 (see 5.7).

Further legislative developments to improve protection   Over the past few years, the Government has taken further legislative steps to improve protection for victims. Thus, the Domestic Violence, Crime and Victims Act (DVCVA) 2004 was enacted to amend, *inter alia*, Part IV of the Family Law Act 1996 (see above) so as to extend the class of persons who can apply for remedies, and to make breach of a non-molestation order a criminal offence (see further below). The DVCVA 2004 also amended the Protection from Harassment Act 1997 to give the court power to make a restraining order with regard to *any* criminal offence, not just harassment (see 5.7). The DVCVA 2004 and, more recently, the Domestic Violence, Crime and Victims (Amendment) Act 2012 have also made changes to the criminal law in order to provide better protection for victims of violence in the home (see further below).

5.2   Domestic violence – the criminal law

Domestic violence is a serious and frequently reported crime which the police treat as seriously as any other crime. Police forces are required to draw up clear policy statements about intervention in domestic violence cases and to have special domestic violence units. Police forces are also required to support victims by, for instance, finding them temporary accommodation and keeping them informed about the case. Police forces are also involved in local domestic violence initiatives; and police domestic violence units work closely with solicitors, Women's Aid and other organisations. They also have powers and duties where children are suffering, or at risk of suffering, violence in the home.

The police have a wide range of powers in respect of domestic violence. Thus, for instance, under the common law they can enter premises to prevent or deal with breaches of the peace, and they have a power of arrest in such circumstances. For instance, under section 17 of the Police and Criminal Evidence Act 1984 a constable can enter premises to make an arrest and/or to save life or limb or to prevent serious damage to property. A perpetrator of violence can be prosecuted for: common assault (s 39 Criminal Justice Act 1988); assault occasioning actual bodily harm (s 47 Offences Against the Person Act 1861); rape (s 1 Sexual Offences Act 2003); sexual assault (s 3 Sexual Offences Act 2003); affray (s 3 Public Order Act 1986); criminal damage (s 1 Criminal Damage Act 1971); and harassment (s 2 Protection from Harassment Act 1997). Under section 51 of the Criminal Justice and Public Order Act 1994 it is an offence to intimidate a witness or to harm, or threaten to harm, a witness. Offences can also be committed under the Telecommunications Act 1984 (which prohibits the sending of grossly offensive, indecent, obscene or menacing communications) and under the Malicious Communications Act 1988 (which prohibits the sending of indecent or grossly offensive letters which are intended to create distress or anxiety). Victims of domestic violence may be entitled to compensation under the Criminal Injuries Compensation Scheme.

In addition to the criminal offences above, there are other criminal law provisions which relate more specifically to domestic violence. Thus, under section 5 of the Domestic Violence, Crime and Victims Act (DVCVA) 2004 it is a criminal offence to cause or allow a child or a vulnerable adult to die or to suffer serious physical harm (equivalent to grievous bodily harm). Prior to 2 July 2012, the criminal offence related only to causing or allowing death, but the Domestic Violence, Crime and Victims (Amendment) Act 2012, which came into force on 2 July 2012, extended the section 5 offence to include causing or allowing serious physical harm. The DVCVA 2004 has also made common assault an arrestable offence under Schedule 1A to the Police and Criminal Evidence Act 1984, so that the police have the power to arrest a person on suspicion of assault and/or battery without an arrest warrant (s 10(1)). Another recent development to give greater protection to actual or potential victims of domestic violence is the introduction of new powers under sections 24–33 of the Crime and Security Act 2010 which give senior police officers the power to issue a domestic violence protection notice (a DVPN). If a DVPN has been issued, a police constable *must* apply, by way of complaint to the magistrates' courts, for a domestic violence protection order (a DVPO), which must contain certain specified provisions, including, *inter alia*, a provision prohibiting a person from molesting the person for whose protection it is made; and it may contain a provision regulating the occupation of the home. Breach of a DVPO is a criminal offence.

There have been further developments with a view to improving protection for victims of domestic violence. Thus, in October 2011 the Government announced a 12-week consultation on the desirability of disclosing information about an individual's history of domestic violence to a new partner, following the highly publicised death of Clare Wood who was murdered by her former partner in Greater Manchester in 2009 (see *Domestic violence disclosure scheme – a consultation*, Home Office, October 2011; and *Domestic violence disclosure scheme – a consultation: summary of responses*, Home Office, March 2012). On 5 March 2012, a one-year pilot scheme was introduced in four police areas to test two types of process for enabling the police to disclose information about previous violent offending by an existing or new partner where this might help protect an individual from further violent offending. The first process would be triggered by a request by a member of the public (the 'right to ask'); and the second by the police where they make a proactive decision to disclose the information in order to protect a potential victim (the 'right to know').

ASBOs and domestic violence   Although an ASBO (an anti-social behaviour order, which can be made under the Crime and Disorder Act 1998), is a civil law order, breach is a criminal offence. ASBOs are not generally used in domestic violence cases except where the violence occurs in the public domain and thereby has an effect on other members of the public. An example of a rare case was *R (Rabess) v Commissioner of the Police for the Metropolis* [2007] EWHC 2008 (Admin) where an ASBO was made against a cohabiting couple to prohibit them from using abusive, insulting, threatening or intimidating language or behaviour towards each other and from using or threatening violence against each other, as members of the local community had been affected by their domestic violence. (For a case-note on *R (Rabess)*, see Burton [2008] CFLQ 95.) The Government is proposing to abolish the ASBO and replace it with two new orders (see *Putting victims first – more effective responses to anti-social behaviour*, Cm 8367, May 2012).

5.3 Family law remedies under Part IV of the Family Law Act 1996

Part IV of the Family Law Act 1996, which was enacted to consolidate the law and to provide remedies for a wider range of victims, gives the family courts jurisdiction to grant the following two remedies to protect victims of domestic violence, including children:

A Non-Molestation Order This is an order containing a provision prohibiting the respondent from molesting a person who is associated with the respondent and/or a relevant child (s 42(1)).

An Occupation Order This is an order made under sections 33, 35, 36, 37 or 38 of Part IV of the Family Law Act 1996 regulating, prohibiting, and governing the occupation of the family home.

The procedural rules for making an application are laid down in Part 10 of the Family Procedure Rules 2010.

According to *Judicial and Court Statistics 2011* (Ministry of Justice, 2012), applications for both non-molestation and occupation orders have fallen, but a greater fall has been seen in occupation orders. Thus, whereas occupation orders accounted for one-third of the orders made in 2002, only one-sixth of the orders were for occupation in 2011.

5.4 Non-molestation orders

Under Part IV of the Family Law Act 1996 all three tiers of the family court have jurisdiction to make a non-molestation order (NMO) prohibiting the respondent from molesting a person who is associated with the respondent and/or from molesting a relevant child (s 42(1)). Most applications are made in county courts. Thus, according to *Judicial and Court Statistics 2011* (Ministry of Justice, June 2012), in 2011 there were 15,573 applications to the county courts for non-molestation orders (a decrease of 13 per cent on 2010).

(i) Applicants A wide range of family members can apply for a NMO, not just spouses and cohabitants, provided the applicant is 'associated' with the respondent and any child is a 'relevant child' (see 5.6 below for definitions). A child can apply, but, if the child is aged under 16, the court must give the child leave (permission) to apply, which it can only grant if the child has sufficient understanding to make the proposed application (s 43). The court is unlikely to grant leave save in the most exceptional circumstances. In fact, there are no reported decisions on applications by children.

An application for a NMO can be made where the parties are an engaged couple or a formerly engaged couple (provided the application is brought within three years of its termination) (s 42(4)). Written evidence of the engagement will be required, unless the court is satisfied that the engagement is evidenced by an engagement ring or an engagement ceremony; or by a gift by one party to the agreement as a token of the agreement (s 44). Parties to a civil partnership agreement (or former agreement) can also apply, and the rules are the same as those which apply to engaged couples (see s 43(4ZA) and s 44(3),(4)).

Orders can be made of the court's own motion (on its own initiative)   The court in any family proceedings (see p. 121) can make a NMO without an application having been made (s 42(2)(c)); and it can also do so in proceedings for an occupation order (s 42(4A)).

(ii) What is 'molestation'?   'Molestation' is not defined in the Act, but is instead determined on a case-by-case basis by the courts. Under the law prior to Part IV of the FLA 1996, the term 'molestation' was interpreted widely to include not just actual or threatened violence, but also pestering (*Vaughan v Vaughan* [1973] 3 All ER 449) and harassment (*Horner v Horner* [1982] Fam 90), and the same approach is taken under Part IV of the FLA 1996. In *C v C (Non-Molestation Order: Jurisdiction)* [1998] 1 FLR 554 Stephen Brown P stated that there must be some conduct which clearly harasses and affects the applicant to such a degree that the intervention of the court is called for. The order can refer to molestation in general and/or to particular acts of molestation (s 48(6)).

(iii) Criteria for making a non-molestation order   When deciding whether to make a NMO, and, if so, in what manner, the court must have regard to all the circumstances of the case, including the need to secure the health, safety and well-being of the applicant and of any relevant child (s 42(5)).

(iv) Orders without notice (ex parte orders)   As urgent action is often needed, the court, where just and convenient to do so, may make an *ex parte* NMO (an order without the respondent being given notice of the proceedings) (s 45(1)). When deciding whether to make an *ex parte* NMO, the court must consider all the circumstances of the case, including (s 45(2)): the risk of significant harm to the applicant or any relevant child by the respondent if an order is not immediately made; and the likelihood of the applicant being deterred or prevented from pursuing the application if an order is not immediately made. The court must also consider: whether there is reason to believe that the respondent is aware of the proceedings but is deliberately avoiding service; and whether the applicant or relevant child will be seriously prejudiced by a delay in effecting service of proceedings or in effecting substituted service. If an *ex parte* NMO is made, the court must give the respondent an opportunity to make representations relating to the order at a full hearing (in other words, *inter partes*), as soon as is just and convenient (s 45(3)).

(v) Terms and duration of the order   A NMO can refer to molestation in general and/or to particular acts of molestation (s 48(6)); and it can be made for a specified period or until further order (s 48(7)). Although the aim of a NMO is to give the parties a temporary breathing space, in *Re B-J (Power of Arrest)* [2000] 2 FLR 443 the Court of Appeal held that an order can be made for an indefinite period in appropriate circumstances.

(vi) Undertakings   Instead of making a NMO the court can accept an undertaking (a promise to the court) from any party to the proceedings (s 46(1)), unless it appears to the court that the respondent has used or threatened violence against the applicant or a relevant child and a NMO is needed so that any breach can be punishable as a criminal offence under section 42A (s 46(3A)). An undertaking carries less of a stigma than a court order as the court does not make findings of fact about the respondent's behaviour and breach is not a criminal offence. Breach of an undertaking is enforceable in the same way as a court order (s 46(4)).

(vii) Variation and discharge   A NMO may be varied or discharged on the application of the respondent or by the applicant for the order (s 49).

(viii) Breach of a non-molestation order   Breach of any term in a NMO, without reasonable excuse, is a criminal offence (s 42A(1)). If the order was made *ex parte* (without notice), there is no criminal offence unless the person concerned was aware of the existence of the order (s 42A(2)). A person found guilty of breaching a NMO can be fined or imprisoned for up to 5 years (s 42A(5)).

5.5   Occupation orders

There may come a point where a victim of domestic violence can no longer tolerate living with the perpetrator and is forced to leave the family home and seek alternative accommodation. In an urgent situation a victim may need to seek accommodation in a refuge (see www.refuge.org.uk). A victim of domestic violence who is forced to leave the home, and/or who cannot seek entry to it, can apply for an occupation order which the family courts have jurisdiction to make under Part IV of the Family Law Act 1996.

Occupation orders are, however, less frequently made than non-molestation orders due to the seriousness of making an order, particularly where the respondent has a property interest in the home. But each case depends on its own facts and the court may decide that the seriousness of a party having no accommodation may outweigh the seriousness of making an order as it did, for example, in *Grubb v Grubb* [2009] EWCA Civ 976 (see p. 114 below). Nevertheless, occupation orders are regarded as a short-term remedy; and in the longer term, a victim may be forced to apply for a divorce (or dissolution of a civil partnership). According to *Judicial and Court Statistics 2011* (Ministry of Justice, June 2012), in 2011 there were 6,100 applications for occupation orders (a decrease of 17 per cent on 2010, when 7,100 applications were made).

Under sections 33 and 35–38 of Part IV of the Family Law Act 1996, the family courts have jurisdiction to make an occupation order (s 39). It can be made by the court on an application, or of the court's own motion in any family proceedings (ss 39(1), (2)). An occupation order does not affect a person's claim to any legal or equitable interest in the home in any subsequent proceedings, including subsequent proceedings under Part IV (s 39(4)). If a respondent is ordered to leave the home immediately, or within a specified time, his or her rights of ownership in the home are not affected.

Variation and discharge   An occupation order may be varied or discharged on an application by the respondent or by the person who made the original application (s 49).

Categories of applicant   Part IV of the Family Law Act 1996 creates two categories of applicant: 'entitled' and 'unentitled'. The court's powers are much wider for entitled applicants.

An 'entitled' applicant is a person who has a right to occupy the home by virtue of a beneficial estate or interest or contract; or by virtue of any enactment giving him the right to remain in occupation; or who has 'home rights' under section 30 of the Act.

A 'non-entitled' applicant is a person who has no right to occupy the home by virtue of a beneficial estate, interest, contract, or enactment, or by having 'home rights' under section 30 of the Act.

Different sections of the Act apply, depending on the parties' status and whether or not they have a property entitlement.

Applications by children   A child can apply for an occupation order, but a child under 16 needs leave of the court to do so which can be granted only if the child has sufficient understanding to make the proposed application (s 43). Applications by children are rare, or virtually non-existent, just as they are for non-molestation orders.

(a)   'Entitled' applicant and 'associated' respondent (s 33)

An entitled applicant (in other words a person with a property interest, see above) can apply for an occupation order if he or she is 'associated' with the respondent and the house is, was or was intended to be the home of both of them (s 33(1)). The term 'associated person' includes a wide range of persons, not just spouses, civil partners and cohabitants, but other family members and also persons living in the same household (see p. 120 for the definition of 'associated person'). Parties to an engagement or civil partnership agreement or to an engagement or civil partnership agreement which has been terminated no less than three years previously (ss 33(2) and (2A)) can apply. Proof of the engagement or civil partnership agreement may be needed in the same way as it is for an application for a non-molestation order (see p. 109 above, and ss 44(3) and (4)).

Powers of the court   The court has wide powers to insert a range of terms in the order (see s 33(3)). Thus, it may: enforce the applicant's entitlement to remain in occupation; require the respondent to allow the application to enter and remain in the home; regulate occupation by either or both parties; prohibit, suspend or restrict the respondent's right to occupy the home except where that right is a section 30 'home right' (see pp. 72 and 73); require the respondent to leave the home or part of it; and exclude the respondent from a defined area in which the home is included. Also, if the respondent has section 30 'home rights' in relation to the home, and the applicant is the other spouse or civil partner, the court can restrict or terminate those rights.

The court has other powers under section 33. Thus, the order may declare that the applicant is an entitled person (s 33(4)). If the applicant has section 30 'home rights', and the respondent is the applicant's spouse or civil partner, the court, where just and reasonable to do so, can, when making an order during the subsistence of a marriage or civil partnership, include a provision in the order that those rights are not to be brought to an end by the death of the other spouse or civil partner or by the termination of the marriage or civil partnership (ss 33(5), (8)).

How the court exercises its powers   When deciding whether to exercise its powers above and, if so, in what manner, the court must first apply the so-called 'balance of harm test' in section 33(7). In other words, it must weigh in the balance the significant harm which is likely to be caused to either party and any relevant child. If it decides that the applicant or any relevant child is likely to suffer significant harm which is greater than that which the respondent or any relevant child is likely to suffer, then the court *must* make an occupation order. 'Harm', in relation to an adult, means ill-treatment (physical or non-physical) and impairment to health (physical or mental). In relation to a child, 'harm' has the same meaning, but also includes impairment to development (physical, intellectual, emotional, social or behavioural) and sexual abuse (see s 63(1)). Where the question of whether the harm suffered by the child is significant turns on the child's health or development, the court must compare the child's health or development with that which could reasonably be expected of a similar child (s 63(3)). If, applying the balance of harm test, the court finds that the balance does not lie in favour of the applicant and/or any relevant child, then it must go on to conduct the discretionary exercise laid down in section 33(6) (see below).

In the following case the Court of Appeal held that the balance of harm test had been incorrectly applied in the circumstances of the case. It also held that occupation orders which overrode proprietary rights were justified only in exceptional circumstances.

▶ *Chalmers v Johns* [1998] EWCA Civ 1452, [1999] 1 FLR 392

The parties were cohabitants whose relationship had always been tempestuous. There had been acts of violence by each party against the other, resulting in minor injuries. Alcohol use, particularly by the woman, had been responsible for much of this. She left the family home with their daughter (aged 7) and moved into temporary council accommodation. She applied for an occupation order under section 33 (as she was a joint tenant of the home with the respondent). Applying the balance of harm test, the judge made an interim order on the basis that the mother and child were likely to suffer significant harm attributable to the father if the order was not made. The father appealed.

The Court of Appeal allowed his appeal, as the judge had incorrectly applied the statutory provisions. The applicant mother and the child were not likely to suffer significant harm attributable to the conduct of the respondent father if the order was not made. There was no real risk of violence or any other harm befalling the child. The Court of Appeal held that the case was one in which the court should exercise its discretion by considering all the circumstances of the case and the prescribed matters in section 33(6). It also stated that occupation orders which overrode proprietary rights (the father was a joint tenant) were justified only in exceptional circumstances. The fact that the final hearing was to take place very shortly weighed against making such a draconian order at an interlocutory hearing, particularly as there was no evidence that any further domestic disharmony could not be managed by the imposition of injunctive orders. The trial judge had not clearly focused upon the alternative nature of the adjoining subsections of section 33(6) and section 33(7), but had treated them as if they were both simultaneously applicable to the facts of the case. Had she directed herself more closely to the statutory language, she would have seen that this was a case which came nowhere near section 33(7).

Each case, however, turns on its own facts, as the Court of Appeal emphasised in the following case where it allowed the husband's appeal against an occupation order as the balance of harm test had not been satisfied on the facts. The case shows the importance of taking into account *all* the relevant children in a family.

▶ *B v B (Occupation Order)* [1999] 1 FLR 715

The wife left the matrimonial home (of which she and her husband were council tenants). She took their baby daughter with her and the husband remained in the home with his 6-year-old son from a previous marriage. The Court of Appeal held that, although the husband's behaviour fully justified an occupation order being made, his position as the full-time carer of his son also had to be taken into consideration. If an occupation order was made, the husband would have to leave the matrimonial home with his son and move into unsuitable temporary council accommodation and his son would have to change schools.

The exceptional nature of occupation orders was also emphasised by the Court of Appeal in *G v G (Occupation Order: Conduct)* [2000] 2 FLR 36, which also held that there was no requirement for a respondent's conduct to be intentional for the court to make an order.

The discretionary exercise under section 33(6)   If, applying the balance of harm test (see above), the balance is not in favour of making the order, then the court must go on to conduct the discretionary exercise under section 33(6), which requires the court, when deciding whether to exercise its powers and, if so, in what manner, to have regard to all the circumstances including:

'(a) the housing needs and housing resources of each of the parties and of any relevant child;

(b) the financial resources of each of the parties;

(c) the likely effect of any order, or of any decision by the court not to exercise any of the powers under s 33(3), on the health, safety or well-being of the parties and of any relevant child; and

(d) the conduct of the parties in relation to each other and otherwise.'

A good example of the application of the discretionary exercise can be found in the following case:

▶ *Grubb v Grubb* **[2009] EWCA Civ 976**

The application for an occupation order arose in the course of divorce proceedings which the husband had initially defended. He had excluded his wife from the matrimonial home by refusing to give her the keys. The wife was granted an occupation order (she had applied under section 33(6), and so there was no need to prove significant harm under section 33(7)). The husband appealed against the order on the basis *inter alia* that the trial judge had failed to recognise the seriousness of the order.

The Court of Appeal dismissed his appeal. Wilson LJ stated that an occupation order was likely to carry its greatest level of seriousness when it was made against a spouse to whom alternative accommodation was not readily available. Taking into account the circumstances of the case, immediate separation was not only 'beneficial' but 'necessary' and the only way of achieving it was to evict the husband, to whom another property was readily available and who in any event had massive resources with which to fund his comfortable accommodation elsewhere.

The following case shows that, even though occupation orders are regarded as serious orders which should not be routinely made, physical violence is not necessarily needed. It also shows that an improper application of the statutory provisions may not necessarily invalidate the exercise of judicial discretion:

▶ *Dolan v Corby* **[2011] EWCA Civ 1664, [2012] 2 FLR 1031**

The parties were cohabitants who were joint tenants of the home in which they had been living for 30 years. The woman applied for *ex parte* non-molestation and occupation orders, alleging verbal and physical abuse by the respondent. The non-molestation order was granted, and the application for the occupation order was set down to be heard *inter partes*.

Although the trial judge found no evidence of physical violence (but merely verbal abuse), an occupation order was made excluding the respondent from the property as the applicant, who had a history of drug abuse and suffered from psychiatric problems, was less able than the respondent to find alternative accommodation.

The respondent appealed on the basis *inter alia* that the trial judge had conflated the discretionary exercise under section 33(6) and the balance of harm test under section 33(7). The Court of Appeal agreed, but held that the conflation had not vitiated the exercise of discretion. Thus, it was held that the Recorder's decision was a discretionary one and could be properly construed under section 33(6) even though he had not considered the provisions separately.

He also argued that, following *Chalmers v Johns* and *G v G (Occupation Order: Conduct)* (see above), occupation orders are draconian orders which should be granted only in exceptional circumstances, and that, as there had been no finding of violence at first instance, he should not have been excluded from the home. However, Black LJ held that *Chalmers v Johns* and *G v G* did not necessitate a finding of violence. The court had to have regard to 'all the circumstances' of the case and the central feature of the case was the psychiatric state of the applicant which was capable of making the case exceptional.

(For another case where an occupation order was made excluding the husband from the jointly owned home for three months where there was no violence, but where the trial judge found that the heated arguments between the husband and wife on marriage breakdown caused their children emotional harm, see *Re L (Children)* [2012] EWCA Civ 721.)

Duration of the order The order may be made for a specified period, or until the occurrence of a specified event, or until further order (s 33(10)). There is no time limit on the duration of the order, as there is for non-entitled applicants.

(b) Non-entitled applicants

Non-entitled applicants (persons with no right to occupy the home – see p. 111 above) must apply under sections 35–38 of Part IV of the Family Law Act 1996. Each section of the Act applies to a particular sort of status relationship as follows:

(i) Non-entitled former spouse/civil partner v entitled former spouse/civil partner (section 35)

Powers of the court These are similar to those in section 33(3) (see above), except that in certain circumstances there are mandatory provisions which must be included in an order (see s 35(3) and (4)). Thus, if the applicant is in occupation of the home, the order *must* contain a provision giving the applicant the right not to be evicted or excluded from the home or any part of it by the respondent for a specified period; and must prohibit the respondent from evicting or excluding the applicant during that period (s 35(3)). If the applicant is *not* in occupation, the orders *must* contain a provision giving the applicant the right to enter into and occupy the home for a specified period; and require the respondent to permit the exercise of that right (s 35(4)). An order *may* also (s 35(5)): regulate the occupation of the home or part of it; prohibit, suspend or restrict the respondent's right to occupy it; require the respondent to leave the home or part of it; and/or exclude the respondent from a defined area in which the home is included.

How the court exercises its powers When deciding whether to make a mandatory provision (in sections 35(3) and (4), see above) and, if so, in what manner, the court must have regard to all the circumstances including the following (s 35(6)):

'(a) the housing needs and housing resources of each of the parties and of any relevant child;
(b) the financial resources of each of the parties;
(c) the likely effect of any order, or of any decision by the court not to exercise any of the powers under [subsection 35(3) and (4)], on the health, safety or well-being of the parties and of any relevant child;
(d) the conduct of the parties in relation to each other and otherwise;
(e) the length of time that has elapsed since the parties ceased to live together;
(f) the length of time that has elapsed since the marriage or civil partnership was dissolved or annulled; and
(g) the existence of any pending proceedings between the parties:– (i) for an order under s.23A or 24 of the Matrimonial Causes Act 1973 (property adjustment orders in connection with divorce proceedings etc); (i(a)) for a property adjustment order under Part 2 of Schedule. 5 to the Civil Partnership Act 2004; (ii) for an order under paragraph 1(2)(d) or (e) of Schedule 1 to the Children Act 1989 (orders for financial relief against parents); or (iii) relating to the legal or beneficial ownership of the dwelling-house.'

Section 35(7) provides that, when deciding whether to include a discretionary provision in an order (a 'section 35(5) provision', see above), and, if so, in what manner, the court must have regard to all the circumstances including the matters in section 35(6)(a)–(d) (see above) and consider 'the balance of harm test' laid down in section 35(8). In other words, if the court decides to make a section 35 order and it appears that if the order does not include a discretionary section 35(5) provision, the applicant or any relevant child is likely to suffer significant harm attributable to conduct of the respondent, the court *must* include a discretionary provision in the order unless it appears to the court that (a) the respondent or any relevant child is likely to suffer significant harm if the provision is included in the order; and (b) the harm likely to be suffered by the respondent or child in that event is as great as or greater than the harm attributable to conduct of the respondent which is likely to be suffered by the applicant or child if the provision is not included (s 35(8)).

Duration of the order   The order must be limited to a specified period not exceeding six months, but can be extended on one or more occasions for a further specified period not exceeding six months (s 35(10)). While the order is in force an applicant is treated as possessing 'home rights' and sections 30(3)–(6) apply (s 35(13)). An order cannot be made after the death of either party; and an order ceases to be effective on either party's death (s 35(9)).

(ii) Non-entitled cohabitant/former cohabitant v entitled cohabitant/former cohabitant (section 36)

The parties can be opposite-sex or same-sex cohabitants/former cohabitants.

Powers of the court   Where the applicant is in occupation of the home, the order *must* give the applicant the right not to be evicted or excluded from the home or any part of it by the respondent for a specified period and prohibit the respondent from evicting or excluding the applicant during that period (s 36(3)). If the applicant is not in occupation, the order *must* give the applicant the right to enter into and occupy the home for a specified period; and require the respondent to permit the exercise of that right (s 36(4)). The order *may* also contain a discretionary provision (s 36(5)): regulating the occupation of the home or part of it by either or both parties; prohibiting, suspending or restricting the respondent's right to occupy it; requiring the respondent to leave the home or part of it; or excluding the respondent from a defined area in which the home is included.

How the court exercises its powers When deciding whether to make a mandatory order under section 36(3) or (4) (see above), and, if so, in what manner, the court must have regard to all the circumstances of the case, including (s 36(6)):

'(a) the housing needs and housing resources of each of the parties and of any relevant child;
(b) the financial resources of each of the parties;
(c) the likely effect of any order, or of any decision by the court not to exercise any of the powers under s 33(3), on the health, safety or well-being of the parties and of any relevant child;
(d) the conduct of the parties in relation to each other and otherwise;
(e) the nature of the parties' relationship and in particular the level of commitment involved in it;
(f) the length of time during which they have cohabited;
(g) whether there are or have been any children who are children of both parties or for whom both parties have or have had parental responsibility;
(h) the length of time that has elapsed since the parties ceased to live together; and
(i) the existence of any pending proceedings for an order under paragraph 1(2)(d) or (e) of Schedule 1 to the Children Act 1989 (orders for financial relief against parents); or relating to the legal or beneficial interest of the dwelling-house.'

When deciding whether to include one or more of the discretionary provisions in section 36(5) (see above) and, if so, in what manner, the court must have regard to all the circumstances including the matters mentioned in section 36(6)(a)–(d) (above); and apply the 'balance of harm' test laid down in section 36(8). In other words, the court must ask whether the applicant or any relevant child is likely to suffer significant harm which is greater than that likely to be suffered by the respondent or any relevant child if a section 36(5) provision is not included in the order. However, even if the balance of harm lies in favour of the applicant and any relevant child, there is no obligation on the court to make an order as there is in an application (under s 35) by an entitled applicant – the balance of harm test is merely part of the discretionary exercise.

Duration of the order The order must be limited so as to have effect for a specified period not exceeding six months, but may be extended on one occasion for a further specified period not exceeding six months (s 36(10)). An order cannot be made after the death of either party; and an order ceases to have effect on either party's death (s 36(9)).

(iii) Neither spouse/civil partner of former spouse/former civil partner is entitled to occupy (section 37)

Either party may apply against the other for an occupation order under section 37 (ss 37(1), (2); s 37(1A)). The order *may* (s 37(3)): require the respondent to permit the applicant to enter and remain in the home or part of it; regulate the occupation of the home by either or both parties; require the respondent to leave the home or part of it; or exclude the respondent from a defined area in which the house is included.

How the court exercises its powers When deciding whether to make an order under section 37(3) and, if so, in what manner, the court must have regard to the factors in section 33(6) and the balance of harm test in section 33(7) (see pp. 112–17 above) as they apply to the exercise by the court of its powers under section 33(3) of the Act (s 37(4)).

Duration of the order The order must be limited to six months, but may be extended on one or more occasion by a further specified period not exceeding six months (s 37(5)).

(iv) Neither cohabitant/former cohabitant entitled to occupy (section 38)

Where both cohabitants or former cohabitants (opposite-sex or same-sex) occupy a house which is the home in which they cohabit or cohabited, but neither party is entitled to occupy the house, either party may apply for an occupation order (ss 38(1), (2)).

Powers of the court The provisions which the order may contain are the same as those for a section 37 order (s 38(3)) (see above).

How the court exercises its powers When deciding whether to include one or more of the discretionary provisions in section 38(3) and, if so, in what manner, the court must have regard to all the circumstances including all of the factors in section 38(4) and the balance of harm test in section 38(5). These provisions are in fact identical to those in section 36(6)(a)–(d) (see p. 117 above), and, as in section 36(7), even if the balance of harm lies in favour of the applicant and any relevant child, there is no obligation on the court to make an order as there is in the case of an entitled applicant.

Duration of the order The order must be limited to a specified period not exceeding six months, but can be extended on one occasion by a further specified period of up to six months (s 38(6)).

(c) Occupation orders: other powers

(i) Undertakings, orders without notice, and enforcement The rules for undertakings, orders without notice, and enforcement are the same as those for non-molestation orders (see 5.4 above), except that the restriction on accepting an undertaking (s 46(3A)) does not apply to occupation orders.

(ii) Attaching a power of arrest Under section 47, the court can attach a power of arrest to an occupation order. The power differs depending on whether the occupation order is made with notice (*inter partes*) or without notice (*ex parte*).

If the order is made with notice and it appears to the court that the respondent has used or threatened violence against the applicant or a relevant child, it *must* attach a power of arrest to one or more provisions of the order, unless it is satisfied that the applicant or any child will otherwise be adequately protected (ss 47(1), (2)). If the order is made without notice, the court *may* attach a power of arrest to one or more provisions of the order, but only if the respondent has used or threatened violence against the applicant or a relevant child, and there is a risk that the applicant or relevant child will suffer significant harm as a result of the respondent's conduct if the power of arrest is not attached to the order immediately (s 47(3)). Although it is usually preferable for a power of arrest to have effect for the same period as the order, it can be made to have effect for a shorter period than the other provisions in the order (see s 47(4) and *Re B-J (Power of Arrest)* [2000] 2 FLR 443).

The effect of a power of arrest is to permit a constable to arrest, without warrant, a person whom he has reasonable cause to suspect is in breach of any provision in an order to which the power of arrest is attached (s 47(6)). The respondent must be brought before a judge or justice of the peace within 24 hours, and, if the matter is not disposed of, the respondent may be remanded in custody or on bail (s 45(7)). A power of arrest can be attached even though the respondent is a minor (see *Re H (Respondent Under 18: Power of Arrest)* [2001] 1 FLR 641 where the Court of Appeal upheld an occupation order which had been made with a power of arrest attached, ordering a 17-year-old boy, who had been violent and abusive to his parents, to leave the home and not return and not enter or attempt to enter it).

(iii) Ancillary powers (section 40)   Where an application is made under sections 33, 35 or 36 (see above), the court has various discretionary ancillary powers under section 40 of the Act. Thus, it can impose repair and maintenance obligations, require a party to pay the rent, mortgage or other outgoings, and impose obligations in respect of the furniture or other contents of the house (for example, grant the use or possession of furniture or other contents, and order a party to take reasonable care of them). It can also require a party to keep the house, furniture and any other contents secure. When deciding whether and, if so, how to exercise its powers under section 40, the court must consider all the circumstances of the case, including the parties' financial needs and resources, and their present and future financial obligations, including their financial obligations to each other and any relevant child (s 40(2)). Ancillary orders are only effective for the duration of the occupation order (s 40(3)).

Once of the problems with these ancillary powers, however, is that the courts have no power to enforce them (see *Nwogbe v Nwogbe* [2000] 2 FLR 74 where the Court of Appeal was strongly critical of this lacuna in the law).

(d)   Breach of an occupation order

Breach of an occupation order is not a criminal offence as it is for breach of a non-molestation order. Instead, civil proceedings for contempt of court will have to be brought and, if contempt is proved, the respondent will be ordered to pay a fine and/or serve a prison sentence. The courts have been increasingly willing to impose prison sentences for breach (see, for instance, *H v O (Contempt of Court: Sentencing)* [2005] 2 FLR 329). However, as the Human Rights Act 1998 and the European Convention for the Protection of Human Rights apply to committal proceedings, the Court of Appeal has held that the greatest possible care must be taken to ensure that the applicable evidential and procedural rules are properly obeyed (see *Hammerton v Hammerton* [2007] 2 FLR 1133).

5.6   Definitions for the purposes of Part IV of the Family Law Act 1996

Sections 62 and 63 of Part IV of the Family Law Act 1996 are important because they define key terms in the Act, including which persons are eligible to apply for orders.

(i) 'Cohabitants' and 'former cohabitants'   The Act applies to both opposite-sex and same-sex cohabitants. Thus, 'cohabitants' are defined as two persons who are neither married to each other nor are civil partners of each other but who are living together as if they were husband and wife or civil partners; but it does not include cohabitants who have subsequently married each other or become civil partners of each other (s 62(1)). As the court favours a purposive approach when construing the Act (in order to give victims protection), it has been held that the term 'cohabitant' can include persons who maintain separate households (see, for example, *G v F (Non-Molestation Order: Jurisdiction)* [2000] 2 FLR 233).

(ii) 'Relevant child' A 'relevant child' is: any child who is living with, or who might reasonably be expected to live with, either party to the proceedings; any child in relation to whom an order under the Adoption and Children Act 2002 or the Children Act 1989 is in question in the proceedings; and any other child whose interests the court considers relevant (s 62(2)). This broad definition highlights the importance of protecting *any* child from domestic violence. Thus, the child need not be related to the applicant, nor be a child of the family.

(iii) 'Associated persons' An applicant for a non-molestation order must be 'associated' with the respondent, and so must an entitled applicant for an occupation order who is not a spouse, civil partner or cohabitant (or a former spouse, civil partner or cohabitant). 'Associated persons' are widely defined as (s 62(3)):

▶ spouses, or former spouses;
▶ civil partners, or former civil partners;
▶ cohabitants, or former cohabitants (opposite-sex or same-sex);
▶ persons who live, or have lived, in the same household, otherwise than merely by reason of one of them being the other's employee, tenant, lodger or boarder;
▶ relatives (see further below);
▶ engaged, or formerly engaged, couples;
▶ parties to a civil partnership agreement (whether or not that agreement has been terminated);
▶ persons who have, or have had, an intimate personal relationship with each other which is or was of significant duration;
▶ in relation to any child, both parties are a parent of the child or have or have had parental responsibility for the child (s 62(4));
▶ parties to the same family proceedings (see definition below) other than proceedings under Part IV FLA 1996.

(iv) A 'relative' A 'relative' in relation to a person is (s 63(1)):

▶ the father, mother, step-father, step-mother, son, daughter, step-son, step-daughter, grandmother, grandfather, grandson or granddaughter of that person or of that person's spouse or former spouse, civil partner or former civil partner; or
▶ the brother, sister, uncle, aunt, niece or nephew (whether of the full blood or of the half blood or by marriage or civil partnership) of that person or of that person's spouse or former spouse, civil partner or former civil partner, and includes, in relation to a person who is cohabiting or has cohabited with another person, any person who would be any of the above relatives if the parties were married to each other or were civil partners of each other.

(v) Adopted children If a child has been adopted, or an adoption agency has power to place the child for adoption by parental consent or by placement order (see Chapter 15), two persons are associated if: one of them is the natural parent of the child (or a parent of such a natural parent); and the other is the child or any person who has become a parent of the child under an adoption order or has applied for an adoption order, or is any person with whom the child has at any time been placed for adoption (ss 62(5), (7)).

(vi) 'Family proceedings'   'Family proceedings' means any proceedings under (ss 63(1), (2)):

- the inherent jurisdiction of the High Court in relation to children;
- Part IV of the Family Law Act 1996;
- Part 4A of the Family Law Act 1996;
- the Matrimonial Causes Act 1973;
- the Domestic Proceedings and Magistrates' Courts Act 1978;
- Part III of the Matrimonial and Family Proceedings Act 1984;
- Parts I, II and IV of the Children Act 1989;
- section 54 of the Human Fertilisation and Embryology Act 2008;
- the Adoption and Children Act 2002;
- Schedules 5–7 to the Civil Partnership Act 2004.

5.7 The Protection from Harassment Act 1997

The Protection from Harassment Act (PHA) 1997 was enacted primarily to provide protection from harassment and other similar conduct arising in the context of 'stalking' (the obsessive harassment of one person by another), but it is sometimes used by victims of domestic violence. The Act creates criminal offences and provides civil remedies (injunctions and damages). It has been amended by the Domestic Violence, Crime and Victims Act 2004 and the Serious Organised Crime and Police Act 2005.

There are a number of important differences between applications under Part IV of the Family Law Act 1996 and the Protection of Harassment Act 1997. Thus, under the PHA 1997: there is no requirement that the parties must be 'associated' persons; the remedies do not specifically relate to occupation of the home; damages can be awarded; and proceedings are not family proceedings.

Section 1(1) of the PHA 1997 prohibits harassment by providing that a person must not pursue a course of conduct which amounts to harassment of another, and which that person knows, or ought to know, amounts to harassment of another. There is no definition of 'harassment' in the Act, but section 7(2) provides that references to harassing a person include alarming a person or causing a person distress. The Act may therefore be used to prosecute persons for acts other than stalking.

Course of conduct   In order for there to be harassment, there must be a 'course of conduct'. A single incident is not enough, as there must be 'conduct on at least two occasions' (s 7(3)(a)). As 'conduct' can include speech (s 7(4)), verbal abuse can constitute harassment. In the following case, the Court of Appeal held that there must be a cogent link between the incidents involved in the 'course of conduct' in order for there to be harassment:

> ▶ *R v Hills* [2001] 1 FLR 580
>
> After the woman left the defendant he was charged with harassment under the 1997 Act. The course of conduct consisted of various assaults during a seven-month period, but centred on two separate and individual assaults which took place approximately six months apart. The defendant was convicted but appealed against his conviction. The Court of Appeal allowed his appeal, holding that a course of conduct requires proof of a cogent link between the two (or more) incidents constituting harassment. As the case centred on two separate and individual incidents, the necessary cogent link between the two assaults had not been

established. The case was held to be far from the stalking type of offence for which the 1997 Act was intended. The Court of Appeal held that, where a couple were frequently coming back together and having sexual intercourse, it was unrealistic to think that the behaviour fell within the stalking category. It applied *Lau v Director of Public Prosecutions* [2000] 1 FLR 799, which concerned two incidents between a girlfriend and a boyfriend, and where it was held that, although two incidents could be enough to establish harassment, the fewer the occasions and the wider they were spread the less likely it would be that a finding of harassment could reasonably be made for the purposes of the Act.

The following case shows that a number of acts of violence over time may not necessarily constitute the offence of harassment, although they may constitute another offence, such as an assault:

▶ *R v Widdows* **[2011] EWCA Crim 1500, [2011] 2 FLR 869**

The defendant had a volatile relationship with a woman who was described as mature but emotionally vulnerable. The relationship involved a significant degree of mutual violence and volatility, with frequent arguments, separations and reconciliations. He was convicted of the section 4 offence of aggravated harassment (see below) in respect of six incidents involving assaults over a 9-month period, culminating in two allegations of rape on the final occasion (of which he was acquitted). He appealed against his conviction.

The Court of Appeal, allowing his appeal, held *inter alia* that, when bringing a charge under section 4, or when summing up to the jury, the concept of harassment must be borne in mind, even though the word 'harassment' is not used in section 4. Adopting Lord Nicholl's description of harassment in *Majrowski v Guy's and St Thomas's NHS Trust* [2006] UKHL 34 as implying 'stalkers, racial abusers, disruptive neighbours, bullying at work and so forth', the Court of Appeal held that the facts of the case (a number of acts of violence spread over 9 months during a close and affectionate relationship) did not satisfy the course of conduct requirement or the requirement that it was conduct amounting to harassment.

The Court of Appeal referred to its earlier ruling in *R v Curtis* [2010] EWCA Crim 123, where, relying on earlier authorities (including *R v Hills* [2001] 1 FLR 580, above), it emphasised, on very similar facts, the need to find that the 'course of conduct' complained of 'amounts to' harassment.

(a) Criminal offences under the Act

The Protection from Harassment Act 1997 creates two levels of criminal offence: the section 2 offence of harassment; and the section 4 offence of aggravated harassment. A person who is found guilty of a section 2 offence is liable to a fine or imprisonment for up to six months (s 2(2)). The section 4 offence applies where a person causes another person to fear on at least two occasions that violence will be used against him or her (s 4(1)). This is an indictable offence and carries stricter penalties than the section 2 offence.

Defences Both offences are subject to two statutory defences: that the course of conduct was pursued for the purpose of preventing or detecting crime; or that the pursuit of the course of conduct was reasonable (see ss 1(3) and 4(3)).

Restraining orders The criminal court has the power to make restraining orders (injunctive-style orders) under section 5 of the PHA 1997. As a result of provisions inserted into the PHA 1997 (by the DVCVA 2004), the criminal courts can now make restraining orders on the conviction of *any* offence, not just the offence of harassment; and they can make a restraining order where a person has been acquitted of harassment if they believe that such an order is necessary to protect a named person from harassment by the defendant in the future (s 5A). The aim of these wider powers is to give victims immediate protection and to save them having to bring a separate civil action.

With respect to duration, a restraining order may be made to have effect for a specified period or until further order (s 5(3)). Breach of an order without reasonable excuse is a criminal offence (s 5(5)) and can result in a fine or imprisonment (for up to five years) (s 5(6)).

(b) Civil remedies

The Protection from Harassment Act 1997 also provides civil remedies. Section 3 creates a statutory tort of harassment by providing that a person who is, or may be, the victim of harassment, as prohibited by section 1 of the Act, can bring a claim in civil proceedings against the person responsible for the harassment (s 3(1)). Damages can be awarded, including damages for any anxiety caused by the harassment and/or any financial loss resulting from the harassment (s 3(2)). In *Singh v Bhakar and Bhakar* [2007] 1 FLR 889 a young Sikh girl (who suffered harassment by her mother-in-law after she joined her husband in his extended family home) obtained damages under section 3 for the depression caused by the maltreatment.

Injunctive protection may also be granted. If the court grants an injunction restraining the defendant from pursuing any conduct which amounts to harassment, and the claimant considers that the defendant has done anything which is prohibited by the injunction, the claimant may apply for the issue of a warrant for the defendant's arrest (s 3(3)). Breach of an injunction restraining the defendant from pursuing any conduct which amounts to harassment is a criminal offence (s 3(6)); it is not punishable as contempt of court (s 3(7)).

In an application for a civil remedy under section 3 the standard of proof is the civil standard of proof (on the balance of probabilities). The court must also ensure that it exercises its powers in compliance with the European Convention for the Protection of Human Rights (for instance the Article 8 right to family life – see Tugendhat J in *Hipgrave and Hipgrave v Jones* [2005] 2 FLR 174).

5.8 Injunctions ancillary to legal proceedings

County courts and the High Court have jurisdiction (under section 38 of the County Courts Act 1984 and section 37 of the Supreme Court Act 1981 respectively) to grant injunctions ancillary to civil proceedings where it is just and convenient to do so. These powers may be useful if a victim of domestic violence is not an 'associated person' for the purposes of Part IV of the Family Law Act 1996 (see p. 120 above). However, the court only has jurisdiction to grant an injunction ancillary to civil proceedings if the claimant has a legal or equitable right which is capable of being protected, such as a cause of action in tort or a proprietary interest. The House of Lords has held that it is not sufficient if another member of the family has such a right (*Hunter v Canary Wharf Ltd* [1997] 2 FLR 342).

Although these powers are rarely used by domestic violence victims because better statutory protection is available to them, they were used to protect social workers involved in a child protection case in *Tameside Metropolitan Borough Council v M (Injunctive Relief: County Courts: Jurisdiction)* [2001] Fam Law 856 where an injunction was granted ancillary to care proceedings to protect the social workers who had been threatened with violence by the children's parents. The local authority's alternative application for injunctive relief under the Protection from Harassment Act 1997 was dismissed as the local authority was not a 'person' for the purposes of that Act.

Summary

▶ Domestic violence is a serious issue and one which the Government and the judiciary are committed to fighting. Both the civil law and the criminal law provide protection for victims. Multi- and inter-agency approaches are adopted. Domestic violence is widely defined, for various purposes, to include not just actual or threatened physical violence but other forms of behaviour such as emotional abuse and coercive and controlling behaviour. Housing law is sometimes relevant. The law also provides protection for children who are victims of domestic violence or who witness it. Specialist domestic violence courts operate in some parts of England and Wales. There are various Acts of Parliament which provide protection for victims of domestic violence, including, in particular, Part IV of the Family Law Act 1996 and the Protection from Harassment Act 1997 (both of which have been amended in recent years to provide more effective protection for victims).

▶ The criminal law provides protection for victims. The police take domestic violence very seriously and have a wide range of common law and statutory law duties and powers for dealing with the problem. The police have been given greater statutory powers to protect victims. .

▶ Under Part IV of the Family Law Act 1996 the family courts have jurisdiction to grant two injunctive-style orders to provide protection for victims of domestic violence: a non-molestation order (NMO); and an occupation order.

▶ A non-molestation order is an order made under section 42 of Part IV of the Family Law Act 1996 which prohibits the respondent from molesting a person who is 'associated' with the respondent and/or from molesting a relevant child. 'Molestation' is not defined in the Act, but has been widely interpreted by the courts. Where urgent action is needed, a NMO can be made without notice (*ex parte*) (s 45). When deciding whether to make a NMO, and, if so, in what manner, the court must take into account all the circumstances of the case, including the need to secure the health, safety and well-being of the applicant and of any relevant child (s 42(5)). The NMO can be made for a specified period or until further order (s 48). Breach of a NMO is a criminal offence. The court can, in certain circumstances, accept an undertaking instead of making a NMO (s 46). A NMO can be varied or discharged (s 49). Breach of any term in a NMO without reasonable excuse is a criminal offence, and can result in a fine or imprisonment (s 42A).

▶ An occupation order, which can be made under sections 33 and 35–38 of Part IV of the Family Law Act 1996, is an order regulating the occupation of the family home. There are two categories of applicant: entitled (persons with a proprietary right); and unentitled (persons with no proprietary right). The court's powers are much wider for entitled applicants (see s 33). An order can be made without notice (*ex parte*) (s 45). Different provisions apply to the making of an order, depending not just on whether or not the applicant is an entitled applicant, but also on his or her status (in other words, whether he or she is a spouse, civil partner, cohabitant, etc.). The court has wide powers to regulate the occupation of the home. For instance, it can exclude a person from the home and/or allow a person to enter into and occupy it. Occupation orders are not, however, routinely made due to the seriousness of excluding a person from his or her home, particularly where he or she has a proprietary right in the home. The criteria which govern the exercise of the court's powers differ depending on the type of applicant and

Summary cont'd

respondent. These criteria are complex. Different criteria apply and the outcome of the so-called 'balance of harm' test differs depending on the type of applicant. The provisions which the court has power to include in an occupation order also differ depending on the type of applicant and respondent. The duration of the order also varies depending on which section of Part IV of the Family Law Act 1996 the applicant falls under. The court can attach a power of arrest to an occupation order (s 47), but breach of an order is not a criminal offence. Instead, civil proceedings can be brought for contempt of court. The court can accept an undertaking instead of making an occupation order (s 46). An order can be varied or discharged (s 49). A child can apply for an occupation order, but leave of the court is needed (s 43).

▶ Sections 62 and 63 of Part IV of the Family Law Act 1996 are important because they define who can apply under the Act and other key terms.

▶ The Protection from Harassment Act 1997 can provide protection for victims of domestic violence. It creates two criminal offences of harassment (the section 2 offence of harassment; and the section 4 offence of aggravated harassment); and a civil tort of harassment for which damages are available (s 3). In order to constitute the offence of harassment, there must be a 'course of conduct', but a series of violent acts may not necessarily constitute harassment. A restraining order (to protect a named person from harassment) can be made under section 5. It can be made on the conviction of *any* offence, not just harassment; and can also be made if a defendant is acquitted of harassment (s 5A). Breach of a restraining order is a criminal offence.

▶ County courts and the High Court have jurisdiction to grant injunctions ancillary to other legal proceedings, provided it is just and convenient to do so and the applicant has a right in law or in equity which is in need of protection. Domestic violence injunctions under these powers are rare because of the statutory protection available for family members, in particular under Part IV of the Family Law Act 1996.

Further reading and references

Burton, '*R (Rabess)* v *Commissioner of the Police for the Metropolis* – "Scream Quietly or the Neighbours will Hear": Domestic violence, "nuisance neighbours" and the public/private dichotomy revisited' [2008] CFLQ 95.

Donovan and Hester, 'Seeking help from the enemy: help-seeking strategies of those in same-sex relationships who have experienced domestic abuse' [2011] CFLQ 26.

Edwards, 'Domestic violence: not a term of art but a state of consciousness' [2011] Fam Law 1244.

Websites

End Violence Against Women: www.endviolenceagainstwomen.org.uk
ManKind Initiative: www.mankind.org.uk
Men's Advice Line: www.mensadviceline.org.uk
National Centre for Domestic Violence: www.ncdv.org.uk
Refuge: www.refuge.org.uk
Women's Aid: www.womensaid.org.uk

Links to relevant websites can also be found at: www.palgrave.com/law/familylaw8e

Part IV

Divorce and its consequences

Chapter 6

Divorce

This chapter deals first with the development of divorce law, and then with the current law governing the obtaining of a divorce. Financial and property matters on divorce are dealt with in Chapter 7. Residence and contact arrangements for children are dealt with in Chapter 11, and financial provision for children in Chapter 12.

6.1 The development of divorce law

This section looks at the development of divorce from the end of the nineteenth century up to the present day. Although some readers may consider this account of the historical development of divorce law to be rather too detailed and rather too archaic, it is included in this chapter because it provides the background to the current law which continues to be very much rooted in the 'old' origins of the law. Thus, in order to understand the current law, it is necessary to look at the earlier law and how it has developed.

(a) The grounds for divorce

Until the mid-nineteenth century the ordinary courts had no jurisdiction to grant decrees of divorce, although the ecclesiastical courts could annul marriages and grant a limited sort of divorce which relieved the spouses of the legal obligation to live together, but did not terminate the marriage. The Christian idea of marriage as an indissoluble life-long union prevailed. Anyone who wished to divorce could only do so by private Act of Parliament, which was a complex, lengthy and expensive procedure available only to a few.

In order to remedy the inadequacies of the Act of Parliament procedure, the Matrimonial Causes Act 1857 was passed permitting judicial divorce on the ground of adultery by the respondent – a ground which was acceptable to the Church because of biblical precedent. In addition to adultery, the petitioner had to prove that there was no collusion, condonation or connivance between the parties. However, divorce was more difficult for wives, as, unlike husbands, they had to prove 'aggravated adultery' (adultery plus an additional factor, such as incest, cruelty, bigamy, sodomy or desertion). After considerable pressure for reform by the female emancipation movement, aggravated adultery was abolished by the Matrimonial Causes Act 1923.

The Matrimonial Causes Act 1937 added three further grounds: cruelty; desertion for a continuous period of at least three years; and incurable insanity. In response to concerns that this more liberal divorce law would undermine the institution of marriage, the 1937 Act introduced an absolute bar on divorce in the first three years of marriage, unless the petitioner could prove exceptional hardship or that the respondent had shown exceptional depravity. The aim of the three-year bar was to deter trial marriages and hasty divorces. Condonation, connivance and collusion remained as bars on divorce.

At the end of the Second World War, there was a sharp increase in the number of people wishing to divorce, and a growing dissatisfaction with the law. It seemed wrong to have to prove a matrimonial offence, thereby apportioning blame, when both spouses might be responsible for marriage breakdown. It seemed wrong for a restrictive divorce law to perpetuate a dead marriage which had completely broken down. It was also easy to abuse the system, for example by fabricating adultery. In response to dissatisfaction with the law, a Royal Commission, the Morton Commission, was established to look at divorce, and in its *Report* in 1956 (Cmd. 9678) it recommended the retention of the matrimonial offence doctrine as the basis for a good divorce law. This was a considerable setback for the proponents of reform, and it was not until the 1960s with the publication of two reports, one by the Church of England and the other by the Law Commission, that proposals for change began to be made. In 1963 the Archbishop of Canterbury appointed a Committee to study divorce, which in its report (*Putting Asunder*, 1966) recommended that the doctrine of the matrimonial offence be abolished and be replaced by a principle of irretrievable breakdown of marriage, which would be proved by holding an inquest into the causes of breakdown. Shortly after the publication of *Putting Asunder*, the Law Commission published a report (*Reform of the Grounds of Divorce: The Field of Choice,* Cmnd. 3123, 1966) in which it stated that the objectives of a good divorce law should be:

> 'To buttress, rather than to undermine the stability of marriage; and when, regrettably a marriage has irretrievably broken down, to enable the empty legal shell to be destroyed with the maximum fairness, and the minimum bitterness, distress and humiliation.'

The Law Commission concluded that a divorce law based on a matrimonial offence failed to satisfy these objectives, and, while it agreed with the Archbishop's Committee that irretrievable breakdown should be the sole ground for divorce, it rejected the Committee's proposal that breakdown should be established by holding an inquest into its causes, as this would be distressing for the parties, expensive, time-consuming and essentially untriable. The Law Commission proposed instead that breakdown should be established on proof of one or more of five facts, three of which would be based on the old matrimonial offences, and the other two on periods of separation. The five facts proposed were: adultery plus intolerability; unreasonable behaviour; desertion for a period of at least two years; two years' separation with consent to the divorce; and five years' separation. The Law Commission also recommended that a new divorce law should incorporate certain policy objectives. It should encourage reconciliation, prevent injustice to economically vulnerable spouses and protect children. It also recommended that the three-year bar on divorce should be replaced with a one-year bar as the three-year bar prolonged poor marriages, encouraged allegations of exceptional hardship or depravity which were difficult to adjudicate, and caused hostility and bitterness between the parties. It also caused duplication of proceedings, as an unhappily married spouse would petition for a decree of judicial separation followed not long afterwards by a petition for divorce. The Law Commission recommended a one-year bar, as it felt that to have no bar at all would undermine the sanctity of marriage.

The Law Commission's recommendations were eventually enacted in the Divorce Reform Act 1969, which came into force on 1 January 1971 (but which was later re-enacted as Part I of the Matrimonial Causes Act 1973). Except for certain amendments (notably the 'clean-break' provisions introduced by the Matrimonial and Family Proceedings Act 1984) the reforms introduced by the Divorce Reform Act 1969 remain the law today. We therefore have a hybrid law of divorce made up of fault and no-fault grounds. The retention of fault means that the matrimonial offence doctrine remains, and in fact is particularly prevalent, as many divorces are sought on the basis of the fault grounds of adultery or unreasonable behaviour – as these enable a petitioner to obtain a 'quick' divorce. The Law Commission's belief that most couples would use the separation grounds has not been realised in practice.

Since the introduction of the current grounds for divorce (in 1971), there has been increasing dissatisfaction with the law. In 2000 a radically new form of divorce was to have been introduced, but it was abandoned because it was found to be unworkable in practice.

(b)   Divorce procedure

Changes to divorce procedure have taken place over the years. Initially, because divorce was considered a serious matter, proceedings were heard only in London and only by senior judges. At one time, divorces were heard in open court with the petitioner giving oral evidence to prove the ground alleged. However, it became increasingly recognised that hearing divorces in open court was not only distressing for the parties, as they would have their intimate marital details exposed in public, but it was also unnecessarily expensive and time-consuming. Divorce was failing to achieve one of its major policy aims, namely the burial of a dead marriage with the minimum of distress and humiliation.

With the huge increase in the divorce rate, particularly after the introduction of the more liberal grounds for divorce by the Divorce Reform Act 1969, the courts became overloaded, even though most undefended divorces were taking as little as ten minutes to be heard. Eventually, a new divorce procedure, the 'special procedure', was introduced with the aim of achieving simplicity, speed and economy. It was initially introduced in 1973 for childless couples divorcing with consent, but was extended in 1975 to all childless couples, except those petitioning on the basis of unreasonable behaviour. In 1977 it was eventually extended to all undefended divorces. The introduction of the 'special procedure' was a radical change in the law, as an undefended divorce became available by what is essentially an administrative procedure, and, in most cases, with neither party being required to attend court. As this procedure has become the norm, the term 'special procedure' is no longer used.

All undefended divorces today are therefore dealt with by what is largely a 'paper exercise'. Thus the judge examines the papers to establish whether the fact alleged in the divorce petition is proved, whether the marriage has irretrievably broken down and whether there is any reason for not granting the divorce. A list of petitioners who satisfy the judge is drawn up and is read out in open court by the judge's clerk, after which the judge pronounces decree nisi of divorce en bloc. This judicial pronouncement is the last vestige of the public hearing of divorce.

6.2   An attempt at reform

In the late 1980s, as a result of increasing dissatisfaction with divorce law, proposals for reform were made. Although these proposals were enacted in Parts I, II and III of the Family Law Act 1996, they were never implemented because the Government concluded that they were unworkable in practice. Since then there has been no attempt to reform the law.

(a)   The background to the proposed reforms

In the 1980s the Booth Committee looked at divorce procedure and made recommendations for reform which included joint applications for divorce, a system of initial hearings in which the parties would be able to reach a settlement or identify areas of dispute, and changes of terminology to make the law more understandable. These proposals were not implemented.

Concerns about the ground for divorce led to proposals for reform by the Law Commission (see *Facing the Future: A Discussion Paper on the Ground for Divorce*, Law Com No. 170, 1988;*Family Law: The Ground for Divorce*, Law Com No. 192, 1990; *Looking to the Future: Mediation and the Ground for Divorce* Cm 2424, 1993;and*Looking to the Future: Mediation and the Ground for Divorce. The Government's Proposals*, Cm 2799, 1995).

The Law Commission was of the view that, although the 1969 reforms were a considerable improvement on the previous law, a major aim of those reforms – to move away from fault – had not been achieved in practice, as most divorces were being sought on the basis of adultery and unreasonable behaviour. It concluded that divorce law was not working well for various reasons. It allowed a divorce to be obtained too quickly and easily without the parties being required to consider the consequences. It did nothing to save marriages. It could make things worse for children. It was unjust and exacerbated bitterness and hostility. It was confusing, misleading, open to abuse, discriminatory and it also distorted the parties' bargaining positions.

Having identified the weaknesses in the law, the Law Commission made proposals for reform which, it claimed, would introduce a truly, and not artificially, no-fault divorce which would encourage the parties to reach agreement and consider and face up to the consequences of marital breakdown. Having discussed various options for reform, the Law Commission concluded that a no-fault model was best. After discussing the advantages and disadvantages of different no-fault models (divorce on proof of marriage breakdown, separation, or divorce by mutual consent, or by unilateral demand), it recommended the retention of irretrievable breakdown as the ground for divorce, but with divorce available at the end of a period of time. The Commission claimed that divorce over a period of time would encourage the parties to co-operate and consider the practical consequences of divorce; and would reinforce the idea that divorce is a process and not an event. It would also fit well with mediation.

(b) The proposed reform – 'divorce over a period of time'

'Divorce over a period of time,' which was enacted as Part II of the Family Law Act 1996, emphasised that divorce is a process, not an event, and introduced no-fault divorce. It required couples, in most cases, to have sorted out ancillary matters (finance, property and children) before being able to obtain a divorce. Parties were to be given more information about divorce, and greater emphasis was to be placed on mediation.

Irretrievable breakdown was to be the sole ground for divorce, which would be proved if: the applicant(s) had made a statement of marriage breakdown; a required period for reflection and consideration had passed; and one or both parties had declared that, having reflected on the breakdown and having considered arrangements for their future, their marriage could not be saved. A series of steps would have to be taken in order to obtain a divorce. An applicant would first have to attend an 'information meeting' at which information about divorce would be given, and marriage counselling provided, if needed. At least three months later, one or both of the parties would have to send a 'statement of marital breakdown' to the court which would then have the power to make directions requiring the parties to attend a meeting at which mediation would be explained, and to make interim ancillary relief orders and interim orders under the Children Act 1989. Once the statement of marital breakdown was lodged with the court, a period for reflection and consideration (9 months in some cases, 15 in others) would have to pass during which the applicant(s) would be required to spend time reflecting on whether their marriage could be saved and, if not, then on making arrangements in respect of ancillary relief and the welfare of any children. At the end of that period, an application for a 'divorce order' could be made, which the court could grant if it was satisfied that: the marriage had irretrievably broken down; the information meeting requirements had been complied with; arrangements for the future had been made; there was no order preventing divorce; and the requirements in respect of the welfare of the children had been satisfied.

The court would be able to make 'orders preventing divorce' where divorce would result in substantial financial or other hardship to the other party, or to a child of the family.

(c) The decision not to introduce the reforms

'Divorce over a period of time' was due to come into force on 1 January 1999, but implementation was suspended until 2000 so that the Government could consider the results of a pilot scheme to see how the information meetings (see above) would work in practice. However, the results of the pilot scheme turned out to be disappointing. Only 7 per cent of those attending information meetings were diverted into mediation and very few couples attended the meetings together. The information meetings had failed to achieve the Government's stated objectives of saving saveable marriages and encouraging mediation. Because the proposals had failed to fulfil the policy objectives in Part I of the Act of saving saveable marriages and, where they had broken down, bringing them to an end with the minimum of distress to the parties and any children, the reforms were never introduced, and Parts I and II of the Family Law Act 1996 were eventually repealed.

The Government's decision not to implement the reforms was greeted with considerable relief by those who believed the proposals to be inherently flawed on the grounds that they were unnecessarily complicated and unworkable in practice. One of the main criticisms was that the reforms placed impractical and impossible demands on divorcing couples. Couples in the throes of marriage breakdown would have found it difficult, and in some cases impossible, to make arrangements for the future. Cretney (1995) thought that the Government seemed 'curiously naive' about what was likely to happen during the period of reflection. He said that some couples would not spend time considering whether their marriage could be saved or making arrangements for the future, but would instead spend time conceiving children, or exploiting their emotional or financial advantage or brooding on their grievances. Freeman (1997) was critical of the length of the divorce process because he thought it would create 'more conflict, more tension, more domestic violence, unnecessary abortions and more children who [would] experience their parents' divorce while still of pre-school years'. Eekelaar (1999) criticised the need for information meetings, and considered them a form of 'social engineering'. The Solicitors' Family Law Association (now called Resolution) considered the new law to be cumbersome and confusing, and said it would create delay and uncertainty, which were contrary to the best interests of divorcing couples and their children.

Thus, despite a more than decade-long attempt at reform, the new divorce law never came to fruition; and there are no current proposals to reform the law. In Scotland, however, where divorce law is similar to that in England and Wales, a simple change to the law has been implemented, so that the five-year separation ground has been reduced to two, and the two-year separation with consent ground reduced to one. The aim of this change was to encourage the use of the separation grounds, and thereby lessen the acrimony and conflict which may be associated with fault-based divorces, and to allow parents and children to move on.

6.3 The current law of divorce: introduction

Statistics on divorce for 2010 in England and Wales

These figures were published in December 2011 by the Office for National Statistics (www.statistics.gov.uk).

▶ There were 119,589 divorces, an increase of 4.9 per cent on 2009. This is the first annual increase in divorces since 2003 (when there were 153,065 divorces).
▶ There were 11.1 divorces per 1,000 married men and women (compared with 10.5 in 2009).
▶ The average duration of marriage was 11.4 years (unchanged from 2009).
▶ 20 per cent of men and 19 per cent of women had been previously divorced (compared with 10 per cent of men and women in 1980).
▶ Men and women aged 40 to 44 had the highest divorce rates of all age groups.
▶ 66 per cent of divorces were granted to wives.
▶ 55 per cent of divorces granted to wives, and 36 per cent of divorces granted to husbands, were based on unreasonable behaviour.
▶ 50 per cent of divorcing couples had at least one child under 16. There were 104, 364 children aged under 16 who were in families where the parents divorced.
▶ The average age at divorce was 41.7 years (for women) and 44.2 years (for men) (compared to 41.5 years and 44.0 years respectively in 2006).

The law of divorce is laid down in the Matrimonial Causes Act (MCA) 1973, Part I of which deals with obtaining a divorce (or an annulment or judicial separation) and Part II with finance and property orders on divorce (and also nullity and judicial separation) (see Chapter 7). Procedural rules governing divorce are found in Part 7 of the Family Procedure Rules (FPR) 2010 (which also applies to annulments, judicial separation, and civil partnership dissolution).

An undefended divorce is obtained by means of what is essentially an administrative exercise. It can be granted in a matter of weeks without the need, in most cases, for either party to attend court. Sorting out ancillary matters (property, finance and children), if the parties cannot reach agreement, takes much longer. Obtaining a divorce is a two-stage process: decree nisi followed by decree absolute. Only on the grant of the decree absolute is the marriage terminated. The procedure for defended divorces is different, but divorces are rarely defended. Under the FPR 2010, the parties to a divorce are called the 'applicant' (formerly known as the 'petitioner') and the 'respondent'.

Jurisdiction The jurisdictional rules for hearing a petition for divorce (or for nullity or judicial separation) in the courts in England and Wales are laid down in section 5(2) of the Domicile and Matrimonial Proceedings Act 1973; and, for divorces involving Member

States of the EU, in Article 3 of Council Regulation (EC) (No. 2201/2003) Concerning Jurisdiction and the Recognition and Enforcement of Judgments in Matrimonial Matters and in Matters of Parental Responsibility (Brussels II Revised). The rules are complex, but in general terms the courts in England and Wales have jurisdiction to grant a divorce if either spouse is domiciled in England or Wales when the proceedings are begun, or is habitually resident in England or Wales throughout the period of one year ending with the date on which proceedings are begun.

In *Mark v Mark* [2005] UKHL 42, [2005] 2 FLR 1193 the House of Lords held that, for the purpose of jurisdiction to entertain a petition for divorce under section 5(2) of the Domicile and Matrimonial Proceedings Act 1973, residence in England and Wales need not be lawful residence. Thus a person can be habitually resident or domiciled in England and Wales even if their presence in the UK is a criminal offence under the Immigration Act 1971.

Difficulties can occur when a couple move out of the jurisdiction of the UK to another country. Thus, for example, in *Munro v Munro* [2008] 1 FLR 1613 Bennett J had to decide whether the wife should be allowed to petition for divorce in England and Wales even though she and her husband had moved to Spain shortly after marrying in England. The husband argued that, as his wife had acquired domicile in Spain, the divorce should be heard in Spain. Applying Brussels II Revised (see above), Bennett J said that cogent evidence was required to prove that by unequivocal intentions and acts either party had abandoned his or her English domicile of origin and acquired a Spanish domicile of choice; and he held on the facts that the English, not the Spanish, court had jurisdiction.

Staying divorce proceedings   The Domicile and Matrimonial Proceedings Act 1973 gives the divorce courts in England and Wales the power to stay divorce proceedings where divorce proceedings are pending in another country (see, for example, *JKN v JCN* [2010] EWHC 843 (Fam) where the High Court granted the husband's application for a stay of proceedings as the court in New York was the more appropriate forum for the divorce).

The 'one-year bar' on divorce   Divorce proceedings cannot be commenced within the first year of marriage (s 3(1) MCA 1973). This is an absolute bar – there is no discretion to waive it. Despite the one-year bar, a divorce petition can be based on matters which happened during the first year of marriage (s 3(2)). A decree of nullity, on the other hand, can be sought during the first year of marriage.

Encouraging reconciliation   As part of the policy objective of divorce law to encourage the saving of saveable marriages, certain provisions in Part I of the MCA 1973 aim to encourage reconciliation. Thus, the court can adjourn divorce proceedings at any stage if there is a reasonable possibility of a reconciliation between the parties (s 6(2)), and certain periods of resumed cohabitation are ignored when establishing whether or not the marriage has irretrievably broken down. Where the applicant for divorce is legally represented, a 'reconciliation statement' must be filed with the divorce petition (see further below).

6.4   The ground for divorce and the five facts

Under Part I of the Matrimonial Causes Act 1973 there is only one ground for divorce: irretrievable breakdown of the marriage (s 1(1)). To establish irretrievable breakdown, the applicant must prove one or more of the following five 'facts' which in common parlance are referred to as the 'grounds' for divorce:

The five facts for divorce

Section 1(2) of the Matrimonial Causes Act 1973 requires the petitioner to prove to the court that:

'(a) the respondent has committed adultery and the petitioner finds it intolerable to live with the respondent;

(b) the respondent has behaved in such a way that the petitioner cannot reasonably be expected to live with the respondent;

(c) the respondent has deserted the petitioner for a continuous period of at least two years immediately preceding the presentation of the petition;

(d) the parties to the marriage have lived apart for a continuous period of at least two years immediately preceding the presentation of the petition ... and the respondent consents to a decree being granted; or

(e) the parties to the marriage have lived apart for a continuous period of at least five years immediately preceding the presentation of the petition.'

If a fact is proved, the court must grant a decree nisi of divorce unless it is satisfied that the marriage has not irretrievably broken down (s 1(4)). The court must be satisfied *both* of irretrievable breakdown and at least one fact. This requirement was described by the Law Commission, when discussing reform (see 6.2 above), as illogical (see, for example, *Richards v Richards* [1972] 1 WLR 1073 and *Buffery v Buffery* [1988] 2 FLR 365 where in each case the Court of Appeal found that irretrievable breakdown had been established, but not unreasonable behaviour).

(a) Adultery (section 1(2)(a))

Adultery involves an act of voluntary heterosexual intercourse between two people who are not married to each other, but at least one of whom is married. Adultery is proved by the respondent admitting the adultery on the acknowledgment of service form (r 7.12(4) FPR 2010).

In addition to adultery, the applicant also must prove that it is intolerable to live with the respondent (s 1(2)(a)). This requirement was added to buttress the stability of marriage (a policy aim of the law), so that an act of adultery would be insufficient on its own to end a marriage. Adultery and intolerability are two separate and unrelated facts (*Cleary v Cleary* [1974] 1 WLR 73). There is no need for an applicant to show that he or she finds it intolerable to live with the respondent in consequence of the adultery; it is sufficient if the applicant genuinely finds it intolerable to do so for whatever reason (*Goodrich v Goodrich* [1971] 2 All ER 1340). As part of the policy objective of divorce law to encourage reconciliation, a petition based on adultery cannot be heard if the parties have lived together for more than six months (in one period, or more than one period, aggregated) after the applicant discovered the adultery (s 2(1)); but a period (or aggregated periods) of living together not exceeding six months is disregarded when determining the question of intolerability (s 2(2)).

(b) Unreasonable behaviour (section 1(2)(b))

The applicant must prove that the respondent has behaved in such a way that he or she cannot reasonably be expected to live with the respondent. Although this fact is referred to as 'unreasonable behaviour', this is a misnomer because, under section 1(2)(b), it is the effect of the respondent's behaviour on the applicant which is relevant, not whether the respondent's behaviour is unreasonable.

In *Livingstone-Stallard v Livingstone-Stallard* [1974] Fam 47 Dunn J adopted the following test for establishing unreasonable behaviour:

> 'Would any right-thinking person come to the conclusion that this husband has behaved in such a way that this wife cannot reasonably be expected to live with him, taking into account the whole of the circumstances and the characters and personalities of the parties?'

This test was approved by the Court of Appeal in *O'Neill v O'Neill* [1975] 1 WLR 1118, and endorsed by the Court of Appeal in *Buffery v Buffery* [1988] 2 FLR 365.

Divorces are granted for a wide range of behaviour, including both acts and omissions. Some behaviour, however, may be too trivial and a decree may be refused, as it was in *Buffery v Buffery* (above) where the wife alleged that her husband was insensitive, never took her out, and that they had nothing to talk about and nothing in common after their children had grown up and left home. Her petition was dismissed, as her husband's behaviour was found to be insufficient to satisfy the behaviour ground. An accumulation of trivial incidents may, however, constitute unreasonable behaviour as they did in *Livingstone-Stallard v Livingstone-Stallard* (above), where Dunn J held that the wife 'was subjected to a constant atmosphere of criticism, disapproval and boorish behaviour on the part of her husband'. However, as each case depends on its own facts, an accumulation of various minor matters will not necessarily result in a decree being granted. In *Butterworth v Butterworth* [1997] 2 FLR 336, for example, the decree of divorce was set aside by the Court of Appeal as the petition was severely defective. The husband had denied the wife's allegations that he was a violent, possessive, sexually demanding and jealous alcoholic who had stopped her going to church. The Court of Appeal stressed that the law of divorce still gave the respondent the right to oppose a divorce, and to have the allegations in the petition properly proved. The Court of Appeal held that the court had not applied the correct test for unreasonable behaviour, or anything like it.

Sometimes the court may have to decide whether to grant a divorce where the behaviour is not the respondent's fault (for example where the respondent is mentally or physically ill). Whether a divorce will be granted will depend on the circumstances of the case, and, although the court will be cognisant of the fact that marriage entails a commitment which includes caring for a sick spouse, it is likely to be sympathetic to the plight of an applicant and the fact that illness can place severe strains on a marriage. A divorce may therefore be granted even though a respondent is not responsible for his or her own 'behaviour' (see, for example, in *Katz v Katz* [1972] 1 WLR 955 where the respondent husband suffered from manic depression).

The parties can live together for up to six months (in one period or more than one period, aggregated) after the last instance of behaviour alleged without losing the right to petition for divorce; and the court must ignore this period when determining whether the applicant can reasonably be expected to live with the respondent (s 2(3)).

(c) Desertion (section 1(2)(c))

The respondent must have deserted the applicant for a continuous period of at least two years immediately preceding the presentation of the petition. To prove desertion there must be: factual separation; an intention by the respondent to desert; no consent by the applicant to the desertion; and no just cause to desert. Constructive desertion is also possible (in other words where a spouse's behaviour is so bad that the other spouse is forced to leave the home). To encourage reconciliation, a period of up to six months' resumed cohabitation does not prevent the desertion from being continuous (s 2(5)). Divorces based on desertion are rare.

(d) Two years' separation with consent to the divorce (section 1(2)(d))

The parties must have lived apart for a continuous period of at least two years immediately preceding the presentation of the petition, and the respondent must consent to the decree being granted. The respondent must have the capacity to consent and must be given such information as will enable him or her to understand the effect of a decree being granted (s 2(7)). Notice of consent is given by the respondent signing to that effect on the acknowledgement of service form (see r 7.12(4) and (6) FPR 2010). Consent may be withdrawn at any time before decree nisi, whereupon the proceedings must be stayed. At any time before decree absolute the respondent can apply to have the decree nisi rescinded if the respondent has been misled by the applicant in respect of any matter which the respondent took into account in deciding whether to give consent (s 10(1)). The respondent can also ask for the decree absolute to be postponed in certain circumstances (see 6.5 below).

The parties must be living in separate households for separation to be established (s 2(6)). This is a question of fact. However, as 'household' does not mean 'house', separation is possible where the parties are living under the same roof (see, for example, *Fuller v Fuller* [1973] 1 WLR 730 where a decree was granted even though the husband lived as a lodger with his wife and her new male friend).

When calculating separation, no account is taken of a period of up to six months (in one period or several periods aggregated) during which the parties resumed living together, but there must still be an aggregated period of actual separation for at least two years (s 2(5)). If the period of resumed cohabitation is more than six months, the two-year period of separation starts to run again.

(e) Five years' separation (section 1(2)(e))

The parties must have lived apart for a continuous period of at least five years immediately preceding the presentation of the petition. The applicant must establish factual separation, but there can be separation even though the spouses live under the same roof. To protect the respondent, the court can delay decree absolute or refuse decree nisi (see 6.5 below). A reconciliation period of up to six months can be ignored, provided the parties have separated for an aggregated period of at least five years, but, if the reconciliation is for more than six months, then the five-year period begins to run again (s 2(5)). In practice, few spouses petition for divorce on this fact because most applicants do not wish to wait for five years to obtain a divorce.

6.5 Protection for respondents

Sections 10 and 5 of the Matrimonial Causes Act 1973 provide protection for respondents who are being divorced on the basis of two or five years' separation. The aim of these provisions is to protect 'innocent' spouses; in other words, those who have committed no matrimonial offence.

(a)   Section 10 Matrimonial Causes Act 1973

Under section 10(2) a respondent to a divorce based on two or five years' separation can ask the court to consider whether his or her financial situation after divorce will be satisfactory. If such an application is made, the court may refuse to grant the decree absolute unless it is satisfied: that the applicant should not be required to make financial provision for the respondent; or that the provision made or to be made by the applicant is reasonable and fair, or the best that can be made in the circumstances (s 10(3)). The court may, however, grant a decree absolute in any event if it is desirable to do so without delay, and it has obtained a satisfactory undertaking from the applicant that he or she will make such financial provision as the court may approve (s 10(4)).

Few applications are made under section 10, but an application may be useful as a tactical manoeuvre to put pressure on an applicant to sort out the parties' financial position, for instance where there may be a problem enforcing an ancillary relief order (see, for example, *Garcia v Garcia* [1992] 1 FLR 256 where a section 10 application was made in order to enforce maintenance payments for a child).

Section 10 applications were sometimes used to provide protection for respondents (particularly wives) who would lose pension entitlement as a result of divorce. However, as the divorce court now has wide powers in respect of pension distribution (see 7.8), there is no longer any need to use section 10 for this purpose.

(b)   Section 5 Matrimonial Causes Act 1973

Under section 5 a respondent to a divorce based on five years' separation has a complete defence to divorce. The aim of this provision is to safeguard the position of 'innocent' spouses who do not wish to be divorced. In practice, however, it is rarely invoked, and even if it is, it rarely succeeds. Under section 5, the court has the power to rescind a decree nisi if the respondent proves that they will suffer grave financial or other hardship if the divorce is granted; and that it would be wrong in all the circumstances to grant the divorce. The alleged hardship must arise as a result of the dissolution of the marriage. Hardship can include the loss of the chance of acquiring a benefit which the respondent might acquire if the marriage were not dissolved (s 5(3)) for example, loss of a right to succeed under the other spouse's will or intestacy. Most of the reported cases have been in relation to pension rights (see, for example *Archer v Archer* [1999] 1 FLR 327), but because of changes to the law on pensions on divorce this is no longer necessary (see 7.8). 'Other hardship' for the purposes of section 5 could include, for instance, hardship that a respondent might suffer as a result of ostracism in the community because of religious or social attitudes to divorce.

Defences under section 5 are extremely rare, and, even where pleaded, may not be successful. In most cases the court will consider it best to end the marriage.

6.6   Divorce procedure

Divorce procedure differs according to whether a divorce is undefended or defended. In practice, virtually all divorces are undefended, because of the futility of defending a divorce. The rules of procedure are laid down in Part 7 of the Family Procedure Rules 2010 ('Procedure for Applications in Matrimonial and Civil Partnership Proceedings').

(a) Undefended divorce

An undefended divorce is obtained by way of what is essentially a paper exercise. There is usually no need for the parties, or their legal representatives (if any), to attend court. Advice about obtaining divorce and downloadable copies of the various forms are available at Directgov (www.direct.gov.uk).

(i) Starting proceedings To start proceedings, an applicant must complete a divorce petition on Form D8 and send it to any divorce county court (r 7.5(1) FPR 2010). The petition must contain the following: information about the applicant and the respondent (name, address, date of birth); details about the marriage; details about any other court proceedings; a statement that the marriage has irretrievably broken down on the basis of at least one of the five facts; details about the children and whether or not a statement of arrangements for children (Form D8A, see 11.3) is attached; details of the legal representative (if any); and details about any co-respondent (in the case of adultery). The final part of the petition concludes with: a 'prayer' by the applicant for the marriage to be dissolved; a claim for costs (if any); and a claim for financial orders (if any) for the applicant and/or any children. The petition must be signed and dated by the applicant (or by the legal representative, if there is legal representation). The petition cannot be presented to the court until one year has expired from the date of the marriage (s 3(1)); but anything that happened during that one-year period (such as unreasonable behaviour or adultery) can be used as evidence in the proceedings (s 3(2)).

Three copies of the petition (Form D8) are sent to the court with three copies of each of the following: the marriage certificate; the statement of arrangements for children (Form D8A); certified copies of any court orders; and any certificate in respect of public funding. Where the applicant is legally represented, the legal representative must, unless the court directs otherwise, file with the application a 'reconciliation statement' stating whether the legal representative has discussed with the applicant the possibility of a reconciliation and given the applicant the names and addresses of persons qualified to help effect a reconciliation (r 7.6 FPR 2010) A fee (currently £340) must be paid when the petition is filed.

(ii) The next stage Once the petition and other documents have been filed in the court, a copy of the petition is served on the respondent accompanied by a 'notice of proceedings' (which explains the effect of the petition and informs the respondent of the procedure involved) and also an 'acknowledgement of service' (Form D10). Form D10 is a question-and-answer form which the respondent must complete, sign and return to the court within eight days of receiving the divorce papers, failing which a further copy of the petition may be served upon the respondent personally. On Form D10 the respondent must state whether the petition has been received, whether the respondent intends to defend the divorce, whether consent to the divorce is given if sought on the basis of two years' separation with consent, and also whether the respondent intends to apply for a financial order and/or for any order in respect of the children.

(iii) Obtaining decree nisi Once the respondent (and any co-respondent) has returned the acknowledgement of service (D10) to the court and it is clear that the respondent does not wish to defend the divorce, the applicant (or legal representative) must file an 'application for decree nisi' (Form D84) (asking the court to review the applicant's paper work and decide whether to grant a decree nisi) (see also r 7.19 FPR 2010). Form D84 must be accompanied by Form D80, which is a written statement and questionnaire in specified form, sworn by the applicant and which provides evidence of the fact(s) relied on. (There are different versions of Form D80, depending on the fact alleged.) These forms will then be given to the judge who will look at all the paperwork and decide whether there is enough evidence on which to grant the divorce. If there are any children aged under 16, or over 16 whom the court directs should be included (for instance, because of disability), the court must consider the proposed arrangements for the children before granting a decree nisi (s 41 MCA 1973 and r 7.25 FPR 2010) (see further at 11.3). The judge may request further information or evidence, if needed.

If satisfied about all the paperwork and that the fact is proved and the marriage has irretrievably broken down, the judge will file a 'certificate of entitlement to a decree' (FormD84A), which is sent to both parties, and informs them of the date, time and place for the formal pronouncement of decree nisi (see r 7.20 FPR 2010). If the judge does not agree on the divorce, the parties will be sent a 'notice of refusal of judge's certificate' (Form D79), which will explain why the judge does not consider it is right to grant a divorce, and will, if necessary, explain whether the judge needs more information and/ or whether a formal court hearing is need.

Pronouncement of decree nisi takes place in open court, but there is no need for the parties and/or any legal representative to attend (see r 7.18 FPR 2010) unless either party wishes to be heard on the question of costs. Pronouncement is a mere formality. The decrees are listed together in batches and collectively read out by the clerk of the court before the judge who agrees by nodding (or are read out by the judge orally). The parties will also be sent Form D84B stating that the judge thinks the proposed arrangements for the children are not a reason for delaying the divorce. (If the parties do not have children, they will also receive Form D84B, which will state that they have no children.) Once the decree nisi has been formally pronounced, the parties will be sent a 'decree nisi' (Form D29), after which the applicant can apply for decree absolute.

(iv) Obtaining decree absolute The grant of decree nisi does not terminate the marriage. It is only terminated on the grant of the decree absolute, which is automatically granted on the application of the applicant, who can apply for it (on Form D36, 'notice of application for decree nisi to be made absolute') six weeks or more after decree nisi (s 1(5) MCA 1973; r 7.32(1) FPR 2010). There is no need to give the respondent notice of the application. A fee must be paid (currently £45). If the applicant fails to apply for decree absolute, the respondent may apply (on Form D11, 'application notice') after three months have passed from the earliest date on which the applicant could apply (s 9(2) MCA 1973). A court fee (currently £90) must be paid. The respondent cannot be granted a decree absolute in these circumstances without a court hearing (r 7.33 FPR 2010). These rules are strict. If a decree absolute is obtained in breach of the rules, the divorce is void (see *Dennis v Dennis* [2000] 2 FLR 231).

If there are children, the divorce cannot be made absolute until the district judge has considered whether the court should exercise any of its powers under section 41 MCA 1973 (r 7.25 FPR 2010; and see 11.3). Where a divorce is sought on either of the separation grounds, a decree absolute can be refused where a respondent has not been satisfactorily financially provided for by the applicant (see 6.5).

The purpose of the gap between decree nisi and decree absolute is to enable a respondent to appeal, and for the Queen's Proctor and other persons to intervene to show just cause why a decree should not be made absolute (s 8 MCA 1973). Intervention by the Queen's Proctor was much more of a possibility under the old divorce law where a decree absolute could be refused if the parties had colluded. Intervention by the Queen's Proctor is now rare (but see *Bhaijii v Chauhan (Queen's Proctor Intervening)* [2003] 2 FLR 485 where the Queen's Proctor opposed the grant of decrees absolute where bogus allegations of behaviour had been made to obtain divorces in respect of five marriages which had been entered into solely for the purpose of circumventing the immigration rules).

(b) Defended divorce

Defended divorce proceedings begin in the same way as an undefended divorce, but the respondent in the acknowledgement of service indicates an intention to defend. Provided various notice requirements have been satisfied (see r 7.12 FPR 2010), there is an exchange of pleadings and the hearing takes place in open court with oral evidence being given and cross-examination of both parties.

6.7 Legal effects of divorce

Once a decree absolute of divorce has been granted, the marriage is dissolved and each party is free to remarry. A decree absolute has other legal consequences. Thus, financial provision and property adjustment orders made under Part II of the Matrimonial Causes Act 1973 in favour of the parties to the marriage take effect, and orders for settlement or variation of a settlement can take effect in respect of any child of the family. All other orders for children take effect as soon as they are made. Divorce also has an effect on a will made by either party to the marriage (see 4.2). Social security and pension rights and taxation are affected, and both parties lose rights under certain matrimonial legislation, in particular rights of occupation of the home ('home rights' – see pp. 72–3). However, as far as children are concerned, each parent retains parental responsibility, and the obligation to provide children with financial support continues (see Chapter 12). Disputes about residence and contact can be settled by way of mediation or, in the last resort, by an application to the court (see Chapter 11).

6.8 The future of divorce

▶ **Stephen Cretney,** *Family Law in the Twentieth Century*, **2003, p. 391**

'English divorce law is in a state of confusion. The theory of the law remains that divorce is a matter in which the State has a vital interest, and that it is only allowed if the marriage can be demonstrated to have irretrievably broken down. But the practical reality is very different: divorce is readily and quickly available if both parties agree, and even if one of them is reluctant he or she will, faced with a divorce petition, almost always accept the inevitable: there is no point in denying that the marriage has broken down if one party firmly asserts it has.'

After the Government's decision not to implement the divorce reforms in Part II of the Family Law Act 1996 (see 6.2), judges, practitioners and academics have continued to voice concerns about the unsatisfactory nature of divorce law. Thus, for example, in July 2001, the Lord Chancellor's Advisory Board on Family Law in its final report regretted the missed opportunity to reform divorce, and urged that serious consideration be given to replacing the current adversarial and partly fault-based divorce regime. It said that the serious defects in the current law identified by the Law Commission still remained. In particular, allegations of adultery and unreasonable behaviour caused unnecessary conflict between the parties, and their distress and anger impacted on children.

The most senior family law judges have also argued for the introduction of no-fault divorce. Thus, the Rt Hon Dame Elizabeth Butler-Sloss (a former President of the Family Division) has described obtaining a divorce on the basis of unreasonable behaviour as a 'hypocritical charade' and said that there is a need to introduce a truly no-fault divorce. Another former President of the Family Division, Sir Nicholas Wall, is also in favour of no-fault divorce (see below).

Allegations of fault also seem contrary to the promotion of the settlement culture which exists in respect of applications for a financial remedy and arrangements for children on divorce. There is also a risk that some parties may be 'steam-rollered' into divorce, because a divorce can be obtained so quickly. As Kay (2004) states:

'Over two-thirds of divorces granted in England and Wales in 2002 were based on facts that clearly have connotations of blame and guilt, and where proceedings can be commenced in haste, without thought for the consequences of the breakdown and the legal ending of marriage. Taken as a whole, these statistics make a compelling case for reform.'

Kay also points out that, although divorce law is acknowledged to be unsatisfactory, it has nevertheless been replicated in virtually the same form for civil partners under the Civil Partnership Act 2004.

The possibility of introducing a purely administrative divorce has been considered from time to time. Cretney, for instance, asked ([2002] Fam Law 900):

'Should we not accept that the routine processing of marriage breakdown is no longer a judicial function and that it should accordingly be removed altogether from the courts and the judicial system, leaving them with more time to deal with the problems that do require their expertise and procedures? If we believe that respect for the law and the legal system is important, and that the 1996 reforms would have made the law even more complex and difficult to understand, should we not begin to ask whether there is not a simpler and better alternative?'

Resolution (the organisation of family lawyers) has campaigned for many years for no-fault divorce to be introduced – because the current law of divorce does not sit well with the non-confrontational approach adopted and promoted in the rest of the family justice system. It has called for reform to be put back on the agenda. Thus, Shepherd [2009] Fam Law 122, for example, has said that 'ending the blame game should be right at the top of the list of priorities for all of us working with those who are having to come to terms with relationship breakdown'. With the increasing emphasis on mediation and settlement, divorce by mutual consent would seem to be a logical development, even though it was somewhat cursorily dismissed by the Law Commission in its 1988 Discussion Paper on the basis that it would undermine the institution of marriage.

There continue to be calls for reform. For instance, in a submission to the Family Justice Review (see further at p. 7) The Law Society in 2011 expressed the opinion that the adversarial grounds for divorce should be removed and a no-fault system introduced; and that there should be no need to show why a marriage has irretrievably broken down when submitting a divorce petition. In the following extract, Sir Nicholas Wall, former President of the Family Division (who retired in December 2012) has also called for reform of the law of divorce:

▶ **Sir Nicholas Wall, former President of the Family Division, 'The President's Resolution address 2012' [2012] Fam Law 817.**

'My position is very simple. I am a strong believer in marriage. But I see no good arguments against no-fault divorce. At the moment, as it seems to me we have a system – so far as divorce itself is concerned – which is in fact administrative, but which masquerades as judicial. No doubt this has its roots in history. In the nineteenth century and for much of the twentieth, divorce was a matter of social status – it mattered whether you were divorced or not, and if you were, it was important to demonstrate that you were the "innocent" party. All that, I think, has gone. Defended divorces are now effectively unheard of. The allegations in a petition under section 1(2)(b) are rarely relevant to any other aspect of the process, and if used in proceedings for ancillary relief have to be separately pleaded, and even then are only relevant if stringent criteria are attached to them. As a student, of course, I grew up with the three Cs – connivance, collusion and condonation. All those have gone. It seems to me, therefore, that the time for no fault divorce has also come.'

In May 2011 Sir Paul Coleridge, a Senior High Court Judge, in a speech to the Christian Charity CARE, described the current law of divorce as being 'no longer fit for purpose' having been designed for 'a wholly different era to deal with a different way of life'. However, despite widespread criticism of the law of divorce, there are no Government proposals to reform it.

6.9 Recognition of an overseas divorce

Part II of the Family Law Act 1986 lays down rules for the recognition in the UK of divorces (and annulments and separations) obtained overseas. The Act makes a distinction between divorces obtained in judicial or other proceedings and those otherwise obtained. Recognition is much broader for divorces obtained in proceedings. An overseas divorce granted in proceedings is recognised in the UK if it is effective under the law of the country where it was obtained, and at the commencement of those proceedings either party was habitually resident or domiciled in that country or was a national of that country (s 46(1)). An overseas divorce obtained otherwise than in proceedings is recognised in the UK if it is effective in the country where it was obtained and at the date it was obtained one or both parties were domiciled there, or one party was domiciled there and the other party was domiciled in a country which recognised the divorce, and in any case neither party was habitually resident in the UK for one year immediately preceding the divorce (s 46(2)).

The English courts have a discretion to refuse recognition of an overseas divorce whether or not it was obtained in proceedings. Thus, for example, they may under section 51(3) refuse to recognise an overseas divorce if reasonable steps have not been taken for giving notice of the proceedings to a party to the marriage (see *Duhur-Johnson v Duhur-Johnson (Attorney-General Intervening)* [2005] 2 FLR 1042 where a Nigerian divorce was refused recognition as a valid overseas divorce because the husband had not taken reasonable steps to give notice of the divorce proceedings to his wife).

An overseas divorce may not be recognised in England and Wales where recognition would be manifestly contrary to public policy (s 52). However, it may be difficult to argue that a divorce should not be recognised on public policy grounds (*per* Thorpe LJ in *Eroglu v Eroglu* [1994] 2 FLR 287, where the wife's claim that her Turkish divorce should not be recognised in England and Wales was dismissed, despite her claim that it had been obtained by fraud). In *H v H (The Queen's Proctor Intervening) (Validity of Japanese Divorce)* [2007] 1 FLR 1318 a Japanese divorce by agreement (a *Kyogirikon*) was recognised as a valid divorce, as there was no reason to refuse recognition on the grounds of public policy.

Recognition of divorces within the EU   Special rules apply to the recognition of divorces within the European Union. Council Regulation (EC) (No. 2201/2003) Concerning Jurisdiction and the Recognition and Enforcement of Judgments in Matrimonial Matters and in Matters of Parental Responsibility (Brussels II Revised) applies (see, for example, *D v D (Nature of Recognition of Overseas Divorce)* [2005] EWHC 3342 (Fam), [2006] 2 FLR 825 where Bodey J made a declaration that the Greek divorce was recognised in England and Wales under Brussels II, which had the effect of dissolving the parties' marital status).

Is a talaq a valid overseas divorce?   A *talaq* is a unilateral Islamic divorce whereby a husband can divorce his wife by merely uttering the words 'I divorce you' three times without being in the presence of another person and without his wife's consent. Whether a *talaq* will be recognised in England and Wales depends on the circumstances of the case. If the *talaq* is obtained in England it will not be recognised as a valid divorce, as divorces obtained in England and Wales other than by court proceedings are not recognised. Thus, in *Sulaiman v Juffali* [2002] 1 FLR 479 a *talaq* pronounced in England, but subsequently registered in Saudi Arabia, was held not to be a valid divorce within the meaning of section 45(1) of the Family Law Act 1986, as it was not obtained in Saudi Arabia. Even though the *talaq* had complied with all the formalities required by Sharia law in Saudi Arabia, it had clearly been obtained in England other than in a court, and thus fell foul of the FLA 1986.

Whether the court in England and Wales will recognise a *talaq* validly made outside the UK depends on the circumstances of the case, and is a matter for the discretion of the court. Thus, for instance, in *El Fadl v El Fadl* [2000] 1 FLR 175, a *talaq* divorce registered with the Sharia court in Lebanon was recognised by the High Court, and, as a result, the wife's petition for an English divorce was dismissed. It was held that recognition was not contrary to public policy, even though such a divorce might offend English sensibilities. Similarly, in *H v H (Talaq Divorce)* [2007] EWHC 2945, [2008] 2 FLR 857, a *talaq* divorce validly announced in Pakistan was upheld by the High Court. Sumner J said that it was important that marriages and divorces recognised in one country should be recognised in another unless there were good reasons for not doing so, especially when there were, as in this case, close links between the two countries and many people moved freely between them. There were no good reasons for refusing to recognise the *talaq* divorce in the circumstances of the case. However, each case depends on its own facts, and in *A v L* [2010] EWHC 460 (Fam) (where the wife petitioned for divorce in the English courts but where her husband claimed they had already been divorced in Egypt by *talaq*), the High Court held that the *talaq* should not be recognised as the husband had deliberately failed to give his wife notice of the Egyptian court hearing.

6.10   Other decrees

Under Part I of the Matrimonial Causes Act 1973 the court has jurisdiction to grant decrees of nullity (see Chapter 2), decrees of judicial separation and decrees of presumption of death.

(a)   Decree of judicial separation

Divorce county courts and the High Court have jurisdiction to grant a decree of judicial separation under section 17 of the Matrimonial Causes Act 1973, provided the applicant can prove one of the five facts in section 1(2) of the MCA 1973 (see p. 136 above). There is no need to prove irretrievable breakdown of marriage. The effect of a decree of judicial separation is not to dissolve the marriage but merely to terminate the obligation of the applicant to continue living with the respondent (s 18(1)) (although the spouses are not obliged to separate).

Where a decree of judicial separation is in force and separation is continuing, the surviving spouse is not entitled to succeed to the deceased spouse's property on his or her intestacy, but judicial separation does not affect a will (s 18(2)).

On the grant of a decree, the court has jurisdiction to make financial orders under Part II of the Matrimonial Causes Act 1973 (see Chapter 7). Divorce is not precluded by a previous judicial separation and the divorce court can treat the decree of judicial separation as proof of one or more of the five facts alleged for divorce (s 4).

Decrees are rarely sought, but a decree may be useful for a spouse who does not wish to divorce or who is precluded from divorcing (for instance, for religious reasons) or who cannot divorce because one year of marriage has not elapsed. In 2011 there were 227 petitions filed for judicial separation, a decrease of 24 per cent on 2010 (*Judicial and Court Statistics 2011*, Ministry of Justice, 2012).

(b)   Decree of presumption of death

Where a spouse is missing and thought to be dead, the other spouse can petition for a decree of presumption of death and dissolution of marriage under section 19 of the Matrimonial Causes Act 1973. If a decree is granted, the applicant can contract a valid new marriage, which remains valid even if the spouse who is presumed dead subsequently reappears. The court will grant a decree if it is satisfied that reasonable grounds exist for supposing the applicant's spouse is dead. A spouse is presumed dead if he or she has not been seen for a continuous period of at least seven years. The applicant must, however, have made reasonable enquiries to establish whether the other spouse is alive.

Summary

▶ Until the mid-nineteenth century the ordinary courts had no jurisdiction to grant decrees of divorce, although the ecclesiastical courts could annul marriages and relieve the spouses of the legal obligation to live together. Anyone who wished to divorce could only do so by private Act of Parliament, but this was a complex, lengthy and expensive procedure. The Matrimonial Causes Act 1857 introduced judicial divorce, with the sole ground being adultery. The Matrimonial Causes Act 1937 extended the grounds for divorce to: adultery; cruelty; three years' desertion;

Summary cont'd

and incurable insanity. It also introduced an absolute bar on divorce in the first three years of marriage. The Divorce Reform Act 1969 introduced new grounds for divorce and replaced the three-year bar on divorce with a one-year bar. These provisions were later re-enacted in Part I of the Matrimonial Causes Act 1973 and remain the law today. All divorces were once heard in open court. The 'special procedure' (an administrative form of divorce) was introduced in the 1970s for all undefended divorces.

▶ In the late 1980s, as a result of increasing dissatisfaction with the law, proposals for reform were made. These proposals were enacted in Parts I, II and III of the Family Law Act 1996, but they were not implemented because they were found to be unworkable in practice. Since then, there has been no new attempt to reform the law despite widespread calls for reform.

▶ The law of divorce is laid down in Parts I and II of the Matrimonial Causes Act 1973. Procedural rules are laid down in the Family Procedure Rules 2010.An undefended divorce can be granted in a matter of weeks without the need, in most cases, for either party to attend court. Sorting out disputes about property, finance and arrangements for any children may take much longer. The jurisdictional rules are complex. Special rules apply to the jurisdiction to hear a divorce in the EU (see Brussels II Revised). The Domicile and Matrimonial Proceedings Act 1973 gives the courts in England and Wales the power to stay divorce proceedings where such proceedings are pending in another country.

▶ There is only one ground for divorce: irretrievable breakdown of marriage (s 1(1) MCA 1973). This is established on proof of one or more of the following five facts: (a) adultery; (b) unreasonable behaviour; (c) desertion for a period of at least two years; (d) two years' separation with consent to the divorce; and/or (e) five years' separation (s 1(2) MCA 1973). There must be proof of irretrievable breakdown *and* at least one of the facts. There is an absolute bar on commencing divorce proceedings within the first year of marriage (s 3(1) MCA 1973), although an applicant can base his or her petition on matters which happened during the first year of marriage (s 3(2) MCA 1973). Respondents to two-year and five-year separation divorces are provided with some protection under the law (see below). Undefended divorces are dealt with under what is an essentially administrative procedure and there is usually no need to attend court. Defended divorces, on the other hand, are heard in open court. Obtaining a divorce is a two-stage process: decree nisi followed by decree absolute. A marriage is terminated only on the grant of decree absolute.

▶ Respondents who are being divorced on the basis of two or five years' separation are afforded some protection by sections 10 and 5 of the MCA 1973. Under section 10 MCA 1973, a respondent can ask the court to consider whether his or her financial situation after divorce will be satisfactory. The court may refuse to grant the decree absolute if it is not satisfied that this is the case, unless it has obtained a satisfactory undertaking from the applicant that he or she will make such financial provision as the court may approve. Few applications are made under section 10, but it can be a useful tactical manoeuvre to put pressure on an applicant to sort out the parties' financial position. Under section 5 MCA 1973, a respondent can ask the court to rescind the decree nisi if the respondent can prove that he or she will suffer grave financial or other hardship if the divorce is granted, and that it would be wrong in all the circumstances to grant the divorce. Applications are rare in practice, and, even when pleaded, may not be successful.

▶ Divorce procedure differs according to whether a divorce is undefended or defended. The rules of procedure are laid down in Part 7 of the Family Procedure Rules 2010. An undefended divorce is obtained by way of what is essentially an administrative paper exercise and there is usually no need for the parties, or their legal representatives, to attend court. The grant of decree nisi does not terminate the marriage; it is terminated only on the grant of decree absolute. Defended divorce proceedings begin in the same way as an undefended divorce, but the parties are required to attend a hearing in open court.

▶ Once a decree absolute has been granted, the marriage is dissolved and each party is free to remarry. Financial provision and adjustment orders made under Part II MCA 1973 also take

Summary cont'd

effect, as do orders for settlement or variation of settlement in respect of any child of the family. As far as children are concerned, each parent retains parental responsibility and the obligation to provide their children with financial support continues.

▶ There has been considerable criticism of the current law of divorce, but there are currently no proposals to reform it. Since the Government's decision not to implement the reforms in Part II FLA 1996, many commentators have continued to voice concerns about the unsatisfactory state of the law. The current law of divorce is considered, by many, to be archaic and out of touch with social reality. There is considerable support for the introduction of a truly no-fault divorce.

▶ Part II of the Family Law Act 1986 lays down rules for the recognition in the UK of divorces obtained overseas. Overseas divorces are more likely to be recognised in the UK if they were obtained in court proceedings.

▶ Under Part I of the MCA 1973 the court has jurisdiction to grant a decree of judicial separation and a decree of presumption of death. A decree of judicial separation terminates the obligation of the applicant to continue living with the respondent. A decree of presumption of death allows a spouse to apply for a dissolution of marriage where the other spouse has been missing for a continuous period of at least seven years and is thought to be dead, provided the applicant has made reasonable enquires to establish whether the other spouse is alive.

Further reading and references

Cretney, 'Marriage, divorce and the courts' [2002] Fam Law 900.
Cretney, 'The Divorce White Paper – some reflections' [1995] Fam Law 302.
Deech, 'Divorce – a disaster?' [2009] Fam Law 1048.
Hasson, 'Setting a standard or reflecting reality? The "role" of divorce law, and the case of the Family Law Act 1996' [2003] IJLP&F 338.
Kay, 'Whose divorce is it anyway? – the human rights aspect' [2004] Fam Law 892.
Shepherd, 'Ending the blame game: getting no fault divorce back on the agenda' [2009] Fam Law 122.
Wall, President of the Family Division, 'The President's Resolution address 2012' [2012] Fam Law 817.

Websites

Directgov: www.direct.gov.uk
The Marriage Foundation: www.marriagefoundation.org.uk

Links to relevant websites can also be found at: www.palgrave.com/law/familylaw8e

Chapter 7

Finance and property on divorce (and on the dissolution of a civil partnership)

This chapter deals with the law relating to financial orders on divorce and on the dissolution of a civil partnership. The statutory provisions and judge-made principles in this chapter also apply to the courts' powers to make financial orders on annulments and judicial separations.

NOTE: The principles in this chapter also apply to financial orders on the dissolution of a civil partnership except that the provisions governing civil partnership are laid down in the Civil Partnership Act 2004 (see 2.10). Thus, with respect to financial provision orders, the law makes no distinction between marriage and civil partnership. For this reason, the words 'divorce' and 'spouse' are interchangeable, respectively, with 'dissolution of a civil partnership' and 'civil partner'.

7.1 Introduction

On marriage breakdown, the parties to the marriage will usually have to distribute and reallocate their property and financial assets, whether it be the home, a pension, investments or other assets. Obtaining a divorce (see Chapter 6) and bringing financial proceedings involve separate court proceedings, and, whereas the divorce itself can be obtained in a matter of weeks, a dispute about financial relief takes much longer.

A settlement culture Despite the number of reported cases, most couples do not litigate about property and finance on divorce, but instead reach agreement with or without the assistance of a lawyer, and/or without resorting to mediation or other alternative dispute resolution (ADR) techniques (see 1.5). If legal advice is sought, solicitors adopt a conciliatory approach. Also, the rules of procedure laid down in the Family Procedure Rules 2010 encourage and promote the use of mediation (see below). However, despite the emphasis on settlement, some couples spend vast sums of money on legal advice. In *Moore v Moore* [2007] 2 FLR 339, for instance, the parties spent £1.5 million on legal fees primarily to decide whether the English or Spanish courts should hear the case. However, judges now have the power to control proceedings in order to encourage the parties to reach agreement and thereby reduce costs.

A wide range of different family situations The courts exercise their discretion over a wide spectrum of family life. In *Dart v Dart* [1996] 2 FLR 286 Butler-Sloss LJ said that the Matrimonial Causes Act 1973 'provides the jurisdiction for all applications for ancillary relief from the poverty-stricken to the multi-millionaire'. Where the parties are wealthy, orders in respect of vast sums of money may be made. At the opposite end of the spectrum, on the other hand, the court may have to consider finance and property issues in the context of State benefits and local authority housing. In low-income cases 'the assessment of the needs of the parties will lean heavily in favour of the children and the parent with whom they live' (*per* Butler-Sloss LJ in *Dart v Dart*, above). Thus, in *B v B (Financial Provision: Welfare of Child and Conduct)* [2001] EWCA Civ 2308, [2002] 1

FLR 555, for example, the parties' sole asset of £124,000 (which represented the proceeds of sale of the matrimonial home) was ordered to be transferred to the wife because of the need to rehouse herself and the child.

Although the same statutory provisions and legal principles apply to all cases, whether they be 'big-money' or 'small-money' cases, Sir Nicholas Wall, former President of the Family Division, in his Presidential speech to Resolution in March 2012 ([2012] Fam Law 817) expressed concern that the law is dominated by decisions made in 'big-money' cases which 'bear no resemblance to the ordinary lives of most divorcing couples and to the average case heard, day in and day out, by district judges up and down the country'. The former President also expressed concern about the disparity in representation between 'big-money' cases and 'smaller' cases. In most 'big-money' cases, the parties were represented by specialist solicitors and sometimes leading counsel. In 'smaller' cases, on the other hand, where there might be no, or inadequate, disclosure, or where there might be an impoverished wife and a better-off husband, then the difficulty was compounded if neither party received sensible advice.

Judicial discretion In England and Wales, the system governing financial relief on divorce (and on the dissolution of a civil partnership) is based on judicial discretion. There is no community of property regime as there is in some European countries, such as in France and Italy, whereby each spouse on marital breakdown is entitled to a fixed share of the matrimonial assets, subject to any agreement to the contrary. Instead, under Part II of the Matrimonial Causes Act 1973, the court has wide powers to redistribute matrimonial assets, and the outcome of each case depends on its own particular facts. The main advantage of a discretion-based system is that the court can tailor the order to fit the facts of the case. Its disadvantages, however, are that it can create uncertainty and unpredictability, and can involve the court in a time-consuming and expensive exercise. It is also difficult for lawyers to advise their clients with certainty as to the likely outcome of their case.

7.2 Procedure for a financial remedy

The rules of procedure governing applications for a financial remedy are laid down in the Family Procedure Rules (FPR) 2010 and in Practice Directions and accompanying Protocols. Part 9 of the FPR 2010 ('Applications for a Financial Remedy') is particularly relevant, but so too are: Part 1 ('Overriding Objective'); Part 2 ('Application and Interpretation of the Rules'); and Part 3 ('Alternative Dispute Resolution: The Court's Powers'). The overriding objective of the FPR 2010 is to enable the court to deal with cases justly, having regard to any welfare issues involved (r 1.1). The Law Society's *Family Law Protocol* also provides guidance on the conduct of applications, as does Resolution's *Code of Practice*.

The party who applies for a financial remedy is called the 'applicant' and the other party the 'respondent'. Cases are heard in the county court seized of the divorce petition; but complex or serious cases can be transferred to the High Court. With the exception of maintenance pending suit and orders to or for the benefit of a child of the family, financial orders do not take effect until the grant of decree absolute.

Encouraging Settlement Part 3 of the FPR 2010 contains rules which aim to encourage and facilitate the use of alternative dispute resolution (ADR) in proceedings for a financial remedy on divorce (and in certain other family proceedings). Under Part 3, the court has a duty to consider, at every stage of the proceedings whether ADR is appropriate (r 3.2); and it can adjourn proceedings to allow ADR to take place (r 3.3). *Practice Direction 3A* and the *Pre-Application Protocol for Mediation Information and Assessment* (see Annex A to the Practice Direction) require any applicant for financial relief (or his or her legal representative) to first of all attend a Mediation Information and Assessment Meeting (MIAM) to see if the dispute can be resolved by mediation. However, in certain circumstances (see Annex C to the Practice Direction), this obligation does not apply (for example, where there is domestic violence, a party is bankrupt, the case needs to be heard urgently, or if there are no mediators available within the vicinity). If mediation is unsuccessful, the parties are required to attend a first appointment followed by a financial dispute resolution (FDR) appointment (see below). Not less than 35 days before the first appointment, both parties must simultaneously exchange with each other and file with the court a financial statement in the form referred to in *Practice Direction 5A* (r 9.14).

The first appointment   The duties of the court at the first appointment are set out in rule 9.15 FPR 2010. The appointment must be conducted with the objective of defining the issues and saving costs (r 9.15(1)). Thus aim of the appointment is to define the issues, and make directions (if needed) so that the parties can endeavour to reach agreement. Both parties must attend, unless the court orders otherwise. The judge has various powers, such as to: direct that further documents be produced; give directions about the valuation of assets; order that the case be adjourned for out-of-court mediation or private negotiation; and make an interim order (r 9.15).

The financial dispute resolution (FDR) appointment   Both parties must attend the FDR appointment personally unless the court orders otherwise (r 9.17(10)). The FDR appointment is a 'meeting held for the purposes of discussion and negotiation' (r 9.17(1)). As the emphasis is on encouraging the parties to settle, they must use their best endeavours to reach agreement on the matters in issue between them (r 9.17(6)). If agreement is not possible, then the case proceeds to a final hearing.

In *Rose v Rose* [2002] 1 FLR 978 Thorpe LJ held that: although the FDR appointment can take many forms. depending on the style and practice of the judge, it should never be superficial or ill-considered; and that, although it is an invaluable tool for dispelling unreasonable expectations, in a finely balanced case it is no substitute for a trial and should not be used to discourage either party from going to trial where the case can only be resolved in such a way. In *S v S (Ancillary Relief: Importance of FDR)* [2008] 1 FLR 944 Baron J stated, *inter alia*, that the FDR procedure must be undertaken in an effective way in every case, because it gives the parties the opportunity to settle the litigation, to air the issues and to have neutral judicial evaluation at a time before costs have denuded assets.

The final hearing   This involves a full trial, which will be heard by a judge who was not involved in the first and FDR appointments.

Staying divorce proceedings to allow the case to be heard in another jurisdiction   In an international case, the court in England and Wales can stay the proceedings if it considers it more appropriate for the matter to be determined in another jurisdiction. For example, in *Bentinck v Bentinck* [2007] 2 FLR 1 proceedings were stayed to allow the Swiss court to determine the matter; and in *Ella v Ella* [2007] 2 FLR 35 to allow the Israeli court to hear the case.

A duty of full and frank disclosure Both parties have an absolute duty to make full, frank and clear disclosure of all their present and likely future assets for, without such disclosure, the court will be unable to exercise its discretion fairly and justly. The duty was summed up by Mostyn J in *NG v SG (Appeal: Non-Disclosure)* [2011] EWHC 3270 (Fam), [2012] 1 FLR 1211 who described non-disclosure as 'a bane which strikes at the very integrity of the adjudicative process' and that without full disclosure 'the court cannot render a true certain and just verdict'.

Failure to make full and frank disclosure is therefore a serious matter and can result in an order being set aside (see 7.12). A costs penalty can also be imposed on a dishonest party (see for instance, *Al-Khatib v Masry* [2002] 1 FLR 1053).

Media attendance Media representatives are permitted to attend financial relief proceedings, unless the judge decides to exclude them or the rules provide otherwise (see r 27.11 FPR 2010 and *Practice Directions 27B and 27C*).

7.3 Financial orders that can be made

Under Part II of the Matrimonial Causes Act 1973 the court has jurisdiction to make the following orders:

(a) maintenance pending suit (s 22);
(b) financial provision orders (s 23): periodic payments orders; lump sum orders; pension attachment orders;
(c) property adjustment orders (s 24): transfer of property; settlement of property; and variation of a settlement; and
(d) pensions orders.

Most cases are not contested or are otherwise made with consent; and the orders most commonly made are property adjustment and lump sum orders.

Judicial and Court Statistics 2011 (Ministry of Justice, 2012)

'In 2011 a total of 80,601 applications for ancillary relief were disposed of; an increase of 2 per cent from the 82,290 recorded for 2010. Of the disposals made in 2011, the majority (70 per cent) were not contested, while a further 24 per cent of orders were made by consent after initially being contested. Most disposals made in 2011 were for property adjustment orders (26,185) or lump sum orders (24,034).'

(a) Maintenance pending suit (section 22)

This is a short-term interim order which exists to bridge the gap between the commencement of proceedings and their final determination. It terminates when the divorce suit is determined (or earlier if the court so orders). Either party can apply for maintenance pending suit. When deciding whether or not to make an order and, if so, in what manner, the court is required make such order as is 'reasonable' (s 22), but in practice it performs a similar exercise to that required by section 25 (see 7.4). The court has a wide discretion and in an appropriate case may make a substantial order (see, for example, *M v M (Maintenance Pending Suit)* [2002] 2 FLR 123 where the wife was awarded £330,000 per annum maintenance pending suit). In an appropriate case, maintenance pending suit can include a sum for legal costs (see, for example, *G v G (Maintenance Pending Suit: Costs)* [2003] 2 FLR 7).

(b)   Financial provision orders (section 23)

The following orders can be made in favour of a spouse, and to or for the benefit of any child of the family aged under 18, or a 'child' over 18 who is undergoing education or training or who has special circumstances (such as a disability) (ss 23(1), 29(1), (3)).

(i) A periodical payments order (maintenance)   An order for periodical payments can be made in favour of a spouse and/or to or for the benefit of any child of the family (s 23(1)(a)). The order can be secured or unsecured. A secured order is one where a capital asset or other property is charged as security for payment (s 23(1)(b)). Secured orders are rare in practice but they are sometimes made where there may be difficulties enforcing an order. Periodical payments made in favour of a spouse automatically terminate if that spouse enters into another marriage after the divorce (s 28(1)), but they do not necessarily terminate if the divorced spouse enters into a cohabitation relationship. However, the fact that a party is cohabiting with a new partner after divorce can be taken into account by the court as one of the factors of the case when it is considering whether and in what form to make an order (see p. 157) and also when it is considering whether to vary or discharge an order (see pp. 187 and 188). Periodical payments made in favour of a spouse terminate on his or her death (s 28(1)).

(ii) A lump sum order   This is an order for payment of a specified sum of money, which can be made in favour of a spouse and/or to or for the benefit of any child of the family (s 23(1)). It can be used to enable a party to meet liabilities or expenses reasonably incurred in maintaining him or herself and/or a child of the family prior to and after an application for a lump order has been made (ss 23(3)). The court can order payment of a whole sum or order it to be paid by instalment (s 23(3)(c)), which can include the payment of interest (s 23(6)). Only one lump sum order can be made: the plural reference to 'lump sums' in s 23(1)(c) is to allow payment by instalment.

The advantage of a lump sum order is that it can be used to affect a 'clean break' between the parties (see 7.5). Sometimes a lump sum will be ordered to represent 'capitalised maintenance' (a sum which can be invested to provide an income). A *'Duxbury* calculation' is sometimes used as a guide to calculate a party's capitalised maintenance needs by taking account of certain variables, such as inflation, life expectancy, income tax, capital growth and income from investments. This calculation is not determinative, however, as it is the section 25 factors which prevail.

A lump sum order made in favour of a *spouse* is a final order which cannot be varied in variation proceedings, unless the circumstances are exceptional. A lump sum order made in favour of a *child*, on the other hand, is not a final order as the court's power to make orders for children is 'exercisable from time to time' (s 23(4)). In practice, however, lump sums in favour of children are rare, although they may sometimes be made in a 'big-money' case.

Adjourning an application where a capital sum will become available in the future   To avoid the potential injustice caused by the finality of a lump sum order, the court can in exceptional circumstances adjourn proceedings where there is a real possibility of capital from a specific source becoming available in the near future, for instance an inheritance or a pension.

(c) Property adjustment orders (section 24)

(i) A transfer of property order (section 24(1)(a)) This order directs a spouse to transfer specified property to the other spouse and/or to or for the benefit of a child of the family. Any property can be transferred, but in practice the order is usually used to transfer the matrimonial home. The transferee may be given a charge over the house for a fixed amount or a percentage of the value which is to be realised at a later date, or may be ordered to pay the transferor a lump sum representing the latter's share in the matrimonial home. A transfer of property is a useful way of effecting a 'clean break' (see 7.5). For example, a spouse could be ordered to transfer investments to the other spouse so that the transferee can live on the income; or be ordered to transfer the matrimonial home to the other spouse with that spouse agreeing to forego any claim for maintenance.

(ii) A settlement of property order (section 24(1)(b)) This order directs a spouse to settle property for the benefit of the other spouse and/or any child of the family. Under a settlement, property is held on trust for certain persons who have an interest in the property. Although such orders are rare in practice, an order may be useful to give the children of the family a roof over their heads during their dependency, but enable the house to be transferred back to the owner once the children become independent. This type of order is known as a '*Mesher* order' (see 7.7).

(iii) A variation of settlement (ante-nuptial or post-nuptial) order (sections 24(1)(c), (d)) The court can vary any ante-nuptial or post-nuptial settlement made by the parties. This order can be made for the benefit of the parties and/or any child of the family. Such orders are rare.

(iv) Order for the sale of property (section 24A) Where the court has made a secured periodical payments, lump sum or property adjustment order, it can also make a further order for the sale of property (or proceeds of the sale of property) in which one spouse has, or both spouses have, a beneficial interest. The power to order sale is a useful enforcement mechanism where there has been, or is likely to be, non-compliance with an order. For example, the court could order that property belonging to a spouse who has failed to pay a lump sum be sold and that the proceeds of sale be paid to the spouse who should have received it (s 24A(2)(a)). The court can defer sale until a specified event has occurred or until a specified period of time has expired (s 24A(4)). It can also order that property be offered for sale to a specified person or persons (s 24A(2)(b)). A third party with an interest in the property in dispute (such as a mortgagee) must be allowed to make representations to the court, and the third party's interest must be included as one of the circumstances of the case when the court performs its discretionary exercise (s 24A(6)).

(d) Pension orders

See 7.8.

7.4   How the court exercises its discretion: the section 25 factors

▶ **Lord Nicholls in** *Miller v Miller; McFarlane v McFarlane* **[2006] UKHL 24, [2006] 1 FLR 1186**

'The 1973 Act gives only limited guidance on how the courts should exercise their statutory powers. Primary consideration must be given to the welfare of any children of the family. The court must consider the feasibility of a 'clean break'. Beyond this the courts are largely left to get on with it for themselves. The courts are told simply that they must have regard to all the circumstances of the case.

Of itself this direction leads nowhere. Implicitly the courts must exercise their powers so as to achieve an outcome which is fair between the parties. But an important aspect of fairness is that like cases should be treated alike. So, perforce, if there is to be an acceptable degree of consistency of decision from one case to the next, the courts must themselves articulate, if only in the broadest fashion, what are the applicable if unspoken principles guiding the court's approach.

This is not to usurp the legislative function. Rather, it is to perform a necessary judicial function in the absence of parliamentary guidance. As Lord Cooke of Thorndon said in *White v White* (1970), there is no reason to suppose that in prescribing relevant considerations the legislature had any intention of excluding the development of general judicial practice.'

▶ **Baroness Hale in** *Miller v Miller; McFarlane v McFarlane* **[2006] UKHL 24, [2006] 1 FLR 1186**

'There is much to be said for the flexibility and sensitivity of the English law of ancillary relief. It avoids the straitjacket of rigid rules which can apply harshly or unfairly in an individual case. But it should not be too flexible. It must try to achieve some consistency and predictability. This is not only to secure that so far as possible like cases are treated alike but also to enable and encourage the parties to negotiate their own solutions as quickly and cheaply as possible.'

As the above extracts show, the court has wide discretionary powers when deciding whether to make an order, and if so in manner. Property law principles, such as the laws of trusts, are not relevant and will not be investigated by the court, except where there is a genuine third-party interest in any property.

In addition to applying the section 25 factors (see below) and considering whether to effect a clean break (see 7.5) the courts must apply the principles laid down by the House of Lords in *White v White*[2000] UKHL 54, [2000] 2 FLR 981 and *Miller v Miller; McFarlane v McFarlane* [2006] UKHL 24, [2006] 1 FLR 1186 (see 7.6), and in any other relevant case-law.

The welfare of the children and the other section 25 factors

When deciding whether to exercise its powers to make orders under Part II of the Matrimonial Causes Act 1973, and, if so, in what manner, the court must consider all the circumstances of the case, but with the first consideration being given to the welfare of any child of the family:

Section 25(1) 'It shall be the duty of the court in deciding whether to exercise its powers, ... and, if so, in what manner, to have regard to all the circumstances of the case, first consideration being given to the welfare while a minor of any child of the family who has not attained the age of eighteen.'

As the duty in section 25(1) applies not just to the parties' own children but to children treated by the parties as children of the family (see s 52(1), children such as step-children are included; but it does not include foster-children placed with the parties by a local authority or voluntary organisation.

When exercising its powers in relation to a party to the marriage, the court must in particular have regard to the following list of factors laid down in section 25(2).

Section 25(2) 'As regards the exercise of the powers of the court in relation to a party to the marriage, the court shall in particular have regard to the following matters –

(a) The income, earning capacity, property and other financial resources which each of the parties to the marriage has or is likely to have in the foreseeable future, including in the case of earning capacity any increase in that capacity which it would in the opinion of the court be reasonable to expect a party to the marriage to take steps to acquire.
(b) The financial needs, obligations and responsibilities which each of the parties to the marriage has or is likely to have in the foreseeable future.
(c) The standard of living enjoyed by the family before the breakdown of marriage.
(d) The age of each party to the marriage and the duration of the marriage.
(e) Any physical or mental disability of either of the parties to the marriage.
(f) The contribution which each of the parties has made or is likely in the foreseeable future to make to the welfare of the family, including any contribution by looking after the home or caring for the family.
(g) The conduct of each of the parties, if that conduct is such that it would in the opinion of the court be inequitable to disregard it.
(h) In the case of proceedings for divorce or nullity of marriage, the value to each of the parties to the marriage of any benefit which by reason of the dissolution or annulment of the marriage, that party will lose the chance of acquiring.'

The weight or importance attached to these factors will depend on the facts of each case. In practice, however, financial needs and financial resources are usually particularly important.

The factors in section 25(2) are not exclusive – other factors can be taken into account, as section 25(2) refers to 'all the circumstances of the case'. Thus, for example, the terms of a pre- or post-nuptial agreement may be taken into account (see 7.9 below). Cultural factors may also be taken into account (see, for example, *A v T (Ancillary Relief: Cultural Factors)* [2004] 1 FLR 977 where the parties were Iranian Muslims bound by Sharia law and where the High Court considered how the matter would be dealt with in Iran).

The following paragraphs consider the factors in section 25(2) in more detail.

(a) *'The income, earning capacity, property and other financial resources which each of the parties to the marriage has or is likely to have in the foreseeable future, including in the case of earning capacity any increase in that capacity which it would in the opinion of the court be reasonable to expect a party to the marriage to take steps to acquire.'* The court has the discretion to take into account any resource, such as business profits, interest on investments, insurance policies, pension rights, welfare benefits, damages for personal injury (*Mansfield v Mansfield* [2011] EWCA Civ 1056, [2012] 1 FLR 117) and a windfall such as lottery prize (*S v AG (Financial Orders: Lottery Prize)* [2011] EWHC 2637 (Fam)). However, as cases are highly fact-specific, whether various resources will be taken into account will depend on the facts of the case. In some cases, the court may have the difficult task of having to decide whether or not a particular resource (such as an inheritance or a resource obtained before marriage) is 'matrimonial' or 'non-matrimonial' property (see p. 168 below).

In an appropriate case, the court may impute a notional earning capacity, or infer that unidentified resources are available from a spouse's expenditure or style of living. Future earning potential is an important consideration when the court is deciding whether to effect a 'clean break' (see 7.5). As future financial resources must be considered, the court may decide to postpone making an order if financial resources are likely to be available in the relatively near future, for instance a pension, an inheritance, or assets tied up in a business which are realisable at a later date.

The impact of a new partner   The court can take into account the fact that a former spouse is living with a new partner, whether a spouse or cohabitant, as this may affect the parties' financial resources and needs under section 25(2)(a). If the new partner is making, or has the potential to make, a financial contribution, then this may be taken into account. In *Grey v Grey* [2010] EWCA Civ 1424, [2010] 1 FLR 1764 the Court of Appeal held that the real question would generally be not what the cohabitant was contributing, but what he or she ought to contribute. It held, referring to the facts of the case, that the judge could not be fair to the husband without investigating whether the man in question was making any financial contribution to the wife's household, and, if not, what his capacity to make a contribution was. It held that the approach in *Fleming v Fleming* [2003] EWCA Civ 1841, [2004] 1 FLR 667 remained sound, and was sufficiently flexible to enable the court to do justice and to reflect social and moral shifts within society. *Grey v Grey* also shows that a stable and committed relationship falling short of cohabitation may, depending on the circumstances, have an impact on the level of spousal maintenance, as, when the case was heard again on its facts (see *Re Grey (No 3)* [2010] EWHC 1055 (Fam), [2010] 2 FLR 1848), the trial judge took account of the wife's new relationship and reduced the maintenance payable.

(b)   *'The financial needs, obligations and responsibilities which each of the parties to the marriage has or is likely to have in the foreseeable future.'*   The financial needs of the parties and any children of the family is a key factor which the court must take into account, as the decision of the House of Lords in *Miller v Miller* (see p. 165) recognised. Financial needs, obligations and responsibilities will vary from case to case, but they include, for example, the provision of accommodation and general living expenses. 'Need' will be a particularly important consideration in a 'small-money' case, especially where there are children of the family, but even in a 'big-money case' need is important and an award can be made which exceeds a party's reasonable needs (see *White v White* (2000), 7.6). In practice, despite the fact that the reported cases are largely 'big-money' cases, in practice most cases are still needs-based. As the meaning of 'needs' has generated uncertainty and there is confusion about the extent to which one spouse should be required to meet the other's needs on marriage breakdown, the Law Commission is currently conducting a project which looks, among other things, at the issue of needs (see p. 96).

Obligations and responsibilities to a new partner or a new family   Such obligations and responsibilities can be taken into account, depending on the facts of the case and applying all the section 25 criteria. As far as the principle of equality laid down in *White v White* is concerned (see 7.6), different approaches have been taken in the case-law. Thus, for example, in *S v S (Financial Provision: Departing from Equality)* [2001] 2 FLR 246 it was held that obligations and responsibilities to a new family could justify a departure from equality, whereas in *H-J v H-J (Financial Provision: Equality)* [2002] 1 FLR 415 Coleridge J held that such an approach would normally be wrong in principle.

(c) *'The standard of living enjoyed by the family before the breakdown of marriage.'* Although this factor must be taken into account, the court is under no duty to attempt to place the parties in the position they would have been in if the marriage had not broken down. In fact, in practice it is often not possible for the parties to enjoy the same standard of living after divorce as they did before it, unless there are substantial assets available for distribution.

(d) *'The age of each party to the marriage and the duration of the marriage.'* These two factors can have an important impact on the court's decision. The needs and resources of a young (and possibly childless) couple are likely to differ significantly from those of an older couple. It may be reasonable, for example, to expect a wife in her twenties or thirties to make her way on her own, but the court is less likely to expect a wife in her forties or fifties to go out and find a job, particularly if she has not worked since marrying or having children.

The duration of the marriage will be an important consideration when the court is considering whether assets (such as inheritances or property accrued before marriage) should be part of the pool of assets available for distribution. Thus, the longer the marriage, the less likely the court will be to categorise different types of property as 'matrimonial' or 'non-matrimonial' (see *Miller v Miller,* 7.6). In other words, the importance of the source of the assets *may* diminish over time. However, as each case depends on its facts and the application of the other factors in section 25, even in the case of a short marriage the court may make a generous award.

Pre-marital cohabitation may count towards the duration of a marriage At one time the courts were unwilling to take pre-marital cohabitation into account when calculating the duration of a marriage because they considered that marital obligations and needs began on marriage, not before (*Foley v Foley* [1981] 22 FLR 215). However, this approach has now changed (as social attitudes to cohabitation have changed), and the court may, in the exercise of its discretion, decide to take a settled and committed period of pre-marital cohabitation into account when calculating the duration of a marriage, particularly where the period of cohabitation has seamlessly and immediately preceded the marriage. In *C v C* [2009] 1 FLR 8, for example, Moylan J took into account the couple's pre-marital cohabitation of approximately four years as to do otherwise would fly in the face of the duty of the court to have regard to all the circumstances of the case.

(e) *'Any physical or mental disability of either of the parties to the marriage.'* This section is self-explanatory and there are no important decided cases on this factor.

(f) *'The contribution which each of the parties has made or is likely in the foreseeable future to make to the welfare of the family, including any contribution by looking after the home or caring for the family.'* Under section 25(2)(f) the court can take into account both financial and non-financial contributions to the home and to the family. The court will not usually favour the 'breadwinner' over the 'homemaker' as this would be contrary to the principles of fairness and non-discrimination expounded by the House of Lords in *White v White* (see 7.6). In *Lambert v Lambert* [2003] 1 FLR 139 Thorpe LJ held that there must be an end to the sterile suggestion that the breadwinner's contribution was more important than that of the homemaker.

(g) *'The conduct of each of the parties, if that conduct is such that it would in the opinion of the court be inequitable to disregard it.'* The court generally takes the view that a certain amount of unpleasantness is to be expected on both sides on the breakdown of a relationship, and that such matters should not affect the outcome of an application for a financial remedy. For this reason, only conduct of an extreme or exceptional kind will be taken into account, as to do otherwise would contradict one of the policy aims of divorce law which is not to apportion blame. The section 25 exercise is regarded as a financial, not a moral, exercise. In *Miller v Miller* (2006) (see 7.6) the House of Lords reaffirmed the 'obvious and gross' test laid down by Lord Denning MR in *Wachtel v Wachtel* [1973] Fam 72 and held that the lower court had been wrong to take into account the husband's alleged responsibility for the marriage breakdown (he had left his wife for another woman), given that it was conduct which fell far short of 'conduct which it would be inequitable to disregard' under section 25(2)(g).

As the case-law shows, only extreme types of conduct will be taken into account, such as, for instance: stabbing a spouse (*H v H (Financial Provision: Conduct)* [1994] 2 FLR 801); violently attacking the wife in the matrimonial home in front of the children (*H v H (Financial Relief: Attempted Murder as Conduct)* [2006] 1 FLR 990); exceptionally malicious and misleading litigation conduct by both parties (*FZ v SZ and Others (Ancillary Relief: Conduct: Valuations)* [2010] EWHC 1630 (Fam), [2011] 1 FLR 64); and sexual assaults and other related offences by the husband on his wife's grandchildren (*K v L* [2010] EWCA Civ 125, [2010] 2 FLR 1467). An accumulation of serious misconduct, such as failing to make full and frank disclosure, dissipating matrimonial assets and abducting a child might constitute conduct for the purposes of section 25(2)(g) (as it did in *Al-Khatib v Masry* [2002] 1 FLR 1053). However, even if the conduct is serious, the court may decide, in the exercise of its discretion, to discount that conduct and take other factors into account (see, for example, *A v A (Financial Provision: Conduct)* [1995] 1 FLR 345, where, even though the depressed and suicidal husband had assaulted his wife with a knife, other factors prevailed). Unless the violence is extremely severe it will not usually be taken into account as conduct under section 25(2)(g) (see, for example, *S v S (Non Matrimonial Property: Conduct)* [2007] 1 FLR 1496).

If the court considers that the conduct is sufficiently serious to be taken into account, it does not necessarily mean that the 'guilty' party will receive nothing. For instance, in *Clark v Clark* [1999] 2 FLR 498 the wife was granted an order even though her conduct was held to be inequitable to disregard (she had refused to consummate the marriage, had transferred her husband's property into her own name and had made him a virtual prisoner in his own home). In *H v H (Financial Provision: Conduct)* [1998] 1 FLR 971, where the husband's conduct was held to be too inequitable to ignore (he had transferred money for three years into a Swiss bank account), Singer J said that the approach to be taken was not to fix a sum as a 'penalty', but to carry out an evaluation based on all the relevant factors taken in the round.

Non-disclosure A failure to make full and frank disclosure (or any other misconduct in respect of the process of the case) may be taken into account. In some cases it may only affect costs (see, for example, *Tavoulareas v Tavoulareas* [1998] 2 FLR 418; and *Young v Young* [1998] 2 FLR 1131), but in a serious case it may affect the size and nature of the award or even lead to the application being dismissed.

Bigamy Although bigamy is a criminal offence and a ground for nullity (see 2.2), a party to a bigamous marriage is not necessarily barred from applying for financial relief on divorce, even though it is the policy of the law not to allow a person to profit from his or her own crime. Whether bigamy will affect an award will depend on the circumstances of the case. Thus, in *Whiston v Whiston* [1995] 2 FLR 268 a bigamist was barred from claiming on grounds of public policy, whereas in *Rampal v Rampal (No. 2)* [2001] 2 FLR 1179 a bigamist was allowed to pursue a claim, on the basis that he had been much less culpable than the bigamist in *Whiston*. In *Ben Hashem v Al Shayif* [2009] 1 FLR 115 Munby J awarded the wife more than £7 million as both parties were aware of the bigamy.

(h) *'In the case of proceedings for divorce or nullity of marriage, the value to each of the parties to the marriage of any benefit which by reason of the dissolution or annulment of the marriage, that party will lose the chance of acquiring.'* On divorce a spouse may lose certain property rights and interests, such as the benefit of a pension, the surrender value of an insurance policy, future business profits, or the right to succeed to the other spouse's estate. The court can take these and other lost benefits into account. It might, for example, decide to increase an order to compensate for the loss of future benefits, or make a deferred lump sum order, or, in an exceptional case, adjourn proceedings. Pensions on divorce are governed by special rules (see 7.8).

7.5 The 'clean break'

A major policy aim of the law governing financial relief on divorce is that a divorced spouse cannot expect a 'meal ticket' for life. For this reason the court is required to determine cases in such a way as to effect, where possible, a 'clean break' between the parties. The clean break was introduced to encourage the parties to put the past behind them and to begin a new life which would not be overshadowed by the relationship which had broken down (*per* Lord Scarman in *Minton v Minton* [1979] AC 593).

> ▶ **Baroness Hale in** *Miller v Miller; McFarlane v McFarlane* **[2006] UKHL 24, [2006] 1 FLR 1186**
>
> 'Section 25A is a powerful encouragement towards securing the court's objective by way of lump sum and capital adjustment (which now includes pension sharing) rather than by continuing periodical payments. This is good practical sense. Periodical payments are a continuing source of stress for both parties. They are also insecure. With the best will in the world, the paying party may fall on hard times and be unable to keep up with them. Nor is the best will in the world always evident between formerly married people. It is also the logical consequence of the retreat from the principle of the life-long obligation. Independent finances and self-sufficiency are the aims. Nevertheless, section 25A does not tell us what the outcome of the exercise required by section 25 should be. It is mainly directed at how that outcome should be put into effect.'

The court encourages the parties to go their separate ways after divorce, provided it is fair in the circumstances. Thus, under section 25A(1), when exercising its powers to make finance and property orders in favour of a spouse, the court must consider 'whether it would be appropriate so to exercise those powers that the financial obligations of each party towards the other will be terminated' as soon after the divorce as the court 'considers just and reasonable'. Whether the court will effect a clean break depends on the facts of the case, and also on the overarching objective of fairness laid down in *White v White* (see 7.6).

The court can effect a clean break between the parties in an application for periodical payments in the following ways:

- by dismissing the application;
- by dismissing the application with a direction that the applicant shall not make any further application (s 25A(3));
- by making a limited-term periodical payments order (s 25A(2));
- by making a limited-term periodical payments order with a direction that no application can be made in variation proceedings for an extension of that term (s 28(1A));
- by ordering a lump sum representing capitalised periodical payments as a means of discharging a party's liability to make further periodical payments (ss 31(7A) and (7B)).

The court also has a duty to consider a clean break in section 31 variation proceedings, when the court can make a limited-term order 'to enable the party in whose favour the order was made to adjust without undue hardship to the termination of those payments' (s 31(7)).

In certain circumstances, the court may decide to make a nominal periodical payments order (such as for £10 per annum), so that there is an order in place which can be varied if circumstances change in the future.

Despite the court's duty to consider a clean break, it may be unwilling to effect one where it makes unrealistic expectations of a spouse's capacity for economic independence. In cases where there is ill-health the court may also be unwilling to effect a clean break (see *Purba v Purba* [2000] 1 FLR 444).

7.6 The discretionary exercise – *White v White* and *Miller v Miller*

There have been two important cases heard by the House of Lords on the question of how the courts should exercise their discretion in financial remedy cases on divorce: *White v White* [2000] UKHL 54, [2000] 2 FLR 981; and *Miller v Miller; McFarlane v McFarlane* [2006] UKHL 24, [2006] 1 FLR 1186. Although both were 'big-money' cases, the principles they laid down apply to all applications for a financial remedy. However, if there is a pre-marital or post-marital agreement in existence, other principles may apply (see p. 177).

(a) *White v White* (2000)

Before the decision of the House of Lords in *White v White* [2000] UKHL 54, [2000] 2 FLR 981 the Court of Appeal had adopted a 'reasonable requirements' ('reasonable needs') approach in 'big-money' cases, whereby an award would be made sufficient to satisfy the other spouse's needs even though it was possible to award more. This approach resulted in wives, in particular, receiving much smaller proportions of the matrimonial assets than their husband.

In the late 1990s, however, the Court of Appeal began to wonder whether the 'reasonable requirements' approach might be causing injustice. Thus, in *Dart v Dart* [1996] 2 FLR 286, for example, where the wife was awarded £4 million of her husband's £400 million fortune, Butler-Sloss LJ questioned whether the courts might be giving too much weight to reasonable needs over the other section 25 criteria. Nonetheless the Court of Appeal in *Dart* held that any challenge to the reasonable requirements approach was a matter for Parliament, not the courts. Although the reasonable needs approach was considered unsatisfactory because it discriminated against wives and prioritised needs when there was no such hierarchy in section 25 (see 7.4 above), it was not until the following case of *White v White* that the reasonable needs approach was overturned:

▶ *White v White* **[2000] UKHL 54, [2000] 2 FLR 981**

After 33 years of marriage the wife obtained a divorce and sought enough capital to set herself up independently in farming, arguing that her equal contribution to the parties' farming business throughout their long marriage justified her claim to an equal share of the assets. Her husband argued that she should only be given enough to satisfy her reasonable needs, applying the approach adopted in earlier decisions of the Court of Appeal (see above). Their overall assets were assessed at approximately £4.6 million.

At first instance, the judge adopted a reasonable needs approach and, on the basis that it was impractical for the wife to continue farming, awarded her one-fifth of their joint assets and ordered that the farming business remain with the husband.

The wife appealed to the Court of Appeal, which allowed her appeal and increased her award to £1.5 million. Butler-Sloss LJ said that cases where a wife was an equal business partner were in a wholly different category from other 'big-money' cases such as *Dart v Dart* (see above) and *Conran v Conran* [1997] 2 FLR 615 where the origin of the wealth was clearly on one side and the emphasis was rightly on contribution, not entitlement. The Court of Appeal also held that it was not the function of the judge to criticise the wife's plans to carry on farming. Both parties appealed to the House of Lords.

The House of Lords held, dismissing the appeals, that, although the judge had been mistaken in regarding reasonable requirements as the determinant factor, the award made by the Court of Appeal was within the ambit of reasonable discretion. The House of Lords, with Lord Nicholls giving the leading opinion, laid down the following statements of principle:

▶ The objective implicit in section 25 is to achieve a fair outcome in financial arrangements on divorce, giving first consideration to the welfare of any children.
▶ Fairness requires the court to take into account all the circumstances of the case. In seeking to achieve a fair outcome, there is no place for discrimination between husband and wife in their respective roles. Fairness requires that their division of labour should not prejudice or advantage either party when considering their contributions to the welfare of the family under section 25(2)(f). If each in their different spheres contributed equally to the family, then in principle it matters not who earned the money and built up the assets. There should be no bias in favour of the money earner as against the homemaker and the child carer.
▶ Before making an order for division of assets, a judge should check his tentative views against the yardstick of equality of division. As a general rule, equality should be departed from only if, and to the extent that, there is good reason for doing so. The need to consider and articulate reasons for doing so will help the parties and the court to focus on the need to ensure the absence of discrimination.
▶ Section 25(2) does not rank the matters listed therein in any hierarchy and other matters may also be important. Financial need is only one of the several factors to be taken into account in determining a fair outcome. When considering section 25(2)(b), confusion will be avoided by courts ceasing to employ the expression 'reasonable requirements' and returning to the statutory language of 'needs', which preserves the necessary degree of flexibility.
▶ Lord Nicholls, who laid down the propositions above, dismissed, however, the idea that there should be a presumption of equality, as this would be an impermissible judicial gloss on section 25, and because the introduction of such a presumption was a matter for Parliament, not the courts.

In *White* the 'reasonable needs or requirements' approach was therefore rejected and replaced by 'a yardstick of equality of division' in order to ensure fairness and abolish discrimination. *White* recognised that marriage is a partnership of equals and that the homemaker should not be discriminated as against the breadwinner. Discrimination was the antithesis of fairness. This was a principle of universal application which was to be applied to all cases, not just 'big-money' cases. In *Miller v Miller* (see p. 165 below), however, Lord Nicholls said that the yardstick of equality was to be applied as an aid, not as a rule.

Reaction to White The decision provoked considerable comment from lawyers and academics. Duckworth and Hodson (2001) thought that the decision would increase the impetus for recognising formal agreements between spouses, especially pre-marital contracts. Although Eekelaar ([2001] Fam Law 30) thought that the equality of sharing approach might deter people from marrying, he considered that the decision in *White* was no great advance in the law because the House of Lords had provided no suggestions as to what sorts of reasons might justify departing from equality. Cretney ([2001] Fam Law 3) was of the opinion that the House of Lords had gone too far. He thought that the House might have been a 'trifle rash' in overturning the settled practice of the courts, particularly in a case which was highly untypical of other 'big-money' cases (both parties were in business together). He also questioned whether such a change of approach should have been taken by the House of Lords at all, but instead should have been a matter for Parliament. Cretney also stated ([2003] CFLQ 303) that the preference in *White* for equal division was expressed in such a muted and confused way that it would be difficult to predict how cases would be decided and that it would increase 'the expense, uncertainty and consequent destructive emotional stress of resolving the consequences of marriage breakdown'. In *Charman v Charman (No. 4)* [2007] EWCA Civ 503, [2007] 1 FLR 1246 (see further at p. 166 below) Sir Mark Potter P said that the decision in *White* had undoubtedly not resolved 'the problems faced by practitioners in advising clients or by clients in deciding upon what terms to compromise'.

Another criticism that might be made is that *White v White* seems riddled with contradictions. Thus, although the House of Lords emphasised the importance of applying the statute (particularly the section 25 factors), in fact it introduced an approach (a 'yardstick of equality') which had no basis in the statute. Also, as the non-discrimination principle articulated in *White* is derived from section 25(2)(f) of the section 25 factors, then the House of Lords appears to have elevated that factor, when it had stressed, in *Piglowska v Piglowski* [1999] 1 WLR 1360, [1999] 2 FLR 763, that there was no hierarchy in section 25. Furthermore, although the House of Lords in *White* said that no gloss must be put on needs in section 25 (as to whether they are reasonable or not), it nonetheless imposed fairness and equality as glosses on the section 25 factors. The relationship between section 25 and the principles enunciated in *White* is therefore unclear. Perhaps any 'glosses' on section 25 should have been left to Parliament, not the House of Lords. It is also rather unsatisfactory that the principles propounded by Lord Nicholls in *White* (namely equality, fairness and non-discrimination) arose in an atypical case, namely one in which both spouses were involved as partners in a family business.

The case-law after White v White and 'special contribution' After *White v White* the courts began to make larger awards (at least in 'big-money' cases), as *White* had removed the requirement that awards should be limited to reasonable needs. As a result, husbands who felt they had been dealt with unfairly began to argue that their special business contribution justified a departure from equality. In other words, they began to argue that, as they had been responsible for the accumulation of matrimonial assets, they should be entitled to more than half of those assets on divorce. This argument was sometimes successful. Thus, in *Cowan v Cowan* [2001] 2 FLR 192, for example, the wife (after a long marriage) was awarded only a 38 per cent share of the assets (worth over £11 million) on the basis that equal division would not be fair in the circumstances, in particular because of the husband's special business talent and the great wealth which he had thereby produced. The Court of Appeal so held even though its approach seemed to contradict the non-discrimination principle laid down in *White*.

After *Cowan v Cowan* (above) courts began to take into account special contributions by husbands as a justification for departing from equality, but this began to create difficulties. Not only did it lead to detailed evidence of contribution being put forward – which increased the length and cost of litigation and was contrary to the policy objective of encouraging agreement – but the courts began to adopt different approaches to contribution. Thus, although some judges accepted special contribution as a justification for departing from equality of division, others began to express concerns about such an approach. Coleridge J, for example, in *G v G (Financial Provision: Equal Division)* [2002] 2 FLR 1143 expressed disquiet about the growing forensic practice of routinely arguing special contribution in 'big-money' cases, which, he said, invited recrimination and was not conducive to settlement.

The difficulties created by *Cowan* (of allowing arguments based on special contribution to justify a departure from equality) were eventually addressed by the Court of Appeal in *Lambert v Lambert* [2003] 1 FLR 139 where it endeavoured to confine the doctrine of exceptional or special contribution, endorsed in *Cowan*, within narrow bounds. In *Lambert*, the husband, whose business had produced more than £26 million, argued that his exceptional business contribution (which had led to the accumulation of the matrimonial assets) justified a departure from equality. His wife, on the other hand, claimed a half-share of the assets on the ground that she had been the principal homemaker and parent during the marriage and that she had played a significant role in her husband's business. At first instance, Connell J, applying *Cowan* (see above), awarded her 37.5 per cent of the assets on the basis that her contribution had been modest, in fact merely 'ornamental', whereas her husband's had been 'really special' or 'exceptional'. The wife appealed, arguing *inter alia* that Connell J had fallen into the trap of gender discrimination by concluding that the husband's contribution justified a departure from equality, and that there had been insufficient consideration of her needs. The Court of Appeal allowed her appeal and awarded her 50 per cent of the assets. Although Thorpe LJ said that there 'must be an end to the sterile assertion that the breadwinner's contribution weighs heavier than the homemaker's', his Lordship cautiously acknowledged that, given the infinite variety of fact and circumstance, special contribution remained a legitimate possibility in exceptional circumstances.

The courts have taken a variety of approaches to the division of matrimonial assets on the basis of special contribution. Thus, for example, in *Norris v Norris* [2003] 1 FLR 1142 Bennett J rejected the wife's claim that she was entitled to half the matrimonial assets on the basis of her exceptional contribution (primary carer of the child, domestic contribution and financial contribution from her inherited wealth). Similarly, in *L v L (Financial Provision: Contributions)* [2002] FLR 642 Connell J rejected the wife's claim that she had played a pivotal role in the success of her husband's business, and instead awarded her only 37 per cent of the matrimonial assets because of her husband's special contribution. However, each case depends on its facts.

(b) Miller v Miller; McFarlane v McFarlane (2006)

In *Miller v Miller* [2006] UKHL 24, [2006] 1 FLR 1186 (heard with *McFarlane v McFarlane*) the House of Lords had the opportunity once again to consider 'the most intractable of problems: how to achieve fairness in the division of property following a divorce' (*per* Lord Nicholls in *Miller*). But this time it had to do so in the light of the principles it had laid down in *White v White* (above). It also had the opportunity (in *McFarlane*) to consider for the first time whether the principles in *White* should apply to the court's power to order periodical payments.

▶ *Miller v Miller; McFarlane v McFarlane* **[2006] UKHL 24, [2006] 1 FLR 1186**

Mr and Mrs Miller had been married for less than three years, and had no children. At the time of the marriage, the husband was an exceptionally successful businessman earning about £1 million a year, whereas the wife was earning £85,000 a year. The matrimonial home was purchased by the husband for £1.8 million and he subsequently bought a second property in joint names in the South of France. During the marriage the husband acquired shares in a new firm which subsequently proved to be extremely valuable. The wife gave up work to concentrate on furnishing their two homes. The husband left his wife for another woman, whom he subsequently married.

At first instance, Singer J ordered the husband to transfer the matrimonial home to his wife and to pay her a lump sum of £2.7 million. The husband appealed to the Court of Appeal, which held, dismissing his appeal, that Singer J had been entitled to take into account the husband's responsibility for the breakdown of the marriage and the wife's legitimate expectation of a higher standard of living. The husband appealed to the House of Lords.

The House of Lords, dismissing the husband's appeal and applying the principles in *White* (see p. 162 above), held *inter alia* that, in an application for financial relief, the redistribution of resources from one party to the other was justified on the basis of the following three principles: needs (generously interpreted) generated by the relationship between the parties; compensation for relationship-generated disadvantage; and sharing of the fruits of the matrimonial partnership. Which of these would be considered first depended on the circumstances of the case. In general it could be assumed that the marital partnership did not stay alive for the purpose of sharing future resources unless this was justified by needs and compensation. The ultimate object was to give each party an equal start on the road to independent living.

The House of Lords also considered the following issues: the role of conduct and the role of special contribution in applications for financial relief; the distinction between matrimonial and non-matrimonial property; and whether periodical payment can be made to provide compensation as well as to meet financial needs (see further at pp. 171–2 below).

Thus in *Miller* the House of Lords held that the following three principles must be applied by the courts when deciding how to distribute resources from one party to the other in an application for a financial remedy: needs (generously interpreted); compensation; and sharing.

In the following case, the Court of Appeal considered the principles laid down by the House of Lords in *White* and *Miller*, including, in particular, special contribution and how the yardstick of equality should be applied:

> ▶ *Charman v Charman* (No. 4) [2007] EWCA Civ 503, [2007] 1 FLR 1246
>
> The wife, who conceded that her husband had made a special contribution to the generation of matrimonial assets (worth about £131 million), sought 45 per cent of the assets but her husband offered her only £20 million. Coleridge J awarded her £48 million, representing 36.5 per cent of the assets, basing his departure from equality both on the husband's special contribution and on the greater risks inherent in the assets remaining with the husband.
>
> The husband appealed to the Court of Appeal arguing, *inter alia*, that: insufficient allowance had been made for his special contribution; and that Coleridge J had erred by incorrectly starting with a premise of equality, instead of starting with the section 25 exercise (and then considering whether there should be a discount for his special contribution).
>
> The Court of Appeal, led by Sir Mark Potter, P, dismissed the appeal; holding *inter alia* that special contribution (which could include non-financial contributions) had survived *Miller/ McFarlane* but that the bar was set very high. With respect to the *White* 'yardstick of equality', Sir Mark Potter P stated that, as it had developed into the 'equal sharing principle' and 'sharing entitlement', the application of the 'yardstick of equality' was no longer postponed to the end of the statutory exercise, Instead the property should be shared equally unless there was good reason not to do so.

A yardstick of equality or a principle of equal sharing?   In *White v White* the House of Lords introduced the notion of a yardstick of equality, but in *Miller* this term was referred to as 'the equal sharing principle' and to 'sharing entitlement'. In *White* the House of Lords held that a judge must conduct the section 25 exercise and then test his or her tentative view against the yardstick of equality; but in *Miller* the House of Lords appeared to adopt an approach whereby the starting point was equality of sharing rather than equality being a yardstick for testing a tentative calculation. In other words, *Miller* seemed to create a presumption of equal sharing and this was the approach adopted by Sir Mark Potter P in *Charman v Charman (No 4)* (above). Thus, the approaches to equality in *White* and *Miller* appeared to be quite different; and to have the potential to produce quite different results.

In cases after *Charman (No. 4)* (above) the approach of the courts was that the *Miller* sharing principle should be determined first and the outcome checked against the parties' needs. In other words, property should be shared equally unless there was good reason to the contrary. However, in *B v B (Ancillary Relief)* [2008] 2 FLR 1627, in which Hughes and Wall LJJ gave the leading judgments, and with whom Sir Mark Potter P concurred, the Court of Appeal indicated that the yardstick of equal division was *not* a sharing principle, but a tool to be used as a check at the *end* of the section 25 exercise, rather than as a principle of sharing operating within the section 25 discretionary exercise. These fine and difficult distinctions (as to whether or not equal sharing is a yardstick or a presumption) have muddied, rather than clarified, the law; and, as a result, have made it more difficult for lawyers to advise their clients. Furthermore, reaction to the needs, sharing and compensation 'formula' has not been positive (see further at pp. 192–4 below). As a result, there have been calls for reform of the law (see 7.14).

(c)   How the court conducts the discretionary exercise after *White* and *Miller*

After the decisions of the House of Lords in *White v White* (see p. 162) and *Miller v Miller*(see p. 165), the court, in an application for a financial remedy, must not only conduct the section 25 exercise, but must also exercise its discretion by taking into account the principle of fairness without discrimination (laid down in *White*) and the 'strands' of needs (generously construed), compensation and sharing (laid down in *Miller*). It must then, it seems, test its tentative conclusions against the yardstick of equality (laid down in *White*).

The trend in the case-law following *White* and *Miller* has been to emphasise the wide discretion of the court and its duty to apply the section 25 factors in order to achieve a fair result. The following propositions can be extracted from the case-law following *White* and *Miller*:

▶ *The section 25 factors prevail* The courts post-*Miller* have been keen to emphasise that the three 'strands' (of needs, compensation and sharing) have not supplanted the requirement that courts must apply the section 25 factors (see 7.4). Thus, for example, in *H v H* [2008] 2 FLR 2092 Moylan J said that the pivotal factor in every application for a financial remedy is to ensure that the order is fair and for all the relevant factors in section 25 to be considered. Only afterwards would there be a consideration of needs, compensation and sharing, if these are relevant at all to the facts of the case.

▶ *Special contribution* This can be taken into account as a reason for departing from equality but only in exceptional circumstances, for otherwise the principles of fairness and non-discrimination may be jeopardised. In *Miller* the House of Lords approved the words of Thorpe LJ in *Lambert* (see p. 164 above), who had acknowledged that special contribution remains a legitimate possibility but only in exceptional circumstances. In *Miller* the House of Lords stated that the question of contribution should be approached in much the same way as conduct. In other words, it should be regarded as a factor leading to a departure from equality of division only in wholly exceptional cases when it would be inequitable to disregard it. In *Charman v Charman (No. 4)* (see p. 166 above) Sir Mark Potter P said that special contribution includes both financial and non-financial contribution. On the basis that section 25(2)(f) of the statutory checklist refers to the ' contribution' made 'to the welfare of the family', contributions other than merely contributions to the purchase of property can be taken into account.

▶ *The courts should adopt a flexible, not formulaic, approach* The courts have emphasised that a flexible, not formulaic, approach should be adopted in an application for financial relief in order to do what is fair in the circumstances (see, for example, *C v C* [2009] 1 FLR 8).

▶ *The three strands of needs, sharing and compensation are not to be elevated into separate 'heads of claim'* In *CR v CR* [2008] 1 FLR 323 Bodey J said that it was important that the three 'strands' should not become elevated into separate 'heads of claim' or 'loss' independent of the MCA 1973, for, if such an approach were to gain momentum, then there would be a real danger of double-counting, which the House of Lords in *Miller* had warned against. In *P v RP* [2007] 1 FLR 2105 Coleridge J warned against the introduction of an approach which separated out and quantified the element of compensation, rather than treating it as one of the strands in the overall requirement of fairness. Coleridge J's warning was endorsed by Sir Mark Potter P in *VB v JP* [2008] 1 FLR 742.

▶ *What constitutes matrimonial property and valuations of matrimonial property must be viewed broadly* In *CR v CR* [2008] 1 FLR 323 Bodey J held that, although matrimonial property must now, post-*Miller*, be identified, the court must strive to take as broad a view as possible of what constitutes matrimonial property. In *H v H* [2008] 2 FLR 2092 Moylan J said that, in approaching valuation issues in respect of matrimonial property, the court must avoid over-artificial constructs of marital and non-marital property which could lead to an unduly formulaic approach. The valuation exercise was an art, not a science. The court was not engaged in a detailed accounting exercise, but in a broad analysis in the exercise of its jurisdiction under the 1973 Act. The purpose of valuations was to assist the court in testing the fairness of the proposed outcome, not to ensure mathematical/accounting accuracy.

▶ *Compensation may not always be a factor to be considered*   Whereas in *Miller/ McFarlane* the House of Lords described Mrs McFarlane's case as a 'paradigm case' for an award of compensation, in many cases compensation is unlikely to be a relevant factor. In fact, it may not even be relevant in a 'big-money' case (see, for example, *McCartney v Mills McCartney* below).

▶ *Sharing yields to a consideration of need where the pool of assets is limited and there are children of the family whose welfare is the court's first consideration* (as Lord Nicholls in *White v White* made clear).

▶ *Sometimes only one of the three strands in Miller may apply*   For instance in *McCartney v Mills McCartney* [2008] 1 FLR 1508 Bennett J held that needs (generously interpreted), not compensation and sharing, was the only relevant strand that applied in the circumstances of the case. Bennett J held that the compensation principle was not in any way engaged (as the wife had exaggerated her case), and neither was the sharing principle (as the marriage had been short and the husband's wealth had been accumulated before they had met).

▶ *Where the assets available for distribution exceed those required to meet the parties' needs*, a party can persuade the court to depart from ordering equal division by arguing that: a special contribution justifies a departure from equality (see pp. 163–5); that the relevant property is 'non-matrimonial' property (see below) and is not therefore subject to the presumption of equal shares; and/or that a term in a marital agreement about property is binding (see 7.9).

(d)   Matrimonial and non-matrimonial property and short and long marriages

In exercising their discretion in an application for financial relief, the courts may sometimes be required (particularly in 'big-money' cases) to consider whether or not to ring-fence certain assets from the pool of assets and treat them as non-matrimonial assets. The law is complex and confusing and it is debatable whether the attempt by the courts to find principles to help in categorising property as 'matrimonial' and 'non-matrimonial' has done anything to help in practice. Depending on the facts of the case, property acquired before marriage and inheritances and gifts received during marriage may be deemed not to be part of the pool of assets to be divided by the court. The length of the marriage will be an important factor when deciding whether or not assets have become or are matrimonial assets. In *Miller v Miller*, however, there were conflicting opinions about matrimonial and non-matrimonial property. Because of the uncertainty about how the courts should treat non-matrimonial property, the Law Commission is currently looking at the issue as part of its project on 'Matrimonial Property, Needs and Agreements' (see p. 196).

Whether property brought into the marriage will be treated as matrimonial or non-matrimonial for the purpose of financial relief proceedings depends on all the circumstances of each case. In *C v C* [2009] 1 FLR 8, for instance, the husband, a property developer, argued that the wife's entitlement should be limited to her needs (generously construed), on the basis that a large proportion, if not most, of his fortune had been acquired prior to their marriage (of 17 years, preceded by approximately 4 years' cohabitation). His wife, on the other hand, who sought half the assets (valued at £22 million), argued that the bulk of those assets had been built up during their relationship. Moylan J, who awarded the wife 40 per cent of the assets, held *inter alia* that the substantial wealth of the husband prior to the commencement of the parties' relationship justified a departure from equality.

In the following case, Mostyn J stated how the court should deal with the question of pre-marital property in financial proceedings on divorce:

▶ *N v F (Financial Orders: Pre-Acquired Wealth)* [2011] EWHC 586 (Fam), [2011] 2 FLR 533

The parties had been married for 16 years and had two children. At the time of the marriage the husband had assets of £21 million. As the husband had left his job as a high-earning banker and taken a job as a schoolteacher, the family had lived off capital. The total assets, at the time of the proceedings, were worth £9.7 million. Mostyn J, awarding the wife 44.7 per cent of the total assets and, making orders for child maintenance, made the following statements about pre-marital property:

▶ Although the treatment of pre-marital property is highly fact-specific and very discretionary, the court's discretion must be exercised consistently and predictably.
▶ The longer the marriage, the easier it was to say, by virtue of the mingling of pre-marital property with the product of the parties' marital endeavours, that the supplier of that property had in effect agreed to share it with his/her spouse.
▶ If the court had decided that the existence of pre-marital property should be reflected in an order, the correct approach was to identify the scale of the non-matrimonial property to be excluded, leaving the matrimonial property alone to be divided in accordance with the equal sharing principle (see *Jones v Jones* [2011] EWCA Civ 41, [2011] 1 FLR 1723).
▶ However, this process was subject to the question of need, the assessment of which could be affected by factors other than the scale of available resources and the marital standard of living.

Even where the marriage is of long duration, the court must consider the source of the assets. Thus, although Baroness Hale in *Miller* had said that the 'importance of the source of the assets will diminish over time', in *Vaughan v Vaughan* [2008] 1 FLR 1108 Wilson LJ held that, despite the long marriage (of nearly 20 years), the judge in the lower court had not properly taken into account the fact that the husband had bought the matrimonial home in his sole name (free of mortgage) three years prior to the marriage.

Inherited assets There are many reported cases on how inherited wealth should be dealt with by the courts in an application for financial relief. In *White v White* (2000) (see p. 162), Lord Nicholls stated that inherited assets stood on a different footing from other assets acquired during marriage, and that fairness generally required that a spouse should be allowed to keep inherited property, unless the other party's financial needs could not otherwise be satisfied. However, whether inherited assets will form part of the matrimonial assets to be divided on divorce will depend on the circumstances of the case (as was recently reiterated by the Court of Appeal in *Robson v Robson* [2011] 1 FLR 751). The needs of the parties and the length of the marriage will be particularly important.

In some cases, inherited property may count for little, but in others it may be of the greatest significance. For example, in *H v H (Financial Provision: Special Contribution)* [2002] 2 FLR 1021 inherited assets were quarantined from the pool of assets to be divided, but in *Norris v Norris* [2003] 1 FLR 1142 and *GW v RW (Financial Provision: Departure from Equality)* [2003] 2 FLR 108 they were taken into account as being part of the pool of assets. The length of the marriage may be important as it was, for example, in *S v S* [2007] EWHC 1975 (Fam), [2008] 1 FLR 944, where the wife's inherited assets were treated as part of the pool of assets to be divided as they had become amalgamated with other assets during the 20-year marriage.

Fairness may require that different types of inheritance be treated differently. For example, in *P v P (Inherited Property)* [2005] 1 FLR 576 Munby J held that the bulk of the matrimonial assets (a farm which had been in the husband's family for generations) should, in the circumstances of the case, be treated differently from a case involving a pecuniary inheritance.

The possibility of a party to the marriage receiving an inheritance in the future may be taken into account but whether it will have a material effect on how the court exercises its distributive powers will depend on the facts of the case (see, for example, *J v J (Financial Orders: Wife's Long-term Needs)* [2011] EWHC 1010 (Fam), [2011] 2 FLR 1280 where the possibility of the husband receiving an inheritance from his parents was taken into account but had no material effect on how the court exercised its distributive powers, due in part to the age of his parents and to the court's assessment of the parties' needs).

The following case, which went to the Court of Appeal, involved inherited assets, and provides a useful exposition of the law:

▶ *K v L (Non-Matrimonial Property: Special Contribution)* [2011] EWCA Civ 550 [2011] 2 FLR 980

After a 21-year relationship, the husband and wife separated. They had three children. The wife was very wealthy, as, about 13 years before she had started cohabiting with the husband, she had inherited shares from her grandfather which, at the date of separation, were worth about £28 million, but which by the date of the trial (3 years after the separation) were worth £57.4 million. Neither the husband nor the wife had worked during the marriage; and they had lived extremely modestly. The husband sought an award of £18 million, but Bodey J awarded him £5 million, plus the matrimonial home, on the basis that this award, plus the husband's existing capital of £300,000, would meet his needs, generously assessed. Bodey J described the wife's inherited wealth as a factor of 'central relevance', but indicated that it was also relevant that this wealth had always been kept separate from their other assets.

The husband appealed to the Court of Appeal, arguing, *inter alia*, that: (i) the award discriminated against his own contribution; and (ii) Bodey J had taken insufficient account of Baroness Hale's proposition in *Miller v Miller; McFarlane v McFarlane* [2006] UKHL 24 that 'the importance of the source of the assets will diminish over time'.

The Court of Appeal dismissed his appeal, with Wilson LJ who gave the only judgment, holding *inter alia* that:

▶ It is of the essence of the judicial function to discriminate between different sets of facts and thus between different claims. The discrimination outlawed by *White v*

White [2000] UKHL 54 is discrimination in the division of labour within the family, in particular between the party who earns the income and the party whose work is in the home, unpaid. Therefore, Bodey J's finding that the wife made a financial contribution to the marriage of great importance did not discriminate between the parties in any unacceptable way: on the contrary it correctly recognised a substantive difference.

▶ The dictum of Lord Nicholls that the importance of the source of assets *may* diminish over time is to be preferred to that of Baroness Hale in *Miller v Miller; McFarlane v McFarlane* (2006) that they *will* do so. In the circumstances of the case, there was nothing to justify a conclusion that, as the marriage proceeded, there was a diminution in the importance of the sources of the parties' entire wealth, at all times ring-fenced by share certificates in the wife's sole name which to a large extent were just kept safely and left to reproduce themselves and to grow in value.

Welstead was critical of the decision in *K v L* and of the law governing financial relief on divorce in general as the following extract shows:

▶ **Welstead, 'The sharing of pre-matrimonial property on divorce: *K v L*' [2012] Fam Law 185, at 189**

'The law relating to ancillary relief oscillates in a schizophrenic manner as attempts are made by the judiciary to find overriding principles, such as the tripartite ones put forward in *Miller v McFarlane*, to guide them through the discretionary morass of section 25 of the Matrimonial Causes Act 1925. No sooner than new principles are articulated, they are followed by decisions which erode them or expand them depending on the viewpoint of the judiciary. *K v L* is yet one more example of such erosion. Its restrictive approach is unlikely to lead to fairer or more certain financial awards. It has, rather, added to the complexities of the law relating to ancillary relief.'

(For other cases where the courts have had to deal with the distinction between matrimonial and non-matrimonial property, see: *Jones v Jones* [2011] EWCA Civ 41, [2011] 1 FLR 1723; *N v F (Financial Orders: Pre-Acquired Wealth)* [2011] EWHC 586 (Fam), [2011] 2 FLR 533; and *AR v AR (Treatment of Inherited Wealth)* [2011] EWHC 2717 (Fam).)

(e)   Big-money cases and periodical payments

Although *White v White* (2000) involved a lump sum, the House of Lords held in the *McFarlane* appeal in *Miller/McFarlane* (2006) that the overriding objective of fairness laid down in *White v White* could also apply to periodical payments in an exceptional case. In *McFarlane* the facts were exceptional as there was a huge surplus of available income after the needs of the parties had been met.

▶ *Miller v Miller; McFarlane v McFarlane* **[2006] UKHL 24, [2006] 1 FLR 1186**

Mr and Mrs McFarlane had been married for 16 years. Both were qualified professionals and, until shortly before the birth of their second child, earned similar sums of money. The wife gave up her highly paid career to care for the family, while the husband continued his professional career, with his annual salary increasing considerably from year to year (and which stood at £750,000 per annum by the time of the hearing). The family had insufficient capital available to achieve a clean break, but the husband earned substantially more than would be needed to meet his own and the wife's budgeted household expenditure. The district judge made a periodical payments order of £250,000 per year (on the basis that fairness required the wife to have a share of her husband's future earnings). This was reduced to £180,000 by the High Court; but the Court of Appeal allowed the wife's appeal in part, restoring the award to £250,000, but limiting the term to 5 years. The Court of Appeal held that in exceptional cases, and on the basis of term rather than joint lives orders, periodical payments could be used to accumulate capital. The wife appealed.

The House of Lords held, upholding the £250,000 award, but removing the 5-year term, that a periodical payments order could be made to afford compensation as well as to meet financial needs. However, a clean break was not to be achieved at the expense of a fair result. Thus, if a claimant was owed compensation and capital assets were not available, the social desirability of a clean break would not be sufficient reason for depriving a claimant of that compensation. There was no reason to limit periodical payments to a fixed term in the interests solely of achieving a clean break.

The House held that the case was a paradigm case for an award of compensation in respect of the significant future economic disparity sustained by the wife, arising from the way the parties had conducted their marriage.

Note: After a change of circumstances (Mr McFarlane's earnings had risen to over £1 million per annum), Mrs McFarlane obtained (in variation proceedings) a 40 per cent increase in periodical payments for herself and the three children (see *McFarlane v McFarlane* [2009] EWHC 891 (Fam)).

Cooke ([2004] Fam Law 906) was critical of the decision in *McFarlane* for extending the principles in *White* to income, as it perpetuated 'dependency and perhaps animosity'.

7.7 The family home on divorce

The future of the family home on divorce will be important, not just because of its financial value but because it provides accommodation for the family. As Lord Nicholls said in *Miller v Miller; McFarlane v McFarlane* (see p. 165 above), the matrimonial home 'usually has a central place in any marriage'. The provision of accommodation will usually be a primary consideration for the court when deciding how to distribute matrimonial assets. The provision of a home for any children will be a particularly important consideration. As Thorpe LJ said in *M v B* [1998] 1 FLR 53, 'it is one of the paramount considerations, in applying the section 25 criteria, to endeavour to stretch what is available to cover the need of each for a home, particularly where there are young children involved'. Thus, the housing needs of both parties and any relevant children will be taken into account, but the outcome will depend on the facts of the particular case.

When deciding what should happen to the home on divorce, the court has various options available. It might, for example, order one spouse to transfer the house, or his or her share of the house, to the other spouse with or without the other spouse making any compensating payment. It might order a transfer but make it subject to a charge in favour of the transferor, representing the value of the transferor's interest in the home which will be realised on sale at a later date. The house might be transferred for the purpose of effecting a clean break (for instance by being transferred to the wife with her forbearing to claim periodical payments).

A Mesher order   This is an order made under section 24(1)(b) MCA 1973 whereby the house is settled on trust for one or both of the spouses in certain shares, but with sale postponed until a future event (such as until the children have reached a particular age or have finished full-time education, or until the death, remarriage or cohabitation of the other spouse). *Mesher* orders were once popular with the courts, but they have become less popular because of their disadvantages. One disadvantage is that a spouse may have insufficient funds from the eventual proceeds of sale to rehouse him or herself, particularly in a declining property market. Another disadvantage is that children may continue to need accommodation after the event triggering sale has occurred and even when they have reached majority. It is possible, however, for the court to take this into account, as it did in *Sawden v Sawden* [2004] EWCA Civ 339, where the Court of Appeal inserted another condition into the *Mesher* order so that the children could remain indefinitely in the home, if they wished, without their father enforcing sale and claiming his 45 per cent of the proceeds of sale. Another disadvantage of *Mesher* orders is that they are contrary to the clean break, as, until sale, the parties are tied together as joint owners, thereby restricting their chances of financial self-sufficiency.

Despite the above disadvantages, the Court of Appeal in *Clutton v Clutton* [1991] 1 WLR 359 said that a *Mesher* order might be appropriate where the family assets were sufficient to provide both parties with a roof over their heads if the matrimonial home were sold at a later date, but where the interest of the parties required the children to stay in the matrimonial home. However, Lloyd LJ stressed that, where there were any doubts about a wife's eventual ability to rehouse herself, then a *Mesher* order should not be made. The Court of Appeal held that a *Martin* order (see below) did not suffer from the same disadvantage. In *B v B (Mesher Order)* [2003] 2 FLR 285 a *Mesher* order was held not to be appropriate because of the wife's inability to generate capital at the date of the suggested *Mesher* triggering event and because it would impose a significant financial burden on her.

A Martin order   This order is similar to a *Mesher* order, except that it gives a spouse a right to occupy the house until his or her death, remarriage or cohabitation, after which the proceeds of sale are divided in certain shares. It therefore provides a more secure solution than a *Mesher* order.

An order for sale   Under section 24A of the MCA 1973 the court can order that the matrimonial home be sold, but this power can only be exercised ancillary to the court's power to make a financial provision or property adjustment order. Thus, for example, the court could order sale of the home so that one of the parties receives a lump sum from the proceeds of sale.

If the house is in joint names the signatures of both parties will be required for sale. However, if it is in the name of one spouse, and there is a danger that the sole owner may sell it before the divorce court has exercised its powers, the non-owner spouse should register his or her 'home rights' (see pp. 72–3). If the house has been sold to defeat an application for a financial remedy, an application can be made under section 37 MCA 1973 to have the transaction set aside (see 7.11).

Tenancies of the home   Section 53 and Schedule 7 to Part IV of the Family Law Act 1996 make provision for the transfer of tenancies on divorce. A tenancy can also be transferred under section 24 MCA 1973.

7.8 Pensions on divorce

A pension is a valuable asset and its loss on divorce can be substantial. Although pension entitlement is something which the divorce courts have always been able to take into account as part of the section 25 discretionary exercise (see 7.4), amendments to the Matrimonial Causes Act 1973 have over the years improved the pension position for persons who are divorcing (or having their civil partnership dissolved). The following options are available in respect of pension entitlement on divorce: (i) 'off-setting'; (ii) a pension attachment order; (iii) a pension sharing order; and (iv) pension compensation orders. The law on pensions, including pensions on divorce, is complex. Only an outline is given here.

(i) 'Off-setting'   To compensate for lost or reduced pension entitlement, the court in the exercise of its section 25 discretionary powers has the power to make compensatory adjustments in respect of the division of matrimonial assets other than the pension. In this way, rights under a pension scheme are left untouched but their value is taken into account by giving a party an appropriately enlarged share of the other party's assets. Off-setting may be useful where pension assets are inaccessible (for example, where they are held outside the jurisdiction). Off-setting can only be used, however, if there are sufficient assets available to compensate for the loss of pension entitlement. If this is not the case then the other options below will have to be considered. Off-setting has the advantage of creating a clean break between the parties, as there will be no need for the parties to have contact with each other in the future.

(ii) Pension attachment orders ('earmarking')   Pension attachment orders can be made under sections 25B–25D of the MCA 1973. Pension attachment involves a pension being 'earmarked' for the other party. If an order is made, then, once the pension becomes payable, the person responsible for the pension arrangement (the trustee or managers of the fund) must pay part of the pension income and/or a lump sum available under the pension arrangement to the other party to the marriage (s 25B(4)). Although the main advantage of a pension attachment order is that the payment is more likely to represent the actual value of the pension once it becomes payable, they have disadvantages. Thus, they undermine the policy of the clean break (as the parties remain financially tied to each other, and either party may apply for variation). It may be difficult for the court to force the pension holder to continue to make payments to the pension fund or to retire by a specified age; and it may be difficult for the court to predict the value of the pension and the needs of the parties at the point in time when the pension becomes payable. Because of these disadvantages, and others, pension sharing orders provide a better solution.

(iii) Pension sharing orders   These orders were introduced in 2000 and are commonly made. A pension sharing order is an order which enables pension benefits to be irrevocably split at the time of divorce, forming two separate pensions, so that one can be allocated to the other spouse to invest as he or she thinks appropriate. The pension sharing order will specify the percentage value to be transferred (s 21A(1)). An order can be made in respect of a pension which is already being paid. The provisions do not apply to the basic State retirement pension. The section 25 guidelines apply when the court is deciding whether to make a pension sharing order and, if so, in what manner.

Pension sharing has the following advantages over off-setting and pension attachment: a clean break can be effected because the pension fund is split at the time of divorce; the order allows the pension assets to be kept separate from other assets on divorce; and it avoids the problems involved in off-setting assets fairly in order to compensate for loss of a pension.

(iv) Pension compensation New sections have been inserted into the MCA 1973 by the Pensions Act 2008 (which came into force on 6 April 2011) to enable Pension Protection Fund (PPF) compensation to be shared or attached in the same way as a pension can be shared or attached.

The exercise of discretion in respect of a pension The court's powers in respect of pension arrangements are governed by the section 25 factors (see 7.4) and the principles laid down in *White v White* and *Miller v Miller* (see 7.6). Section 25B(1) expressly requires the court when conducting its section 25(2) exercise to have regard to: any benefits under a pension arrangement which a party to the marriage has or is likely to have; and any benefits under a pension arrangement which, by reason of the divorce (or annulment), a party to the marriage will lose the chance of acquiring. When considering any benefits under a pension arrangement, there is no requirement that the courts take into consideration only those benefits which will be available in the foreseeable future (s 25B(1)). A pension can also be taken into account under section 25(2)(a) as a 'financial resource' which a party has or is likely to have in the future. If retirement is reasonably imminent, the court may decide to adjourn the proceedings.

7.9 Agreements about property and finance

Divorcing couples are encouraged to reach agreement about legal issues arising on divorce whether they be in respect of property, finance or children. It is better for them to reach an amicable agreement rather than to engage in costly, hostile, unpredictable and emotionally stressful litigation. Many couples reach agreement of their own accord, but others may do so with the assistance of ADR and/or lawyers (see 1.5).

Couples can also enter into more formal written agreements about finance and property, and they may do this before and during marriage, and on marriage breakdown. However, such agreements are not automatically binding, because the divorce court retains a supervisory jurisdiction in respect of such agreements.

The following agreements are considered in this section: (a) consent orders; (b) separation agreements; and (c) pre- and post-nuptial agreements. There has been discussion about reforming the law relating to marital agreements(see p. 182 below).

(a) Consent orders

An agreement about finance and property on divorce can be incorporated into a consent order, which the court has jurisdiction to make under section 33A of the Matrimonial Causes Act 1973. A consent order can contain only those orders which the court has power to make under Part II of the 1973 Act. In order to enable the court to exercise its discretion to make a consent order, the parties must provide the court with prescribed information. Failure to do so may result in the order being set aside (see pp. 190–1). Although consent orders are based on an agreement, the general principles of contract law do not determine the outcome of a case. Instead, it is the consent order itself which determines the rights and duties of the parties

When considering whether to make a consent order, the court does not just 'rubber-stamp' the proposed agreement. It considers all the circumstances and applies the section 25 factors, the clean-break provisions and the approaches laid down in the case-law. However, the court will usually approve the agreement, as the fact that it has been drawn up and agreed to by the parties, usually with legal advice, is *prima facie* proof of its reasonableness. The terms of a consent order can be varied in variation proceedings, but only in respect of periodical payments (see pp. 186–8 below). Consent orders may be set aside in some circumstances, for example if there has been non-disclosure.

The Law Commission in its Consultation Paper on *Marital Property Agreements* (CP 198) stated (at para 3.15) that it was not aware of any dissatisfaction with the practice of the courts in making consent orders.

(b) Separation agreements

A separation agreement is an agreement made in contemplation of imminent separation, or following separation, which seeks to make financial arrangements for the period of separation and any subsequent divorce. It can be made before or after proceedings for financial relief have been commenced, and it can be made with or without legal advice. The law relating to separation agreements is distinct from that relating to pre- and post-nuptial agreements (see below). The reason for this is that, whereas pre-nuptial and post-nuptial agreements have historically been treated as immoral (as they made provision for future separation and divorce) and were therefore void, separation agreements were treated with much less suspicion because they catered for the situation where the relationship had already run its course.

Sections 34–36 of the Matrimonial Causes Act 1973 govern separation agreements. Such agreements are not automatically binding, because the divorce court retains a supervisory role with regard to such agreements. Thus, the court has power under section 35(2) to vary, revoke or insert new terms into an agreement if the terms of the agreement (or omission of terms) do not allow for a change of circumstances; or where there is no provision in the agreement for proper financial arrangements with respect to any child of the family. Also, any provision in an agreement restricting the right of either party to apply to the court for an application for a financial remedy is void (s 34(1)).

A separation agreement does not give rise to an enforceable legal contract (see Thorpe LJ in *Xydhias v Xydhias* [1999] 1 FLR 683), with the result that the agreement cannot exclude, or oust, the jurisdiction of the court in financial relief proceedings; and either spouse can ask the court to ignore some, or all, of the terms in the agreement and make a different order.

Private agreements have the advantages of promoting amicable settlement and avoiding the uncertainty and cost of litigation. For these reasons, in the following case of *Edgar v Edgar*, the Court of Appeal held that a formal separation agreement, entered into with competent legal advice, should generally be enforced unless there are good and substantial grounds for concluding that an injustice will be done by holding the parties to the terms of their agreement.

▶ *Edgar v Edgar* (1981) 2 FLR 19

The parties entered into a separation agreement in which the husband, a multi-millionaire, agreed to pay his wife a lump sum of £100,000 and in which she agreed to seek no further provision. The wife entered into the agreement despite her solicitor's advice that she would obtain a better settlement in divorce proceedings. Later in ancillary relief proceedings on divorce she was granted a lump sum of £760,000. The husband appealed to the Court of Appeal.

The Court of Appeal held, allowing his appeal and setting the order aside, that the wife was bound by the terms of the original agreement. There was no evidence that she had been exploited. She had received legal advice and there had been no adverse conduct by her husband during negotiations leading up to the agreement. A large disparity between the sum agreed and the sum that she might have been awarded in divorce proceedings was insufficient on its own for the court to ignore the agreement. The court acknowledged that it had a duty to exercise its discretionary powers under section 25, but Ormrod LJ held that it was an important general principle that 'formal agreements, properly and faithfully arrived at with competent legal advice' should not be displaced unless there were 'good and substantial grounds' for concluding that an injustice would be done by holding the parties to the terms of their agreement. Ormrod LJ said that 'good and substantial grounds' included whether there was pressure from one side, exploitation of a dominant position, inadequate knowledge, bad legal advice or an unforeseen change of circumstances. His Lordship said that 'the existence of a freely negotiated bargain entered into at the instance of one of the parties and affording him or her everything for which he or she has stipulated must be a most important element of conduct which cannot lightly be ignored'.

Baroness Hale in *MacLeod* (see further below) explicitly endorsed Ormrod LJ's analysis above, stating that, although the courts 'must be alive to the risk of unfair exploitation of superior strength', 'the fact that the agreement is not what a court would have done cannot be enough to have it set aside'.

Edgar v Edgar therefore emphasised the important policy objective of achieving finality, and the undesirability of opening up arrangements which have already been settled by the parties. The approach in *Edgar v Edgar* is still followed, with the result that a spouse will not be permitted to resile from an agreement without good reason. Thus, for example, in *G v G (Financial Provision: Separation Agreement)* [2004] 1 FLR 1011 the agreement was upheld (even though it had been drawn up without legal advice and at a time when emotional pressures were high and judgment was likely to be clouded), as both parties had had previous experience of marital breakdown and had from the outset of their marriage elected to regulate their affairs contractually.

(c)   Pre- and post-nuptial agreements

A pre-nuptial agreement (a 'pre-nup') is an agreement made before marriage which seeks to regulate the couple's financial affairs during their marriage or to determine the division of their property in the event of divorce or separation. A post-nuptial agreement (a 'post-nup') is a similar agreement but one made during marriage. Historically, the law treated such agreements with suspicion and considered them to be immoral, as spouses had a duty to live together and marriages could not be terminated by divorce, except in restricted circumstances. Thus, the rule (laid down in *Hyman v Hyman* [1929] AC 601) was that any agreement made in contemplation of marital breakdown was contrary to public policy. For this reason, agreements which made arrangements about provision for future separation and divorce were held to be void and could not be enforced as a valid contract. Separation agreements, on the other hand, were treated differently (see above).

Although pre- and post-nuptial agreements were considered to be contrary to public policy, they could be taken into account by the divorce court as one of the circumstances of the case when it was conducting the section 25 exercise (see 7.4). However, until relatively recently, the courts accorded little weight to such agreements. In 1995, for instance, Thorpe J (as he was then) stated in *F v F (Ancillary Relief: Substantial Assets)* [1995] 2 FLR 45 (where the husband had sought to rely on pre-nuptial contracts drawn up in Germany) that such agreements were of 'very limited significance' in England and Wales. As a result, Thorpe J refused to attach any significant weight to the German contracts, even though they might be strictly enforced against the wife in Germany.

However, although the courts would often refuse to recognise pre-nuptial agreements, they showed a greater willingness to accept and recognise post-nuptial agreements as they were considered to be more like separation agreements which were not contrary to public policy (see above). In fact, there were two strands of case-law depending on whether the agreement was pre-nuptial or post-nuptial, as the two types of agreement were considered to be conceptually distinct (see Baroness Hale in *MacLeod* below). However, this distinction has now been eroded by the majority of the Supreme Court in *Radmacher v Granatino* (see below) which held that there is no conceptual difference between them.

In recent years there has been a change of attitude and the benefits of such agreements have been increasingly recognised as an important part of the settlement culture, particularly as they are often entered into and upheld in other European jurisdictions.

The law in this area has developed rapidly in a series of recent cases. A key case was the case of *MacLeod v MacLeod* [2008] UKPC 64, [2009] 1 FLR 641 where the Judicial Committee of the Privy Council (with Baroness Hale giving the leading opinion) held that post-nuptial (not pre-nuptial agreements) were no longer void. However, the Privy Council (affirming *Edgar v Edgar*, above) nonetheless held that it was still open to the divorce court to set aside any agreement which was unfairly entered into or which failed to make sufficient provision generally or where there had been a change of circumstances. The case involved an appeal from the Isle of Man, but, because the Manx legislation governing matrimonial law has its equivalent in the Matrimonial Causes Act 1973, the decision was also relevant to the law in England and Wales. The Privy Council, with Baroness Hale giving the leading opinion, held that the post-nuptial agreement entered into by the husband and wife was, on the facts of the case, a valid and enforceable agreement. Baroness Hale stated that:

> 'Post-nuptial agreements…are very different from pre-nuptial agreements. The couple are now married. They have undertaken towards one another the obligations and responsibilities of the married state.…There is nothing to stop a couple entering into contractual financial arrangements…as this couple did as part of their 2002 agreement.'

Following *MacLeod,* and its rejection of the *Hyman* (1929) rule of public policy, it became more likely that *post*-marital agreements would be upheld by the courts. Thus, for example, in *S v S (Ancillary Relief)* [2009] 1 FLR 254 Eleanor King J relied on a post-marital agreement as compelling evidence that a concluded agreement had been reached between the parties and should be upheld.

However, it is the Supreme Court's decision in the landmark case of *Radmacher v Granatino* (see below) which now represents the most authoritative statement of the current law on both pre-nuptial and post-nuptial agreements. The majority in *Radmacher* swept away the distinction between pre-nuptial and post-nuptial agreements established in *MacLeod*, holding that neither form of marital agreement was contrary to public policy *per se* and that the courts should apply the same principles to both. Thus the rule in *Edgar v Edgar* (see p. 177 above) and *MacLeod v MacLeod* (see above) on post-nuptial agreements now applies equally to pre-nuptial agreements. In *Radmacher*, Baroness Hale, who had held in *MacLeod* that there was a clear distinction between pre- and post-nuptial agreements, found herself dissenting with the majority in *Radmacher* which held that there was no distinction between the two types of agreement.

▶ *Radmacher (Formerly Granatino) v Granatino* [2010] UKSC 42, [2011] 1 FLR 1851

The wife (a German heiress said to be worth in excess of £100 million) and her French husband married in London in 1998 and had two children. Three months before the marriage they entered into a pre-nuptial contract which was signed in Germany in front of a notary in compliance with all the legal requirements and formalities under German law, the terms of which stipulated that the effects of the marriage should be governed by German law and the matrimonial regime of a separation of property, and that in the case of the marriage ending by divorce or death neither party should have a claim against the separate property of the other. The parties divorced in England in 2007 and the husband applied for a financial remedy, basing his claim on needs, not compensation and sharing (see *Miller*, at p. 165 above). The wife argued that the pre-nuptial contract was binding.

Baron J refused to recognise and enforce the pre-nuptial contract as it 'fell foul' of a number of safeguards, including the fact that the husband had received no independent legal advice, there had been no disclosure by the wife, and there was no provision for the two children of the marriage. But as the contract would have been binding in their respective home countries (Germany and France), Baron J held that it would not be right to ignore it and, in assessing the husband's needs, awarded him a lump sum of £5.56 million with a further £504,000 paid by the wife to provide a home for him in Germany to have contact with the two children, and periodical payments for the children of £70,000 per annum. The wife appealed to the Court of Appeal.

The Court of Appeal (with Thorpe LJ giving the leading judgment) allowed the wife's appeal as far as the financial provision for him as husband was concerned, but not as father. It held that, although Baron J had correctly held that pre-nuptial settlements were not binding *per se*, but were a factor to be taken into account, she had not taken into account certain factors, including *inter alia* that: the contract was standard practice and would have been binding in the parties' home countries; and that the husband had chosen not to seek independent legal advice. There was no good reason not to hold the husband to the agreement. The husband appealed to the Supreme Court.

The Supreme Court (with Lord Phillips giving the leading opinion) dismissed the husband's appeal and upheld the decision of the Court of Appeal by a majority of 8 to 1 (with Baroness Hale dissenting). It held that:

1. The rule that it is the court, not any prior agreement between the parties, that determines what will happen to the parties' financial arrangements upon divorce, still prevails. Thus, the court is not obliged to give effect to a pre- or post-nuptial agreement, but must decide how much weight to accord such an agreement, and decide whether it is fair or just to depart from it.
2. In relation to the argument that agreements providing for future separation are no longer contrary to public policy, no distinction should be drawn between pre- and post-nuptial agreements. The Privy Council was wrong in *MacLeod v MacLeod* (see above) to hold that a post-nuptial agreement is a contract but that an ante-nuptial agreement is not. Regardless of whether one or both are contracts, the court should apply the same principles when considering ante-nuptial agreements as apply to post-nuptial agreements.

3. The rebuttable presumption that courts should give effect to post-nuptial agreements (see *Edgar v Edgar*, p. 177 above, and *MacLeod v MacLeod*, above) now applies equally to pre-nuptial agreements. Thus, the court should give effect to any nuptial agreement that was freely entered into by each party with a full appreciation of its implications unless in the circumstances of the case it would not be fair to hold the parties to their agreement.

4. If an ante- or post-nuptial agreement is to carry full weight, both parties must enter into it of their own free will, without undue influence or pressure, and informed of its implications. The circumstances of the parties at the time of the agreement would be relevant. An important factor might be whether the marriage would have gone ahead without an agreement, or without the terms agreed.

5. The contents of a pre-nuptial agreement must be fair. The question of fairness will depend upon the facts of the particular case, but, by way of guidance, the factors to be considered include :

   ▶ A nuptial agreement cannot be allowed to prejudice the reasonable requirements of any children of the family.

   ▶ The court should accord respect to the decision of a married couple as to the manner in which their financial affairs should be regulated. It would be paternalistic and patronising to override their agreement simply on the basis that the court knows best.

   ▶ There is nothing inherently unfair in parties making express agreement as to the disposal of non-matrimonial property and there may be good objective justification for doing so (such as obligations towards existing family members).

   ▶ The longer the marriage has lasted, the more likely it is that the couple's circumstances would have changed over time in ways or to an extent that either could not be or simply was not envisaged, giving more scope for what had happened over the years to make it unfair to hold them to the agreement.

   ▶ Of the three strands in *Miller v Miller* (needs, compensation and sharing), it is the first two (needs and compensation) which could most readily render it unfair to hold the parties to an agreement.

Applying the above principles to the facts, the Supreme Court held that the ante-nuptial had not been tainted by the lack of independent legal advice, disclosure or negotiations. The needs of the husband were not a factor that rendered it unfair to hold him to the terms of the agreement, subject to making provision for the needs of the children of the family. There was no compensation factor in this case and the husband had agreed that he was not entitled to share in a portion of the wife's inherited wealth. Overall, it would be unfair to depart from the ante-nuptial agreement.

Baroness Hale dissented for the following reasons:

▶ Couples were not entirely free to determine for themselves all the legal consequences of marriage. Their mutual duty to support one another and their children was part of an irreducible minimum of matrimony.

▶ Although the law of marital agreements was a mess, it was the task of Parliament, with the help of the Law Commission, to review and reform the law, not a court hearing a particular case with very unusual features.

▶ Although the test to be applied to marital agreements proposed by *MacLeod* had been too strict, the test suggested by the majority in the present case was an impermissible gloss upon the courts' statutory duties, in that it introduced a presumption or starting point.

▶ The test to be applied to any and all marital agreements should be the same: 'Did each party freely enter into an agreement, intending it to have legal effect and with a full appreciation of its implications? If so, in the circumstances as they now are, would it be fair to hold them to their agreement?'

▶ The husband's appeal should have been allowed, because, although there was nothing in the circumstances in which the agreement had been made to make it unfair, the husband's role as father to the children was a relevant factor even after the children attained their majority, and would at the least have justified providing him with a home for life.

The principles that now govern both pre- and post-marital agreements were summarised in the following words of Lord Phillips who gave judgment for the majority in *Radmacher*:

LORD PHILLIPS: 'A court when considering the grant of ancillary relief is not obliged to give effect to nuptial agreements – whether they are ante-nuptial or post-nuptial. The parties cannot, by agreement, oust the jurisdiction of the court. The court must, however, give appropriate weight to the agreement.

...Under English law it is the court that is the arbiter of the financial arrangements between the parties when it brings a marriage to an end. A prior agreement between the parties is only one of the matters to which the court will have regard.

...The court should give effect to a nuptial agreement that is freely entered into by each party with a full appreciation of its implications unless in the circumstances prevailing it would not be fair to hold the parties to their agreement.'

This approach is very similar to that taken by Ormrod LJ in *Edgar v Edgar* in 1981 (see p. 177) with regard to separation agreements. Consequently, a pre-marital or post-marital agreement will be upheld by the court provided it was fairly entered into at the time it was made and subsequent circumstances have not rendered it unfair. Scherpe ([2011] CFLQ 513), commenting on *Radmacher*, explains that courts must apply a two-stage fairness test: 'a procedural fairness' stage which looks at the time when the agreement was made; and a 'substantive fairness' stage where the scrutiny is focused on the actual content of the agreement. Thus, the outcome of the Supreme Court's decision in *Radmacher* is that the courts are now more likely to recognise pre-marital and post-marital agreements provided they are fairly made, and where it is fair to uphold the agreement, applying the principles which apply to applications for financial relief on divorce.

Some of the points made by Baroness Hale in her dissenting opinion seem to have considerable force, particularly as she was the sole family law expert who heard the case in the Supreme Court. Her view that the majority's approach constituted an 'impermissible gloss on the courts' statutory duty in section 25 (see 7.4) has some strength in it. In other words, it is arguable that the majority in *Radmacher* engaged in 'judicial law-making' when the matter was one for the Law Commission and Parliament to address. Furthermore, according to Harris, George and Herring ([2011] Fam Law 367), 'the judgment seems to risk making agreements all but enforceable while by-passing the kinds of safeguards which any legislative scheme would almost certainly have included'. Harris *et al.* also argue that, while arguments based on respect for individual autonomy, which formed the policy basis for the decision of the majority, 'have an inherent attraction', it also needs to be recognised that marriage is a legally regulated status and that marriage and civil partnership, 'as social institutions, inevitably involve a degree of compromise between personal autonomy and state regulation'. As Baroness Hale stated in her dissenting opinion, 'the parties are not entirely free to determine all [the] legal consequences for themselves'.

The first reported case post-*Radmacher* was *Z v Z (No 2) (Financial Remedies: Marriage Contract)* [2011] EWHC 2878 (Fam) where Moor J, referring to *Radmacher*, upheld the pre-nuptial agreement, but went on to make financial provision for the wife's needs.

In *V v V (Prenuptial Agreement)* [2011] EWHC 3230 (Fam) the Court of Appeal held that the district judge had erred in according too little weight to a Swedish pre-nuptial agreement. However, in *Kremen v Agrest (No.11) (Financial Remedy: Non-Disclosure: Post-Nuptial Agreement)* [2012] EWHC 45 (Fam) Mostyn J gave no weight whatsoever to a post-marital agreement made in Israel (which would have left the wife with approximately £1.5 million when the total assets were assessed at £20 to £30 million) as there had been a material absence of independent legal advice and disclosure. Also, in *GS v L (Financial Remedies: Pre-Acquired Assets: Needs)* [2011] EWHC 1759 (Fam) a Spanish post-marital agreement was not upheld by King J.

A marital agreement made abroad The fact that an agreement has been made abroad does not mean that it will necessarily be binding, but, as the Supreme Court stated in *Radmacher v Granatino* (above), the fact that an agreement was made abroad may be relevant to the important question of whether or not the parties *intended* the agreement to be binding (see also, Charles J in *V v V* [2011] EWHC 3230 (Fam)).

(d) Reform to make marital agreements binding

As a result of the decision of the Supreme Court in *Radmacher v Granatino* (2010) (see above), the rule of public policy that rendered marital agreements void if they made financial provision for a future separation or divorce no longer applies, so that agreements can now be upheld provided they are procedurally and substantively fair. Thus, the court retains a supervisory jurisdiction to decide whether the terms of the agreement should be binding in the circumstances of the case. The question now is whether legislation should be introduced to make them binding.

Before the decision in *Radmacher* there had been discussion for many years about introducing legislation to make pre-marital contracts legally binding, subject to certain safeguards. For instance, in its 1998 discussion paper, *Supporting Families* (Home Office), the Government discussed this proposal, but its proposals were taken no further. In 2004, Resolution (the organisation of family lawyers) recommended that the section 25 factors should be amended to give the court a duty to treat pre-marital agreements as legally binding, subject to the overriding safeguard of significant injustice to either party or to any minor child of the family (see *A More Certain Future – Recognition of Pre-Marital Agreements in England and Wales*). In July 2007 a Pre-Nuptial Agreement Bill to provide for the enforceability of pre-nuptial agreements was introduced into the House of Commons by Quentin Davies MP as a Private Member's Bill, but this was not taken forward. The most recent development, however, is that the Law Commission, the Government's reform body, has been looking at marital agreements (both pre-marital and post-marital), and also at other related issues, with a possible view to reform (see 7.14).

There are arguments both for and against making marital agreements legally binding, some of which are as follows:

Arguments for making marital agreements legally binding

▶ It would remove some of the uncertainty and unpredictability created by the current discretionary system governing financial relief on divorce, as the parties, not the courts, would be responsible for regulating their financial and property matters on divorce.

> ▶ It would reduce the need for costly, time-consuming and unpredictable litigation.
> ▶ It would respect the autonomy of the parties to choose how to regulate their own affairs.
> ▶ It would bring the law in England and Wales into line with Europe and other countries where marital agreements are binding.
> ▶ It would bring the law into line with the increasing emphasis on settlement and agreement in family matters.
>
> **Arguments against making marital agreements legally binding**
>
> ▶ It may be unjust and unfair to make them legally binding, for instance where unforeseen events happen in the marriage which are not catered for in the agreement (for instance the birth of children, ill-health, loss of a job, or receipt of a windfall).
> ▶ It may be unjust to make them legally binding where there was unfairness at the time when the agreement was made (such as non-disclosure, duress, mistake and inequality of bargaining power).
> ▶ There may be problems drafting agreements, and lawyers may risk having negligence claims brought against them for failing to draft them appropriately.
> ▶ The birth of children may cause problems, because, although it may be appropriate for a spouse to contract out of any financial obligation to the other spouse, the parental obligation to support and maintain children cannot be terminated by agreement.
> ▶ It may be difficult to draft legislation to protect against injustice and unfairness; and any new legislation may itself lead to greater complexity and to litigation.

(For a discussion of the advantages and disadvantages of making marital property agreements binding, see para 5.88 of the Law Commission's consultation paper, *Marital Property Agreements* (LCCP No 198, 2011).)

Matters to be addressed   Discussion of reform will have to address a range of matters such as: Should agreements be in a prescribed form? Should there be a compulsory requirement that the parties must seek independent legal advice? Should there be a time limit between the agreement and the marriage? On what grounds should they be set aside, for instance if they fail to make satisfactory financial provision? What about changes of circumstances, such as the birth of children, illness or loss of employment?

The Law Commission's project on marital agreements   In October 2009 the Law Commission began a project on the status and enforceability of marital property agreements, but its consultation paper (*Marital Property Agreements*, LCCP No. 198) was not published until January 2011 because of the need to wait for the Supreme Court's decision in *Radmacher* (see above). The consultation paper discussed options for reform and asked consultees whether there should be legislative reform to 'enable couples effectively to contract out of ancillary relief, and out of the court's discretion, by entering into an agreement in a prescribed form and subject to appropriate safeguards' (para 1.11). The major question for the project was: 'whether or not the law relating to marital property agreements should be changed so as to allow such agreements to oust the jurisdiction of the courts in ancillary relief, and if so to what extent' (para 4.62).

The consultation period closed on 11 April 2011, but was extended to cover two other related issues: needs and non-matrimonial property. However, in its supplementary consultation paper (*Matrimonial Property, Needs and Agreements*, LCCP No. 208), (see further p. 196 below), the Law Commission stated (at para 1.10) that those who had responded to its consultation on marital property agreements (above) had shown considerable support for the introduction of qualifying nuptial agreements, provided there were safeguards to protect the financially weaker party. One reason why the marital agreements project was extended to look at needs was that the Law Commission considered that it should not be possible, in a marital agreement, to contract out of provision for needs, and that such a restriction would provide an important safeguard for qualifying nuptial agreements (see para 1.12, LCCP No. 208, above).

7.10 Enforcing financial orders

Financial orders can be enforced in various ways. The law on enforcement is complex. Only an outline is given here. The Law Commission will be conducting a project on the enforcement of financial orders on divorce after it has completed its current project on 'Matrimonial Property, Needs and Agreements' (see further at p. 196 below).

(a) Enforcing orders for payment of money

Procedures for enforcing orders for payment of money include:

▶ *A judgment summons* The spouse who wishes to enforce payment of a financial order can apply for a judgment summons, which requires the other party to attend before a judge to be examined as to his or her means At the hearing, the judge will make such order as he or she thinks fit in relation to the arrears or outstanding payment. There is a power to commit a spouse to prison for non-payment in certain circumstances.

▶ *A warrant of execution against goods* This authorises an enforcement officer to seize and sell enough of the other spouse's goods to pay off the debt (excluding basic goods for domestic needs). It is a commonly used enforcement procedure.

▶ *A garnishee order* This order ring-fences funds in the debtor's bank account equivalent to the sum of money owed and directs that it is paid directly to the spouse. This type of order can only be issued once. Thus, if there are insufficient funds in the debtor's bank account, the order will fail and cannot be used again.

▶ *Appointment of receiver* A court may appoint an individual to receive and protect rents, profits and other proceeds of property belonging to the defaulting spouse, or of a business carried on by that spouse, for the satisfaction of the debt. This is an exceptional remedy.

▶ *A charging order* A court may issue a charge over one of the defaulting party's property assets (for example, shares or a house) so that any debt owed is secured against that property. Once a court has issued a charging order, a spouse can apply for an order for sale of the property so that the property can be sold and the debt paid out of the proceeds of sale.

▶ *A writ of sequestration* This is a process for dealing with contempt of court whereby the defaulting spouse's assets are seized until the order is complied with. It prevents the defaulting spouse from dealing with property until the default has been made good. It is a complex and expensive procedure.

▶ *An attachment of earnings order* This is only of use when the defaulting spouse is employed. A court can order that payments from the defaulter's earnings be paid to the collecting officer of the court.

▶ *Registration of a periodical payments order in the magistrates' family proceedings court* Once registered, it can be enforced as a magistrates' court order (for example by warrant of distress, attachment of earnings, a fine or imprisonment).

(b) Enforcing property adjustment orders

Property adjustment orders are most commonly made in respect of the family home. If a spouse fails to cooperate in completing the required formalities for a transfer of the home to the other spouse, an application can be made to the court for an order that, unless the transfer is completed within a specified time, then the document will be executed by a judge. In the case of a section 24A order for sale, if a spouse refuses to vacate the home, an application can be made to the court for an order requiring that spouse to give up possession so that the sale can proceed (r 9.24 FPR 2010).

7.11 Protecting matrimonial property pending an application for financial relief

The following orders allow property to be protected pending an application for financial relief. As these orders are considered to be severe orders, they are granted only as a last resort and only in exceptional circumstances.

(i) A freezing order If there is a danger that a spouse may dispose, or attempt to dispose, of assets in order to defeat an application for financial relief (for example by selling them, giving them away, or sending them out of the UK), an application can be made for a 'freezing order' to freeze those assets. The application can be made under section 37 of the Matrimonial Causes Act 1973 or under the High Court's inherent jurisdiction. The applicant must prove that there is a real risk that the respondent is likely to move or dissipate assets with the intention of defeating the applicant's claim for a financial remedy on divorce unless restrained from doing so by the court (see, for instance, *ND v KP (Asset Freezing)* [2011] EWHC 457 (Fam), [2011] 2 FLR 662). Overseas assets can be frozen, unless there are likely to be problems enforcing the order in a foreign court. The order will not usually freeze all the defendant's assets, but only the maximum amount of property likely to be awarded in the financial relief proceedings.

(ii) A search and seize order This order, which can only be made by the High Court, allows a named person to enter premises to search for and seize documents which might be useful as evidence in an application for financial relief. The aim of the order is to ensure that the respondent does not dispose of evidence which may be useful at the hearing for financial relief. Strict rules apply to the grant of an order and to the way in which the entry and search powers can be exercised.

(iii) Preventing a party leaving the jurisdiction Where there is a risk that a party may leave the jurisdiction of the court before an application for a financial remedy on divorce has been dealt with, a writ *ne exeat regno* can be sought which directs an officer of the court to arrest the respondent and bring him or her before a judge.

(iv) Impounding a passport The court can make an order impounding a party's passport pending the disposal of a financial remedy claim, but, as this involves a restriction on a person's liberty, the power will be exercised with caution and for as short a period as possible. The applicant must show that the respondent is likely to leave the jurisdiction unless restrained, and that this would materially prejudice his or her case. If these requirements are satisfied, then an order impounding a passport will be held

to represent a proportionate public policy-based restraint on freedom of movement founded on the personal conduct of the respondent. These principles were applied in *Young v Young* [2012] EWHC 138 (Fam) where Mostyn J held that impoundment of the husband's passport was lawful.

7.12 Challenging a financial order

A financial order can be challenged by: (a) applying for a rehearing; (b) applying for variation or discharge; (c) appealing; and/or (d) applying to have the order set aside.

(a) Applying for a rehearing

Where a party considers that there was something fundamentally wrong with the way in which the case was heard (for example, there was non-disclosure or misrepresentation), an application can be made for a rehearing. Sometimes an appeal court will order a rehearing because a financial order is fundamentally flawed.

(b) (b) Variation or discharge

Under section 31(1) of the Matrimonial Causes Act 1973 the court has wide powers to vary or discharge an order (whether or not made by consent) or to temporarily suspend any provision in an order and revive any provision in an order so suspended The most common applications for variation are in respect of an increase or decrease in periodical payments due to a change of circumstances. The court will list a Financial Dispute Resolution (FDR) appointment in the same way as a first application for financial relief. If an agreement cannot be reached in the FDR, the case will proceed to a full hearing.

The powers under section 31(1) (see above) apply only to the following orders (s 32(2)):

- maintenance pending suit or interim maintenance;
- periodical payments (secured or unsecured);
- a lump sum order payable by instalments (including in exceptional circumstances, the lump sum itself – see *Westbury v Sampson* [2002] 1 FLR 166);
- any deferred order made by virtue of section 23(1)(c) (lump sum) which includes provision made by virtue of section 25B(4) or section 25C (provision in respect of pension rights);
- any order for a settlement of property under section 24(1)(b) or for a variation of settlement under section 24(1)(c) or (d) above, being an order made on or after the grant of a decree of judicial separation;
- an order for the sale of property under section 24A;
- a section 24B pension sharing order made before decree absolute.

There is no power to vary a lump sum order (except where it is payable in instalments) or to vary a property adjustment order (except in the very limited circumstances set out in section 31(4) where an order has been made on judicial separation). In other words, lump sum orders and property adjustment orders are 'once and for all' orders. The reason for the final nature of these orders is to create certainty and bring about finality in litigation, so that the parties can make plans for the future without worrying about whether an order will be overturned. Lump sum orders and property adjustment orders can, however, be appealed against or set aside (see further below).

How the court exercises its powers When exercising its powers under section 31(1), the court must consider all the circumstances of the case, but must give first consideration to the welfare of any child of the family aged under 18 and to any changes of circumstance, including any change in any of the matters to which the court was required to have regard when making the original order (s 31(7)). The court must also consider whether to effect a clean break. In other words, it must consider whether it is appropriate to bring periodical payments to an end immediately or to vary a periodical payments order so that payments will be made for a limited term sufficient to enable the payee to adjust without undue hardship to the termination of those payments (s 31(7)(a)). The court also has power to remit payment of all or part of any arrears due under any periodical payments order, including maintenance pending suit and interim maintenance (s 31(2A)). Where a periodical payments order is for a limited term, it can extend the term, unless the original order prohibited it (s 28(1A)).

For the purpose of effecting a clean break, the court can substitute periodical payments with one of the following orders: a lump sum order; a property adjustment order; a pension sharing order; or a direction that the person in whose favour the original order discharged or varied was made is not entitled to make any further application for a periodical payments order or an extension of the period to which the original order is limited by any variation made by the court (see s 31(7B)).

The court has a wide discretion in section 31 proceedings. The principles laid down by the House of Lords in *White* and *Miller* (see 7.6) apply (see for instance *VB v JP* [2008] 1 FLR 742 where periodical payments to the wife were increased on the basis that she was entitled to an element of compensation for loss of earning capacity, applying *Miller*). In *North v North* [2008] 1 FLR 158 Thorpe LJ said that in any application under section 31 the applicant's needs were likely to be the dominant or magnetic factor, but that it did not follow that the respondent would inevitably be held responsible for any and all established needs.

Cohabitation and variation Cohabitation after divorce may be taken into account in section 31 proceedings as one of the circumstances of the case, and may result in the reduction or termination of periodical payments. This is in contrast to the position with marriage after divorce, when section 28 of the MCA 1973 provides that periodical payments automatically terminate.

Whether cohabitation will be taken into account in section 31 proceedings will depend on the facts of the case. In *K v K (Periodical Payments: Cohabitation)* [2006] 2 FLR 468 Coleridge J held that the law should keep up with changing social conditions and the court should give considerable weight to cohabitation after divorce. Here, the wife's settled cohabitation for three years had reduced her dependency on her former husband and was held to constitute a relevant circumstance under section 31(7)(b). Coleridge J stated, however, that this was 'a troubling and messy area of the law' and that the current legislation 'enacted against an utterly different social fabric [was] not adequate to deal with it'. However, in *Grey v Grey* [2009] EWCA 1424, [2010] 1 FLR 1764 Thorpe LJ said that, although he was sympathetically attracted by Coleridge J's philosophy in *K v K* (for a revised approach to cohabitation on the basis that it was now perceived as normal, commonplace and as acceptable as marriage), any change in the law must come from Parliament. Thorpe LJ said that, in the meantime, the approach adopted in the Court of Appeal must apply (as in *Fleming v Fleming* [2003] EWCA Civ 1841, [2004] 1 FLR 667). In other words, post-divorce cohabitation is not to be equated with marriage post divorce, but the court, in assessing the impact of cohabitation, should have regard to the overall circumstances, including the financial consequences of the case. Wall LJ in *Grey* also stated that he could find 'no warrant for equating in this context remarriage with cohabitation, a word which itself presents problems of definition'; and he did not consider that it was open to the courts to add a gloss to the existing provisions by equating cohabitation with remarriage without legislative sanction.

(c) Appeals and permission to appeal out of time

Appeals are allowed if there has been a procedural irregularity, or the judge has taken into account irrelevant matters or ignored relevant matters, or has otherwise reached a conclusion which is plainly wrong (*G v G* [1985] 1 WLR 647). The aim of this rule is to promote finality in litigation. It also recognises that, with discretionary judicial decision-making, such as that in financial relief proceedings on divorce, there is a wide band within which a decision may be reasonable even though a party may not agree with it. The mere fact that a party is not happy with the outcome of a case is not of itself sufficient ground for bringing an appeal.

If the date for lodging the appeal has passed, an application for leave to appeal out of time will be required. Appeals out of time are often combined with an application to set aside the original order (see p. 190 below). As the courts are unwilling to reopen litigation unless it is really necessary (because it increases costs and extends the duration of the conflict), leave to appeal out of time will not be granted unless the principles laid down in the following case are satisfied.

▶ *Barder v Barder (Caluori Intervening)* [1988] AC 20,[1987] 2 FLR 480

A consent order was made in full and final settlement, in which the husband agreed to transfer his half-share in the matrimonial home to his wife. Four weeks after the order was made, but outside the time limit for lodging an appeal, the wife killed the children and committed suicide. The husband sought leave to appeal out of time against the order (it could not be varied under section 31 as it was a property order), arguing that the basis on which the order had been made had been fundamentally altered by the unforeseen change of circumstances – the death of his wife and children.

The House of Lords held that he should be granted leave to appeal out of time and that the order should be set aside. Lord Brandon said, however, that leave to appeal should be granted only where the following four conditions were satisfied:

▶ the new events relied on had invalidated the fundamental basis or assumption on which the original order had been made, so that, if leave to appeal were granted, the appeal would be certain or very likely to succeed;
▶ the new events had occurred within a relatively short time of the original order being made – probably less than a year;
▶ the application for leave to appeal had been made promptly; and
▶ the grant of leave would not prejudice third parties who had acquired in good faith and for valuable consideration an interest in the property subject to the order.

Thus, not every application will result in permission to appeal being granted and an order being set aside. There must be a material change of circumstances which has undermined or invalidated the basis of the order. The 'Barder principles' are strict in order to promote finality in litigation and to ensure that the courts are not swamped by meritless applications. In *Richardson v Richardson* [2011] EWCA Civ 79, [2011] 2 FLR 244, where the Court of Appeal held, *inter alia*, that the wife's early death was not a *Barder* event, Thorpe LJ stated that cases in which a *Barder* event, as opposed to a vitiating factor, can be successfully argued are extremely rare and should be regarded as such by the specialist profession.

The supervening event must be an unforeseeable event In *Barder* (above) it was held that the supervening event must be unforeseen. For example, in *Maskell v Maskell* [2003] 1 FLR 1138 the Court of Appeal held that becoming unemployed two months after an order was made was not a *Barder* event, as it was foreseeable. Foreseeability of the event was also fatal to the claim in *S v S (Ancillary Relief: Consent Order)* [2002] 1 FLR 922 where the wife and her legal advisers should have known that the decision of the House of Lords in *White v White* was foreseeable and that its impact was unavoidable.

Examples of situations where appeals out of time have been brought

Appeals out of time are claimed in a wide range of situations, for instance where there is unforeseen death or serious illness (*Amey v Amey* [1992] 2 FLR 89; *Reid v Reid* [2004] 1 FLR 736); or misrepresentation (*Ritchie v Ritchie* [1996] 1 FLR 898). They are often brought with respect to changes in property valuations, or fluctuations in the value of property (such as investments), or where a former spouse is alleged to have unexpectedly remarried or cohabited after divorce.

Changes in property valuations A change in respect of a property valuation (upward or downward) or a misrepresentation as to valuation is sometimes used as a ground for an appeal out of time, but the court will usually hold that this does not constitute a 'Barder event' (see for instance, *B v B* [2008] 1 FLR 1279; *Walkden v Walkden* [2009] EWCA Civ 627, and *S v S (Ancillary Relief: Application to Set Aside Order)* [2009] EWHC 2377 (Fam), [2010] 1 FLR 993).

Fluctuations in the value of property such as investments In *Cornick v Cornick* [1994] 2 FLR 530 (where the wife applied to set aside an order on the basis of a dramatic upward change in share prices) Hale J (as she was then) said that the case-law did not 'suggest that the natural processes of price fluctuation, whether in houses, shares or other property, and however dramatic' provided grounds for setting an order aside. Hale J said that, only where there had been a misvaluation or mistake at the trial might an order be set aside. The fact that an order was unfair was an insufficient ground on its own. Hale J's dicta were applied by Thorpe LJ in *Myerson v Myerson (No. 2)* [2009] 2 FLR 147 where the husband (a victim of the global economic downturn, the 'credit crunch') failed in his claim to appeal out of time. Had he succeeded, it would have opened the floodgates to many other claimants

Unexpected remarriage or cohabitation In some cases unexpected marriage or cohabitation has been held to be a *Barder* event as it was, for example in *Williams v Lindley* [2005] 2 FLR 710 where the wife became engaged within one month of a lump sum being ordered in her favour. However, each case depends on its facts; and in *Dixon v Marchant* [2008] 1 FLR 655 a majority of the Court of Appeal, distinguishing *Williams v Lindley*, refused to accept the husband's argument that his former wife's remarriage (7 months after a consent order had been made) was a *Barder* event.

How the court exercises its powers once permission to appeal has been granted

In *Smith v Smith* [1991] 2 FLR 432 the Court of Appeal stated that the correct approach was to start the section 25 exercise from the beginning and consider what order should be made on the basis of the new facts. In *Smith* a lump sum order had been made in favour of a wife, which represented half the family assets, but six months later she committed suicide leaving her whole estate, including the lump sum, to her daughter. Applying the section 25 guidelines to the new facts (that she would have had only a few months to live), Butler-Sloss LJ reduced the lump sum.

(d) Setting the original order aside

An application can be made to set aside an order which has been made on an improper basis (for example, because of non-disclosure, fraud, duress or misrepresentation, or where changes of circumstances have occurred which were unforeseen when the original order was made). An application to set an order aside will often be made in conjunction with an appeal out of time (see above). Because of the need for finality in litigation, the courts will not usually set aside an order unless the circumstances are exceptional.

Applications are sometimes made where there has been non-disclosure. This occurred in the following case, which lays down the approach to be adopted by the court in applications to set aside an order.

▶ *Jenkins v Livesey (Formerly Jenkins)* **[1985] 1 AC 424, [1985] 1 FLR 813**

A clean-break consent order was made, in which the parties agreed that the husband would transfer to his wife his half-share in the matrimonial home, on her foregoing all claims to ancillary relief. Three weeks after the house had been transferred, the wife remarried and two months later put the house up for sale. The husband appealed out of time, asking for the consent order to be set aside on the grounds of misrepresentation and non-disclosure.

The House of Lords allowed his appeal and held that parties who wished the court to exercise its discretionary powers under Part II of the 1973 Act were under a duty in contested or consent proceedings to make full and frank disclosure of all material matters, so that the court could exercise its discretion properly. However, because of the importance of encouraging a clean break, orders should not be lightly set aside. They should only be set aside if the failure to make full and frank disclosure led the court to make an order which was substantially different from the one it would have made had there been full and frank disclosure. As the wife's engagement was a material circumstance directly relevant to the parties' agreement about ancillary relief, she was under a duty to disclose it before the agreement was put into effect by means of the consent order. Her failure to disclose the engagement invalidated the order. The order was set aside, and the case remitted for a rehearing.

The House of Lords stressed that non-disclosure of itself is not a sufficient ground for an order to be set aside. Like applications for appeals out of time, where the policy objective of finality is also upheld, the circumstances must be such that a fundamentally different order would have been made had the circumstances been known.

Thus, in *Jenkins v Livesey (formerly Jenkins)* the House of Lords held that not every breach of the duty of full and frank disclosure would necessarily result in an order being set aside. It has to be shown that the non-disclosure had led the court to make an order which was substantially different from that which would have been made had there been full disclosure.

Each case depends on its facts. For instance, in *Harris v Manahan* [1997] 1 FLR 205 the Court of Appeal refused to set aside a consent order where the applicant had received poor legal advice. In *I v I (Ancillary Relief: Disclosure)* [2009] 1 FLR 201, although there had been non-disclosure on the part of the husband (by failing to disclose his intention to change his employment), Charles J refused to set aside the order as disclosure would have made no difference to the terms of the order.

7.13 An application for a financial remedy after a foreign divorce

Under Part III of the Matrimonial and Family Proceedings Act 1984, a person who has divorced overseas can apply for financial relief in England and Wales provided the court in England and Wales has granted leave to apply, which it can only grant if there is a substantial ground making the application (s 13(1)). Once leave has been granted, sections 17 and 18 provide that the court can exercise its powers under Part II of the Matrimonial Causes Act 1973 having regard to the section 25 factors (see 7.4) and applying the principles laid down in the case-law (see 7.6).

Granting leave to apply   When deciding whether to grant leave, the court must consider whether England and Wales is the appropriate venue for the application (s 16(1)) and it must have regard to a number of specified matters (s 16(2)), such as: the connection the parties have with England and Wales, the country where they were divorced and any other country; and any financial benefit the applicant or any child of the family has received or is likely to receive by agreement or by operation of law in another country. Consideration of these matters in section 16 acts as a filter to prevent unmeritorious applications

The following case is the leading case on applications to seek leave to apply for financial relief in the courts in England and Wales after a foreign divorce. The Supreme Court held that hardship and injustice are factors that can be taken into account by the court, but they are not necessary preconditions for granting leave to apply for financial relief.

▶ *Agbaje v Agbaje* [2010] UKSC 13, [2010] 1 FLR 1813

The parties, a Nigerian couple, had spent most of their long marriage in Nigeria but had acquired British citizenship and spent time living in England. After their separation, the wife made her home in England. When the husband began divorce proceedings in Nigeria, the wife subsequently filed for divorce in England and also cross-petitioned for judicial separation in Nigeria. In the Nigerian proceedings she sought maintenance and property settlement orders (there was no jurisdiction to transfer property). The Nigerian court declined to stay its proceedings, and granted a divorce and awarded her a life interest in the matrimonial home (worth £83,000) and a lump sum of £21,000 as maintenance for life. The husband retained assets worth £616,000, including two London properties. The wife applied for financial relief in the English courts under Part III of the MFPA 1984. She was granted leave on the ground that, if leave were refused, she would suffer real hardship. In the substantive application, Coleridge J, finding that the parties had a real connection with

England and holding that it was appropriate for the English court to make an order, awarded her £275,000 from the sale of the English property on condition that she transferred her interest in the Nigerian property to her husband.

The Court of Appeal allowed the husband's appeal on the basis that Coleridge J had failed to address the issue of comity (respect for the law and courts of the other jurisdiction) and to explain why the case was an exceptional case which justified the wife having a 'second bite of the cherry'. It held that the parties' connection with Nigeria was more significant than with England; and Nigeria was the appropriate forum for resolving the wife's claims. Serious injustice had not been done to her by the Nigerian court. Thus, although it was plain that she would suffer real hardship in England and Wales, comity commanded respect for the overseas order. The wife appealed to the Supreme Court.

The Supreme Court, unanimously allowing her appeal and restoring the order made by Coleridge J, held *inter alia* that:

▶ The principal object of the filter mechanism is to prevent wholly unmeritorious claims being pursued to oppress or blackmail a former spouse.

▶ Section 16 does not require the court to consider 'whether it is appropriate for an order to be made', but whether it would be appropriate for an order to be made by a court in England and Wales.

▶ Part III contains no express reference to hardship, injustice or exceptionality. Hardship and injustice are not preconditions, although they will both be relevant factors for the court to take into consideration under both sections 16 and 18.

▶ A mere disparity between the award made by the foreign court and that which would be awarded on an English divorce will be insufficient to trigger the application of Part III. A court will not lightly characterise foreign law, or the order of a foreign court, as unjust.

▶ The amount of financial provision will depend on all the circumstances of the case and there is no rule that it should be the minimum amount required to overcome injustice (*A v S (Financial Relief after Overseas US Divorce and Financial Proceedings*) [2002] EWHC 1157 (Fam), [2003] 1 FLR 431 disapproved).

On the facts, Lord Collins, delivering the judgment of the Supreme Court, concluded that 'it was not so much that there was a very large disparity between what the wife received in Nigeria and what she would have received in England, but that there was also a very large disparity between what the husband received and what the wife received such as to create real hardship and a serious injustice.'

Agbaje v Agbaje was applied in *Traversa v Freddi* [2011] EWCA Civ 81, [2011] 2 FLR 272 where the husband, who was working as a waiter in England, successfully appealed against the refusal of leave to bring proceedings for financial relief in the courts in England and Wales after his wife had divorced in Italy.

7.14 Reforming the law

(a) Criticism of the law

There has been considerable criticism of the law on financial remedies, not just the statutory provisions but also the principles laid down by the House of Lords in *White v White* and *Miller v Miller*; *McFarlane v McFarlane* (see 7.6). As a result there have been calls for reform from judges, lawyers and academics. For instance, Resolution (the organisation of family lawyers) has called for reform ([2007] Fam Law 203), and Nicholas Mostyn QC has strongly criticised the law for its continuing uncertainty ([2007] Fam Law 573).

Much of the criticism relates to the discretionary system for dealing with financial remedies, which, despite having the advantage of flexibility, creates difficulties in respect of certainty, consistency and predictability. The decisions of the higher courts have also failed to make the law clearer. In fact Sir Mark Potter P in *Charman v Charman (No. 4)* [2007] EWCA Civ 503, [2007] 1 FLR 1246 was of the opinion that the decision in *White v White* had undoubtedly not resolved 'the problems faced by practitioners in advising clients, or by clients in deciding upon what terms to compromise'. According to Welstead ([2012] Fam Law 185), since 2006, 'the courts, have been engaged in a constant struggle to understand the limitations of, and attempt to apply, the tripartite principles of fairness outlined by the House of Lords in *Miller v Miller; McFarlane v McFarlane* ... when making financial awards on divorce'. In Welstead's opinion, it is the principle of equal division which has 'caused the greatest headache for the judiciary, particularly where the only assets in existence at the end of a marriage were acquired by one of the spouses prior to the marriage'.

White and *Miller* have therefore been criticised for muddying rather than clarifying the law. For instance, what is 'special contribution' and when is it to be taken into account? What should be regarded as 'matrimonial' or 'non-matrimonial' property? To what extent will the length of a marriage affect whether an inheritance, for example, is to be part of the matrimonial assets to be divided? What is the starting point in applications for a financial remedy? Does equality apply as a yardstick to test the conclusion which has been tentatively reached by a judge after conducting the section 25 exercise, or is there a principle of equality which acts as a starting point in an application for a financial remedy?

In *RP v RP* [2007] 1 FLR 2105 Coleridge J was strongly critical of the decision in *Miller*. He said that although *Miller* was a 'high profile case' which had sent 'seismic reverberations throughout the whole [family justice] system', the case had created 'very real uncertainty as to outcome' and, as a result, the 'consensual disposal of individual cases in this huge and, sadly, ever growing area of litigation' had become 'that much harder to achieve and that much more costly'. Coleridge J said that 'considerable confusion' still existed. In particular, Coleridge J said that the word 'compensation' did not appear in the statute, and that 'talk of "compensation"' in respect of the circumstances of the case in *RP* had 'added nothing except confusion and the real risk of double counting'.

As two of the three strands laid down in *Miller* (compensation and sharing) are not mentioned in the list of statutory factors in section 25 of the MCA 1973, the House of Lords may also be criticised for introducing changes to the law by means of judicial law-making when it is Parliament's responsibility to change the law. As Cretney said (in *Family Law in the Twentieth Century*, 2003), the decision in *White* and *Miller/McFarlane* 'may come close to the imposition by the judiciary of the community of property neither Parliament nor any official advisory body had ever accepted as the basis of English matrimonial law'.

According to Elizabeth Cooke (the current Law Commissioner responsible for family law reform), crucial issues of principle which were left unresolved by the House of Lords in *White* and *Miller* have left the operation of section 25 of the MCA 1973 the subject of considerable uncertainty (see [2007] CFLQ 98). She said that, as divorce is common, then the principles which apply to financial relief should be clear enough to be applied without recourse to litigation so that the parties can work matters out for themselves, or with the help of a mediator or lawyer. Determining what is, or is not, matrimonial property (for the purpose of distributing property in ancillary proceedings on divorce) remains uncertain and unpredictable. As Cooke (above) says, although 'the concept of non-matrimonial property is firmly embedded in law and practice...we do not know how it is defined'. In Europe, on the other hand, community of property regimes define the term 'matrimonial property'.

Determining the question of special contribution is also difficult to predict. What sorts of contribution are 'special' and how will other factors, such as the duration of the marriage, impact on the issue? As Coleridge J said, '[f]rom the summit of the mountain, the House of Lords has pronounced some of the principles which underlie the "special contribution" issue', but '[t]hey are silent on how to apply them' (see *Charman v Charman (No 2)* [2006] EWHC 1879 (Fam), [2007] 1 FLR 593).

There has also been concern about the trend since the decision in *White* to give wives greater shares of property on divorce in big-money cases. For example, at a public lecture in 2009, Baroness Deech called for an end to the idea that women deserve half of their husband's wealth on divorce. She said that '[t]he notion that a wife should get half of the joint assets of a couple after even a short, childless marriage has crept up on us without any parliamentary legislation to this effect' (see [2009] Fam Law 1140).

These uncertainties and difficulties in the law have been seen by some commentators as sufficiently serious to justify the need for reform of the law.

(b) Discussion of reform

Discussions of reform have focused on three main options for reform: making marital agreements binding; introducing a presumptive 50:50 split of matrimonial assets; and introducing a set of policy objectives to help govern the exercise of judicial discretion. These three options for reform were considered as long ago as 1991 by the Family Law Committee of the Law Society (see *Memorandum: Capital Provision on Divorce*, Law Society, 1991), but the proposals were not taken forward.

At the end of the 1990s, there was renewed discussion of reform when the Government considered these three options for reform in its consultation paper, *Supporting Families* (Home Office, 1998). These discussions were taken further by the Lord Chancellor's Ancillary Relief Advisory Group (chaired by the Rt Hon Lord Justice Thorpe), but the group concluded that there was a need for research and wide consultation, which should encompass both social and public policy issues (see *Report of the Lord Chancellor's Advisory Group on Ancillary Relief*, July 1998). Some of the Advisory Group, however, urged the retention of the status quo.

In July 2003, the Family Law Committee of the Law Society published a report (*Financial Provision on Divorce: Clarity and Fairness – Proposals for Reform*) in which it recommended *inter alia* that section 25 of the Matrimonial Causes Act 1973 should have incorporated in it a series of guidelines for the sharing of assets. The Family Law Committee was of the view, however, that pre-marital contracts should not be given binding status but that the courts should continue to consider them as a factor to be taken into account.

(c) Options for reform

Four options for reform of financial relief have been discussed over the years: (i) the introduction of a 50:50 split of matrimonial assets; (ii) the introduction of a set of general principles; (iii) the introduction of a formula for calculating financial relief; and (iv) making marital agreements binding (see also pp. 182–4).

(i) A 50:50 split of marital assets Equal division of matrimonial assets on divorce (subject to any agreement to the contrary) is common throughout Europe and exists in some states in the USA and also in New Zealand. However, while a 50:50 split has the advantage of certainty, it may create unfairness and hardship, in particular for poorer families who might find themselves with insufficient funds to rehouse themselves. The possibility of introducing a 50:50 split in England and Wales has been discussed from time to time, but, although there have been no proposals to change the law, there has been a move towards equality of division of assets in 'big-money' cases. In fact, Cretney has claimed that: 'English law now has, by virtue of judicial decision rather than legislation, a matrimonial regime of community of property' ([2003] CFLQ 403). According to Cooke ([2007] CFLQ 98), community of property was part of the thinking behind the yardstick of equality idea laid down by the House of Lords in *White v White* (see p. 162).

(ii) A set of general principles Another possible reform that has been mooted is whether the Matrimonial Causes Act 1973 should be amended to include a set of general principles which would supplement the application of the section 25 factors. Although section 25 contains a list of factors which the courts must take into account, there is no express articulation of the principles and policies which govern the distribution of assets on divorce, other than that the child's welfare is the court's first consideration. There is no mention of any policy of fairness or whether marriage is a partnership of equals or whether there should be no discrimination between husbands and wives. The Scottish legislation on financial relief on divorce, which is similar to that in England and Wales, includes a set of general principles which the courts must take into account when exercising their discretion. Thus, the Family Law (Scotland) Act 1985 makes financial orders available for the following purposes:

(1) fair sharing of matrimonial or partnership property;
(2) to take account of economic advantages and disadvantages;
(3) the fair sharing of the economic burden of looking after children;
(4) enabling a dependent partner to adjust to loss of support; and
(5) relieving serious financial hardship.

The introduction of a similar set of principles in England and Wales has been mooted from time to time. Thus, in 1998 the Government in its discussion paper, *Supporting Families* (Home Office, para 4.49), suggested the following set of general principles: seek first to promote the welfare of children by meeting their housing needs and those of their primary carer; take into account any written agreement about financial arrangements; divide any surplus so as to achieve a fair result, recognising that fairness will generally require the value of the assets to be divided equally between the parties; and try to determine financial relationships at the earliest date practicable. However, the Lord Chancellor's Advisory Group on Ancillary Relief, which reported in 1998, said that it would not be appropriate to adopt a set of principles like those in Scotland, but it was in unanimous agreement that there was a strong case for codifying in legislation the principles that are applied by the courts in England and Wales (*Report of the Lord Chancellor's Advisory Group on Ancillary Relief*, 1998). More recently, the Law Commission has discussed the option of introducing a set of principles (see *Matrimonial Property, Needs and Agreements*, LCCP No. 208, September 2012, below).

It is questionable, however, whether a set of principles would actually improve the law. In fact, the judge-made principles enunciated by the House of Lords in *White* and *Miller* have done little to stem the criticism emanating from lawyers, judges and academics about the unsatisfactory nature of the law. Instead, the principles have arguably led to obfuscation, rather than clarification, of the law.

(iii) A formula for calculating financial relief   Another possible option for reform which has been more recently discussed is the introduction of a formula for calculating financial relief. Thus, for instance, Eekelaar has proposed a 'standard model' (in other words a formula) which could be used for calculating financial relief on divorce (see [2010] Fam Law 359). The Law Commission in its supplementary consultation paper, *Matrimonial Property, Needs and Agreements*, LCCP No. 208, discussed the possibility of introducing a formula to help determine how assets should be distributed on divorce (and on civil partnership dissolution). It looked, for instance, at the American Law Institute's Principles of the Law of Family Dissolution ('the ALI Principles'), which sets out a formulaic approach to financial relief, but which allows for departures where there is substantial injustice. It also looked at the Canadian formulaic approach.

Although a formulaic approach, unlike a discretionary approach, has the disadvantage of being inflexible, the availability of an intellectually coherent formula would create greater certainty and predictability and give couples some idea of what they could expect to receive, or have to pay out, with respect to financial provision on divorce. It would help couples to make informed agreements about finance and property arrangements on divorce. It would also avoid the problem of couples having to bargain in the shadow of the law. In fact, most couples have no access to the discretionary approach laid down in the Matrimonial Causes Act 1973, and developed by the judges in the case-law, as they cannot afford to go to court.

(d)   The work of the Law Commission

The Law Commission, the Government's law reform body, is currently looking at some aspects of the law on finance and property on divorce (and on civil partnership dissolution) with a review to reform of the law in England and Wales.

Matrimonial Property, Needs and Agreements   The Law Commission is conducting a project on matrimonial property, needs and agreements on divorce (and on the dissolution of a civil partnership). The project initially involved only marital property agreements (see pp. 183–4 above), but was extended to cover needs and non-matrimonial property. Its provisional proposals are set down in *Matrimonial Property, Needs and Agreements – A Supplementary Consultation Paper* (LCCP No. 208), which was published on 11 September 2012. This document is long (123 pages) and extremely complex, arguably more complex than the law it is seeking to reform.

With respect to needs (see Parts 3–5 of the Consultation Paper), the Law Commission states that, although needs are 'an important focus of virtually all financial provision cases' (para 1.22), there is no definition of what 'needs' means and no clear answer as to why needs should be met (para 1.23), and for how long (para 3.28). According to the Law Commission, this is particularly unsatisfactory as, 'although the law on financial orders is built on the assumption that there is a judge who will exercise discretion, most couples will not access that discretion' (para 3.35) and, as a result, 'it is not clear how they are to find out what the law is' (para 3.35). With increasing numbers of persons bringing their own case as litigants in person (due to the lack of legal aid), this is particularly concerning.

In Part 4 of the Consultation Paper, the Law Commission looks at the issue of need and at the policy choices which should be made in order to provide a principled basis to the question of needs. It looks, for instance, at the question of why needs should be met at all and at developments in other jurisdictions, such as in the USA, France and Canada. It considers issues such as formulaic approaches to calculating financial relief, and the question of whether maintenance paid to women undermines their independence. In fact, Baroness Deech has argued that 'no maintenance should be payable unless the claimant spouse is unable to work or has the care of young children' (see 'What's a woman worth? The maintenance law', October 2009, Gresham College Lecture, available at www.gresham.ac.uk/lectures-and-events). Other issues the Law Commission looks at are the relationship between needs and compensation, and needs and sharing. The Law Commission asks consultees about a range of issues relating to need (see paras 4.113–118), such as whether they favour a principled reform of spousal support, and, if so, whether it should take the form of a reformed discretionary approach or a formulaic calculation. The Law Commission also recommends, in addition to statutory reform, the use of authorised guidance on financial relief for courts and divorcing couples, which could be made available, for instance, on the internet.

Part 6 of the Consultation Paper deals with the issue of non-matrimonial property, in other words property that may be outside the pool of assets available for distribution on divorce, such as, for example, an inheritance, a gift or property acquired before marriage. However, as the Law Commission says (para 6.1), unlike the question of needs, which is important in every divorce (and every dissolution of a civil partnership), the issue of non-matrimonial property is more limited as not everyone has any such property. The Law Commission states that the following problems are associated with non-matrimonial property:

- The range of property within the term 'non-matrimonial property' is unclear.
- It is not known how long it takes for 'non-matrimonial' property to become 'matrimonial'.
- There is a difference of opinion as to whether the existence of non-matrimonial property should lead the court to adjust (if it sees fit) the proportions in which property is shared (see *Charman v Charman (No. 4)* [2007] EWCA Civ 503, [2007] 1 FLR 1246; and *Robson v Robson* [2010] EWCA Civ 1171, [2011] 1 FLR 751); or whether the non-matrimonial property should simply be excluded from the sharing exercise and the rest shared equally (see *Jones v Jones* [2011] EWCA Civ 41, [2011] 1 FLR 1723).
- There are no rules as to what happens when non-matrimonial property changes over time, for instance when it is sold and other property is bought with the proceeds or when the owner or the other spouse invests in the property during marriage.

Having discussed the various issues relating to non-matrimonial property, the Law Commission makes a range of provisional proposals and asks consultees for their views. For instance, it proposes that non-matrimonial property should be defined as property held in the sole name of one party to the marriage and which is received as a gift or inheritance or was acquired before the marriage; and that it should no longer be subject to the sharing principle on divorce except where it is required to meet the other party's needs. (For a full list of the Law Commission's other proposals with respect to non-matrimonial property and its proposals with respect to needs, see Part 7 of the consultation paper.)

The consultation period terminated on 11 December 2012. Once the responses to the consultation have been processed, the Law Commission aims to produce a report in autumn 2013 in which it will make its final recommendations. (For an article by Elizabeth Cooke, the Law Commissioner with responsibility for the project, see [2012] Fam Law 323.)

The enforcement of financial orders   The Law Commission will be conducting a project on the enforcement of financial orders made under the Matrimonial Causes Act 1973 (and under the Civil Partnership Act 2004 and the Children Act 1989), once it has completed its project above. It has chosen to conduct the project on enforcement because of the financial hardship that can be caused to adults and children if orders cannot be enforced; and because of the complexity of the current law. The project is not likely to be completed until autumn 2015.

(e)   Reform: the future

Despite discussions of reform, there is no consensus as to what form any reform should take, except for the fact that there is support for making marital agreements binding; and the Law Commission has made provisional proposals with respect to two other issues, namely needs and non-matrimonial property. The Law Commission, however, is not looking at a wholesale reform of the law, and to that extent it may be regarded as merely 'tinkering' with the law.

Although the discretionary system for dealing with financial relief on divorce (and on the dissolution of a civil partnership) creates uncertainty, there is a danger that making the discretionary system more rule-based may remove the flexibility which is its great strength. According to Harris (2008), the uncertainty of the law may encourage parties to negotiate:

> '[The paradox in *Miller v Miller*] is that in failing to achieve greater certainty the judges have both secured a powerful incentive for parties to negotiate rather than litigate (which incentive would be weakened if the law were more certain) and, further, have reduced the incentive for parties to incur costs and prolong cases by haggling over detailed facts.'

What is clear from discussions of reform is that it will be extremely difficult to reform the law in order to produce a fair, just and effective system for adjusting finance and property matters on relationship breakdown which is both predictable and also flexible enough to deal with the infinite variety of family circumstances. Reforms of child support have been riddled with the same problems (see Chapter 12). In *Miller v Miller* Baroness Hale spoke of the need for flexibility but for the law not to be 'too flexible'. This is the source of the difficulty. Rigid rules have their advantages and disadvantages. Flexibility also has its advantages and disadvantages. But so too does a compromise. As the Law Commission in its consultation paper on *Matrimonial Agreements* (LCCP No. 198, 2011) points out, any reform of the law will be a 'major undertaking' (see para 5.61). Also, perhaps the shortest, truest, and most understandable paragraph in the whole of the Law Commission's 123-page supplementary consultation paper (*Matrimonial Property, Needs and Agreements*, LCCP No. 208, 2012) on needs and non-matrimonial property is a simple seven-word sentence which merely states that: 'Each of these issues is very difficult' (para 1.21).

Finally, despite the difficulty of deciding on the nature of any reforms, many practitioners, judges and academics believe that reform is needed. It will be interesting to see what the outcome of the Law Commission's consultation on matrimonial property, needs and agreements will be, and whether the Government will decide to make any proposals for reform in the light of the Law Commission's final report. Whether such a piecemeal approach to reform is the best way forward may be questionable, but, on the other hand, wholesale reform of the law would be a major, and perhaps too radical, a task to undertake, and there may be more pressing concerns on the Parliamentary agenda.

Summary

▶ On the breakdown of a marriage it will usually be necessary for the parties to redistribute their property and financial assets. There is an emphasis on settlement and most couples reach agreement without going to court. However, others spend vast sums of money on legal costs. If the parties cannot reach agreement, financial provision and property adjustment orders can be applied for on divorce (and on nullity or judicial separation) in an application for financial relief under Part II of the Matrimonial Causes Act 1973. The same rules apply on civil partnership dissolution under the Civil Partnership Act 2004.

▶ The procedure for a financial remedy is laid down in the Family Procedure Rules 2010 and in Practice Directions and accompanying Protocols. The emphasis is on reducing delay and costs, which is done by facilitating agreement and allowing the court to have control over the conduct of proceedings. An applicant for financial relief must attend a Mediation Information and Assessment Meeting (MIAM) to see if the dispute can be resolved by mediation. The respondent may also be invited to attend. If mediation is unsuccessful, both parties must attend a first appointment followed by a financial dispute resolution appointment at which the district judge will help the parties reach agreement. If this is not possible, then the case will proceed to a full hearing. The court can stay proceedings if it considers it more appropriate for the matter to be determined outside England and Wales. The parties are under a duty to make full, frank and clear disclosure of all their current and future assets. The media are permitted to attend financial relief proceedings, unless the district judge or the rules of court provide otherwise.

▶ The court can make the following orders in financial relief proceedings: maintenance pending suit (s 22); financial provision orders (s 23); property adjustment orders (s 24); orders for the sale of property (s 24A); and pension orders (ss 25B–D).

▶ When considering whether to make an order, and, if so, in what manner, the court must have regard to all the circumstances of the case, first consideration being given to the welfare of any child of the family who has not attained the age of 18 (s 25(1). When exercising its powers in relation to the parties to the marriage the court must in particular have regard to a list of factors laid down in section 25(2), which includes, for instance, the financial needs and resources of the parties, their standard of living, their ages, the length of the marriage, serious misconduct, etc.

▶ The court must apply the clean-break provisions laid down in Part II of the Matrimonial Causes Act 1973 when making any financial order in favour of a spouse in financial relief proceedings (s 25A) and also in variation proceedings (s 31(7)). The policy of the clean break encourages the parties to put their past behind them and go their separate ways after divorce, but the court's powers are subject to the section 25 factors (see above,) and the principles laid down in the case-law, in particular, *White v White* and *Miller v Miller* (see below).

▶ In addition to applying the section 25 factors (see above) and the clean-break provisions (see above), the court in financial relief proceedings must apply the principles laid down by the House of Lords in *White v White* (2000) and *Miller v Miller* (2006). Although these were 'big-money' cases, the principles they laid down apply to all applications for financial relief. In *White v White* the House of Lord overturned the principle laid down by the Court of Appeal in earlier cases that financial relief was limited to satisfying the parties' reasonable needs or requirements. In *White*, the House of Lords held that: the objective in financial relief proceedings is fairness; there must be no discrimination between husbands and wives; and before making an order for financial relief, the court should check its tentative views against the 'yardstick of equality'. The House of Lords in *Miller v Miller* (2006) endorsed the principles laid down in *White v White* (2000) and identified the following three guiding general principles which apply in financial relief proceedings: needs (generously construed); compensation; and sharing. The trend in the case-law following *White* and *Miller* has been to emphasise the wide discretion of the court and its duty to apply the section 25 factors in order to achieve a fair result. In some cases, it has been argued that special contribution (such as special business skills in creating the wealth) is a justification for not ordering equal, or near-equal, division of matrimonial assets. In exercising their discretion, the courts may have to consider whether or not to ring-fence certain assets (such as an inheritance) and treat them as non-matrimonial assets. The length of the marriage will be an important factor as to whether or not property is non-matrimonial or matrimonial.

▶ Various financial orders can be made in respect of the family home. Tenancies can also be transferred under section 24 of the Matrimonial Causes Act 1973 or under section 53 and Schedule 7 of the Family Law Act 1996.

▶ The court has a range of powers which it can exercise in respect of pensions on divorce, namely 'off-setting', making a pension attachment order, or making a pension sharing order. The court's powers in respect of pension arrangements are governed by the section 25 criteria and the principles in *White v White* and *Miller v Miller* (see above).

▶ Married couples can make agreements about their financial arrangements should they divorce. The divorce court has jurisdiction to make consent orders (an order incorporating an agreement about matrimonial property incorporating the sorts of orders which the court can make under Part II of the MCA 1973). Parties to a marriage can enter into a separation agreement (which agreements are governed by ss 34–35 MCA 1973). Parties to a marriage are also free to enter into a pre-nuptial (pre-marital) or post-nuptial (post-marital) agreement in which they can make arrangements about the distribution of their assets on divorce. The Supreme Court in *Radmacher v Granatino* (2010) laid down the following principles which now govern *both* pre-nuptial and post-nuptial agreements: the courts continue to have a supervisory role to play in scrutinising such agreements; and the courts can give effect to an agreement provided it is fairly entered into by each party with a full appreciation of its implications unless in the circumstances prevailing it would not be fair to hold the parties to the agreement.

▶ Financial orders can be enforced in a variety of ways. The Law Commission is to look at the law governing the enforcement of orders for financial relief.

▶ Two orders allow matrimonial property to be protected pending an application for financial relief: a 'freezing order' (which can be granted under section 37 MCA 1973 or under the High Court's inherent jurisdiction) to freeze assets; and a 'seek and search order' to gain entry to premises to take out and copy evidence relevant to financial relief proceedings. These orders are granted only in exceptional circumstances because of their severity. The court can lawfully impound a passport provided it is really necessary and is a proportionate response.

▶ A financial order can be challenged in the following ways: by asking for a rehearing; by applying to have the order varied or discharged under section 31; by appealing against the order (which may require an application for permission to appeal out of time); or by applying to have the order set aside. Appeals out of time and applications to set orders aside are granted only in exceptional circumstances because of the policy objective of achieving finality in litigation. The court will not grant permission to appeal out of time unless the *Barder* principles are satisfied. An application to set aside an order will not be granted unless the original order is fundamentally unsound (such as due to non-disclosure, misrepresentation, fraud, or mistake).

Summary cont'd

▶ An application for permission to seek financial relief in the courts in England and Wales after a foreign divorce can be sought under Part III of the Matrimonial and Family Proceedings Act 1984, but the court in England and Wales must first grant leave to apply. In *Agbaje v Agbaje* (2010) the Supreme Court laid down the rules which apply to leave applications, in particular that hardship and injustice are factors that can be taken into account by the court but which are not necessary preconditions for granting leave to apply.

▶ The law on financial relief on divorce has been criticised for many years, largely because of its uncertainty and unpredictability; and because the decisions of the House of Lords in *White v White* (2000) and in *Miller v Miller* (2006) have not helped to resolve these problems. Reforms have been discussed, such as: a presumption in favour of a 50:50 split of matrimonial property; making marital agreements legally binding; the introduction of a set of policy guidelines to govern the exercise of judicial discretion; and a formula for calculating financial relief. The Law Commission has conducted a consultation exercise looking at whether legislation should be enacted to make marital agreements binding, but this project was extended in 2012 to look at two other issues, namely needs and non-matrimonial property.

Further reading and references

Barlow and Smithson, 'Is modern marriage a bargain? Exploring perceptions of pre-nuptial agreements in England and Wales' [2012] CFLQ 304.

Barton, '*White* v *White* and co: the not-so-well-off and a 'balance of needs' [2012] Fam Law 963.

Chandler, '"The law is now reasonably clear": the courts' approach to non-matrimonial assets' [2012] Fam Law 163.

Cooke, '*White* v *White* – a new yardstick for the marriage partnership' [2001] CFLQ 81.

Cooke, '*Miller/McFarlane*: law in search of discrimination' [2007] CFLQ 98.

Cooke, 'The Law Commission's consultation on marital property agreements' [2011] Fam Law 145.

Cooke, 'Pre-nups and beyond: what is the Law Commission up to now?' [2012] Fam Law 323.

Cretney, 'Community of property imposed by judicial decision' (2003) LQR 349.

Cretney, 'Private ordering and divorce – how far can we go?' [2003] Fam Law 399.

Deech, Baroness, 'What is a woman worth?' [2009] Fam Law 1140.

Eekelaar, '*Miller* v *Miller*: The descent into chaos' [2005] Fam Law 870.

Eekelaar, 'Financial and property settlement: a standard deal?' [2010] Fam Law 359.

Harris, George, Herring, 'With this ring I thee wed (terms and conditions apply)' [2011] Fam Law 367.

Harris, 'Financial orders after divorce: a category error?' [2012] Fam Law 860.

Hitchings, 'The impact of recent ancillary relief jurisprudence in the 'everyday' ancillary relief cases' [2010] CFLQ 93.

Miles, '*Charman* v *Charman* (No 4) – making sense of need, compensation and equal sharing after *Miller/McFarlane*' [2008] CFLQ 378.

Miles and Probert (eds), *Sharing Lives, Dividing Assets*, 2009, Hart Publishing.

Scherpe, 'Fairness, freedom and foreign elements: marital agreements in England and Wales after *Radmacher* v *Granatino*' [2011] CFLQ 513.

Scherpe, 'Marital agreements and matrimonial property' [2012] Fam Law 865.

Scherpe (ed), *Marital Agreements and Private Autonomy in Comparative Perspective,* Hart Publishing, 2012.

Wall, President of the Family Division, 'The President's Resolution address 2012' [2012] Fam Law 817.

Welstead, 'The sharing of pre-matrimonial property on divorce: *K* v *L*' [2012] Fam Law 85.

Websites

Law Commission: www.lawcommission.gov.uk

Links to relevant websites can also be found at: www.palgrave.com/law/familylaw8e

Part V

Children and parents

Chapter 8
Children

This chapter provides a general introduction to the law relating to children. It looks in particular at children's rights, both in domestic law and under the UN Convention on the Rights of the Child and the European Convention for the Protection of Human Rights. It considers, in particular, the child's right to make autonomous decisions and the landmark case of *Gillick v West Norfolk and Wisbech Health Authority* [1986] AC 112, [1986] 1 FLR 224. The law governing the corporal punishment of children by parents and teachers is considered, and also the right of children to participate in family law proceedings. Finally, the use of the inherent jurisdiction and wardship in children's cases is considered.

8.1 Introduction

(a) Children's rights

During the twentieth century there was an increasing recognition and acceptance of the fact that children have rights. A major impetus for this was the children's liberationist movement in the USA in the 1960s and 1970s, which generated debate about the extent to which children should have rights. The children's liberationists took the view that children had the right to enjoy certain freedoms, in particular the right to be free to make decisions about themselves. Radical liberationists took the view that children had the right to enjoy the same freedoms as adults. However, others took a more moderate view, arguing that children have a right not to be forced into adulthood, and have rights to be protected and cared for. Also to give children too much autonomy might undermine parental authority and have adverse repercussions for children themselves.

Some theorists have argued that it is theoretically difficult to talk about children's rights because children can only have rights if they have the necessary competence, or will, to make decisions. Some writers have preferred instead to talk about children's 'interests' (for instance, Eekelaar, 1986) or to view children's rights in terms of the obligations which adults owe them (for instance, O'Neill, in Alston *et al*, 1992). Children therefore need adults to champion their rights.

Some writers have attempted to classify children's rights or interests. Thus, Freeman (1983), for example, proposed four categories of rights: welfare rights; protective rights; rights grounded in social justice; and rights based on autonomy. Eekelaar (1986) suggested that children have three types of interest: basic; developmental; and autonomy interests. Basic and developmental interests, he said, would prevail over autonomy interests where this was necessary to protect a child.

One of the key dilemmas in the context of children's rights is the extent to which children should have rights of self-determination or autonomy. Whereas some would argue in favour of greater autonomy for children, the law must strike a balance and recognise that, although children should have greater rights of self-determination as they near adulthood, they also need the protection of the law.

(b) Children's Commissioners

England and Wales each has a Children's Commissioner to act as a champion for children. The powers and duties of the English Commissioner are laid down in Part I of the Children Act (CA) 2004 and those of the Welsh Commissioner in the Care Standards Act (CSA) 2000. However, whereas the Welsh Commissioner has a duty to 'to safeguard and promote the *rights* and welfare of children' (s 72A CSA 2000), the general function of the English Commissioner is merely to promote an 'awareness of the views and *interests* of children in England' (s 2(1) CA 2004). The lack of any reference to the word 'rights' in the statutory provisions governing the role of the English Commissioner has been criticised by various commentators (such as Clucas [2005] Fam Law 290, and Fortin [2006] Fam Law 757) and also by the *Review of the Office of the Children's Commissioner (England)* (see below).

The Children's Commissioners in the different parts of the UK are responsible for promoting the UN Convention on the Rights of the Child (the UNCRC) (see 8.2). From time to time, they submit reports to the UN Committee on the Rights of the Child whose task it is to ensure the implementation of the UNCRC in signatory states. In 2008 the joint reports of the UK Children's Commissioners identified youth justice, immigration, the use of restraint in institutions, and child poverty as some of the worst injustices suffered by children in the UK. In their 2011 report, two of their main concerns were the high level of persistent poverty across the UK and the impact that Government spending cuts might have on children.

In 2010, the Office of the Children's Commissioner of England was the subject of an independent review conducted by John Dunford and commissioned by the Secretary of State for Education. The review set out 46 recommendations, all of which were accepted in principle by the Government (see John Dunford, *Review of the Office of the Children's Commissioner (England)*, Cm 7981, November 2010). The *Review* stated that the role of the Children's Commissioner had been disappointing. Like some of the commentators above, the review blamed this mainly on the limited remit of the Commissioner to promote children's interests rather than their rights. For this reason, the *Review* recommended that the role of the Children's Commissioner should be rights-based. It also recommended that the Commissioner should have a stronger role to promote children's rights in order for the Government to meet its commitment to implement the UNCRC. (The *Review* is available at www.education.gov.uk/publications.)

Provisions in the Children and Families Bill 2012–2013 (which was presented to Parliament in February 2013) aim to strengthen the role of the Children's Commissioner.

8.2 The UN Convention on the Rights of the Child 1989

The UN Convention on the Rights of the Child 1989 (the UNCRC) was created with the aim of encouraging governments worldwide to recognise the importance of children in society and the fact that children have rights. It is the most ratified UN convention, with the USA and Somalia being the only two UN members who have not ratified it. It covers the social, economic and civil rights of children and young people, as well as their protection from abuse, discrimination, exploitation, abduction and armed conflict.

Although the UK has ratified the UNCRC, it does not have the same force in the UK as the European Convention for the Protection of Human Rights (the ECHR). This is because it has not been incorporated into all the legal systems in the UK. However, in Wales, the Rights of Children and Young Persons (Wales) Measure 2011, which received Royal Assent in March 2011, places a duty on Welsh Ministers to have due regard to the UNCRC. Up till April 2014 the duty to have regard to the UNCRC applies when ministers are making decisions about new policy or changing existing policies, but from May 2014 it will apply when they are exercising any of their functions. The Measure, *inter alia*, also places a duty on Welsh ministers to take appropriate steps to promote knowledge and understanding of the UNCRC among the public, including children; and it gives ministers powers to make orders which will amend legislation in order to improve children's rights.

Another drawback of the UNCRC is that there is no special court under the Convention, like the European Court of Human Rights, to which aggrieved children and other persons can go to enforce its provisions. However, despite these drawbacks, the UNCRC can be used in legal arguments before the courts, and judges also take it into account when making their decisions. The UK Government also takes it into account when considering new policies relating to children. The UNCRC has become increasingly important in the UK, due in part to the rights-based culture created in the UK by the implementation of the Human Rights Act 1998.

The following articles of the UNCRC lay down key principles, namely non-discrimination (Art 2); the best interest of the child (Art 3); and the right to life (Art 6):

UN Convention on the Rights of the Child 1989

Article 2(1)

'States Parties shall respect and ensure the rights set forth in the present Convention to each child within their jurisdiction without discrimination of any kind, irrespective of the child's or his or her parent's or legal guardian's race, colour, sex, language, religion, political or other opinion, national, ethnic or social origin, property, disability, birth or other status.'

Article 3(1)

'In actions concerning children, whether undertaken by public or private social welfare institutions, courts of law, administrative authorities or legislative bodies, the best interests of the child shall be a primary consideration.'

Article 6

'1. States Parties recognise that every child has the inherent right to life.
2. States Parties shall ensure to the maximum extent possible the survival and development of the child.'

Under the UNCRC children have rights, *inter alia* to: freedom of expression (Art 13); freedom of association and peaceful assembly (Art 15); a private and family life (Art 16); freedom of thought, conscience and religion (Art 14); education (Art 28); minority rights (Art 30); rest and leisure (Art 31); an adequate standard of living (Art 27); protection against economic exploitation (Art 32); and social security benefits (Art 26).

Children also have a right to contact with both parents on a regular basis, except when a court decides that it is contrary to their best interests (Art 9). States Parties must also protect children from all forms of abuse, neglect, maltreatment, exploitation and sexual abuse while in the care of their parents or other persons (Art 19). Children must be protected against: drugs (Art 33); sexual exploitation (Art 34); other forms of exploitation (Art 36); abduction (Art 35); and cruel, inhuman or degrading treatment or punishment (Art 37). The UNCRC also lays down rights for refugee children (Art 22) and disabled children (Art 23), as well as rights to health care and medical provision for children (Art 24).

The UNCRC recognises the importance of the family unit and the importance of parents in the upbringing of their children. It provides that respect must be afforded to the responsibilities, rights and duties of parents, members of the extended family or community and others who are legally responsible for children (Art 5). It also recognises the importance of both parents having common responsibilities for the upbringing and development of their children, and having the primary responsibility for bringing them up (Art 18). Parents and others responsible for children must ensure that the child's living conditions are the best that can be secured in the circumstances (Art 27(2)), and States Parties must take all appropriate measures to recover maintenance for children from parents having financial responsibility (Art. 27(4)).

The UN Committee on the Rights of the Child   This Committee is responsible for monitoring the implementation of the UNCRC in Member States (see Arts 43 and 44). It does so by responding, by way of report, to periodic reports submitted (approximately every five years) by Member States about children's rights in their State. This reporting mechanism puts pressure on Member States to change their law when the UN Committee's Report (which is put into the public domain) criticises them for failing to promote the rights and best interests of children. In July 2007, the UK Government submitted its consolidated third and fourth Report to the UN Committee, whose responses to the UK Report were published in October 2008. In its Report on the UK, the UN Committee expressed concerns about a wide range of children's issues, including, for example, the treatment of young offenders in the youth justice system, child poverty, bullying and exclusion in schools, and the fact that the UK still permitted corporal punishment of children by their parents. The next UK periodic report is due to be submitted to the UN Committee in January 2014.

8.3   The European Convention for the Protection of Human Rights

Although the European Convention for the Protection of Human Rights (the ECHR) makes no express provision for, or reference to, children, they nonetheless have rights under the Convention. The European Court of Human Rights (the ECtHR) has recognised the importance of the best interests of the child. Thus, for instance, in *Johansen v Norway* (1997) 23 EHRR 33 it held that 'particular weight should be attached to the best interests of the child ... which may override those of the parent'. In *Scott v UK* [2000] 1 FLR 958, which concerned the question of whether a mother's Article 8 rights had been breached by a local authority which had applied to free her child for adoption, the ECtHR stated that 'consideration of what is in the best interests of the child is always of crucial importance'.

With respect to the application of the ECHR in the courts in England and Wales, the ECHR has played a greater role in public law cases (such as in care proceedings) as a result of the Human Rights Act 1998 which gives particular protection to victims whose human rights have been breached by a public authority (see 1.8). In private law cases (such as in contact and residence disputes), on the other hand, human rights arguments are not used much, even though the courts as public authorities have obligations under the HRA 1998 to ensure that their judgments comply with the ECHR and to take into account the decisions of the ECtHR. For instance, as Choudhry and Herring point out (2010, p. 203), and also Fortin (see below), the reasoning of the House of Lords in *Re G (Children)* [2006] UKHL 43, [2006] 2 FLR 629 (see pp. 232–3 below) would have been very different if the decision had been decided in accordance with Article 8 of the ECHR (the right to family life).

Despite the fact that human rights are now being used more than they used to be in children's cases, Fortin claims that they are not being used enough ([2011] FamLaw176). Even in public law cases, where judges make 'very free use' of the ECHR, Fortin says that children's rights are 'simply spliced onto the parents' rights as if they were identical', and this precludes any analysis of the child's own rights under the Convention. She also criticises the approach of the ECtHR to children's rights, for although it clearly recognises children's rights when dealing with applications by children (see, for instance, *A v United Kingdom (Human Rights: Punishment of Child)* at 8.5 below), it has 'a record of producing an astonishingly inconsistent response to the child's individual status'. Fortin concludes: 'For lawyers working in the field of child law, the new rights framework imposed by the HRA has undoubtedly had a strong influence on the legal principles applying to children – but in a disappointingly patchy fashion'.

8.4 The autonomy of children – the *Gillick* case

As children grow older, particularly as they near adulthood, it is important that they become more autonomous in the sense that they are able to make decisions for themselves. The case of *Gillick v West Norfolk and Wisbech Health Authority* [1986] AC 112, [1986] 1 FLR 224 was a landmark case with respect to the autonomy of children in that it gave greater recognition to children's right to self-determination, in particular in the context of medical treatment. The decision was also relevant to parental rights as it held that it was preferable to use talk about parental responsibility, rather than parental rights.

▶ *Gillick v West Norfolk and Wisbech Health Authority* **[1986] AC 112, [1986] 1 FLR 224**

A Department of Health and Social Security (DHSS) circular was sent to doctors advising them that they would not be acting unlawfully if in exceptional circumstances they prescribed contraceptives to girls under the age of 16 without first obtaining parental consent, provided they did so in good faith. Mrs Gillick, an ardent Roman Catholic with teenage daughters, brought an action against the DHSS and her local hospital authority seeking a declaration that the circular was illegal on two grounds. First, it enabled doctors to break the criminal law by causing or encouraging unlawful sexual intercourse under the Sexual Offences Act 1956. Secondly, the circular was inconsistent with her parental rights. Mrs Gillick was successful in the Court of Appeal. The defendants appealed to the House of Lords.

The House of Lords held, allowing the appeal, that:

(i) There was no rule of absolute parental authority over a child until a fixed age, but that parental authority dwindled as the child grew older and became more independent. The law recognised parental rights only in so far as they were needed for the child's protection, so that it was more appropriate to talk of duties and responsibilities than rights. Parental rights, if any, yielded to the right of the child to make his or her own decisions if of sufficient understanding and intelligence. Consequently a girl under 16 did not merely by reason of her age lack legal capacity to consent to contraceptive treatment.

(ii) Neither had any offence under the Sexual Offences Act 1956 been committed, as the *bona fide* exercise of a doctor's clinical judgment negated the necessary mental element required for that offence.

> **LORD SCARMAN:** 'The underlying principle of the law was exposed by Blackstone [in his *Commentaries on the Laws of England*] and can be seen to have been acknowledged in the case-law. It is that parental right yields to the child's right to make his own decisions when he reaches a sufficient understanding and intelligence to be capable of making up his own mind on the matter requiring decision.'

Gillick was applied and upheld in the following case, despite the applicant's argument that, with the coming into force of the Human Rights Act 1998, *Gillick* could no longer be considered good law. The case focused on the question of medical confidentiality between doctors and children.

> ▶ *R (Axon) v Secretary of State for Health* **[2006] EWHC 37 (Admin), [2006] 2 FLR 206**
>
> The applicant, a mother of teenage daughters, applied in judicial review proceedings for the following declarations: (i) that a doctor is under no obligation to keep confidential the advice or treatment he proposes to give a young person aged under 16 in respect of contraception, sexually transmitted infections and abortion, and should therefore not provide such advice and treatment without a parent's knowledge unless to do so might prejudice the child's physical or mental health so that it was in the child's best interests not to do so; and (ii) that the Department of Health's *Best Practice Guidance for Doctors and Other Health Professionals on the Provision of Advice and Treatment to Young People Under 16 on Contraception, Sexual and Reproductive Health* (2004) was unlawful because it violated parents' rights under Article 8 of the ECHR.
>
> Silber J dismissed the application, holding that the *Gillick* case (above) was determinative of these issues. There was no different rule on waiving confidentiality when abortion advice or treatment was being discussed from when contraceptive advice or other treatment was under consideration. Silber J held that the very basis and nature of the information which a medical professional received relating to the sexual and reproductive health of any patient of whatever age deserved the highest degree of confidentiality. The proposed limitation on the young person's right to confidentiality might well be inconsistent with the current trend towards a 'keener appreciation of the autonomy of the child and the child's consequential right to participate in the decision-making-process'. The guidelines laid down in *Gillick* did not infringe parental rights under the ECHR. Not only did a young person have his or her own right to respect for family life, and a significant and compelling right to confidentiality of health information under the ECHR which would compete with, and potentially override, any right to parental authority, but also the right to parental authority dwindled as a child matured. The 2004 *Guidance* was not unlawful. *Gillick* did not establish as a matter of law that a medical professional should regard it as an exceptional practice, or unusual, to offer contraceptive advice or abortion advice or treatment to young people without first involving a parent.
>
> Silber J stated, however, that nothing in his judgment was intended to encourage young people to seek or to obtain advice or treatment on sexual matters without first informing their parents and discussing matters with them.

In *Axon* the challenge to *Gillick* on the basis that it infringed a parent's right to family life under Article 8 of the ECHR therefore failed, and *Gillick* remains a landmark decision in the development of children's rights. It led to the phrases '*Gillick* competency' and a '*Gillick* competent child', terms used to denote a child who is old enough and mature enough to be able to make an informed decision.

The impact of Gillick *on the ChildrenAct 1989*   The recognition in *Gillick* that children have a voice that should be heard, particularly where they are sufficiently old and mature, was incorporated into some of the provisions of the Children Act 1989. This was due in part to the fact that *Gillick* was decided when the Law Commission was engaged in consultation and discussion about reforming and consolidating the law on children which eventually led to the enactment of the Children Act 1989. Thus, section 1(3)(a) of the Act 1989 provides that in section 8 order proceedings (see 10.4) and in care and supervision proceedings (see 14.7) the court must have regard to the ascertainable wishes and feelings of the child concerned, considered in the light of his age and understanding. A child can apply for section 8 orders with leave of the court (s 10(8)), which the court can grant if the child has sufficient understanding to make the application; and a child with sufficient understanding to make an informed decision can refuse to consent to a medical or psychiatric examination, or other assessment (s 38(6)). In other words, the Children Act 1989 incorporates the concept of '*Gillick* competency'.

However, although *Gillick* had an impact on the Children Act 1989 and the views and wishes of children of sufficient intelligence and understanding are given greater recognition, a child does not necessarily have the final say as it is always open to the court to overrule, or discount, a child's wishes. Furthermore, although there are many references to the welfare of the child in the Children Act 1989, nowhere is there any reference to children's 'rights'. Thus, for example, children are not usually party to court proceedings, and a child's consent is not needed to his or her removal from the UK or change of surname.

Gillick – its progeny Although *Gillick* was hailed as a landmark case for children's rights, it did not give them absolute rights. In fact, the House of Lords in *Gillick* stressed that, as far as contraception was concerned, it was only in exceptional cases that there would be no parental involvement. Subsequent case-law shows that the scope of children's autonomy rights depends on the circumstances in which they are being exercised. Thus, even the wishes of a '*Gillick* competent' child (a child who is mature and intelligent enough to make an informed decision) can be overridden, as the child's welfare is the court's paramount consideration. Thus, whether or not the wishes of a *Gillick* competent will prevail will depend on the nature and seriousness of the decision to be taken.

(a) Autonomy rights and medical treatment

Section 8(1) of the Family Law Reform Act 1969

Consent by persons over 16 to surgical, medical and dental treatment.
'8(1)The consent of a minor who has attained the age of sixteen years to any surgical, medical or dental treatment which, in the absence of consent, would constitute a trespass to his person, shall be as effective as it would be if he were of full age; and where a minor has by virtue of this section given an effective consent to any treatment it shall not be necessary to obtain any consent for it from his parent or guardian.'

The issues of autonomy rights of children and *Gillick* competency have been considered in several cases where young persons have *refused* to consent to medical treatment. In these cases the courts have overridden their wishes and authorised the treatment, even though the young person concerned was mature enough to make an informed decision, and even though section 8 of the Family Law Reform Act 1969 above provides that 16- and 17-year-olds can consent to surgical, medical and dental treatment. The following three cases provide examples:

▶ *Re R (A Minor) (Wardship: Medical Treatment)* **[1992] Fam 11**

R, a girl aged 15 who had a serious mental illness, had been placed in an adolescent psychiatric unit. The local authority applied in wardship (see 8.7) for her to be given psychiatric treatment without her consent.

The Court of Appeal allowed the application, holding that she was not *Gillick* competent as her mental state fluctuated from day to day, but, even if she had been, the court would still have had the power to override her refusal. Lord Donaldson MR was also of the opinion that a *Gillick* competent child's refusal to have treatment could be overridden if a person with parental responsibility gave consent. The Court of Appeal held that a *Gillick* competent child could consent to medical treatment, but where such a child refused to give consent, then consent could be given by someone else with parental responsibility, including the court.

▶ *Re W (A Minor) (Medical Treatment: Court's Jurisdiction)* **[1993] 1 FLR 1**

W, a 16-year-old girl, suffered from anorexia nervosa. Her condition was rapidly deteriorating, but she refused treatment. The local authority applied to the court under its inherent jurisdiction (see 8.7) for it to authorise medical treatment for the girl, despite her refusal.

The Court of Appeal held, authorising the treatment, that the court has jurisdiction to override a *Gillick* competent child's refusal to consent to medical treatment, despite the provisions of section 8 Family Law Reform Act 1969 (which allows 16- and 17-year-olds to give valid consent to surgical, medical and dental treatment), as the court under its inherent *parens patriae* jurisdiction had theoretically limitless powers extending beyond the powers of natural parents. Nolan LJ said: 'In general terms the present state of the law is that an individual who has reached the age of 18 is free to do with his life what he wishes, but it is the duty of the court to ensure so far as it can that children survive to attain that age.'

▶ *South Glamorgan County Council v W and B* **[1993] 1 FLR 574**

An interim care order had been made in respect of a severely disturbed 15-year-old girl with a direction under section 38(6) Children Act 1989 that she receive a psychiatric examination and assessment. When she refused to consent to the examination and assessment, the court under its inherent jurisdiction overrode her wishes and gave the local authority permission to take the necessary steps for her to be treated and assessed. The court so decided, despite the fact that section 38(6) expressly states that a child of sufficient understanding to make an informed decision can refuse to submit to the examination or other assessment, and notwithstanding the fact that she was *Gillick* competent. The court had the power to override the wishes of a mature minor in respect of medical treatment, despite statutory provisions in the Children Act 1989 to the contrary.

In *Re M (Medical Treatment: Consent)* [1999] 2 FLR 1097 Johnson J, following *Re W* (above), authorised an urgent heart transplant operation for a 15-year-old girl, despite her refusal to give consent. In several cases the High Court has authorised treatment where young people have refused life-saving medical treatment because of their religious beliefs (see, for example, *Re E (A Minor) (Wardship: Medical Treatment)* [1993] 1 FLR 386; and *Re P (Medical Treatment: Best Interests)* [2004] 2 FLR 1117).

The cases show that, even if children are '*Gillick* competent', their wishes can be overridden. Thus, while children may have greater rights of self-determination than they used to have, they do not have absolute autonomy, particularly where they are refusing treatment. On reaching the age of 18, on the other hand, they are free to choose what to do with regard to their medical treatment, even though it may not be in their best interests. According to Gilmore and Herring ([2011] Fam Law 175), 'a great injustice in both [*Re R* and *Re W*, above] was that the children's abilities to refuse treatment were never properly ascertained'. The approach to competency described above may need in a future case to be considered in the light of the Mental Capacity Act 2005 which applies not only to adults but also to 16- and 17-year-olds and which covers both capacity to refuse treatment and capacity to consent (see Cave [2011] CFLQ 431).

What if the child is nearly an adult?   In *Re P (Medical Treatment: Best Interests)* [2004] 2 FLR 1117 Johnson J held, *obiter dicta*, that where a child is nearly an adult the court will give very careful consideration to the child's wishes about medical treatment; and that there could be cases where the refusal of a child approaching 18 would be determinative. Nonetheless, Johnson J granted the hospital leave to administer blood or blood treatments to a young Jehovah's Witness (aged 17) who objected, as did his parents, to the doctors using medical treatment involving blood or blood products on the ground of his religious beliefs.

(b)   Autonomy rights and human rights

In the following two cases the court had to consider the autonomy of children in the context of their human rights, as it did in the *Axon* case (see p. 210 above). In both cases, teenage girls claimed that their human rights under the European Convention for the Protection of Human Rights (the ECHR) had been breached.

▶ *Re Roddy (A Child) (Identification: Restriction on Publication)* **[2004] 2 FLR 949**

Angela Roddy (aged 16 at the time of the hearing) had given birth to a baby at the age of 12; and she had been in care of the local authority. Her baby was adopted despite her refusal to consent to adoption. On her reaching 16, the care order was discharged, on her application, and she wished to publish an account of her experiences in a national newspaper. The local authority applied to prevent publication, but Munby J refused the application, holding that she should be permitted to publish her story subject to conditions imposed to preserve the anonymity of the father and baby.

Munby J, referring to *Gillick* (see pp. 209–10 above), held that the same principles which applied in other areas of adolescent decision-making also applied to the question of whether a minor could exercise her right to freedom of expression under Article 10 of the ECHR and choose to waive her right to privacy under Article 8. He held that it was the court's duty to defend the right of the child (who had sufficient understanding to make an informed decision) to make his or her own choice.

▶ *R (On the Application of Begum) v Headteacher and Governors of Denbigh High School* **[2006] UKHL 15**

The claimant, a Muslim girl, claimed that her school had breached her right to freedom of religion under Article 9 of the ECHR because she had been excluded from school for wearing a *jilbab* (a form of Muslim dress which covers the arms and legs) rather than the *shalwarkameez* (tunic and trousers) which was permitted by her school. She also claimed that the school had breached her right to education under Article 2 of Protocol 1 to the ECHR because she had been excluded from school. Her claim failed at first instance, but she was successful in the Court of Appeal. However, the House of Lords unanimously allowed the school's appeal, with the majority holding that her Article 9 right had not been breached. Lord Nicholls and Baroness Hale, on the other hand, held that her Article 9 right had been breached but that the breach was proportionate and justifiable on the facts (in particular, because the school had taken thorough steps to ensure that its school uniform policy did not offend the religious beliefs of Muslim children who attended the school, and those of their families).

8.5 The corporal punishment of children

Article 37(a) of the UN Convention on the Rights of the Child 1989

'No child shall be subjected to torture or other cruel, inhuman or degrading treatment or punishment...'

Article 19(1) of the UN Convention on the Rights of the Child 1989

'States Parties shall take all appropriate legislative, administrative, social and educational measures to protect the child from all forms of physical or mental violence, injury or abuse, neglect or negligent treatment, maltreatment or exploitation, including sexual abuse, while in the care of parent(s), legal guardian(s) or any other person who has the care of the child.'

Article 3 of the European Convention for the Protection of Human Rights

'No one shall be subjected to torture or to inhuman or degrading treatment or punishment.'

Corporal punishment of children by their parents is permitted in certain very limited circumstances, but it is outlawed in all schools.

(a) Corporal punishment of children by their parents

The development of society's attitude to the corporal punishment of children by their parents shows how differently children are treated today. At one time it was acceptable for parents to beat their children, whereas today they may commit a criminal offence if they inflict corporal punishment on them.

Physical chastisement of a child can also constitute significant harm for the purposes of the Children Act 1989 and result in a child being the subject of a care or supervision order (see 14.7). Each case depends on its fact and the court may decide, however, that the corporal punishment is not significant enough to constitute significant harm as it did, for instance, in *Re MA (Children) (Care Proceedings: Threshold Criteria)* [2009] EWCA Civ 853 where the Court of Appeal held that the harm was insufficient to justify the intervention of the State and disturb the autonomy of the parents.

The corporal punishment of children by parents is not completely outlawed in England and Wales, as the defence of reasonable chastisement can be used in certain restricted circumstances. This defence originated in the case of *R v Hopley* (1860) 2 F&F 202 where Cockburn CJ held that the beating of a boy aged 13 by a teacher was 'reasonable' even though the boy later died. In many European countries, however, there is a total ban on parents using corporal punishment. Sweden, for instance, imposed a ban in 1979, and other countries have outlawed it (for example, Austria, Croatia, Cyprus, Denmark, Finland, Germany, Iceland, Latvia, Norway, Romania and Ukraine). Over the years there has been increasing pressure to outlaw it in the UK, in particular by organisations such as End All Corporal Punishment of Children and the National Society for the Prevention of Cruelty to Children (NSPCC). The UN Committee on the Rights of the Child in its periodic reports on the UK (see p. 206 above) has been critical of the lack of an absolute ban on corporal punishment in the UK.

Pressure to change the law At the end of the 1990s the UK Government came under increasing pressure to change the law in part because of the following decision by the European Court of Human Rights:

> ▶ *A v United Kingdom (Human Rights: Punishment of Child)* [1998] ECHR 85, [1998] 2 FLR 959
>
> The applicant, a boy aged 9, was beaten with a garden cane on a number of occasions by his step-father. The step-father was charged with assault occasioning actual bodily harm (under section 47 Offences Against the Persons Act 1861), but was acquitted because, although it was not disputed by the defence that the step-father had caned the boy on a number of occasions, the jury accepted his defence of 'reasonable chastisement'. The applicant claimed before the European Court of Human Rights (ECtHR) that the UK was in breach of Article 3 of the ECHR (the right not to be subjected to torture or to suffer inhuman or degrading treatment or punishment) and Article 8 (the right to a private and family life).
>
> The ECtHR unanimously held that the UK was in breach of Article 3, because the reasonable chastisement defence did not give a child sufficient protection. It said that the ill-treatment must attain a minimum level of severity in order to fall within Article 3. On the facts, the step-father's ill-treatment of the child had reached that level taking into account the age of the child and the severity of the treatment. It held that the following factors were particularly important when establishing whether punishment was sufficiently severe to constitute ill-treatment for the purposes of Article 3: the nature and context of the defendant's treatment; its duration; its physical and mental effects in relation to the age and personal characteristics of the victim; and the reasons given by the defendant for administering the punishment.
>
> Having concluded that there was a breach of Article 3, it held that there was no need to consider Article 8. The applicant was awarded £10,000 by way of damages.

As a result of the decision in *A v UK*, the UK Government was obliged to consider reforming the law. However, it was not obliged to impose a complete ban on corporal punishment as the breach of Article 3 in *A v UK* related to the degree of severity of the ill-treatment and to the unsatisfactory nature of the reasonable chastisement defence. The step-father's use of corporal punishment was not of itself a breach of Article 3.

In January 2000, the Government published a consultation document (*Protecting Children, Supporting Parents: A Consultation Document on the Physical Punishment of Children*, Department of Health) in which it said that, while harmful and degrading treatment of children could never be justified, it did not consider the right way forward was to make all physical punishment by parents unlawful. It said that there was 'a common-sense distinction between the sort of mild physical rebuke which occurs in families, and which most loving parents consider acceptable, and the beating of a child' (para 1(5)). The Government said that it was considering introducing a statutory definition of the defence of 'reasonable chastisement' based on the criteria laid down in *A v UK* (nature of the treatment, its context, duration etc.). However, with the coming into force of the Human Rights Act 1998 (see 1.8) it was no longer necessary to change the law as the courts in the UK were obliged to take account of the ruling in *A v UK* in any event due to its obligations under section 2(2) of the HRA 1998. In fact, before the HRA 1998 had come into force, the decision in *A v UK* had already been applied in *R v H (Reasonable Chastisement)* [2001] 2 FLR 431, where the Court of Appeal held that, when juries were considering the reasonableness or otherwise of reasonable chastisement, they must be instructed by the judge to consider the criteria laid down in *A v UK*.

In November 2001, the Government published its conclusions on the responses to its consultation document (above) (*An Analysis of Responses to Protecting Children, Supporting Parents: A Consultation Document on the Physical Punishment of Children*). It concluded (at para 76) that it did not believe that 'any further change to the law at this time would command widespread public support or that it would be capable of consistent enforcement'. It said that the guidance issued by the Court of Appeal in *R v H* (above) was sufficient to provide the protection guaranteed by Article 3 of the ECHR. It did say, however, that it intended to keep the defence of reasonable chastisement under review.

The Government's refusal to change the law did not command widespread support, and further pressure was put on the Government to change the law. At the end of 2004 renewed attempts were made to prohibit parents from using corporal punishment, but proposals for an absolute ban were defeated in the House of Commons. However, a last-minute amendment to the Children Bill 2004 by Lord Lester of Herne Hill was accepted by the Government, which resulted in the enactment of section 58 of the Children Act 2004.

Section 58 of the Children Act 2004 This provision does not outlaw all forms of corporal punishment, as it allows parents (and other persons *in loco parentis*) to raise the defence of reasonable chastisement if they are charged with the offences of common assault or battery against a child. However, section 58 has removed the availability of the reasonable chastisement defence where the accused is charged with wounding, causing grievous bodily harm, assault occasioning actual bodily harm, or cruelty to a person under the age of 16.

When section 58 was going through Parliament, the Government promised to conduct a review after it had been in force for two years. The results of the review were published in October 2007 (*Review of Section 58 of the Children Act 2004*, Cm 7232, Department for Children, Schools and Families), but, on the basis of its findings, the Government concluded that it did not intend to change the law to outlaw corporal punishment completely. It considered that, through the enactment of section 58, it had met its international obligations under the UNCRC and the European Convention for the Protection of Human Rights. The Government found, as part of its review, that parents were using corporal punishment less, but that 52 per cent of parents (compared with 88 per cent in 1998) still favoured retaining the right to use it. The Government accepted, however, that there appeared to be a lack of understanding about what the law did and did not allow. It said that it would do more to help with positive parenting; and also ask the Crown Prosecution Service and the police to monitor the situation with regard to the use of reasonable punishment.

In early 2010, the Government commissioned Sir Roger Singleton to produce an independent report on corporal punishment. His report, which was published in March 2010, recommended, *inter alia*, that the Government should 'continue to promote positive parenting strategies and effective behaviour management techniques directed towards eliminating the use of smacking' and that 'parents who disapprove of smacking should make this clear to others who care for their children'.

Should corporal punishment by parents be outlawed completely? Despite the restrictions imposed by section 58 on the corporal punishment of children, some people and some organisations are in favour of it being outlawed completely (for example the NSPCC, Save the Children, the Children's Rights Alliance, and the Children's Commissioners throughout the UK). The UN Committee on the Rights of the Child has also recommended it be outlawed in the UK. Thus in its report on the UK in October 2002 at (para 38(a)), it recommended that the UK should '[w]ith urgency adopt legislation ... to remove the 'reasonable chastisement' defence and prohibit all corporal punishment in the family and in any other contexts not covered by existing legislation'.

Although there are arguments for allowing parents to administer reasonable and moderate corporal punishment (such as that parents should have the choice, and it does not harm children), there are strong arguments for outlawing it completely, such as that: condoning corporal punishment creates a culture of abuse which can result in children being harmed, sometimes very seriously; the current law breaches children's human rights; and the current law is confusing. Whether it will be banned completely remains to be seen, but there are no current proposals to do so.

(b) Corporal punishment in schools

Corporal punishment of children is banned in all schools (by s 548 Education Act 1996). It was banned first of all in State schools (s 47 Education (No. 2) Act 1986), and later in independent schools. Use of physical force or punishment by a teacher on a schoolchild can therefore give rise to criminal or civil liability, and there is no defence of reasonable chastisement. However, in certain circumstances teachers are permitted to use reasonable restraint on a schoolchild (s 550A Education Act 1996).

The following case was highly influential in leading to the abolition of corporal punishment in State schools:

▶ *Campbell and Cosans v UK* **(1982) 4 EHRR 293**

Two mothers from Scotland claimed that the use of corporal punishment in State schools breached their sons' rights not to suffer inhuman and degrading treatment under Article 3 of the ECHR.

The ECtHR found no breach of Article 3 – as the boys had not been punished or threatened with punishment – but held that there had been a breach of Article 2 of Protocol 1 to the ECHR, which provides that '[n]o person shall be denied the right to education', and that 'the State shall respect the right of parents to ensure such education and teaching in conformity with their own religious and philosophical convictions'. The ECtHR held that Jeffrey Cosans' right to education had been breached as he had been suspended from school for nearly a year, because his parents objected to corporal punishment. It also held that the applicants' rights had been breached, because corporal punishment was not in conformity with their philosophical convictions.

In *Costello-Roberts v UK* (1993) 19 EHRR 112 the applicant boy claimed that the corporal punishment he had suffered at his independent school breached Articles 3, 8 and 13 of the ECHR. His claim failed, but in September 1999 corporal punishment in independent schools was abolished.

In the following case, on the other hand, parents and teachers at certain Christian schools objected on religious grounds to the abolition of corporal punishment in schools in England and Wales:

> ▶ *R (Williamson) v Secretary of State for Education and Employment and Others* [2006]
> **UKHL 15, [2005] 2 FLR 374**
>
> Head teachers, teachers and parents at certain Christian independent schools in England claimed in judicial review proceedings that the ban on corporal punishment in schools breached their rights to freedom of religion under the ECHR. They claimed that it was a tenet of their fundamental Christian belief that parents (and teachers) should be able to administer physical punishment to children. They wished teachers to be able to administer reasonable chastisement because they believed it was conducive to the moral well-being of children. They claimed that section 548 of the Education Act 1996 did not completely abolish the use of corporal punishment in independent schools, and that, if it did so, it was a breach of Article 9(1) (right to freedom of religion) and Article 2 of Protocol No. 1 ECHR, which provides that '[n]o person shall be denied the right to education' and that 'the State shall respect the right of parents to ensure such education and teaching in conformity with their own religious and philosophical convictions'. Their application was rejected at first instance. Their appeal was dismissed by the Court of Appeal, and so they appealed to the House of Lords.
>
> The House of Lords held, dismissing their appeal, that there was no breach of the ECHR. Section 548 of the Education Act 1996 did not breach their rights to freedom of religion under Article 9(1) because the ban complied with Article 9(2), which permits freedom of religion to be limited by law where 'necessary in a democratic society ... for the protection of the rights and freedoms of others'. The statutory ban pursued a legitimate aim (to protect children from physical violence) and the means used to achieve that aim were appropriate and not disproportionate.

8.6 Children and family proceedings

> **Article 12 of the UN Convention on the Rights of the Child 1989**
>
> '1. States Parties should assure to the child who is capable of forming his or her own views the right to express those views freely in all matters affecting the child, the views of the child being given due weight in accordance with the age and maturity of the child.
> 2. For this purpose, the child shall in particular be provided the opportunity to be heard in any judicial and administrative proceedings affecting the child, either directly, or through a representative or an appropriate body, in a manner consistent with the procedural rules of national law.'

The first paragraph of Article 12 of the UN Convention on the Rights of the Child above draws attention to the right of children, who are capable of forming their own views, to express those views in matters which affect them and for weight to be given to those views in accordance with their age and maturity. It is very similar to the notion of 'Gillick competency' (see further at 8.4 above) and to section 1(3)(a) of the Children Act 1989 which requires the court in most children's proceeding to take into account 'the ascertainable wishes and feelings of the child concerned (considered in the light of his age and understanding)' (see further at p. 267). It is the second paragraph in Article 12 (above), however, which is particularly important to the question of the voice of the child in family proceedings.

The rules with respect to children in family proceedings differ depending on whether the proceedings are private law or public law proceedings. Private law proceedings involve private individuals (such as parents and children), whereas public law proceedings involve a public authority (such as a local authority social services team in care or supervision proceedings).

(a) Private law

(i) Making an application to the court A child can apply for a section 8 order under the Children Act 1989 (such as a residence or contact order, see 10.4), but only with leave of the court, which the court can grant if it considers the child has sufficient understanding to make the application (s 10(8) CA 1989). Although the test of sufficient understanding is that of *Gillick* competence (see 8.4 above), only older teenagers are likely to be held to have the required sufficiency of understanding (see, for example, *Re C (Residence: Child's Application for Leave)* [1995] 1 FLR 927). Children can also bring proceedings under other legislation, such as for a non-molestation order under Part IV of the Family Law Act 1996 (see 5.4). They can also bring proceedings under the inherent jurisdiction of the court (see 8.7). In practice, however, applications to the court in any matter are extremely rare.

(ii) Rights of representation for children The usual way in which the voice of the child is conveyed to the court in private law proceedings (such as for residence and contact) is by means of a welfare report prepared by a Children and Family Reporter (an officer of Cafcass – see 1.7). Children do not have party status in family proceedings, or the legal representation that accompanies it, unless the court exercises its power under rule 16.2 of the Family Procedure Rules (FPR) 2010 which provides that the court may make a child a party to proceedings if it considers it is in the best interests of the child to do so. If it does so decide, then it *must* appoint a Children's Guardian for the child unless it is satisfied that such an appointment is not necessary to safeguard the child's interests (r 16.3) The Children's Guardian will work in tandem with the lawyer acting for the child.

(iii) Separate representation of children There has been increasing concern in the last few years that children in private family proceedings (particularly for residence and contact) are not being given the opportunity to instruct their own solicitor without having to do so via a Children's Guardian (see above). Thus, although the child or the child's solicitor can ask the court for leave to remove the Children's Guardian (so that the child can instruct the lawyer directly) (see r 16.6), in practice this rarely happens.

Practice Direction 16A – Representation of Children This *Practice Direction* (which supplements Part 16 of the FPR 2010 which deals with 'Representation of Children and Reports in Proceedings Involving Children') provides, among other things, that making a child party to the proceedings is 'a step that will be taken only in cases which involve an issue of significant difficulty and consequently will occur in only a minority of cases'; and that the court should consider whether an alternative might be preferable (Part 4, s 1, para 7.1). Para 7.2 of the *Practice Direction* provides guidance on the circumstances where it might be justifiable to make an order that the child should have separation representation, such as where: there is an intractable residence or contact dispute; where the child has a standpoint or interest which is inconsistent with or not capable of being represented by any of the adult parties; the child's views cannot be adequately met by a report to the court; an older child is opposing a proposed course of action; or where there are complex medical, mental health or other issues which necessitate separate representation of the child. The *Practice Direction* also draws attention to the fact that granting separate representation to a child may cause delay (see para 7.3).

The following case concerned children having the right to instruct their own lawyer in private family law proceedings:

▶ *Mabon v Mabon and Others* [2005] EWCA Civ 634, [2005] 2 FLR 1011

Three teenage boys (aged 13, 15 and 17), who were living with their father on the breakdown of their parents' relationship, wished to be separately represented in court proceedings involving a residence dispute between their parents. The boys had three younger siblings, who were living with the mother, but the mother sought residence orders against the father in respect of all six children. A Cafcass officer filed a report and was appointed Guardian of all six children. During the trial, however, the three oldest boys contacted a solicitor. At the residence hearing the boys' solicitor applied under the Family Procedure Rules 1991 (now replaced by FPR 2010) for them to be separately represented, but the application was refused. The boys appealed to the Court of Appeal.

The Court of Appeal unanimously allowed their appeal, holding that the judge had been plainly wrong. Thorpe LJ said that it was unthinkable to exclude young men from knowledge of and participation in legal proceedings that affected them so fundamentally. He said that, in the case of articulate teenagers, courts must accept that the right to freedom of expression and participation in family life outweighed the paternalistic judgment of welfare, and that the case provided a timely opportunity to recognise the growing acknowledgment of the autonomy and consequential rights of children. Thorpe LJ said that in individual cases trial judges must equally acknowledge this shift of approach when they made a proportionate judgment of the sufficiency of the child's understanding.

Mabon v Mabon was applied in *Re C (Abduction: Separate Representation of Children)* [2008] 2 FLR 6 and *W v W (Abduction: Joinder as Party)* [2009] EWHC 3288 (Fam) [2010] 1 FLR 1342 where the children were granted separate representation in cases brought under the Hague Convention on Abduction (see 13.4).

In most cases, however, the court will usually consider that the child's views and best interests will be sufficiently safeguarded by asking for a welfare report (under s 7 of the Children Act 1989). Participating in court proceedings can be a harrowing and traumatic experience for children. They may be also exposed to the risk of having to make a choice between parents, or of being manipulated by a parent. The courts are therefore keen to ensure that children are protected from the potentially harmful effect of being involved in court proceedings. Allowing children to participate in family proceedings can also add to the delay and cost of the trial. In the following case a different approach was taken to that in *Mabon*:

▶ *Re N (Contact: Minor Seeking Leave to Defend and Removal of Guardian)* [2003] 1 FLR 652

Coleridge J held that an 11-year-old boy who wished to defend the contact proceedings did not have sufficient understanding to participate and give instructions on his own behalf without a Children's Guardian. Complex issues were involved against a background of a long and stormy contact dispute. The child would not be able to understand the issues involved. Consequently he did not have sufficient understanding to participate. Coleridge J held that the test of competence was 'not whether the child was capable of articulating instructions but whether the child was of sufficient understanding to participate as party in the proceedings, in the sense of being able to cope with all the ramifications of the proceedings and giving considered instructions of sufficient objectivity'.

Whybrow (2004), commenting on *Re N*, said that the test of competence was set high and 'would render many adults incapable of conducting their family litigation, let alone children'.

The Court of Appeal has held that there is no objection to a service, such as the National Youth Advocacy Service (www.nyas.org.uk), representing a child in private law proceedings, such as in a contact dispute (see *Re H (National Youth Advocacy Service)* [2007 1 FLR 1028).

(b) Public law cases

In public law proceedings (such as for care and supervision orders) the system of representation for children operates with a Children's Guardian and a solicitor acting side by side. Thus, children involved in public law proceedings are party to the proceedings. This has been so since the mid-1970s when the practice of using guardians *ad litem* to put forward the voice of the child was introduced as a result of the recommendations made in the wake of the Maria Colwell Inquiry in 1974.

(c) The voice of the child in family proceedings

Despite the fact that Article 12(2) of the UN Convention on the Rights of the Child 1989 (see p. 218 above) requires a child to be given the opportunity to be heard in legal proceedings, and section 1(3)(a) of the Children Act 1989 requires the court to have regard to 'the ascertainable wishes and feelings of the child concerned (considered in the light of his age and understanding)' (see p. 267), there has been concern that children are not being listened to enough in family proceedings; and that judges should be more willing to allow them to be separately represented by their own lawyer (see, for example, Macdonald [2008] Fam Law 648; [2009] Fam Law 40). In *Mabon v Mabon* (see above) Thorpe LJ said that 'in the twenty-first century, there is a keener appreciation of the autonomy of the child and the child's consequential right to participate in decision-making processes that fundamentally affect his family life'. In *Re D (A Child) (Abduction: Rights of Custody)* [2006] UKHL 51,[2007] 1 FLR 961 Baroness Hale also drew attention to the growing importance of listening to the views of children:

> '[T]here is now a growing understanding of the importance of listening to children in children's cases. It is the child, more than anyone else, who will have to live with what the court decides. Those who do listen to children understand that they often have a point of view which is quite distinct from that of the person looking after them. They are quite capable of being moral actors in their own right. Just as the adults may have to do what the court decides whether they like it or not, so may the child. But that is no more reason for failing to hear what the child has to say than it is for refusing to hear the parent's views.'

In the last few years, there has been a growing interest and increased debate about reforming the law governing the voice of the child in family proceedings, something which has been promoted in part by the Family Justice Council (see [2008] Fam Law 431). However, although there is considerable support for the idea that children should be more involved in family proceedings, the difficult question concerns the extent to which they should be involved. For some children it may be distressing to hear the details of their parents' case in court. As Thorpe LJ warned in *Mabon* (see above), if direct participation in proceedings 'would pose an obvious risk of harm to the child, arising out of the continuing proceedings, and, if the child is incapable of comprehending that risk, then the judge is entitled to find that sufficient understanding has not been demonstrated'. Thorpe LJ said, however, that judges also have to be 'equally alive to the risk of emotional harm that might arise from denying the child knowledge of and participation in the continuing proceedings'. There are also time and resource implications in permitting children to be separately represented. In fact, in *Re A (Contact Order)* [2010] EWCA Civ 208, [2010] 2 FLR 577, where the trial judge's decision that there should be no separate representation of the child was upheld by the Court of Appeal, Thorpe LJ held that orders for the separate representation of children should in the present conditions of restricted funding for the family justice system be issued very sparingly.

There is concern not just about whether separate representation should be more widely available for children in private family proceedings, but whether children's voices are being sufficiently heard at all. Thus, a child's wishes and feelings may be overlooked by parents who are involved in a difficult conflict, and in some cases the court may decide not to commission a welfare report.

A breach of human rights?   Refusing to allow a child to participate in family proceedings, with or without a Children's Guardian, may be a breach of the child's human rights under Article 12 of the UNCRC (see p. 218 above) or one of the following rights guaranteed under the ECHR: Article 6 (the right to a fair trial); Article 8 (the right to family life); Article 10 (the right to freedom of expression); and Article 12 (the right to an effective remedy). In *Re A (Contact: Separate Representation)* [2001] 1 FLR 715 Butler-Sloss P recognised that there were cases where children needed to be separately represented, and cases where she suspected that the voices of children had not always been sufficiently heard. She said that the courts' attitude to separate representation needed to change as a result of Articles 6 and 8 of the ECHR. However, although the European Court of Human Rights has not ruled on the need for separate representation in children's cases, in two cases brought against Germany involving contact disputes it was critical of the German courts' failure to hear the children's views (see *Elsholz v Germany* [2000] 2 FLR 486; *Sahin v Germany* [2002] 1 FLR 119).

The UN Committee on the Rights of the Child (see p. 208) has expressed concern about the failure of the UK courts to allow children to be represented in private law proceedings.

Separate representation of children – reform   Although section 41(6A) of the Children Act 1989 permits rules of court to be drawn up to allow children to have separate representation in section 8 order proceedings (such as in residence or contact proceedings – see 10.4), these rules have never been made but merely discussed. In 2006, the Government consulted on the question of allowing separate representation of children in private law proceedings but said that only a small proportion of section 8 proceedings would be suitable for separate representation (see *Consultation Paper, Separate Representation of Children* (CP/20/06, 2006). The responses to the consultation were published in July 2007 (*Separate Representation of Children: Summary of Responses to a Consultation Paper*, CP(R)20/06), and the Government said that it proposed to extend jurisdiction for deciding whether a child should be made a party to family proceedings to all levels of court. It also proposed that children would be provided with information during proceedings to help them cope with anxieties and uncertainties; and that, subject to agreement with the judiciary, children who wished to speak to a judge or magistrate should be able to do so. Although these proposals were not introduced, there is some evidence to show that the number of children for whom the courts order separate representation has increased (see [2009] Fam Law 466).

The Family Justice Review in its *Final Report* in November 2011 (see further at p. 7) suggested that children and young people should be given the opportunity to have their voices heard in cases that are about them, if they so wished; and that separate representation of children was an area that needed to be kept under review. Thus, for example, in the Executive Summary to the *Report* (see p. 6, para 8), it was stated, with respect to the child's voice, that:

'Children's interests are central to the operation of the family justice system. Decisions should take the wishes of children into account and children should know what is happening and why. People urged us to consider the need to take great care in consulting children, and for this to be handled sensitively and to take into account the child's age and understanding.'

In February 2012, the Government fully endorsed these proposals, stating that the new Family Justice Board will consider how children can be best supported to make their views known and be taken into account in decisions that affect them (*The Government Response to the Family Justice Review: A system with children and families at its heart*, Cm 8273, February 2010). In its *Response* the Government stated (at p. 11, para 29):

'At the individual level more consistency is needed in how children are involved in the court processes which affect their lives. This needs to be done with great care and sensitivity, by practitioners who understand how to best communicate with and listen to children depending on their age and circumstances.'

Judicial interviews of children   In the last few years there has been discussion about whether judges should interview children in order to discover their views. In New Zealand, for instance, the courts have adopted this practice, subject to certain guidelines ([2008] Fam Law 809). Senior members of the judiciary are in favour of judicial interviews of children in appropriate cases, but, as yet, no specific measures have been introduced to make provision for this. Nonetheless, in some cases, judges have interviewed children and endorsed this practice. Thus, for example, in *Re G (Abduction: Children's Objections)* [2010] EWCA Civ 1232, [2011] 1 FLR 1645, a case brought under the Hague Convention on Abduction involving a 13-year-old child, Thorpe LJ endorsed the view that interviewing a child was a viable option for the judiciary and he was critical of the fact that a judicial interview with the child had not been suggested by the High Court at first instance. Although he said that it was 'highly unusual' to meet a child before deciding an appeal, he nevertheless endorsed the approach of the Family Justice Council which had forcefully expressed the view that judges should be meeting with children and hearing their voices.

(d)   Children giving evidence in family proceedings

In *Re W* [2010] UKSC 12, [2010] 1 FLR 1485 the Supreme Court held that there was no longer a presumption or even a starting point against children giving oral evidence in family proceedings. Although *Re W* was a care proceedings case, this approach also applies to other family proceeding cases. In response to *Re W*, a set of guidelines (*Guidelines in relation to children giving evidence in family proceedings*) were produced by the Family Justice Council Working Party on Children Giving Evidence, chaired by Thorpe LJ, which were endorsed by Sir Nicholas Wall, President of the Family Division. The guidelines were drawn up for the benefit of the judiciary, lawyers and professionals who have to deal with applications for children to give evidence in family proceedings. The guidelines (which are available at www.judiciary.gov.uk.) are lengthy and detailed, but in deciding whether a child should give evidence, the court's principal objective should be to achieve a fair trial. The age and maturity of the child are, for example, considerations that the court has to take into account. Evidence by video link is possible, depending on the circumstances.

8.7 Protection for children in wardship and under the inherent jurisdiction

(a) Introduction

The inherent jurisdiction, of which wardship is a part, is an ancient jurisdiction deriving from the right and duty of the Crown as *parens patriae* (parent or protector of the realm) to take care of persons who are unable to care for themselves, which includes not just children, but also incapacitated adults (for instance in the context of marriage, see pp. 34–5). Only the High Court has jurisdiction in wardship and under the inherent jurisdiction.

(i) Applications by local authorities   Before the Children Act 1989 came into force, local authorities would choose to use the inherent jurisdiction to take children into care, even though statute made provision for this. The Children Act 1989 changed that practice, so that a local authority could no longer use the inherent jurisdiction to: place a child in its care or under its supervision (s 100(2)(a)); accommodate a child in care (s 100(2)(b)); make a child a ward of court (s 100(2)(c)); or determine a question about any aspect of parental responsibility for a child (s 100(2)(d)).

However, a local authority is not totally precluded from invoking the inherent jurisdiction, as it can ask the High Court to give it leave to invoke it (s 100(3) CA 1989). The High Court can grant such leave if it is satisfied that the result which is wanted cannot be achieved by any other order, and there is reasonable cause to believe that the child will suffer significant harm if the inherent jurisdiction is not exercised (s 100(4)). Local authorities have sometimes successfully invoked the inherent jurisdiction in cases where children need medical treatment (see 9.7). Hospitals and health authorities sometimes invoke the jurisdiction in difficult medical cases in order to ask the court to authorise or terminate a child's medical treatment.

(ii) Applications by private individuals   With respect to applications by private individuals, although there is no express prohibition in the Children Act 1989 against them using wardship and the inherent jurisdiction, they are now rarely invoked, as the Children Act 1989 introduced two new orders (the prohibited steps and specific issue orders, see 10.7 and 10.8) which allow judges to exercise similar powers to those which the High Court can exercise under its inherent jurisdiction. Thus, as in local authority cases, the inherent jurisdiction and wardship are now a residual jurisdiction which provide a safety net for children in complex and difficult cases and cases which cannot be resolved under the Children Act 1989, for example difficult medical cases (see 9.7), some international child abduction cases (see 13.10), and some forced marriage cases (see 2.6). However, even cases which could be dealt with under the Children Act 1989 may sometimes be dealt with by using wardship, for instance, where the parents are engaged in a particularly bitter and ongoing dispute about a child as the parents were in *T v S (Wardship)* [2011]

EWHC 1608 (Fam), [2012] 1 FLR 230 (see below). Such uses of wardship are, however, rare as the circumstances must be exceptional before the court will intervene by way of wardship rather than making an order under the Children Act 1989.

(iii) Section 8 orders   As proceedings under the inherent jurisdiction and in wardship are 'family proceedings' for the purpose of the Children Act 1989, the High Court can make any section 8 order (see 10.4) in the proceedings, except where the child is in care, when only a residence order can be made (s 9(1)). As a section 8 order cannot be made in favour of a local authority on an application by a local authority when a child is in care (ss 9(1) and (2)), a local authority wishing to resolve a question about a child in care (such as in respect of medical treatment) must apply for leave to invoke the inherent jurisdiction (see above).

(b) Wardship

Wardship is part of the inherent jurisdiction of the High Court. The essence of wardship is that, once a child is made a ward of court, the situation is frozen and the court stands *in loco parentis* for the child. Consequently, as the court has parental responsibility for the child, any major step in the child's life requires the court's prior consent. Thus, for example, a ward cannot marry, be adopted, leave the jurisdiction, or receive serious medical treatment without the consent of the court. It is this supervisory role of the court which distinguishes wardship from the inherent jurisdiction, and is sometimes the reason why it is used in children's cases. For instance, in *T v S (Wardship)* [2011] EWHC 1608 (Fam), [2012] 1 FLR 230 Hedley J held that wardship should be continued with respect to a 4-year-old child whose parents were involved in an incessant and serious conflict about how their parental responsibility was to be exercised, as wardship would enable the court to retain care and control of the child and parental responsibility would rest with the court save insofar as it was prepared to delegate its exercise to the parents.

Wardship is also useful in urgent situations, as the High Court acquires powers in respect of the child automatically on the issue of the initial application. For this reason wardship is useful in some abduction cases (see 13.10). It has also been used in forced marriage cases (see 2.6).

The governing principle in wardship proceedings is that the welfare of the child is the court's paramount consideration (s 1(1) CA 1989). Provided the High Court has jurisdiction to make the child a ward of court, it can exercise a wide range of powers. Thus, under the Children Act 1989, it can: make any section 8 order; make a section 37 direction that a local authority make enquiries about a child; appoint a guardian for the child; and make orders for financial provision under Schedule 1. It also has the power to grant injunctions. Although the wardship jurisdiction is theoretically limitless, in some situations the court will refuse to exercise it (for instance, where it will undermine a statutory power; or in immigration and asylum cases) (see below). Inappropriate uses of wardship are therefore not permitted. The court will also refuse to exercise jurisdiction where the child has never been habitually resident or present in the UK (see, for example, *H v H (Jurisdiction to Grant Wardship)* [2011] EWCA Civ 796), but in forced marriage cases wardship has sometimes been used to protect a child who is a victim of a forced marriage but who is not currently resident in the UK (see 2.6).

(c) The inherent jurisdiction

The High Court has a general inherent power to protect children (and incapacitated adults) which is independent of the wardship jurisdiction. The inherent jurisdiction is sometimes used to obtain the court's permission to allow or refuse medical treatment, for example: to arrange medical treatment for a 16-year-old anorexic girl in care (*Re W (A Minor) (Medical Treatment: Court's Jurisdiction)* [1993] Fam 64); to give blood transfusions to a child whose parents object to treatment on religious grounds (*Re O (A Minor) (Medical Treatment)* [1993] 2 FLR 149); and to obtain guidance on the treatment of a severely handicapped child (*Re J (A Minor) (Medical Treatment)* [1992] 2 FLR 165).

The inherent jurisdiction is also sometimes used in forced marriage cases (see 2.6) and in abduction cases (see 13.10). It has also been be used in the case of vulnerable adults, in other words where a person lacks mental capacity (see, for example, *A Local Authority v E* [2008] 1 FLR 978, which involved a 19-year-old woman with a severe learning difficulty who had been made the subject of a care order at the age of 15).

The inherent jurisdiction has sometimes been used to fill in gaps in the law in order to protect the best interests of children, as it was in *Re D (Unborn Baby)* [2009] EWHC 446 (Fam), [2009] 2 FLR 313 where Munby J made an order under the inherent jurisdiction in respect of an unborn baby, because the Children Act 1989 and the wardship jurisdiction could not be invoked in respect of an unborn child. In this case the local authority successfully applied for an anticipatory declaration under the inherent jurisdiction declaring that it could lawfully remove a baby at birth from her mother because there was a serious and likely risk that the mother would seriously harm the child. The inherent jurisdiction was also invoked in *Re C (Abduction: Separate Representation of Children)* [2008] 2 FLR 6 where the child concerned was too old to come within the jurisdiction of the Hague Convention on Abduction, and in *Re U (Abduction: Nigeria)* [2010] EWHC 1179 (Fam), [2011] 1 FLR 354, where the children concerned were removed to a country which was not a signatory to the Hague Convention on Abduction (see 13.10).

(d) Limits on the use of wardship and the inherent jurisdiction

In addition to the restrictions placed on local authorities (see p. 224 above), the High Court may refuse to exercise the inherent jurisdiction or to make a child a ward of court even though the inherent jurisdiction and wardship are theoretically limitless. Thus, for example, in *Re F (In Utero)* [1998] Fam 122 the High Court refused to make an unborn child a ward of court, as to do so would place an unjustifiable fetter on the rights of the child's mother. In some cases, the court will refuse to make a child a ward of court because public interests prevail, such as in the context of immigration control:

> ▶ *S v S* [2009] 1 FLR 241
>
> The mother of the child was resisting deportation as a failed asylum seeker. The mother's cousin began wardship proceedings in respect of the child, but Munby J dismissed the application, holding that the High Court cannot, even in the exercise of its inherent jurisdiction, make orders which in any way impinge upon or prevent the Secretary of State exercising powers lawfully conferred by statute in the context of immigration and asylum (following *R v Secretary of State for the Home Department ex parte T* [1995] 1 FLR 293; and *Re A (Care Proceedings: Asylum Seekers)* [2003] 2 FLR 921). Munby J held that, in the circumstances of the case, the wardship proceedings were not serving any useful or permissible purpose.

(e) Protecting children from media intrusion and harmful publication

Applications to the High Court in wardship or under its inherent jurisdiction are sometimes made in order to obtain an injunction to protect a child from harmful media attention and exposure (see, for example, *Re Z (A Minor) (Freedom of Publication)* [1996] 1 FLR 191; and *Nottingham City Council v October Films Ltd* [1999] 2 FLR 347). However, jurisdiction may be refused on the ground that freedom of speech prevails, as the following case shows:

▶ *R (Mrs) v Central Independent Television plc* [1994] **Fam 192**

A child was made a ward of court, on the application of her mother, in order to prevent a television programme being broadcast which discussed the child's father's conviction and imprisonment for indecency. The decision of the High Court was overturned by the Court of Appeal. Waite LJ stated that no child, simply by virtue of being a child, is entitled to a right of privacy or confidentiality. As the programme had nothing to do with the care or upbringing of the child, there was nothing to put in the balance against the freedom to publish.

The Human Rights Act 1998 gives particular priority to the right to freedom of speech under Article 10 of the ECHR (see s 12(4) HRA 1998) and the High Court in children's cases must weigh this in the balance when considering the child's Article 8 right to a private and family life, and the child's welfare.

The following decision of the House of Lords is the leading case on preventing publication in order to protect a child:

▶ *Re S (Identification: Restriction on Publication)* [2004] **UKHL 47, [2005] 1 FLR 591**

The guardian of an eight-year-old child obtained an injunction under the inherent jurisdiction to restrain publication of the identity of the child's mother who had been charged with the murder of the child's older brother. The judge in the High Court (on the application of the newspaper) modified the injunction so that the newspaper could, in reports of the criminal trial, publish the identity of the mother and the deceased brother and reproduce their photographs. This decision was upheld by the Court of Appeal. The child appealed to the House of Lords, arguing that his right to respect for his private and family life under Article 8 of the ECHR meant that he was entitled to protection against harmful publicity concerning his family.

The House of Lords unanimously dismissed his appeal, holding that cases decided before the Human Rights Act 1998 on the existence and scope of the High Court's inherent jurisdiction to restrain publicity no longer need to be considered. The foundation to restrain publicity now derives from rights under the ECHR. However, the case-law on the inherent jurisdiction is not wholly irrelevant, as it might remain of some interest in regard to the ultimate balancing exercise to be carried out under the provisions of the ECHR. Article 8 was engaged in the case, but the child would not be involved in the trial as a witness or otherwise. The impact of the trial on the child would be indirect. Competing rights of freedom of the press under Article 10 were also engaged but were not outweighed by the rights of the child under Article 8. Given the weight traditionally given to the importance of open reporting of criminal proceedings, it had been important for the judge, in carrying out the exercise required by the ECHR, to begin by acknowledging the force of the argument under Article 10 before considering whether the right of the child under Article 8 was sufficient to outweigh it.

The House of Lords referred to the UN Convention on the Rights of the Child, which protects the privacy of children directly involved in criminal proceedings, but not children indirectly affected by criminal trials.

There have been other cases where the court has refused to make a child a ward of court because freedom of speech prevails. Thus, for example, it was refused in *Re X (A Minor) (Wardship: Jurisdiction)* [1975] Fam 4 where an application was made to ward a child for the purpose of prohibiting the publication of a book containing references to the salacious behaviour of her deceased father which might harm her if the book came to her knowledge. Wardship was refused on the ground that freedom of speech and freedom of publication prevailed over the child's welfare. (For another case involving wardship and restricting publication, see *Re Stedman* [2009] 2 FLR 852; and for a case involving autonomy of the child and freedom to publish, see *Re Roddy (A Child) (Identification: Restriction on Publicity)* [2004] 2 FLR 949, at p. 213 above.)

Summary

▶ It has been increasingly recognised and accepted that children have rights. Some theorists, however, have argued that it is not appropriate to talk about children's 'rights' (because children lack the necessary competence to have rights) and that it is better to talk about children's 'interests' or in terms of the obligations that adults owe them. A particularly difficult dilemma is the extent to which children should have rights of self-determination, in other words autonomy rights. The law must, however, strike a balance between allowing children greater rights of self-determination and ensuring that they are protected by the law. The Children's Commissioners throughout the UK act as champions for children, and have a statutory responsibility to promote the UN Convention on the Rights of the Child.

▶ The UN Convention on the Rights of the Child 1989 (the UNCRC) has been ratified by the UK, but it does not have the same force in the UK as the European Convention for the Protection of Human Rights (the ECHR). This is because it has not been incorporated into UK law (which needs an Act of Parliament) and it does not have its own court to enforce its provisions. However, arguments based on the UNCRC can be used persuasively in court, and judges sometimes refer to it in their decisions. The Government also takes it into account when considering new policies relating to children. The UN Committee on the Rights of the Child is responsible for monitoring the implementation of the UNCRC and produces periodic reports on children's rights, or the lack of them, in Member States.

▶ Children have rights under the European Convention for the Protection of Human Rights (ECHR). The European Court of Human Rights (ECtHR) has recognised that a child's best interests are paramount and can sometimes prevail over parental interests. The ECHR has played a greater role for children in England and Wales since the coming into force of the Human Rights Act 1998. Human rights are used in legal argument and by judges when making decisions, but there are some concerns that they are not being used enough.

▶ *Gillick v West Norfolk and Wisbech Health Authority* (1986) was a landmark case with respect to the autonomy of children in that it gave greater recognition to the right of children to make their own decisions, not just with regard to medical treatment but in other contexts. The case gave rise to the phrases 'Gillick competency' and the 'Gillick competent child' (a child who is old and mature enough to make an informed decision). It also emphasised that it is better to talk about parental responsibilities rather than parental rights, a recommendation which was implemented in the Children Act 1989.

▶ *Gillick* did not, however, give children absolute rights and subsequent cases have shown that children do not always have the final say about medical treatment, or about any other matter, particularly if a proposed course of action is not in their best interests. For instance, in cases where children have refused medical treatment (*Gillick* was about consent), the courts have overridden their wishes notwithstanding that the children have been 'Gillick competent' and section 8 of the Family Law Reform Act 1969 provides that 16- and 17-year-olds can give valid consent to surgical, medical and dental treatment (see, for example, *Re R (A Minor) (Wardship: Medical Treatment)* (1992) and *Re W (A Minor) (Medical Treatment: Court's Jurisdiction)* (1993)). In *R (Axon) v Secretary of State for Health* (2006) it was held that *Gillick* was still good law after the enactment of the Human Rights Act 1998 as its guidelines about medical treatment and parental consent did not infringe parental rights to a private and family life (under Article 8 ECHR). *Gillick* had an impact on the content of the Children Act 1989 as some of its provisions require the court to listen to the wishes and feelings of a '*Gillick* competent child' (see, for example, section 1(1)(a)).

▶ Children's autonomy rights have sometimes been considered in the context of their human rights, as they were, for example, in *Re Axon* above (with respect to medical treatment), *Re Roddy (A Child) (Identification: Restriction on Publication)* (2004) (with respect to publishing a story), and *R (On the Application of Begum) v Headteacher and Governors of Denbigh High School* (2006) (with respect to wearing religious clothing in school).

▶ Parents are not prohibited from using corporal punishment on their children, but section 58 of the Children Act 2004 has outlawed the defence of reasonable punishment for all criminal charges except common assault or battery. Corporal punishment is prohibited in all State and independent schools (by section 548 Education Act 1996).

▶ The rules concerning the representation of children in public law proceedings are different from those which apply in private law proceedings. In public law proceedings (such as for care and supervision orders), a child is automatically made a party to the proceedings and is represented through a Children's Guardian. In private law proceedings (such as for a residence or contact order), a child can be made a party to those proceedings and be represented through a Children's Guardian or can instruct a solicitor without such a person, but this is at the discretion of the court (see Part 16 of the Family Procedure Rules 2010 and *Practice Direction 16A – Representation of Children*). The usual way in which the voice of the child is conveyed is through a welfare report prepared by a Cafcass officer (see section 7 Children Act 1989).

▶ There is some concern that, despite Article 12(2) of the UNCRC and section 1(3)(a) of the Children Act 1989, that the voice of the child is still not being sufficiently heard in private law proceedings. The Government has consulted on the question of allowing separate representation of children in private law proceedings, but no reforms have been made. There has been discussion about judges interviewing children in order to discover their views, and this is a practice which is sometimes used now, but only rarely.

▶ The presumption that children should not give oral evidence in care proceedings (and also in family law proceedings) was overturned by the Supreme Court in *Re W* (2010), and guidelines about this change in the law have been drawn up by the Family Justice Council and approved by the President of the Family Division.

▶ The High Court has an inherent jurisdiction (which includes wardship) to protect children. This is a parental type of jurisdiction. The welfare of the child is the court's paramount consideration in such cases (s 1(1) CA 1989). The High Court's powers are not invoked as often as they once were, following changes introduced by the Children Act 1989. Thus, there are restrictions on local authorities using the inherent jurisdiction and wardship, although they do sometimes invoke them in difficult medical cases involving children. Wardship is useful in complex cases where urgent action is needed, such as in some international child abduction cases and forced marriage cases. It is also useful where the court wishes to retain a supervisory role with respect to a child. The High Court may refuse to exercise its inherent powers and wardship where other interests prevail over the child's welfare, for instance where there is a need to uphold immigration policy or freedom of speech.

Further reading and references

Alston, Parker and Seymour (eds), *Children, Rights and the Law*, 1992, Clarendon Press.

Barton, '*A* v *UK* – The thirty thousand pound caning – An "English vice" in Europe' [1999] CFLQ 63.

Butler-Sloss, Baroness, 'A child's place in the big society' [2010] Fam Law 938.

Caldwell, 'Common law judges and judicial interviewing' [2011] CFLQ 41.

Cave, 'Maximisation of minors' capacity' [2011] CFLQ 431.

Choudhry and Herring, *European Human Rights and Family Law*, 2010, Hart Publishing.

Edwards, 'Imaging Islam ... of meaning and metaphor symbolising the jilbab – *R (Begum)* v *Headteacher and Governors of Denbigh High School*' [2007] CFLQ 247.

Eekelaar, 'The emergence of children's rights' (1986) 6 OJLS 161.

Eekelaar, 'The importance of thinking that children have rights' (1992) 6 IJLF.

Eekelaar, 'The interests of the child and the child's wishes: the role of dynamic self-determinism' (1994) 8 IJLF 42.

Fenwick, 'Clashing rights, the welfare of the child and the Human Rights Act' (2004) 67(6) *Modern Law Review* 889.

Fortin, *Children's Rights and the Developing Law* (3rd edn), 2009, Cambridge University Press.

Fortin, 'A decade of the HRA and its impact on children's rights' [2011] Fam Law 176.

Gilmore, 'Children's refusal of treatment: the debate continues' [2012] Fam Law 973.

Gilmore and Herring, 'Children's refusal of medical treatment: could *Re W* be distinguished?' [2011] Fam Law 715.

Gilmore and Herring, '"No" is the hardest word: consent and children's autonomy' [2011] CFLQ 4.

Hendrick, 'When should the judge and the child meet?' [2011] Fam Law 1148.

Hunter, 'Close encounters of a judicial kind: "hearing" children's "voices" in family law proceedings' [2007] CFLQ 283.

Huxtable, '*Re M (Medical Treatment: Consent)* – time to remove the "flak jacket"' [2000] CFLQ 83.

Macdonald, 'Bringing rights home for children: arguing the UNCRC' [2009] Fam Law 1073.

Macdonald, 'The voice of the child – still a faint cry?' [2008] Fam Law 648.

Macdonald, 'The child's voice in private law: loud enough?' [2009] Fam Law 40.

McFarlane, Mr Justice, 'Mental capacity: one standard for all ages' [2011] Fam Law 479.

Parkinson and Cashmore, *The Voice of the Child in Family Disputes*, 2008, Oxford University Press.

Taylor, 'Reversing the retreat from *Gillick*? *R (Axon)* v *Secretary of State for Health*' [2007] CFLQ 81.

Wall, Rt Hon Lord Justice, 'Separate representation of children' [2007] Fam Law 124.

Walsh, 'Enhancing the participation of children and young people in family proceedings: starting the debate' [2008] Fam Law 431.

Whybrow, 'Children, guardians and rule 9.5' [2004] Fam Law 504.

Websites

Association of Lawyers for Children: www.alc.org.uk

Children are Unbeatable! Alliance: www.childrenareunbeatable.org.uk

Children's Commissioner (for England): www.childrenscommissioner.gov.uk

Children's Commissioner (for Wales): www.childcom.org.uk

Children's Rights Alliance for England: www.crae.org.uk

Coram Children's Legal Centre: www.childrenslegalcentre.com

Department for Education: www.education.gov.uk

End All Corporal Punishment of Children: www.endcorporalpunishment.org

Websites cont'd

National Youth Advocacy Service: www.nyas.net
NSPCC: www.nspcc.org.uk
UN Convention on the Rights of the Child: www.unicef.org/crc

Links to relevant websites can also be found at: www.palgrave.com/law/familylaw8e

Chapter 9

Parents

This chapter deals with the law governing parenthood. It considers first of all the different sorts of parent and the importance of parents. It next considers the issue of parentage, and then looks at parental responsibility and the various rights, duties and responsibilities that parents have. It concludes by looking at parenthood in the context of assisted reproduction, in particular with respect to surrogacy arrangements.

9.1 Introduction

(a) Who is a parent?

Most children are brought up by parents with whom they have a biological link, but some children are brought up by a person with whom they have no such link, such as a step-parent, a foster-parent, a guardian (see 9.8), an adoptive parent (see Chapter 15) or a special guardian (see 15.14).

The word 'parent' is not defined in the Children Act 1989 (see Chapter 10). In *Re G (Children) (Residence: Same-Sex Partner)* [2006] UKHL 43, [2006] 2 FLR 629 (below) Baroness Hale considered the meaning of the term 'parent' and said that parents could be classified as 'legal' and/or 'natural' parents and that a person could be, or could become, a natural parent in one of the following three ways: by genetic parenthood (where the parent provides the gametes which produce the child); by gestational parenthood (where the parent conceives and bears the child); or by social and psychological parenthood. Baroness Hale said that in the great majority of cases the child's mother would combine all three types of natural parenthood, and the father would combine two.

The importance of the biological bond between parent and child The weight to be accorded to the biological bond (the 'blood tie') between parent and child has been a question which the courts have sometimes had to address. The courts have generally recognised that it is usually in a child's best interests for the child to be brought up, where possible, by natural (biological) parents. However, although the courts regard natural parenthood as an important and significant factor in determining what is in the best interests of a child, they have been unwilling to describe it as a presumption as the following case (concerning a residence dispute between lesbian partners) shows:

▶ *Re G (Children) (Residence: Same-Sex Partner)* **[2006] UKHL 43, [2006] 2 FLR 629**

CG and CW were a lesbian couple who had two daughters (full sisters) by artificial insemination (by an unknown donor). CG was the children's genetic and gestational mother. When their relationship broke down CW applied for contact and shared residence. A shared residence order was made with CG (the biological mother) being granted a 70 per cent share. When CG moved to Cornwall in breach of a court order requiring the children to live in Leicester, Bracewell J made an order changing the children's primary place of residence to that of CW, as she had no confidence that CG would promote the 'essential close relationship' with

CW and her family. CG's appeal to the Court of Appeal was dismissed and so she appealed to the House of Lords on the basis, *inter alia*, that it was wrong for the courts below to have attached no significance to the fact that she was the children's genetic and gestational mother.

The House of Lords unanimously overturned the decision of the Court of Appeal and reversed the children's living arrangements so that their primary home was once more with CG, the biological mother. It held that it was contrary to the welfare of the children to remove them from their biological mother.

BARONESS HALE: 'I am driven to the conclusion that the courts below have allowed the unusual context of this case to distract them from principles which are of universal application. ... [T]he fact that CG is the natural mother of these children in every sense of that term, while raising no presumption in her favour, is undoubtedly an important and significant factor in determining what will be best for them now and in the future. Yet nowhere is that factor explored in the judgment below ...'

LORD NICHOLLS: '[The welfare of the child] is the court's paramount consideration. In reaching its decision the court should always have in mind that in the ordinary way the rearing of a child by his or her biological parent can be expected to be in the child's best interests, both in the short term and also, importantly, in the longer term. I decry any tendency to diminish the significance of this factor. A child should not be removed from the primary care of his or her biological parents without compelling reasons. Where such a reason exists the judge should spell this out explicitly.'

In the following case, which involved a residence dispute between a child's father and maternal grandmother, the Supreme Court reaffirmed the central message of *Re G*, which is that the child's welfare is the paramount consideration. It held that the correct interpretation of *Re G* was that there should be no presumption in favour of the natural parent as such a presumption would detract from an examination of what is in a child's best interests.

▶ *Re B (A Child) (Residence)* [2009] UKSC 5, [2010] 1 FLR 551

The child, a boy (H) aged 4, whose parents had separated before his birth, had lived from birth with his maternal grandmother. H's mother had lived with him and her mother intermittently but eventually left and did not return. The father's application for a residence order in respect of H (as by this time he had married and his new wife was expecting their child) was refused as the justices found no compelling reasons to disrupt the continuity of care that the grandmother had provided for H. The circuit judge and the Court of Appeal allowed the father's appeal as the justices had erred in law and been plainly wrong in giving disproportionate weight to maintaining the status quo. Applying *Re G* (above), in particular the observations of Lord Nicholls, it held that the court should always bear in mind that, ordinarily, the rearing of a child by his or her biological parent could be expected to be in his or her best interests. The grandmother appealed to the Supreme Court.

The Supreme Court unanimously allowed her appeal. Lord Kerr, giving the leading opinion, held that the justices had not been plainly wrong as they had recognised that H's welfare was the paramount consideration and had carefully evaluated the evidence before them, correctly weighing up the various competing factors. It held that:

1) The circuit judge and the Court of Appeal had misinterpreted *Re G*. In that case, when Lord Nicholls said that courts should keep in mind that the interests of a child will normally be best served by being reared by his or her biological parent, he was doing no more than reflecting common experience that, in general, children tend to thrive when brought up by parents to whom they have been born. All consideration of the importance

of parenthood in private law disputes about residence must be firmly rooted in an examination of what is in the child's best interests. This is the paramount consideration. It is only as a contributor to the child's welfare that parenthood assumes any significance. In common with all other factors bearing on what is in the best interests of the child, it must be examined for its potential to fulfil that aim.

2) Any discussion of a child's right to be brought up by its natural parents is misplaced. The only consideration for the court is the child's welfare; to talk of a child's rights detracts from that consideration.

3) On the facts of the case, in deciding where H's best interests lay, the justices had therefore been right to give significant weight to maintaining the status quo in H's living arrangement.

Everett and Yeatman ([2010] CFLQ 290), who discussed *Re G* and *Re B*, concluded that 'the crucial factor should be the love and commitment shown by the adults in the child's life, not the source of that love, be it genetic or social'. Bainham ([2010] Fam Law 394) has questioned whether the rejection in *Re G* and *Re B* and in other higher court decisions of a rights-based approach in private law disputes is correct.

Step-parents Many children are brought up by step-parents. A step-parent is not a biological parent but a parent created by marriage or civil partnership. Step-parents have legal obligations towards their step-children, including the duty to provide financial support. With respect to a step-child, step-parents can obtain parental responsibility (see 9.5) and apply for section 8 orders (see 10.4). They can also apply to be a special guardian (see 15.14) or an adoptive parent (see Chapter 15) of their step-child.

Foster-parents Foster-parent are persons who act *in loco parentis* for a child on a fairly settled basis. There are two types of foster-parent: those who care for children under a private fostering arrangement; and those who look after children in local authority care. Although they have no 'automatic' parental responsibility in law, they nonetheless have an obligation to care for the child as they have a delegated form of parental responsibility under section 3(5) of the Children Act 1989. They can, however, acquire parental responsibility by means of a residence order (see 10.5), a special guardianship order (see 15.14), or by adoption (see Chapter 15).

(b) The importance of parents

Governments, past and present, recognise the importance of parents and that good parenting improves the life chances of children. They also recognise that parents need support, and sometimes advice and guidance. The current Government has expressed its commitment to promoting good parenting by providing advice and support. It wants parenting advice and support to be considered the norm and it regards good parenting, particularly in the first five years of a child's life, as a key factor influencing social mobility (see *Opening doors, breaking barriers: a strategy for social mobility*, HM Government, 2011; and *Parenting matters: early years and social mobility*, Chris Paterson, Centre Forum, 2011).

The judiciary also recognise the importance of parents (as has been seen above); and so do various statutory provisions. Thus, under the Children Act 1989 parents have, for instance, an automatic right to bring proceedings for a section 8 order (see 10.8 and

10.10), whereas other persons need leave of the court to apply. They also have a right to contact if their child is in care, unless this is contrary to the child's best interests (see 14.8). The adoption legislation also recognises the importance of a child's natural parents, notably in respect of their right to consent or refuse to consent to their child's adoption (see 15.9).

The importance of parents is also recognised in the decisions of the European Court of Human Rights (the ECtHR) which, by virtue of the Human Rights Act 1998, must be taken into account by the courts in England and Wales. For instance, in *Kosmopolou v Greece (Application No. 60457/00)* [2004] 1 FLR 800 the ECtHR held that the bond between a child and his parents amounts to a right to family life under Article 8, and that this right arises from the moment of the child's birth and cannot be broken by subsequent events, other than in exceptional circumstances. The ECtHR held that the mutual enjoyment of each other's company by parent and child constitutes a fundamental element of family life, even if the relationship between the parents has broken down; and that any interference must be justified under Article 8(2), applying the principle of proportionality and the principle of the best interests of the child.

Courts and public authorities in the UK must abide by the provisions of the ECHR, as a result of their obligations under the HRA 1998 (see 1.8), and must therefore do their best to foster co-operation between parents in order to maintain the bond between parent and child (see also *Johansen v Norway* (1997) 23 EHRR 33; and *K and T v Finland* [2001] 2 FLR 707). Thus, for instance, the failure of a court in England and Wales to enforce a contact order, or the failure of social services to allow a parent to have contact with a child in care, might amount to a breach of a parent's and a child's right to family life under Article 8 of the ECHR.

The importance of parents is also recognised in the UN Convention on the Rights of the Child 1989 (see 8.2). Thus Article 5 provides that 'States Parties shall respect the responsibilities, rights and duties of parents'; and Article 18(1) requires States Parties to 'use their best efforts to ensure recognition of the principle that both parents have common responsibilities for the upbringing and development of the child, and that parents or guardians have the primary responsibility for the upbringing and development of the child'.

9.2 Parentage

(a) Establishing parentage

Sometimes it may be necessary to establish a child's parentage. For example, a man may need to prove that he is the father so that he can seek an order under the Children Act 1989 (for example, a parental responsibility order, or a contact or residence order). A mother may need to prove paternity so that the father can be required to pay child maintenance. Parentage may also need to be proved for the purpose of amending a birth certificate, establishing inheritance rights or for immigration reasons.

(i) Presumptions of parentage Certain presumptions exist in respect of parentage. Under the presumption of legitimacy, a child born to a married woman is presumed to be the child of the married couple. This presumption applies to any child conceived or born during marriage, or born within the normal gestation period if the marriage is terminated by divorce or death. Under the presumption of birth registration, the entry

of a man's name on the birth register as a child's father is *prima facie* evidence that he is the father (s 10 Births and Deaths Registration Act 1953).

These presumptions, however, are of much less relevance today as parentage can be established with virtually 100 per cent certainty by means of DNA profiling. In fact, the Court of Appeal in *Re H and A (Paternity: Blood Tests)* [2002] EWCA Civ 383, [2002] 1 FLR 1145 held that such presumptions should not be relied on when scientific tests can be carried out (see below).

(ii) Directing a scientific test   Provisions governing the use of scientific tests for determining parentage in civil proceedings are laid down in sections 20–25 of the Family Law Reform Act 1969. Special provisions exist under the Child Support Act 1991 in respect of determining parentage for child support purposes.

Section 20(1) of the Family Law Reform Act 1969

'In any civil proceedings in which the parentage of any person falls to be determined, the court may, either of its own motion or on an application by any party to the proceedings, give a direction –

(a) for the use of scientific tests to ascertain whether such tests show that a party to the proceedings is or is not the father or mother of that person; and

(b) for the taking, within a period specified in the direction, of bodily samples from all or any of the following, namely, that person, any party who is alleged to be the father or mother of that person and any other party to the proceedings;

and the court may at any time revoke or vary a direction previously given by it under this subsection.'

'Bodily sample' means a sample of bodily fluid or bodily tissue taken for the purpose of scientific tests (s 25). The scientific test must be carried out by an accredited body (s 20(1A)) and the result must be reported to the court (s 20(2)). The court can draw such inferences as appear proper in the circumstances if a person fails to comply with any step required for the purpose of giving effect to a section 20 direction for scientific testing (s 23(1)) (see, for instance, *Re P (Identity of Mother)* [2011] EWCA Civ 795, where a 15-year-old girl refused to give consent to give bodily samples for DNA testing in order to establish her maternity).

Consent is required (section 21)   Adults and persons aged 16 or over must give their consent to a bodily sample being taken (s 21(1)). The consent of a young person aged 16 or 17 is effective as if he or she were an adult (s 21(2)). If the child is under 16, then the person with care and control of the child must give consent, but, if this is not forthcoming, the court can give consent, provided it is in the child's best interests to do so (s 21(3)). In *Re P (Identity of Mother)* (see above), it was felt appropriate to obtain the consent of the 15-year-old girl whose maternity was in dispute.

The approach of the courts   The approach of the courts is laid down in the following case in which Thorpe LJ stated the principles which apply to an application for a scientific test:

▶ *Re H and A (Paternity: Blood Tests)* [2002] EWCA Civ 383, [2002] 1 FLR 1145

The applicant applied for contact with, and parental responsibility for, twins who were living with their mother and her husband. He believed that he was their father, as he had had a sexual relationship with the mother. When the mother challenged his claim to paternity he applied for blood samples to be taken from the twins with the court's consent (under section 23(1)(b) FLRA 1969). The judge refused the application, because of the possible disastrous disintegrative effects upon the mother's family unit if the applicant was proved to be the father. The father appealed.

The Court of Appeal allowed his appeal and remitted the case for a retrial, as there had been fundamental flaws in the judge's assessment of the individual factors which had to be brought into the essential balancing exercise. Thorpe LJ held that the following two principles applied to cases on establishing parentage:

▶ That the interests of justice are best served by the ascertainment of the truth; and
▶ That the court should be provided with the best available science and not be confined to such unsatisfactory alternatives as presumptions and inferences.

In parentage cases, the interests of justice and the child's right to know the truth are important considerations but they are subject to the child's welfare, which is the court's paramount consideration. Thus, the general principle is that scientific tests should be ordered unless it would be contrary to the child's best interests.

The child's rights and best interests   A child has a right to be cared for by his or her parents and a right to know his or her true identity. Thus, according to the UN Convention on the Rights of the Child, a child has 'as far as possible, the right to know and be cared for by his parents' (Art 7(1)). States Parties must 'respect the right of the child to preserve his or her identity, including...family relations' (Art 8(1)); and, if a child is illegally deprived of some or all of the elements of his or her identity', States Parties must 'provide assistance and protection with a view to speedily re-establishing his or her identity' (Art 8(2)). In *Re H (Paternity: Blood Tests)* [2001] 2 FLR 65 Ward LJ, referring to Article 7(1), stated that 'every child has a right to know the truth unless his welfare clearly justifies the cover-up'. The right to family life (guaranteed by Article 8 ECHR, see p. 15) may also provide a justification for the truth to be known.

▶ *Re T (Paternity: Ordering Blood Tests)* [2001] 2 FLR 1190

The applicant, who believed he had fathered a child during a sexual relationship with a friend's wife, wanted blood tests to be taken for DNA sampling to prove his paternity as a preliminary to applying for parental responsibility and contact. He relied on the right to family life in Article 8 of the ECHR. Bodey J ordered the tests to be taken, as it was in the child's best interests to be sure about his father's identity, and suspicions about the child's identity were already in the public domain. Bodey J balanced the rights of the adults and the child under Article 8, but held that the child's right to know his true identity carried most weight. Any interference with the mother's and her husband's rights to family life under Article 8 was proportionate to the legitimate aim of providing such knowledge to the child.

Refusing to direct a scientific test   Although the court will usually direct a scientific test (because it is usually in the child's best interests to know the truth), it may refuse to do so where it is contrary to a child's best interests. For example, in *Re D (Paternity)* [2007] 2 FLR 26 a test was refused as it was not in the best interests of the child (a boy aged 11 who was not *Gillick* competent) due to the turbulence in his life and his strong resistance to scientific testing. A test was also refused in *Re J (Paternity: Welfare of Child)* [2007] 1 FLR 1064, as the undoubted advantage of the child learning the truth was outweighed by the impact that the process of revealing the child's paternity would have on the child's mother and family upon whom the child was dependent.

Fortin has argued ([2009] CFLQ 336) that, although the idea of children having a right to know their origins appears to be reasonable, there are risks involved, and that it may not necessarily be in a child's best interests to know his or her parent. She states that the child's human right to know his or her parents is not an absolute right; and that when 'dealing with applications from putative fathers, it is arguable that the domestic courts are extending a child's right to know beyond its appropriate boundaries'.

Paternity fraud   Where a person fraudulently assures another person that he or she is the child's parent, but knows this is not so, then that person may be liable under the tort of deceit to pay damages to the wronged person. In *A v B (Damages: Paternity)* [2007] 2 FLR 1051, for example, the claimant was successful in obtaining damages against the defendant mother who had repeatedly and fraudulently assured him that he was the child's biological father, with the result that he had provided maintenance for both the mother and child for several years. Such claims, however, are rare.

(b)   Declarations of parentage

A declaration of parentage may be required, for instance, to impose (or deny) a child maintenance obligation; or for the purpose of establishing citizenship, nationality or inheritance rights; or to amend a birth certificate.

Under section 55A of the Family Law Act 1986 a person domiciled in England and Wales, or habitually resident in England and Wales for at least one year, can apply for a declaration of parentage (or of non-parentage). Persons seeking to establish that they are a parent or that a named person is their parent have an unqualified right to apply (s 55A(4)), whereas other persons must prove a sufficient personal interest in the determination of the application before the court can hear their case (s 55A(3)).

The court can refuse to hear an application which is not in the child's best interests (s 55A(3)); and, if it does so, then it can order that no further application may be made without leave of the court (s 55A(6)).

The child's involvement in proceedings   A failure to involve a child in proceedings for a declaration of status may be a breach of the child's human rights as the following case shows:

> ▶ *Re L (Family Proceedings Court) (Appeal: Jurisdiction)* [2005] 1 FLR 210
>
> A girl (aged 15), who had learned that her parentage was in doubt, applied for permission to appeal a declaration of parentage which had been made under section 55A of the FLA 1986 for the purposes of child support. She alleged breaches of her rights under Article 6 ECHR (right to a fair trial) and Article 8 ECHR (right to family life), as the declaration affecting her status had been made without reference to her or her mother. She had not been a party to proceedings, had not been given notice of proceedings, and had not been given the opportunity to be heard or to make representations.
>
> Munby J held that it was not disputed that she was fully entitled to invoke what she correctly described as a basic and fundamental human right. Information about one's biological father went to the very heart of a person's identity (*per* Scott Baker J in *Rose v Secretary of State for Health and Human Fertilisation and Embryology Authority* [2002] 2 FLR 962). As her human rights had been infringed the decision could not stand. She had not been given a fair hearing or a fair trial (Art 6), and the declaration breached her rights under Article 8. She was entitled to have the order made by the family proceedings court set aside.

Adoption – declaration of parentage   A declaration of parentage may be useful in the context of adoption, as it was in *M v W (Declaration of Parentage)* [2007] 2 FLR 270 where the petitioner, an adopted adult, applied for a declaration of parentage in respect of his natural father who had died in Australia and with whom he had never had any contact. Hogg J, granting the declaration, drew attention to the importance of adopted persons knowing about their background and said that the declaration would be of assistance to the petitioner, and his children, in relation to medical conditions or genetic make-up. Furthermore, the declaration would not affect the validity of the adoption order.

(c)   Declarations of legitimacy or legitimation

Under section 56 of the Family Law Act 1986 a person may apply to the High Court or a county court for a declaration in respect of legitimacy or legitimation. An application under this provision can only be made by a child. The court can make a declaration that: the applicant is the legitimate child of his or her parents; or that the applicant has (or has not) become a legitimated person.

9.3   Parental responsibility

This section looks at parental responsibility and shows how some persons have such responsibility without the need to acquire it, but how other persons, including unmarried fathers, can acquire it.

> **Section 3(1) of the Children Act 1989**
>
> 'In this Act 'parental responsibility' means all the rights, duties, powers, responsibilities and authority which by law a parent of a child has in relation to the child and his property.'

The law governing parental responsibility is laid down in the Children Act 1989 and in related case-law. 'Parental responsibility', not 'parental rights', is the term used in the Children Act to describe parental interests in children. 'Responsibility' was chosen as the preferred term in order to reflect the idea that children are persons to whom duties are owed rather than persons over whom power is wielded. As Lord Scarman had said in *Gillick* (see 8.4), parental rights are derived from parental duty.

The Family Justice Review (FJR) in its final report (*Family Justice Review: Final Report*, Ministry of Justice, 2011) (see further at p. 7) stated that the nature of parental responsibility needed to be better understood, and it recommended that the Government should find ways of strengthening the importance of a good understanding of parental responsibility in the information it gives to parents. The Government accepted the FJR's recommendations and in its response stated that it recognised that 'parents are not always aware of the concept or significance of parental responsibility, nor of the adverse impact on children of prolonged parental conflict', and that it would therefore consider 'how best to raise awareness of parental responsibility and to support parents in focusing on their child's needs, both in terms of timing and channels of communication' (*The Government Response to the Family Justice Review*, Department of Education and Ministry of Justice, 2012, para 65).

(a) Who has parental responsibility?

Some persons have 'automatic' parental responsibility (PR), whereas other persons have to acquire it. The advantage of having PR is that it allows parents (and other persons who acquire it) to make important decisions about the child.

(i) 'Automatic' parental responsibility Over the years, the list of persons who have 'automatic' PR has lengthened due in part to the introduction of civil partnership and to changes in the law governing assisted fertilisation under the Human Fertilisation and Embryology Act 2008 (HFEA 2008).

The Children Act 1989 (CA 1989) provides that the following persons have 'automatic' PR for the child:

- *Married parents* (s 2(1)).
- *An unmarried mother* (s 2(2)).
- *A mother and her civil partner who is a parent by virtue of section 42 of the Human Fertilisation and Embryology Act 2008 (HFEA 2008)* (s 2(1A)(a)).
- *The mother and her female partner who is a parent by virtue of section 43 HFEA 2008* (s 2(1A)(b)).
- *A mother who is parent by virtue of section 43 HFEA 2008* (s 2(2A)) (a mother who has a child by assisted reproduction).

(ii) Persons who can acquire parental responsibility The Children Act 1989 enables the following persons to acquire PR:

- *An unmarried father* (s 4).
- *A step-parent (whether by marriage or civil partnership)* (s 4A) (see, for instance, *Re R (Parental Responsibility)* [2011] EWHC 1535 (Fam); [2011] 2 FLR 1132, but where PR was refused on the facts).

▶ *A female non-biological parent in a same-sex female relationship* (s 4ZA) (see, for instance, *T v T* [2010] EWCA Civ 1366 where the mother's civil partner was granted PR).

Other persons   Parental responsibility (PR) can be acquired by other persons by means of: a residence order (see 10.5); a special guardianship order (see 15.14); or an adoption order (see Chapter 15). Local authorities have a limited kind of PR when a child is in care (see Chapter 14); and the court has PR when a child is a ward of court (see 8.7).

More than one person can have PR for a particular child (s 2(5) CA 1989); and PR does not terminate when another person acquires it (s 2(6)), except in the case of adoption which involves a complete legal transfer of PR (see Chapter 15). It is not lost when a child goes into local authority care; and it does not terminate on parental separation, or on the legal termination of a marriage or civil partnership. It terminates when a child reaches the age of majority or if a child is adopted. It can, in some circumstances, be terminated by a court order (see p. 244 below).

(b)   The exercise of parental responsibility

Persons with parental responsibility (PR) can act independently of each other in meeting such responsibility except where the law requires the consent of both parents (and other person(s) with PR), such as when: removing the child from the UK; consenting to the child's adoption; deciding on the child's education; changing the child's surname; consenting to serious or irreversible medical treatment; and consenting to the child's marriage if he or she is under the age of majority.

If the parents cannot agree or consent is not forthcoming, then the court's consent can be obtained by applying for a specific issue order (see 10.8) or by invoking the wardship or inherent jurisdiction of the High Court (see 8.7). Serious medical treatment may need the consent of the court even if both parents are in agreement about the treatment (see 9.7).

Persons with PR are prohibited from exercising it in a way which is incompatible with a court order made under the Children Act 1989 (s 2(8)). Where persons who share PR cannot agree on a particular course of action an application can be made for a section 8 order (see 10.4) or, in some cases, to the High Court under its wardship or inherent jurisdiction (see 8.7).

In certain circumstances, a person who is caring for the child (but who does not have PR for that child) may (subject to the provisions of the Children Act 1989) 'do what is reasonable in all the circumstances of the case for the purpose of safeguarding or promoting the child's welfare' (s 3(5) CA 1989). This provision enables, for example, a doctor to act without parental or judicial consent in an emergency. As Munby J said in *R (G) v Nottingham City Council* [2008] 1 FLR 1660, doctors and midwives do not have to stand idly by waiting for a court order if a premature baby desperately needs to be put in a special unit or placed on a ventilator.

Parental responsibility is not transferable   A person with PR cannot surrender or transfer any of that responsibility, although he or she may arrange for some or all of it to be met by one or more persons acting on his or her behalf (s 2(9)), including another person with PR (s 2(10)). Thus it is lawfully permissible to place the child with a person acting *in loco parentis* (for example a child-minder or babysitter) or with someone else with PR. However, as a person with PR cannot escape liability under the criminal or civil law by delegating that responsibility to another person (s 2(11)), the onus is on parents to make proper arrangements for their children.

9.4 Unmarried fathers and parental responsibility

(a) Unmarried fathers do not have 'automatic' parental responsibility

An unmarried father does not have parental responsibility (PR) for his child just because he is the child's natural parent (s 2(2)). Thus, unless he has acquired PR (see further below), his rights with respect to his child are limited. For instance, he has no legal right to consent to his child's adoption or removal from the UK.

The reason why unmarried fathers were not given 'automatic' PR by the Children Act 1989 was because of concerns that it might not be in the best interests of some children and mothers. The rationale for not giving unmarried fathers automatic PR was explained by Balcombe LJ in *Re H (Illegitimate Child: Father: Parental Rights) (No. 2)* [1991] 1 FLR 214:

> 'The position of the natural father can be infinitely variable; at one end of the spectrum his connection with the child may be only the single act of intercourse (possibly even rape) which led to conception; at the other end of the spectrum he may have played a full part in the child's life from birth onwards, only the formality of marriage to the mother being absent. Considerable social evils might have resulted if the father at the bottom of the spectrum had been automatically granted full parental rights and duties.'

A similar view was taken by the European Court of Human Rights (the ECtHR) in *McMichael v UK (Application No. 16424/90)* (1995) 20 EHRR 205 where it held that, compared with married fathers, unmarried fathers inevitably vary in their commitment and interest in, or even knowledge of, their children. However, the ECtHR held that, as a general rule, unmarried fathers who had an established family life with their children should be able to claim rights of contact and custody equal to those of married fathers. In the following case, however, the ECtHR held that the lack of automatic PR for unmarried fathers in the UK did not breach their human rights:

▶ *B v UK* [2000] 1 FLR 1

An unmarried father without PR complained that his inability to obtain a declaration that his child had been unlawfully removed from the UK (because he had no custody rights) was a breach of his right to family life under Article 8 ECHR and was therefore discriminatory under Article 14 ECHR.

The ECtHR dismissed his claim and held that unmarried fathers in the UK are not discriminated against because they have no automatic PR. It held that, as the relationship between unmarried fathers and their children varies from ignorance and indifference to a close stable relationship indistinguishable from the conventional family-based unit, the UK Government had an objective and reasonable justification for the difference in treatment between married and unmarried fathers with regard to the automatic acquisition of parental rights.

Since the implementation of the Children Act 1989 there has been increasing concern about unmarried fathers not having 'automatic' PR and about the injustices it may cause.

As a result, in December 2003 the law was changed to give PR automatically to unmarried fathers who are registered on their child's birth certificate with the mother (see below).

(b) The unmarried father – acquiring parental responsibility

An unmarried father can acquire parental responsibility (PR) for his child by: joint birth registration with the mother (see below); making a PR agreement with the mother (see below); obtaining a PR order (see below); obtaining a residence order (see 10.4); becoming the child's guardian on the mother's death (see 9.8); adopting the child (see Chapter 15); obtaining a special guardianship order (see 15.14); or by marrying the mother (s 1 Legitimacy Act 1976). Once a father has acquired PR he has the same rights as a married father, except that his PR can be terminated by the court (except where he has acquired it by adoption or marriage). In this respect, unmarried fathers are still discriminated against.

(i) Acquiring parental responsibility by birth registration   Under sections 4(1)(a) and 4(1A) of the Children Act 1989 an unmarried father has PR for his child if he is registered with the child's mother on the child's birth certificate under sections 10(1)(a)–(c) and 10A(1) of the Births and Deaths Registration Act 1953. These provisions came into force in December 2003. Acquiring PR in this way is not, however, permanent, as it can be terminated by court order. There have been proposals to introduce compulsory joint birth registration by unmarried parents (see p. 248 below).

(ii) Acquiring parental responsibility by agreement with the child's mother   Under section 4(1)(b) CA 1989 an unmarried father can enter into a PR agreement with the mother and thereby acquire PR for his child. The agreement is made on a prescribed form (available at HM Courts' Service) which must be signed by both parties, witnessed and then registered in the Principal Registry of the Family Division. There is no judicial scrutiny of the agreement, but PR acquired in this way can be revoked by court order. A local authority has no power to stop the mother of a child in care from entering into a PR agreement with the child's father (*Re X (Parental Responsibility Agreement: Children in Care)* [2000] 1 FLR 517).

(iii) Acquiring parental responsibility by parental responsibility order   An unmarried father can apply to the court under section 4(1)(c) CA 1989 for an order giving him PR. When considering whether or not to grant the order, the child's welfare is the court's paramount consideration (see s 1(1)). The other welfare principles apply, but not the welfare checklist (see p. 267). In *Re H (Minors) (Local Authority: Parental Rights) (No. 3)* [1991] Fam 151 Balcombe LJ held that the following three factors are important when the court is considering whether to make an order:

▶ the degree of commitment which the father has shown towards the child;
▶ the degree of attachment which exists between the father and the child; and
▶ the father's reasons or motivation for applying for the order.

The Court of Appeal has stated, however, that these factors are only a starting point and that other factors can be taken into account (see *Re H (Parental Responsibility)* [1998] 1 FLR 855). Even where these three factors are satisfied, the court may nonetheless decide that making a PR order is contrary to the child's best interests (as it was held to be, for example, in *Re B (Role of Biological Father)* [2008] 1 FLR 1015).

As the court recognises the important status conferred by a PR order, it will usually make the order unless it is clearly contrary to the child's welfare. Thus, PR orders have been made even where there is acrimony between the parents (*Re P (A Minor) (Parental Responsibility Order)* [1994] 1 FLR 578) or where PR cannot be exercised (*Re H (A Minor) (Parental Responsibility)* [1993] 1 FLR 484). Failure to provide maintenance may not of itself provide a reason for refusing an order (*Re H (Parental Responsibility: Maintenance)* [1996] 1 FLR 867). In *Re S (Parental Responsibility)* [1995] 2 FLR 648 the Court of Appeal stated that, as a PR order granted an important status, it was wrong to place an undue and false emphasis on the rights, duties and powers that come with PR because any abuse of its exercise could be controlled by making a section 8 order under the Children Act 1989 (see 10.4).

Despite the willingness of the courts to make a PR order (as it confers an important status), an order may be refused in an exceptional case, as it was, for example, in *Re H (Parental Responsibility)* [1998] 1 FLR 855) where the father had physically harmed the child; and in *Re P (Parental Responsibility)* [1998] 2 FLR 96, where the father was found to be in possession of obscene pictures of young children.

(c) Termination and revocation of parental responsibility agreements and orders

Termination   Parental responsibility (PR) agreements and parental responsibility orders terminate when the child reaches 18, unless terminated earlier by court order (ss 91(7), (8) CA 1989).

Revocation   A person who has acquired PR under section 4(1) CA 1989 (by birth registration, agreement or court order) can have it revoked by a court order made under section 4(2A) on an application made by any person with PR for the child or, with leave (permission) of the court, the child (s 4(3)). The court can only grant leave to the child if he or she has sufficient understanding to make the application (s 4(4)).

In revocation applications the child's welfare is the court's paramount consideration (s 1(1)). Each case depends on its own facts, but PR will only be revoked in exceptional circumstances. Thus, as PR confers an important status, there is a strong presumption in favour of its continuance. It cannot be terminated, for instance, where a mother is dissatisfied with the father. Cases where it was revoked include, for instance, *Re P (Terminating Parental Responsibility)* [1995] 1 FLR 1048) (where the child suffered severe non-accidental injuries as a very young baby at the hands of the father who had shown no attachment or commitment to the child) and *Re F (Indirect Contact)* [2007] 1 FLR 1015 (where the father had a history of serious and uncontrollable violence). Although revocation of the father's PR in these cases seemed appropriate in the circumstances, it is possible to argue that the law continues to discriminate against unmarried fathers because it would not have been possible for the court to remove the PR of the fathers had they been married. Thus, in *Re M (A Minor) (Care Order: Threshold Conditions)* [1994] 2 AC 424, [1994] 2 FLR 577 for example, the married father had murdered the mother in the presence of the children, but there was no question of him losing his PR.

9.5 Step-parents and other persons – acquiring parental responsibility

(a) Step-parents

Under section 4A of the Children Act 1989 a step-parent (whether by marriage or civil partnership) can acquire parental responsibility (PR) for a step-child by means of a PR agreement or a PR order. Other ways of acquiring PR are by means of a special guardianship order (see 15.14), a residence order (see 10.5), or an adoption order (see Chapter 15).

(i) A parental responsibility agreement (section 4A(1)(a)) The child's parent(s) who have PR may enter into an agreement with the step-parent to provide for the latter to have PR for the child. This involves filling in a prescribed form (s 4A(2)). The agreement takes effect once it has been received and recorded at the Principal Registry of the Family Division.

(ii) Parental responsibility order (section 4A(1)(b)) The court may, on the application of a step-parent, order that the step-parent shall have PR for the child. The welfare of the child is the court's paramount consideration (under section 1(1) CA 1989) and the other principles in section 1 apply, other than the welfare checklist.

(iii) Termination of parental responsibility A step-parent's PR (whether acquired by agreement or court order) can be terminated by the court on the application of any person with PR or, with leave of the court, the child (s 4A(3)). The court can grant leave to the child to apply for termination of the order, provided it is satisfied that the child has sufficient understanding to make the proposed application (s 4A(4)).

(b) The female non-biological parent in a same-sex female relationship

A female non-biological parent in a same-sex female relationship can acquire PR in relation to the child by joint birth registration or by way of a PR agreement or PR order (s 4ZA CA 1989, inserted by the Human Fertilisation and Embryology Act 2008). PR acquired in any of these ways can be terminated by court order (s 4ZA(5)).

(c) Other persons

Persons other than those above can acquire parental responsibility (PR) by obtaining a residence order (see 10.5), a special guardianship order (see 15.14), or an adoption order (see Chapter 15).

In *Re A (Joint Residence: Parental Responsibility)* [2008] 2 FLR 1593, for example, an unmarried man acquired PR by way of a residence order (made under section 12(4) in his and the mother's favour) because he was unable to apply for a PR order for, although he had been at the child's birth and had lived with the child and the mother for two years before the relationship had broken down, he was subsequently found not to be the biological father. The trial judge made a joint residence order under section 12(2) CA 1989, as this was the only way in which he could obtain PR, and the decision was upheld by the Court of Appeal as a legitimate means by which PR could be acquired.

9.6 Parental responsibility and parental rights

The definition of 'parental responsibility' in section 3(1) of the Children Act 1989, which defines it as 'all the rights, duties, powers, responsibilities and authority which by law a parent of a child has in relation to the child and his property', is not very helpful as it does not define its precise nature and scope. This must be deduced instead from statute and case-law.

(a) What rights do parents have?

Despite the emphasis on parental responsibility in the Children Act 1989, parents do have rights. They have a right, for instance, to bring proceedings under the Children Act 1989 and to challenge a local authority's decision to institute care and supervision proceedings. In fact section 3(1) (see above) mentions the word 'rights' in its definition of parental responsibility, and in the *Gillick* case (see further at 8.4) Lord Scarman, while recognising that 'responsibility' was a more appropriate term than 'rights', nevertheless stated that parental rights clearly existed, but that the law had never treated such rights as 'sovereign or beyond review and control'.

Parental have a wide range of rights. They also have duties to their children, in particular a duty to provide maintenance (see Chapter 12). Some parental rights are also duties. For example, a parent has both a right and a duty to register the child's birth. Unmarried fathers without PR have some, but not all, of the rights below.

Parental rights are not absolute   Parents' rights are not absolute, as they are subject to the principle that the child's welfare is the court's paramount consideration. Parental wishes can therefore be overridden by the court. In *Re Z (A Minor) (Freedom of Publication)* [1996] 1 FLR 191 Sir Thomas Bingham MR said that if a parental decision 'is in accord with that of the devoted and responsible parent, well and good', but that, if not, then 'it is the duty of the court ... to give effect to its own judgment'.

Thus, the court can restrain a parent from doing any act which might adversely affect the child's welfare. For example, parental consent to adoption can be dispensed with if this is in the child's best interests; and in applications for orders under the Children Act 1989 the child's welfare, not parental wishes, is paramount. In the context of medical treatment for a child, parental wishes can be overridden (see 9.7 below); and children who suffer significant harm can be taken into local authority care, whereupon PR is not removed from the child's parents, but the local authority is 'in the driving seat' (see Chapter 14).

(b) Important parental rights

The following parental rights are particularly important:

(i) A right to the physical possession of the child   The criminal and civil law relating to child abduction (see Chapter 14), and the restriction in section 13 of the Children Act 1989 on removing a child from the UK (when the child is subject to a residence order) show that parents have a right to physical possession of their child. This right is also evidenced by the fact that under the Children Act 1989 a parent can ask a local authority to hand the child back if the child is not subject to a care or emergency protection order. The right to physical possession also includes the right to decide where the child lives. Thus,

for example, when a child is accommodated in local authority care under a voluntary arrangement a local authority cannot place the child in accommodation against parental wishes (see *R v Tameside Metropolitan Borough Council ex parte J* [2000] 1 FLR 942). The right to physical possession also includes the right to decide on travel and emigration, although this right is subject to certain controls and safeguards.

(ii) A right to have contact with the child   The section 8 contact order (see 10.6) and the presumption of reasonable contact with a child in local authority care (see 14.8) show that parents have a right to contact with their child. But this right is not an absolute or fundamental right as it can be terminated by court order where it is in the child's best interests. However, the law encourages parent–child contact, as contact is generally considered to be beneficial for the child. As contact is also considered to be a right of the child (see p. 295), then contact is not just a parental right but also a parental duty, provided this is in the child's best interests.

(iii) A right to decide on education   Parents have a legal duty to ensure that a child of compulsory school age receives efficient full-time education (suitable to the child's age, ability and aptitude, and to any special needs) either by regular attendance at school or otherwise (s 7 Education Act 1996). The words 'or otherwise' in section 7 permit parents to lawfully educate their children at home, provided it is an efficient and suitable education. Children in the state education system must be educated in accordance with parental wishes so far as this is compatible with the provision of efficient instruction and training and the avoidance of unreasonable public expenditure (s 9 Education Act 1996).

(iv) A right to choose the child's religion   Parents have a right to choose the child's religion (if any), at least until the child becomes '*Gillick* competent' (see further at 8.4). Parents have the right to choose to remove their child from religious instruction and school assemblies. The importance of religion is also reflected in statutory provisions relating to fostering and adoption placements, as the local authority and adoption agency must take into consideration the child's religious beliefs and background. However, parental rights with respect to their child's religious beliefs are not absolute, and in some circumstances the best interests of the child will prevail (for instance in the context of religious objections to medical treatment (see 9.7) and with regard to corporal punishment in schools (see 8.5).

(v) A right to consent to medical treatment   (see 9.7 below).

(vi) A right to consent to the child's marriage or civil partnership   Where a child is aged over 16 but under 18, the child's parents and other persons with parental responsibility must give their consent to the marriage or civil partnership. However, failure to do so is unlikely to invalidate the marriage or civil partnership.

(vii) A right to choose the child's surname and to register the child's birth   Although a child traditionally takes the father's surname, this is not a legal requirement as a parent can choose any surname for the child. If there is a residence order in force, then the surname of the child who is the subject of that order cannot be changed without the *written* consent of all persons with parental responsibility, or otherwise with permission of the court (s 13(1) Children Act 1989).

Parents have a statutory duty to register the child's birth under the Births and Deaths Registration Act 1953. If the mother and father are married either parent can register the child's birth. If they are not married, only the unmarried mother can register the birth, and the registrar is not permitted to enter the name of any person as the child's father in the register, unless: both parents attend together and make a joint request to register the birth; or one of them makes a request to register the child's birth and provides a statutory declaration acknowledging paternity. If both unmarried parents are registered on the birth certificate the father has parental responsibility for the child with the mother (see p. 243 above). If a child is legitimated by the parents' subsequent marriage, the parents must re-register the child's birth (s 9 Legitimacy Act 1976).

Compulsory birth registration for unmarried couples The Labour Government introduced reforms (under section 56 and Schedule 6 of the Welfare Reform Act 2009) to make joint birth registration compulsory for unmarried couples (subject to certain safeguards), but these reforms have not been implemented. The aim of this reform was not only to give unmarried fathers parental responsibility (which can be acquired by birth registration, see p. 243 above), but also to promote the involvement of both unmarried parents in the child's upbringing. (For the background to the reforms, see the White Paper, *Joint Birth Registration: Recording Responsibility*, Cm 7293, 2008.) Wallbank ([2009] CFLQ 267) has challenged the assumption that a child's welfare is necessarily best served by having two parents with parental responsibility.

Birth registration by female couples   Since 1 September 2009 (as a result of amendments made to the Births and Deaths Regulations 1987 by the Human Fertilisation and Embryology Act 2008), female couples have been able to register the birth of their child conceived as a result of fertility treatment, and with both female parents' names being included on the birth certificate. These provisions apply only to female couples who had fertility treatment on or after 6 April 2009.

(viii) A right to consent to the child's adoption   Parents with parental responsibility have a right to consent to their child's adoption, although consent may be dispensed with in certain circumstances (see Chapter 15).

(ix) A right to discipline the child and to administer reasonable punishment   A parent has a right and a duty to discipline a child, but the use of certain forms of corporal punishment is a criminal offence (see 8.5).

(x) Other rights   Parents have other rights. Thus, they can administer the child's property and enter into contracts on the child's behalf. They have a right to appoint a guardian for the child (see 9.8). They also have rights to apply for court orders in respect of their children (see Chapter 10); and a right to apply for child support (see Chapter 12).

9.7 Parents and children – medical treatment

The *Gillick* case (see 8.4) did not remove the right and duty of parents to consent to their child's medical treatment. In fact the Department of Health and Social Security circular, which was the subject of Mrs Gillick's wrath, stated that doctors should act on the presumption that parents should be consulted before contraceptives were prescribed to teenage girls.

If a child is a mature minor (in other words he or she is 'Gillick competent'), then parental consent to medical treatment may not be needed. Also, section 8 of the Family Law Reform Act 1969 provides that young persons aged 16 or 17 have a statutory right to give valid consent to medical, dental or other treatment (see p. 211). However, despite these principles, the court has the power to override the wishes of children of whatever age and maturity, and those of parents, if it considers the medical treatment, or the withdrawal of medical treatment, is in the best interests of the child.

(a) Disputes between parents and doctors about a child's medical treatment

Although a failure to obtain parental consent can result in a medical practitioner being liable for assault under the civil and/or criminal law, parental rights in medical matters are not absolute as their wishes can be overridden by the court. Where there is a dispute between the medical profession and parents the court will be asked to intervene. The usual procedure is for the hospital or National Health Service Trust to seek a declaration from the High Court under its inherent jurisdiction (see 8.7). Another option, which is used less often, is to apply for a section 8 specific issue order under the Children Act 1989 (see 10.8), which requires leave of the court to apply if the applicant is not the child's parent or guardian.

If doctors treat, or fail to treat, a child in defiance of parental wishes, this may be a breach of the right to family life of the parent and child under Article 8 of the ECHR. For example, in *Glass v UK (Application No. 61827/00)* [2004] 1 FLR 1019 (where doctors, in contravention of the mother's wishes, stopped giving medical treatment to her child who was severely mentally and physically disabled) the ECtHR held that the UK was in breach of Article 8, and awarded the mother and child damages. It held that the NHS trust should have sought the intervention of the court before deciding to withdraw medical treatment in contravention of the mother's wishes.

(b) The governing principles in disputes between doctors and parents

The following principles are applied by the court in cases where parents are in dispute with the medical profession:

- The best interests of the child are paramount.
- The matter is to be decided by adopting an objective approach.
- Each case depends on its own particular facts.
- There is a very strong presumption in favour of prolonging life, but there is no obligation on the medical profession to give treatment which would be futile. In *Re J (A Minor) (Wardship: Medical Treatment)* [1991] 1 FLR 366 Lord Donaldson MR said that account had to be taken of the pain and suffering and quality of life which the child will experience if life is prolonged, and the pain and suffering involved in the proposed treatment.

Thus, the court has to conduct a balancing exercise and weigh up the advantages and disadvantages of giving, or withholding, medical treatment in order to decide what is in the child's best interests. While the courts accord great respect to parental wishes, which are usually put into the balancing exercise, such wishes never prevail over the best interests of the child (but for a rare case where they seemed to do so, see *Re T (Wardship: Medical Treatment)* [1997] 1 FLR 502 below).

There are many reported cases involving disputes between parents and the medical profession about the medical treatment of children. Each case depends on its own special facts, applying the principle that the child's welfare is the court's paramount consideration. The following are some examples from the case-law:

▶ *Re B (A Minor) (Wardship: Medical Treatment)* **[1990] 3 All ER 927**

A baby born with Down's syndrome was ordered to have a life-saving operation to remove an intestinal blockage where the parents refused to consent to the operation.

▶ *Re R (A Minor) (Blood Transfusion)* **[1993] 2 FLR 757**

A specific issue order was granted on the application of a local authority ordering that a child with leukaemia be given medical treatment (including blood transfusions) despite the parents' religious objections as they were Jehovah's Witnesses.

▶ *Re T (Wardship: Medical Treatment)* **[1997] 1 FLR 502**

The parents (medical professionals) refused to give consent to their child having a life-saving liver transplant, as they did not wish to care for the child. The court under its inherent jurisdiction, applying the welfare principle, refused to overrule the parents' refusal to consent.

▶ *Local Authority v SB, AB and MB* **[2010] EWHC 1744 (Fam), [2010] 2 FLR 1203**

The parents of a boy aged 6 with a rare and progressive brain disease refused to consent to the boy having surgery as had been recommended in a medical report. Sir Nicholas Wall P, referring to *Re T* above, held that the decision about surgery was for the child's parents as they were the only people with parental responsibility. The question of the boy undergoing surgery was currently a matter between his parents and the hospital. As neither the hospital nor the parents were inviting the court to decide that issue there was no issue for the court to decide.

▶ *Re C (HIV Test)* **[1999] 2 FLR 1004**

A specific issue order was granted on the application of the local authority, so that an HIV test could be carried out on a baby, despite the mother and father's refusal to consent to the test.

▶ *A National Health Service Trust v D* **[2000] 2 FLR 677**

A declaration was granted that the child need not be ventilated, and this was held not to breach Article 2 (right to life) and Article 3 (the right not to suffer inhuman and degrading treatment) of the ECHR.

▶ *Re A (Conjoined Twins: Medical Treatment)* **[2001] 1 FLR 1**

Conjoined twins were ordered to be separated despite their parents' wishes to the contrary, and the fact that separation would inevitably lead to the death of the weaker twin.

▶ *Portsmouth NHS Trust v Wyatt and Wyatt, Southampton NHS Trust Intervening* **[2005] 1 FLR 21**

Hedley J made declarations that further aggressive treatment to prolong the life of a seriously ill one-year-old child was not in her best interests, despite her parents' wishes to the contrary (but see *Portsmouth NHS Trust v Wyatt and Wyatt, Southampton NHS Trust Intervening* [2005] 2 FLR 480 where the restriction was lifted as the child showed signs of improvement).

▶ *NHS Trust v A* **[2008] 1 FLR 70**

The parents of a 6-month-old child refused to consent to the child having a life-saving bone marrow transplant on religious grounds, and because they did not want her to suffer further. The doctors and the child's guardian were in favour of the treatment. Holman J granted the declaration sought by the NHS trust, holding that the question of whether the court should consent to the treatment in the face of disagreement was to be decided by the application of an objective test based on the best interests of the child, considered in the widest sense.

(c)   Seriously invasive medical treatment

Where the medical treatment of a child is seriously invasive the court's consent may be needed. For instance, sterilisation of a child usually requires the prior sanction of the High Court under its inherent or wardship jurisdiction (although an application by way of specific issue order was permitted in *Re HG (Specific Issue Order: Sterilisation)* [1993] 1 FLR 587).

In *Re B (A Minor) (Wardship: Sterilisation)* [1988] AC 199 the House of Lords authorised the sterilisation of a mentally retarded 17-year-old girl under the wardship jurisdiction. In *Re D (A Minor) (Wardship: Sterilisation)* [1976] Fam 185, on the other hand, sterilisation was refused, because the court felt that the girl might be able to give informed consent to the operation at a later date. Consent of the court may not be required, however, where sterilisation is needed for therapeutic reasons, such as to treat cancer of the womb.

(d)   Where parents cannot agree about medical treatment

The consent of the court may be needed in respect of certain types of medical treatment of a child where the child's parents cannot agree between themselves about the treatment. This is so even though section 2(7) of the Children Act 1989 provides that each parent with parental responsibility can act independently of the other. Medical treatment, such as circumcision and immunisation, may, for example, need the court's consent if the child's parents cannot agree about the treatment. The following cases are examples:

▶ *Re J (Specific Issue Orders: Child's Religious Upbringing and Circumcision)* [2000] 1 FLR 571

A Muslim father applied for a specific issue order under section 8 of the Children Act 1989 so that his son (aged 5) could be circumcised, as the child's mother, a Christian, objected to it. The Court of Appeal held that a parental dispute about circumcision is one of the exceptional cases where a disagreement between those who possess parental responsibility must be determined by the courts. The father's application was refused, as the best interests of the child prevailed over the parents' religious beliefs and wishes.

   (See also *Re S (Specific Issue Order: Religion: Circumcision)* [2005] 1 FLR 236 where a Muslim mother's application for a specific issue order authorising her son's circumcision (which the Hindu father had objected to) was refused, as the child might be able to make his own informed choice about circumcision when he was older).

▶ *Re C (Welfare of Child: Immunisation)* [2003] 2FLR 1095

Fathers who had parental responsibility and contact rights were granted specific issue orders ordering that their daughters be immunised with the MMR vaccine, despite the mothers' opposition. Immunisation was held to be in the girls' best interests, applying the welfare principle in section 1(1) of the Children Act 1989. It was not a breach of the mothers' right to family life under Article 8 ECHR, because Article 8(2) allowed a court to interfere with the rights of parents and children in order to protect the health of a child.

(e)   Disputes between parents and children about medical treatment

See 8.4.

9.8 Appointing a guardian for a child

(a) Appointing a guardian for the child

The aim of guardianship is to ensure that there is a person who can exercise parental responsibility for a child on the death of the child's parents. Appointment of a guardian is governed by sections 5 and 6 of the Children Act 1989.

(i) Appointment of a guardian by a parent, guardian or special guardian (section 5) A parent with parental responsibility, a guardian, or a special guardian can appoint a guardian for the child. Two or more persons may do so jointly. The appointment must be: made in writing, and be dated and signed by the person making the appointment. Special provisions apply if the appointer is unable to sign the document, whether made in a will or otherwise.

Revocation, disclaimer and termination of appointment (section 6) An appointment can be revoked by a subsequent appointment or by a written instrument revoking the appointment. An appointment (excluding one made in a will or codicil) can be revoked by the instrument being destroyed, provided it is the appointer's intention to revoke the appointment. An appointment made in a will or codicil is revoked if the will or codicil is revoked.

A person who is appointed as a guardian (other than by an appointment made by the court) can disclaim the appointment by an instrument in writing signed by him or her and made within a reasonable time of first knowing about the appointment. An appointment made by an individual (not the court) is revoked if the person appointed is the spouse or civil partner of the appointer and the marriage or civil partnership is terminated by divorce or dissolution.

Any appointment of a guardian (by an individual or by the court) can be terminated by court order on the application of any person with parental responsibility for the child (including a local authority) or on the application of the child concerned, provided the court has given the child leave to apply. The court also has the power to terminate the appointment of its own motion in any family proceedings, in other words without any application having been made.

(ii) Appointment by the court (section 5) The court can order that an applicant be appointed as a guardian of a child if: the child has no person with parental responsibility; or a residence order has been made with respect to the child in favour of a parent, guardian, or special guardian, who has died while the order was in force; or where there is no residence order and the child's only surviving special guardian has died. The court cannot appoint a guardian if a residence order was also made in favour of a surviving parent of the child. The court can also appoint a guardian under section 5 of its own motion in any family proceedings, in other words without any application for an appointment having been made.

When exercising its powers to decide whether to appoint a guardian the child's welfare is the court's paramount consideration and the 'no-delay' (s 1(2)) and the 'no-order' provisions (s 1(5)) apply (see 10.3). As proceedings for the appointment of a guardian are family proceedings (see s 8(4)), the court can instead of, or in addition to, appointing a guardian, make a section 8 order under the Children Act 1989 (see 10.4).

Termination of court order (section 6)   A court order appointing a guardian can be terminated by the court on the application of any person with parental responsibility for the child (including a local authority) or on the application of the child concerned, with leave of the court; or by the court of its own motion in any family proceedings.

(b)   Effects of guardianship

The appointment of a guardian takes effect on the appointer's death provided no other person has parental responsibility for the child. As a guardian has parental responsibility for the child (see 9.3), he or she must ensure that the child is cared for and provided for and is educated. A guardian has a right to apply for orders under the Children Act 1989 (see Chapter 10) and to consent to the child's adoption (see Chapter 15). However, a guardian has no legal duty to provide financial support for the child (as this might deter people from becoming a guardian); and has no right to succeed to the child's estate on the child's intestacy.

9.9   Parenthood – assisted reproduction

Assisted reproduction is governed by the Human Fertilisation and Embryology Acts 1990 and 2008 (HFEA 1990 and 2008). The 2008 Act, which was enacted primarily in response to new technological and scientific developments, is relevant to family lawyers because Part 2 contains provisions governing the law of parenthood. These provisions, which came into force on 6 April 2009, extend the rules on parenthood to include lesbian couples, whether or not they are civil partners.

(a)   Who is the child's mother?

The woman who is carrying (or has carried) a child as a result of fertility treatment (the placing in her of an embryo or of sperm and eggs), and no other woman, is treated as the child's mother (s 33(1) HFEA 2008). This rules applies whether or not the woman was in the UK or elsewhere at the time of the treatment (s 33(3)).

(b)   Who is the child's 'father' or 'other parent'?

The rules differ depending on the status of the couple's relationship.

(i) Married couples   The husband is automatically recognised as the legal father of a child born as a result of his wife having fertility treatment, unless he did not consent to the treatment (s 35(1) HFEA 2008). This rule applies, whether or not the wife was in the UK or elsewhere at the time of the treatment (s 35(2)).

(ii) Unmarried couples   Under sections 36 and 37 HFEA 2008, where the woman has a child as a result of insemination in a UK licensed clinic and the couple have in place (at the time of the transfer of the sperm or embryo which results in conception) current notices of the man stating that he consents to being treated as the father of any child resulting from the assisted reproduction, then he is the legal parent of the child. The parties must not be within the degrees of prohibited relationship with each other (s 37(1)(e)).

(iii) Lesbian couples who are civil partners   If the child was conceived before 6 April 2009, the non-birth mother in a lesbian civil partnership has no 'automatic' recognition as a parent and has no 'automatic' parental responsibility. If she wishes to acquire parental responsibility she will have to do so by means of a parental responsibility agreement or parental responsibility order, or by a residence order, a special guardianship order, or an adoption order.

If the child is conceived on or after 6 April 2009, section 42 HFEA 2008 provides that, where a female civil partner gives birth to a child conceived as a result of donor insemination (whether the woman was in the UK or elsewhere) she is the mother of the child; and her civil partner is automatically the other parent in law unless she did not consent to the treatment. In other words, the legal position is the same as for married couples (see above). If the civil partner did not consent, she may acquire parental responsibility in relation to the child in the ways listed above.

(iv) Lesbian couples who are not civil partners   Sections 43 and 44 HFEA 2008 make provision in respect of lesbian couples who are not civil partners. The law is the same as that for lesbian civil partners (see above), except for the requirement that the mother's lesbian partner will only be the other parent in law if the child was conceived at a licensed clinic in the UK. If the child was conceived outside the UK or at home, or the partner did not consent to the treatment, she can acquire parental responsibility in one of the ways listed above.

(c)   Deceased persons

Sections 39 and 40 of HFEA 2008 enable a man to be registered on the child's birth certificate as the father of a child conceived after his death using his sperm or using an embryo created with his sperm before his death. It also enables a man to be registered as the father of a child conceived after his death using an embryo created using donor sperm before his death. Registration of the child does not confer upon the child any legal status or rights as a consequence of the registration. The father must give written consent to registration of his name on the birth register.

Section 46 of HFEA 2008 lays down similar provisions in respect of a deceased lesbian partner (whether or not that partnership had been registered as a civil partnership).

(d)   Consent and assisted reproduction

Consent is an essential requirement in the law governing assisted reproduction, not just for the purpose of acquiring parenthood (see above), but also for the purpose of consenting to the fertility treatment itself. The issue of consent was considered in the following case in respect of section 12 HFEA 1990, which requires the genetic parent's consent to *in vitro* fertilisation (IVF). The same approach is likely to be taken under section 37 HFEA 2008 which deals with the agreed fatherhood conditions.

▶ *Evans v Amicus Healthcare Ltd; Hadley v Midland Fertility Services Ltd* [2004] 1 FLR 67

In each appeal the female claimant had undergone IVF treatment with her respective partner, but after the relationship had broken down the male partner had withdrawn his consent to the treatment and to the storage of the embryos, and wished them to perish. The claimants argued that the court had the power to override the withdrawal of consent and to permit the embryos to be used. Each claimant sought an injunction to restore the man's consent. They also sought a declaration of incompatibility under the Human Rights Act 1998 arguing that the relevant provisions in the HFEA 1990 were in breach of the ECHR.

Wall J held that the court had no power to override the unconditional statutory right of either party to withdraw or vary consent to the use of embryos in connection with IVF treatment at any time before implantation in the woman. Where consent had originally been given for treatment together with a named partner it was neither effective nor valid once the parties had ceased to be together. HFEA 1990 did not breach the claimants' right to family life under Article 8 ECHR. As HFEA 1990 was enacted with sound policy reasons for requiring treatment to be consensual throughout, any interference by the State was both lawful and proportionate. There was no breach of Article 12 (right to marry and found a family) and Article 14 (discrimination in respect of a Convention right). Nor was there a breach of Article 2 (right to life), as an embryo is not a person in English law.

Note: Ms Evans (who had received IVF treatment prior to the surgical removal of her ovaries due to a pre-cancerous condition but whose partner subsequently refused to consent to their use when their relationship broke down) sought leave to appeal to the Court of Appeal, but leave was refused (see [2004] EWCA (Civ) 727). She subsequently applied to the ECtHR (see *Evans v UK (Application No 6339/05)* [2007] 1 FLR 1990) claiming that the requirement of the father's consent to the continued storage and implantation of the fertilised eggs breached her rights under Articles 8 and 14 ECHR, and the rights of the embryos under Article 2. However, the ECtHR held by a majority of 13–4 that there had been no breach of her human rights or those of the embryos.

In the following case it was held that, where a man and a woman separate before a successful implantation takes place, even though it started out as a 'joint enterprise', the man may not be the legal father of the child. The case related to section 28(3) of HFEA 1990, but the same approach is likely to be taken under HFEA 2008.

▶ *Re R (IVF: Paternity of Child)* [2005] 2 FLR 843

The mother and her unmarried partner sought fertility treatment involving donor sperm. The man signed the prescribed documents acknowledging that he intended to become the legal father of any child born as a result of the treatment. An implantation was successful, but the mother failed to inform the clinic after the pregnancy was confirmed that she had separated from her partner. Her former partner obtained a declaration of paternity but the Court of Appeal allowed the mother's appeal. The man appealed to the House of Lords.

The House of Lords dismissed his appeal, and held that, in conferring the relationship of parent and child on people who were related neither by blood nor marriage, the rules must be applied very strictly. If the 'joint' enterprise of fertility treatment had ended by the time the successful treatment had begun (because by that stage the couple had separated), the man was not the legal father of the resulting child.

9.10 Surrogacy

(a) Introduction

Some couples may resort to surrogacy to have a child. Under a surrogacy arrangement a surrogate mother acts as the birth mother for the commissioning parent(s) and she agrees to hand the child over soon after the child's birth. The practice of surrogacy is governed by the Surrogacy Arrangements Act 1985. Under the Act a surrogate mother is defined as a woman who carries a child in pursuance of an arrangement made before she began to carry the child, and with a view to any such child being handed over to, and parental responsibility being met (so far as practicable) by, another person or persons (s 1(2)).

Surrogacy arrangements between private individuals are permitted in England and Wales (s 2(2) SRA 1985), but commercial surrogacy is prohibited. Thus, it is a criminal offence to set up a surrogacy agency commercially and to advertise and to negotiate a surrogacy arrangement for money (s 2(1)) (although payment of money may in some circumstances be authorised retrospectively by the court – see further below).

Surrogacy can raise difficult legal, ethical and practical problems. For instance, the surrogate mother may decide not to hand over the child (see, for example, *Re P (Surrogacy: Residence)* [2008] 1 FLR 177). Difficulties can also arise when a couple enter into a commercial surrogacy arrangement abroad and wish to apply for a parental order in the court in England and Wales. In *Re IJ (Foreign Surrogacy Agreement: Parental Order)* [2011] EWHC 921 (Fam), [2011] 2 FLR 646 Hedley J drew attention to the legal difficulties which can arise, including immigration issues, and he warned of the danger of parties relying on the advice of overseas agencies who may not fully understand the legal position in England and Wales.

The following case, in which McFarlane J laid down some principles which should be borne in mind in future cases, provides a good example of the complexities that can arise in a surrogacy cases. His Lordship expressed concern that surrogacy agencies, such as COTS, which was involved in the case, were not covered by any statutory or regulatory provision. Given that COTS was unaware of the domicile requirements to apply for a parental order (see further below) and had not realised that it was unlawful to take a child abroad for an adoption, McFarlane J said that it had to be asked whether some form of inspection or authorisation should be required in order to improve the quality of advice offered to couples who sought to have a child through surrogacy.

▶ *Re G (Surrogacy: Foreign Domicile)* [2007] EWHC 2814 (Fam), [2008] 1 FLR 1047

A surrogacy arrangement was entered into whereby an English surrogate mother agreed to give birth to a surrogate child for a married couple living in Turkey. The child was conceived using the egg of the surrogate mother and the Turkish husband's sperm. The surrogate mother's estranged husband had not given written consent to the insemination due to lack of communication between the couple. The Turkish parents came to England and (as a precursor to returning to Turkey where they would apply to adopt the child) they applied for a section 30 parental order under HFEA 1990. However, as they had failed to satisfy the domicile requirements in section 30(3)(b) of the Act (because of the short time they had spent in the UK), McFarlane J instead made an order under section 84 of the Adoption and Children Act 2002, which confers parental responsibility on a prospective adopter.

In respect of the issue of consent to insemination by the estranged husband of the surrogate mother, McFarlane J held that, pursuant to section 28 of the 1990 Act, the common law position applied and that the father was to be treated for all purposes as the child's father. The fact that there had been no written consent did not necessarily mean that the father had not consented for the purposes of section 28(2). The term 'consent' was not confined to the narrow meaning argued for by COTS. It was necessary for the court to look more widely than simply at whether the husband had signed the form at the clinic. McFarlane J listed the principles which should be borne in mind in trying to ensure that lessons were learned for the future:

> ▶ Non-commercial surrogacy arrangements where neither of the commissioning parents is domiciled in the UK are to be discouraged, as it is not open to them to apply for a parental order under section 30 (see below).
> ▶ Surrogacy agencies must ensure they are fully familiar with the basic legal requirements.
> ▶ Any application for a parental order under section 30 involving an international element should be transferred to a nominated inter-country adoption county court or the High Court.
> ▶ Any court hearing an application for a parental order under section 30 must ensure that the qualifying conditions required of the applicants are met.
> ▶ Where a surrogate mother is married, but separated from her husband, all reasonable attempts should be made before the surrogacy process begins, in order to establish whether or not her husband consented to the proposed arrangement.
> ▶ The court can make orders as to costs, as costs should not be borne by the British taxpayer in such cases.

(b)   Surrogacy and parenthood

As the rules on parenthood in surrogacy cases are the same as those which apply in non-surrogacy cases (see 9.2 above), the birth mother (the surrogate) is the legal parent of the child. However, it is possible for legal parenthood to be transferred from the surrogate mother to the commissioning parents by means of a parental order (see below).

(c)   Surrogacy and parental orders

The commissioning parents of a surrogacy arrangement can apply for a parental order which the court has jurisdiction to make under section 54 of the Human Fertilisation and Embryology Act 2008 (which came into force on 1 September 2009 and replaced section 30 of HFEA 1990). As section 54 does not differ in substance from section 30 (other than to extend the law to civil partners), the case-law on section 30 remains relevant. The law is therefore unaffected by the 2008 Act, except that welfare is now the paramount, not the first, consideration (following the importation of section 1 of the Adoption and Children Act 2002 into section 54 of the 2008 Act by SI 2010 No 985). Applications for a parental order must be made in the High Court.

The effect of a parental order is to provide for the child to be treated in law as the child of the applicants (s 54(1)). Where an application is made, a Children's Guardian (an officer of Cafcass – see 1.7) will be appointed by the court to conduct a welfare inquiry. On issuing the order, the court notifies the General Register Office of Births, which re-registers the birth, and the new birth record supersedes the original one.

Section 54(1) provides that the court can make a parental order if the child has been carried by a woman who is not one of the applicants as a result of the placing in her of an embryo or sperm and eggs or her artificial insemination, the gametes of at least one of the applicants were used to bring about the creation of the embryo, and the preconditions in section 54(2) and (8) are satisfied (see below).

Applicants for an order   The applicants must be: a married couple; a couple who are civil partners of each other; or a couple (opposite- or same-sex) who are living with each other as partners in an enduring family relationship and who are not within the prohibited degrees of relationship in relation to each other (s 54(2)). Thus, single persons cannot apply. A parental order can be made, however, if one of the couple has died after the surrogacy arrangement (*A v P (Surrogacy: Parental Order: Death of Applicant)* [2011] EWHC 1738 (Fam)

Preconditions to be satisfied   In addition to the above requirements, the following conditions must also be satisfied before the court can consider whether to make a parental order:

▶ The application must be made within six months of the child's birth (s 54(3)).
▶ At the time of the application and of the making of the order the child's home must be with the applicants; and one or both parties must be domiciled in a part of the UK or in the Channel Islands or in the Isle of Man (s 54(4)). (In *Re K (Minors: Foreign Surrogacy)* [2010] EWHC 1180 (Fam), [2011] 1 FLR 533, for example, the court had no jurisdiction as the children, who had been born as a result of a commercial surrogacy arrangement in India, were still living there.)
▶ At the time of making the order both applicants must have attained the age of 18 (s 54(5)).
▶ The court must be satisfied that both the woman who carried the child, and any other person who is a parent of the child but is not one of the applicants (including any man who is the father by virtue of section 35 or 36 or any woman who is a parent by virtue of section 42 or 43) have freely, and with full understanding of what is involved, agreed unconditionally to the making of the order (s 54(6)). Agreement is not required if they cannot be found or are incapable of giving agreement; and the agreement of the mother who carried the child is ineffective if given less than six weeks after the child's birth (s 54(7)). (See, for instance, *D and L (Surrogacy)* Re [2012] EWHC 2631 (Fam) where a parental order was made on the application of a couple who were male civil partners even though the surrogate mother could not be found.)
▶ The court must be satisfied that no money or other benefit (other than for expenses reasonably incurred) has been given or received by either of the applicants for or in consideration of: the making of the order, any agreement required by section 54(6) (see above), the handing over of the child to the applicants, or the making of arrangements with a view to the making of the order, unless authorised by the court (s 54(8)). (On authorising payment retrospectively, see below.)

The child's welfare is the court's paramount consideration   If the above preconditions are satisfied, the court will then go on to exercise its discretion to decide whether or not to make the order, applying the principle that the child's lifelong welfare is the court's paramount consideration. In *Re L (Commercial Surrogacy)* [2010] EWHC 3146 (Fam), [2011] 1 FLR 1423, where Hedley J retrospectively authorised payments made in excess of reasonable expenses with respect to a surrogacy arrangement made in the USA and made a parental order, his Lordship said that the effect of the importation of the paramountcy principle into applications for a parental order was for the balance between public policy considerations and welfare to weigh decisively in favour of welfare; and that it would only be in the clearest case of an abuse of public policy that the court would be able to withhold an order if welfare considerations supported it being made.

Authorising payments   As commercial surrogacy arrangements are outlawed in the UK (see above), couples from the UK may choose to go abroad for the purpose of having a surrogate child. On their return they may decide to apply for a parental order which the court cannot consider making unless it is willing to authorise any payments which were made in excess of reasonable expenses (see s 54(8), above).

When considering whether payments should be retrospectively authorised, the court will ask three questions: was the sum paid disproportionate to reasonable expenses; were the applicants acting in good faith and without 'moral taint' in their dealings with the surrogate mother; and were the applicants a party to any attempt to defraud the authorities? The court will also take into account the following policy issues: that the commercial arrangement was not being used to circumvent UK childcare laws (for example, by giving people who would not have been approved as adoptive parents a right to a parental order); that payments were not simply being used to buy a child overseas; and that the sums of money were not such that they might overbear the will of a surrogate carrier.

In the following cases, payments were retrospectively authorised by the court. They show that, although the aim of section 54(8) is to prevent the commercialisation of surrogacy, the paramountcy of the child's welfare will usually result in unauthorised surrogacy payments being retrospectively authorised.

▶ *Re C (Application by Mr and Mrs X Under s.30 of the Human Fertilisation and Embryology Act 1990)* [2002] 1 FLR 909

£12,000 paid to the surrogate mother by the commissioning parents (because they did not wish her to work during pregnancy) was authorised by Wall J as being expenses reasonably incurred.

▶ *Re X and Y (Foreign Surrogacy)* [2009] 1 FLR 733

The applicants (a married couple from the UK who had entered into a surrogacy agreement with a married woman in the Ukraine who had produced twins for them) were granted a parental order by Hedley J despite having paid the surrogate mother. Hedley J authorised the payments, applying *Re C* above and finding that the three questions (see above) were satisfied and that the paramountcy of the child's lifelong welfare prevailed over the policy considerations (see above).

▶ *Re S (Parental Order)* [2009] EWHC 2977, [2010] 1 FLR 1156

Hedley J granted a parental order to a married couple who had entered into a commercial surrogacy arrangement in California and who had paid $23,000 to the surrogate carrier. They had entered into the agreement in good faith without realising that it would not be recognised in England and Wales. Hedley J made clear that, without the order, the surrogate carrier would remain the legal mother and, if she were married, her husband would be the lawful father. The parental order was clearly important for the long-term well-being of the new family; and the policy issues (see above) did not militate against an order being made.

▶ *Re X and Y (Parental Order: Retrospective Authorisation of Payments)* [2011] EWHC 3147 (Fam)

The British parents entered into a surrogacy arrangement with a clinic in India to whom they paid about £27,000. Sir Nicholas Wall P authorised the payment and made a parental order, holding that: the applicants were entirely genuine; the conditions in section 54 had been met; the payments were not disproportionate; and it was plainly in the children's interests to be brought up by the applicants as their parents.

▶ *Re D and L (Surrogacy)* [2012] EWHC 2631 (Fam)

Baker J granted a parental order to the male civil partner applicants even though they had paid for the services of a surrogate mother using the services of a clinic in India (and even though the mother had not given her consent as she could not be found). Although the payment was accepted as being beyond the 'reasonable expenses' permitted by section 54(8), Baker J held that the court was under a duty to place the welfare of the children first and therefore retrospectively authorised the payments which had been made.

Section 54 proceedings are family proceedings   As section 54 proceedings for a parental order are family proceedings for the purposes of the Children Act 1989 (s 54(9)(a)) the court may make any section 8 order under the Children Act 1989 (for instance, a residence or contact order) in those proceedings, either on an application or of its own motion.

Setting aside a parental order   There is no power to set aside a parental order under HFEA 2008. However, in *G v G (Parental Order: Revocation)* [2012] EWHC 1979 (Fam), [2013] 1 FLR 286, where an application was made by Mr G to set aside a parental order (on the ground of procedural flaws and on the basis that at the time of the order the mother had a concealed intention to separate and raise the child alone), Hedley J, refusing to set aside the order, drew parallels between the revocation of a parental order and that of an adoption order, holding that guidance could be derived from the relevant authorities (in particular, *Re M (Minors) (Adoption)* [1991] 1 FLR 458 which concerned an application for revocation on the basis of 'mistake' by one of the parties as to the factual basis of the application). Thus, the bar to set aside a parental order (like an adoption order) is set very high. Here the facts of the case were not such that the parental order should be set aside, although Hedley J stated that, in the light of the novelty of the application, he would be minded to grant permission to appeal to the Court of Appeal if it was sought, as it would be in the public interest for the case to be considered at the appellate level.

Summary

▶ Most children are brought up by parents with whom they have a biological link, although some are brought up by step-parents, foster-parents, guardians, adoptive parents or special guardians. The Government recognises the importance of parents and is keen to support them. The courts have held that the biological bond between parent and child is a significant and important factor, but that this is not a presumption, as the overriding principle is that the welfare of the child is the court's paramount consideration. The importance of parents is recognised in the UN Convention on the Rights of the Child 1989 and is reflected in the jurisprudence of the ECtHR which has held that the mutual enjoyment of each other's company by parent and child constitutes a fundamental element of family life.

▶ Various legal presumptions exist in respect of parentage, but such presumptions are of little relevance today as parentage can be established, by DNA testing, with virtually 100 per cent certainty. The courts have held that scientific tests, rather than legal presumptions, should be used to prove parentage. Provisions governing the use of scientific tests for determining parentage are laid down in the Family Law Reform Act 1969. The consent of the child is needed (if aged 16 and over), or the consent of the person with the care and control of the child if the child is aged under 16. If consent is not forthcoming the court can give consent. Although the courts have held that it is normally in the best interests of the child to know his or her origins, and for the truth to come out, this is subject to the overriding principle that the child's welfare is the court's paramount consideration. A declaration of parentage can be made under section 55A of the Family Law Act 1986; and a declaration of legitimacy under section 56 of the Family Law Act 1986.

▶ The law governing parental responsibility (PR) is laid down in the Children Act 1989. The following persons have 'automatic' PR (see s 2 CA 1989): married parents; an unmarried mother; a mother and her civil partner who is a parent by virtue of section 42 of HFEA 2008; a mother and her female partner who is a parent by virtue of section 43 HFEA 2008; a mother who is parent by virtue of section 43 HFEA 2008 (a mother who has a child by assisted reproduction).

▶ An unmarried father does not have 'automatic' PR for his children, but can acquire it by making a PR agreement with the mother or obtaining a PR order from the court or by joint birth registration with the mother (s 4 CA 1989). It is also possible to obtain PR: under a residence order; or by becoming the child's guardian on the mother's death; by adopting the child; by obtaining a special guardianship order; or by marrying the mother (s 1 Legitimacy Act 1976). When considering whether to make a PR order the court will take into account the welfare principles in section 1 of the Children Act 1989 (except the welfare checklist) and also: the degree of commitment which the father has shown towards the child; the degree of attachment which exists between the father and the child; and the father's reasons or motivation for applying for the order. An unmarried father who has acquired PR (and other persons who do not possess it 'automatically') can have it revoked where such a step is in the best interests of the child (except where he has aquired PR by adoption or marriage).

▶ A step-parent can acquire PR by means of a PR agreement or PR order (s 4A CA 1989). A female non-biological parent in a lesbian relationship can acquire PR in relation to the child by joint birth registration or by way of a PR agreement or PR order (s 4ZA CA 1989). Other persons can acquire PR by means of a residence order, a special guardianship order or an adoption order.

▶ Parents have certain rights and duties at common law and under statute, but parental rights are not absolute. These include the right to: choose where the child lives; have contact with the child; decide on the child's education; choose the child's religion; consent to the child's medical treatment; consent to the child's marriage or civil partnership; choose the child's surname and register the child's birth; consent to the child's adoption; discipline the child; administer the child's property and enter into contracts on the child's behalf; appoint a guardian for the child; and bring legal proceeding in respect of the child.

▶ Parents are responsible for consenting to their child's medical treatment except that, in some circumstances, a '*Gillick* competent' child may be able to give consent. Disputes between parents and doctors about the medical treatment of a child can be decided by the High Court under its inherent jurisdiction or in wardship, or by making an application for a section 8 specific issue order under the CA 1989. The best interests of the child are paramount in these cases and, while parental wishes are respected by the courts, they do not prevail. Serious and irreversible operations on the child (such as sterilisation and circumcision) may need the consent of the court. Disputes between parents about medical treatment can be decided by means of a specific issue order under section 8 of the CA 1989, or by the High Court in the exercise of its inherent or wardship jurisdiction. A prohibited steps order under section 8 of the Children Act 1989 can be used to prevent the other parent making a decision about a child's medical treatment or taking steps with respect to medical treatment.

▶ A guardian can be appointed (by a private individual or by the court) under sections 5 and 6 of the Children Act 1989. The aim of guardianship is to ensure that there is a person available to exercise parental responsibility for the child should the child's parents die.

▶ The Human Fertilisation and Embryology Acts 1990 and 2008 govern assisted reproduction. The woman who is carrying (or has carried) a child as a result of the placing in her of an embryo or of sperm and eggs, and no other woman, is treated as the mother of the child. If the couple are married, the husband is automatically recognised as the legal father of the child. If the couple are not married and the man states that he consents to being treated as the father of any child resulting from the assisted reproduction, then he is the legal parent of the child. If the couple are in a lesbian relationship and the non-birth mother wishes to acquire parental responsibility, she has to either enter into a parental responsibility agreement with the mother or apply to the court for parental responsibility (whether or not the couple are civil partners). Consent is an essential requirement in respect of the law governing assisted reproduction, not just for the purpose of acquiring parenthood but for the purpose of consenting to the fertility treatment itself.

Summary cont'd

▶ Some couples may decide to have a child by way of a surrogacy arrangement. Surrogacy raises difficult legal, ethical and practical problems. Commercial surrogacy is unlawful in the UK and is punishable as a criminal offence under the Surrogacy Arrangements Act 1985. The commissioning parents of a surrogate arrangement can apply for a parental order under section 54 of the Human Fertilisation and Embryology Act 2008 which has the effect of transferring legal parenthood from the surrogate mother to the commissioning parents. Only couples, not single persons, can apply, namely: a married couple; a civil partnership couple; and a cohabiting (same-sex or opposite-sex) couple who are living in an enduring family relationship and who are not within the prohibited degrees of relationship. Certain preconditions (laid down in section 54) must be satisfied first, after which the court will consider whether or not to make the order, applying the principle that the child's welfare is the paramount consideration. There are many reported cases involving commercial surrogacy agreements entered into overseas involving payment (which is outlawed in the UK) but where the court has retrospectively authorised the payment (under section 54(8)), and made the parental order, because this has been held to be in the best interests of the child.

Further reading and references

Bainham, 'Is legitimacy legitimate?' [2009] Fam Law 673.

Bainham, 'Rowing back from *Re G*? Natural parents in the Supreme Court' [2010] Fam Law 394.

Bainham, 'Is anything now left of parental rights?', Chapter 2 in Probert, Gilmore and Herring (2009), below.

Blain and Worwood, 'Alternative families and changing perceptions of parenthood' [2011] Fam Law 289.

Bridge, 'Religion, culture and conviction: the medical treatment of children' [1999] CFLQ 217.

Diduck ' "If only we can find the appropriate terms to use the issue will be solved": law, identity and parenthood' [2007] CFLQ 458.

Downie, '*Re C (HIV Test)* – the limits of parental autonomy' [2000] CFLQ 197.

Eekelaar, 'Are parents morally obliged to care for their children?' (1991) OJLS 340.

Eekelaar, 'Parental responsibility: State of nature or nature of the state?' (1991) JSWFL 37.

Eekelaar, 'Rethinking parental responsibility' [2001] Fam Law 428.

Everett and Yeatman, 'Are some parents more natural than others?' [2010] CFLQ 290.

Fortin, 'Accommodating children's rights in a post Human Rights Act era' (2006) *Modern Law Review* 299.

Fortin, 'Children's rights to know their origins – too far, too fast?'[2009] CFLQ 336.

Gamble and Ghevaert, 'International surrogacy: payments, public policy and media hype' [2011] Fam Law 504.

Harris and George, 'Parental responsibility and shared residence orders: parliamentary intentions and judicial interpretations' [2010] CFLQ 151.

Horsey, 'Challenging presumptions: legal parenthood and surrogacy arrangements' [2010] CFLQ 499.

Probert, Gilmore and Herring (eds), *Responsible Parents and Parental Responsibility,* 2009, Hart Publishing.

Smith, 'Clashing symbols? Reconciling support for fathers and fatherless families after the Human Fertilisation and Embryology Act 2008' [2010] CFLQ 42.

Wallbank, ' "Bodies in the shadows": joint birth registration, parental responsibility and social class' [2009] CFLQ 267.

Websites

Advice Now: www.advicenow.org.uk

Families Need Fathers: www.fnf.org.uk

Family and Parenting Institute: www.familyandparenting.org

Human Fertilisation and Embryology Authority: www.hfea.gov.uk

Links to relevant websites can also be found at: www.palgrave.com/law/familylaw8e

Chapter 10

The Children Act 1989

10.1 The Children Act 1989

The Children Act 1989 contains provisions governing both the private and the public law relating to parents and children. The Act came into force in 1991, but there have been many important amendments.

(i) Influences on the Act and its principles and policies   The Children Act 1989 was an important Act not only because it consolidated much of the civil law relating to children, but because it introduced new principles and policies. Government reports and public inquiries relating to the management of child abuse by social workers and other agencies had a considerable influence on the Act. Of particular importance was *The Report of the Inquiry into Child Abuse in Cleveland 1987* (Cm 412, 1988), which severely criticised the over-zealous intervention of local authority social services in children's cases in Cleveland in the North East of England. The *Report* had an important influence on the public law provisions of the Act, in particular in respect of emergency protection of children and the importance of promoting inter-agency co-operation.

The *Gillick* case (see 8.4) also had an impact on the Act, which gives children of sufficient age and understanding the right to bring proceedings and to have their views taken into account by the court. The Act also introduced the concept of 'parental responsibility', not parental rights (partly as a result of *Gillick*) in order to stress the positive ongoing nature of parental involvement in bringing up children and to remove the adversarial undertones of the word 'rights'. Another aim of the Act was to provide a flexible court structure and a flexible range of orders available in all family proceedings involving children (and which can be made on an application or by the court of its own motion).

(ii) Strengths and weaknesses   The Children Act 1989 has generally been considered to be a 'successful' Act (and this was recognised by the inquiry which followed the tragic death of Victoria Climbié –see 14.5). However, it has been criticised by some commentators for not bringing children's interests sufficiently to the fore (see Freeman, 1998) and for failing to include any reference to children's rights (see Fortin, 2006). A major problem with proceedings under the Act, however, is that of delay. Delays can be particularly long in child protection and adoption cases, but the Government is proposing to take steps reduce delay.

(iii) Amendments to the Act   New provisions have been inserted into the Children Act 1989 over the years. Thus, it has been amended to allow unmarried fathers to acquire parental responsibility by birth registration (see 9.4); and step-parents to acquire parental responsibility for a step-child (see 9.5). New provisions on special guardianship have been inserted into the Act (see 15.14); and also in respect of the facilitation and enforcement of contact (see 11.6). In 2009, changes were made extending the duration of residence orders; and new provisions were inserted governing the parental responsibility of a female civil partner who has had a child by assisted reproduction. Amendments have also been made to the public law provisions of the Act, for instance in respect of provisions concerning children leaving care (see further in Chapter 14).

(iv) Proposals for reform: a 'child arrangements order'   The Family Justice Review (FJR, see further at p. 7) recommended in its *Final Report* in 2011 that a new order, a 'child arrangements order', should be introduced to replace residence and contact orders (which are available under section 8 CA1989) so as to move away from loaded terms such as residence and contact and to focus more on the practical issues involved in the day-to-day care of a child (see para 112 of the *Final Report*). The Government has accepted the FJR's recommendation (see *The Government Response to the Family Justice Review,* Department of Education and Ministry of Justice, February 2012) and in September 2012 it published draft legislation on child arrangement orders (and on several other family justice matters), which will repeal the current provisions relating to residence and contact orders. The draft legislation defines a child arrangements order as 'an order regulating arrangements relating to with whom a child should live, spend time, or have other types of contact, or when a child should live, spend time or have other contact with a person'.

10.2   An overview of the Act

Parts I to V of the Children Act 1989 are the parts most relevant to family lawyers (see below). Part XII ('Miscellaneous and General') is also important because it includes provisions about the effect and duration of orders (s 91), privacy for children in certain proceedings (s 97), restrictions on the use of the wardship jurisdiction (s 100), and the interpretation section of the Act (s 105). The following schedules are also important: Schedule 1 (Financial Provision for Children); Schedule 2 (Local Authority Support for Children and Families); and Schedule 3 (Supervision Orders).

The main provisions of the Children Act 1989 are as follows:

Children Act 1989

Part I Introductory

The welfare principle and other principles applicable in proceedings under the Act (s 1). Parental responsibility (ss 2–4A). Appointment of guardians for children (ss 5 and 6). Welfare reports (s 7).

Part II Orders with respect to children in family proceedings

Section 8 orders (residence, contact, specific issue and prohibited steps) and the powers of the court in respect of these orders (ss 9–14), including provisions relating to the enforcement and facilitation of contact (ss 11A–11P). Special guardianship orders (ss 14A–14G). Orders for financial relief for children (s 15 and Schedule 1). Family assistance orders (s 16). Risk assessments (s 16A).

Part III Local authority support for children and families

Local authority services for children in need, their families and others (ss 17–19). Payments and vouchers in respect of children in need (ss 17A and B). Provision of accommodation for children in need (ss 20 and 21). The duties of local authorities in relation to children looked after by them (ss 22 and 23). Advice and assistance for children (s 24). Advice and assistance for children and young persons who have left care (ss 23A–E, ss 24A–D). Secure accommodation (s 25). Independent reviewing officers (ss 25A–C). Case reviews (s 26). Co-operation between local authorities (s 27). Advocacy services for children (s 27A). Consultation with local education authorities (s 28). Recoupment of cost of providing services (s 29).

> **Part IV Care and supervision**
>
> Care orders, supervision orders and education supervision orders (ss 31–40). Care plans (s 31A).
>
> **Part V Protection of children**
>
> Child assessment orders (s 43). Emergency protection orders (ss 44–45). Police removal of children (s 46). Local authority duty to investigate (s 47). Power to assist in discovery of children who may be in need of emergency protection (s 48).

10.3 The welfare principles

Important principles are laid down in section 1 of the Children Act 1989 which apply to most court applications involving children, whether brought by private individuals or by public authorities. These principles are as follows:

(a) The welfare principle (section 1(1))

The paramountcy of the child's welfare is the governing principle in children's cases.

> **Section 1(1) of the Children Act 1989**
>
> 'When a court determines any question with respect to—
>
> (a) the upbringing of a child; or
> (b) the administration of a child's property or the application of any income arising from it,
>
> the child's welfare shall be the court's paramount consideration.'

The child's welfare is the paramount consideration in private law proceedings (such as for residence and contact orders) and in public law proceedings (such as for care and supervision orders). The Act does not expressly require the welfare principle to be applied in applications for leave (permission) to apply for a section 8 order (see 10.4) or in applications for financial relief for children under section 15 and Schedule 1 (see 12.3), but in practice the court will consider the child's welfare as part of its statutory obligation to consider all the circumstances of the case.

The paramountcy of the child's welfare is enshrined in Article 3(1) of the UN Convention on the Rights of the Child 1989. It is also recognised by the European Court of Human Rights, even though there is no express reference to children in the European Convention for the Protection of Human Rights (see 1.8).

(b) The 'welfare checklist' (section 1(3))

Section 1(3) contains a list of factors (a 'welfare checklist') which creates a framework for the exercise of judicial discretion in the application of the welfare principle above. The court must have regard to the checklist when deciding whether to make, vary or discharge a section 8 order in contested proceedings (s 1(4)(a)), and when deciding whether to make, vary or discharge a special guardianship order, a care order, or a supervision order (s 1(4)(b)). Thus, the checklist must be applied in private law proceedings and in public law proceedings (except in emergency protection proceedings, as to apply the checklist might hinder emergency action).

Section 1(3) of the Children Act 1989

'... a court shall have regard in particular to—

(a) the ascertainable wishes and feelings of the child concerned (considered in the light of his age and understanding);

(b) his physical, emotional and educational needs;

(c) the likely effect on him of any change in his circumstances;

(d) his age, sex, background and any characteristics of his which the court considers relevant;

(e) any harm which he has suffered or is at risk of suffering;

(f) how capable each of his parents, and any other person in relation to whom the court considers the question to be relevant, is of meeting his needs;

(g) the range of powers available to the court under this Act in the proceedings in question.'

'Harm' in section 1(3)(e) has the same meaning as it has in section 31 of the Act (see 14.7); and also includes harm caused by seeing or hearing the ill-treatment of another person. Witnessing or hearing domestic violence can therefore constitute harm.

The list in section 1(3) is not exclusive – other factors may be taken into account – and the factors are not listed in any hierarchy of importance. Furthermore, as the Act does not refer to section 1(3) as a 'checklist', a judge is not required 'to read out the seven items in s 1(3) and pronounce his conclusion on each' (*per* Staughton LJ in *H v H (Residence Order: Leave to Remove from Jurisdiction)* [1995] 1 FLR 529). In *B v B (Residence Order: Reasons for Decision)* [1997] 2 FLR 602, Holman J held that, although it is not always necessary or appropriate for a judge to go through the checklist item by item, it does represent an extremely useful and important discipline for judges to ensure that all the relevant factors and circumstances are considered and balanced. In *Re G (Children) (Residence: Same-Sex Partner)* [2006] UKHL 43, [2006] 2 FLR 629 Lord Nicholls said that in a 'difficult or finely balanced case it is a great help to address each of the factors in the list, along with any others which may be relevant, so as to ensure that no particular feature of the case is given more weight than it should properly bear'.

A failure to consider one or more of the factors in the checklist may provide a successful ground for an appeal.

(c)   The 'minimum intervention principle' (section 1(5))

This principle laid down in section 1(5) was introduced as part of the general policy of the Children Act 1989 to place the primary responsibility for children on their parents.

Section 1(5) of the Children Act 1989

'Where a court is considering whether or not to make one or more orders under this Act with respect to a child, it shall not make the order or any of the orders unless it considers that doing so would be better for the child than making no order at all.'

The aim of section 1(5) is to discourage courts making unnecessary orders and to ensure that orders are made only if they will positively improve the child's welfare.

Section 1(5) was at one time interpreted by some commentators and judges as creating a presumption in favour of making no order, in other words a 'no-order' principle. However, in *Re G (Children) (Residence Order: No Order Principle)* [2006] 1 FLR 771 Ward LJ in the Court of Appeal held that this was an incorrect interpretation, as section 1(5) did not create a presumption either way. It merely required the court to ask whether making an order would be better for a child than making no order at all.

(d) The 'no-delay' principle (section 1(2))

Section 1(2) of the Act recognises that delay is harmful for a child.

Section 1(2) of the Children Act 1989

'In any proceedings in which any question with respect to the upbringing of a child arises, the court shall have regard to the general principle that any delay in determining the question is likely to prejudice the welfare of the child.'

To avoid delay, the progress of cases is determined by the court, which must draw up a timetable for section 8 order proceedings (s 11) and for care and supervision proceedings (s 32). The court can give directions, and the rules of court make provision, to avoid delay. Children's issues must be determined as soon as possible so that minimum disruption is caused to the child's life and the child is not left in limbo. Despite repeated attempts to reduce delay, it continues to be a problem, particularly in child protection and adoption cases, but the Government in 2012 announced changes to reduce the delays endemic in the family justice system.

10.4 Section 8 orders

Section 8 of the Children Act 1989 makes provision for the following orders which can be used in a wide range of different situations involving children:

- **A residence order** (determining with whom the child should live);
- **A contact order** (determining whom the child should visit or stay with);
- **A prohibited steps order** (preventing an action in respect of parental responsibility being taken);
- **A specific issue order** (determining an issue arising in respect of parental responsibility).

The Family Justice Review and the Government have recommended that two of the above orders – residence orders and contact orders – should be replaced by a new 'child arrangements order' (see p. 265 above).

Applicable principles   When considering whether or not to make, vary or discharge any section 8 order, the court must apply the welfare principle (s 1(1)) and the welfare checklist (s 1(3)); it must also apply the other provisions in section 1 of the Act, namely the no-delay (s 1(2)) and the no-order (s 1(5)) provisions (see above).

Applicants   Some persons have an 'automatic' right to apply for a section 8 order, whereas other persons, and children, need the court's permission to apply (see 10.10). Restrictions exist with regard to applications by local authorities (see below).

General provisions The court can: make interim section 8 orders (s 11(3)); attach directions and conditions to a section 8 order (s 11(7)); and grant a section 8 order without the other party being given notice of the proceedings (if urgent action is needed).

Restrictions Section 9 lays down the following restrictions which apply to section 8 orders:

- A court cannot make any section 8 order (other than a residence order) with respect to a child who is in local authority care (s 9(1)).
- A local authority cannot apply for a residence or contact order and no court shall make such an order in favour of a local authority (s 9(2)). This prohibition is to prevent local authorities using section 8 orders instead of a care or supervision order.
- A local authority foster-parent (or a person who was a foster-parent at any time during the previous six months) cannot apply for leave (permission) to apply for a section 8 order with respect to a foster-child unless the foster-parent has the consent of the local authority; or is the relative of the child; or the foster-child has lived with the foster-parent for at least one year preceding the application (s 9(3)).
- A court cannot make a specific issue order or a prohibited steps order with a view to achieving a result which could be achieved by making a residence or contact order; or in any way which is denied to the High Court (by section 100(2)) in the exercise of its inherent jurisdiction with respect to children (s 9(5)).
- Unless the circumstances are exceptional, a court cannot make a specific issue order, contact order or prohibited steps order to last after the child has reached the age of 16 (s 9(6)).
- Unless the circumstances are exceptional, a court cannot make any section 8 order if the child has already reached the age of 16 (s 9(7)).

10.5 Residence orders

> **A residence order** is an order 'settling the arrangements to be made as to the person with whom the child is to live' (s 8(1)).

(For residence orders on family breakdown, see 11.4.)

Residence orders were introduced by the Children Act 1989 to replace custody orders, with the aim of removing the claim right implicit in, and the adversarial undertones of, the term 'custody'. The emphasis on residence rather than custody was intended to reinforce the fact that both parents have a continuing role to play in relation to a child. With a residence order it is a question of where the child should live, rather than to whom the child belongs.

In addition to the general provisions and restrictions which apply to section 8 orders (see above), the following provisions in the Children Act specifically apply to residence orders:

- The court can make a 'shared' or 'joint' residence order in favour of two or more persons who live in different households (s 11(4)) (see further at p. 289).
- If a residence order is made there are restrictions on changing the child's surname and taking the child out of the UK (ss 13(1) and (2)).

▶ If, under a residence order, the child is to live with one of two parents who each has parental responsibility for him, the order ceases to be effective if the parents live together for a continuous period of more than six months (s 11(5)).

▶ The court can impose a condition (or conditions) on a residence order (s 11(7)).

Local authorities and residence orders A residence order is the only section 8 order that can be made in respect of a child in local authority care (s 9(1)), as to permit otherwise would undermine a local authority's statutory powers. However, a residence order cannot be applied for by, or be made in favour of, a local authority (s 9(2)), as this would allow a local authority to gain parental responsibility for a child by means other than a care order.

Residence orders and parental responsibility A residence order does not affect the parental responsibility of any other person who possesses such responsibility. Thus, parental responsibility is retained and continues whether or not a residence order is made.

If a residence order is made in favour of an unmarried father without parental responsibility, the court must also make an order under section 4 (see pp. 243–4) giving him that responsibility (s 12(1)). The same rules applies where a residence order is made in favour of a female civil partner who is a parent of a child by virtue of assisted reproduction or artificial insemination, but who does not have parental responsibility; the court must then make an order under section 4ZA giving her that responsibility (s 12(1A)) (see 9.5)

Where the court makes a residence order in favour of any person who is not the parent or guardian of the child concerned, then that person has parental responsibility for the child while the order is in force (s 12(2)), except for having the right to agree, or refuse to agree, to the making of an adoption order; or to appoint a guardian (s 12(3)).

10.6 Contact orders

> A **contact order** is an order 'requiring the person with whom the child lives, or is to live, to allow the child to visit or stay with the person named in the order, or for that person and the child otherwise to have contact with each other' (s 8(1)).

(For contact orders on family breakdown, see 11.5).

The Children Act 1989 introduced the term 'contact' to replace that of 'access' in order to stress the importance of children maintaining links with their parents and other family members on family breakdown.

The welfare principles and general provisions and restrictions which apply to section 8 orders (see above) also apply to contact orders. In respect of local authorities, a contact order cannot be made in respect of a child in care, and cannot be applied for by, or be made in favour of, a local authority (ss 9(1) and (2)). Contact in care is governed by section 34 of the Children Act (see 14.8). A contact order ceases to be effective if the parents live together for a continuous period of more than six months (s 11(6)).

New provisions governing the enforcement and facilitation of contact were brought into force on 8 December 2008 (see 11.6).

10.7   Prohibited steps orders

> A **prohibited steps order** is an order 'that no step which could be taken by a parent in meeting his parental responsibility for a child, and which is of a kind specified in the order, shall be taken by any person without the consent of the court' (s 8(1)).

The prohibited steps order (PSO), like the specific issue order (see 10.8 below), gives the court powers similar to those which before the Children Act 1989 were available only to the High Court under its inherent jurisdiction (see 8.7).

A PSO is a flexible injunctive type of order which can be used in a wide range of circumstances, for example to prohibit: a parent taking a child out of the UK; or making a unilateral decision about the child's medical treatment or education; or changing the child's surname.

In addition to the general provisions and restrictions which apply to section 8 orders (see p. 269 above), a PSO cannot be made to achieve the same result which could be achieved by making a residence or contact order, and cannot be made in any way which is denied to the High Court (by section 100(2)) in the exercise of its inherent jurisdiction with respect to children (s 9(5)).

As a PSO is an order prohibiting 'a step which could be taken by a parent in meeting his parental responsibility' for a child, it cannot be used to restrict anything other than some aspect of parental responsibility. For example, it cannot be used to restrict publicity about a child, since this is not within the scope of parental responsibility (this must be dealt with by the High Court under its inherent jurisdiction); or to prohibit a parent from occupying the family home (see, for example, *Re D (Prohibited Steps Order)* [1996] 2 FLR 273).

10.8   Specific issue orders

> A **specific issue order** is an order 'giving directions for the purpose of determining a specific question which has arisen, or which may arise, in connection with any aspect of parental responsibility for a child' (s 8(1)).

A specific issue order (SIO) can be made to settle any dispute which has arisen, or which may arise, in respect of the exercise of parental responsibility. It is a flexible order which can be used in a wide range of different situations, for example to settle a dispute arising in respect of a child's education or medical treatment, or a decision to move a child abroad, or to change a child's surname. A SIO (like a prohibited steps order) gives the court powers similar to those of the High Court under its inherent and wardship jurisdictions (see 8.7). In addition to the general provisions and restrictions which apply to section 8 orders (see p. 269 above), a SIO, like a prohibited steps order, cannot be made to achieve the same result which could be achieved by making a residence or contact order, and cannot be made in any way denied to the High Court (by section 100(2)) in the exercise of its inherent jurisdiction with respect to children (s 9(5)).

With respect to local authorities, a SIO cannot be made in relation to a child in care (s 9(1)). A local authority will instead have to seek leave to invoke the court's inherent jurisdiction to decide the matter (ss 100(2)–(5)). A SIO cannot be made to deem a child to be in need for the purposes of Part III of the Children Act 1989 (see 14.6), as this is not an 'aspect of parental responsibility' for the purposes of the order – the appropriate remedy is judicial review (see *Re J (Specific Issue Order: Leave to Apply)* [1995] 1 FLR 669).

10.9 Power of the court to make section 8 orders of its own motion

In any family proceedings in which a question arises with respect to the welfare of any child, the court may make a section 8 order with respect to the child if (s 10(1)): a person is entitled to apply for a section 8 order with respect to the child; a person has been given leave (permission) of the court to make the application; or the court considers that the order should be made even though no such application has been made.

'Family proceedings' are defined in sections 8(3) and (4) as being proceedings under the:

- inherent jurisdiction of the High Court in relation to children;
- Parts I, II and IV of the Children Act 1989;
- Matrimonial Causes Act 1973;
- Schedule 5 to the Civil Partnership Act 2004;
- Adoption and Children Act 2002;
- Domestic Proceedings and Magistrates' Courts Act 1978;
- Schedule 6 to the Civil Partnership Act 2004;
- Part III of the Matrimonial and Family Proceedings Act 1984;
- Family Law Act 1996;
- sections 11 and 12 of the Crime and Disorder Act 1998.

Thus section 8 orders can be made in a wide range of proceedings involving children, for example in divorce proceedings, adoption proceedings, and proceedings for non-molestation orders and occupation orders in domestic violence cases.

10.10 Applicants for section 8 orders

In addition to having the power to make a section 8 order of its own motion in any family proceedings (see above), the court may make an order with respect to a child on the application of a person who is entitled to apply or a person who has been granted leave (permission) by the court to do so (s 10(2)).

(a) Applicants not needing leave of the court

(i) Any section 8 order The following persons can apply for any section 8 order without needing leave of the court (s 10(4)): a parent, guardian, or special guardian of the child (s 10(4)(a)); a step-parent who has parental responsibility for the child under section 4A (s 10(4)(aa)); and a person in whose favour a residence order is in force with respect to the child (s 10(4)(b)).

(ii) Residence or contact order The following persons are entitled to apply for a residence or contact order without needing leave of the court (s 10(5)): a married person or civil partner (whether or not the marriage of civil partnership is subsisting) in relation to

whom the child is a child of the family (ss 10(5)(a), (aa)); any person with whom the child has lived for at least three years, which period need not be continuous but must not have begun more than five years before, or have ended more than three months before, applying for the order (ss 10(5)(b), (10)); any person who has the consent of each person in whose favour a residence order was made; any person who has the consent of the local authority when a child is in care; and any other person who has the consent of each person (if any) who has parental responsibility for the child (s 10(5)(c)).

An application for a residence order can be made in respect of a child who is the subject of a special guardianship order, but only with leave of the court (s 10(7A)).

(iii) Residence order (local authority foster-parents and relatives)   A local authority foster-parent is entitled to apply without leave of the court for a residence order with respect to the child if the child has lived with him/her for a period of at least one year immediately preceding the application (s 10(5A)). The same rule applies to a relative of a child (s 10(5B)).

(b)   Applicants needing leave of the court

Certain persons need leave (permission) of the court to apply for a section 8 order.

(i) Children   A child needs leave of the court to apply, which the court may grant only if it is satisfied that the child has sufficient understanding to make the proposed application (s 10(8)). The court can take into account the likelihood of the proposed application succeeding, and, on that basis, refuse leave even if the child has sufficiency of understanding (see Johnson J in *Re H (Residence Order: Child's Application for Leave)* [2000] 1 FLR 780). Applications for leave are heard in the High Court. There has been conflicting judicial opinion as to whether the child's welfare is paramount in leave applications; but in *Re C (Residence) (Child's Application for Leave)* [1995] 1 FLR 927 Stuart-White J considered these divergent views and concluded that the child's welfare is an important, but not a paramount, consideration. This approach was subsequently adopted by Johnson J in *Re H (Residence Order: Child's Application for Leave)* (above).

(ii) Other persons   In leave applications by persons other than children the court must have particular regard to (s 10(9)): the nature of the proposed application; the applicant's connection with the child; any risk of the proposed application disrupting the child's life to such an extent that he would be harmed by it; and (where the child is being looked after by a local authority) the local authority's plans for the child's future and the wishes and feelings of the child's parents.

The welfare principle does not apply (*Re A and W (Minors) (Residence Order: Leave to Apply)* [1992] Fam 182, [1992] 2 FLR 154). The application will be refused if it is frivolous or vexatious, or otherwise an abuse of the court. The case must disclose a real prospect of success, and there must be a serious issue to be tried and a good arguable case (*per* Wall J in *Re M (Minors) (Contact: Leave to Apply)* [1995] 2 FLR 98). Leave was granted, for example, in *Re J (Leave to Issue Application for Residence Order)* [2003] 1 FLR 114 (to allow a grandmother to apply for a residence order); and in *Re H (Leave to Apply for Residence Order)* [2008] EWCA Civ 503, [2008] 2 FLR 848 (to allow a married couple to apply for a residence order after they had been adjudged to be too old to apply for an adoption order in respect of a child whose half-sibling they were already legally bringing up).

Applications by grandparents   There has been discussion from time to time about whether grandparents should be able to apply for a section 8 order without leave of the court. However, the Family Justice Review (FJR) (see p. 7) in its *Final Report* in 2011 recommended that the leave requirement should remain in order to prevent 'hopeless or vexatious applications that are not in the interests of the child' (see para 110 of the Executive Summary). The Government agreed with this recommendation (see its *Response*, 2012) but stated that it was committed to ensuring that children have meaningful relationships with family members who are important to them following family separation, where it is in their best interests and safe. The Government said that, as a matter of good practice, supporting a child's ongoing relationships with their grandparents and wider family members should be considered when making arrangements for a child's future.

10.11 Other orders under the Children Act 1989

A wide range of orders other than section 8 orders can be made by the courts under the Children Act 1989.

(a) Part I orders

Parental responsibility orders (section 4)   The court can make an order giving the following persons parental responsibility: an unmarried father (s 4); the other female parent where the mother has had a child by assisted reproduction or artificial insemination (s 4ZA); and a step-parent (s 4A).

Order appointing a guardian of a child (section 5)   The court can appoint a person to be a guardian of a child (see 9.8).

Order for a welfare report (section 7)   When considering any question with respect to a child under the Children Act 1989, the court may request a report from a Cafcass officer (see 1.7) or from a local authority officer (or such other person as the authority considers appropriate) on such matters relating to the child as are required to be dealt with in the report (s 7(1)).

(b) Part II orders (orders with respect to children in family proceedings)

The following orders are orders which can be made in family proceedings under Part II of the Children Act 1989:

(i) Section 8 orders   (See 10.4-10.8 above.)

(ii) Contact activity directions and conditions etc (sections 11A–11P)   The family courts have various powers to facilitate and enforce contact orders (see 11.6).

(iii) Special guardianship orders (sections 14A–14G)   A special guardianship order (a SGO) is an order giving a person parental responsibility for a child which, for the duration of the order, can be exercised to the exclusion of the parental responsibility of any other person (apart from another special guardian). SGOs are sometimes used as an alternative to adoption (see 15.14).

(iv) Orders for financial relief (section 15 and Schedule 1)   The family courts have jurisdiction to make finance and property orders for children under Schedule 1 (see 12.3).

(v) Family assistance orders (section 16)   Under section 16 the court in family proceedings can make a family assistance order (FAO), which is an order requiring a Cafcass officer or a Welsh family proceedings officer or an officer of the local authority to assist, advise and befriend any person named in the order (s 16(1)) A FAO is a short-term alternative to a section 8 order, but it may also be used when a section 8 order has already been made but where additional support is required.

The following persons can be named in a FAO: any parent, guardian or special guardian of the child; any person with whom the child is living or in whose favour a contact order is in force with respect to the child; and the child (s 16(2)). A FAO cannot be made without the consent of all those persons named in the order (other than the child) (s 16(3)). It may direct the person(s) named in the order to take such steps as may be so specified with a view to enabling the officer concerned to be kept informed of the address of any person named in the order and to be allowed to visit any such person (s 16(4)). The order can be made to last for up to 12 months (s 16(5)). An order cannot be made against a local authority officer unless the local authority agrees and the child concerned lives (or will live) in its area (s 16(7)).

If the court makes a FAO which is to be in force at the same time as a section 8 order (see above) with respect to a child, the order may direct the officer concerned to report to the court on such matters relating to the section 8 order as the court may require (including whether the section 8 order should be varied or discharged) (s 16(6)).

Section 16 has been amended to make FAOs useful for the purpose of facilitating contact (see 11.6). Thus, if the court makes a FAO with respect to a child which is to be in force at the same time as a contact order, the order may direct the officer concerned to give advice and assistance as regards establishing, improving and maintaining contact to such of the persons named in the order as may be specified (s 16(4A)).

The *Practice Direction 12M – Family Assistance Orders: Consultation* provides that, before making a FPO, the court must obtain the opinion (oral or written) of a Cafcass officer or Welsh family proceedings officer as to whether it is in the best interests of the child for an order to be made; and, if so, how the order should operate and for what period. The *Practice Direction* also provides that, before making a FAO, the court must give any person whom it proposes to name in the order the opportunity to comment upon any opinion given by that officer.

(c)   Part IV orders (care and supervision)

(i) Care and supervision orders (section 31)   Where a child is suffering, or is likely to suffer, significant harm, the court can, if certain threshold criteria are satisfied and the child's welfare requires it, make a care order placing the child in the care of a local authority, or a supervision order placing the child under the supervision of a local authority officer or probation officer (s 35) (see 14.7).

(ii) Order for contact with a child in care (section 34)   Where a child is in local authority care the authority must allow parents and certain other persons reasonable contact with the child, and the court can make orders in respect of such contact, including the termination of contact (see 14.8).

(iii) Education supervision order (section 36)   Where a child of compulsory school age is not being properly educated, the court can, on the application of a local education authority, make an education supervision order in favour of that authority (see, for example, *Essex County Council v B* [1993] 1 FLR 866). These orders are rarely made.

(iv) Order that a local authority investigate the child's circumstances (section 37)   Where in any family proceedings a question arises in respect of the child's welfare and it may be appropriate for a care or supervision order to be made, the court may direct that a local authority undertake an investigation into the child's circumstances (s 37(1)). The Court of Appeal has held that it is for the courts, not local authorities, to determine whether the requirements for making a section 37 order are satisfied and whether directions should be made under section 37 (see *Lambeth LBC v TK and KK* [2008] 1 FLR 1229).

(d)   Part V orders (protection of children)

(i) Child assessment order (section 43)   Where there is reasonable cause to suspect that a child is suffering, or is likely to suffer, significant harm and an assessment of the child's health and development or of the way in which the child is being treated is needed, the court can make a child assessment order (see 14.9).

(ii) Emergency protection order (section 44)   Where there is reasonable cause to believe that a child is likely to suffer significant harm, the court can in certain circumstances make an emergency protection order, which authorises the removal from, or retention of the child in, certain accommodation (see 14.9).

(e)   A section 91(14) order restricting an application to the court

Section 91(14) of the Children Act 1989 provides that, when disposing of any application under that Act, the court (whether or not it decides to make an order) can order that no application for an order under the Act of any specified kind may be made with respect to the child by any person named in the order without the court's permission. The aim of a section 91(14) order is to prevent unnecessary and disruptive court applications which may be detrimental to the child's best interests. It gives the court power to prevent a party from making repeated and unreasonable applications to the court. However, an order does not impose an absolute bar on applying to the court, as it can be lifted by the court where the applicant can show a need for renewed judicial investigation into the matter. Because of the human rights and natural justice implications of prohibiting access to the courts, there are strict controls on the exercise of the courts' power to make a section 91(14) order (see below).

The approach of the courts   The courts are greatly aware of the severity of making a section 91(14) order, and will only do so if there is a clear evidential basis for making it. The leading case is *Re P (Section 91(14) Guidelines) (Residence and Religious Heritage)* [1999] 2 FLR 573 where Butler-Sloss LJ in the Court of Appeal laid down the following guidelines governing the exercise of the court's discretion to make a section 91(14) order:

1. 'Section 91(14) should be read in conjunction with s.1(1) which makes the welfare of the child the paramount consideration.

2. The power to restrict applications to the court is discretionary and in the exercise of its discretion the court must weigh in the balance all the relevant circumstances.

3. An important consideration is that to impose a restriction is a statutory intrusion into the right of a party to bring proceedings before the court and to be heard in matters affecting his/her child.

4. The power is therefore to be used with great care and sparingly, the exception and not the rule.

5. It is generally to be seen as a useful weapon of last resort in cases of repeated and unreasonable applications.

6. In suitable circumstances (and on clear evidence), a court may impose the leave restriction in cases where the welfare of the child requires it, although there is no past history of making unreasonable applications.

7. In cases under para (6) above, the court will need to be satisfied first that the facts go beyond the commonly encountered need for a time to settle to a regime ordered by the court and the all too common situation where there is animosity between the adults in dispute or between the local authority and the family and secondly that there is a serious risk that, without the imposition of the restriction, the child or the primary carers will be subject to unacceptable strain.

8. A court may impose the restriction on making applications in the absence of a request from any of the parties, subject, of course, to the rules of natural justice such as an opportunity for the parties to be heard on the point.

9. A restriction may be imposed with or without limitation of time.

10. The degree of restriction should be proportionate to the harm it is intended to avoid. Therefore the court imposing the restriction should carefully consider the extent of the restriction to be imposed and specify, where appropriate, the type of application to be restrained and the duration of the order.

11. It would be undesirable in other than the most exceptional cases to make the order *ex parte.*'

There are many reported cases where an appeal against the making of a section 91(14) order has been allowed by the Court of Appeal on the ground that the lower court had failed to apply the above guidelines appropriately (see for example, *Re G (A Child)* [2010] EWCA Civ 470; and *Re A (Contact: Section 91(14))* [2009] EWCA Civ 1548).

A section 91(14) order can be made against *both* parties to the litigation (see, for example, *Re N (Section 91(14))* [2009] EWHC 3055 (Fam), [2010] 1 FLR 1110, where the litigation between the parents concerning the child (aged 8) had been continuous since he was 2 years old).

Human rights As a result of their obligations under the Human Rights Act 1998 (see 1.8) the courts must ensure that making a section 91(14) order does not infringe a person's rights under the ECHR, in particular Article 6 (a right of access to the court) and Article 8 (a right to family life). In the leading case of *Re P (Section 91(14) Guidelines) (Residence and Religious Heritage)* [1999] 2 FLR 573 (see above), although the Court of Appeal held that making a section 91(14) order did not breach Article 6 ECHR (as it was only a partial restriction on disallowing a claim before the court), it ruled that, because of the severity of making an order, the court should specify what type of court applications are restricted and for how long.

Summary

▶ The Children Act 1989 (CA 1989) contains much of the civil law, private and public, relating to children. The Act consolidated much of the civil law relating to children and introduced new policies and principles. Influences on the Act included *The Report of the Inquiry into Child Abuse in Cleveland 1987* (Cm 412, 1988) and the *Gillick* case (2006). There have been many amendments to the Act, and there are new proposals to amend the Act to replace the section 8 residence and contact orders with a new 'child arrangements order'.

▶ The following Parts of the Act are particularly important. Part I ('Introductory'); Part II ('Orders with Respect to Children in Family Proceedings'); Part III ('Local Authority Support for Children and Families'); Part IV ('Care and Supervision'); and Part V ('Protection of Children'). Part XII ('Miscellaneous and General') is also important as it includes provisions on: the effect and duration of orders (s 91); privacy for children in certain proceedings (s 97); restrictions on the use of the inherent jurisdiction (s 100); and the interpretation of the Act (s 105). The following schedules are also important: Schedule 1 ('Financial Provision for Children'); Schedule 2 ('Local Authority Support for Children and Families'); and Schedule 3 ('Supervision Orders').

▶ Section 1 of the Act lays down the following principles: the welfare principle (s 1(1)); the no-delay principle (s 1(2)); the 'welfare checklist' (s 1(3)); and the minimum intervention principle (s 1(5)). The welfare checklist must be applied in contested section 8 order proceedings, special guardianship proceedings and in care and supervision proceedings (s 1(4)).

▶ The court can make the following 'section 8 orders': a residence order; a contact order; a prohibited steps order; and a specific issue order. The welfare principles (see above) apply when the court is considering whether or not to make, vary or discharge any of these orders. An order can be made on application or by the court of its own motion in any family proceedings. Some persons have an automatic right to apply but other persons, including the child, need leave (permission) of the court (s 10).

▶ A residence order is an order 'settling the arrangements to be made as to the person with whom the child is to live' (s 8(1)). The court can also make a 'shared' or 'joint' residence order (s 11(4), and see p. 289). If a residence order is made, there are restrictions on changing the child's surname or taking the child out of the UK (s 13(1) and (2)). The court can impose a condition (or conditions) on a residence order (s 11(7)). Special rules apply to residence orders and local authorities (s 9(1) and (2)).

▶ A contact order is an order 'requiring the person with whom the child lives, or is to live, to allow the child to visit or stay with the person named in the order, or for that person and the child otherwise to have contact with each other' (s 8(1)). The same provisions which apply to residence orders and other section 8 orders apply, such as the welfare principle and the rules on applicants. Provisions governing the enforcement and facilitation of contact are found in sections 11A–11P. A contact order cannot be made in respect of a child in local authority care.

▶ A prohibited steps order is an order 'that no step which could be taken by a parent in meeting his parental responsibility for a child, and which is of a kind specified in the order, shall be taken by any person without the consent of the court' (s 8(1)). The same rules which apply to residence orders and other section 8 orders apply.

▶ A specific issue order is an order 'giving directions for the purpose of determining a specific question which has arisen, or which may arise, in connection with any aspect of parental responsibility for a child' (s 8(1)). The same rule which apply to residence orders and other section 8 orders apply.

▶ The court in family proceedings can make a section 8 order on an application, or on its own motion in any family proceedings (s 10(1) and (2)). 'Family proceedings' are defined in sections 8(3) and (4).

Summary cont'd

▶ There are two sorts of applicant for a section 8 order: persons who can apply as of right (namely parents and guardians with or without parental responsibility); and persons who need leave (permission) of the court to apply (see s 10). Children can apply with leave of the court (s 10(8)). There has been discussion about giving grandparents the right to apply without leave, but the Family Law Review and the Government have rejected this.

▶ Under Part I of the Act, the court can make: a parental responsibility order (s 4); an order appointing a guardian of a child (s 5); and an order for a welfare report (s 7). Under Part II, in addition to section 8 orders, the court can make: a special guardianship order (ss 14A–G); orders for financial relief (s 15 and Schedule 1); and a family assistance order (s 16). Provisions with respect to facilitating and enforcing contact are found in sections 11A–11P. Cafcass officers and Welsh family proceedings officers have a duty under Part II to conduct risk assessments of children (s 16A). Under Part IV, the court can make a range of public law orders including, in particular, care and supervision orders (sections 32 and 35 – see Chapter 14). Under Part V the court can make a child assessment order (s 43), and an emergency protection order (s 44) (see Chapter 14). Under section 91(14) the court can also make an order restricting an application under the Children Act 1989, subject to strict requirements being satisfied.

Further reading and references

Fortin, 'Children's rights – substance or spin?' [2006] Fam Law 757.
Freeman, 'The next Children's Act' [1998] Fam Law 341.
Mitchell, *Children Act Private Law Proceedings: A Handbook* (3rd edn), 2012, Jordans.

Websites

Legislation: www.legislation.gov.uk

Links to relevant websites can also be found at: www.palgrave.com/law/familylaw8e

Chapter 11

Children on family breakdown

11.1 Introduction

This chapter deals with the law governing arrangements for children when parental relationships break down. The law is laid down in the Children Act 1989 (see also Chapter 10). After divorce, civil partnership dissolution or parental separation, parents continue to have parental responsibility for their children (see 9.3); and they also have a duty to make financial provision (see Chapter 12). Despite the legal provisions and the number of reported cases, most separating couples make their own arrangements for the care of their children without resorting to court proceedings. It is generally recognised that it is better for both parents and children if parents resolve matters themselves, rather than bringing court proceedings.

This introductory section deals with a range of matters relating to the law on family breakdown. Two key areas of controversy are whether a presumption of shared parenting should be introduced (see pp. 283-4), and whether the courts are adopting the correct approach in cases where a parent wishes to relocate to another country with the child (see 11.9). This section starts, however, by looking at the Family Justice Review's discussions of the law.

(i) The Family Justice Review's recommendations on the law relating to family breakdown The Family Justice Review (FJR) (see further at p. 7) has recently looked at family law, including the law relating to families when parental relationships break down. In its *Final Report*, published in November 2011, the FJR identified various ways in which the current processes relating to private family law on parental separation fall short:

> ***Family Justice Review: Final Report* (November 2011, Ministry of Justice), paras 105 and 106 of the Executive Summary**
>
> '**105.** Our current processes fall short in many ways.
>
> ▶ Many parents do not know where to get the information and support they need to resolve their issues without recourse to court.
> ▶ There is limited awareness of alternatives to court, and a good deal of misunderstanding.
> ▶ Too many cases end up in court, and court determination is a blunt instrument.
> ▶ The court system is hard to navigate, a problem that is likely to become even more important as proposed reductions in legal aid mean more people represent themselves.
> ▶ There is a feeling (which may or may not be right) that lawyers generally take an adversarial approach that inflames rather than reduces conflict.
> ▶ Cases are expensive and take a long time.
>
> **106.** There are more fundamental issues that go beyond process.
>
> ▶ Children say they do not understand what is going on and do not have enough opportunity to have their say.
> ▶ There is a lack of understanding about parental responsibility, both legally and more generally: some mistakenly think the balance of parental responsibility shifts following separation, with one parent assuming full responsibility for their child.
> ▶ This goes with the difficulty for all involved in assuring that children retain a relationship with both parents, and others, including grandparents, after separation where this is safe. Some have a perception that the system favours mothers over fathers.'

The FJR made a wide range of recommendations to address the above issues in order to 'set out a clear process for separation that emphasises shared parental responsibility, provides information, manages expectations and helps people to understand the costs they face at each stage'; and with the emphasis throughout on 'enabling people to resolve their disputes safely outside court wherever possible' (para 107, Executive Summary). With respect to the law relating to children and parents on family breakdown, the FJR's recommendations included, among other things: the introduction of 'Parenting Agreements' in which parents would set out arrangements for their children post separation; a new 'child arrangements order' to replace residence and contact orders (see p. 265); a greater role for mediation; more opportunities for children to have their voice heard; and better measures for the enforcement of orders. However, the FJR has argued against the introduction of a legislative presumption of shared parenting (see pp. 283–4 below).

The Government accepted the FJR's recommendations, except for the proposal that shared parenting should be implemented (see Part F 'Changes to private FJR's law', *The Government Response to the Family Justice Review: A system with children and families at its heart*, February 2012, Cm 8273, Ministry of Justice and Department for Education).

The Children and Families Bill 2012–2013 contains measures relating to the FJR's proposals, including measures relating to shared parenting. It also aims to speed up court processes to reduce the delays endemic in children's cases. The Bill was debated in the Commons in February 2013 and sent to the Public Bill Committee for scrutiny.

(ii) The impact of family breakdown on children   Children may suffer emotionally when their parents' relationship breaks up. They may suffer fear, anger, withdrawal, grief, depression and guilt. Research on children of divorced parents (by the Centre of Longitudinal Studies, based on the National Child Development Study, July 2008) found that divorce was not a single event in a child's life but a process which could begin years before the parents separated and which could have repercussions that reverberated through childhood and into adulthood. According to the report, children from separated families tended to do less well at school and in their subsequent careers. They were more likely to experience the break-up of their own partnerships; and more likely to have higher levels of alcohol consumption and problem-drinking in adulthood. They were also likely to have poorer levels of general health; and a small minority of young adults developed serious mental health problems associated with parental divorce. (The report is available at: www.cls.ioe.ac.uk.)

(iii) Reaching agreement and keeping cases out of the court   Because of the emotional impact that divorce and parental separation can have on children (and parents), it is better if parents make amicable arrangements for their children on family breakdown. Most parents make their own arrangements, but some fail to reach agreement and end up having to apply to the court for residence and/or contact orders. Going to court, however, can be costly, time-consuming, unpredictable and traumatic; and the judge may decide to refuse to make the order sought or make a different order. Also, having a court order does not necessarily guarantee that the other parent will comply with it.

Lawyers who deal with residence and contact disputes on family breakdown adopt a conciliatory, not a litigious, approach, because of the benefits of reducing hostility and bitterness where children are involved. Mediation and other forms of alternative dispute resolution (ADR) are increasingly being promoted as a much better way of resolving parental disputes than going to court (see 1.4). The following words of Baroness Hale in a case on shared residence orders and housing (see further at p. 92) acknowledge the importance of agreement where children are concerned:

▶ **Baroness Hale of Richmond in** *Holmes-Moorhouse v London Borough of Richmond-upon-Thames* **[2009] UKHL 7, [2009] 1 FLR 904**

'The reality is that every effort is made, both before and during any family proceedings, to encourage the parents to agree between themselves what will be best for their children. There are many good reasons for this. The parents know their own children better than anyone. They also know their own circumstances, what will suit them best, what resources are available and what they can afford. Agreed solutions tend to work much better and last much longer than solutions imposed by a court after contested proceedings. The contest is likely to entrench opposing viewpoints and inflame parental conflict. Conflict is well known to be bad for children. Not only that, the arrangements made when the couple separate are bound to have to change over time, as the children grow up and their own and their parents' circumstances change. Parents who have been able or helped, through mediation or in other ways, to agree a solution at the outset are more likely to be able to negotiate those changes for themselves, rather than to have to return to court for further orders.'

Despite the fact that it is better if disputes about children on family breakdown are kept out of the court, many thousands of children continue to be the subject of parental disputes on family breakdown. Thus, according to *Judicial and Court Statistics 2011* (Ministry of Justice, 2012), the number of children involved in private law applications rose to a peak in 2009, but fell to 109,656 in 2011, a similar level to that last seen in 2006. The total number of children involved in private law applications in 2011 was 109,656, a 13 per cent decrease on 2010 when 126,220 were involved.

(iv) Cafcass and children on family breakdown   Cafcass performs important functions with respect to children on family breakdown (see 1.7). One of its main functions is to provide officers for the court in children's cases. Of particular importance is the Children and Family Reporter who has a duty to provide a welfare report if requested by the court (see below). Cafcass officers also perform an important conciliatory role in endeavouring to help parents reach agreement about arrangements for their children. They also have to conduct risk assessments; and they have various obligations in respect of facilitating contact (see 11.6). A Children's Guardian, an officer of Cafcass, may be appointed by the court (under r 16.3 of the Family Procedure Rules 2010) to represent the interests of a child who has been made a party to family proceedings.

(v) Welfare reports   The court has the power to order a welfare report under section 7 of the Children Act 1989 by a Cafcass officer (see above). A welfare report is important as it provides an independent assessment of the case. The recommendations in the report are particularly important where a case is finely balanced; and judges must not depart from those recommendations without giving reasons. Failure to give reasons may provide grounds for an appeal (as it did in *Re M (Residence)* [2004] EWCA Civ 1574, [2005] 1 FLR 656 where the Court of Appeal ordered a retrial). If the court decides to reject a clear conclusion and recommendation made in the report, it must allow the Cafcass officer to give oral evidence (see *Re R (Residence Order)* [2009] EWCA Civ 445, where the Court of Appeal held, by a majority, that the judge had erred in law in not hearing

the Cafcass officer). However, where there is no clear recommendation in a report, it is not necessary for the court to adjourn proceedings to hear the officer (*Re C (Section 8 Order: Court Welfare Officer)* [1995] 1 FLR 617).

(vi) The voice of the child   Children do not have automatic party status in residence and contact proceedings, but children have been increasingly given rights of separate representation (see 8.6).

(vii) Family disputes involving matters of parental responsibility in the EU   Jurisdiction with regard to disputes between parents living in different Member States of the European Union is governed by Council Regulation (EC) (No. 2201/2003) Concerning Jurisdiction and the Recognition and Enforcement of Judgments in Matrimonial Matters and in Matters of Parental Responsibility (Brussels II Revised). Article 8(1) provides that: 'The courts of a Member State shall have jurisdiction in matters of parental responsibility over a child who is habitually resident in that Member State at the time the court is seised'. The aim of Article 8(1) is to ensure that, in relation to matters of parental responsibility (including applications for residence and contact), that jurisdiction rests with the courts of the child's habitual residence; although Article 12 provides a limited opportunity for parents to elect for the jurisdiction of the court seised with the divorce proceedings if that is, *inter alia*, in the best interests of the child (see, for instance, *Bush v Bush* [2008] EWCA Civ, [2008] 2 FLR 1437).

In *Re I (A Child)* [2009] UKSC 10, [2010] 1 FLR 361 the Supreme Court unanimously held that Article 12 of Brussels II (Revised) can apply where a child is habitually resident outside the EU, as nothing in Article 12 limits jurisdiction to children resident in the EU. In *Re I* the English mother wished to enforce contact with her son who was living with his paternal grandmother and aunt in Pakistan (after his father had removed him there in breach of an undertaking to return him to the UK). On the facts of the case, it was held to be in the best interests of the child for the case to be heard in the UK.

(vii) Shared parenting   There has been discussion in the last few years about the possibility of introducing a presumption of shared parenting. In 2011, a Private Members' Bill, the Shared Parenting Orders Bill 2010–2012, was put before Parliament to promote shared parenting but it went nowhere. Another Private Member's Bill on shared parenting, the Children (Access to Parents) Bill 2012–2013, had its first reading in the House of Commons in June 2012, but was withdrawn in the following November. There has been considerable resistance in some quarters to the introduction of a statutory presumption of shared parenting, particularly by single mothers. Some academics have also argued against it. For instance, Maclean has stated (at [2011] Fam Law 669) that 'to legislate for all, rather than putting the welfare of each child in each situation first, seems at best foolhardy and at worst downright dangerous'.

The Family Justice Review (FJR) (see above and at p. 7), as part of its consideration of parental responsibility, also looked at the possibility of legislative reform to introduce shared parenting. However, in the light of reforms which had taken place in Sweden and Australia, the FJR warned against introducing legislation which created a perception and expectation that there was an assumed parental right to substantially shared or equal time for both parents. In its final report (*Family Justice Review: Final Report* , Ministry of Justice, November 2011) it concluded that: 'no legislation should be introduced that creates or risks creating the perception that there is a parental right to substantially shared or equal time for both parents' (para 5.76). In the Foreword to the *Final Report*, David Norgrove, Chair of the FJR, stated that the Panel believed strongly that most children benefit from a relationship with both parents post separation, but that the best way to achieve this was 'through parental education and information combined with clear, quick processes for resolution where there are disputes'. (For commentators who supported the FJR's recommendation against shared parenting, see Fehlberg [2012] Fam Law 709; and Nickols [2012] Fam Law 573.)

Alleged difficulties relating to Australian reforms introducing shared parenting was one reason why the FJR rejected the idea of introducing a shared parenting presumption in England and Wales. But Bryant CJ, an Australian judge (see [2012] *International Family Law* 269), while recognising that Australia had made some mistakes, was of the view that it might be wrong to exclude the possibility of reforms in England and Wales just because of the Australian experience. Parkinson (see [2012] Fam Law 758) claimed that none of the arguments made by the FJR about the Australian experience could be supported by the available evidence.(See also Rhoades [2012] CFLQ 158.)

The UK Government accepted most of the FJR's proposals but not its arguments against shared parenting (see *The Government Response to the Family Justice Review: A system with children and families at its heart* Cm 8273, Ministry of Justice and Department for Education, February 2012). However, the Government said that it was mindful of the lessons which must be learnt from the Australian experience and that it would therefore consider very carefully how legislation could be framed to avoid the pitfalls of the Australian experience. Between June and September 2012, the Government conducted a consultation on shared parenting to consider four options for amending section 1 of the Children Act 1989 in order to enshrine shared parenting in the law (see *Cooperative parenting following family separation: Proposed legislation on the involvement of both parents in a child's life*, Department for Education, 13 June 2012). The Government's preferred option is the introduction of a legislative provision which 'requires the court to work on the presumption that a child's welfare is likely to be furthered through safe involvement with both parents – unless the evidence shows this not to be safe or in the child's best interests'.

(The FJR recommended the introduction of Parenting Agreements and a new order, a 'child arrangements order', to replace residence and contact orders (see p. 265), which the Government is proposing to introduce in order to help promote the notion of shared parenting.)

11.2 Human rights and family breakdown

The Human Rights Act 1998 requires courts (including family courts) to comply with the European Convention for the Protection of Human Rights (the ECHR) and to take into account the decisions of the European Court of Human Rights (the ECtHR) (see 1.8). In *Hoppe v Germany (Application No. 28422/95)* [2003] 1 FLR 384 the ECtHR identified the following general principles which courts must take into account when exercising their powers in the context of children on family breakdown:

▶ The mutual enjoyment by parent and child of each other's company constitutes a fundamental element of family life, even if the parents' relationship has broken down; and any measures which hinder such enjoyment amount to an interference with Article 8 (the right to family life).

- The task of the ECtHR is not to substitute itself for the domestic authorities in the exercise of their responsibilities regarding custody and access, but to review, in the light of the ECHR, their decisions in the exercise of their margin of appreciation.
- In determining whether the interference into family life is necessary in a democratic society for the purposes of Article 8(2) (see 1.8), consideration of what lies in the best interests of the child is of crucial importance. A fair balance must be struck between the child's interests and those of the parent, and, in striking such a balance, particular importance must be attached to the best interests of the child, which, depending on their nature and seriousness, may override those of the parent.
- In cases concerning a person's relationship with his or her child there is a duty to exercise exceptional diligence in view of the risk that the passage of time may result in a *de facto* determination of the matter.
- The manner in which Article 6 (the right to a fair and public hearing) applies to proceedings before courts of appeal depends on the special features of the proceedings viewed as a whole.
- It is not a breach of Article 6 if proceedings involving children are heard in private.
- The court must avoid delay in reaching a final decision.

In *Sahin v Germany; Sommerfeld v Germany(Application Nos. 30943/96 and 31871/96)* [2003] 2 FLR 671 the ECtHR held that, although national authorities enjoy a wide margin of appreciation when deciding on custody matters, a stricter scrutiny is called for regarding any further limitations, such as restrictions placed on parental rights of access. As regards hearing a child in court on the issue of access, the ECtHR held that domestic courts are not always required to hear the child. It depends on the facts of each case, having regard to the age and maturity of the child concerned.

11.3 The duty to children in divorce and civil partnership dissolution proceedings

An important policy objective of the law of divorce is to protect children. In furtherance of this objective, the applicant for divorce must file with the court a Statement of Arrangements for Children (Form D8A), a form setting out required information about any children under 16, or under 18 who are at school or college or are training for a trade, profession or vocation. The Statement of Arrangements includes details, for instance, relating to the child's home, education and training, childcare, maintenance, contact and health. The applicant must sign the form and, where possible, the respondent must agree with the information on it. The applicant must state on the form whether he or she intends to apply for any section 8 order under the Children Act 1989. (The form is available at www.justice.gov.uk and directgov.uk.)

As a divorce cannot be made absolute until the district judge has considered arrangements for the children (see r 7.25 Family Procedure Rules 2010), the purpose of the Statement of Arrangements is to enable the court to fulfil its duty under section 41(1) which requires it to consider whether, in the light of the actual or proposed arrangements made for the children, it should exercise any of its powers under the Children Act 1989 with respect to any of the children (for these powers, see Chapter 10). If the court is satisfied with the arrangements, the district judge will certify to that effect. If not, then the district judge can direct that further evidence be filed, or order a welfare report, or order the parent(s) to attend court. If the child's interests require it, and the court is not able to exercise any of its powers under the Children Act 1989 without further consideration of the case, the district judge can direct that the decree of divorce should not be made absolute (s 41(2)). In practice, however, this rarely happens.

The same rules above apply if there are children involved in the dissolution of a civil partnership, except that, instead of section 41 MCA 1973, the relevant provision is section 63 of the Civil Partnership Act 2004.

11.4   Residence disputes

An unresolvable dispute about residence arrangements for a child on family breakdown can be decided by making an application for a residence order, which the High Court, county courts and magistrates' family proceedings courts have jurisdiction to make under section 8 of the Children Act 1989 (see also 10.5).

Residence disputes often go hand in hand with contact disputes, as the non-resident parent may wish to have contact with the child (see 11.5). Other parental disputes (for example about education, medical treatment, taking a child out of the UK, and changing the child's name) can be decided by making an application for a prohibited steps or specific issue order (see 10.7 and 10.8). Some parents enter into disputes about financial provision for their children on family breakdown (see Chapter 12).

Residence (and contact) orders made in England and Wales can be enforced in other parts of the UK under section 25 of the Family Law Act 1986.

(a)   A residence order

A residence order is an order 'settling the arrangements to be made as to the person with whom a child is to live' (s 8(1) Children Act 1989, and see further at 10.5). Before the Children Act 1989 came into force unresolvable parental disputes about children on family breakdown were decided by way of custody proceedings. However, in discussions leading up to the Children Act the Law Commission was critical of the term 'custody' because it created a parental claim right and therefore had the potential to increase hostility and bitterness between parents which was detrimental for children. The Children Act 1989 therefore introduced residence orders to replace custody orders, with the aim of placing the emphasis on a child's living arrangements, not on which of the parents had a greater claim to the child. The idea was to encourage the view that parents have responsibilities for their children, not claims to them, an idea that was partly influenced by Lord Scarman's preference (in the *Gillick* case – see 8.4) for the term 'responsibility' rather than 'rights'.

In 2012 the Family Justice Review recommended that residence and contact orders should be replaced with a new order, 'a child arrangements order' (see p. 265). The Government, in response, said that it saw 'value in changing the emphasis of court orders to focus on the practical arrangements for caring for the child, and remove the current emphasis on the labels "contact" and "residence"' (*Family Justice Review Final Report*, Ministry of Justice and Department of Education, February 2012). The Government aims to bring forward legislation on this issue at the earliest opportunity.

Applicants   The child's parents (married or unmarried, and whether or not the father has parental responsibility) can apply. Other persons (including the child) can apply, but only with leave (permission) of the court (see further in Chapter 10).

Applicable principles   See below.

Other powers   The court can: attach a condition to a residence order (s 11(7)); order a welfare report (s 7); and direct that a local authority investigate the child's circumstances (s 37). It can also make a shared residence order (s 11(4)) (see p. 289 below).

Duration   The order can be made to last until the child reaches the age of 18 (s 91(10)).

(b)   How the court exercises its powers in residence order proceedings

When exercising its powers to decide whether or not to make a residence order the court must apply the principles in section 1 of the Children Act 1989 (see 10.3). Thus, it must apply the welfare principle (s 1(1)), the no-delay principle (s 1(2)) and the minimum intervention principle (s 1(5)). In contested proceedings it must also apply the s 1(3) 'welfare checklist'.

The welfare checklist   (section 1(3))
In addition to considering the paramountcy of the child's welfare (s 1(1)), the court in contested residence proceedings must apply the factors listed in section 1(3) of the Children Act 1989. The list is not exhaustive — other factors can be taken into account — and the factors are not in any hierarchy of importance. Under section 1(3) the court must take into account the following factors:

Section 1(3)(a) The child's wishes in the light of the child's age and understanding   If the child is sufficiently mature and intelligent enough (in other words he or she is '*Gillick* competent' – see 8.4), then the child's wishes may determine the matter, all other things being equal. The child's wishes are ascertained by a Cafcass Children and Family Reporter or a Welsh family proceedings officer, who has a duty to report to the court and to consider the best interests of the child; and who may be cross-examined on the report. The court also has the power to appoint a Children's Guardian to represent the child, and to permit the child to be represented by his or her own solicitor without a Children's Guardian (see 8.6). A failure to give any real effect to a child's wishes may provide grounds for an appeal as it did, for instance, in *Re R (Residence Order)* [2009] EWCA Civ 445 where the Court of Appeal held by a majority that the judge had erred in not giving any real effect to the wishes of the child, aged 9.

Section 1(3)(b) The child's physical and emotional needs   The child's physical and emotional needs might include, for instance, the emotional and psychological attachment a child has to a particular parent, and also a child's housing needs. In earlier case-law the courts took the view that it was usually better for young children, particularly babies, to be brought up by their mother (an approach which was endorsed by the House of Lords in *Brixey v Lynas* [1996] 2 FLR 499). Over the years, however, as the courts have given increasing recognition to the importance of fathers, they are likely to consider the child's emotional and psychological attachment to *both* parents, not just the mother. In respect of the child's needs, the fact that one parent is wealthier than the other is likely to count for little.

Section 1(3)(c) The likely effect on the child of a change of circumstances   This is similar to the 'continuity of care' or 'status quo' factor which was an important consideration in the case-law prior to the Children Act 1989 when there was no welfare checklist in the relevant legislation. However, in *Re F (Shared Residence Order)* [2009] EWCA Civ 313 the Court of Appeal held that it was better, since the enactment of the Children Act 1989, to address the factors in the welfare checklist rather than to rely on any presumption of fact that might arise from status quo arguments. (For cases where the status quo prevailed, see, for example, *Re B (Residence Order: Status Quo)* [1998] 1 FLR 368 (as the father had cared for the 8-year-old child since the age of two); and *Re C (Residence)* [2008] 1 FLR 826 (as the child had spent all his life in his mother's care and had a strong and beneficial bond with her).)

Under section (1)(3)(c) the court may be unwilling to disrupt existing residence arrangements if to do so would split up brothers and sisters, disrupt schooling arrangements, or result in the child losing contact with relatives and friends.

Section 1(3)(d) The age, sex, background and any of the child's characteristics which the court considers relevant The child's religious preferences, racial and cultural background, health and disabilities can, for example, be considered under section 1(3)(d).

Section 1(3)(e) Any harm the child has suffered or is at risk of suffering 'Harm' has the same meaning as it has in section 31 of the CA 1989 (see p. 384) and also includes harm caused by 'hearing or seeing the ill treatment of another'. Thus, witnessing domestic violence can constitute harm.

Religious beliefs Making a residence order in favour of a parent with extreme religious beliefs will not necessarily constitute harm. In *Re R (A Minor) (Residence: Religion)* [1993] 2 FLR 163, for example, a residence order was made in favour of the father, as the mother had died, even though he was a member of the Exclusive Brethren, an extreme religious sect in which members are not allowed to mix socially with anyone outside the fellowship (the court also made a supervision order in favour of the local authority to ensure the child's safety). In *M v H (Education: Welfare)* [2008] EWHC 324 (Fam), [2008] 1 FLR 1400 Charles J held *inter alia* that the fact that one parent was a Catholic and the other a Jehovah's Witness was not of itself relevant in the circumstances of the case. However, if the religion is deemed to be harmful, the court will take it into account, as it did in *Re B and G (Minors) (Custody)* [1985] FLR 493 where the court described the views held by members of the Church of Scientology as 'immoral and obnoxious' and denied the father and step-mother the care of the children in preference to the mother and step-father who had left the church.

A refusal to make a residence order in favour of a particular parent on the basis of his or her religious beliefs may constitute a breach of the European Convention for the Protection of Human Rights. But each case depends on its facts. In *Palau-Martinez v France (Application No. 64927/01)* [2004] 2 FLR 810 the ECtHR held that an order granting residence to the child's father, not the mother, because of her religious convictions (she was a Jehovah's Witness), breached the mother's right to a private and family life under Article 8 and was discriminatory under Article 14. On the other hand, in *Ismailova v Russia (Application No 37614/02)* [2008] 1 FLR 533 the ECtHR upheld the decision of the Russian courts to deprive the mother of custody because of the effect of her religion on the children.

Steps the court can take when there is a risk of harm If the court is concerned about making a residence order because of a risk of harm, it can make an interim residence order, or back up the residence order with another order, such as a specific issue order, a prohibited steps order, a family assistance order, or a section 37 direction that the local authority investigate the case (see further in Chapter 10). Cafcass has a duty under section 16A of the Children Act 1989 to make risk assessments where it believes that a child might be at risk of significant harm (see p. 300 below).

Section 1(3)(f) How capable each parent is of meeting the child's needs The court might consider, for example, whether a parent can provide accommodation, love, emotional security, intellectual stimulation, and care during working hours.

Section 1(3)(g) The range of powers available to the court under the Children Act 1989 As proceedings for a residence order are themselves family proceedings (s 8(3)), the court can make other orders on an application or of its own motion, for example: any other section 8 order; a section 16 family assessment order; an order appointing a guardian; or a section 37 direction that a local authority investigate the child's circumstances (for more on these orders, see Chapter 10).

(c) Shared residence orders (section 11(4))

Under section 11(4) of the Children Act 1989 the court can make a 'shared' residence order, (a SRO) which is a residence order 'made in favour of two or more persons who do not themselves all live together', and which specifies 'the periods during which the child is to live in the different households concerned'. The phrase 'shared residence' must be distinguished from 'joint residence' which is the term used where a residence order is made in respect of two people who live together in the same household, such as two grandparents (see, for example, *Re K (Shared Residence Order)* [2008] EWCA Civ 526, [2008] 2 FLR 380). 'Equal' residence is where the child spends equal amounts, or roughly equal amounts, of time with each parent or other carer (see, for example, *Re N (A Child: Religion: Jehovah's Witness)* [2011] EWHC 3737 (Fam), where it was held that the child's welfare required that the child spend broadly equal time with each parent in order to try to guard against the risk that the different religious perspectives of the parents would predominate).

In discussions leading up to the drafting of the Children Act 1989, the Law Commission had said that residence orders should be flexible enough to accommodate a wide range of situations, and that, although shared arrangements would rarely be practicable, evidence from the USA showed that they could work well in some circumstances. The Law Commission saw no reason why shared residence orders (SROs) should be actively discouraged, and said that the aim of introducing shared residence was to 'lower the stakes' in disputes over children so that parents did not see themselves as having 'won or lost'. The aim was to reinforce the notion of shared parenting. The courts have adopted this approach. Thus, in *Re P (Shared Residence Order)* [2005] EWCA Civ 1639, [2006] 2 FLR 347 Wall LJ said that a SRO had the advantage of emphasising the fact 'that both parents are equal in the eyes of the law, and that they have equal duties and responsibilities as parents'. His Lordship also said that a shared order 'can have the additional advantage of conveying the court's message that neither parent is in control and that the court expects parents to co-operate with each other for the benefit of their children'.

In cases decided shortly after the Children Act 1989 came into force, judges were reluctant to make SROs because they were of the view that shared residence arrangements might create uncertainty and insecurity for children (although they were sometimes made for the purposes of giving parental responsibility to a partner who was not the biological parent but who was performing a parental role). In *Re H (A Minor) (Shared Residence)* [1994] 1 FLR 717, for example, the Court of Appeal held that SROs should only be made in exceptional circumstances. Over the years, however, judges have become more willing to make them, so that today they are no longer unusual and there is no need for the circumstances to be exceptional, as the following case shows:

▶ *D v D (Shared Residence Order)* [2001] 1 FLR 495

A pattern had been established on marriage breakdown whereby the three children spent substantial periods of time with each parent, but where the arrangements were subject to a high degree of animosity between the parents, and frequent legal proceedings had been brought to sort out the details. The father applied for a SRO, which was granted at first instance. The mother appealed. The Court of Appeal dismissed her appeal, and held that, contrary to earlier case-law, it was not necessary to show that exceptional circumstances existed before SRO could be granted; and neither was it probably necessary to show a positive benefit to the child. What must be shown is that the order is in the child's best interests in accordance with the welfare principle in section 1 of the Children Act 1989. Here, on the facts, it was necessary to make a SRO to lessen the animosity between the parties.

In *Re A (Joint Residence: Parental Responsibility)* [2008] EWCA Civ 867, [2008] 2 FLR 1593, Sir Mark Potter P, who gave the leading judgment, stated:

> 'It is now recognised by the court that a shared residence order may be regarded as appropriate where it provides legal confirmation of the factual reality of a child's life or where, in a case where one has the primary care of a child, it may be psychologically beneficial to the parents in emphasising the equality of their position and responsibilities.'

In *Re AR (A Child: Relocation)* [2010] EWHC 1346, [2010] 2 FLR 1577 Mostyn J went so far as to say that a SRO 'is nowadays the rule rather than the exception, even where the quantum of care undertaken by each parent is decidedly unequal' but in *T v T* [2010] EWCA Civ 1366 Black LJ was of the view that Mostyn J's approach in *Re AR* went too far, and that whether or not a joint or shared residence order should be granted depended on a determination of what was in the child's best interests in the light of all the factors in the case.

Concern has been expressed about the trend towards making SROs for the purpose of encouraging cooperative parenting (see, for instance, Bevan ([2012] Fam Law 862 who refers to evidence from Sweden given by Newnham [2011] CFLQ 251).

How the court exercises its powers in shared residence order cases When deciding whether or not to make a SRO, the court must apply the welfare principles in section 1(1) of the Children Act 1989 (see 10.3). There is no presumption of shared residence, however. Although the outcome of each case depends on its own facts, the following propositions about SROs can be extracted from the case-law:

▶ It is not necessary to show exceptional or unusual circumstances before a SRO can be granted (*D v D (Shared Residence Order*, above).

▶ There is no requirement that a child should be spending time evenly, or more or less evenly, in the two homes before a SRO can be made (*Re F (Shared Residence Order)* [2003] EWCA Civ 592, [2003] 2 FLR 397; and endorsed in *Re W (Shared Residence Order)* [2009] EWCA Civ 370, [2009] 2 FLR 436).

▶ The court will be alert to discern any malign intent on the part of a parent to use a shared residence application for the purpose of disrupting or interfering with the other parent's role in the management of the child's life (*Re K (Shared Residence Order)* [2008] EWCA Civ 526, [2008] 2 FLR 380).

▶ Although it may be appropriate to make a SRO in a case where there is likely to be a problem facilitating or enforcing contact, the court is unlikely to make such an order where there is little contact between the parties (*A v A (Shared Residence)* [2004] EWHC 142 (Fam), [2004] 1 FLR 1195).

▶ A SRO can be made even though there is a substantial geographical distance between the parents, as the order must reflect the underlying reality of where the children live their lives (see, for example, *Re F (Shared Residence Order)* [2003] EWCA Civ 592, [2003] 2 FLR 397 where one parent lived in England and the other in Scotland).

▶ A lack of co-operation and goodwill between the parties is not necessarily a bar to making a SRO (see, for example, *Re R (Residence: Shared Care: Children's Views)* [2005] EWCA Civ 542, [2006] 1 FLR 491).

▶ A SRO may be made even where there is hostility between the parties (see, for example, *Re AR (A Child: Relocation)* [2010] EWHC 1346, [2010] 2 FLR 1577 where the parents were described as being 'at loggerheads').

▶ Although the inability of the parents to work in harmony is not by itself a reason for making a SRO, a possible consequence of the parents' inability to work in harmony (namely a deliberate and sustained marginalisation of one parent by the other) may sometimes be so (*Re W (Shared Residence Order)* [2009] EWCA Civ 370, [2009] 2 FLR 436).

▶ It is wrong in law to make a contact order if a SRO has been made (*Re W (Shared Residence Order)* [2009] EWCA Civ 370, [2009] 2 FLR 436).

Examples from the law reports   There are many cases in the law reports where SROs have been made:

▶ *A v A (Shared Residence)* [2004] EWHC 142 (Fam), [2004] 1 FLR 1195

A SRO was made (even though the parents were not able to co-operate), as the children had been spending 50 per cent of their time with each parent. Wall J made a SRO partly to reflect the fact that the parents are equal in the eyes of the law, and have equal duties and responsibilities towards their children.

▶ *Re C (A Child)* [2006] EWCA Civ 235

The Court of Appeal described the case as 'a paradigm' case where a SRO should be granted. The child had a strong attachment to both parents and was happy and confident in both homes, which were proximate to each other and close to the child's school. The child had a real familiarity with both homes and a sense of belonging in each, and he had a clear perception that he had two homes. There was a post-separation history of the child's care being shared.

▶ *Re M (Residence Order)* [2008] EWCA Civ 66, [2008] 1 FLR 1087

Wall LJ held that it was 'a paradigm case' for a SRO. The children needed to be kept together, they wished to spend time with each parent and needed to enjoy the benefits of being with both parents. The parents were clearly sufficiently cooperative and lived geographically close.

Shared residence order or defined contact? The court may, depending on the circumstances, decide that it is sufficient to make an order for defined contact rather than a SRO. This was considered in *Re K (Shared Residence Order)* [2008] EWCA Civ 526, [2008] 2 FLR 380 where the father applied to have contact with the child increased (from 40 to 50 per cent) and also applied for a SRO. The Court of Appeal had to decide whether a SRO or an order for defined contact should be made. It held that the court should decide on the division of time the child is to spend with each parent and then determine whether that time should be effected by a SRO or a contact order. The Court of Appeal held that a SRO was more appropriate in the circumstances of the case. The court must make either a SRO *or* a defined contact order (not both), as the Court of Appeal has held that it is a contradiction in terms to grant a contact order to a person who already has a SRO (*Re W (Shared Residence Order)* [2009] EWCA Civ 370, [2009] 2 FLR 436).

Making a shared residence order as a means of acquiring parental responsibility A SRO can be made for the purpose of conferring parental responsibility on a person who does not possess it and who is not otherwise able to apply for it (see, for example, *Re A (Shared Residence: Parental Responsibility)* [2008] EWCA Civ 867, [2008] 2 FLR 1503 where a SRO was made to confer parental responsibility on a man who was not the child's biological father, but who had, with the mother, brought the child up on the assumption he was).

Shared residence orders and housing The House of Lords in *Holmes-Moorhouse v London Borough of Richmond-upon-Thames* [2009] UKHL 7, [2009] 1 FLR 904 (see further at p. 92) held that, when deciding whether to make a SRO, the court must take into account any housing needs of the parties and the fact that there is a shortage of local authority housing and that housing authorities have limited resources. The House of Lords held that a family court should not make a SRO unless it appeared reasonably likely that both parents would have accommodation in which the child could reside. Baroness Hale said that the family court 'should not use a residence order as a means of putting pressure upon a local housing authority to allocate their resources in a particular way'.

(d) Attaching a condition to a residence order and restricting residence

The court can attach a condition to a residence order (s 11(7)), but it usually only does so in exceptional circumstances. Placing a condition on a residence order which requires a person to live in a particular place is even more exceptional, as such a restriction is considered to be 'an unwarranted imposition upon the right of a parent to choose where he/she will live within the UK' (*per* Baroness Hale in *Re G (Children)* [2006] UKHL 43, [2006] 2 FLR 629). But each case depends on its facts; and in *B v B (Residence: Condition Limiting Geographic Area)* [2004] 2 FLR 979 a condition was imposed that the mother and child live within a specified geographic area, as the mother had made two applications to remove the child to Australia and her prime motive in moving the child's residence from the south to the north of England was to escape from the child's father.

11.5 Contact disputes

Article 9(3) of the UN Convention on the Rights of the Child 1989

'States Parties shall respect the right of the child ... to maintain personal relations and direct contact with both parents on a regular basis, except if it is contrary to the child's best interests.'

(a) Introduction

Contact arrangements are best settled by the parents themselves, but if they cannot reach agreement, and mediation or collaborative law fail, then an application can be made to the court for a contact order under section 8 of the Children Act 1989. Despite the number of contact orders, most parents in fact make their own contact arrangements. Research by Hunt and Macleod of the Oxford Centre for Family Law and Policy found that less than one in 10 parents applied to the court for contact arrangements to be settled (*Outcomes of Applications to Court for Contact Orders After Parental Separation or Divorce*, 2008, available on the Ministry of Justice website). Their research also found that, even if cases did go to court, most parties reached agreement (it was rare for the court to have to make a final ruling). Also, most cases ended with face-to-face contact; and contact typically involved overnight stays, at least fortnightly.

It is better if parents reach agreement about contact, because research has shown that parents who turn to the law to settle serious contact disputes risk making matters worse (see Trinder *et al.*, *Making Contact: How Parents and Children Negotiate and Experience Contact After Divorce*, Joseph Rowntree Foundation, [2002] Fam Law 872). It has been recognised by the judiciary and by the Government that contact cases are best dealt with outside the courts. Wall J (as he was then), speaking at a conference on contact, said (see [2003] Fam Law 275):

> 'The law, which of necessity, operates within the discipline of defined orders is, in my judgment, ill-suited to deal with the complex family dynamics inherent in disputed contact applications. Arrangements for contact stand more prospect of enduring if they are consensual. Wherever possible, contact disputes should be dealt with outside the courtroom.'

Amendments have been made to the Children Act 1989 to improve the facilitation and enforcement of contact (see 11.6 below).

(i) Human rights and contact The European Court of Human Rights (the ECtHR) recognises the importance of contact between parents and children as part of the right to family life under Article 8 ECHR (see, for example, *Johansen v Norway* (1997) 23 EHRR 33). In *Kosmopolou v Greece (Application No. 60457/00)* [2004] 1 FLR 800 the ECtHR held that:

> '[T]he mutual enjoyment by parent and child of each other's company constitutes a fundamental element of family life, even if the relationship between the parents has broken down, and domestic measures hindering such enjoyment amount to an interference with the right protected by Art. 8 of the Convention.'

Thus the ECtHR takes the view that, unless the circumstances of the case are exceptional, the mutual enjoyment by parent and child of each other's company constitutes a right to family life under Article 8. In *Hansen v Turkey (Application No. 36141/97)* [2004] 1 FLR 142, for example, the ECtHR held that the failure of the Turkish authorities to take realistic coercive measures against the father (who had custody) to allow the mother to have access to the child was a breach of her right to family life under Article 8. As the Human Rights Act 1998 requires courts in the UK to take account of the decisions of the ECtHR, they must ensure that they order contact and enforce it, unless it is contrary to the child's best interests. The ECtHR has held, however, that the duty on national authorities to enforce and facilitate contact is not absolute. The question to be asked is whether the national authorities concerned have taken all the necessary steps to enforce and facilitate contact that could reasonably be demanded in the circumstances of the case (see, for example, *Zadwadka v Poland (Application No. 48542/99)* [2005] 2

FLR 897; and *Kaleta v Poland (Case No. 11375/02)*, [2009] 1 FLR 927). Each case therefore depends on its facts. Thus, for instance, in *Glaser v UK* (2001) 33 EHRR 1, [2001] 1 FLR 153 the ECtHR rejected a complaint that the UK authorities were in breach of the ECHR by failing to take adequate steps to enforce contact against a mother.

Delay in the court process in respect of enforcing contact may constitute a breach of Article 6 (the right to a fair trial) as it did in *Adam v Germany (No 44036/02)* [2009] 1 FLR 560 where the ECtHR held that the rights of the child's father and paternal grandparents had been breached under Article 6 due to the avoidable delays and protracted nature of the proceedings to enforce contact with the child (which had been going on for more than four years).

(ii) Contact – difficult areas Contact disputes are 'among the most difficult and sensitive cases' which the courts have to deal with (*per* Wall LJ at [2005] Fam Law 26). Contact disputes are often lengthy and intractable. Cases sometimes drag on for years, which not only takes up court time but is contrary to the best interests of children (see, for instance, *Re A-H (Contact Order)* [2008] EWCA Civ 630 where, after five years, the contact question had not been resolved). There have also been problems with contact in the context of domestic violence (see p. 297 below), and in respect of the enforcement and facilitation of contact (see 11.6). There has also been increasing pressure by proponents of children's rights, including the UN Committee on the Rights of the Child (see p. 208), for children's views to be heard more in contact cases and for children to have separate representation (but see *Re S (Contact: Children's Views)* [2002] EWHC 540 (Fam), [2002] 1 FLR 1156 where a contact order was refused because of the views of the two children who were aged 14 and 16). Although an intractable parental contact case may be a suitable case for separate representation of the child involved, in practice separate representation is rarely exercised.

(iii) Contact and child maintenance Some parents may make a link between contact and child maintenance (child support). For example, a mother may decide that, as the father is not paying maintenance, then he should have no or limited contact, or a father may think that, because he is paying maintenance, then he has a right to contact. The Family Justice Review (see p. 7) has stated, however, that there should be no link of any kind between contact and maintenance. A similar view was put forward by Wilson LJ, in *Re B (Contact: Child Support)* [2006] EWCA Civ 1574, [2007] 1 FLR 1949, who stated that it would be 'positively unlawful' to consider the consequences of statutory provisions regarding payment of child support when making orders for contact or residence, 'because it would be to introduce a consideration unrelated to the child's welfare'.

However, despite concerns about linking contact and maintenance, there is a danger that the Government's proposed reforms of the child maintenance system (to encourage parents to make their own child maintenance agreements) may result in some parents making a link between child maintenance and contact, which may be detrimental to children. Thus, in its consultation paper, *Strengthening families, promoting parental responsibility: the future of child maintenance* (Cm 7990, 2011, Department of Work and Pensions, 2011) the Government stated that it aims to promote 'family-based arrangements' for contact and maintenance, in order to encourage collaboration, avoid antagonistic disputes, and minimise the negative impacts of parental separation on children's well-being. (For a discussion of whether there should be some sort of legal linkage between the payment of child maintenance and contact, see Douglas ([2011] Fam Law 491.)

(b) Contact orders

Where a contact dispute cannot be settled by agreement, with or without the help of mediation or collaborative law, an application can be made for a contact order which the High Court, county courts and magistrates' family proceedings courts have jurisdiction to make under section 8 of the Children Act (CA) 1989 (see further at 10.6). A contact order is an order 'requiring the person with whom a child lives, or is to live, to allow the child to visit or stay with the person named in the order, or for that person and the child otherwise to have contact with each other' (s 8(1) CA 1989).The term 'contact' was introduced by the Children Act to replace that of 'access', because 'contact' was considered to be a more child-centred term in that a contact order allows a child to have contact rather than giving a parent a right to have access.

Applicants   The child's parents (married or unmarried, and whether or not the father has parental responsibility) can apply. Other persons (including the child) can apply, but only with leave of the court (see further at 10.6).

Other powers   The court can order a welfare report on the child (s 7); and direct that a local authority investigate the child's circumstances (s 37). The court can also attach a condition to a contact order (s 11(7)), but its power to do so is not unlimited. For example, a condition cannot be attached to a contact order for the purposes of ousting a person from the family home (see *Re K (Contact: Condition Ousting Parent from Family Home)* [2011] EWCA Civ 1075).

Duration   A contact order cannot be made to last beyond the child's sixteenth birthday, unless there are exceptional circumstances (s 9(7)).

A welfare report   The court may order that a Cafcass officer prepare a welfare report for the purposes of the contact proceedings (under s 7 CA 1989). The recommendations in the report are an important consideration for the court when reaching its decision (see p. 282 above).

(c) How the court exercises its discretion in contact cases

When considering whether to make a contact order and, if so, in what manner, the court must apply the welfare principle (s 1(1)), the 'minimum intervention' principle (s 1(5)), the no-delay principle (s 1(2)) and, in a contested application, the section 1(3) welfare checklist (see further at 10.3). (For an analysis of the reported contact cases from 1994 to 2010, see Kaganas [2011] CFLQ 63.)

(i) Contact as a right of the child   Like the UN Convention on the Rights of the Child and the European Court of Human Rights (see p. 293 above), the courts in England and Wales have also referred to contact as a right of the child. As Sir Stephen Brown P said in *Re W (A Minor) (Contact)* [1994] 2 FLR 441, it is 'quite clear that contact with a parent is a fundamental right of a child, save in wholly exceptional circumstances'. Cogent reasons will therefore be needed to deprive a child of contact (see *Re H (Contact Principles)* [1994] 2 FLR 969. In *Re R (A Minor) (Contact)* [1993] 2 FLR 762 Butler-Sloss LJ stated that it 'is a right of a child to have a relationship with both parents wherever possible' and

that 'in general the parent with whom the child does not live has a continuing role to play, which is recognised by s 2(1) of the Children Act 1989'.

In most cases the court will usually decide that it in the child's best interests for the non-resident parent to have contact. Due to the importance attached to a child knowing his or her natural parent, the court may decide to order contact even where the father is absent, for instance, because he is in prison (*A v L (Contact)* [1998] 1 FLR 361). Because of the importance of contact for children, the Court of Appeal has emphasised that the court should explore all options before contact is terminated (*Re W (Contact)* [2007] EWCA Civ 753, [2007] 2 FLR 1122). The European Court of Human Rights has also recognised the importance of contact between parents and children (see p. 293 above). Gilmore (2008) has argued, however, that it is not contact *per se* that is beneficial for the child but the nature and quality of the contact.

(ii) A presumption or assumption in favour of contact?   Although contact is considered to be a right of the child (see above), and is considered to be beneficial to a child, Thorpe LJ in *Re L,V, M and H* [2000] 2 FLR 334 (which involved contact and domestic violence – see p. 298 below) said that, although there was a 'universal judicial recognition of the importance of contact to a child's development', he was wary of talking of presumptions in the context of contact because it might 'inhibit or distort the rigorous search for the welfare solution'. For this reason, he preferred to talk about an 'assumption' in favour of contact or an assumption that contact is beneficial. Thorpe LJ was in no doubt, however, 'of the secure foundation for the assumption that contact benefits children'.

(d)   Types of contact

Different types of contact may be ordered depending on the circumstances. Section 8(1) of the Children Act 1989 provides that the child can visit, stay or otherwise have contact with the parent or other named person. Direct contact (visiting or staying contact) will usually be ordered, unless there are cogent reasons to the contrary affecting the child's welfare (such as where there is violence). Instead of ordering direct contact, especially where it is of significant duration, the option of applying for a shared residence order (see p. 289 above) should be considered.

Sometimes the court will order indirect or supervised contact (the word 'otherwise' in section 8(1) allows this). The court may decide to add a condition to a contact order (under section 11(7)) to specify what arrangements are to take place (for instance indirect contact by letter, birthday cards, Christmas cards or telephone conversations). Indirect contact was ordered, for example in: *Re P (Contact: Indirect Contact)* [1999] 2 FLR 893 (the father was a former drug addict who had just been released from prison); *Re L (Contact: Genuine Fear)* [2002] 1 FLR 621 (the mother was genuinely and intensely frightened of the father, so that direct contact would cause the child emotional harm); and in *Re F (Indirect Contact)* [2006] EWCA Civ 1426, [2007] 1 FLR 1015 (the father had a history of serious and uncontrollable violence).

Where there is a risk that contact may be harmful for the child, supervised contact can be ordered whereby contact takes place in the presence of a third party. Sometimes it takes place in a contact centre run under the auspices of the National Association of Child Contact Centres, where children can enjoy contact with one or both parents (and other family members) in a comfortable and safe environment. Although a judge has a positive duty to promote contact and must look at any alternative options available before refusing contact, in some cases an order of no contact may be ordered (as in *Re K (Children: Refusal of Direct Contact)* [2011] EWCA Civ 1064, [2012] 1 FLR 195 where the father had committed sexual offences against children; and in *Re J (Refusal of Contact)* [2012] EWCA Civ 720 where there were findings against the father of physical and emotional abuse to the mother and her extended family, including threats of rape of the mother's sisters and a threat to abduct the child). In an exceptional case, the court may decide not only to order that there be no contact, but it may also make an order under section 91(14) of the Children Act 1989 (see p. 276) that no further application can be made to the court without leave of the court (as it did, for example, in *Re T (A Child: One Parent Killed by Other Parent)* [2012] 1 FLR 472 where the father, a paranoid schizophrenic, had stabbed and killed the 2-year-old child's mother).

(e) Parental hostility to contact

As contact is considered to be a right of a child and beneficial for a child, the courts are reluctant to allow contact to be thwarted because of parental hostility to it. In *Re H (A Minor) (Contact)* [1994] 2 FLR 776 Butler-Sloss LJ said that it was important that there should not be 'a selfish parents' charter' whereby a parent could make such a fuss about contact that it could prevent the court ordering it. Only in highly exceptional cases would contact be refused because of a parent's strong opposition and hostility to contact (see, for example, *Re J (A Minor) (Contact)* [1994] 1 FLR 729 where the mother's hostility to contact with the father caused the child stress).

Over the years the courts began to increasingly realise, however, that some parents had genuinely held reasons for being intractably hostile to contact, for instance because of fear that the child might suffer violence (see *Re H (Contact: Domestic Violence)* [1998] 2 FLR 42). Courts began to take allegations of domestic violence and hostility to contact more seriously. However, in cases where there is hostility to contact, but contact is in the best interests of the child, the court now has stronger enforcement powers (see 11.6).

(f) Contact and domestic violence

For many years allegations of domestic violence were not taken as seriously as they might have been in contact cases. There were various reasons for this, such as that research on domestic violence had tended to concentrate on adult victims rather than children; and the courts were of the view that, as children had a right to contact and contact was beneficial to them, then contact should usually be ordered. The courts were also distrustful of mothers who made allegations of violence by fathers, and considered that they were merely being hostile to contact; and they were keen to ensure that children were brought up having a positive image of a father, even where there were allegations of violence. Furthermore, there was nothing expressly about domestic violence in the Children Act 1989.

Increasing concern began to be voiced, however, that the courts had perhaps created too high a threshold for a denial of contact, and that contact was being ordered in cases even though there was a risk of violence. An important impetus for a change of approach was psychiatric research which showed that domestic violence could have a harmful emotional impact on children. Another impetus for change was the publication of a report by Radford (*Unreasonable Fears? Child Contact in the Context of Domestic Violence: A Survey of Mothers' Perception of Harm*, 1999, Women's Aid), which provided evidence of children being physically and sexually abused as a result of contact being ordered; and which recommended the introduction of a rebuttable presumption against residence and direct or unsupervised contact in cases where there was a risk of violence.

In June 1999 a consultation paper by the Children Act Sub-Committee of the Advisory Board on Family Law (*Contact Between Children and Violent Parents: The Question of Parental Contact in Cases where there is Domestic Violence*) was published, proposing guidelines for good practice in contact cases where there were allegations of domestic violence. But the consultation paper was not in favour of introducing a legislative presumption against contact in domestic violence cases, which existed in some countries. The Government began to acknowledge that domestic violence had not been fully or appropriately handled by the courts in contact cases, and that something needed to be done. In a report to the Lord Chancellor (*The Question of Parental Contact in Cases where there is Domestic Violence*, 2002) it was recommended that: guidelines for good practice should be drawn up; professionals involved should be better informed and better trained; and there should be more research into contact and domestic violence.

As a result of the concerns voiced about contact and domestic violence, the courts began to take domestic violence more seriously in contact cases and would order indirect or supervised contact, or refuse contact, where there was violence (see, for example, *Re M (Contact: Violent Parent)* [1999] 2 FLR 321; and *Re K (Contact: Mother's Anxiety)* [1999] 2 FLR 703). The courts began to take the view that, where there was evidence of domestic violence, a father would have to show a future track record of proper behaviour, including taking up the offer of indirect contact, before successfully gaining direct contact (see dicta of Wall J in *Re O (Contact: Imposition of Conditions)* [1995] 2 FLR 124, approved by Cazalet J in *Re S (Violent Parent: Indirect Contact)* [2000] 1 FLR 481).

It was the following case, however, which was particularly important in the development of the law in contact cases where there were allegations of domestic violence. In this case the Court of Appeal considered the Report by the Children Act Sub-Committee (see above) and a joint report by two child psychiatrists, Dr Sturge and Dr Glaser, in which they stated that domestic violence involved a significant failure in parenting and that, where it was proved, the balance should tip against contact with the abusive parent unless that parent: fully acknowledged the inappropriateness of the violence; recognised its likely ill-effects on the child; had a genuine interest in the child's welfare; and was fully committed to making reparation to the child.

▶ *Re L (Contact: Domestic Violence); Re V (Contact: Domestic Violence); Re M (Contact: Domestic Violence); Re H (Contact: Domestic Violence)* **[2000] 2 FLR 334**

The fathers in the four conjoined appeals appealed against a judge's refusal to allow them direct contact with their children against a background of domestic violence. The violence or threats of violence had been proved, the fears of the resident parents were reasonable, and serious issues arose as to the risk of emotional harm to the children.

The Court of Appeal, dismissing all four appeals, laid down the following principles which were to be applied in contact cases where there were allegations of domestic violence:

▶ Judges and magistrates need to have a heightened awareness of the existence, and consequences for children, of exposure to domestic violence.

- ▶ Allegations of domestic violence which might affect the outcome of a contact application must be adjudicated upon and found proved or not proved.
- ▶ Where domestic violence is proved, there is not, nor should there be, a presumption of no contact. As a matter of principle, domestic violence cannot of itself constitute a bar to contact.
- ▶ Domestic violence is a highly relevant and important factor, among others, which must be taken into account by the judge when carrying out the difficult and delicate balancing exercise of discretion, applying the welfare principle in section 1(1) of the Children Act 1989, and the welfare checklist in section 1(3).
- ▶ Where domestic violence is proved, the court should weigh in the balance the seriousness of the violence, the risks involved and the impact on the child against the positive factors, if any, of contact between the parent found to have been violent and the child.
- ▶ Where domestic violence is proved, the following factors, among others, are of particular significance: the extent of the violence; its effect upon the primary carer; its effect upon the child; and, in particular, the ability of the offender to recognise his past behaviour, to be aware of the need for change, and to make genuine attempts to change it.
- ▶ In respect of Article 8 of the ECHR (the right to family life), where there is a conflict between the rights and interests of a child and those of a parent, the child's interests must prevail under Article 8(2).
- ▶ On an application for interim contact, when allegations of domestic violence have not been adjudicated upon, the court should give particular consideration to the likely risk of harm (physical or emotional) to the child if contact is granted or refused. The court should ensure, as far as it can, that any risk of harm to the child is minimised, and that the safety of the child and the residential parent is secured before, during and after any such contact.

The message which came out of *Re LVMH* was that courts and lawyers needed to be more aware of domestic violence and its effect on children. After *Re LVMH*, courts began to take allegations of violence in contact cases seriously, and, where violence was proved, they would consider ordering indirect or supervised contact, or, in an extreme case, no contact. According to Kaganas ([2000] CFLQ 311, at 311), what *Re LVMH* did was 'to rein back, in domestic violence cases, what was a very strong trend to prioritise contact between children and non-resident parents and to downgrade the risks to which such contact might expose mothers and children'.

Other developments   In response to concerns about children and domestic violence, the definition of 'harm' in the welfare checklist in section 1(3) of the Children Act 1998 (see 10.3) was redefined to include 'impairment suffered from seeing or hearing the ill-treatment of another'. Cafcass was also given an increased role to monitor domestic violence and conduct risk assessments (see below). Another development was the introduction of a new form (C1A) which must be completed in proceedings for *any* section 8 order under the Children Act 1989 so as to ensure that safety issues are prioritised throughout the proceedings and are brought to the attention of the court.

A practice direction was also issued (see now *Practice Direction 12J – Residence and Contact Orders: Domestic Violence and Harm*, which supplements the Family Procedure Rules 2010) laying down rules of practice to be adopted in any family proceedings where there is an application for a residence or contact order and there is an allegation, or other reason to suppose, that a child or party has experienced domestic violence perpetrated by another party, or that there is a risk of domestic violence. A failure to follow the fact-finding requirements of the *Practice Direction* may provide grounds for a successful appeal as it did in *Re Z (Unsupervised Contact: Allegations of Domestic Violence)* [2009] EWCA Civ 430, [2009] 2 FLR 877 where, although the Cafcass officer had reported risks of violence, the judge decided that a fact-finding hearing should not go ahead. (See also *Re W (Children: Domestic Violence)* [2012] EWCA Civ 528 where the Court of Appeal allowed the father's appeal because the judge had not discharged his obligation, either explicitly or implicitly, to examine the factors set out in paragraphs 26 and 27 of *Practice Direction 12J*.)

Risk assessments (section 16A Children Act 1989)   Cafcass officers (see 1.7), when exercising any of their functions in respect of any of the orders that can be made under Part II of the Children Act 1989 (see 10.2), and who suspect that the child concerned is at risk of harm, must make a risk assessment in relation to the child and make that assessment available for the court (ss 16A(1), (2)). The assessment must be presented to the court even if the officer concludes that there is no risk of harm to the child; as the fact that a risk assessment has been carried out is a material fact which should be placed before the court (see *Practice Direction 12 – Children Act 1989: Risk Assessments Under Section 16A*, which supplements the Family Procedure Rules 2010).

11.6 Enforcing and facilitating contact

> ▶ **Baroness Hale in *Re G (Children) (Residence: Same-Sex Partner)* [2006] UKHL 43, [2006] 2 FLR 629**
>
> 'Making contact happen and, even more importantly, making contact work is one of the most difficult and contentious challenges in the whole of family law. It has recently received a great deal of public attention. Courts understandably regard the conventional methods of enforcing court orders as a last resort: fining the primary carer will only mean that she has even less to spend on the children; sending her to prison will deprive them of their primary carer and give them a reason to resent the other parent who invited this. Nor does punishment address the real sources of the problem, which may range from a simple failure to understand what the children need, to more complex fears resulting from the parents' own relationships.'

The courts in England and Wales must take effective steps to enforce contact, otherwise they risk being in breach of the European Convention for the Protection of Human Rights and the UN Convention on the Rights of the Child. Enforcement remains difficult in some cases, however, even though the court now has wider powers to enforce and facilitate contact.

(a) Enforcing and facilitating contact

In order to improve the enforcement and facilitation of contact, sections 11A–11P were inserted into the Children Act 1989 to give the courts new and wider powers to enforce and facilitate contact and to resolve child contact disputes.

(i) The background to the new provisions   In 2002 the Children Act Sub-Committee of the Lord Chancellor's Advisory Board on Family Law, chaired by Wall J, published *Making Contact Work: A Report to the Lord Chancellor on the Facilitation of Arrangements for Contact Between Children and Their Non-Residential Parents and the Enforcement of Court*

Orders for Contact. The report made various recommendations, including: providing more information about contact; giving Contact Centres extra funding to facilitate contact; promoting mediation, conciliation and negotiation; amending the provisions governing family assistance orders; giving courts the power to refer a parent to a psychiatrist or psychologist, or to an education programme; imposing community service orders for breach of contact orders; and awarding financial compensation to parents who suffered financial loss as a result of loss of contact. Many of these recommendations were incorporated in the new law.

Two years later, in 2004, the Government published a consultation paper, *Parental Separation: Children's Needs and Parents' Responsibilities* (Cm 6273), in which it acknowledged that the current system for enforcing and facilitating contact was not working well. The consultation paper was followed, in 2005, by the White Paper, *Parental Separation: Children's Needs and Parents' Responsibilities, Next Steps* (Cm 6452), which recommended various reforms to improve the enforcement and facilitation of contact, including, for example, a wider range of services to support contact, a greater role for Cafcass in the promotion and enforcement of contact, additional powers for the court before making contact orders, changes to family assistance orders to make them better suited to being used in difficult contact cases, and a greater role for mediation.

(ii) The new provisions Many of the above recommendations were enacted in Part 1 of the Children and Adoption Act 2006, which inserted sections 11A–11P into the Children Act 1989. These provisions came into force in December 2008. In addition to giving the courts additional powers when dealing with applications for contact orders, the provisions placed a number of new duties on Cafcass officers (including monitoring compliance with contact orders, contact activities and enforcement, and reporting back to the court). The provisions also give the courts more flexibility in dealing with breaches of contact orders.

Under sections 11A–11P the following steps can be taken to enforce and facilitate contact.

Contact activity directions and conditions In order to facilitate contact, the court at the interim stage of a contact dispute can make a 'contact activity direction' (under s 11A) directing a party to the proceedings to take part in a specified activity which promotes contact with the child. Contact activities can include: classes; counselling; guidance; information and advice about contact; and information about mediation.

A contact activity, which a judge may decide to order a parent to participate in, is a Separated Parent Information Programme (PIP), a programme delivered by approved providers which is designed to help parents focus on their children's needs and improve relationships with their former spouse or partner in order to come to amicable arrangements about contact. The Programme is delivered by a variety of providers (such as National Family Mediation (NFM) and NRS Child Contact Centre), and is managed by Cafcass (see 1.7). When considering whether to make a contact activity direction, the child's welfare is the court's paramount consideration.

When making or varying a contact order, the court can include a 'contact activity condition' (under s 11C) in the order, requiring the person with whom the child lives (or is to live) and/or a person with a right to contact under a contact order (or a condition under a contact order) to take part in an activity that will promote contact with the child. The condition will specify the activity and the activity provider.

Before making a contact activity direction or condition, the court must be satisfied that (s 11E): the activity is appropriate in the circumstances; the activity provider is suitable to provide the activity; and the proposed activity is in a place to which the person subject to the direction or condition can reasonably be expected to travel. Before making the direction or condition, the court must obtain and consider information about the person who is to be subject to the direction or condition; and consider the likely effect of the direction or condition on that person. This may include information about any conflict with the person's religious beliefs and any interference with that person's work or education arrangements. The court can ask a Cafcass officer to provide this information.

The court can ask a Cafcass officer to monitor a person's compliance with a contact activity direction or condition; and to report to the court on any failure to comply (s 11G). Financial assistance may be available to persons who are required to undertake a contact activity (s 11F).

Monitoring contact orders (section 11H)   The court can ask a Cafcass officer to monitor compliance with a contact order (or an order varying contact) and report to the court on such matters relating to compliance as the court may specify. The court can make the request when making or varying a contact order or in any subsequent contact proceedings. This monitoring role can only last for up to 12 months.

Warning notices (section 11I)   When a court makes a contact order (or varies a contact order) it must attach a warning notice to the order providing information about the consequences of failing to comply with the order.

Enforcement orders (sections 11J–11N)   If the court is satisfied beyond reasonable doubt that a contact order has been breached without reasonable excuse, it can make an 'enforcement order' imposing an unpaid work requirement (community service) on the person in breach (see s 11J), unless that person proves on the balance of probabilities that he or she has a reasonable excuse for failing to comply with the contact order.

The following persons can apply for an enforcement order: the person who for the purpose of a contact order is the person with whom the child lives (or is to live); the person whose contact with the child is provided for in the contact order; any person subject to a condition in a contact order (made under s 11(7)(b)) or to a contact activity condition (made under s 11C); or the child concerned (but only with leave of the court, which it can grant if the child has sufficient understanding to make the application). Schedule A1 to the Children Act 1989 makes further provision in respect of enforcement orders.

An enforcement order cannot be made unless the person concerned has received a copy of a warning notice (see above); and it cannot be made against a person aged under 18 at the time of the breach (s 11K).

Before making an enforcement order the court must be satisfied that (s 11L): the order is necessary to secure compliance with the contact order; and that the likely effect of the order on the person in breach is proportionate to the seriousness of the breach. It must also be satisfied that the provision for the person to work under an unpaid work requirement can be made in the local justice area in which the person in breach resides, or will reside. The court must obtain and consider information about the person and the likely effect of the order on that person before making the order. The provisions about seeking information are the same as those for obtaining information before making a contact activity or direction. When making the order, the court must take into account the welfare of the child who is the subject of the contact order.

Compensation for financial loss (section 110)   A person who breaches a contact order can be ordered by the court to pay compensation for financial loss resulting from the breach (such as the cost of a holiday or outing for the child). The following persons can apply for compensation: the person who, for the purposes of the contact order, is the person with whom the child lives (or is to live); the person for whom contact is provided for in the contact order, or a person subject to a section 11(7)(b) contact condition or a section 11C contact activity condition; or the child concerned (but only with leave of the court, which it can grant if the child has sufficient understanding to make the application). The amount of compensation must not exceed the amount of the applicant's financial loss. In determining the amount payable, the court must take into account the financial circumstances of the person in breach; and, in exercising its powers, the court must take into account the child's welfare. A compensation order cannot be made against a person aged under 18 at the time of the breach (s 11P).

(b)   Other measures with respect to enforcing and facilitating contact

The following powers are also available for the purpose of promoting the enforcement and facilitation of contact, but, with the introduction of the new provisions above, they are less likely to be used.

(i) Family assistance order (section 16)   A family assistance order (FAO – see further at 10.11) can be made under section 16 of the Children Act 1989 for the purpose of facilitating contact in a difficult contact case. Thus, a FAO can be made (when a contact order is in force) directing a Cafcass officer or a local authority officer to give advice and assistance with regard to establishing, improving and maintaining contact to such persons as are specified in the FAO (s 16(4A)).

(ii) Contempt of court   Breach of a contact order is contempt of court, punishable by fine or imprisonment, although, with the introduction of the new enforcement measures above, contempt of court is now less likely. Although imposing a fine or a prison term is a rather unsatisfactory measure in family cases (as fining a parent reduces the amount of money available for the child, and sending a parent to prison may be emotionally damaging for the child), the courts have sometimes imposed fines and prison sentences for breaches of contact orders (see, for example, *Re S (Contact Dispute: Committal)* [2004] EWCA Civ 1790, [2005] 1 FLR 812). The Court of Appeal has warned, however, that a custodial sentence should not be imposed where a fine is appropriate (see *Re M (Contact Order)* [2005] EWCA Civ 615, [2005] 2 FLR 1006). In *Re L-W (Enforcement and Committal: Contact); CPL v CH-W and Others*[2010] EWCA Civ 1253, [2011] 1 FLR 1095, where a committal order against the father was set aside in the circumstances of the case, Munby LJ held that committal should not be used unless it is a proportionate response to the problem nor if some less drastic remedy will provide an adequate solution.

Contempt proceedings must comply with Article 6 (the right to a fair trial) and Article 8 (the right to family life) of the ECHR. Thus, for example, in *Re K (Contact: Committal Order)* [2002] EWCA Civ 1559, [2003] 1 FLR 277 a mother successfully appealed against her committal to prison for 42 days for breach of a contact order as there had been a breach of Article 6 (as she had had no legal representation) and Article 8 (as the court had failed to consider the fact that committal would separate her from her children).

(iii) Transfer residence to the other parent Where there are protracted difficulties in enforcing contact the court may in exceptional circumstances decide that the child's residence should be transferred from the parent who is hostile to contact to the non-resident parent (as it did, for example, in *V v V (Contact: Implacable Hostility)* [2004] EWHC 1215 (Fam), [2004] 2 FLR 851 where Bracewell J transferred residence to the father because the mother's behaviour constituted emotional abuse of the children). However, a transfer of residence will be ordered only in the last resort and where it is not contrary to the child's best interests. In *Re A (Residence Order)* [2009] EWCA Civ 1141 [2010] 1 FLR 1083, for example, the transfer of residence from the mother to the father was held to be premature and too risky for the children concerned. On the other hand, in *Re W (Residence: Leave to Appeal)* [2010] EWCA Civ 1280, [2011] 1 FLR 1143 the Court of Appeal refused to grant the mother leave to appeal against the trial judge's decision to transfer residence of her 3-year-old child to the paternal grandmother as she had continually flouted court orders for her to comply with a contact order in favour of the father.

11.7 Changing a child's name on family breakdown

On family breakdown the parent with whom the child lives may wish to change the child's surname (perhaps because of a desire to sever ties with the other parent or for the child to acquire a step-parent's surname). However, there are restrictions on changing a child's surname, but not first name (see *Re H (Child's Name: First Name)* [2002] EWCA Civ 190, [2002] 1 FLR 973). A child's surname can changed by a person with parental responsibility for the child provided every other person with parental responsibility gives consent. However, if there is a residence order in force with respect to the child, then *written* consent is required (s 13(1)(b) CA 1989). Written consent to a change of surname is also required if a child is in local authority care (s 33(7) CA 1989). If consent is not forthcoming, then the court's consent will be needed.

A dispute about a child's surname can be settled by making an application for a specific issue order (see 10.8), or, if a residence order is in force, by making an application under section 13. Where a change of name appears imminent, then a prohibited steps order (see 10.9) may be necessary to stop the change of surname. When considering an application for a change of surname, the child's welfare is the court's paramount consideration (s 1(1)), and the section 1(3) welfare checklist applies if the application is by way of a specific issue or prohibited steps order (see s 1(4)). Although the Children Act 1989 does not require the court to consider the welfare checklist in an application for a change of surname under section 13, the court is likely to perform the same sort of exercise.

The courts take the view that changing a child's surname is a serious matter (*Dawson v Wearmouth* [1999] AC 308, [1999] 1 FLR 1167); and that the child's wishes, not those of the parent, may prevail. In *Re C (Change of Surname)* [1998] 2 FLR 656 the Court of Appeal held that good reasons have to be shown before a judge will allow a change of name. In *Re W; Re A; Re B (Change of Name)* [1999] 2 FLR 930 Butler-Sloss LJ said that a desire to change a child's name, because the applicant parent did not have the same name as the child, will generally not carry much weight.

The court will take into account cultural and religious circumstances when deciding whether to permit a change of surname, but even then it may be unwilling to permit a change (see, for example, *Re S (Change of Names: Cultural Factors)* [2001] 2 FLR 1005 where Wilson J refused to give the mother permission to change the child's Sikh names to Muslim names after she had moved back into a Muslim community on family breakdown). A change of surname may, however, be permitted where there is a need to protect a child against the risk of abduction (see, for example, *Re F (Contact)* [2007] EWHC 2543 (Fam) where the father had made repeated threats to abduct the children).

In *Re R (Surname: Using Both Parents')* [2001] EWCA Civ 1344, [2001] 2 FLR 1358 it was suggested that parents should be encouraged to use the Spanish custom of combining the paternal and maternal surnames as a way of avoiding surname disputes.

11.8 Relocation on family breakdown

(a) Removing a child lawfully from the UK

On family breakdown, a parent may wish to take the child temporarily or permanently out of the UK. A parent can do this, provided he or she is not in breach of any statutory provision or court order and has obtained the necessary consents.

Obtaining the necessary consents   A parent who wishes to take a child out of the UK must obtain the consent of everyone with parental responsibility for the child, otherwise he or she may commit the criminal offence of child abduction or kidnapping (see 13.3) or be in contempt of court (if there is a court order prohibiting the child's removal). Oral consent to take the child abroad is usually sufficient, unless there is a court order to the contrary, or there is a residence order in force, when *written* consent is needed (see above) except if the holder of the residence order wishes to go abroad for less than one month (s 13(1)(b) CA 1989). If consent is not forthcoming then the court's permission to leave the UK will have to be obtained. Such applications are known as 'relocation applications'.

(b) International relocation applications

After family breakdown, a parent may wish to take the child out of the UK, perhaps to start a new relationship, or to take up a new job, or to move back to his or her country of origin. The other parent may refuse to agree to this, perhaps because of the difficulty of maintaining contact, or because of a fear that the child will not be returned. Where the necessary consents to taking the child out of the UK are not forthcoming (see above), the court's permission must be sought in order to avoid committing a criminal offence or being in contempt of court.

Permission to leave the UK (to relocate) with a child can be sought by applying for a specific issue order (see 10.8), or, if a residence order is in force, by applying under section 13(1) CA 1989. The court must apply the welfare principle in section 1(1) and the other welfare principles in section 1 of the Children Act 1989 (see 10.3). The court will usually ask a Cafcass officer to prepare a report, but they are not invariably ordered and a failure to do so will not necessarily be a sufficient ground for an appeal (see *Re R (Leave to Remove: Contact)* [2010] EWCA Civ 1137, [2011] 1 FLR 1336).

The voice of the child   The child's views can be taken into account in a relocation application. The usual way in which the child's voice is put before the court is by way of a Cafcass report. Separate representation of the child is permitted but is rarely exercised in practice. The child's wishes may be an important consideration in tilting the balance one way or the other if the child is mature enough to understand the situation. Thus, for instance, in *Re W (Leave to Remove)* [2008] EWCA Civ 538, [2008] 2 FLR 1170 the Court of Appeal allowed the mother's appeal, and granted her permission to take the children to Sweden, on the ground *inter alia* that the judge had failed to sufficiently consider the wishes of the three children (aged 11, 13, and 15), who were particularly intelligent, mature and sophisticated for their ages, and who supported the proposed move to Sweden.

The approach of the courts in relocation applications   The approach of the courts is to allow a reasonable and properly thought-out application, unless this is clearly incompatible with the child's welfare. This approach was laid down by the Court of Appeal in *Poel v Poel* [1970] WLR 1469 and has been upheld by the courts in subsequent cases, notably in *Payne v Payne* [2001] EWCA Civ 1166, [2001] 1 FLR 1052 (see below) even though some parents (usually fathers), as well as lawyers and academics, have argued that this approach is wrong. With the coming into force of the Human Rights Act 1998, parents began to argue that the approach in *Poel* and *Payne* breached their human rights and those of the child. They also argued that the approach was contrary to the welfare principle in section 1(1) of the Children Act 1989 because it failed to treat the child's welfare as the court's paramount consideration. Thus, for example, in *Re A (Permission to Remove Child from Jurisdiction: Human Rights)* [2000] 2 FLR 225 the father argued that, if permission was given to allow the mother to take their child to New York, it would breach his right to family life under Article 8 of the ECHR. However, the Court of Appeal, dismissing his appeal, held that Article 8(2) required the court to balance such rights where they were in conflict. It held that the test laid down in *Poel v Poel* (above) was not in conflict with the ECHR. In fact, Buxton LJ doubted whether difficult balancing questions of this nature fell within the purview of the ECHR at all.

Payne v Payne: the leading case   In *Payne v Payne*, which is the leading case in relocation applications, the Court of Appeal reviewed the long line of authority on relocation applications in the light of the new obligations imposed on the courts by the Human Rights Act (HRA) 1998.

▶ *Payne v Payne* [2001] EWCA Civ 1166, [2001] 1 FLR 1052

The mother (the primary carer) applied for permission to remove the daughter (aged 4) permanently from the UK to live with her in New Zealand. The father opposed the application and applied for a residence order. The father and paternal grandmother had regular and exceptionally good staying contact with the child. The mother's application was granted at first instance, applying the principle in *Poel* (namely, to allow a reasonable and properly thought-out application unless it is clearly incompatible with the child's welfare). The father appealed arguing that: contact between children and non-residential parents had increased in importance since the decision in *Poel*; the principles in relocation applications were inconsistent with the Children Act 1989, as they created a presumption in favour of the applicant; and the court's approach was inconsistent with the HRA 1998.

The Court of Appeal dismissed his appeal, holding that there was no conflict between the case-law governing relocation applications and the European Convention for the Protection of Human Rights, and the Children Act 1989. It held that the proposition in *Poel* (that a reasonable application would be allowed) did not amount to a presumption in favour of the primary carer. The child's welfare is always the court's paramount consideration, and the welfare checklist in section 1(3) CA 1989 (see 10.3) should be used by a judge when carrying out the welfare test.

Butler-Sloss P said that, although the reasonable proposals of the residential parent wishing to live abroad carried great weight, they had to be scrutinised carefully so that the court could be satisfied that there was a genuine motivation for the move and not an intention to terminate contact between the child and the other parent. Her Ladyship said that the effect on the child of a denial of contact with the non-resident parent and his family was an important consideration, and that the opportunity for continuing contact between the child and the parent left behind in the UK might be a very significant factor.

Thorpe LJ agreed with Ward LJ in *Re A (Permission to Remove Child from Jurisdiction: Human Rights)* (see above) that the advent of the ECHR in domestic law by the HRA 1998 did not necessitate a revision of the fundamental approach to relocation applications formulated by the Court of Appeal and consistently applied over so many years. Thorpe LJ said that 'in a united family the right to family life is a shared right', but that 'once a family unit disintegrates the separating members' separate rights can only be to a fragmented family life'. In the present case the mother's right to mobility under Article 2 of Protocol 4 of the European Convention was another relevant right to be considered. Thorpe LJ said that he did not consider that a reasonable request by the primary carer created a legal presumption of permission to relocate. He also proposed a 'discipline' which the courts should use in relocation cases (see below).

The 'discipline' which courts should use Thorpe LJ in *Payne* suggested that the following framework or 'discipline' should be used by the courts when deciding relocation applications:

'(a) Pose the question: is the mother's application genuine in the sense that it is not motivated by some selfish desire to exclude the father from the child's life? Then ask is the mother's application realistic, by which I mean founded on practical proposals both well researched and investigated? If the application fails either of these tests refusal will inevitably follow.

(b) If however the application passes these tests then there must be a careful appraisal of the father's opposition: is it motivated by genuine concern for the future of the child's welfare or is it driven by some ulterior motive? What would be the extent of the detriment to him and his future relationship with the child were the application granted? To what extent would that be offset by extension of the child's relationships with the maternal family and homeland?

(c) What would be the impact on the mother, either as the single parent or as a new wife, of a refusal of her realistic proposal?

(d) The outcome of the second and third appraisals must then be brought into an overriding review of the child's welfare as the paramount consideration, directed by the statutory checklist in so far as appropriate.'

The principles laid down in *Payne* were endorsed by the Court of Appeal in *Re G (Leave to Remove)* [2007] EWCA Civ 1497, [2008] 1 FLR 1587 where the father sought leave to appeal against the trial judge's decision to grant the mother leave to relocate to Germany, on the basis that judges were misapplying *Payne* in that they were inappropriately prioritising the impact of refusal on the primary carer, and were disregarding modern views on the importance of co-parenting. The Court of Appeal refused permission to appeal. Thorpe LJ, giving judgment, held that it was not possible to argue that the principles in *Payne* were being widely misunderstood or misapplied by trial judges; but he said that he did recognise that relocation cases were very difficult for trial judges and that often the balance between grant and refusal was a very fine one.

In *Re H (A Child)* [2007] EWCA Civ 222, [2007] 2 FLR 317 Thorpe LJ said that a fundamentally important part of the judge's task in deciding a finely balanced relocation case was to assess the impact on the caring parent of a decision to refuse permission to relocate. He said that this was 'often the most important single task that confronts the judge'. In *Re B (Leave to Remove: Impact of Refusal)* [2004] EWCA Civ 956, [2005] 2 FLR 239 Thorpe LJ said that 'each case turned on its own facts, but that the applicant's explanation for fundamental relocation is the core of every case'.

Despite considerable concern and criticism about the approach to relocation adopted in *Payne v Payne* (see further below), it remains good law as the following decision of the Court of Appeal shows:

▶ *Re W (Relocation: Removal Outside Jurisdiction)* **[2011] EWCA Civ 345, [2011] 2 FLR 409**

The Australian mother sought leave to return to Australia with the two children, aged 12 and 8, after having been in the UK for many years. The parents had never married or lived together as a couple, and the father did not have parental responsibility. There had been little contact with the father for some time and the mother was concerned about the father's use of drugs and alcohol. There was evidence that the mother was suffering from postnatal depression, although her main reason for seeking to relocate was that she thought that she and the children would have a better life in Australia. The Cafcass reports favoured relocation, and the children were keen to move. In fact they appeared more interested in relocating than in developing a better relationship with their father. However, despite accepting that the mother had a genuine motivation, that she would be devastated by a refusal to relocate and that reasonable proposals were in place for the practicalities of the move, the trial judge nonetheless refused leave to relocate on the basis that relocation would effectively end the children's relationship with their father. The mother appealed to the Court of Appeal.

The Court of Appeal, allowing her appeal and granting her leave to remove the children to Australia, held that the judge had misdirected himself in law, in that he had failed to have regard to the full list of considerations in *Payne*, and, in particular, had given too little weight to the mother's well-being and the effect on her of a refusal of leave when considering the children's welfare. Consequently, his decision to refuse leave to relocate was plainly wrong.

(For a comment on *Re W*, and also *K v K* (see further below), see Gilmore [2011] Fam Law 970.)

Practical matters While each relocation application turns on its own facts, practical matters (such as housing, education, contact arrangements and potential cultural difficulties for the child) will be important (see, for example, *Re F (Leave to Remove)* [2005] EWHC 2705 (Fam), [2006] 1 FLR 776 where the mother's application to remove the child to Jamaica was refused on the basis, *inter alia*, of her failure to make adequate plans in respect of supporting herself and the child and in respect of the child's schooling; and because there were insufficient funds available to pay for regular airfares for contact visits to the father).

However, where the primary carer is returning to a completely familiar home life after a brief absence, the Court of Appeal has held that the bar in respect of practical matters is set relatively low (see *Re F and H (Children: Relocation)* [2007] EWCA Civ 692, [2008] 2 FLR 1667 where the mother was granted permission to return to Texas with the children after a relatively brief absence from her home city, her family and all that was familiar). But, even if the caring parent is returning to his or her homeland, the application will not necessarily be allowed, as each case depends on its own facts (see *Re H (Removal from Jurisdiction)* [2007] EWCA Civ 222, [2007] 2 FLR 317 where the American mother's application to move back to the USA with the child (aged 5) and her new husband failed, as, although it was clear that if leave was refused the mother would be distressed and unhappy in the short term, there was no risk of her compromising the care of the child).

The psychological impact of relocation In *Re B (Leave to Remove: Impact of Refusal)* [2004] EWCA Civ 956, [2005] 2 FLR 239 Thorpe LJ, with whom May and Scott Baker LJJ agreed, said that it was important to give great weight to the emotional and psychological well-being of the primary carer, and not merely take note of the impact on the primary carer of refusing the application to relocate. However, in respect of possible mental harm to the applicant, it was held in *Re G (Removal from Jurisdiction)* [2005] EWCA Civ 170, [2005] 2 FLR 166 that an applicant is not required to prove that he or she will suffer psychological damage if permission to relocate is refused – all that is required is that a refusal will have an impact on the applicant's sense of well-being and that this will be transmitted to the children. In *R v R (Leave to Remove)* [2004] EWHC 2572 (Fam), [2005] 1 FLR 687 Baron J refused the mother's application to remove the children to France on the basis, *inter alia*, that the mother (who had psychiatric problems) did not have the necessary emotional stability to establish a new life in another country.

The psychological impact of relocation on the children will be an important consideration under the welfare test. Thus, for example, in *Re B (Leave to Remove)* [2008] EWCA Civ 1034, [2008] 2 FLR 2059 the mother's application to remove the children of the marriage to Germany was refused as there was strong oral evidence from a psychologist that relocation to Germany would have a very negative effect on the children and would severely damage their relationship with their father.

Cultural and religious objections to relocation Cultural and religious objections to a parent relocating outside the UK will not usually be allowed to prevail over the primary consideration of the child's welfare. Thus, in *Re A (Leave to Remove: Cultural and Religious Considerations)* [2006] EWHC 421 (Fam), [2007] 2 FLR 572 Hedley J allowed the child's mother to relocate with her son (aged 9) to The Netherlands where she lived with her new husband, despite the father's arguments that his son should remain in England for religious and cultural reasons (in particular, so that he could succeed to the mantle of head of the family group).

Shared care and relocation applications The following decision of the Court of Appeal is an important case for its discussion of *Payne v Payne*. It also shows that the courts take a different approach to relocation from that in *Payne* when there is no primary carer as both parents share care of the child. Thus, the *Payne* 'discipline' does not apply where equal or roughly equal shared care arrangements are in place. Instead the judge must exercise his or her discretion to grant or refuse the application by applying the statutory checklist in section 1(3) of the Children Act 1989.

▶ **K v K (Relocation: Shared Care Arrangement) [2011] EWCA Civ 793**

The care of the two children (aged 4 and 2) was shared as both parents were working part-time. The children spent six consecutive days with the father and eight with the mother each fortnight (though some of these days also involved time with a nanny).

The mother sought leave to relocate with the children to Canada on marriage breakdown as she was unhappy and isolated in London, was not getting on well with the father's family, and wanted additional support from her own family. The Cafcass report, while describing the case as finely balanced, recommended that there be no relocation in the immediate future, but that it might be best for the children in three to four years. The trial judge granted leave to relocate, and the father appealed arguing that: the judge had failed to give reasons for departing from the Cafcass recommendations; the judge had directed herself by reference to *Payne* (a primary carer case) when she should have been guided by the decision of Hedley J in *Re Y (Leave to Remove from Jurisdiction)* (a shared care case); and the judge's analysis had been one-sided, in that she had looked only at the mother's case and not adequately addressed his case.

The Court of Appeal allowed the appeal, and remitted the case for a retrial before a different judge. All three judges concluded that the only principle to be extracted from *Payne v Payne* was the paramountcy principle. Black LJ described the welfare principle as being the only 'authentic principle' found in *Payne* and as 'the only truly inescapable principle in the relocation jurisprudence'. Her Ladyship stated that judges were not at liberty to ignore the 'valuable guidance' contained in *Payne*, but that it must be taken into account as guidance not as a rigid principle. Black LJ also said that an important point which must always be borne in mind is how highly fact-specific relocation applications are. Moore-Bick LJ said that the controversy which surrounds *Payne* is the result of a failure to distinguish between legal principle and guidance. His Lordship warned against an unduly mechanistic application of the guidance and reminded the court that, while the decision in *Payne* is binding, the only principle of law enunciated in *Payne* is that the welfare of the child is paramount, and all the rest is merely guidance.

George, commenting on *K v K* (see [2012] CFLQ 108) wondered why the Court of Appeal felt it necessary to emphasise the welfare principle so much when that principle is clearly encapsulated in statute. Eaton, commenting on *K v K* ([2011] Fam Law 1093) stated that, 'though without explicitly doing away with *Payne* (as of course it could not do so), the Court of Appeal has made [a review to the Supreme Court] unnecessary', and that '[t]he golden thread running through all the judgments is that the *Payne* guidance is subordinate to a welfare assessment – in every case'.

Another case involving shared care was *C v C (International Relocation: Shared Care Arrangement)* [2011] EWHC 335 (Fam), [2011] 2 FLR 701 where Theis J refused to permit the mother to relocate to Florida as the parents had an agreed shared care arrangement. Theis J held that the approach in *Payne* must be modified by the approach adopted in *Re Y (Leave to Remove from Jurisdiction)* [2004] 2 FLR 330 where Hedley J had refused permission for the mother to relocate to Texas as the child had been brought up in Wales in a Welsh-speaking environment under an equal parenting arrangement.

Contact and relocation In some cases the court has made a contact order when granting leave to relocate (see *AP v TD (Relocation: Retention of Jurisdiction)* [2010] EWHC 2040 (Fam), [2011] 1 FLR 1851), but in *Re R (Leave to Remove: Contact)* [2010] EWCA Civ 1137, [2011] 1 FLR 1336 Wilson LJ held that, although a contact order is occasionally made by way of attachment to a grant of leave, it is contrary to principle since the court is, if only for practical reasons, surrendering its control over the child to the foreign court.

(c)　Is the approach in relocation cases the correct one?

The approach to international relocation as laid down by the Court of Appeal in *Poel v Poel* and endorsed in *Payne v Payne* (see above) has been the subject of considerable debate and increasing criticism. It is felt that that resident parents (often mothers) are favoured too much over the other parent and that the resident parent's welfare, not that of the child, seems to be the primary consideration. In other words, the courts place too much emphasis on the wishes and proposals of the parent who wishes to relocate rather than looking at the best interests of the child from the point of view of having the benefit of maintaining a relationship with both parents. There is also concern that courts are denying children their right to contact with both parents, usually their father. Also, *Poel v Poel* was decided in the 1970s when different conceptions of parenthood prevailed in that mothers were usually responsible for the day-to-day care of children and were granted custody, whereas today both parents are often engaged in parenting.

Spon-Smith (2004) claims that the conventional approach to relocation applications is not supported by American research (by Braver *et al.*, 2003) which shows that children do not necessarily benefit from moving to a new location which is distant from the other parent. Hayes (2006) argues that trial judges are being prevented by strong rulings from the Court of Appeal from exercising their discretion in relocation cases in a broad and principled manner. She claims that the 'discipline' recommended in *Payne*, and entrenched in subsequent Court of Appeal judgments, is misguided as it places a gloss on the welfare principle, it narrows the proper application of that principle and is biased in favour of the residential parent (who is almost invariably the mother). Herring and Taylor (2006) claim that principles adopted in relocation cases fail to take adequate account of the impact of human rights reasoning. Geekie (2008) argues that the approach in relocation cases seems to be at odds with the approach adopted in shared residence cases where the approach has been to shake off 'the shackles of a dated approach to shared parenting'. Pressdee (2008) argues that Thorpe LJ's approach in *Payne* needs to be applied with greater flexibility. Thomas ([2010] Fam Law 982) has argued for 'greater weight to be placed on the best interests of the child being found in the stability and continuity of home, education, community, culture and wider family rather than the relationship abroad with one parent'.

Some countries take a different view to relocation. For instance, the New Zealand Court of Appeal in *D v S* [2002] NZFLR 116 has rejected *Payne v Payne* as the leading precedent in relocation cases on the basis that it puts the mother's needs above those of the child. (For a comparative study of relocation in England New Zealand, see George [2011] CFLQ 178.) The debate on relocation in England and Wales has also focused on the Washington Declaration on International Family Relocation 2010, which includes a non-exhaustive list of 13 factors for the court to consider when deciding on a child's best interests in a relocation dispute. Mostyn J in *Re AR (A Child: Relocation)* [2010] EWHC 1346, [2010] 2 FLR 1577 was of the view that the Washington Declaration provided 'a more balanced and neutral approach to a relocation application'. His Lordship was also of the opinion that a review of the ideology of *Poel/Payne* by the Supreme Court is urgently needed. However, in *Re H (Leave to Remove)* [2010] EWCA Civ 915, [2010] 2 FLR 1875, where the father argued *inter alia* that the Washington Declaration should replace the guidance in *Payne*, the Court of Appeal held that, while the Declaration might prove a valuable means of harmonising the approaches to relocation applications in different jurisdictions, it could not replace the guidance in *Payne*.

However, despite the widespread concern and criticism of the approach to relocation applications, recent decisions of the Court of Appeal, such as those in *Re W (Relocation: Removal Outside Jurisdiction)* (above) and *K v K (Relocation: Shared Care Arrangement)* (above), show that *Payne* remains good law except where a child is subject to a shared, or almost shared, care arrangement (for a discussion of these cases, see George [2012] CFLQ 108).

(d) Temporary removals from the UK

Sometimes a parent may wish to take the child temporarily out of the UK (for instance for a holiday). In some cases the court's permission will be needed. Thus, if a residence order is in force and the primary carer wishes to take the child out of the UK temporarily for more than one month, then the written consent of all persons with parental responsibility is needed, or otherwise the consent of the court (see s 13(1)(b) CA 1989). In the following case, the Court of Appeal considered how the courts should deal with applications for temporary removal:

> ▶ *Re A (Temporary Removal from Jurisdiction)* [2004] EWCA Civ 1587, [2005] 1 FLR 639
>
> The child (aged 4) spent five nights a week with the mother and two nights with the father under the terms of a shared residence order. The mother applied for permission to take the child to South Africa for two years to carry out research for her doctorate. The judge, applying the principles in *Payne v Payne* (above), refused the application. The Court of Appeal allowed the mother's appeal, as the judge had erred in holding that the considerations which govern decisions about applications for permanent removal of the child should also apply, without modification, to applications for temporary removal. The considerations relevant to an application for permission to relocate permanently were not automatically applicable to applications for temporary removal. Thorpe LJ said: 'The more temporary the removal, the less regard should be paid to the principles stated in *Payne v Payne.*'

Thus, the approach in *Payne* is unlikely to apply, particularly where the temporary removal is for a short duration. In fact, in the light of subsequent authorities on shared care and relocation (see p. 309 above), it is surprising that the approach in *Payne* was held to apply at all in the above case, as the parties had a shared care arrangement.

Practical safeguards to ensure the child's return   If there is a risk that a parent will not return after a temporary stay outside the UK, the court in England and Wales can impose certain safeguards. Thus, it may: impose a condition on a court order; require an undertaking to be given to the court; require the parties to enter into a notarised agreement containing provisions about returning the child; require 'mirror' orders (orders equivalent to English orders) to be applied for in the foreign court; order a parent to swear on the Holy Qur'an before a Shariah Court that the child will be returned; and/or order a parent to provide a sum of money as surety for the child's return (see, for example, *Re L (Removal from Jurisdiction: Holiday)* [2001] 1 FLR 241).

The following case provides an example of the court imposing a range of practical safeguards to ensure the children's return:

> ▶ *Re S (Leave to Remove from Jurisdiction: Securing Return from Holiday)* **[2001] 2 FLR 507**
>
> The court wished to ensure that the mother would return the children after taking them to India on holiday. She was ordered: to return them by a certain date and not to return them to India without the father's written permission; to deposit the children's passports with her solicitors in India; to provide the father with copies of the airline tickets and the children's visas from the Indian High Commission; to seek only short tourist visas (that order to be served on the Indian High Commission); and not to seek Indian passports or Indian citizenship for the children while in India. The children were made wards of court, and the court made declarations that their habitual residence was England and Wales and that they were British citizens.

The approach in *Re S* above was followed in *Re DS (Removal from Jurisdiction)* [2009] EWHC 1594 (Fam) where a mother wished to take the child to India for a family wedding, but where the child was at risk because the mother had on a previous occasion been a month late in returning from India to the UK. She was granted leave to make the trip on the basis of a range of undertakings and a declaration as to the child's citizenship and habitual residence.

11.9 Relocation within the UK

Moving a child from England and Wales to another part of the UK (Scotland or Northern Ireland), unlike moving a child *from* the UK (see 11.8 above), does not require the oral or written consent of the other parent or anyone else with parental responsibility whether or not a residence order is in force. Neither is it a criminal offence under the Child Abduction Act 1984 (see 13.3), although it could constitute the offence of kidnapping.

(i) Steps to prevent removal   A parent (or other person with parental responsibility) who wishes to prevent the other parent (or person with parental responsibility) from moving the child from England and Wales to another part of the UK can apply under the Children Act 1989 for a prohibited steps or residence order (with a condition attached to the residence order under section 11(7)) or apply to make the child a ward of court (see 8.7).

(ii) Resolving a dispute about removal   An unresolvable dispute between parents (and other persons with parental responsibility for a child) about a child's removal to another part of the UK can be determined by applying for a residence order or specific issue order under the Children Act 1989 (see 10.5 and 10.8). In such a case the court must apply the welfare principle and the welfare checklist and the other principles in section 1 of the Children Act 1989 (see 10.3). The Court of Appeal has held that a dispute about relocation within the UK must be decided by adopting a similar approach to that laid down in *Payne v Payne* (see p. 306 above), but that the test is less stringent than that for external relocations (*per* Thorpe LJ in *Re H (Children: Residence Order: Condition)* [2001] EWCA Civ 1338, [2001] 2 FLR 1277 where a condition restricting relocation was upheld).

(iii) Restricting residence   The Court of Appeal has held that an order, or condition in an order, restricting a primary carer's right to choose where he or she lives should only be made in exceptional circumstances (see, for example, *Re E (Residence: Imposition of Conditions)*

[1997] 2 FLR 638; and *Re B (Prohibited Steps Order)* [2007] EWCA Civ 1055, [2008] 1 FLR 613, where the Court of Appeal allowed the mother's appeal against a prohibited steps order which had prohibited her from changing the child's residence from England and Wales to Northern Ireland). The House of Lords also adopted the same approach in *Re G (Children) (Residence: Same-Sex Partner)* [2006] UKHL 43, [2006] 2 FLR 629 (see further at p. 232 above). Thus, the courts must acknowledge that the primary carer has reasonable freedom to choose where he or she resides with the child in the UK.

(iv) Relocation and shared residence   In *Re L (Shared Residence: Relocation)* [2009] EWCA Civ 20, [2009] 1 FLR 1157 (where there was a shared residence order and the mother wished to move from London to Somerset), the Court of Appeal held, dismissing her appeal, that a shared residence order is not an automatic bar to relocation, as it may well be in the child's best interests to relocate notwithstanding the existence of such an order. It held that the correct approach to relocation in the context of shared residence is for the court to look at the underlying factual substratum in welfare terms bearing in mind the tension which may well exist between a parent's freedom to relocate and the welfare of the child which may militate against relocation. (See also *Re F (Internal Relocation)* [2010] EWCA Civ 1428, [2011] 1 FLR 1382 where the mother's application by means of a specific issue order to move the four children (who were subject to a shared caring arrangement) to the Orkney Islands in Scotland (as she had strong Scottish connections) was refused at first instance and on appeal on the basis of the circumstances of the case which militated against her being granted permission.)

Summary

▶ The law governing arrangements for children on family breakdown is laid down in the Children Act 1989. Parents retain parental responsibility for their children on family breakdown (see further at 9.6). For finance and property arrangements for children on parental separation, see Chapter 12.

▶ The Family Justice Review has made various recommendations to improve the law governing children and families on family breakdown (such as the introduction of 'Parenting Agreements' and a new child arrangements order). These recommendations have been accepted by the Government, except for the FJR's recommendation that there should be no change to the law regarding shared parenting (see further below).

▶ Many children experience parental relationship breakdown; and this may have an adverse effect on some of them. It is therefore better for children (and parents) if the parties reach agreement about arrangements for their children on family breakdown. Going to court is regarded as the last resort, and other forms of dispute resolution are being increasingly promoted.

▶ Cafcass performs various important functions on family breakdown, namely: making reports for the court if needed; helping parents to reach agreement about contact; and conducting risk assessments. Welfare reports have an important role to play in children's cases.

▶ Jurisdiction in family disputes involving matters of parental responsibility in the EU is governed by Council Regulation (EC) (No. 2201/2003) Concerning Jurisdiction and the Recognition and Enforcement of Judgments in Matrimonial Matters and in Matters of Parental Responsibility (Brussels II Revised).

▶ There has been discussion in the last few years about introducing a presumption of shared parenting. Although the Family Justice Review was opposed to this, the Government is considering introducing legislative reform to promote shared parenting, subject to safeguards.

Summary cont'd

▶ In cases dealing with children's disputes on family breakdown (for instance in respect of residence and contact), the family courts must ensure that they comply with the ECHR and the jurisprudence of the ECtHR as a result of their obligations under the Human Rights Act 1998.

▶ An applicant for a divorce (or civil partnership dissolution) must complete a Statement of Arrangements for Children, a form which is looked at by the district judge, who must consider whether to exercise any of the court's powers under the Children Act 1989 (see s 41 Matrimonial Causes Act 1973; and s 63 Civil Partnership Act 2004)). In exceptional circumstances the divorce or dissolution can be postponed, but this is unusual.

▶ An unresolvable dispute about which parent a child should live with on family breakdown can be settled by making an application for a residence order under the Children Act 1989 (see also Chapter 10). The welfare of the child is the court's paramount consideration (s 1(1)) and the other welfare principles in section 1 apply. A shared residence order can be made (s 11(4)). Once a residence order is made, no person can change the child's surname or remove the child from the UK (except for up to one month) without the *written* consent of all persons with parental responsibility, or otherwise with permission of the court (ss 13(1), (2)). A shared residence order can be made under section 11(4) and these are increasingly being made. The courts have developed a range of principles which apply when considering whether or not to make the order. The court has the power to attach a condition to a residence order under section 11(7).

▶ An unresolvable dispute about contact can be determined by an application for a contact order under section 8 of the Children Act 1989. The court must apply the welfare principles in section 1 of the Act. Direct contact, indirect contact, supervised contact and an order of no contact are possible options for the court. Hostility to contact by residential parents has caused difficulties for the court. Domestic violence is a serious factor to be considered by the court, and various steps have been put in place to improve protection for children who may suffer domestic violence in the context of contact. The ECtHR recognises the importance of contact between parents and children as part of the right to family life under Article 8 ECHR.

▶ New provisions in the Children Act 1989 (ss 11A–11P) have been enacted to improve and resolve contact difficulties on family breakdown, which include: contact activity directions and conditions; monitoring contact orders; warning notices; enforcement orders; and compensation orders. Other measures for promoting the enforcement and facilitation of contact include: a family assistance order; proceedings for contempt of court; and transferring residence of the child.

▶ A dispute about a child's surname can be decided by making an application for a specific issue order, or, if a residence order is in force, by making an application under section 13 of the Children Act 1989. The child's welfare, not the parents' wishes, prevails in such proceedings.

▶ Where a parent who wishes to take a child out of the UK cannot obtain the consent of the other parent and/or other persons with parental responsibility, then he or she will have to make a relocation application in order to avoid committing a criminal offence or being in contempt of court. The parent who wishes to relocate can apply to the court for permission to leave the UK either by applying for a specific issue order, or, if a residence order is in force, by making an application under section 13 of the Children Act 1989. The child's welfare is the court's paramount consideration (see s 1(1) CA 1989).

▶ The 'discipline' for deciding relocation applications was laid down by the Court of Appeal in *Payne v Payne* (2001) and this is still the leading case despite various concerns, such as that the approach in *Payne* favours mothers rather than fathers, is contrary to the best interests of children, and is out of line with modern views of parenthood. However, the Court of Appeal has recently emphasised that the primary consideration is the *welfare* of the child and that the *Payne* 'discipline' is merely guidance. *Payne* does not apply where the parents have a shared care arrangement.

Summary cont'd

▶ *Payne* is unlikely to apply to an application to take a child temporarily out of the UK (for example, for a holiday), unless it is for a considerable period of time. A range of practical safeguards are available for ensuring that a child is returned after a temporary removal.

▶ Moving a child from England and Wales to another part of the UK does not require the oral or written consent of the other parent or anyone else with parental responsibility whether or not a residence order is in force. Neither is it a criminal offence under the Child Abduction Act 1984, although it could constitute the offence of kidnapping. A person who wishes to prevent a child moving to another part of the UK can apply for a prohibited steps order, a residence order (with a condition attached) or apply to make the child a ward of court.

▶ An unresolvable dispute between parents (and other persons with parental responsibility for a child) about a child's removal to another part of the UK can be determined by applying for a residence order or specific issue order under the Children Act 1989. The welfare principles in section 1 of the Children Act 1989 apply. The court will adopt a similar approach to that adopted in *Payne v Payne* (above), but the test is likely to be less stringent than that for relocation to places outside the UK. A shared residence order is not necessarily a bar to permitting a relocation within the UK, subject to the relocation being in the child's best interests.

Further reading and references

Bevan, 'What's in a name? A practitioner's view on reform of residence orders' [2012] Fam Law 862.

Brasse, District Judge, 'The *Payne* threshold: leaving the jurisdiction' [2005] Fam Law 780.

Braver *et al.*, 'Relocation of children after divorce and children's best interests: new evidence and legal considerations' (2003) 17(2) *Journal of Family Psychology* 206.

Bryan, Chief Justice of the Family Court of Australia 'An Australian perspective on the Family Justice Review' [2012] *International Family Law Journal* 269.

Butler *et al.*, *Divorcing Children: Children's Experience of Their Parents' Divorce*, 2003, Jessica Kingsley.

Douglas, 'Contact is not a commodity to be bartered for money' [2011] Fam Law 491.

Douglas and Ferguson, 'The role of grandparents in divorced families' (2003) *International Journal of Law, Policy and the Family* 41.

Eaton, 'Relocation after *K* v *K*' [2011] Fam Law 1093.

Fehlberg, 'Legislating for shared parenting: how the Family Justice Review got it right' [2012] Fam Law 709.

Fortin, Richie and Buchanan, 'Young adults' perceptions of court-ordered contact' [2007] CFLQ 211.

Freeman, 'Relocation and the child's best interests' [2010] *International Family Law* 248.

Geekie, 'Relocation and shared residence: one route or two?' [2008] Fam Law 446.

George, 'Practitioners' views on children's welfare in relocation disputes: comparing approaches in England and New Zealand' [2011] CFLQ 178.

George, 'Reviewing relocation? *Re W (Relocation: Removal Outside Jurisdiction)* [2011] EWCA Civ 345 and *K* v *K (Relocation: Shared Care Arrangement)* [2011] EWCA Civ 793' [2012] CFLQ 108.

Gilmore, 'The *Payne* saga: precedent and family law cases' [2011] Fam Law 970.

Gilmore, 'Contact/shared residence and child well-being: research evidence and its implications for legal decision-making' [2006] *International Journal of Law, Policy and the Family* 344.

Gilmore, 'Court decision-making in shared residence order cases: a critical examination' [2006] CFLQ 478.

Gilmore, 'Disputing contact: challenging some assumptions' [2008] CFLQ 285.

Gilmore, 'The assumption that contact is beneficial: challenging the "secure foundation"' [2008] Fam Law 1226.

Further reading and references cont'd

Harris and George, 'Parental responsibility and shared residence orders: parliamentary intentions and judicial interpretations' [2010] CFLQ 151.

Hayes, '*Dawson* v *Wearmouth* – What's in a name? A child by any other name is surely just as sweet?' [1999] CFLQ 423.

Hayes, 'Relocation cases: is the Court of Appeal applying the correct principles?' [2006] CFLQ 351.

Henaghan, 'Relocation cases: the rhetoric and the reality of a child's best interests: a view from the bottom of the world' [2011] CFLQ 226.

Herring and Taylor, 'Relocating relocation' [2006] CFLQ 517.

Humphreys and Harrison, 'Focusing on safety – domestic violence and the role of child contact centres' [2003] CFLQ 237.

Hunt, Masson and Trinder, 'Shared parenting: the law, the evidence and guidance from Families Need Fathers' [2009] Fam Law 831.

Johnson, 'Shared residence orders: for and against' [2009] Fam Law 131.

Kaganas, 'Regulating emotion: judging contact disputes' [2011] CFLQ 63.

Kaganas, '*Re L (Contact: Domestic Violence); Re V (Contact: Domestic Violence); Re M (Contact: Domestic Violence); Re H (Contact: Domestic Violence)*: Contact and domestic violence' [2000] CFLQ 311.

Murch with Keehan, *The Voice of the Child in Private Family Law Proceedings*, 2003, Family Law.

Newnham, 'Shared residence: lessons from Sweden' [2011] CFLQ 251.

Nickols, 'A presumption of shared parenting: long awaited or misguided?' [2012] Fam Law 573.

Perry, '*Payne* v *Payne* – leave to remove from the jurisdiction' [2001] CFLQ 455.

Pressdee, 'Relocation, relocation, relocation; rigorous scrutiny revisited' [2008] Fam Law 220.

Reece, 'UK women's groups' child contact campaign: "so long as it is safe"' [2006] CFLQ 538.

Relocation and Leave to Remove, A Report by Custody Minefield (www.thecustodyminefield.com), December 2009.

Rhoades, 'Legislating to promote children's welfare and the quest for certainty' [2012] CLQ 158.

Spon-Smith, 'Relocation revisited' [2004] Fam Law 191.

Thomas, 'Gain a new country but lose a child' [2010] Fam Law 982.

Thomas LJ, 'Relocation development' [2010] Fam Law 565.

Thorpe LJ, 'Relocation: the search for common principles' [2010] *International Family Law* 242

Trinder, 'Shared residence: a review of recent research evidence' [2010] Fam Law 1192.

Wall J, 'Making contact' [2003] Fam Law 275.

Wall LJ, 'Making contact work in 2009' [2009] Fam Law 590.

Worwood, 'International relocation – the debate' [2005] Fam Law 621.

Websites

Association for Shared Parenting: www.sharedparenting.org.uk

Cafcass: www.cafcass.gov.uk

Custody Minefield, The: www.thecustodyminefield.com

Families Need Fathers: www.fnf.org.uk

Family and Parenting Institute: www.familyandparenting.org

National Association of Child Contact Centres: www.naccc.org.uk

Links to relevant websites can also be found at: www.palgrave.com/law/familylaw8e

Chapter 12

Financial provision for children

All parents have a duty to provide financial support for their children, and this obligation continues when parental relationships break down. Financial provision for children is usually in the form of maintenance, but the family courts also have power to make lump sum and property orders for the benefit of a child.

12.1 Child maintenance

Child maintenance is regular financial support towards a child's everyday living costs whereby the parent who does not have the main day-to-day care of the child pays specified sums of money to the parent or person who has the main day-to-day care.

(a) The development of the law

Until April 1993, child maintenance disputes were heard by the courts, which had discretionary powers to make maintenance orders for children according to the circumstances of each case. However, in 1990, as a result of dissatisfaction with the court-based system, radical new proposals were made to move most child maintenance disputes from the courts into a Government agency, the Child Support Agency(CSA) (see the White Paper, *Children Come First*, Cm 1264). The case for reform was based on various arguments, for example that the discretion-based court system was resulting in arbitrary and unpredictable awards and that it was 'unnecessarily fragmented, uncertain in its results, slow and ineffective' (para 2, *Children Come First*). Also, the fact that many fathers were failing to fulfil their maintenance obligations meant that the cost was being thrown onto the State, and consequently onto the taxpayer. The welfare needs of children were not being sufficiently protected.

The proposed changes were passed into law by the Child Support Act 1991, which: transferred the task of assessing, reviewing, collecting and enforcing child maintenance from the courts to the CSA; prohibited the courts from making maintenance orders for children where the CSA had jurisdiction to make a maintenance assessment; and introduced a formula for calculating child maintenance. Right from the beginning, and up till the present day, the scheme has been riddled with problems. Despite amendments to the scheme (such as changes to the formula and the introduction of a 'departures' system to permit the CSA to depart from the formula where assessments produced unfair results), problems and criticisms have continued.

At the end of the 1990s, due to dissatisfaction with the scheme, the Labour Government made proposals to simplify and speed up the system (see *Children First: A New Approach to Child Support*, Cm 3992, 1998; and *New Contract for Welfare: Children's Rights and Parents' Responsibilities*, Cm 4349, 1999). These changes were brought into force in March 2003 by way of amendment to the Child Support Act 1991, the most radical change being the simplification of the formula in order to make it easier for parents to understand and easier and quicker for the CSA to administer. Despite these changes, however, problems continued, in particular in respect of enforcement of payments, delays in maintenance assessments and errors in calculation. By July 2006, £3 billion was owed in unpaid child support. In 2003, a new £456 million computer system was introduced but that also had major problems. By July 2006, the CSA had a backlog of 300,000 cases.

In February 2006, as a result of the catalogue of failings, the Government commissioned Sir David Henshaw to investigate the scheme and make suggestions for reform. In his report (*Recovering Child Support: Routes to Responsibility*, Cm 6894, DWP, 2006) he identified major failings in the system and recommended it be replaced with a completely new system where the emphasis would be on parents making private maintenance agreements and where difficult cases would be dealt with by a new body with tougher enforcement powers. In July 2006, the Government's response to the Henshaw Report was presented to Parliament (*A Fresh Start: Child Support Redesign*, Cm 6895, DWP). This was followed in December 2006 by a White Paper (*A New System of Child Maintenance*, Cm 6979, DWP) setting out a new child support system which would empower parents to take responsibility for making their own maintenance agreements but which would have radically strengthened enforcement powers in cases of non-compliance.

As a result of the above discussions and recommendations, changes to the child support system were made (by the Child Maintenance and Other Payments Act (CMOPA) 2008, which came into effect on 23 July 2008) in order to encourage parents to make their own child maintenance agreements, to strengthen collection and enforcement procedures, and to improve the assessment process. The CMOPA 2008 created a new body, the Child Maintenance and Enforcement Commission (CMEC), with responsibility for the work of the Child Support Agency and for 'Child Maintenance Options', a new information and support service. However, as part of the Government's reforms of QUANGOs, the CMEC was abolished on 1 August 2012 and its work transferred to the 'Child Maintenance Group' within the Department for Work and Pensions (www.dwp.gov.uk), which now manages the child maintenance system in Great Britain. It funds information and support for separating parents, including the Child Maintenance Options service; and is responsible for running the statutory child maintenance scheme which is currently run by the Child Support Agency but which is being gradually transferred to the new Child Maintenance Service.

Discussions of reform have continued. Thus, in January 2011, the Coalition Government published a Green Paper on the future of the child maintenance system (*Strengthening families, promoting parental responsibility: the future of child maintenance*, Cm 7990, DWP). This was followed, in July 2012, by the publication of a consultation paper (*Public consultation. Supporting separated families; securing children's futures*, Cm 8399, DWP), setting out the Government's vision for transforming the child maintenance system so that the emphasis is placed on supporting families to make their own arrangements. For parents who, despite support, are unable to come to a collaborative arrangement, the Government aims to 'provide a new statutory service that will be both faster and more up-to-date than the current CSA schemes' (para 7 of the Ministerial Foreword).

Despite the various reforms, CSA data for the first quarter of 2012 showed that more than 5,000 past and current CSA cases remain over £50,000 in arrears. The data also showed increases in the use of enforcement powers against parents who refuse to pay. For instance, the number of deduction orders made had trebled since 2009. (Data is available at www.childmaintenance.org.)

(b) Maintenance options

Separated parents have three options with respect to making child maintenance agreements. They can make a private 'family-based arrangement'; they can apply to the CSA; and they can apply to the court for a consent order containing an agreement about child maintenance (see pp. 175–6). However, in certain limited circumstances, parents can apply for 'top-up' maintenance from the court (for example for school fees, provision for disabled children etc.) (see p. 325). Parents can also make applications to the court for lump sum and property orders for the benefit of a child (see 12.2 and 12.3).

Detailed information and guidance (including maintenance calculation tools and details of organisations that can help) are available on the following government websites: the Department of Work and Pensions (www.dwp.gov.uk); Directgov (www.directgov.uk); and Child Maintenance Options (www.cmoptions.org).

Note: Although the Government is in the process of winding down the CSA and transferring its statutory powers to the new Child Maintenance Service, this chapter continues to refer to the CSA.

A private 'family-based' agreement Parents can make their own private agreements about child maintenance. The problem with this option is that, as the agreement is not legally binding, enforcement may be a problem and so may varying the agreement when circumstances change. There is also the problem that the amount of maintenance agreed upon may be inadequate. Guides and a maintenance calculator etc. are available on the Child Maintenance Options website (see above). If the agreement breaks down or is considered to be unsatisfactory, either parent can use the Child Support Agency (see below) or 'Maintenance Direct', a service whereby the CSA calculates how much and how often payments should be made, but where the parents themselves set up and manage payments.

The Government's child support scheme

The Department for Work and Pensions (DWP) is responsible for the child maintenance scheme. It funds information and support for separating parents and runs the statutory child maintenance scheme, currently operated through the Child Support Agency (CSA) but whose responsibilities are gradually being transferred to a new Child Maintenance Service (CMS) where the focus will be on parents making 'family-based arrangements'. The Government intends the transfer of responsibilities to be completed by 2014.

The powers and duties of the CSA are laid down in the Child Support Act (CSA) 1991, which remains the relevant Act governing child support maintenance, even though it has been amended many times over the years.

The welfare of the child Unlike court applications, the welfare of the child plays a limited role in applications for child support under the CSA 1991. Thus, a duty to consider the welfare of any child arises only in respect of discretionary decisions made by the CSA or any of its officers (s 2). As section 2 applies to *any* child affected by a decision, the duty is not limited to children for whose benefit the maintenance is being sought but can include, for example, children in the payer's own household and the payer's own children from a new relationship (see *Brookes v Secretary of State for Work and Pensions* [2010] EWCA Civ 420, [2010] 2 FLR 1038).

(i) Applicants and 'qualifying' children

An application to the CSA can be made by the parent (or person who is responsible for the main day-to-day care of the child, such as a grandparent) or by the parent without day-to-day care of the child, provided:

▶ the child is under 16 or is under 19 (and in full-time education, not higher than A-level or its equivalent; or in receipt of Child Benefit) (s 55);

▶ the applicant (parent or other person) has the main day-to-day care of the child and lives in the UK; and the parent without the main day-to-day care lives in the UK, or works in the civil service, the armed forces or for a UK-based company (see s 4); and

▶ no court order is in place from before April 2003, or there is a court order from after April 2003 but it was set up more than 12 months before the application.

Where the parent with the main day-to-day care is on benefits, then he or she can choose to arrange child maintenance by means of any of the options listed above (at p. 320). Child maintenance has no effect on State benefits, including council tax or housing benefit and tax credit award.

(ii) How is child support maintenance calculated?

The CSA calculates the amount of maintenance using four different rates, depending on the payer's income. In summary, these rates (at the time of writing) are as follows:

▶ **The Basic Rate** applies if the payer's net weekly income is at least £200 (after certain deductions). The payer will pay the following percentage of net weekly income as child support: 15 per cent for one child; 20 per cent for two children; and 25 per cent for three or more children.

▶ **The Reduced Rate** applies if the payer's net weekly income is more than £100 but less than £200. The payer will pay a flat rate of £5 a week on the first £100 of net income, plus a percentage of net weekly income over £100 of: 25 per cent for one child; 35 per cent for two children; and 45 per cent for three or more children.

▶ **The Flat Rate** (which is £5 no matter how many children are involved) applies if the payer's net weekly income is between £5 and £100 or he/she (or his/her partner) is in receipt of certain prescribed benefits. If he or she has a partner, then the payer pays half the flat rate (£2.50 a week). If both members of a couple in receipt of Income Support or Jobseeker's Allowance are non-resident parents and both have a child, then they each pay child maintenance at a flat rate of £2.50.

▶ **The Nil Rate** applies in some cases, such as where the person who would be liable to maintenance payments: has a net weekly income of less than £5; is a student in full-time education; is under 16; is in prison; or is living in a care home or independent hospital and receiving help with the fees.

The Default Rate This rate applies where the information needed to calculate child maintenance cannot be obtained straight away. It is currently £30 per week for one child, £40 for two children, and £50 for three or more children).

Special rules apply in the following situations:

▶ A smaller sum of child maintenance is paid if there are relevant 'other children' living with the person responsible for paying maintenance (for example, step-children of the payer or children from a new relationship). In such cases, a lower amount of net weekly income is used for calculating maintenance. Thus, the payer's income is reduced by: 15 per cent if there is one relevant other child; 20 per cent if there are two; and 25 per cent if there are three or more.

▶ If care of a child is shared by both parents for 52 or more nights a year, a discount is made when calculating the basic or reduced rate of maintenance.

▶ Where the maximum amount of net weekly income that can be taken into account when making an assessment is exceeded, then the parent with date-to-day care of the child can apply to the court (see 12.2 and 12.3) for 'top-up' maintenance, which, if granted by the court, can be collected by the CSA.

▶ Variations from the formula (upward or downward) are permitted in certain clearly defined circumstances (see Sch 4B, Part 1, CSA 1991). An upward variation can be made for special expenses incurred by the payer, such as contact costs, looking after a disabled child, boarding school fees, and some prior debts. A variation upwards may be permitted on the application of the parent with care if the assessment does not property reflect the payer's true circumstances (for instance, where the payer has a lifestyle which is inconsistent with the level of income which has been, or would be, used for the maintenance calculation). A variation application can be made at any time.

(iii) How is child support maintenance paid?

The payer can pay child maintenance directly to the other parent (known as 'Maintenance Direct') or use the CSA's collection service. The CSA will usually give the payer the choice of paying by direct debit or standing order, or by a voluntary deduction from earnings order (whereby the payer's employer takes payment from earnings and pays it to the CSA); and it will stipulate the intervals when payment is to be made (s 29).

(iv) How are child support maintenance payments enforced?

Enforcement has proved to be one of the major difficulties of the child support system. The following enforcement measures are currently available when a payer defaults with respect to a maintenance assessment made by the CSA:

▶ *A deduction from earnings order (section 31)* This order, which is made by the CSA and is usually the first step it takes, instructs the payer's employer to make deductions of maintenance from the payer's earnings or pension and send them to the CSA which then passes the payments onto the parent (or person) with care of the child. An employer who fails to comply with the order, without good reason, can be taken to court and fined.

▶ *A deduction order (see sections 32A–32F)* A 'regular' deduction order (s 32A) is an order made by the CSA which orders the deduction of regular payments of child maintenance from a deposit or other account held by the defaulter (for example, a bank or a building society account). A 'lump sum deduction order' (ss 32E and 32F) requires a deposit-taker of a deposit or savings account held by the defaulter to pay the CSA any outstanding arrears of child maintenance.

▶ *A liability order (section 33)* If it is not appropriate to make the above orders, or such an order is ineffective, the CSA can apply to the magistrates' court for a liability order. Once the order is made, the CSA can then take various steps to ensure payment, for example: by arranging for sale and seizure of the defaulter's goods by a bailiff; by obtaining a third-party debt order in the county court freezing the funds in the defaulter's bank or building society; or by charging and selling the defaulter's property to make payment. As the CSA can enter a liability order on the Register of Judgments, Orders and Fines, the order can affect the defaulter's credit rating. It has been held that the magistrates' court has no power to challenge the actual assessment (s 33(4); and see *Farley v Secretary of State for Work and Pensions* [2006] UKHL 31, [2006] 2 FLR 1243; and *Child Support Agency v Learad; Child Support Agency v Buddles* [2008] EWHC 2193 (Admin), [2009] 1 FLR 31). In *R (Joplin) v Child Maintenance and Enforcement Commission* [2010] EWHC 1623 (Admin), [2010] 2 FLR 1510 it was held that considerations of the welfare of any children (see pp. 320–1 above) should ideally be taken into account before an application is made for a liability order, and that any such consideration should be properly minuted and taken in a robust and transparent way.

▶ *An avoidance of disposition order (section 32L)* This order, which the CSA can apply for, is an order restraining or setting aside the disposal or transfer of assets made with the intention of avoiding payment of child support maintenance. The CSA must prove that a person: has failed to pay an amount of child support maintenance; and, with the intention of avoiding payment of child support maintenance, is about to make a disposition or to transfer out of the jurisdiction or otherwise deal with any property.

▶ *Other measures: removal of a driving licence and imprisonment* If the above enforcement measures fail, more severe measures can be imposed. Thus the CSA can apply to the magistrates' court for an order removing a defaulter's driving licence for up to two years (or preventing the defaulter from obtaining one) if there is wilful refusal or culpable neglect in respect of paying child maintenance (ss 39A and 40B). In the last resort, a defaulter may be committed to prison, on proof of wilful refusal or culpable neglect to make payment (s 40).

Human rights and enforcement measures

Any of the enforcement measures above must, however, be human rights compliant. In *Karoonian v CMEC; Gibbons v CMEC* [2012] EWCA Civ 1379 the Court of Appeal condemned the CMEC (CSA) for giving two fathers suspended jail sentences without giving them the right to defend themselves. Ward LJ said that the procedures adopted did not comply with the right to a fair trial under Article 6 of the European Convention for the Protection of Human Rights and were flawed. His Lordship condemned the lack of robustness and confusion in the current legal practices as 'obnoxious' and 'unreasonable' and said that the procedures adopted did not comply with the rights to a fair trial and were flawed.

A parent cannot institute court proceedings to enforce maintenance

Legal actions have been brought in the courts by parents to challenge the CSA's failure to enforce the payment of arrears of child support, but their claims have been dismissed for policy reasons and on the basis that the Child Support Act 1991 provides a complete code for child support maintenance, including its enforcement. The following cases provide examples:

> ▶ *R (On the Application of Kehoe) v Secretary of State for Work and Pensions* [2005] **UKHL 48, [2005] 2 FLR 1249**
>
> After various enforcement measures taken by the CSA had failed, the mother brought judicial review proceedings seeking a declaration of incompatibility under section 4(2) of the Human Rights Act 1998 on the basis that the enforcement provisions of the CSA 1991 were incompatible with her right to a fair trial under Article 6 ECHR, as they precluded a parent from bringing enforcement proceedings in the court in her own name or on behalf of her children. She also sought a declaration that the delay by the CSA constituted a breach of her Article 6 rights; and she claimed damages under section 7 HRA 1998. After her claim failed at first instance and on appeal to the Court of Appeal, she appealed to the House of Lords.
>
> The House of Lords by a majority dismissed her appeal, holding that the claimant had no substantive right in domestic law which was capable in Convention law of engaging the guarantees that were afforded with regard to 'civil rights and obligations' by Article 6(1). Enforcement was exclusively a matter for the CSA. As Article 6(1) was not engaged, the CSA could not be said to have acted unlawfully within the meaning of section 7 HRA 1998; and accordingly the claimant had no remedy under that Act.
>
> Baroness Hale, however, dissented, on the basis that the case involved the civil rights of children:
>
> > '[I]f I am right that the children's civil rights to be properly maintained by their parents are engaged, it follows that the public authority which is charged by Parliament with securing the determination and enforcement of their rights is under a duty to act compatibly with their Article 6 right to the speedy determination and effective enforcement of those rights. ... Just as the courts, as public authorities, have to act compliantly with the Convention rights, so does the Agency.'

The mother took her case to the ECtHR (see *Kehoe v UK (Application No 2010/06)* [2008] ECHR 528, [2008] 2 FLR 1014) but her claim was unanimously dismissed as there had been no breach of Article 6 ECHR (the right to a fair trial).

In the following case the High Court adopted a similar approach to that taken by the House of Lords in *Kehoe*.

> ▶ *Treharne v Secretary of State for Work and Pensions* [2008] EWHC 3222 (QB), [2009] 1 **FLR 8**
>
> The applicants were adults who had been denied child maintenance owed to them during their minority, because of failures on the part of the CSA to take steps to enforce payment. They argued that the CSA's maladministration had violated their right to family life under Article 8 ECHR, and they sought damages. Their claim failed. Cranston J, dismissing their appeal, held that the failure of the CSA to function effectively and to enforce the maintenance assessments could not found a claim for damages, as Article 8 ECHR did not include an economic right to reasonably regular maintenance from the State.

In the following case a claim in negligence was made against the CSA for failing to enforce arrears of child support maintenance, but, like the cases above, the claim failed:

> ▶ *R (Rowley) v Secretary of State for Work and Pensions* [2007] EWCA Civ 598, [2007] 2 FLR 945
>
> The mother and her three children sued the CSA in negligence for failure to enforce the child maintenance due. Their claim failed. The Court of Appeal held that there was no assumption of responsibility on the part of the Secretary of State; and to impose a duty of care in negligence would not be an incremental development of the law but a massive extension of it. The CSA 1991 provided a set of remedies; and to impose a duty of care in negligence would be inconsistent with the statutory scheme.

Rowley was essentially a policy decision to stop a flood of claims being brought by aggrieved parents and children.

Making a complaint   Any person who is dissatisfied with the service provided by the CSA can make a complaint to the CSA. If still not satisfied, a complainant can write to the Independent Case Examiner, who has a duty to investigate the complaint (but not if it involves a matter of law). A complaint can also be made to the Ombudsman.

Appeals An appeal can be made to the Child Support Appeal Tribunal (s 20). Appeals on matters of law can be taken to the Child Support Commissioner (s 24), from whom there is a further right of appeal on a question of law to the Court of Appeal (s 25).

(d)   The Child Support Act 1991 and the role of the courts

The court has jurisdiction under the Child Support Act 1991 to order child maintenance in the following situations (s 8): to 'top up' a maintenance assessment where a maximum assessment is in force; for school fees and fees for advanced education or training for a trade, profession or vocation; for a disabled child; for a child who is not a 'qualifying child' under the CSA 1991; when making, varying and enforcing a consent order which embodies child maintenance; when enforcing a parental agreement about child maintenance; where maintenance is required from the person who has care of the child; and where the CSA has no jurisdiction to make a maintenance calculation (for example, because the parent is not habitually resident in the UK).

The courts have jurisdiction to make lump sum and property orders for children (see 12.2 and 12.3 below), whether or not an application for child support is made to the CSA.

12.2   Finance and property orders for children from the court

(a)   Introduction

The family courts have jurisdiction to make finance and property orders for children under the following Acts of Parliament: the Domestic Proceedings and Magistrates' Courts Act 1978; the Matrimonial Causes Act 1973; the Civil Partnership Act 2004; and the Children Act 1989. Applications for child maintenance can only be heard in the courts if the CSA has no jurisdiction to deal with maintenance, but, as the child maintenance provisions now place a greater emphasis on parents making their own private arrangements, it is possible for parents to apply to the court for a consent order (see pp. 175–6) containing an agreement about child maintenance.

Applications can be made to the court for lump sum orders and property orders to or for the benefit of a child, but, because of the cost of bringing proceedings and the need for sufficient resources against which orders can be made, applications are usually only made where substantial assets are involved (see, for example, *Re C (Financial Provision)* [2007] 2 FLR 13 where capital provision of £2 million was ordered for a child).

(b)   Orders for children on divorce and on civil partnership dissolution

Under Part II of the Matrimonial Causes Act 1973 the divorce court has jurisdiction to make the following orders to or for the benefit of any child of the family: periodical payments orders (maintenance), provided the CSA 1991 does not preclude it; and lump sum orders (s 23). It also has the power to make the following property orders to or for the benefit of a child of the family (s 24): a transfer of property order; a settlement of property order; an order varying an ante-nuptial agreement; a post-nuptial settlement for the benefit of the child; and an order for the sale of property (s 24A). These orders can also be made on the annulment of a marriage or on judicial separation (for more on these orders, see Chapter 7).

These orders can be made for 'a child of the family', which includes the parties' own child, any step-child and a privately fostered child (but not a child in local authority care). A 'child of the family' means: a child under 18; or a child over 18 who is, will be, or would be (if an order were made) receiving instruction at an educational establishment or undergoing training for a trade, profession or vocation, or where special circumstances justify an order being made (s 29).

When exercising its discretion, the court must consider all the circumstances of the case, including in particular (s 25(3)): the child's financial needs, income, earning capacity (if any), property and other financial resources; any physical or mental disability of the child; and the manner in which the child is expected to be educated or trained. It must also take into account factors (a)–(d) of the statutory checklist in section 25(2) MCA 1973 (see p. 156).

Where the court is exercising its powers against a spouse in favour of a child of the family who is not that person's child (such as a step-child) the court must also consider (s 25(4)): whether that spouse assumed any responsibility for child maintenance, and, if so, the extent to which, and the basis upon which, he or she assumed such responsibility and the length of time for which that party discharged such responsibility; whether in assuming and discharging such responsibility that party did so knowing that the child was not his or her own; and the liability of any other person to maintain the child.

Similar provisions to those above apply in respect of the dissolution (annulment or separation) of a civil partnership (see s 72(1) and Sch 1 to the Civil Partnership Act 2004).

Consent orders Spouses and civil partners can apply for a consent order in respect of financial arrangements for their children (including child support maintenance), which the court has jurisdiction to make under the MCA 1973 and the CPA 2004. A consent order is a private agreement about financial provision and/or property arrangements for the parties and/or their children which is considered by the court and made into a court order (see further at pp. 175–6). The advantage of a consent order is that (unlike a private arrangement about financial provision for a child) it can be enforced by the court if breached.

(c) Orders for children during a marriage or civil partnership

Finance and property order can be sought from the magistrates' court or county court to or for the benefit of children during the subsistence of a marriage or civil partnership, but applications are virtually non-existent as married couples and civil partners are unlikely to take such steps during the subsistence of their relationship, and, in any event, child maintenance can be sought using the various options listed on p. 320 above. At one time, however, when divorce was uncommon, these powers were exercised more often.

(i) In the family proceedings court Under the Domestic Proceedings and Magistrates' Courts Act 1978, family proceedings courts can make periodical payments orders and lump sum orders for parties to a marriage and children of the family. Lump sums are limited to a maximum sum (s 2(3)). An applicant spouse must prove that the other spouse (the respondent) (s 1): (a) has failed to provide reasonable maintenance for the applicant; (b) has failed to provide, or to make a proper contribution towards, reasonable maintenance for any child of the family; (c) has behaved in such a way that the applicant cannot reasonably be expected to live with the respondent; or (d) has deserted the applicant.

The statutory criteria which the court must apply when exercising its discretion are similar to those which must be applied by the divorce court in proceedings for financial relief (see 7.4), but with the additional requirement that the magistrates must consider whether to exercise any of their powers under the Children Act 1989 (s 8).

Similar provisions apply to civil partnerships under section 72(3) and Schedule 6 to the Civil Partnership Act 2004.

(ii) In the county court Under section 27 of the Matrimonial Causes Act 1973 either spouse can apply to the county court for reasonable maintenance (periodical payments and lump sums) on the ground that the other spouse has: (a) failed to provide reasonable maintenance for the applicant; or (b) has failed to provide, or to make a proper contribution towards, reasonable maintenance for any child of the family (s 27(1)).

Similar provisions apply to civil partnerships (see s 72(1) and Sch 5 to the Civil Partnership Act 2004).

12.3 Finance and property orders for children under the Children Act 1989

Under section 15 and Schedule 1 to the Children Act 1989 the family courts have jurisdiction to make periodical payments orders, lump sum orders and property orders to or for the benefit of children aged under 18, and for some 'children' aged over 18. The court can only make these orders on an application, unless it is making, varying or discharging a residence order (para 1(6)), or the child is a ward of court (para 1(7)), when it can make any of these orders of its own motion.

Importance of Schedule 1 for cohabiting couples and their children

Schedule 1 is particularly important for cohabitants and their children, because, unlike married couples and civil partners, it is the only jurisdiction of the courts available to them if they wish to make applications about property and/or finance for the benefit of their children on family breakdown.

Who is a 'parent' against whom an application can be made for financial provision under Schedule 1?

The persons against whom an application can be made under Schedule 1 are confined to: biological parents; persons who have become parents by operation of law (such as by adoption or pursuant to the provisions of the Human Fertilisation and Embryology Acts 1990 and 2008); and persons otherwise included by paragraph 16 of Schedule 1 (namely a spouse or civil partner who had treated the child as a child of the family). An application under Schedule 1 cannot be made against a person merely by reason of that person being a social or psychological parent of the child. Thus, for example, in *T v B (Parental Responsibility: Financial Provision)* [2010] EWHC 1444 (Fam), [2010] 2 FLR 1966, Moylan J held that a former lesbian partner who was not the civil partner of a mother whose child was conceived by artificial insemination by an unknown donor was not a 'parent' for the purposes of Schedule 1 even though she was clearly a social and psychological parent of the child and she had acquired parental responsibility by virtue of having obtained a shared residence order.

(a) Orders under paragraph 1

On an application by a parent, guardian or special guardian of a child, or by any person in whose favour a residence order is in force with respect to a child, the court may make any of the following orders against either or both parents of a child (including a step-parent) (paras 1(1), (2)):

▶ a periodical payments order (maintenance);
▶ a lump sum order, provided that such an order may be made to enable expenses in connection with the birth or maintenance of the child, which were reasonably incurred before the making of the order, to be met (Sch 1, para 5(1));
▶ a settlement of property order;
▶ a transfer of property order.

These orders can be made in favour of the applicant for the benefit of the child, or in favour of the child – except for a settlement of property order, which can only be made for the benefit of the child. The county court and the High Court can make any of these orders, but the magistrates' family proceedings courts have no jurisdiction to make: transfer and settlement of property orders; secured periodical payments orders (see p. 153); and lump sum orders above a specified maximum amount (para 1(1)).

The powers conferred under paragraph 1 may be exercised at any time (para 1(3)). Periodical payment orders can be varied and discharged (see para (c) below). The court can make further periodical payments orders and lump sum orders with respect to a child who has not reached the age of 18, but it cannot make more than one settlement of property order and more than one transfer of property order (para 1(5)). This is so, even though paragraph 1(3) provides that the power to make such orders can be 'exercised at any time' (see *Phillips v Peace* [2004] EWHC 3180 (Fam), [2005] 2 FLR 1212).

(b) Orders under paragraph 2

The court may make periodical payments orders and lump sum orders for a child aged over 18 against one or both parents (but not against a step-parent or foster-parent –

para 16). These orders can be made on the application of a child aged over 18 who is, will be, or (if an order were made) would be receiving instruction at an educational establishment or undergoing training for a trade, profession or vocation (whether or not while in gainful employment). The court can also make an order where special circumstances exist. An application under paragraph 2 cannot be made by any person if, immediately before the child reached the age of 16, a periodical payments order was in force with respect to the child (para 2(3)). No order can be made under paragraph 2 if the applicant's parents are living with each other in the same household (para 2(4)).

(c) Variation and discharge of periodical payments

Periodical payments orders made under Schedule 1 can be varied or discharged on the application of any person by or to whom payments were required to be made (paras 1(4) and 2(5)). In exercising these powers, the court must have regard to all the circumstances of the case, including any change in any of the matters to which the court was to have regard when making the order (para 6(1)).

(d) Agreements about maintenance

Under paragraph 10(3) of Schedule 1 to the Children Act 1989 the court has jurisdiction to alter the terms of an agreement about maintenance where it appears just to do so having regard to all the circumstances in cases: where there has been a change of circumstances; or where the agreement does not contain proper financial arrangements with respect to the child. In *Morgan v Hill* [2006] EWCA Civ 1602, [2007] 1 FLR 1480 the Court of Appeal held that it was not necessary to demonstrate that such an agreement was massively inadequate in order to obtain a judicial award greater than the agreed settlement.

(e) The exercise of judicial discretion in Schedule 1 proceedings

Each case depends on its own facts, but, when deciding whether to exercise its powers to make orders under paragraphs 1 and 2, and, if so, in what manner, the court must have regard to all the circumstances, including the following (para 4(1)):

'(a) the income, earning capacity, property and other financial resources which the applicant, parents and the person in whose favour the order would be made has, or is likely to have, in the foreseeable future;
(b) the financial needs, obligations and responsibilities which the persons named in (a) have or are likely to have in the foreseeable future;
(c) the financial needs of the child;
(d) the income, earning capacity (if any), property and other financial resources of the child;
(e) any physical or mental disability of the child; and
(f) the manner in which the child is being, or is expected to be, educated or trained.'

Where the court is exercising its powers under paragraph 1 against a person who is not the child's mother or father (such as in the case of a step-child), the court must also consider (para 4(2)):

'(a) whether that person has assumed responsibility for the child's maintenance and, if so, the extent to which and the basis on which that responsibility was assumed and the length of the period during which he met that responsibility;
(b) whether he did so knowing that the child was not his child;
(c) the liability of any other person to maintain the child.'

(f) The approach of the courts

The court adopts the following approach in applications under Schedule 1 to the Children Act 1989:

(i) The child's welfare   Although paragraph 4(1) does not expressly refer to the child's welfare, and the paramountcy principle in section 1(1) CA 1989 does not apply (see s 105(1) CA 1989), the child's welfare is nonetheless taken into account as part of the court's duty to have regard to all the circumstances; and the child's welfare is 'a constant influence on the discretionary outcome' (*per* Thorpe LJ in *Re P (Child: Financial Provision)* [2003] EWCA Civ 837, [2003] 2 FLR 865, approving Hale J in *J v C (Child: Financial Provision)* [1999] 1 FLR 152).

(ii) The child's standard of living   Although paragraph 4 of Schedule 1 makes no mention of the child's standard of living as a factor to be taken into account, the court may take it into account in an appropriate case (see *Re P (Child: Financial Provision)* [2003] EWCA Civ 837, [2003] 2 FLR 865 where Thorpe LJ, approving Hale J in *J v C (Child: Financial Provision)* (above), said that the child was entitled to be brought up in circumstances which bore some sort of relationship to the father's current resources and present standard of living). (See also *F v G (Child: Financial Provision)* [2004] EWHC 1848 (Fam), [2005] 1 FLR 261.)

(iii) The child's entitlement under Schedule 1   The entitlement to financial provision under Schedule 1 arises only during the child's dependency (or until the child has finished full-time education), unless the child's circumstances are special (for example if the child has a disability). For this reason, the court will usually make orders to last during the child's dependency or until the child has finished full-time education (see, for example, *Re P (Child: Financial Provision)* (above); and *Re S (Unmarried Parents: Financial Provision)* [2006] EWCA Civ 479, [2006] 2 FLR 950). This also applies to the provision of a home for the child (see below).

(iv) A home for the child   In respect of the home, the court will usually make a settlement of property order (a '*Mesher* type' property adjustment order – see p. 173) settling the home on the primary carer for the benefit of the child, so that ownership reverts back to the owner at the end of the child's dependency or full-time education. For example, in *J v C (Child: Financial Provision)* [1999] 1 FLR 152, where the father had won £1.4 million on the National Lottery, Hale J made an order requiring the father to purchase a house for the child to live in with her mother which would be held on trust for the child's benefit throughout her dependency and revert back to her father when she reached the age of 21 or finished full-time education, whichever was later.

Even if the parent who owns the home is very wealthy, the court may not necessarily order an outright transfer of the home to the other parent for the benefit of the child (see, for example, *MT v OT(Financial Provision: Costs)* [2007] EWHC 838 (Fam), [2008] 2 FLR 1311 where the father was worth £40 million). Each case depends on its own set of facts. Thus, for example, in *Re N (Payments for Benefit of Child)* [2009] EWHC 11 (Fam), [2009] 1 FLR 1442 Munby J held *inter alia* that the district judge had erred in principle in ordering that the home be settled until the child reached 21 or completed tertiary education. Munby J said that the long-established general principle is that, absent special or exceptional circumstances such as disability, children are not entitled to provision under Schedule 1 except during their dependency or for their education. Special or exceptional circumstances apart, dependency ceased at majority.

(v) Financial provision for the benefit of the child   The courts will guard against claims disguised as being for the benefit of a child when they are really for the benefit of the parent who is caring for the child (*per* Thorpe LJ in *Re P (Child: Financial Provision)*, above, approving Hale J in *J v C (Child: Financial Provision)*, above).

(vi) A broad-brush approach   In *Re P (Child: Financial Provision)* (above) the Court of Appeal held that a broad-brush assessment should be adopted in claims under Schedule 1, but that the starting point is to decide on the home that the respondent should provide for the child. It also held that a broad common-sense assessment of the amount of periodical payments should be taken, but that, in making that assessment, the judge should recognise the responsibility, and often the sacrifice, of the parent who was the primary, or perhaps the exclusive, carer of the child.

(vii) 'Benefit' can include the provision of legal costs   As the phrase 'benefit for the child' has been given a wide meaning by the courts, an order can include a sum to cover legal costs even though this may also benefit a parent. For example, in *Re S (Child: Financial Provision)* [2004] EWCA Civ 1685, [2005] 2 FLR 94, the Court of Appeal held that it could include the cost of the mother travelling to the Sudan to see her child and to pursue legal proceedings there, even though this might be for the benefit of the mother as well as the child. (See also *MT v T* [2006] EWHC 2494 (Fam), [2007] 2 FLR 925; and *R v F (Schedule 1: Child Maintenance: Mother's Costs of Legal Proceedings)* [2011] 2 FLR 991 where in both cases lump sums towards legal costs involving the child were ordered.)

(viii) The court has jurisdiction under Schedule 1 after a clean-break order has been made on divorce   The court so held in *MB v KB* [2007] EWHC 789 (Fam), [2007] 2 FLR 586 in respect of an application for a lump sum order, but it held that the circumstances had to be exceptional.

(ix) There is no jurisdiction to make provision for a car for a child's benefit   In *PK v BC (Financial Remedies: Schedule 1)* [2012] EWHC 1382 (Fam) the mother's application under Schedule 1 for a lump sum for a car and for housing provision for the child's benefit was dismissed, as there was no jurisdiction to make provision for a car, or, if there was jurisdiction, the court should certainly decline to exercise it

12.4   The voice of the child in financial proceedings

In *Morgan v Hill* [2006] EWCA Civ 1602, [2007] 1 FLR 1480 Thorpe LJ said that in exceptional cases brought under Schedule 1 to the Children Act 1989 (see above) the court should consider separate representation of the child. In *Re S (Unmarried Parents: Financial Provisions)* [2006] EWCA Civ 479, [2006] 2 FLR 950 Thorpe LJ said that the facts in *Re S* provided, in his opinion, 'a neat illustration of the advantages of ensuring separate representation for the child' in some cases brought under Schedule 1. Here the child's father and mother were engaged in an intense and bitter battle and Thorpe LJ said that it was easy to see how in such circumstances 'the crux of the case can be lost to view unless there is some advocate there to urge constantly the needs and interests of the child' for whom the award is largely designed.

In practice, however, children are rarely listened to or represented in financial proceedings, even though they may be significantly affected by the decision (for example, when the court is considering whether or not the family home should be transferred to a parent for the benefit of the child).

Summary

▶ All parents have a duty to maintain their children, and all children have a right to be maintained.

▶ In April 1993, child maintenance disputes were removed, for the most part, from the courts and into a Government agency, the Child Support Agency (CSA) with maintenance being assessed according to a mathematical formula. Over the years, the CSA has been riddled with problems (including, for instance, delays, errors in calculation and problems with enforcement), and many amendments to the law have been made. The Government is currently looking at reforming the law to place an even greater emphasis on parents making their own agreements about maintenance; and it is in the process of moving statutory child support responsibilities from the CSA into a new Child Maintenance Service.

▶ Parents have three options available with respect to arrangements for child maintenance. They can: make a private 'family-based' agreement; apply to the CSA; or apply to the court for a consent order. In certain limited circumstances, parents can apply to the court for 'top-up' maintenance. They can apply to the family courts for lump sum and property orders.

▶ If a parent fails to provide maintenance, and the parents cannot agree on the matter, then an application can be made to the CSA, which has the power under the Child Support Act 1991 to calculate, collect and enforce child support maintenance. The calculation is based on percentages of the non-resident parent's net weekly income and the number of qualifying and relevant other children. Deductions are made for shared care. Variations are permitted in certain limited and exceptional circumstances. The CSA is responsible for enforcing payments and can make deduction from earnings orders and deduction orders. It can apply to the court for liability orders and avoidance of disposition orders. Other measures against failure to pay child maintenance include the removal of a driving licence, and, in the last resort, imprisonment. Parents cannot apply to enforce child support maintenance in the courts as that is a matter for the CSA under the Child Support Act 1991.

▶ Maintenance for children can be sought from the courts in certain cases (for example, in school fees cases, where a child is disabled, where the parents are wealthy, or where the CSA does not have jurisdiction). Parents can apply to the court for a consent order incorporating their agreement about child maintenance.

▶ Periodical payments, lump sum, and property adjustment orders can be sought for children on divorce (and on nullity and judicial separation) under Part II of the Matrimonial Causes Act 1973. The same orders can be sought under section 72(1) and Schedule 5 to the Civil Partnership Act 2004 on the dissolution (annulment or separation) of a civil partnership.

▶ During marriage, a parent may seek periodical payments (maintenance) and/or a lump sum for a child from the magistrates' family proceedings courts under the Domestic Proceedings and Magistrates' Courts Act 1978. Civil partners can do the same under section 72(3) and Schedule 6 to the Civil Partnership Act 2004. Periodical payments, lump sums and property adjustment orders for the benefit of children can also be sought during marriage from the county court and the High Court under section 27 MCA 1973 (and during a civil partnership under section 72(1) and Schedule 5 to the CPA 2004). In practice these powers are rarely exercised.

Summary cont'd

▶ Orders for financial relief (periodical payments, lump sums, settlements and transfers of property) can be sought under section 15 and paragraph 1 of Schedule 1 to the Children Act 1989 by parents, guardians, special guardians and persons with a residence order in their favour. 'Children' aged over 18 can apply under paragraph 2.

▶ In an exceptional case, a child may be separately represented in a financial provision case, but such a practice is extremely rare.

Further reading and references

Department for Work and Pensions, *Public consultation. Supporting separated families; securing children's futures*, Cm 8399, July 2012.

Websites

Child Maintenance Options: www.cmoptions.org
Department for Work and Pensions: www.dwp.gov.uk
Directgov: www.direct.gov.uk

Links to relevant websites can also be found at: www.palgrave.com/law/familylaw8e

13.1 Introduction

Child abduction is a distressing consequence of family breakdown. Due to the increasing numbers of 'international families' and increasing family breakdown, child abduction is also an increasing phenomenon, and a global one. According to a survey by Lowe and Stephens [2011] Fam Law 1216, there has been a significant increase globally in applications made to the central authorities which deal with child abduction under the Hague Convention on Abduction. Thus, in 2008 the number of applications was 45 per cent higher than in 2003. They also found that most abductors were mothers (69 per cent in 2008 compared with 68 per cent in 2003). Figures available from the Foreign and Commonwealth Office show a significant increase in the number of British children abducted by a parent and taken overseas (213 reported cases in 2010). It is particularly concerning that there has been an increase in abductions to countries which are not parties to the Hague Convention on Abduction as it is much more difficult to get children back from such countries. In 2010, the Foreign and Commonwealth Office handled 97 non-Hague Convention cases.

The courts in England and Wales deal not only with international child abduction cases but they also hear 'relocation' applications by parents wishing to take a child lawfully out of the UK or to another part of the UK (see 11.8 and 11.9). The courts can also make: orders preventing parents and other persons from taking a child out of the UK; orders declaring that the removal of a child from the UK is wrongful; and orders asking for information about an abducted child to be disclosed to the court.

Advice about child abduction can be obtained from the following bodies: the International Child Abduction and Contact Unit (ICACU) (the central authority in England and Wales for Convention and Brussels II Revised purposes); the Foreign and Commonwealth Office (which deals with non-Convention cases); and the Reunite International Child Abduction Centre (a UK charity specialising in international child abduction). (Website addresses for these bodies can be found at the end of this chapter.)

13.2 Preventing abduction

Where there is a risk of abduction, preventative measures should be taken as it may be difficult to find and return a child to the UK once the child has been abducted. In addition to being vigilant, the following preventative measures can be taken.

(a) Police assistance

As child abduction is a criminal offence (see 13.3 below), a parent (or any other person) who believes that a child has been (or is about to be) abducted can seek police assistance. The police have various powers. Thus, they can arrest any person who is abducting or is suspected of abducting a child. They can also institute a 'port alert' whereby details of the child and the abductor are sent by the police national computer to UK ports and airports to prevent the child leaving the country. An application for a port alert must be *bona fide* and there must be a real and imminent danger of abduction.

(b)   A court order

Where there is a risk of abduction a court order can be useful. Not only is breach of a court order contempt of court (see, for example, *Re A (Abduction: Contempt)* [2008] EWCA Civ 1138, [2009] 1 FLR 1), but a court order may be useful if a parent wishes to institute court proceedings abroad or seek the assistance of various agencies abroad. Although a court order is not needed to institute a port alert (see above), it provides useful evidence of a genuine risk of abduction. An order is also useful for passport purposes (see p. 336 below).

(i) Section 8 orders under the Children Act 1989   A useful range of orders is available under section 8 of the Children Act 1989 (see 10.4). For example, a prohibited steps order could be sought so as to prohibit a child being removed from the UK; or a specific issue order could be sought to decide whether a parent and child should be permitted to leave the UK. A residence order under the Children Act 1989 can be useful, as a child who is subject to a residence order cannot be lawfully removed from the UK without the *written* consent of every person with parental responsibility (s 13(1)(b)) – except for a period of up to one month by a person who has the residence order (s 13(2)). Similar restrictions exist in respect of taking a child in care out of the UK (see s 33(7) CA 1989).

Although a section 8 order can be made if a child has already been abducted, the court may be reluctant to make one if there is likely to be a problem enforcing the order abroad (*Re D (Child: Removal from Jurisdiction)* [1992] 1 WLR 315). Where urgent action is needed the court can make a section 8 order *ex parte* (without the respondent being given notice of the proceedings) (see, for example, *Re J (Abduction: Wrongful Removal)* [2000] 1 FLR 78). In an exceptional case, where there is a risk of abduction, the court can impose a direction on a residence order (under section 11(7) CA 1989).

(ii) Wardship   An alternative to a section 8 order (above) is to have the child made a ward of court (see 8.7). There are two main advantages of wardship over a section 8 order. One is that wardship takes effect immediately on the application being made, so that any attempt to abduct the child may be contempt of court. The other advantage is that, as the High Court exercises a supervisory role over the ward, no major step in the child's life (such as removing the child out of the UK) can be taken without the court's consent. However, wardship is used only in exceptional cases, for instance where other legal remedies are not available or where the situation is particularly urgent. Thus, for example, in *Re S (Wardship)* [2010] EWCA Civ 465, [2010] 2 FLR 1960 the child was warded on the application of a local authority which was concerned that the child was at risk of significant harm. She had been taken by her mother to live with the father and his family in Spain, and, as both parents had been complicit in the child's removal to Spain, the case did not come within the Hague Convention on Abduction.

(iii) Other powers of the court   The court has power under the inherent jurisdiction and under statute to order a person to disclose a child's whereabouts (see s 33 Family Law Act 1986; s 24A Child Abduction and Custody Act 1985; and *Re H (Abduction: Whereabouts Order to Solicitors)* [2000] 1 FLR 766). The county court can authorise an

officer of the court, or a police constable, to take charge of a child and deliver the child to a named person. The High Court can make a 'seek and find' order requiring the Tipstaff (the High Court's enforcement officer) to find the child and deliver the child as directed by the court; or a 'seek and locate' order requiring the Tipstaff to locate the child's whereabouts. It can also make an order permitting media publicity about the child; or requiring any person to disclose information about the child to the court; or requesting the disclosure of an address from a Government department or agency.

Under the Family Law Act 1986, the court can order: the surrender of a passport (s 37); the recovery of a child (s 34); and can restrict the removal of a child from the UK (s 35). The High Court can also make a declaration under section 8 of the Child Abduction and Custody Act 1985, on an application made for the purposes of Article 14 of the Hague Convention, that the removal of any child from, or his retention outside, the UK was wrongful under Article 3 of the Hague Convention.

(iv) Enforcing a court order in another part of the UK   Under the Family Law Act 1986 a court order relating to a child made in England and Wales can be recognised and enforced in another part of the UK without the merits of the case being considered afresh. Once registered, the court in the other part of the UK has the same powers of enforcement as if it had made the order. However, a parent and any other interested party can object to enforcement on the ground that the original order was made without jurisdiction; or that, because of a change of circumstances, the original order should be varied. Although the court in the other part of the UK can stay proceedings or dismiss the application (ss 30 and 31), it is likely to enforce the order.

(c)   Passport control

Children are now required to have their own passport. At one time, they could be named on a parent's passport. To prevent abduction, a parent (or other person with parental responsibility) can contact the UK Identity and Passport Service and object to the child being issued with a passport. It will require a court order as proof of a risk of abduction before it will respond to such a request.

Where there is a risk of abduction, a restriction can be placed on the child's or the likely abductor's passport. The court can order a UK passport to be surrendered where an order restricting removal is in force (s 37 Family Law Act 1986; and see *Re A (Return of Passport)* [1997] 2 FLR 137). It can also order the surrender of a non-UK passport, under its inherent jurisdiction (see 8.7, and *Re A-K (Foreign Passport: Jurisdiction)* [1997] 2 FLR 569). A section 8 order under the Children Act 1989 (see 10.4) can be made conditional on a suspected abductor depositing his passport with a solicitor or with the court.

(d)   Curfews and electronic tagging

In a highly exceptional case the court may make a curfew order supported by electronic tagging. Thus, for example, in *Re A (Family Proceedings: Electronic Tagging)* [2009] EWHC 710 (Fam), [2009] 2 FLR 891 the parents agreed that, when the child was with the mother, the mother should on an interim basis be subject to a curfew supported by electronic tagging. Here the mother had twice abducted the child to her country of origin and the child had been returned pursuant to proceedings under the Hague Convention. Parker J made an interim order giving effect to the parties' agreement and laid down guidelines in respect of electronic tagging.

(e)   Unmarried fathers and child abduction

Unmarried fathers may find themselves in a vulnerable position if they have no parental responsibility (see 9.4) and their child has been, or is at risk of being, abducted. In such cases, it is important for the unmarried father to take immediate and urgent legal steps to protect himself and/or the child, for otherwise he may find himself deprived of any effective right of recourse to the Hague Convention on Abduction. Thus, he should consider obtaining a parental responsibility order (see 9.4), which can be obtained *ex parte* in an emergency; and he should also consider obtaining a declaration under section 8 of the Child Abduction and Custody Act 1985 that he has 'rights of custody' for the purposes of the Hague Convention (which is what the unmarried father did in *A v B (Abduction: Rights of Custody: Declaration of Wrongful Removal)* [2008] EWHC 2524 (Fam), [2009] 1 FLR 1253 when he discovered that the child's mother, a French national, was about to take their child to France). Another option for unmarried fathers is to apply for a section 8 order under the Children Act 1989 (see 10.4).

The courts have taken a broad view of what constitutes 'custody rights' in the case of an unmarried father for the purpose of making a declaration under section 8 CACA 1985 (see *Re W; Re B (Child Abduction: Unmarried Father)* [1999] Fam 1, [1998] 2 FLR 146); and *Practice Note (Hague Convention – Application by Fathers without Parental Responsibility) 14 October 1997* [1998] 1 FLR 491). If, for instance, a father has been caring for the child, even though he has no parental responsibility in law, this may be sufficient for him to have 'custody rights' for the purpose of the Hague Convention on Abduction. Each case, however, depends on its facts. In *Re C (A Child) (Custody Rights: Unmarried Fathers)* [2002] EWHC 2219 (Fam), [2003] 1 FLR 252, where the unmarried father was concerned that the mother might take the child to Ireland, Munby J refused to make a declaration under section 8 CACA 1985 as there was nothing in the case-law to suggest that an unmarried father without parental responsibility could acquire rights of custody within the meaning of the Hague Convention in circumstances where a mother had remained the primary carer.

Thus, despite a purposive interpretation of 'rights of custody', the court will not necessarily hold that an unmarried father has rights of custody for Hague Convention purposes, even if he has shared care of the child for a considerable length of time (see *Re J (Abduction: Acquiring Custody Rights by Caring for Child)* [2005] 2 FLR 791).

The European Court of Human Rights (ECtHR) held in *B v UK* [2000] 1 FLR 1 that it is not discriminatory (under Article 14 ECHR) in conjunction with the right to family life (under Article 8 ECHR) for the court to hold that an unmarried father without parental responsibility does not come within the scope of the Hague Convention on the ground that he has no right of custody. In *B v UK* an unmarried father without parental responsibility, whose child had been removed from the UK without his consent, argued that the UK Government was in breach of Articles 14 and 8 because he was treated differently from other fathers. His application failed. The ECtHR held that there was an objective and reasonable justification for the different treatment of the father in this case.

13.3   Abduction – the criminal law

A person who abducts, or attempts to abduct, a child from the UK may commit a criminal offence under the Child Abduction Act 1984 or under the common law.

(a) The Child Abduction Act 1984

Persons 'connected with a child' (s 1) and 'other persons' (s 2) can commit a criminal offence under this Act.

(i) Persons 'connected with a child' Under section 1 it is an offence for a person 'connected with a child' under 16 to take or send the child out of the UK without the 'appropriate consent'. A person 'connected with a child' is (s 1): a parent (including an unmarried father if there are reasonable grounds for believing he is the father); a guardian; a special guardian; any person with a residence order in their favour; and any person with custody of the child. 'Appropriate consent' means the consent of: the mother; the father (with parental responsibility); a guardian; a special guardian; any person with a residence order in force in their favour; and any person with custody of the child (s 1(2)(a)).

'Appropriate consent' can include the court's consent where it is required under Part II of the Children Act 1989 (ss 1(2)(b), (c)) (for example, where a residence order is in force – see s 13 CA 1989). However, a person with a residence order in force with respect to the child does not commit a criminal offence if he or she takes the child out of the UK for less than one month, unless this is in breach of another court order (s 1(4)).

It is a defence under the Act if the accused believed that the other person consented to the abduction, or would have consented had he or she been aware of all the circumstances; or the accused was unable to communicate with the other person despite taking reasonable steps to do so (s 1(5)). It is also a defence if the other person unreasonably refused consent to the child being taken out of the UK (but this defence does not apply if the person refusing consent has a residence order in his or her favour; or the person taking or sending the child out of the UK did so in breach of a court order) (s 1(5A)).

(ii) 'Other persons' Under section 2 a person who is not 'connected with a child' under section 1 (above) commits the offence of child abduction if, without lawful authority or reasonable excuse, he or she takes or detains a child under the age of 16 so as to remove the child from the lawful control of any person having lawful control of the child; or so as to keep the child out of the lawful control of any person entitled to lawful control (s 2(1)). An unmarried father without parental responsibility comes under section 2, unless he is the child's guardian, or has a residence order in his favour, or has custody of the child. An unmarried father, however, has a defence if he can prove that he is the child's father, or that at the time of the alleged offence he reasonably believed he was the child's father (s 2(3)(a)). It is also a defence if the accused believed that at the time of the alleged offence the child had reached the age of 16 (s 2(3)(b)). The mental state for an offence under section 2 is an intentional or reckless taking or detention of a child (see *Foster and Another v Director of Public Prosecutions* [2004] EWHC 2955 (Admin)).

The courts have taken a strong line in punishing those convicted of child abduction and have been willing to impose long prison sentences even where the defendant abductor has been the primary carer of the child for many years (as a result of the abduction. (See *R v Kayani; R v Solliman* [2011] EWCA Crim 2871 where the Court of Appeal also drew attention to the illogical disparity between prison sentences for offences under the 1984 Act (where the maximum is seven years) and those for kidnapping (where a life sentence is possible); and invited the Law Commission to address the question of whether cases where children were removed from one parent by the other should be treated as kidnapping offences.)

(b) The offence of kidnapping

A person who abducts a child unlawfully may commit the common law offence of kidnapping (see, for example, *R v D* [1984] AC 778). Where the child is under 16 and the person removing the child is a person 'connected with' the child under section 1 of the Child Abduction Act 1984 (above), the consent of the Director of Public Prosecutions is needed to bring a prosecution (s 5 CAA 1984). The offence is rarely used, but may be relevant where an abduction involves a child aged over 16 – as such a child does not come within the scope of the 1984 Act above (but see *R v Kayani; R v Solliman* above).

13.4 The Hague Convention on Abduction

(a) Introduction

The UK is a Contracting State to the Hague Convention on the Civil Aspects of International Child Abduction 1980 (the 'Hague Convention'), which has been implemented into UK law by Part I of the Child Abduction and Custody Act 1985. The text of the Convention and a list of Contracting States are available on Reunite's website (www.reunite.org).

Article 1 of the Hague Convention on the Civil Aspects of International Child Abduction 1980

'The objects of the present Convention are –

(a) to secure the prompt return of children wrongfully removed to or retained in any Contracting State; and
(b) to ensure that rights of custody and of access under the law of one Contracting State are effectively respected in the other Contracting States.'

(i) The policy of the Convention The Hague Convention is based on the policy that children should be swiftly returned to their country of habitual residence. It is also based on the principle of 'comity', a principle of international law which requires courts to respect the laws of foreign jurisdictions. Thus, the presumption lies in favour of returning a child; and it is generally assumed that, if a country is a party to the Convention, then the child's case will be dealt with in a welfare-oriented way. Another policy objective of the Convention is to deter abductions. As Baroness Hale has said, the 'message should go out to potential abductors that there are no safe havens among the Contracting States' (see *Re M (Abduction: Zimbabwe)* [2007] UKHL 55, [2008] 1 FLR 251).

The objects of the Convention were described by Baroness Hale and Lord Wilson in the following extract:

▶ *Baroness Hale and Lord Wilson in Re E (Children) (Abduction: Custody Appeal)* [2011] UKSC 27 [2011] 2 FLR 758:

'The first object of the Hague Convention is to deter either parent (or indeed anyone else) from taking the law into their own hands and pre-empting the result of any dispute between them about the future upbringing of their children. If an abduction does take place, the next object is to restore the children as soon as possible to their home country, so that any dispute can be determined there. ... Factual disputes of this nature are likely to be better able to be resolved in the country where the family had its home.'

(ii) How the Convention works   The scheme of the Convention is to provide a speedy extradition-type remedy whereby Contracting States agree to return abducted children to their country of habitual residence so that the parental custody (or residence) dispute can be dealt with there. In this sense it is a provisional remedy, for Convention proceedings are not concerned with the merits of a custody issue (Article 19). That is a matter for the court in the child's country of habitual residence. In *C v B (Abduction: Grave Risk)* [2005] EWHC 2988 (Fam), [2006] 1 FLR 1095 Sir Mark Potter P said that it was essential that the court hearing a return application did not usurp the function of the 'home' court by considering broader welfare considerations instead of confining itself to those matters which went to the establishment of the defence being relied upon under Article 13 of the Convention. The central question in Hague Convention proceedings is therefore whether the child should be returned to the *court* of his or her habitual residence, so that the custody issue can be considered there, and not whether the child should be returned to a particular *person*.

As the Convention is concerned with breaches of custody *rights*, not custody orders, it is not necessary to have a court order to invoke it. Applications under the Convention are heard by the Family Division of the High Court which can also make declarations that a removal or retention of a child outside the UK is wrongful under Article 3.

(iii) Central Authorities   The Convention works by establishing a network of Central Authorities which are required to co-operate with each other, and promote cooperation among the competent authorities in their respective States, in order to secure the prompt return of children and to achieve the other objects of the Convention (Art 7). Central Authorities have various duties under the Convention which include: discovering the child's whereabouts; preventing further harm to the child by taking provisional measures; securing the child's voluntary return; exchanging information; and providing information. The Central Authority for England and Wales is the International Child Abduction and Contact Unit (ICACU) based in the Office of the Official Solicitor at the Ministry of Justice. It is responsible for making administrative arrangements under the Convention in order to secure the return of abducted children and to enforce rights of access. It also provides advice and assistance.

(iv) Speed is of the essence   In abduction cases any delay is contrary to the child's best interests – because the longer the situation remains undecided the more difficult it will be to disturb the status quo. Because of the importance of speed, Convention proceedings are summary. The court will not, for example, investigate the parent's marital situation or examine the child's welfare. Cases are usually heard and decided upon on the basis of written evidence (such as a Cafcass report) rather than oral evidence. In EU abduction cases (see pp. 442–4), Article 11(3) of Brussels II Revised provides that a return application under the Hague Convention must be completed within 6 weeks unless exceptional circumstances make this impossible.

(v) The welfare of the child   The welfare of the child is not paramount in Hague Convention cases because 'it is presumed under the Convention that the welfare of children who have been abducted is best met by return to their habitual residence' (*per* Butler-Sloss LJ in *Re M (A Minor) (Child Abduction)* [1994] 1 FLR 390). Nevertheless, as Baroness Hale emphasised in *Re M (Abduction: Zimbabwe)* [2007] UKHL 55, [2008] 1 FLR 251, the Convention is child-centred, as it is principally directed towards the protection of children, not adults. As Baroness Hale pointed out, the Preamble to the Convention states that the Contracting

States are 'firmly convinced that the interests of *children* are of paramount importance in matters relating to the custody of children'. (On the issue of the child's welfare, see also *Neulinger and Shuruk v Switzerland* (ECtHR) and *Re E* (Supreme Court) below.)

(vi) Human rights and the Hague Convention The European Court of Human Rights (the ECtHR) has held that a failure by a national authority (under domestic or international law) to secure the return of an abducted child may amount to a breach of the right to family life under Article 8 ECHR (see 1.7); and that national authorities must take positive measures to enable parents to be reunited with the child, unless contrary to the child's best interests. Breaches of Article 8 were found, for example, in *Gil and Aui v Spain (Application No. 56673/00)* [2005] 1 FLR 190; and in *Maire v Portugal (Application No. 48206/99)* [2004] 2 FLR 653.

In *Neulinger and Shuruk v Switzerland (App No 41615/07)* [2011] 1 FLR 122 the ECtHR held (by 16 votes to 1) that there had been a breach of the mother's and the child's right to family life under Article 8 ECHR because a return order had been made even though the mother had raised the Article 13(b) defence under the Hague Convention that the child would suffer a grave risk of harm if the child was ordered to be returned to Israel. The decision caused considerable concern among lawyers and judges in the UK as it seemed contrary to the approach adopted in the UK courts. In other words, the approach adopted by the ECtHR in *Neulinger*, which required national courts to base their decisions on the best interests of the child and to conduct an in-depth examination of the facts, seemed diametrically opposed to the approach adopted by the UK courts where the priority is to effect the speedy return of a child to his or country of habitual residence so that the matter can be dealt with there.

The concerns raised by the decision of the ECtHR in *Neulinger* were addressed by the UK Supreme Court in the following case:

▶ *Re E (Children) (Abduction: Custody Appeal)* [2011] UKSC 27 [2011] 2 FLR 758

After the mother wrongfully removed the two children (aged 6 and 4) from Norway to England, the father applied to the High Court in England and Wales for the summary return of the children to Norway under the Hague Convention. The mother and the children's half-sister opposed the father's application, relying on the Article 13(b) grave risk of harm defence (based on the father's alleged long-term abusive behaviour towards the mother and his generally angry approach to the children).

Pauffley J in the High Court concluded that it was overwhelmingly in the children's best interests to return to Norway for their futures to be decided there. The mother's and half-sister's appeal to the Court of Appeal was dismissed, but it granted them permission to appeal to the Supreme Court where they argued *inter alia* that the current approach to the Article 13(b) defence, at least in the courts of England and Wales, did not properly respect the requirement that the best interests of the child should be a primary consideration; and they claimed that their appeal was supported by the decision of the ECtHR in *Neulinger* (see above).

The Supreme Court dismissed the appeal. Baroness Hale and Lord Wilson, giving judgment for the Supreme Court, held, *inter alia* that, although the best interests of the child had not expressly been made a primary consideration in Hague proceedings, there was a general underlying assumption that the best interests of the child would be best served by a prompt return to the child's country of habitual residence (although this assumption was rebuttable in certain circumstances).

(For the Supreme Court's discussion of the Article 13(b) defence (grave risk of harm), see pp. 355–6.)

Thus, the Supreme Court concluded that the decision in *Neulinger* did not require the UK courts to adopt a change of approach in Hague Convention cases. It concluded that both the Hague Convention and Brussels II Revised (see below) had been devised with the best interests of children generally, and of the individual children involved in such proceedings, as a primary consideration. It held that, if the court faithfully applied the provisions of the Hague Convention and Brussels II Revised, then it would also be complying with Article 3(1) of the UN Convention on the Rights of the Child. Also, the decision in *Neulinger* did not require a departure from the normal summary process, provided that the decision made was not arbitrary or mechanical.

Although in *X v Latvia (Application No 27853/09)* [2012] 1 FLR 860 the ECtHR once again stated that the determination of Hague Convention cases required an in-depth examination of the facts, in *Re S (A Child) (Abduction: Rights of Custody* [2012] UKSC 10 [2012] 2 FLR 442 (see pp. 356–7 below), Lord Wilson nonetheless reiterated the point that had been made in *Re E* (above) with respect to *Neulinger* that neither the Hague Convention nor Article 8 of the ECHR required the court to conduct an in-depth examination.

(vii) Access (contact) rights Although Article 21 of the Convention provides that access rights may be secured, it confers no power on the courts to determine access matters, or to recognise or enforce foreign access orders. It merely provides for executive cooperation between Central Authorities for the recognition and enforcement of such access rights as national laws allow. The International Child Abduction and Contact Unit (ICACU) will provide assistance with finding a solicitor, legal aid and instituting section 8 proceedings under the Children Act 1989. If a foreign access order is in force, an application can be made to have it recognised and enforced in the courts in England and Wales under the European Convention on the Recognition and Enforcement of Decisions Concerning Custody of Children 1980 (see *Re A (Foreign Access Order: Enforcement)* [1996] 1 FLR 561); or under Brussels II Revised if EU Member States are involved (see *Re S (Brussels II Revised: Enforcement of Contact Order)* [2008] 2 FLR 1358 where Wood J recognised a Polish contact order but refused to enforce it).

(viii) Breach of a return order Breach of a return order made under the Hague Convention can be contempt of court provided there has been deliberate disobedience of the court order applying the criminal standard of proof. But each case depends on its facts (see, for instance, *Re A (Abduction: Contempt)* [2008] EWCA Civ 1138, [2009] 1 FLR 1).

(b) The Hague Convention and abductions within the EU: Brussels II Revised

Where a child has been abducted within the European Union, it is also necessary to take into account the provisions of Council Regulation (EC) (No. 2201/2003) Concerning Jurisdiction and the Recognition and Enforcement of Judgments in Matrimonial Matters and in Matters of Parental Responsibility (Brussels II Revised), which takes precedence over the Hague Convention with respect to Member States of the EU. Article 11 of the Regulation aims to harmonise the application of the Hague Convention in EU Member States by setting out details of procedure that are binding on the courts. As Schulz (2008) explains, while the Hague Convention contains provisions aimed at 'a quick clarification of the *factual* situation (return of the child)', Brussels II Revised contains provisions aimed at 'a quick clarification of the *legal* situation'; in other words, it enables a final decision about custody to be taken in the court of the State of the child's habitual residence even if the child is not being returned under the Hague Convention (see further below). The central authority in England and Wales for the purposes of Brussels II Revised is the International Child Abduction and Contact Unit (ICACU).

The following provisions in Brussels II Revised apply in Hague Convention cases involving EU Member States:

▶ The court is required in every case to hear the views of the child unless this appears inappropriate having regard to the age or degree of maturity of the child (Art 11(2)).

▶ Proceedings for the return of a child under the Hague Convention must be completed within 6 weeks unless 'exceptional circumstances make this impossible' (Art 11(3)).

▶ The court may not make a non-return order (if a defence of grave risk to the child has been made out under Article 13(b) of the Hague Convention–see pp. 355–7) if it is established that adequate arrangements have been made to ensure the protection of the child after his or her return (Art 11(4)).

▶ The court cannot refuse to return a child unless the person who requested the return of the child has been given an opportunity to be heard (Art 11(5)).

▶ Brussels II Revised allows a custody decision made in the child's home Member State to 'trump' a non-return order made in the Member State to which the child has been abducted (see below).

Brussels II Revised and non-return orders under the Hague Conventions Brussels II Revised provides protection for a parent whose child has been abducted, as Articles 11(6)–(8) allow the court in the child's home State to order the child's return even if the court in the country to which the child has been abducted makes a non-return order under the Hague Convention (provided the order was made on the basis of a successful Article 13 defence, see 13.8). (See for example, *Re RC and BC (Child Abduction) (Brussels II Revised: Article 11(7)* [2009] 1 FLR 574; *Re RD (Child Abduction) (Brussels II Revised: Articles 11(7) and 19)* [2009] 1 FLR 586; and *Rinau (Case C-195/08)* [2008] 2 FLR 1495.) Thus, Brussels II Revised 'accepts the parallel continuation of return and custody proceedings in two different Member States, regardless of the ultimate outcome of the Hague Convention return proceedings' (Schulz, 2008). In other words, despite a court ordering the non-return of a child in Hague Convention proceedings, the court of habitual residence can revisit the issue and override that decision. Article 11(7) of Brussels II Revised therefore permits a custody decision made in another Member State of the EU to take precedence over a decision made under the Hague Convention. Custody decisions can 'trump' Hague Convention orders. Thus, for example, in *Vigreux v Michel* [2006] EWCA Civ 630, [2006] 2 FLR 1180 the Court of Appeal held that McFarlane J had erred in law in refusing the mother's application for return of the child to France under the Hague Convention when she had already been granted sole parental responsibility for the child by a French court. Thorpe LJ held that the case was one in which the policy of the Hague Convention buttressed by the provisions of Brussels II Revised powerfully outweighed the Article 13 defence.

With respect to a child living in England and Wales, even though a court in another EU country has refused to order the child's return to England and Wales under the Hague Convention, Article 11(7) of Brussels II Revised enables custody issues with respect to the child to be heard in the court England and Wales. Article 11(8) of the EU regulation permits the court to make an order for return. As, for the purposes of Articles

11(7) and (8), the child's welfare is the court's first consideration, the court can conduct a full welfare inquiry and full hearing. For example, in *M v T (Abduction: Brussels IIR Art 11(7))* [2010] EWHC 1479 (Fam), [2010] 2 FLR 1685, after the Lithuanian court had refused to return the child to the UK under the Hague Convention, Charles J in Article 11(7) proceedings ordered that the father should have contact with the child in England or Lithuania and that the mother should be permitted to live permanently with the child in Lithuania (applying *Payne v Payne*, see pp. 307–8). (See also *AF v T and A* [2011] EWHC 1315, where the English court examined the custody of the child with respect to residence and contact under the Children Act 1989 subsequent to a non-return decision made by the German court under the Hague Convention.)

(c)   The voice of the child in Hague Convention cases

As Hague Convention proceedings are summary and speed is of the essence, the usual way in which the voice of the child is heard is by means of a written report compiled either by a Cafcass officer (see 1.7) or by another professional who has interviewed the child. There is no obligation on the judge to hear oral evidence even where an Article 13(b) defence (child's objection to return) is being argued (*per* Sir Mark Potter P in *Re M (Abduction: Child's Objections)* [2007] EWCA Civ 260, [2007] 2 FLR 72). In some cases the judge may wish to speak to the child, and this is a practice which, although not common, is more common than it once was. In exceptional circumstances the child may have separate legal representation (see below).

Although the child's voice may be put before the court, it does not necessarily mean that the child's views will be taken into account. Thus, in *C v B (Abduction: Grave Risk)* [2005] EWHC 2988 (Fam), [2006] 1 FLR 1095, for example, the views of the 9-year-old child, whose mother did not wish to return to Australia, were put before the court by means of a Cafcass report, but Sir Mark Potter P held that, while the child was of sufficient maturity to have his views taken into account, those views (anger with his father and concerns about his mother) did not provide a sufficient basis on which to withhold an order of return for him and his 5-year-old sister.

Separate representation of the child in Hague Convention proceedings   The court has the power to permit children to intervene in Hague Convention proceedings. The test to be applied when deciding whether a child should be separately represented is whether separate representation will add enough to the court's understanding of the issues arising under the Hague Convention to justify the intrusion, expense and the delay that may result (*per* Baroness Hale in *Re M (Abduction: Zimbabwe)* [2007] UKHL 55, [2008] 1 FLR 251).

Although separate representation remains the exception rather than the rule, there has been an increasing trend to permit children to be separately represented. Thus, for example, in *Re C (Abduction: Separate Representation of Children)* [2008] EWHC 517 (Fam), [2008] 2 FLR 6 Ryder J directed that all four articulate siblings (aged 9, 11, 13 and 16), who vigorously objected to being returned to France, be joined as parties and that the three younger children be represented by a guardian *ad litem*. Ryder J (applying the test for separate representation laid down by Baroness Hale in *Re M* above and the approach taken by the Court of Appeal in *Mabon v Mabon* (see p. 320)) held that there would be little additional delay and expense in allowing separate representation; and the younger three children were able to make submissions and defences distinct from those put forward by the mother. However, a different approach was taken in *Re H (Abduction)* [2006] EWCA Civ 1247, [2007] 1 FLR 242 where the Court of Appeal refused permission to allow a girl (aged 15) to be made a party to Hague Convention proceedings as they were summary proceedings where speed is of the essence. Wall LJ said that there were material differences between the question of separate representation for a child in a welfare enquiry under the Children Act 1989 and in summary proceedings under an international convention where the welfare enquiry is to take place elsewhere.

Where a child has a distinctive point of view which needs to be heard separately from that of the defaulting parent, the court may decide to grant separate representation, as it did to a 14-year-old boy in *Re L (Abduction: Child's Objections to Return)* [2002] EWHC 1864 (Fam), [2002] 2 FLR 1042. (For other cases where children were granted separate representation, see *Re S (Abduction: Children's Representation)* [2008] EWHC 1798 (Fam), [2008] 2 FLR 1918; and *Re B (Separate Representation)* [2007] EWCA Civ 1463.)

Are children being heard enough in Hague Convention proceedings? There has been increasing concern that children are not being heard enough in Hague Convention cases, and that more children should be separately represented. Baroness Hale in *Re D (A Child) (Abduction: Rights of Custody)* [2006] UKHL 51, [2007] 1 FLR 961 said that, 'whenever it seems likely that the child's views and interests may not be properly presented to the court, and in particular where there are legal arguments which the adult parties are not putting forward, then the child should be separately represented'.

In respect of abductions within the EU, a failure to hear a child may breach Article 11(2) of Brussels II Revised (see p. 342 above), which requires courts in Member States, when applying Articles 12 and 13 of the Hague Convention, to ensure that the child 'is given the opportunity to be heard during the proceedings unless this appears inappropriate having regard to his or her age or degree of maturity'. Although Brussels II Revised applies only to EU cases, Baroness Hale in *Re D* (above) held that, as the obligation to hear a child is a principle of universal application and consistent with the UK's obligations under Article 12 of the UN Convention on the Rights of the Child (see 8.2), the obligation to hear a child applies not just to EU cases but to all Hague Convention cases. Her Ladyship held that it created a presumption that a child would be heard unless this appeared inappropriate. She warned, however, that listening to a child does not mean that the court should necessarily give effect to those views.

In *Re F (Abduction: Joinder of Child as Party)* [2007] EWCA Civ 393, [2007] 2 FLR 313, however, Thorpe LJ said that *Re D* (above) was not to be interpreted as having the effect of lowering the bar with respect to granting party status to the child; and that there remained a need to demonstrate that a case was sufficiently exceptional. Thorpe LJ said that '[h]earing the child is one thing and giving the child party status is quite another'. In *Re F* the Court of Appeal refused leave for the child (aged 7) to be joined in the proceedings, despite the mother's argument that the judge had not observed her obligation to hear the child under Article 11 of Brussels II Revised. The Court of Appeal held that this refusal did not breach the child's human rights under Articles 6 (right to a fair hearing) and 8 (right to family life) of the European Convention for the Protection of Human Rights.

In addition to a slight move towards children being permitted to be separately represented in Hague Convention cases, several cases have also drawn attention to the desirability of judges talking to children face to face (see, for example, *De L v H* [2009] EWHC 3074 (Fam), [2010] 1 FLR 1229; and *Re G (Abduction: Children's Objections)* [2010] EWCA Civ 1232, [2011] 1 FLR 1645). The *President's Practice Note (Guidelines for Judges Meeting Children Who are Subject to Family Proceedings)* [2010] 2 FLR 1872, which applies to all family proceedings, also applies to abduction cases.

(d) Construing the Convention

As the Hague Convention on Abduction is an international legal instrument, the courts in England and Wales have stressed the importance of it being construed uniformly by courts in Contracting States (see, for example, *per* Lord Browne-Wilkinson in *Re H (Minors) (Abduction: Acquiescence)* [1998] AC 72). To promote uniformity of construction, the Hague Conference has an International Child Abduction Database (INCADAT) of leading Convention case-law from Hague Contracting States.

The courts in England and Wales adopt a purposive approach when construing the Convention. In *Re B (A Minor) (Abduction)* [1994] 2 FLR 249 Waite LJ said that the Convention was 'to be construed broadly as an international agreement according to its general tenor and purpose, without attributing to any of its terms a specialist meaning which the word or words in question would have acquired under the domestic law of England'. In *Hunter v Murrow (Abduction: Rights of Custody)* [2005] EWCA Civ 976, [2005] 2 FLR 1119 the Court of Appeal held that the Convention was a living instrument to be interpreted and applied as necessary to keep pace with social and other trends. It also held that questions involving the construction or interpretation of the Convention were to be answered according to the international jurisprudence of the Contracting States, not simply according to the law of a particular jurisdiction.

In *Re M (Abduction: Zimbabwe)* [2007] UKHL 55, [2008] 1 FLR 251 the House of Lords warned that the courts should not add additional words to the Convention (in that case, an additional test of 'exceptionality' to the circumstances under which a court should refuse to order the return of an abducted child). Baroness Hale, who gave the leading opinion, said that, as the Convention 'itself contains a simple, sensible and carefully thought out balance between various considerations, all aimed at serving the interests of children by deterring, and, where appropriate, remedying international child abduction', then further elaboration with 'additional tests and checklists is not required'.

'The Convention itself contains a simple, sensible and carefully thought out balance between various considerations, all aimed at serving the interests of children by deterring and, where appropriate, remedying international child abduction. Further elaboration with additional tests and checklists is not required.'

Baroness Hale said that, while the court is entitled to take into account the various policy aspects of the Convention (see p. 339 above), that was 'the furthest one should go in seeking to put a gloss on the terms of the Convention'. This approach to the Convention was also reiterated by Baroness Hale and Lord Wilson in *Re E (Children) (Abduction: Custody Appeal)* [2011] UKSC 27, [2011] 2 FLR 758 (see p. 341 above) who held that the exceptions to the obligation to return are by their very nature restricted in their scope and do not need any extra interpretation or gloss.

In *Re F (Abduction: Rights of Custody)* [2008] EWHC 272 (Fam), [2008] 2 FLR 1239 Sir Mark Potter P said that Baroness Hale's express disapproval of the 'exceptionality' test over and above the express requirements of the Hague Convention applied to all Hague Convention cases, including those brought under Brussels II Revised.

13.5 The Hague Convention – jurisdiction

To come within the jurisdiction of the Hague Convention, the child must be under 16 and have been habitually resident in one Contracting State and taken to another. If the child has reached the age of 16 by the time of the hearing, the High Court can consider the case under its inherent jurisdiction (see 8.7). The Convention does not apply to an unborn child (*Re F (Abduction: Unborn Child)* [2006] EWHC 2199 (Fam), [2007] 1 FLR 627). To come within the scope of the Convention, there must also have been a breach of a right of custody (see 13.6 below).

(a)   Habitual residence

Habitual residence, not domicile, is the connecting factor used in the Hague Convention. Thus, the child must have been habitually resident in one Contracting State and moved to another Contracting State. If the child is not, or has ceased to be, habitually resident in a Contracting State, there can be no wrongful removal or retention of the child for the purposes of Article 3(a); and the child will fall outside the scope of the Convention. 'Habitual residence' is not defined in the Convention – its meaning must be determined by the principles laid down in the case-law. In the following case Lord Brandon laid down the principles which apply to the question of habitual residence:

▶ *Re J (A Minor) (Abduction: Custody Rights)* [1990] 2 AC 562, *sub nom C v S (A Minor) (Abduction)* [1990] 2 FLR 442

The parents cohabited in Australia and had a son (aged about 2). The parents' relationship broke down, and, without informing the father, the mother left Australia and flew to England with the child, where it was her settled intention to remain and to make a long-term home for herself and the child. Five days after her departure the father applied to the Australian court for sole custody and guardianship of the child, which was granted. The Australian court later made a declaration that the child's removal from Australia was wrongful under Article 3 of the Hague Convention. A month after the mother's departure, the Australian authorities applied to the English High Court under the Hague Convention for the child's immediate return to Australia.

The House of Lords refused the application for return on the ground that there had been no wrongful removal or retention for the purposes of Article 3. There had been no wrongful removal because, under the law of Western Australia, the father possessed no custody rights capable of being breached at the time when the mother left Australia (as he was not married to the mother). There was no wrongful retention, as the child had ceased to be habitually resident in Australia before the Australian court had made the custody order, because the mother had a unilateral right to determine the child's place of habitual residence, and her settled intention to come to England had terminated the child's habitual residence in Australia.

In respect of habitual residence Lord Brandon said that:

▶ Habitual residence is to be understood according to its ordinary and natural meaning.
▶ Whether a person is or is not habitually resident in a particular country is a question of fact to be decided by reference to all the circumstances of the case.
▶ There is a significant difference between a person ceasing to be habitually resident in country A, and subsequently becoming resident in country B. A person may cease to be habitually resident in country A in a single day, if he leaves it with a settled intention not to return but to take up long-term residence in country B. But an appreciable period of time and a settled intention are needed for a person to become habitually resident in country B. During that 'appreciable period of time' the person will have ceased to be habitually resident in country A, but not yet have become habitually resident in country B.
▶ In the case of a child of the same age as the child in this case, and who is in the sole lawful custody of his mother, the child's habitual residence will be the same as hers.

In *R v Barnet London Borough Council ex parte Shah* [1983] 2 AC 309 Lord Scarman said that habitual residence is the country adopted voluntarily and for a settled purpose as part of the regular order of a person's life, whether of short or long duration.

There have been many reported abduction cases involving the issue of habitual residence, from which the following propositions can be extracted:

Habitual residence

Habitual residence may be established even after a short period of residence, provided there is a settled intention to reside in that country (see, for example, *Re S (Habitual Residence)* [2009] EWCA Civ 1021 where seven to eight weeks' residence in London plus an intention to reside there was sufficient to establish habitual residence in England and Wales). In *Al Habtoor v Fotheringham* [2001] EWCA Civ186, [2001] 1 FLR 951 Thorpe LJ said that habitual residence could be acquired 'even if the person's move was intended to be fulfilled within a comparatively short duration, or was only on a trial basis'.

A short visit to a country does not necessarily start a period of habitual residence(see, for example, *Re A (Abduction: Habitual Residence)* [1998] 1 FLR 497 where a three-week visit to Greece for what was akin to a holiday was held not to be an 'appreciable period of time' to create a new habitual residence).

A child may have no habitual residence at all (see *W and B v H (Child Abduction: Surrogacy)* [2002] 1 FLR 1008 where a Californian couple's application in England for the return of twins born of an English surrogacy arrangement was refused under the Hague Convention as the twins were not habitually resident in California or England).

A dependent child will not necessarily have the same habitual residence as a parent (see *Al Habtoor v Fotheringham* (above) (a case brought in wardship, not under the Hague Convention) where the High Court refused jurisdiction as the applicant mother's nine-year-old child remained habitually resident in Dubai, even though the mother was habitually resident in England).

It is not necessary for a person to remain continuously present in a particular country in order for him or her to retain residence there (*per* Millet LJ in *Re M (Abduction: Habitual Residence)* [1996] 1 FLR 887).

Moving to another Contracting State for educational reasons may not constitute a change of habitual residence (see *TPC v JMJ* [2009] EWHC 638 (Fam) where the children were held to be habitually resident in Spain even though they had come to England for 14 months, with the father's consent, in order to improve their English).

(b) Wrongful removal and retention

To come within the scope of the Convention, there must be wrongful removal from, or wrongful retention in, a Contracting State. Wrongful removal and wrongful retention are mutually exclusive concepts (*Re H; Re S (Minors) (Abduction: Custody Rights)* [1991] 2 FLR 262). Wrongful removal occurs when a child is wrongfully removed from his place of habitual residence in breach of a right of custody. Wrongful retention occurs when, at the end of a period of lawful removal, a parent refuses to return the child. Removal and retention are only wrongful if done in a breach of a right of custody (see below).

A declaration of wrongful removal   Under section 8 of the Child Abduction and Custody Act 1985 the High Court, on an application made for the purposes of Article 15 of the Hague Convention by any person appearing to the court to have an interest in the matter, may make a declaration that the removal of a child from, or his retention outside, the UK is wrongful within the meaning of Article 3 of the Hague Convention. In *Re C (Child Abduction) (Unmarried Father: Rights of Custody)* [2002] EWHC 2219 (Fam), [2003] 1 FLR 252 Munby J said that the grant of declaratory relief under Article 15 is always a matter of discretion, but in the normal case where an applicant succeeds in persuading the court that a child has been wrongfully removed, and seeks a declaration to assist his prospects of obtaining substantive relief in the requested State, he can normally expect to have the court's discretion exercised in his favour.

13.6 The Hague Convention – rights of custody

Article 3 of the Hague Convention on the Civil Aspects of International Child Abduction 1980

'The removal or retention of a child is to be considered wrongful where –

(a) it is in breach of rights of custody attributed to a person, an institution or any other body, either jointly or alone, under the law of the State in which the child was habitually resident immediately before the removal or retention; and
(b) at the time of removal or retention those rights were actually exercised, either jointly or alone, or would have been so exercised but for the removal or retention.'

The existence of a right of custody is crucial to establishing whether the Convention applies, as removal or retention are only wrongful if there has been breach of such a right. The rights of custody mentioned in Article 3(a) above may arise in particular by operation of law, or by reason of a judicial or administrative decision. Article 5(a) provides that for the purposes of the Convention 'rights of custody' 'shall include rights relating to the care of the person of the child and, in particular, the right to determine the child's place of residence'.

In *Re P (Abduction: Consent)* [2004] EWCA Civ 971, [2004] 2 FLR 1057 the Court of Appeal held that the court's task under Article 3 is to establish the custody rights of the parent under the law of the relevant State, and then to consider whether those rights are rights of custody for the purposes of the Hague Convention. In *Re T (Abduction: Rights of Custody)* [2008] EWHC 809 (Fam), [2008] 2 FLR 1794 Coleridge J held that it was particularly important that issues like rights of custody should be clearly settled by the foreign law, either directly by reference to statute or other written material, or by reference to the foreign court's previous decisions.

(a) A purposive construction of custody

In order to give effect to the overriding policy objective of the Hague Convention that children should be expeditiously returned to their country of habitual residence, the courts have adopted a purposive construction of 'rights of custody' and interpreted it broadly to include not just legal custody, but *de facto* (factual) custody. In other words, where a person has no custody rights in law, but is exercising rights of a parental or custodial nature, this can constitute custody. In this way, unmarried fathers without legal custody (or without parental responsibility) have been held to have custody rights. A broad view of custody was taken by the Court of Appeal in the following case:

> ▶ *Re B (A Minor) (Abduction)* **[1994] 2 FLR 249**
>
> The parents were cohabitants living in Australia. The mother, who was a heroin addict, left
> Australia and went to England, leaving the child with the father and maternal grandmother.
> Later, the grandmother took the child to England and failed to return the child to Australia,
> which was in breach of an agreement made between the mother and father that the child
> would be returned within six months. The father, who had been an exemplary parent (but
> who had no legal custody), applied to the English High Court for an immediate return order
> under Article 12. The judge ordered the child's immediate return to Australia. The mother
> appealed to the Court of Appeal.
>
> The Court of Appeal, by a majority, dismissed her appeal and held that, as the purposes
> of the Convention were, in part, humanitarian, it had to be construed broadly as an
> international agreement according to its general tenor and purpose, without attributing to
> any of its terms a specialist meaning which the sort of words in question might have acquired
> under the domestic law of England. The expression 'rights of custody', in most cases, had
> to be interpreted to give it the widest sense possible in order to accord with the objective of
> returning children to their country of habitual residence. Rights of an inchoate nature were
> sufficient to create rights of custody. The removal and retention of the child were held to be
> wrongful, and the child was ordered to be returned to Australia.

Although the facts in *Re B* were similar to those in *Re J sub nom C v S* (see p. 347 above), the majority of the Court of Appeal adopted a purposive construction and held that the father possessed *de facto* custody rights (he had cared for the child), which were sufficient to bring him within the scope of the Convention. Peter Gibson LJ, however, dissented as he considered that the Court of Appeal was bound by the decision of the House of Lords in *Re J sub nom C v S*, as the facts of that case were indistinguishable other than for the fact that the mother in *Re B* had perpetuated a cruel deceit on the father.

The court can possess a right of custody   Removal or retention of a child can be wrongful where it breaches a 'right of custody' possessed by the court. The House of Lords so held in *Re H (Abduction: Rights of Custody)* [2002] 2 AC 291, [2000] 1 FLR 374 where it overturned the trial judge's refusal to order that the mother return the child to Ireland (on the basis that the father had no custody rights), as the Irish court possessed custody rights in the child as an 'institution or other body' to which rights of custody could be attributed within the meaning of Article 3. It held that 'rights' should be given a wide interpretation and that the power to determine a child's place of residence could itself be characterised as a right. In *A v B (Abduction: Rights of Custody: Declaration of Wrongful Removal)* [2008] EWHC 2524 (Fam), [2009] 1 FLR 1253 Bodey J confirmed that the courts can have rights of custody and made a declaration under section 8 of the Child Abduction and Custody Act 1985 to that effect. If a child is made a ward of court, the wardship court acquires rights of custody in the child, which enables it to invoke the Hague Convention if the child is abducted from England (*Re S (Brussels II Revised: Enforcement of Contact Order)* [2008] 2 FLR 1358).

(b)   Seeking a determination about rights of custody

Under Article 15 of the Hague Convention the court in England and Wales can seek a determination from the authorities of the State of the child's habitual residence as to whether or not removal of the child was a breach of a right of custody under the law of that country. In *Re T (Abduction: Rights of Custody)* [2008] EWHC 809 (Fam), [2008] 2 FLR 1794 Coleridge J said that it was important that issues like rights of custody be very clearly settled by the foreign law; and that it would be highly invidious for the English court to trespass into such an area unless it was unavoidable. In *Re T* Coleridge J ordered that there should be a determination by the court in Oregon, USA, as to whether the father had rights of custody (as the mother had argued that he had no such rights).

The status of an Article 15 ruling   The House of Lords held in *Re D (Abduction: Rights of Custody)* [2006] UKHL 51, [2007] 1 FLR 961 that an Article 15 ruling from a requesting State is conclusive as to the parties' rights under the law of the requesting State, unless the circumstances are exceptional (for example where a ruling was obtained by fraud or in breach of the rules of natural justice). It held that a foreign court was much better placed than the English court to understand the true meaning and effect of its own laws in Hague Convention terms; and only if its characterisation of the parent's rights was clearly out of line with international understanding of the Convention's terms should the court in the UK decline to follow it. In *Re D* the House of Lords held that the Court of Appeal had been wrong not to consider itself bound by a ruling of the Romanian court (which had held that the mother's removal of the child from Romania to the UK had not been wrongful, as the father had lost rights of custody on divorce under Romanian law).

13.7   The Hague Convention – return of children

Under the Hague Convention a person (institution or other body) claiming that a child has been removed or retained in breach of a right of custody can apply for assistance in securing the child's return from the Central Authority in the Contracting State of the child's habitual residence, or in any other Contracting State (Art 8). The central authority of the State where the child is present must take all appropriate measures to effect the voluntary return of the child (Art 10). But, if effecting a voluntary return is not possible, then court proceedings will have to be brought.

As the Convention is based on the presumption that an abducted child should be returned to his country of habitual residence, so that the court there can decide on his or her future, the court hearing a return application must order the child's return if the application is made during the first 12 months after the wrongful removal or retention (Art 12). After that 12-month period, the court must also order the child's return, unless the child is 'settled in its new environment' (Art 12) (see below). The duty to return a child is, however, subject to any defence being successfully argued (see below). Because speed is of the essence in abduction cases, judicial and administrative authorities in a Contracting State are required to act expeditiously in return proceedings (Art 11, and see also Brussels II Revised at p. 342 above).

13.8   The Hague Convention – defences to a return application

(a)   Introduction

In addition to defences based on the court having no jurisdiction to hear the application (for example, because the child is not habitually resident in a Contracting State, or there is no custody right – see above), the following defences are expressly laid down in the Convention.

Defences under the Hague Convention

▶ The child is now settled in his new environment (Art 12).
▶ Consent (Art 13(a)).
▶ Acquiescence (Art 13(a)).
▶ Grave risk that the child's return will expose the child to physical or psychological harm or otherwise place him in an intolerable situation (Art 13(b)).
▶ The child objects to being returned and has attained an age and degree of maturity at which it is appropriate to take account of his views (Art 13).
▶ Where return of the child would not be permitted by the fundamental principles of the requested State relating to the protection of human rights and fundamental freedoms (Art 20).

In EU abductions these defences have to be considered in the light of Brussels II Revised (see p. 342 above).

A high threshold for defences The courts in England and Wales have set a high threshold for defences in order not to frustrate the Convention's primary objective, which is to effect the return of abducted children and restore the factual situation which existed before the wrongful removal or retention. Thus, the courts are reluctant to refuse to order return, and constantly emphasise that the underlying aim of the Convention is that the welfare of children is best determined by the court of the child's habitual residence. The alleged abductor therefore has a heavy burden to establish a defence; and, even if a defence is proved, the court retains an overriding discretion to order the child's return.

The overriding discretion of the court A successful defence based on habitual residence or lack of a custody right will mean that the case does not come within the scope of the Convention, and that will be the end of the matter. In respect of the other defences, a successful defence will not necessarily result in the court refusing to order the child's return. This is because Article 18 of the Hague Convention gives the court an overriding discretion to decide whether or not to order return.

Before the decision of the House of Lords in *Re M (Abduction: Zimbabwe)* [2007] UKHL 55, [2008] 1 FLR 251 (see below), a long line of Court of Appeal authorities had held that, even if a defence was established, the court should order return unless there was something special or exceptional about the case, but in *Re M* Baroness Hale said that it was neither necessary nor desirable to import an additional gloss of 'exceptionality' into the plain wording of the Convention, as the circumstances in which return may be refused were themselves exceptions to the general rule. This was also reiterated by Baroness Hale and Lord Wilson, giving judgment for the Supreme Court in *Re E* (see p. 341 above).

(b)   The child is now settled in his or her new environment (Article 12)

Article 12 provides that a court hearing a return application must order the child's return if 12 months have passed since the wrongful removal or retention, unless it can be shown that the child is settled in his or her new environment. 'New environment' means the total physical, social, emotional and psychological experience of the child. Each case depends on its facts (see, for example, *Re H and L (Abduction: Acquiescence)* [2010] EWHC 652 (Fam) [2010] 2 FLR 1277 where the father's application for a return order was refused as the children were found to be settled in England; and the father had also acquiesced in their removal). However, even if it is proved that the child is settled in his or her new environment, the court has a discretion under Article 18 of the Hague Convention to order return, as the leading case on Article 12, shows:

> ▶ *Re M (Abduction: Zimbabwe)* [2007] UKHL 55, [2008] 1 FLR 251
>
> Two girls (aged 13 and 10), born in Zimbabwe to Zimbabwean parents, lived in Zimbabwe with their father after their parents separated. Four years later their mother wrongfully removed them secretly to the UK where she sought asylum. This was refused, but the mother and the children remained in the UK where the two girls became well settled in their local church and school. The father discovered their whereabouts about six months later but did not seek their return under the Hague Convention until about two years later.
>
> Despite finding that the two children were settled in the UK and that they objected to return (under Article 12), Wood J ordered their immediate return, applying the principle that only in exceptional cases should the court exercise its overriding discretion to refuse to order an immediate return once a defence was made out. The mother's appeal to the Court of Appeal (where she argued *inter alia* that Wood J had fallen into error by applying a test of 'exceptionality' at the discretion stage) was dismissed; and so she appealed to the House of Lords, where the children were joined as parties (having regard to the principles laid down in *Re D (Abduction: Rights of Custody)* [2006] UKHL 51, [2007 1 FLR 961. In addition to the arguments raised before the Court of Appeal, the mother raised the issue of whether the Court of Appeal had been right in *Cannon v Cannon* [2004] EWCA Civ 1330, [2005] 1 FLR 169 to hold that, even if settlement was established under Article 12, the courts retained a discretion under Article 18 to order return.
>
> The House of Lords (with Baroness Hale giving the leading opinion, and Lord Rodger dissenting) held that the courts have a discretion to order that a child be returned, even if the child is settled in his or her new environment for the purposes of Article 12. Baroness Hale said that such a construction recognised the flexibility in the concept of settlement, which might arise in a variety of circumstances and to very different degrees; and it acknowledged that late application may be the result of active concealment of where the child has gone. It also left the court with all options open.
>
> Baroness Hale ruled that it was wrong to import any exceptionality into the exercise of discretion under the Hague Convention. She also said that the policy considerations of swift return and comity would carry less weight the longer the abducted child had been in the UK; but that in settlement cases 'the policy of the Convention would not necessarily point towards return'.
>
> Applying the above approach to the facts of the case, the House of Lords allowed the mother's appeal and refused to order that the children be returned to Zimbabwe.

(For a case commentary on *Re M*, see Schuz [2008] CFLQ 64.)

(For a case where the discretion under Article 18 was exercised, see *F v M and N (Abduction: Acquiescence: Settlement)*[2008] EWHC 1525 (Fam),[2008] 2 FLR 1270 where Black J, applying *Re M*, ordered the child's return to Poland even though it had been established that she was settled in England for the purposes of Article 12.)

(c) Consent (Article 13(a))

The court can refuse to order return if it can be proved that the applicant for a return order consented to the child's removal or retention. Consent is a question of fact, but it must be clear, unequivocal and informed (*Re P (Abduction: Consent)* [2004] EWCA Civ 971, [2004] 2 FLR 1057). The principles that apply to acquiescence (see below) also apply to consent.

Each case turns on its own facts. In *M v M (Abduction: Consent)* [2007] EWHC 1404 (Fam), [2007] 2 FLR 1010, for example, Sumner J refused to order the children's return to Greece as the mother had proved by clear and cogent evidence that the father had consented to her bringing the children to the UK. In *Re K v K (Abduction: Consent)* [2009] EWHC 2721 (Fam) it was found that the father had consented to the mother taking the child from Ireland to visit their maternal grandmother in England, and so his application for the return of the children to Ireland was dismissed. In *A v T (Relocation: Consent)* [2012] EWHC 3882 (Fam) the mother's argument that that father had given unequivocal consent to the children's removal to England was accepted and the court exercised its discretion to refuse to order the children's return to Sweden.

(d) Acquiescence (Article 13(a))

The person who removed or retained the child has a defence to a return application if it can be proved that the applicant acquiesced in the removal or retention. The following case, which is the leading case on acquiescence, shows that an attempt to reach a voluntary agreement for a child's return does not necessarily of itself amount to acquiescence:

▶ *Re H (Abduction: Acquiescence)* **[1998] AC 72, [1997] 1 FLR 87**

The parents were strict Orthodox Jews, who were married and lived in Israel. The mother took the children to England without the father's consent. The father contacted his local Beth Din (a religious court of law), and it entered its own summons for the children's return, which the mother ignored. The Beth Din later ordered the father to take whatever steps he saw fit, and six months after the children had been removed from Israel he invoked Hague Convention proceedings in the High Court in England. The mother argued that he had acquiesced in the children's removal by failing to make a prompt application. The High Court ordered the children's return, but the Court of Appeal allowed the mother's appeal, holding that the father had acquiesced, applying its earlier decision in *Re A (Minors) (Abduction: Custody Rights)* [1992] Fam 106, [1992] 2 FLR 14 where by a majority it had applied an objective test to establish acquiescence, and had held that acquiescence could be signified by a single act or communication, even though that act or communication appeared to be at variance with the general course of a parent's conduct. The father appealed to the House of Lords.

The House of Lords held, allowing his appeal and ordering the children's return to Israel, that the objective test of acquiescence laid down by the Court of Appeal in *Re A* was wrong. The correct approach was that adopted by Balcombe LJ who had dissented in *Re A*. Applying this approach, it was clear that the father had not acquiesced in the children's retention in England.

Lord Browne-Wilkinson laid down the following principles on acquiescence:

▶ Whether the wronged parent has acquiesced in the removal or retention of a child depends on his or her actual state of mind. The test is subjective.
▶ The subjective intention of the wronged parent is a question of fact for the trial judge to determine in all the circumstances of the case, the burden of proof being on the abducting parent.
▶ But there is one exception, namely: where the wronged parent's words or actions clearly and unequivocally show and have led the other parent to believe that the wronged parent is not asserting or going to assert his right to the summary return of the child and are inconsistent with such return, justice requires that the wronged parent be held to have acquiesced.

Although each case depends on its own facts, the following approaches to acquiescence have been taken in the case-law:

> *A custody application made in the child's country of habitual residence is a strong indication that there is no acquiescence (Re F (A Minor) (Child Abduction)* [1992] 1 FLR 548).
>
> *Making long-term plans for contact may indicate acquiescence (Re S (Abduction: Acquiescence)* [1998] 2 FLR 115).
>
> *Bringing proceedings for contact in the English courts, even though brought in ignorance of the Convention, may indicate acquiescence (Re B (Abduction: Acquiescence)* [1999] 2 FLR 818).
>
> *A willingness to be involved in negotiations to sort out what is best for a child and the parties does not necessarily amount to acquiescence, even if no agreement is reached (Re I (Abduction: Acquiescence)* [1999] 1 FLR 778); *as negotiations at the early stage of a difficult broken relationship are to be encouraged (P v P (Abduction: Acquiescence)* [1998] 2 FLR 835).
>
> *Consenting to full and final residence orders being made in England and Wales may constitute acquiescence (Re D (Abduction: Acquiescence)* [1998] 1 FLR 686).
>
> *Mere inaction does not necessarily on its own amount to acquiescence (AF v MB-F (Abduction: Rights of Custody)* [2008] EWHC 272 (Fam), [2008] 2 FLR 1239).
>
> *It is not necessarily a prerequisite for establishing acquiescence that a parent has correct advice or detailed knowledge of his or her rights under the Convention; what is important that the applicant knew that he/she could bring a return application but chose to accept the situation as it was (B-G v B-G* [2008] EWHC 688 (Fam), [2008] 2 FLR 965).

(e) Grave risk of harm, or otherwise placing the child in an intolerable situation (Article 13(b))

For this defence to succeed, it must be proved that there is a grave risk that return will expose the child to physical or psychological harm or otherwise place the child in an intolerable situation (Article 13(b)). In the following case, the Supreme Court considered (for the first time) the approach to the interpretation and application of the grave risk of harm defence:

> ▶ *Re E (Abduction: Evaluation of Welfare: Protective Measures)* [2011] UKSC 27, [2011] 2 FLR 758
>
> The case involved an application by the father for his two children (aged 6 and 4) to be returned to Norway. The mother's Article 13(b) defence was that her mental health was so fragile that if she were ordered to return the children there was a grave risk that they would be exposed to psychological harm and/or placed in an intolerable situation by virtue of the impact upon them of the deterioration in her mental health. She argued in relation to Article 13(b) that the requirement laid down by the courts in England and Wales (namely for 'clear and compelling evidence' of a 'grave risk of harm or other intolerability which must be measured as substantial, not trivial and of a severity which is much more than is inherent in the inevitable disruption, uncertainty and anxiety which follows an unwelcome return') was a gloss on the wording of the Hague Convention and imported a higher than normal standard of proof and a more restrictive meaning than the words of the Convention required. (For her other arguments, see p. 341.)

The Supreme Court held, *inter alia*, with respect to the Article 13(b) defence that:

▶ There was no need for Article 13(b) to be construed narrowly, as the exceptions to the obligation to return are by their very nature restricted in their scope. They do not need any extra interpretation or gloss.

▶ In relation to Article 13(b) the burden of proof lies with the 'person, institution or other body' which opposes the child's return. The standard of proof is the ordinary balance of probabilities but the court will be mindful of the limitations involved in the summary nature of the Hague Convention process. It will rarely be appropriate to hear oral evidence of the allegations made under Article 13(b) and thus neither those allegations nor their rebuttal are usually tested in cross-examination.

▶ The risk to the child must be 'grave', not just 'real'.

Each case depends on its own facts. The Article 13(b) defence was argued, for instance, in the following cases but was not accepted and the children were ordered to be returned: *Re S (Abduction: Intolerable Situation: Beth Din)* [2000] 1 FLR 454 (religious discrimination against women who were Orthodox Jews which would breach the right to family life of the mother and children under Article 8 ECHR); *Re S (Abduction: Custody Rights)* [2002] EWCA Civ 908, [2002] 2 FLR 815l (terrorism in Israel); *Re W (Abduction: Domestic Violence)* [2004] EWHC 1247 (Fam), [2004] 2 FLR 499 (mother subjected to regular abuse, which included violence, threats with a firearm and demeaning sexual practices, but no evidence that the child had suffered distress); and *TB v JB (Abduction: Grave Risk of Harm)* [2001] 2 FLR 515 (alleged physical and sexual violence inflicted on the mother and physical abuse of the children).

For cases where the Article 13(b) grave risk of harm defence was accepted, see, for example: *Re D (Article 13b: Non-Return)* [2006] EWCA Civ 146, [2006] 2 FLR 305 (return to Venezuela refused); and *Klentzeris v Klentzeris* [2007] EWCA Civ 533, [2007] 2 FLR 996 (return to Greece refused).

Allegations of domestic violence Whether allegations of domestic harm will constitute a grave risk of harm will depend on the circumstances of the case. Return may be ordered even where serious domestic violence is alleged, as the court in England and Wales will presume that the courts in the foreign jurisdiction will be able to provide and implement protective measures. The following case, which went to the Supreme Court and which involved allegations of domestic violence, affirmed the approach adopted in the earlier Supreme Court case of *Re E* (see above):

▶ *Re S (Abduction: Art 13 Defence) (Reunite International Child Abduction Centre Intervening)* **[2012] UKSC 10, [2012] 2 FLR 442**

The father applied for return of the child (aged 2), who had been wrongly removed to the UK from Australia by the mother. The mother raised a defence under Article 13(b) on the basis of alleged abusive behaviour by the father towards her and of the potential detriment to her mental health if she was compelled to return. Charles J accepted the mother's Article 13(b) defence and exercised his discretion to refuse to order the child's return. The Court of Appeal allowed the father's appeal and ordered return. The mother appealed to the Supreme Court.

The Supreme Court, allowing her appeal, held *inter alia* (with Lord Wilson giving the judgment of the court) that the critical question and the effect of *Re E* (see above) was what would happen if, with the mother, the child were returned. The Court of Appeal had failed to appreciate that the mother's fears about the father's likely conduct rested on much more than disputed allegations. Equally, it had paid scant regard to the unusually powerful nature of the medical evidence about the mother. Overarchingly, it had failed to recognise that the judgement about the level of risk which was required to be made by Article 13(b) was one which fell to be made by the trial judge and that it should not be overturned unless, whether by reference to the law or to evidence, it had not been open to him to make.

The grave risk defence and abductions in the European Union In an abduction involving two Contracting States to the Hague Convention which are also Member States of the European Union, Article 11(4) of Brussels II Revised provides that a court 'cannot refuse to return a child on the basis of the grave risk defence under art. 13(b) if it is established that adequate arrangements have been made to secure the protection of the child after his or her return' (see, for example, *F v M (Abduction: Grave Risk of Harm)* [2008] EWHC 1467 (Fam), [2008] 2 FLR 1263).

(f) Child objects to being returned (Article 13)

The court may refuse to order return if it finds that the child objects to being returned; *and* the child has attained an age and degree of maturity at which it is appropriate to take account of the child's views. The court has a discretion as to the amount of weight to be given to the child's views, but will bear in mind the policy of the Convention that abducted children should be returned to their country of habitual residence. The weight to be attached to the child's objections will depend on the age and maturity of the child.

In *AF v MB-F (Abduction: Rights of Custody)* [2008] EWHC 272 (Fam), [2008] 2 FLR 1239 (see further below) Sir Mark Potter P, summarising the earlier case-law, said that the court must consider the following questions when considering this defence:

▶ Are the objections made out?
▶ Has the child reached an age and degree of maturity at which it is appropriate to take account of his or her views?
▶ Have those views been shaped or coloured by undue influence or pressure directly or indirectly exerted by the abducting parent to an extent which requires such views to be disregarded or discounted?
▶ What weight should be placed on the child's objections in the light of any countervailing factors, and in particular the policy considerations of the Hague Convention (namely that deterrence of abductors and the welfare interests of children are generally best served by making of an order for prompt return; and the need to respect the judicial processes of the requesting State)?

A two-stage approach is adopted in determining whether the exception in Article 13 is made out: a factual stage; and a discretionary stage. At the first stage, the court must be satisfied of the nature of the child's objection, the child's maturity, strength of emotion and independence of view. If these are satisfied, then the 'gate' is opened to the exercise of judicial discretion. The court will be vigilant to ascertain and assess the reasons for the child not wishing to return; and, although Article 12 requires the child to be returned to the *State* of habitual residence, not to the person requesting the child's return, the court can consider the fact that a child is objecting to returning to a parent rather than to a State.

At what age will a child's objections be taken into account?   Although the original aim of the Hague Convention was to permit the views of mature adolescents to be taken into account, the trend over the years has been to take into account the views of much younger children. In *Re W (Abduction: Child's Objections)* [2010] EWCA Civ 520, [2010] 2 FLR 1165, where Black J in the High Court had taken into account the objections of two children aged 6 and 8 and refused to order their return to Ireland, Wilson LJ in the Court of Appeal expressed concern that lowering the age at which a child's objections could be taken into account might gradually erode the policy of the Convention to return children swiftly to their country of habitual residence. However, Wilson LJ drew attention to the safeguard in the expectation set out in *Re R (Child Abduction: Acquiescence)* [1995] 1 FLR 716 that, in the discretionary exercise, the objections of an older child would deserve greater weight than those of a younger child. In *Re G (Abduction: Children's Objections)* [2010] EWCA Civ 1232, [2011] 1 FLR 1645 the Court of Appeal warned of the dangers of refusing to listen to the objections of articulate adolescent children. In *Re M (Abduction: Child's Objections)* [2007] EWCA Civ 260, [2007] 2 FLR 72 the Court of Appeal accepted the objections of the child (an intelligent girl aged 8) and refused to order her return to Serbia on the basis of the exceptional and unusual circumstances of the case.

How the child's views are conveyed to the court   The usual way in which the child's objections are put before the court is by way of a report by a Cafcass officer (see 1.7), but in some cases the court may allow the child to be made a party to the proceedings and be separately represented, particularly if the child has an independent point of view which needs to be put before the court. There has been an increasing trend for judges to meet to children face to face (see, for instance, *De L v H (Abduction: Child's Objections)* [2009] EWHC 3074 (Fam), [2010] 1FLR 1229; and *Re G (Abduction: Children's Objections)*, above).

13.9   The European Convention

The European Convention on the Recognition and Enforcement of Decisions Concerning Custody of Children 1980 (the 'European Convention') was implemented into UK law by Part II of the Child Abduction and Custody Act 1985. The text of the Convention is laid down in Schedule 2 to that Act.

The European Convention is rarely used in abduction cases because it deals only with the enforcement of custody and access *orders*, whereas the Hague Convention deals with custody *rights*. Although the European Convention has been largely superseded by the Hague Convention and by Brussels II Revised (see pp. 342–4 above), it may be useful where the Hague Convention does not apply (for instance to enforce an access order or where the person who has wrongly removed or retained the child has sole custody). Only an outline of the European Convention is provided here.

The European Convention deals with the recognition and enforcement of custody decisions where there has been 'improper removal of a child', by allowing any person who has obtained a custody decision in a Contracting State to apply to a central authority in another Contracting State to have that decision recognised or enforced in that State (Article 4). In no circumstances may the original foreign custody decision be reviewed as to its substance (Article 9(3)). 'Improper removal' is defined as 'the removal of a child across an international frontier in breach of a decision relating to his custody which has been given in a Contracting State and which is enforceable in such a State' and includes:

(i) the failure to return a child across an international frontier at the end of a period of the exercise of the right of access to the child or at the end of any other temporary stay in a territory other than that where the custody is exercised; and (ii) a removal which is subsequently declared unlawful within the meaning of Article 12 (Art 1(d)).

Decisions on access, and custody decisions dealing with access, can also be recognised and enforced under the Convention subject to the same conditions which apply to custody decisions, but the competent authority of the State addressed may fix the conditions for the implementation and exercise of the right of access, taking into account, in particular, undertakings given by the parties on this matter (Art 11). Where there is no decision as to access, or where recognition or enforcement of a custody decision has been refused, the central authority of the State addressed may apply to its own competent authorities for a decision on the right of access if the person claiming a right of access so requests (Art 11(3)).

Grounds for refusal to register an order   The court can refuse to register an order, and thereby fail to recognise and enforce it (see Arts 9 and 10). However, it is unlikely to do so, as the aim of the Convention, like the Hague Convention, is to foster international cooperation to effect the return of abducted children. Article 9 lays down procedural grounds for refusing to register an order. Article 10 lays down substantive grounds for refusing to recognise and enforce an order. Where the court is considering whether to refuse to register an order on the basis that it is no longer in accordance with the child's welfare due to a change of circumstances, it must ascertain the child's views (unless it is impracticable to do so having regard to his age and understanding) (Art 15(1)).

There are few reported cases on the European Convention because it is rarely invoked in the courts in England and Wales, but it was invoked by: grandparents (unsuccessfully) who wished to enforce a French access order in *Re L (Abduction: European Convention: Access)* [1999] 2 FLR 1089); and by a father (unsuccessfully) who wished to enforce a Swedish custody order in *T v T (Abduction: Forum Conveniens)* [2002] 2 FLR 544. In *Re A (Foreign Access Order: Enforcement)* [1996] 1 FLR 561 a French access order was recognised and enforced in England by the English courts.

The central authority which deals with the enforcement of orders under the European Convention in England and Wales is the International Child Abduction and Contact Unit (ICACU).

13.10   Non-Convention cases

If a child is abducted out of the UK to a country which is not party to the Hague Convention (or the European Convention), the 'left-behind' parent is in a precarious position because there is no network of Contracting States which can work together to effect the child's return. A parent will have to endeavour to reach an amicable settlement with the abducting parent; or commence legal proceedings in the country to which the child has been taken, which can be difficult and expensive. Bringing court proceedings in countries with Islamic legal systems can be particularly difficult as the father's interests may prevail over those of the child and mother. Although wardship or the inherent jurisdiction *may* provide a remedy in England and Wales, even though the child is not present in the jurisdiction (see 8.7), it may not necessarily do so. Thus, for example, in the tragic case of *Al Habtoor v Fotheringham* [2001] EWCA Civ 186, [2001] 1

FLR 951 the Court of Appeal held there was no jurisdiction to hear the mother's case in wardship because the child was resident in Dubai and was not a British national.

Where a child is brought into the UK from a non-Convention country, a return application can be made to the High Court in wardship proceedings or under the inherent jurisdiction (see 8.7), or in section 8 order proceedings under the Children Act 1989 (see 10.4). (For examples of the inherent jurisdiction, see *Re F (Abduction: Removal Outside Jurisdiction)* [2008] EWCA Civ 842, [2008] 2 FLR 1649; and *Re U (Abduction: Nigeria)* [2010] EWHC 1179 (Fam), [2011] 1 FLR 354.)

The High Court has a wide discretion in any of these proceedings, and, unlike Hague Convention proceedings, there is no presumption in favour of ordering return. Thus the court can choose to investigate the merits of the case or exercise a 'summary jurisdiction' (in other words order the child's immediate return without conducting a full investigation of the merits) (see further below).

The governing principles in non-convention cases   The principles applicable in non-Convention cases were laid down by the House of Lords in the following case, which is the leading case:

▶ *Re J (A Child) (Child Returned Abroad: Convention Rights)* **[2005] UKHL 40, [2005] 2 FLR 802**

The mother took the child to England from Saudi Arabia. The father applied under section 8 of the Children Act 1989 for a specific issue order for the return of the child to Saudi Arabia, but the trial judge refused the application. The father appealed to the Court of Appeal, which unanimously allowed his appeal. The mother appealed to the House of Lords, which allowed her appeal, and restored the orders made by the trial judge. The House of Lords held that the trial judge and the Court of Appeal had been wrong to leave out of account the absence of a jurisdiction in the home country to enable the mother to bring the child back to England without the father's consent.

Baroness Hale, who gave the leading opinion, laid down the following principles and approaches to be applied in non-Convention cases for the summary return of children:

▶ The child's welfare is paramount and the specialist rules and concepts of the Hague Convention are not to be applied by analogy in non-Convention cases.
▶ Each case depends on its facts. In some cases summary return will be in the child's best interests but in others it will not.
▶ In having to make a decision whether or not to order summary return, a judge might find it convenient to start from the proposition that it was likely to be better for a child to return to his home country for any dispute about his future to be decided there. Any case against his doing so had to be made.
▶ It should not be assumed that allowing a child to remain in the UK while his future was decided here inevitably means that he will remain here for ever.
▶ An important variable is the degree of connection of the child with each country. This does not involve applying the technical concept of habitual residence, but to ask in a common-sense way with which country the child has the closer connection. In determining this issue of the child's 'home country', the child's nationality, where he has lived for most of his life, first language, race or ethnicity, religion, culture and education are relevant matters. A closely related factor is the length of time that the child has spent in each country. Uprooting a child from one environment and bringing him to a completely unfamiliar one, especially if that has been done clandestinely, may well not be in the child's best interests. But if the child is already familiar with the UK, and had been here for some time without objection, it might be less disruptive for him to remain a little longer while his medium- and longer-term future are decided.

▶ The relevance of the fact that the legal system of the other country is different from that in the UK depends on the facts of each case. It is wrong to say that the future of the child should be decided according to the conception of child welfare which exactly corresponds with that which is current in England and Wales. In a world which values difference, one culture is not inevitably to be preferred to another. For this reason, English law does not start from any *a priori* assumptions about what is best for any individual child. The court must consider the individual child and weigh in the balance the checklist of factors in section 1(3) of the Children Act 1989 (see 10.3). If there is a genuine issue between the parents as to whether it is in the best interests of the child to live in the UK or elsewhere, it is relevant whether that issue is capable of being tried in the courts of the country to which he is to be returned. If those courts have no choice but to do what the father wishes, without hearing the mother, then the English courts must ask themselves whether it is in the child's best interests to enable the dispute to be heard. The absence of a 'relocation' jurisdiction in the other country may be a decisive factor, unless it appears that the mother may not be able to make a good case for relocation. There may be cases where the connection of the child and the family with the other country is so strong that any difference between the legal systems in the UK and the other country should carry little weight.

▶ These considerations above must not, however, stand in the way of a swift and unsentimental decision to return the child to his home country, even if that country is very different from the UK. The concept of welfare in the UK is capable of taking cultural and religious factors into account in deciding how a child should be brought up. It also gives great weight to the child's need for a meaningful relationship with both parents.

However, although the child's welfare is the paramount consideration in non-Convention cases, Baroness Hale stated *obiter* in *Re M (Abduction: Zimbabwe)* [2007] UKHL 55, [2008] 1 FLR 251 (a Hague Convention case – see p. 353) that in non-Convention cases the court has 'the power to order the immediate return of the child to a foreign jurisdiction without conducting a full investigation of the merits'. Her Ladyship said:

'Thus there is always a choice to be made between summary return and a further investigation. There is also a choice to be made as to the depth into which the judge will go in investigating the merits of the case before making that choice. One size does not fit all. The judge may well find it convenient to start from the proposition that it is likely to be better for a child to return to his home country for any disputes about his future to be decided there. A case against his doing so has to be made. But the weight to be given to that factor and to all the other relevant factors, some of which are canvassed in *Re J* (see above), will vary enormously from case to case.'

Human rights, Sharia law and abductions   In the following case the mother abducted the child from the Lebanon and, when her application for asylum in England was refused, she claimed that deporting her and her son back to the Lebanon would infringe their human rights. Their claim before the House of Lords was successful, and the House also emphasised the importance of the separate representation of the child. Baroness Hale also considered that the child's human rights were of greater weight than those of his mother.

▶ *EM (Lebanon) v Secretary of State for the Home Department* **[2008] UKHL 64, [2008] 2 FLR 2067**

The Lebanese mother had obtained a divorce in the Lebanon because of her husband's violence. Under Sharia law, which was applicable in Lebanon, the father (who had only seen their son on the day of his birth) retained custody of the child and would be entitled to physical custody once the child reached the age of 7, with contact with the mother entirely at the father's discretion. When the child reached 7, the authorities sought to enforce the transfer of the child to the father, whereupon the mother went into hiding and fled with the child to England where she sought asylum. Her application was rejected and she appealed, arguing in the House of Lords that deporting her and the child back to Lebanon would infringe their Article 8 right to respect for family life and her Article 14 right to non-discrimination under the European Convention for the Protection of Human Rights (ECHR). By the time of the hearing, the child was aged 12.

The House of Lords held, allowing the appeal that:

▶ The threshold test for determining whether returning a person to a State not bound by the ECHR will involve a breach of their Article 8 ECHR right is a stringent one. There must be a flagrant breach of the right, such as will completely deny or nullify it in the destination country. Serious or discriminatory interference with the right protected is insufficient.

▶ In no meaningful sense could occasional supervised visits by the mother to her child at a place other than her home, even if such visits could be ordered, be described as family life. The effect of return would thus be to destroy the family life of the mother and child as it was now lived.

▶ The lower courts had been disadvantaged by the absence of representations on behalf of the child. The hearing before the House of Lords had underscored the importance of ascertaining and communicating to the court the views of a child such as the child in this case. In the great majority of cases, the interests of the child, although calling for separate consideration, are unlikely to differ from those of the applicant parent. If there is a genuine conflict, separate representation may be called for, but advisers should not be astute to detect a conflict where the interests of parent and child are essentially congruent.

Per **BARONESS HALE**: 'The violation of the child's right was of greater weight than that of the mother's. The very essence of his right would be destroyed if he were returned and removed from her, with no justification possible under Article 8(2) since the reasons for its destruction were purely arbitrary and paid no regard to his interests. There had been no family life between the child and his father or paternal family in the Lebanon, and so the circumstances were quite different from the general run of child abduction cases where it is the abduction, rather than the return, that interferes with that family life.'

Summary

▶ Child abduction is an increasing problem and a global one. The courts in England and Wales deal with a range of issues relating to abduction, such as: international abduction cases; hearing 'relocation' applications (see 11.8); making orders preventing removal from the UK; and making orders declaring that a removal is wrongful. The Central Authority for England and Wales for child abduction purposes is the International Child Abduction and Contact Unit (ICACU), based in the Official Solicitor's Department of the Ministry of Justice.

▶ Where there is a risk of abduction, preventative measures can be taken, such as: seeking police assistance (which can include the implementation of a 'port alert'); making an application for court order under section 8 of the Children Act 1989 or under the wardship or inherent jurisdiction of the High Court; or seeking the assistance of the UK Identity and Passport Service. Unmarried fathers without parental responsibility are in a vulnerable situation and should consider applying for a court order if there is a risk of their child being abducted. Child abduction is a criminal offence under the Child Abduction Act 1984 and under the common law offence of kidnapping. Under the 1984 Act a child can be lawfully taken out of the UK provided there is no court order prohibiting removal and every person with parental responsibility consents.

Summary cont'd

▶ The Hague Convention enables Contracting States to work together to return children who have been wrongfully removed from their country of habitual residence or wrongfully retained in another Contracting State in breach of a right of custody. The Convention has been implemented into UK law by Part I of the Child Abduction and Custody Act 1985. The policy of the Convention is for children to be speedily returned to their country of habitual residence so that the court in that country can decide on the future arrangements for the child. The Central Authority for England and Wales for the purposes of the Convention is the International Child Abduction and Contact Unit (ICACU). In Hague Convention cases brought before the UK courts, the welfare of the child is regarded as an important consideration, but not the paramount consideration (as the policy aim of the Convention is to have the child speedily returned to his or her own country). This is despite the fact that the European Court of Human Rights has held otherwise. The courts in the UK also take the view that Hague Convention proceedings do not need to be investigated in depth on their merits but are summary proceedings (again because of the policy aim above, and again even though the ECtHR has held to the contrary).

▶ Where a child has been abducted within the EU, the EU regulation, Brussels II Revised, must also be taken into account.

▶ The voice of the child is usually heard in Hague Convention proceedings by means of a Cafcass report, but in exceptional cases the court may allow the child to be separately represented. Judges have also increasingly adopted the practice of interviewing children.

▶ The UK courts adopt a purposive approach to construing the Convention, but the senior judiciary have said that the courts should not add additional words to the Convention's provision.

▶ To come within the jurisdiction of the Hague Convention the child must be under 16 and have been wrongly removed from a Contracting State to another Contracting State (or wrongfully retained in that Contracting State) in breach of a right of custody. The child must have been habitually resident in a Contracting State. 'Habitual residence' is not defined in the Convention – its meaning must be determined by the principles laid down in the case-law.

▶ The removal or retention of a child will be considered wrongful where it is in breach of a custody rights under the law of the State in which the child was habitually resident immediately before the removal or retention (Art 3). The courts in the UK have adopted a purposive approach to the meaning of 'custody'.

▶ Guidance and assistance about seeking the return of a child can be sought from the Central Authority in the Contracting State of the child's habitual residence or in any other Contracting State (Art 8).

▶ There are specific 'defences' or exceptions to return laid down in the Convention, namely that: the child is now settled in his new environment (Art 12); the other parent consented or acquiesced in the removal or retention of the child (Art 13(a)); there is a grave risk that the child's return will expose the child to physical or psychological harm or otherwise place him in an intolerable situation (Art 13(b)); the child objects to being returned and has attained an age and degree of maturity at which it is appropriate to take account of his views (Art 13); or where return of the child would not be permitted by the fundamental principles of the requested State relating to the protection of human rights and fundamental freedoms (Art 20). With EU abductions these defences must be considered in the light of Brussels II Revised. Even if a defence is established, the court has an overriding discretion to order return (see Art 18), because of the policy objective that abducted children should be speedily returned to their country of habitual residence so that their future can be determined there.

▶ The European Convention on the Recognition and Enforcement of Decisions Concerning Custody of Children 1980 was implemented into UK law by Part II of the Child Abduction and Custody Act

1985. It is rarely used in abduction cases because it deals with the enforcement of custody and access *orders*, whereas the Hague Convention deals with custody *rights*. The Convention has been largely superseded by the Hague Convention and by Brussels II Revised.

▶ Where a child is wrongfully brought into England and Wales from a non-Convention country, the court will decide whether the welfare of the child requires it to order the child's return. There is no presumption in favour of return, as there is in Hague Convention cases; and the court has a discretion to decide whether or not to hear the case on its merits.

Further reading and references

Beevers, 'Child abduction: inchoate rights of custody and the unmarried father' [2006] CFLQ 499.

Lamont, 'The EU: protecting children's rights in child abduction' [2008] IFL 110.

Lowe and Stephens. 'Operating the 1980 Hague Abduction Convention: the 2008 statistics' [2011] Fam Law 1216.

McEleavy, 'Evaluating the views of abducted children: trends in appellate case-law' [2008] CFLQ 230.

Schuz, 'Habitual residence of children under the Hague Child Abduction Convention – theory and practice' [2001] CFLQ 1.

Schuz, 'In search of a settled interpretation of Article 12(2) of the Hague Child Abduction Convention' [2008] CFLQ 64.

Schulz, 'Guidance from Luxembourg: First ECJ judgment clarifying the relationship between the 1980 Hague Convention and Brussels II Revised' [2008] IFL 221.

Websites

Foreign and Commonwealth Office: www.fco.gov.uk/travel

INCADAT (Hague Convention Child Abduction Database): www.incadat.com

International Child Abduction and Contact Unit (ICACU): www.officialsolicitor.gov.uk/os/icacu.htm

Reunite (the International Child Abduction Centre): www.reunite.org

UK Identity and Passport Service: www.homeoffice.gov.uk/agencies-public-bodies/ips/

Links to relevant websites can also be found at: www.palgrave.com/law/familylaw8e

Chapter 14

Child protection

14.1 The practice of child protection

(a) Personnel involved in child protection

In addition to lawyers, many other personnel are involved in the task of providing protection for children and services for children in need. The emphasis is on a multi-agency and inter-agency approach. Of particular importance are local authority social workers who have a statutory responsibility to work together with other agencies and relevant partners to protect children and to make provision for children in need. Their responsibilities are laid down in the Children Acts 1989 and 2004 and in rules of practice, regulations and various guidances (see in particular *Working Together to Safeguard Children*(2006) which local authorities have a statutory obligation to comply with). Cafcass (see 1.7) performs an important function by providing Children's Guardians in public law proceedings under the Children Act 1989, whose role is to safeguard the welfare of the child in court proceedings involving local authorities. Voluntary agencies, such as the National Society for the Prevention of Cruelty to Children (NSPCC), also provide services to protect and assist children and their families.

(b) The task of child protection – getting the balance right

Social workers engaged in child protection have a difficult task as they must take adequate steps to protect children but at the same time ensure that they are not too intrusive into family life. As social services departments are public authorities for the purposes of the Human Rights Act 1998 (see 1.8), they must exercise their powers and duties in line with the European Convention for the Protection of Human Rights. Thus, they must respect the rights of children and parents to enjoy a private and family life (Art 8), while also ensuring that children do not suffer inhuman and degrading treatment (Art 3). Local authorities can have their acts or omissions challenged in the courts under the HRA 1998 and in other ways (see 14.11).

Social workers are sometimes criticised for not intervening enough to protect children; and there is considerable media coverage and concern when children are failed by the system. The Victoria Climbié case was such a case, and it led to reforms of the child protection system by the Children Act 2004. Another case where social workers, and other persons working with children, were criticised was that of Baby Peter who was seen 60 times in eight months by different agencies but who died in 2007 aged 17 months as a result of serious injuries inflicted by his mother, her boyfriend and the lodger. As a result of Baby P's death and a perceived failure of the child protection system, Lord Laming (who had conducted the Victoria Climbié Inquiry in 2003) was asked by the Government to review the system and to prepare a report on how effectively children were being safeguarded after the reforms introduced following the Victoria Climbié Inquiry. Lord Laming's report, *The Protection of Children in England: A Progress Report*, March 2009, HC 330, made various recommendations including, for instance, changes in the training and recruitment of social workers.

Whereas social workers were criticised for failing to intervene to protect Victoria Climbié and Baby P, they are sometimes criticised for being too interventionist as they were in the 'Cleveland affair' in the 1980s when more than 100 children suspected of being the victims of sexual abuse were removed from their homes by social workers on the evidence of two paediatricians without other agencies being consulted. The report of the public enquiry set up to investigate the matter (*Report of the Enquiry into Child Abuse in Cleveland 1987*, Cm 412, 1987) recommended, *inter alia*, better inter-agency co-operation to protect children and better safeguards for parents and children where emergency intervention was needed. The *Report* had a considerable impact on the drafting of the Children Act 1989, in particular in respect of achieving the right balance between family autonomy and State intervention.

The courts must also endeavour to achieve the correct balance between intervention and non-intervention. Thus, as Baroness Hale said in *Re S-B (Children)* [2009] UKSC 17, [2010] 1 FLR 1161, 'on the one hand, children need to be protected from harm; but on the other hand, both they and their families need to be protected from the injustice and potential damage to their whole futures done by removing children from a parent who is not, in fact, responsible for causing any harm at all'. The courts, like other public authorities, also have obligations under the Human Rights Act 1998 to comply with the European Convention for the Protection of Human Rights (see 1.8). For example, removing a child from his or her family under a care order without good cause would be a breach of Article 8.

Despite the need to respect the right to family life, it is sometimes necessary for children to be removed from home and placed in the care of a local authority, with the child being looked after, for instance, by a relative or foster-carer. However, taking a child into care is a step of last resort as it is regarded as a drastic measure. Also, children in care often fare less well socially and educationally than other children. Many turn to crime. Some children have even suffered abuse in the care system itself (see the Waterhouse Report, *Lost in Care*, 2000). In order to improve the life chances of children in care, reforms of the law have been introduced to increase the number of children in care who are placed for adoption (see Chapter 15).

14.2 The Children Act 2004

The Children Act 2004 was, in part, a response to the tragic death in February 2000 of Victoria Climbié, aged 8, who died from malnutrition and hypothermia after suffering months of torture and neglect, despite being in regular contact with social workers and other agencies. The inquiry into her death, chaired by Lord Laming, found grave errors on the part of social services and criticised social workers and other agencies for failing to intervene (*Laming Report on the Inquiry into the Death of Victoria Climbié*, Cm 5730, 2003). Lord Laming found the legislation, namely the Children Act 1989, to be fundamentally sound but that there had been gaps in its implementation. The failure related to a lack of good practice, and organisational and management problems. There was poor co-ordination and a failure to share information, and there was no-one with a strong sense of accountability.

After the publication of various Government papers in response to the *Laming Report* (for example, *Every Child Matters: The Next Steps*, 2004; and *Keeping Children*

Safe, 2003), reforms to improve the practice of child protection were implemented by the Children Act 2004, namely to provide better integrated services and better multi-disciplinary practice. Key developments under the Children Act 2004 included the creation of Children's Trusts and Local Safeguarding Children Boards (LSCBs). Children Trusts were created in order to bring together all the services for children and young people in an area, with the aim of improving outcomes for children and young people by providing a better integrated and more responsive service. LSCBs are statutory bodies which have a duty to co-ordinate local arrangements and services to safeguard children and to ensure their effectiveness. The parties who must work together to protect children are prescribed by the CA 2004, and include local authorities, National Health Service bodies, the police, Cafcass and other agencies. Thus the Act requires local authorities to promote inter-agency co-operation (s 10); and agency organisations and individuals involved must ensure that their functions are discharged with regard to the need to safeguard and promote the welfare of children (s 11). 'Contact Point', a database on all children in England and Wales, was also set up under the Act, but it was scrapped by the new Coalition Government in April 2010.

14.3 The European Convention for the Protection of Human Rights and Child Protection

As local authorities and courts are public authorities under the Human Rights Act (HRA) 1998, they must exercise their powers and duties in compliance with the European Convention for the Protection of Human Rights and Fundamental Freedoms (ECHR) (see 1.8). The decisions of the European Court of Human Rights (ECtHR) must be taken into account by the courts (s 2(1) HRA 1998) and are also relevant to social work practice. A local authority social services department which is found to be in breach of the ECHR can be ordered to pay damages under the HRA 1998 for breach of a Convention right (s 8 HRA 1998).

(i) The right to family life   Article 8 of the ECHR guarantees a right to respect for family life. The aim of Article 8 is to protect individuals against arbitrary action by public authorities. There are also positive obligations inherent in 'respect' for family life. Local authorities must ensure that any interference in family life is lawful, proportionate and necessary, otherwise they risk breaching Article 8. The presumption in favour of keeping children in their families, unless contrary to their best interests, is recognised by the ECtHR. For example, in *Haase v Germany (Application No. 11057/02)* [2004] 2 FLR 39 the ECtHR held that:

▶ authorities should make a careful assessment of the impact of proposed care measures on parents and children, and of the alternatives to taking children into public care;

▶ following a removal into care, a stricter scrutiny is called for in respect of any further limitations by the authorities, for example in respect of restrictions on parental rights and access;

▶ taking a child into care should normally be regarded as a temporary measure to be discontinued as soon as circumstances permit, and any measures of implementation of temporary care should be consistent with the ultimate aim of reuniting the child with the natural parent;

▶ taking a newborn baby into public care at the moment of its birth is an extremely harsh measure, for which there must be extraordinarily compelling reasons.

In *Hokkanen v Finland* (1995) 19 EHRR 139, [1996] 1 FLR 289 the ECtHR held that a 'fair balance has to be struck between the interests of the child in remaining in public care and those of the parent in being reunited with the child', but that in carrying out the balancing exercise 'the best interests of the child ... may override those of the parent'. The ECtHR has held that public authorities must aim to seek to restore the child to his or her family as soon as is practicable; and that any measure which hinders this (such as prohibiting contact or placing the child a long way away) may violate Article 8 (see, for example, *KA v Finland* [2003] 1 FLR 696).

However, each case depends on its facts. In *Johansen v Norway* (1997) 23 EHRR 33 the ECtHR held that the mother's right to family life had been breached (because she had been deprived of her parental and access rights when her daughter had been taken into care and placed with foster-parents with a view to adoption); but in *Söderbäck v Sweden* [1999] 1 FLR 250 the ECtHR distinguished *Johansen* on its facts and found no breach of Article 8.

(ii) Newborn babies Taking a newborn baby into care may violate Article 8 (see *K and T v Finland*(2001) 36 EHRR 255, [2001] 2 FLR 707; and *P, C and S v* UK (2002) 35 EHRR 31, [2002] 2 FLR 631). But, as each case depends on its facts and the welfare of the child always prevails, the court may hold that such intervention is in the child's best interests. Thus, in *Re M (Care Proceedings: Judicial Review)* [2003] EWHC 850 (Admin), [2003] 2 FLR 171 (where the parents sought an injunction to restrain the local authority from commencing emergency protection or care proceedings in respect of their unborn child) Munby J held, dismissing the application, that, although the ECtHR had made it clear that removing a child from his mother at or very shortly after birth was a draconian measure requiring exceptional justification, there are cases where the need for such highly intrusive intervention is imperatively demanded in a baby's interests.

In *Re D (Unborn Baby)* [2009] EWHC 446 (Fam), [2009] 2 FLR 313 Munby J held that the local authority would not be acting unlawfully by removing the child from the mother at birth, despite the mother's right to family life under Article 8. In the highly unusual circumstances of the case (the mother had attempted to kill her other child), Munby J held that the very exceptional step of not engaging the parents fully and frankly in the pre-birth planning process was entirely justified. Munby J applied the approach adopted in *Venema v Netherlands(Application No 35731/97)* [2003] 1 FLR 552 (and in *Haase v Germany (Application No 11057/02)* [2004] 2 FLR 39), where the ECtHR held that it would not be a breach of the Convention to remove a newborn baby provided the public authority had considered all the circumstances of the case and there had been a careful assessment of the impact of the proposed care measure on the parents and child, and possible alternatives had been considered.

(iii) The right to family life – the principle of proportionality An important principle applicable to the Article 8 right to family life is that of proportionality. In other words, local authorities and the courts must ensure that any intervention into family life, by court order or otherwise, is a proportionate response to a legitimate aim, for otherwise they risk being in breach of Article 8. For example, it might be a disproportionate response for a local authority to apply to take a child into care before it has exhausted its support

obligations, or to remove a child without giving the parent(s) an opportunity to improve their parenting skills.

The following two cases provide examples of the principle of proportionality being applied. In the first case, the local authority's response had been disproportionate in the circumstances, whereas in the second case it had not.

▶ *Re C and B (Care Order: Future Harm)* [2001] 1 FLR 611

The Court of Appeal, allowing the appeal, held that full care orders in respect of two children (and permission for the local authority to refuse parental contact) was not a proportionate response in the circumstances. The local authority should have taken time to explore other options. There had been too much speed in the circumstances. Hale LJ, referring to the jurisprudence of the ECtHR on the need for interference to be necessary and proportionate to the legitimate aim, held that, while intervention in the family can be appropriate, cutting off contact and a relationship between a child and his family is only justified by the overriding necessity of the child's best interests.

▶ *Re W (Removal into Care)* [2005] EWCA Civ 642, [2005] 2 FLR 1022

Care orders were made in respect of 5-year-old twins on the basis of a care plan whereby they would remain at home with their parents. As this did not work well, a decision was taken to remove them from their home, and the local authority applied to free them for adoption. The parents, in response, applied to discharge the care orders and sought an injunction under section 8 of the HRA 1998 to enable the twins to return. Their applications failed. The judge held that there had been no breach of section 8, as the local authority's response was a proportionate and legitimate response to the deterioration of the home situation. The decision was upheld by the Court of Appeal.

(iv) Procedural fairness and human rights Procedural fairness is required at all stages of the child protection process, otherwise a local authority or the court may be in breach of the ECHR and the HRA 1998. Procedural fairness is required under Article 6 (the right to a fair trial) and Article 8 (the right to family life). A breach of procedural fairness could include, for instance, failing to involve parents sufficiently in the decision-making process, failing to conduct appropriate enquiries, or failing to give reasons for a decision. Local authorities engaged in child protection may infringe the rights of parents and children under Articles 6 and 8 of the ECHR 'unless overall they conduct themselves with such integrity, transparency and inclusiveness as to satisfy the parents' rights, necessarily to be construed in a wide sense, to a fair hearing and to respect for their private and family life' (*per* Wilson LJ in *Re J (Care: Assessment: Fair Trial)* [2006] EWCA Civ 545, [2007] 1 FLR 77).

Procedural fairness was considered in the following cases:

▶ *Re L (Care: Assessment: Fair Trial)* [2002] EWHC 1379 (Fam), [2002] 2 FLR 730

The mother, whose child was the subject of care proceedings, was not permitted to attend meetings between the local authority, the psychiatrist and the guardian when concerns about her parenting were expressed. No minutes of the meeting were taken and the mother was not informed of the outcome. Munby J held that the right to procedural fairness under Article 6 ECHR was not confined to the judicial process, but to all stages of the process, both in and out of court. Munby J emphasised certain principles of good social work practice. Social workers must notify parents of material criticisms, and advise them how to remedy their behaviour. All professionals involved should keep clear, accurate and full notes and the local authority should make full and frank disclosure of all key documents at an early stage of proceedings. They should provide reports; and parents should be able to make representations, and have the right to attend meetings held by the professionals involved.

▶ *P, C and S v UK* (2002) 35 EHRR 31, [2002] 2 FLR 631

The ECtHR held that the removal of the baby at birth under an emergency protection order breached the parents' right to family life under Article 8 ECHR and their right to a fair trial under Article 6 ECHR, as they did not have legal representation in the care and freeing for adoption proceedings. The child's right to family life was also held to be breached even though she was represented in the proceedings. The ECtHR stressed that emergency measures to remove a child from a situation of danger must be properly justified by the circumstances, and parents must have procedural protection, as part of the right to family life under Article 8, not just under Article 6.

▶ *Re J (Care: Assessment: Fair Trial)* [2006] EWCA Civ 545, [2007] 1 FLR 77

The Court of Appeal held that the way in which the local authority had reached its decision and communicated its care plan had fallen short of the proper standard of fairness and transparency expected of a local authority in care proceedings (because, *inter alia*, the mother had not been invited to comment on the concerns that were inclining the local authority towards adoption rather than a residential assessment). However, the Court of Appeal held that, while the local authority's conduct lacked fairness and transparency, it was not sufficiently substantial to constitute an infringement of the mother's rights under Article 6 or Article 8 ECHR.

▶ *G v N County Council* [2009] 1 FLR 774

The local authority removed the child from the mother after a statutory review which the mother did not attend. She was successful in obtaining a declaration under the HRA 1998 that the local authority had acted unlawfully in breaching her substantive and procedural rights under Article 8 ECHR, and also those of the child. McFarlane J held *inter alia* that the action taken by the local authority had not been proportionate or procedurally fair, and had failed to involve the mother in the process at all.

The ECtHR has held that parents must have access to the information which the local authority relies on for taking measures of protective care (*Venema v The Netherlands (Application No. 35731/97)* [2003] 1 FLR 552). It has also held that a care order must be capable of convincing an objective observer that it is based on a careful and unprejudiced assessment of all the evidence with the distinct reasons for the care measures being explicitly stated, and with all the case material being available to the parents concerned, even if they have not requested it (*KA v Finland* [2003] 1 FLR 696; and see also *K and T v Finland* (2001) 36 EHRR 255, [2001] 2 FLR 707).

(v) Procedure for human rights claims A complaint arising under the HRA 1998 before a final care order is made should normally be made in the care proceedings by the court dealing with those proceedings (*per* Sir Mark Potter P in *Westminster City Council v RA, B and S* [2005] EWHC 970 (Fam), [2005] 2 FLR 1309). In *Re S and W (Care Proceedings)* [2007] EWCA Civ 232, [2007] 2 FLR 275 Wall LJ endorsed this approach and said that 'it would be wholly undesirable to have separate proceedings for a care or supervision order under Part IV of the Children Act 1989 running concurrently with proceedings for judicial review'.

14.4 The UN Convention on the Rights of the Child 1989 and child protection

The UN Convention on the Rights of the Child 1989 (the UNCRC) (see 8.2) contains various articles which are relevant to child protection. The courts in England and Wales and the European Court of Human Rights sometimes refer to the UNCRC when making decisions about children and families. Under the UNCRC, States Parties must:

▶ take all measures to protect children from all forms of abuse while in the care of their parents, guardians and any other person (Art 19);
▶ ensure the child such protection and care as are necessary for the child's well-being, taking into account the rights and duties of his or her parents or others with parental responsibility, and to this end take all appropriate legislative and administrative measures (Art 3(2));
▶ ensure that a child shall not be separated from his or her parents against their will, except when competent authorities subject to judicial review determine that such separation is necessary for the best interests of the child; and all interested parties must be given an opportunity to participate in the proceedings and make their views known (Art 9(1)).

Other articles are also relevant, for example Article 34 (right to be protected from sexual exploitation and abuse) and Article 40(4) (right to care, guidance, supervision, counselling and foster-care).

14.5 The Children Act 1989

The Children Act 1989 is the key Act governing the duties and powers of the courts and of local authorities to take steps to protect children and to provide for children in need. Local authorities have powers and duties: to provide support for children in need under Part III; to seek care and supervision orders under Part IV; and to apply for emergency protection orders and child assessment orders under Part V. Local authorities also have investigative powers and duties (under s 47).

(a) The policy objectives of the Children Act 1989

The practice of child protection under the Children Act 1989 is based on the following policy objectives:

(i) Keeping children in their families A major policy objective is that parents, not local authorities, have primary responsibility for children and that children should be kept in their families unless this is contrary to their best interests. Social services and the courts must carry out their functions on the basis of the presumption that intervention in family life is a serious matter and is only justified where it is a legitimate, necessary and proportionate response in the circumstances. The presumption in favour of keeping children in their families is also recognised by the European Court of Human Rights (see 14.3 above).

Wall LJ in *Re L and H (Residential Assessment)* [2007] EWCA Civ 213, [2007] 1 FLR 1370 held that the following words of Lord Templeman in *Re KD (A Minor) (Ward: Termination of Access)* [1988] AC 806, [1988] 2 FLR 139 underlie the Children Act 1989:

'The best person to bring up a child is the natural parent. It matters not whether the parent is wise or foolish, rich or poor, educated or illiterate, provided the child's moral and physical health are not endangered. Public authorities cannot improve on nature. Public authorities exercise a supervisory role and interfere to rescue a child when the parental tie is broken by abuse or separation.'

Thus, even if the parents have learning difficulties or intellectual deficits, that of itself is unlikely to result in a child being removed from their care. In *Re L (Children) (Care Proceedings: Significant Harm)* [2006] EWCA Civ 1282, [2007] 1 FLR 1068 the Court of Appeal held that the courts did not, nor ever should, remove children from their parents on the basis that substitute parents would provide a greater intellectual stimulus. Such social engineering was wholly impermissible. The parental presumption was applied, for instance, in *Re D (Care: Natural Parent Presumption)* [1999] 1 FLR 134, where it was held that the child, who was subject to a care order, should be placed with his father rather than his grandmother (even though this would separate him from his siblings). It was also applied in the following case:

> ▶ **Re H (Care Order: Contact) [2008] EWCA Civ 1245, [2009] 2 FLR 55**
>
> The Court of Appeal allowed the appeal against a care order in respect of a 10-year-old child because, not only had the trial judge failed to consider the child's wishes in the light of her age and understanding, but, more importantly, the judge had erred in failing to perpetuate the fundamental importance of a relationship and life with a parent if at all possible. The child had expressed a strong desire to be reunited with her mother with whom she had a strong relationship. The Court of Appeal ordered that the care order be replaced with a residence order in favour of the mother, but with a supervision order to last for 12 months.

The Children Act reinforces the policy of keeping children in their families, where possible, in the following ways:

- ▶ Under section 1(5) the court can make an order (for example, a care or supervision order) only if 'it considers that doing so would be better for the child than making no order at all'.
- ▶ Rules and regulations governing social work practice require local authorities to work in partnership with parents to promote and safeguard the welfare of children in order to prevent them being taken into care.
- ▶ Removing a child from his parents is a serious matter, which can only be effected by a court order and only on proof that the child is suffering, or is likely to suffer, significant harm; and only after a thorough investigation and consideration of all the evidence. The only exception where no prior judicial authority is needed is where a police officer can remove a child in certain circumstances (see pp. 402–3).

The need for a court order before a child can lawfully be removed from a parent was shown in the following case:

> ▶ **R (G) v Nottingham City Council [2008] EWHC 152 (Admin), [2008] 1 FLR 1660**
>
> Two days after his birth the child had been removed from his mother (who was aged 18, had been in care and had a history of alcohol and drug abuse and self-harm). No court orders had been passed to the medical team involved in the birth. In judicial review proceedings brought

by the mother Munby J made an order that the baby be reunited with his mother, on the ground that removing a child requires prior judicial authorisation. Munby J held that the only time a social worker can intervene without a court order is where it is necessary to protect a baby from immediate violence at the hands of a parent or other person.

Note: After the baby had been returned to the mother, an interim care order was made later that day (which was upheld by the Court of Appeal). The baby was placed in foster-care with the mother having supervised contact; but, as this proved unsatisfactory, an order for no contact for a limited period was subsequently made.

(ii) Working in partnership with parents In order to promote the presumption that children should be kept in their families, local authorities are required to work in partnership with parents and to involve them as fully as possible. The guidance, *Working Together to Safeguard Children*, establishes two key policy objectives governing good social work practice: the importance of inter-agency co-operation; and the importance of encouraging partnership and participation with parents. Families are encouraged to participate in the decision-making process. A failure to involve parents and children sufficiently in the process, without good reason, may breach the ECHR.

(iii) Inter-agency co-operation Another policy aim of the Children Act 1989, and of the Children Act 2004, is that of inter-agency co-operation, whereby the various agencies (for example, social services, local education authorities and health authorities) must consult with each other and be willing to provide help if this is in the best interests of a child . As part of this emphasis on inter-agency co-operation, section 27 CA 1989 provides that local authorities, local education authorities, local housing authorities and local health authorities (or National Health Service Trusts) have a right to request help from each other and have a reciprocal duty to provide it, except where this is incompatible with their own statutory obligations. Under section 27, for example, a social services department could ask a local housing department to provide accommodation for a child leaving care. The importance of communication and information sharing about children was emphasised in both the *Cleveland Report* (see p. 366 above) and the *Laming Report on the Victoria Climbié Inquiry* (Cm 5730). The findings of the *Laming Report* led to the enactment of the Children Act 2004, in which a greater emphasis is placed on inter-agency co-operation (see 14.2).

(b) Local authority powers and duties under the Children Act 1989 – an overview

Local authorities have a wide range of powers and duties under the Children Act 1989. They have a duty to make such inquiries as are necessary to enable them to decide whether to take any action to safeguard or promote the welfare of the child (see s 47). Furthermore, if in any family proceedings (for example residence or contact proceedings) a question arises with respect to the child's welfare, and the court considers it may be appropriate for a care or supervision order to be made, it can order that a local authority investigate the child's circumstances (s 37). If, however, access to the child is thwarted or the local authority has concerns about the child's safety, it can consider applying for an emergency protection order (s 44) or asking the police to intervene (s 46).

If, following initial inquiries, the child is assessed as not being at risk of significant harm, then local authority social services will have to decide whether or not the child and family need support under Part III of the Children Act 1989. If, on the other hand, the child is, or is at risk of, suffering significant harm, then the local authority will have to consider taking steps to protect the child, such as emergency protection measures under Part V of the Children Act 1989 (see 14.9) or care and supervision proceedings under Part IV (see 14.7).

14.6 Part III of the Children Act 1989 – support for children in need

(a) Introduction

Under Part III of the Children Act 1989 local authorities have a duty to provide support for children in need and their families. 'Family' for this purpose includes not just parents and children, but any person with parental responsibility or any other person with whom the child is living (s 17(10)). Services can only be provided, however, with a view to safeguarding or promoting the welfare of a child in need (s 17(3)). Part III duties include the provision of services (ss 17–19) and the provision of accommodation (ss 20 and 21). Local authorities have duties to children 'looked after' by them (ss 22 and 23) and must provide advice and assistance (s 24); and in some cases secure accommodation (s 25). They must hold case reviews, co-operate with each other and consult with and request help from other authorities within the local area (such as housing, local education and health authorities)), and provide advocacy services (see ss 26–30). Schedule 2 to the Children Act lists the services which local authorities can provide for children in need and their families.

The provision of support under Part III may obviate the need to bring care or supervision proceedings. Help and support for children in their home is the preferred option, with compulsory intervention by court order being the last resort. However, although the Children Act 1989 lays down a duty to safeguard and promote the welfare of children, the provision of services is a discretionary matter and is dependent on the allocation and availability of resources, which are often limited. For these reasons, it may be difficult to bring a successful legal challenge against a local authority for failing to make provision under Part III of the Act.

Local authorities have various duties to children in need under Part III, which include the duty to:

▶ safeguard and promote the child's welfare (s 22(3));
▶ consult the wishes and feelings of the child, his or her parents, any person who has parental responsibility for the child, and any other relevant person (s 22(4));
▶ provide accommodation and maintenance for a child (s 23(2));
▶ maintain the child in other respects apart from providing accommodation (s 23(1)(b));
▶ promote contact (Sched 2, para. 4);
▶ provide 'after care' for children who leave care (s 24(1)).

(b) Who is a 'child in need'?

A child is a 'child in need' for the purposes of Part III if (s 17(10)):

'(a) he is unlikely to achieve or maintain, or to have the opportunity of achieving or maintaining, a reasonable standard of health or development without the provision of services by a local authority under [Part III];

(b) his health or development is likely to be significantly impaired, or further impaired, without the provision for him of such services; or

(c) he is disabled.'

A child is 'disabled' if he is blind, deaf or dumb or suffers from mental disorder of any kind or is substantially and permanently handicapped by illness, injury or congenital deformity or such other disability as may be prescribed; 'development' means physical, intellectual, emotional, social or behavioural development; and 'health' means physical or mental health (s 17(11)).

(c) The Part III general duty

The general duty of local authorities to children in need is laid down in section 17(1):

Section 17(1) of the Children Act 1989

'It shall be the general duty of every local authority, in addition to the other duties imposed on them by [Part III]:

(a) to safeguard and promote the welfare of children within their area who are in need; and

(b) so far as is consistent with that duty, to promote the upbringing of such children by their families, by providing a range and level of services appropriate to those children's needs.'

The scope of the general duty in section 17(1) was considered by the House of Lords in the following case in which all three appeals raised the question of whether social services departments were under a duty to provide accommodation for children in need and their families under the Children Act 1989 when local housing authorities were not able to house or rehouse them:

▶ *R (G) v Barnet London Borough Council; R (W) v Lambeth London Borough Council; R (A) v Lambeth London Borough Council* [2003] UKHL 57, [2004] 1 FLR 454

In each appeal, a mother argued that section 17(1) required a local authority to assess and meet the needs of a particular individual child in need. As one of the local authorities had adopted a policy of providing accommodation for children in need, but not their parents, the House of Lords had to consider two questions: did section 17(1) create a duty to consider and assess the needs of a particular child; and could a local authority meet a child's needs for accommodation by providing accommodation for the child alone, not for both mother and child, when it would cost no more to provide accommodation for them both?

The House of Lords held, dismissing all three appeals, that section 17(1) sets out duties of a general character which are intended to be for the benefit of all the children in need in the local social services authority's area in general, and not for each and every individual child in need. As a result, a local social services authority was not under a duty to provide accommodation for families so that children could be housed with their families. Although social services could provide accommodation for a child in need and his family, this was not the principal or primary purpose of the legislation. Housing was the function of the local housing authority. An obligation under section 17(1) to provide housing would turn social services departments into housing authorities and thereby subvert the powers and duties of housing authorities under the housing legislation.

(d) Services for children in need

The general duty of local authorities laid down in section 17(1) above is facilitated by the performance of specific duties and powers laid down in Part I of Schedule 2 to the Act (s 17(2)), which include, for example: the identification and assessment of children in need; advertising available services; keeping a register of and providing services for disabled children; preventing neglect and abuse; providing accommodation for those who are ill-treating or are likely to ill-treat children, in order to reduce the need for criminal or civil proceedings; reintegrating children in need with their families; and promoting contact between a child and his family. The services provided under section 17 may include the provision of accommodation and giving assistance in kind or in cash (s 17(10)). Local authorities have a duty under section 20 (see below) to provide accommodation for children in need and their families; and a duty to provide day care for certain children (s 18).

Before determining what (if any) services to provide for a particular child in need, a local authority must, so far as is reasonably practicable and consistent with the child's welfare, ascertain the child's wishes and feelings regarding the provision of those services, and give due consideration to those wishes and feelings, having regard to the child's age and understanding (s 17(4A)).

(e) Children in need – the provision of accommodation

(i) The duty to provide accommodation As part of their general duty to safeguard and promote the welfare of children in their area, local authorities have a duty under the Children Act 1989 (ss 20–25) to provide accommodation for children in need and their families. The duty to provide children in need with accommodation is laid down in s 20(1).

Section 20(1) of the Children Act 1989

'Every local authority shall provide accommodation for any child in need within their area who appears to them to require accommodation as a result of –

(a) there being no person who has parental responsibility for him...;
(b) his being lost or having been abandoned; or
(c) the person who has been caring for him being prevented (whether or not permanently, and for whatever reason) from providing him with suitable accommodation or care.'

Before providing accommodation, the local authority must, so far as is reasonably practicable and consistent with the child's welfare, ascertain the child's wishes and feelings regarding the provision of accommodation; and give due consideration to those wishes and feelings (having regard to the child's age and understanding) (s 20(6)). However, the child's wishes are not necessarily determinative (see *Liverpool City Council v Hillingdon London Borough Council and AK* [2009] EWCA Civ 43, [2009] 1 FLR 1536). The local authority must also draw up a written care plan for the child. A child who is accommodated is described as being 'looked after' by the local authority, whereupon the local authority has certain statutory duties with respect to the child (ss 23–30). Children who are in care under a court order are also described as being 'looked after' and similar duties are owed to them under the same provisions.

Accommodation can be provided by the local authority by placing the child with another family, with a relative, with some other suitable person, or in a children's home (s 23(2)). Any family member, relative and any other person providing accommodation for a child is described as being a local authority foster-parent (s 23(3)).

Accommodation must also be provided for a child aged 16 or over if a local authority considers the child's welfare is likely to be seriously prejudiced without it (s 20(3)). Accommodation in a community home can be provided for someone aged 16 to 21 if it will safeguard or promote his or her welfare (s 20(5)) (see, for example, *Re T (Accommodation by Local Authority)* [1995] 1 FLR 159 where the court held that the local authority had erred in refusing a 17-year-old girl accommodation as it had failed to consider her future welfare).

A local authority has no duty, however, to provide accommodation if a person with parental responsibility objects, and he or she is able to provide accommodation or arrange for it to be provided (s 20(7)). The only exception is where a person with a residence order or who has care of the child under a court order agrees to the child being accommodated by the local authority (s 20(9)). Any person with parental responsibility may remove the child from local authority accommodation at any time without giving notice (s 20(8)), except where the child is aged 16 or over and agrees to being provided with accommodation (s 20(1)). As the arrangement is voluntary the local authority must comply with the wishes of persons with parental responsibility, unless the child is suffering, or is likely to suffer, significant harm, in which case a care or supervision order or an emergency protection order will be applied for. As the right to decide where the child lives remains with the parents, it has been held that the local authority has no power to remove a child to different accommodation if this is contrary to parental wishes (see *R v Tameside Metropolitan Borough Council ex parte J* [2000] 1 FLR 942 where it was held that the local authority had no power to move a seriously disabled 13-year-old girl from a residential home into foster-care, as this was contrary to her parents' wishes).

The extent of the duty to provide children in need with accommodation as part of the general duty under section 17 of the Children Act 1989 was considered by the House of Lords in *R (G) v Barnet London Borough Council and Related Appeals* (2003) (see p. 375 above).

(ii) Providing teenage children with accommodation   Local authority social services and local authority housing departments are required to co-operate with each other about the provision of accommodation (ss 27 and 47 CA 1989; and s 213A Housing Act 1996). However, the interface between the Children Act 1989 and the housing legislation can sometimes cause difficulties which may result in challenges by way of judicial review. The *Homelessness Code of Guidance for Local Authorities* (2002) advises that, once it appears to a local housing department that a 16- or 17-year-old child may be homeless, then it must accommodate the child under section 188 HA 1996 pending clarification of whether the local children's services authority owes a duty to provide the child with accommodation under section 20 CA 1989. If the criteria in section 20 are met, then the local authority social services department, not the local housing authority, is responsible for assessing the child.

The House of Lords in *R(M) v Hammersmith and Fulham London Borough Council* [2008] UKHL 14, [2008] 1 FLR 1384 held that a social services department cannot shirk its responsibility for a child under section 20 CA 1989 by passing that responsibility over to the local housing authority; and that, if the criteria in section 20 (see above) are met, then social services, rather than the housing department, should take responsibility, because the young person would have needs over and above their housing needs that could be better met by social services. However, in *R(M)* the applicant (an 18-year-old girl) was unsuccessful in obtaining a declaration that the local authority owed her duties under the Children Act, not the Housing Act, as the House of Lords held that a 'looked after' child under section 22(1) CA 1989 did not include a child who had been provided with accommodation by the local housing authority, but who had not been drawn to the attention of the children's services department or provided with any accommodation or any other services by the social services authority.

R(M) was applied in *R(W) v North Lincolnshire Council* [2008] EWHC 2299 (Admin) [2008] 2 FLR 2150 where a boy aged under 18 successfully challenged the local authority's decision that it would not accommodate him under section 20 CA 1989 on his release from a young offenders' institution. The judge held, referring to *R(M)*, that he was an eligible child under section 20 as he had been accommodated and supported by the local authority's social services department at various times before he was 16.

The duty to provide accommodation under section 20 and the power to provide it under section 17(6) were also considered in the case of *R (G) v Southwark London Borough Council* [2009] UKHL 26, [2009] 2 FLR 380, below, where the House of Lords held that a local authority's children's services unit cannot purport to have fulfilled its duties to a homeless child merely by referring the case to the local housing authority under Part VII of the Housing Act 1996 (see 4.11). The case dealt with the construction of section 20(1) CA 1989. In other words, was the local authority entitled to distinguish between 'requiring accommodation' and requiring 'help with accommodation'? Baroness Hale stated that the question for the House of Lords was: if a child aged 16 or 17, who is thrown out of the family home, presents himself to a local children's services authority and asks to be accommodated under section 20 CA 1989, is it open to the authority to arrange instead for him to be accommodated by the local housing authority under the homelessness provisions of Part VII of the Housing Act 1996?

▶ *R (G) v Southwark London Borough Council* **[2009] UKHL 26, [2009] 2 FLR 380**

A 17-year-old young man who could genuinely not continue living with his mother applied to the local authority's social services department requesting accommodation under section 20 CA 1989 and an assessment under section 17 CA 1989. Despite his claim that he should be accommodated under section 20(1)(c) (which would entitle him to the wide range of services available to him as a 'looked after child' until he was 21 (see s 22(1)), and would mean that he would thereafter qualify as a 'former relevant child'), the local authority said that he did not need accommodation under section 20 but only '*help* with accommodation' under section 17. The Court of Appeal, by a majority, dismissed his appeal, holding that the distinction made in the relevant *Circular* (between a child who required help with accommodation under section 17 and one requiring accommodation under section 20) was lawful, even though the distinction was not expressly drawn in the Children Act 1989. The local authority had therefore been entitled to decide in the circumstances that the applicant only needed help with accommodation, and to refer him to the housing department. He appealed to the House of Lords.

The House of Lords held, allowing his appeal, that he should have been provided with care by his local authority under the Children Act 1989 and not just provided with accommodation by the homeless persons unit under Part VII of the Housing Act 1996. Parliament had decided the circumstances in which the duty to accommodate arose, and then decided what the duty involved. It was not for the local authority to decide that, because they did not like what the duty to accommodate involved or did not think it appropriate, that they did not have to accommodate at all. The local authority was not entitled to 'side-step' the duty under section 20(1) CA 1989 by giving the accommodation a different label.

Section 27 CA 1989 Act empowered a children's authority to ask other authorities (including any local housing authority) for 'help in the exercise of any of their functions' under Part III; and the requested authority had to provide that help if it was compatible with its own statutory or other duties and did not unduly prejudice the discharge of any of its own functions. A local children's authority could not use section 27 to avoid its responsibilities by 'passing the buck' to another authority; but could ask another authority to use its powers to help the children's authority discharge theirs (for example a children's authority could ask a housing authority to make a certain amount of suitable accommodation available for it to use in discharging its responsibility to accommodate children under section 20). The great flexibility provided by section 23(2) CA 1989 as to the ways in which accommodation could be provided for children being looked after by an authority, which included the power to make 'such other arrangements as ... seem appropriate to them', supported the court's construction of section 20(1).

Is the child under the age of 18? The duty to provide accommodation, except where a child is leaving care (see below) is owed to children and young people under the age of 18. There are many cases where age is disputed, particularly in respect of persons arriving in the UK unaccompanied. In *R (A) v Croydon London Borough Council; R (M) v Lambeth London Borough Council* [2009] UKSC 8, [2010] 1 FLR 959 (which involved whether two unaccompanied asylum seekers were under the age of 18), the Supreme Court held that, where social workers disputed a person's claim to be under the age of 18 for the purposes of section 20(1), the question of age was an objective fact which, in the event of a challenge, was to be determined by the court, not by social workers as the lower courts had held.

(iii) Providing accommodation for persons leaving care If a child has been looked after by a local authority for more than a prescribed period of 13 weeks when he or she attains the age of 18, then at that date that person becomes a 'former relevant child' in respect of whom the local authority has a range of powers and duties under the leaving care provisions, which include the provision of accommodation until the age of 21 or, in some cases, until the age of 24 or until that person has finished full-time further or higher education (see ss 24A and 24B CA 1989).

14.7 Part IV of the Children Act 1989 – care and supervision

(a) Introduction

Voluntary arrangements provided under Part III of the Children Act 1989 may not work in some cases; or it may come to the notice of a local authority that a child is suffering, or is at risk of suffering, harm. In such circumstances a local authority social services department may have to intervene by bringing proceedings for a care or supervision order under Part IV of the Act, or by taking emergency action under Part V (see 14.9). The court has jurisdiction to hear an application for a care or supervision order if the child is habitually resident, or resident, in England and Wales (ss 1 and 3 Family Law Act 1986), and the child is aged under 17 (s 31(3) CA 1989).

Although the National Society for the Prevention of Cruelty to Children (NSPCC) has standing to apply for a care or supervision order (s 31(9)), in practice applications are brought by local authority social workers who have a statutory responsibility to protect children and a duty to investigate cases where a child is suffering, or is at risk of suffering, significant harm (ss 37 and 47).

(i) Care order or supervision order? Although the same threshold criteria apply to care and supervision orders (see pp. 383–5 below), the orders are completely different in that a care order places the child in the care of a local authority whereas a supervision order places the child under the supervision a local authority or a probation officer.

As a care order is a more draconian order than a supervision order (because the child may be removed from his or her home and possibly placed for adoption), there must be cogent and strong reasons to make a care order rather than a supervision order (*per* Hale J in *Oxfordshire County Council v L (Care or Supervision Order)* [1998] 1 FLR 70). Making a care order where a supervision order would be sufficient to protect a child might also be a breach of human rights (see below).

In *Re T (Care Order)* [2009] EWCA Civ 121, [2009] 2 FLR 574 the Court of Appeal said that there were two main reasons for making a care order rather than a supervision order: that the local authority needed the power not only to remove the child instantly but also to plan for long-term placement outside the family without prior judicial sanction; or that it was necessary for the local authority to share parental responsibility with the parents. On the facts, the Court of Appeal in *Re T* held that: there were no strong and cogent reasons for making a care order, the more draconian of the two orders; and that, applying human rights considerations, it was preferable to make a supervision order as this was a sufficient and proportionate response in the circumstances.

As care and supervision proceedings under Part IV of the Children 1989 are 'family proceedings' for the purposes of the Children Act 1989 (s 8(3)), the court can make a section 8 order (for instance a residence or contact order, see 10.4) instead of a care or supervision order, either on an application or of its own motion.

The court has no power to compel a local authority to institute care or supervision proceedings. All it can do is make a direction under section 37 of the Children Act 1989 that the local authority investigate the child's circumstances.

(ii) Human rights and care and supervision orders A care order must be a proportionate and legitimate response to the circumstances of the case, for otherwise a local authority may be in breach of the European Convention for the Protection of Human Rights and the Human Rights Act 1998. Thus, for example, making a care order where a supervision order would be adequate to protect the child might offend the principle of proportionality and be a breach of the right to family life under Article 8 ECHR.

In *Re W (Children) (Care: Interference With Family Life)* [2005] EWCA Civ 642, [2005] 2 FLR 1022 Thorpe LJ stated that, whenever a local authority took any step as draconian as the removal of a child, the local authority must have 'due regard to the parents' European Convention rights and the Convention rights of the children' and removal 'was only lawful if it could be justified on both the heads of legality and proportionality'. In *Re T (Care Order)* (see above) the Court of Appeal reiterated the rule that human rights considerations required the court to make the less draconian supervision order rather than the more draconian care order, unless the child's welfare required a care order to be made; and a care order, rather than a supervision order, was a sufficient and proportionate response to the risk presented to the child.

The European Court of Human Rights has held as a guiding principle that a care order should be regarded as a temporary measure to be discontinued as soon as circumstances permit, and that any measures implementing temporary care should be consistent with the ultimate aim of reuniting the natural parent and the child (see *Olsson v Sweden (No. 1)* (1988) 11 EHRR 259). However, this principle is subject to the best interests of the child. The ECtHR has also held that, whereas authorities enjoy a wide 'margin of appreciation' in assessing the necessity of taking a child into public care, a stricter scrutiny is required in respect of any further limitations, including restrictions placed on parental rights of access (*K and T v Finland* (2001) 36 EHRR 255, [2001] 2 FLR 707; *R v Finland (Application No. 34141/96)* [2006] 2 FLR 923).

(iii) The court cannot dictate how a care order is implemented If the court makes a care order, it cannot dictate how the local authority should implement it, as to do so would circumscribe the wide discretionary powers entrusted to local authorities by Parliament. However, there are certain controls on local authorities. Thus, for example, a local authority must supply the court with a care plan containing proposals about future arrangements for the child (see pp. 390–2 below) and the court must ensure that the care plan is the best solution for the child and is human rights compliant (see *Hokkanen v Finland* (1995) EHRR 139, [1996] 1 FLR 289).

Reducing delay in care cases The Government, in response to the Family Justice Review (see p. 7), has proposed reforms to speed up care cases in order to reduce the delays which are endemic in the system. The proposals are contained in the Children and Families Bill 2012–2013 which will introduce a statutory six-month time limit for the completion of non-exceptional care cases. It also proposes to remove the requirement for interim care and supervision orders to be renewed every month by the judge and instead permit the judge to set the length and renewal requirements of interim orders for a period which the judge considers appropriate, up to the six-month time limit. The Bill had its second reading in the House of Commons in February 2013.

Government statistics According to Government statistics, the number of public law applications made by local authorities continues to increase.

> ***Judicial and Court Statistics 2011*, Ministry of Justice, 2012**
>
> 'The number of children involved in public law applications made by local authorities jumped from 19,760 in 2009 to 25,810 in 2010 following the publicity surrounding the Baby P case. Since then the numbers have increased further, and there were 29,492 children involved in public law applications in 2011; an increase of 13 per cent compared with 2010.'

(b)   Care and supervision proceedings procedure

Rules of procedure and preparation and case management for care and supervision proceedings are found in Part 12 of the Family Procedure Rules 2010 and its related practice directions (*Practice Direction 12A – Public Law Proceedings Guide to Case Management, April 2010*), available at www.justice.gov.uk. Proceedings normally commence in the magistrates' family proceedings court, but can be transferred to a county court or the High Court, or to another family proceedings court. The local authority, the child and any person with parental responsibility are automatically parties to the proceedings, but other persons can be joined as parties with leave (permission) of the court. When considering whether to grant leave, the court exercises its powers in the same way as it does in leave applications for a section 8 orders (s 10(9)). In *Re W (Care Proceedings: Leave to Apply)* [2004] EWHC 3342 (Fam), [2005] 2 FLR 468, for example, the child's aunt was refused leave to be a party to care proceedings. However, even a person who has an automatic right to participate can be barred from participating in exceptional circumstances, as the married father was in *Local Authority v M, F and M and M* [2009] EWHC 3172 (Fam), [2010] 1 FLR 1355, for, although he was in prison, he represented a real and substantial risk to the children and the mother.

An unmarried father without parental responsibility has no automatic right to be joined as a party but is entitled to notice of the proceedings and is likely to be given leave by the court to participate unless there is good reason to the contrary. A refusal to do so might breach the father's right to family life under Article 8 ECHR (see, for example, *McMichael v UK (Application No. 16424/90)* (1995) 20 EHRR 205 where the ECtHR held that a failure to allow an unmarried father without parental responsibility to participate in a Scottish children's hearing was a breach of Article 8).

The Children's Guardian   In care and supervision proceedings the child will be represented by a solicitor and a Children's Guardian (an officer of Cafcass – see 1.7), which the court must appoint unless no Guardian is needed to safeguard the child's interests (s 41(1) and r 12.6 FPR 2010). The role of the Guardian is to protect and safeguard the best interests of the child in the proceedings. In *Re S and W (Care Proceedings)* [2007] EWCA Civ 232, [2007] 2 FLR 275 Wall LJ said that 'one of the Guardian's functions is fearlessly to protect the children concerned against local authority incompetence and maladministration, as well as poor social work practice'.

The Guardian must be independent of the parties, in order to prevent a conflict of interest arising. In addition to having a general duty to safeguard the child's interests in the manner prescribed by the rules of court (s 41(2)(b)), the Guardian has specific duties which include: ascertaining the child's wishes and whether the child has sufficient understanding; investigating the circumstances; interviewing persons involved; inspecting records; and appointing professional assistance. The Guardian has a right to examine and copy local authority records relating to a child, which can be admitted in evidence (s 42), such as minutes of a child protection conference or a report compiled by an area child protection committee (*Re R (Care Proceedings: Disclosure)* [2000] 2 FLR 75). When the investigation has been completed, the Guardian must make a written report advising what should be done in the best interests of the child. The report usually has a considerable influence on the court's decision.

Children can give oral evidence in care proceedings   In *Re W (Children) (Abuse: Oral Evidence)* [2010] UKSC 12, [2010] 1 FLR 1485, which concerned the question of whether a 14-year-old girl should give oral evidence in relation to serious sexual abuse, the Supreme Court unanimously held that there was no longer a presumption or even a starting point against children giving evidence in care proceedings. Baroness Hale (who gave the leading opinion) was of the opinion that the existing presumption could not be reconciled with the ECHR, in particular Article 6 (the right to a fair trial) and Article 8 (the right to a family life). The Supreme Court held that the essential test is whether justice can be done to all the parties without questioning the child. (For a discussion of *Re W*, see Hall [2010] CFLQ 499.)

However, although children can now be called to give oral evidence in care proceedings, it is likely to be the exception rather than the rule, and will depend on a range of factors, including, in particular, the welfare of the child considered in the light of his or her age and understanding. *Guidelines in relation to children giving evidence in family proceeding*, endorsed by the former President of the Family Division, Sir Nicholas Wall, were published in December 2011 (see [2012] Fam Law 79).

The judge may meet with the child   In the last few years, it has been recognised that it is permissible for judges in family proceedings (include care and supervision proceedings) to meet with children and interview them (see *Guidelines for Judges Meeting Children Who Are Subject to Family Proceedings* [2010] Fam Law 654). In *Re A (Fact-Finding Hearing: Judge Meeting with Child)* [2012] EWCA Civ 185, [2012] 2 FLR 369 (where five children made very serious allegations regarding sexual abuse and where the 10-year-old child wished to speak to the judge) the Court of Appeal provided guidance to judges on speaking to children in family proceedings.

(c)   The 'threshold criteria'

When exercising its powers in care and supervision proceedings, the court must first be satisfied that the 'threshold criteria' in section 31(2) (see below) are established. If they are, the court must next decide whether it is in the child's best interests to make a care or supervision order, or a different order, or no order at all. When conducting the second part of the exercise, the court must apply the welfare principle (s 1(1)), the welfare checklist (s 1(3)), the 'minimum intervention principle' (s 1(5)) and the no-delay principle (s 1(2)) (see 10.3). The court must also apply the European Convention for the Protection of Human Rights as a result of its obligations under the Human Rights Act 1998 (see 1.8). Article 6 (the right to a fair trial) and Article 8 (the right to family life) are particularly important as these two articles 'affect both the test and the process for intervening in the family lives of children and their parents' (*per* Baroness Hale in *Re S-B (Children)* [2009] UKSC 17, [2010] 1 FLR 1161).

In *Re B (Children) (Sexual Abuse: Standard of Proof)* [2008] UKHL 35, [2008] 2 FLR 141 (see further at p. 387 below), Baroness Hale held that, although the court has to ask two questions ('Has the threshold been crossed?' and 'If so, what will be best for the child?'), care proceedings are not a two-stage process, because threshold issues and welfare issues can be interconnected. Baroness Hale said that the purpose of a split hearing was not to split matters into a threshold stage and a welfare stage, but 'to separate out those factual issues which are capable of swift resolution so that the welfare professionals have a firm foundation of fact upon which to base their assessments of family relationships and parenting ability'.

If the threshold criteria are established, the court is under no obligation to make a care or supervision order. Whether it will do so depends on a detailed assessment of the child's welfare in all the circumstances of the case. Thus, for example, in *Re K; A Local Authority v N and Others* [2005] EWHC 2956 (Fam), [2007] 1 FLR 399, although the threshold criteria were satisfied, Munby J refused to make a supervision order, applying the 'minimum intervention' principle in section 1(5) CA 1989. If the court decides to make a residence order, instead of a care or supervision order, it must also make an interim supervision order, unless the child's welfare is safeguarded without it (s 38(3)). The court must also consider the arrangements that the local authority has made, or proposes to make, in respect of contact (see 14.8) and invite the parties to the proceedings to comment on those arrangements (s 34(11)). Expert evidence is important and the court will also consider the recommendations of the Children's Guardian (see above).

The 'threshold criteria' are laid down in section 31(2) of the Children Act 1989.

Section 31(2) of the Children Act 1989

'A court may only make a care order or a supervision order if it is satisfied –

   (a) that the child concerned is suffering, or is likely to suffer, significant harm; and
   (b) that the harm, or likelihood of harm, is attributable to –
      (i) the care given to the child, or likely to be given to him if the order were not made, not being what it would be reasonable to expect a parent to give him; or
      (ii) the child's being beyond parental control.'

'Harm' means ill-treatment or the impairment of health or development including impairment of the child's health or development as a result of seeing or hearing the ill-treatment of another person (s 31(9)). It can therefore include, for example, seeing or hearing domestic violence. 'Development' means physical, intellectual, emotional, social or behavioural development. 'Health' means physical or mental health, and 'ill-treatment' includes sexual abuse and forms of ill-treatment which are not physical. Where the question of whether the harm is significant turns on the child's health or development, the child's health or development must be compared with that which could reasonably be expected of a similar child (s 31(10)).

(i) 'Significant' harm The word 'significant' is not defined in the Children Act 1989. Whether harm is 'significant' will depend on the circumstances of the case. The guidance, *Working Together to Safeguard Children*, however, provides social workers with guidance on what constitutes 'significant harm'.

The difference between 'harm' and 'significant' harm was considered in *Re MA (Children) (Care Proceedings: Threshold Criteria)* [2009] EWCA Civ 853, [2010] 1 FLR 431, where the Court of Appeal held that, given the underlying philosophy of the Children Act 1989, the harm must be significant enough to justify the intervention of the state and disturb the autonomy of the parents to bring up their children by themselves in the way they choose. It must be significant enough to enable the court to make a care or supervision order if the welfare of the child so demanded. The Court of Appeal held that Article 8 of the European Convention for the Protection of Human Rights also informed the meaning of 'significant'. An evaluative judgment was essential. Wall LJ acknowledged that the line between significant harm and harm was a fine one, and referred to the dictionary definition of 'significant' as 'considerable, noteworthy or important'. The Court of Appeal held that the decision on its facts could have gone either way, but that, where the balance was a fine one (as it was in the case), then it was 'a classic case for trusting the judgment of the trial judge' (*per* Hallett LJ). The Court of Appeal, by a majority, therefore upheld the decision of the trial judge not to make a care order. The decision has been strongly criticised as being wrong (for instance, by

Keating [2011] CFLQ 115; and Hayes J, Hayes M and Williams [2010] Fam Law 166). In the earlier case of *Re L (Care: Threshold Criteria)* [2007] 1 FLR 20 Hedley J held *inter alia*, dismissing the care application, that it was not the provenance of the state to spare children all the consequences of defective parenting; and that significant harm for the purposes of section 31(2) must be something unusual, and more than commonplace human failure or inadequacy.

(ii) Care and the reasonable parent (section 31(2)(b)(i))   Where the court has to consider whether the threshold criteria are satisfied by evaluating parental performance this requires an objective assessment applying the standard of the hypothetical 'reasonable' parent. In *Re K; A Local Authority v N and Others* [2005] EWHC 2956 (Fam), [2007] 1 FLR 399 Munby J said that the court 'must always be sensitive to the cultural, social and religious circumstances of the particular child and family, particularly when the parents have recently, or comparatively recently, arrived from a foreign country with different standards and expectations from those in this country'. In this case the young girl (aged 16) and her family were Kurdish Muslims from Iraq.

(iii) When must the threshold criteria be satisfied?   The date on which the threshold criteria must be satisfied is when the local authority first intervened, in other words at the date of the application or, if temporary protective arrangements (such as an emergency protection order) have continuously been in place, the date on which those arrangements were initiated (*Re M (A Minor) (Care Order: Threshold Conditions)*[1994] 2 AC 424, 1994] 2 FLR 577). However, in establishing that the threshold has been crossed at the date of intervention, the local authority can rely upon information acquired after that date; and it can also rely on later events if they are capable of proving the state of affairs at the date of intervention (*Re G (Care Proceedings: Threshold Conditions)* [2001] EWCA Civ 968, [2001] 2 FLR 1111).

(d)   The standard of proof in care and supervision proceedings

The standard of proof is of considerable importance in care and supervision proceedings. If it is set too high, then there is a danger that a child will continue to suffer significant harm. If it is set too low, then there is a danger that a child will be removed from the care of his parents when he or she has not suffered, or is not at risk of suffering, significant harm. As Ryder J stated, the problem is 'how to balance the need to protect families from any disproportionate interference by the state with the imperative to protect children against harm' ([2008] Fam Law 30).

As care and supervision proceedings are civil proceedings, the local authority must prove the facts alleged (the threshold criteria) on the balance of probabilities. The test is whether, on the evidence, it is more likely than not that the facts took place. There have been several cases in the House of Lords and the Supreme Court which have considered the standard of proof in care and supervision proceedings. The first of these was *Re H and Others (Minors) (Sexual Abuse: Standard of Proof)* (see below), which was a case about whether there was a *future* risk to the other children in the family after the eldest daughter had alleged she had been sexually abused by the mother's cohabitant.

> ▶ *Re H and Others (Minors) (Sexual Abuse: Standard of Proof)* [1996] AC 563, *sub nom*
> *Re H and R (Child Sexual Abuse: Standard of Proof)* [1996] 1 FLR 80
>
> The local authority applied for care orders in respect of three girls (aged 13, 8 and 2) after
> the eldest daughter (aged 14) had alleged that she had been sexually abused by her mother's
> cohabitant. He had been charged with rape but acquitted. The applications for care orders
> were dismissed at first instance and by the Court of Appeal, as the threshold conditions in
> section 31(2) were not satisfied, as it could not be established to the requisite high standard of
> proof that the 14-year-old daughter's allegations were true. The local authority appealed to
> the House of Lords.
>
> The House of Lords held by a majority, dismissing the local authority's appeal, that
> the standard of proof in care proceedings was the ordinary civil standard of balance of
> probability, but that the more improbable the event, the stronger the evidence had to be
> before, on the balance of probability, the occurrence of the event would be established. Lord
> Nicholls said that a conclusion that a child is suffering, or is likely to suffer, harm 'must be
> based on facts, not just suspicion'. The House of Lords unanimously rejected, however, a
> submission that 'likely' in the phrase 'likely to suffer harm' meant probable, but held that
> 'likely' meant likely in the sense of a real possibility, a possibility that could not sensibly be
> ignored having regard to the nature and gravity of the feared harm in the particular case.

Some commentators were critical of the decision of the majority in *Re H* because, for
instance, it created a complicated standard of proof for allegations of serious abuse.
Hemingway and Williams (1997) described the reasoning as flawed, and said that
the decision would create a real danger that some children would not be afforded the
protection they deserved.

In the later case of *Re S-B (Children)* [2009] UKSC 17, [2010] 1 FLR 1161 (see further
at pp. 389–90 below) Baroness Hale said that, when establishing whether the threshold
criteria are established, 'the law has drawn a clear distinction between probability as
it applies to past facts and probability as it applies to future predictions'. In *Re S-B* her
Ladyship stated:

> 'Past facts must be proved to have happened on the balance of probabilities, that is, that it is
> more likely than not that they did happen. Predictions about future facts need only be based
> upon the degree of likelihood that they will happen which is sufficient to justify preventive
> action. This will depend upon the nature and gravity of the harm: a lesser degree of likelihood
> that the child will be killed will justify immediate preventive action than the degree of
> likelihood that the child will not be sent to school.'

The leading case on the standard of proof of past facts is *Re B (Children) (Sexual
Abuse: Standard of Proof)* [2008] UKHL 35, [2008] 2 FLR 141 (see below) where the
House of Lords held that the standard of proof for establishing the threshold criteria
in respect of past facts is the simple balance of probabilities, no more and no less.
In *Re B* the House of Lords refused to follow its earlier decision in *Re H and Others
(Minors) (Sexual Abuse: Standard of Proof)* [1996] AC 563, *sub nom Re H and R (Child
Sexual Abuse: Standard of Proof)* [1996] 1 FLR 80 (but refused to overrule it), in which
it had held that there had to be a 'real possibility' of harm in order for the threshold
criteria to be satisfied. In *Re B* the House of Lords held that there was no 'heightened
civil standard' and no legal rule that 'the more serious the allegation, the more cogent
the evidence needed to prove it'.

▶ *Re B (Children) (Sexual Abuse: Standard of Proof)* [2008] UKHL 35, [2008] 2 FLR 141

The mother had two children, aged 16 and 17, by a previous marriage, and two other children, aged 9 and 6, with her current husband (from whom she was separated). Allegations of sexual abuse and assault, some of which were certainly false, were made by the mother and the elder daughter (R) against the elder son, and by the elder daughter against her step-father (Mr B), and by the elder son against his mother. The two younger children were placed with foster-carers and care proceedings were instituted. These proceedings were transferred to the High Court by which time only the allegations against Mr B remained in issue. Charles J ruled that he was unable to make a finding as to whether Mr B had abused R. He said that he could not make a properly founded and reasoned conclusion that it was more likely than not that R was, or was not, sexually abused by Mr B. He said that his answer to which of these two possibilities was more likely would be a guess. On the basis, however, that he was unable to conclude that there was no real possibility that Mr B had sexually abused R, Charles J said that he had therefore come to the conclusion that there was a real possibility that he had done so. Charles J gave leave to appeal to the Court of Appeal. The Court of Appeal dismissed the appeal and gave leave to appeal to the House of Lords.

The House of Lords, dismissing the appeal, held in respect of the standard of proof in care proceedings that:

▶ The standard of proof in finding the facts necessary to establish the threshold under section 31(2) or the welfare considerations in section 1 of the 1989 Act is the balance of probabilities.

▶ There is no logical or necessary connection between seriousness and probability. In the context of care proceedings, this point applies with particular force to the identification of the perpetrator. It may be unlikely that any person looking after a baby would take him by the wrist and swing him against the wall, causing multiple fractures and other injuries. But once the evidence is clear that that is indeed what has happened to the child, it ceases to be improbable. Someone looking after the child at the relevant time must have done it. The inherent improbability of the event has no relevance to deciding whether the event actually took place.

BARONESS HALE: 'I wish to announce loud and clear that the standard of proof in finding the facts necessary to establish the threshold under s 31(2) or the welfare considerations in section 1 of the 1989 Act is the simple balance of probabilities, neither more nor less. Neither the seriousness of the allegation nor the seriousness of the consequences should make any difference to the standard of proof to be applied in determining the facts. The inherent probabilities are simply something to be taken into account, where relevant, in deciding where the truth lies.'

LORD HOFFMANN: 'I think that the time has come to say, once and for all, that there is only one civil standard of proof and that is proof that the fact in issue more probably occurred than not.'

In *Re B* the House of Lords held that the balance of probabilities test also applies to the second stage of proceedings, in other words where the threshold has been crossed and the court is deciding what order, if any, to make, applying the principle that the welfare of the child is the court's paramount consideration in section 1(1) and the welfare 'checklist' of factors in section 1(3) (see 10.3). Section 1(3)(e) in the checklist refers to 'any harm which he has suffered or is at risk of suffering'. In *Re M and R (Minors) (Sexual Abuse: Expert Evidence)* [1996] 4 All ER 239 the Court of Appeal held that section 1(3)(e) should be interpreted in the same way as section 31(2)(a) of the threshold criteria, in other words that the court must reach a decision based on facts, not on suspicions and doubts. In *Re B* the House of Lords agreed with this approach. In *Re O and N; Re B* [2003] UKHL 18, [2003] 1 FLR 1169 Lord Nicholls had also approved of this approach.

In *Re B* the House of Lords was asked by the Children's Guardian to overrule its earlier decision in *Re H* (see p. 386 above) on the basis that, when taken in combination with *Lancashire County Council v B* [2000] 1 FLR 583 and *Re O and N; Re B* [2003] UKHL 18, [2003] 1 FLR 1169 (see further below), it produced illogical results. However, the House of Lords refused to do so because it considered the principle in *Re H* (that decisions should be made on facts, rather than on mere suspicions) remained 'thoroughly convincing' and provided an essential safeguard against unjustified intervention in family life. The House of Lords in *Re B* also rejected the argument that there was a conflict between *Re H* and the later authorities of *Lancashire v B* (see below) and *Re O and N*, as it said courts can and must distinguish between cases where no significant harm has been proved (as in *Re H*) and those where significant harm has been proved but the actual perpetrator cannot be identified (as in *Lancashire v B*; and *Re O and N*). *Re H* therefore remains good law. As Baroness Hale said in *Re S-B (Children)* [2009] UKSC 17, [2010] 1 FLR 1161:

> 'All are agreed that *Re B* reaffirmed the principles adopted in *Re H* while rejecting the nostrum, "the more serious the allegation, the more cogent the evidence needed to prove it", which had become a commonplace but was a misinterpretation of what Lord Nicholls had in fact said.'

(For a case commentary on *Re B* and the standard of proof, see Keating [2009] CFLQ 230.)

In *Re S-B (Children)* UKSC [2009] 17, [2010] 1 FLR 1161 (see further at pp. below) Baroness Hale said that the House of Lords in its earlier decisions had established the following three propositions which had not been questioned since *Re H* was decided:

1. '[I]t is not enough that the court suspects that a child may have suffered significant harm or that there was a real possibility that he did. If the case is based on actual harm, the court must be satisfied on the balance of probabilities that the child was actually harmed.

2. [I]f the case is based on the likelihood of future harm, the court must be satisfied on the balance of probabilities that the facts upon which that prediction was based did actually happen. It is not enough that they may have done so or that there was a real possibility that they did.

3. [H]owever, if the case is based on the likelihood of future harm, the court does not have to be satisfied that such harm is more likely than not to happen. It is enough that there is "a real possibility, a possibility that cannot sensibly be ignored having regard to the nature and gravity of the feared harm in the particular case" (*per* Lord Nicholls [in *Re H*]).'

(e)   Shared care, uncertain perpetrators and the threshold criteria

When proving the threshold criteria, what must be proved is that 'the harm, or likelihood of harm, is attributable to ... the care given to the child, or likely to be given to him if the order were not made, not being what it would be reasonable to expect a parent to give to him' (see s 31(2)). The emphasis is on harm, not on identifying the perpetrator, or potential perpetrator, of the alleged harm. In the following case the House of Lords held that uncertainty about the identity of the perpetrator of the alleged harm did not prevent the threshold criteria being proved:

▶ *Lancashire County Council v B* [2000] 1 FLR 583

A young baby (child A) suffered harm as a result of being shaken, but it was impossible to prove whether A's parents or the child-minder, who also had a child (child B), was responsible. The Court of Appeal held that the threshold criteria in section 31(2)(b)(i) (lack of reasonable care) were satisfied in respect of child A, but not in respect of child B (because she had suffered no harm), even though it was unclear whether the parents or the child-minder were responsible for A's injuries. Child A's parents appealed to the House of Lords, arguing that the harm suffered by their child had to be attributable to their care, and that the continuation of the care proceedings infringed their right to family life under Article 8 ECHR.

The House of Lord unanimously dismissed their appeal, as the threshold conditions had been met. A majority of the House of Lords said that, under section 31(2)(b)(i) the court had to be satisfied that the harm suffered by the child was attributable to 'the care given to the child', which normally referred to the care given by parents or other primary carer. However, their Lordships said that different considerations applied in cases of shared care where the child suffers harm but the court is unable to identify which of the carers provided the deficient care. They held that the words 'care given to the child' in section 31(2)(b)(i) embraced the care given by *any* of the carers, and that the threshold conditions could be satisfied where there was no more than a possibility that the parents were responsible for inflicting the injuries. This interpretation, their Lordships said, was necessary to permit the court to intervene to protect a child at risk where the individual responsible for harming the child could not be identified. In other words, the interpretation was necessary to avoid the risk of a child remaining wholly unprotected.

The House of Lords stressed that in an uncertain perpetrator case the fact that it had not been proved that the parents had been responsible for the child's injuries could be taken into account at the 'welfare stage' once the threshold conditions had been met. The House of Lords held that there had been no breach of Article 8 ECHR as the steps taken by the local authority had been those reasonably necessary to pursue the legitimate aim of protecting the child from injury.

The standard of proof and possible perpetrators   In *Re S-B (Children)* [2009] UKSC 17, [2010] 1 FLR 1161, which concerned the issue of uncertain perpetrator(s) in the context of bruising to a 4-week old baby and where the mother and the father were the possible perpetrators, the Supreme Court, with Baroness Hale giving the leading opinion, held that the test to be applied to the identification of perpetrators was that of the balance of probabilities as laid down in *Re B (Children) (Sexual Abuse: Standard of Proof)* [2008] UKHL 35, [2008] 2 FLR 141 (above), even though *Re B* was not a case which was directly concerned with the identification of perpetrators. Baroness Hale said the test is 'the balance of probabilities, nothing more and nothing less'. Although her Ladyship in *Re S-B* recognised that it might be difficult for a judge to decide, even on the balance of probabilities, who had caused the harm to the child, there was no obligation to do so, as the threshold criteria were concerned with a finding of harm, not who caused the harm. Baroness Hale agreed with Wall LJ's approach in *Re D (Care Proceedings: Preliminary Hearing)* [2009] EWCA Civ 472, [2009] 2 FLR 668 that judges should not strain to identify the perpetrator as a result of the decision in *Re B*. In *Re D* Wall LJ said that, although the House of Lords in *Re B* had established that the standard of proof to be applied to all findings of fact in care proceedings was the 'simple balance of probabilities' test, that rule did not require a court to come to a conclusion as to which of two people was more likely than not to be the perpetrator in order to satisfy the threshold criteria. Wall LJ said that two parents could, for example, be possible perpetrators.

In *Re S-B*, however, Baroness Hale stated that, even if it was not possible for the judge to identify a perpetrator or perpetrators, it was important for the judge to identify 'the pool of possible perpetrators', as this would sometimes be necessary in order to fulfil the 'attributability' criterion. Her Ladyship said that, if the harm had been caused by someone outside the home or family (for example at school or in hospital or by a stranger), then it was not attributable to parental care unless it would have been reasonable to expect a parent to have prevented it. Baroness Hale also addressed the question of what should be done about the risk that a judge might make a mistake and wrongly identify someone as the perpetrator, stating that, while she recognised that judges can make mistakes, nevertheless a judge 'must remain alive to the possibility of mistake and be prepared to think again if new evidence emerges which casts new light on the evidence which led to the earlier findings'. Her Ladyship said that it was 'well settled that a judge in care proceedings is entitled to revisit an earlier identification of the perpetrator if fresh evidence warrants this' (and she referred to *Re I (A Child)* [2009] UKSC 10, [2010] 1 FLR 361 where the Supreme Court had witnessed an example of this).

The welfare stage and several possible perpetrators In *Re O and N; Re B (Minors)* [2003] UKHL 18, [2003] 1 FLR 1169 the House of Lords unanimously held that in uncertain perpetrator cases, where the judge had found that the child had suffered significant harm at the hands of his parents or carer but was unable to identify which parent or carer had caused the harm, the preferred interpretation of the Children Act was that the court should proceed at the welfare stage of care proceedings on the footing that each of the possible perpetrators be treated as such (but see also *Re S-B* above).

(For other cases on uncertain perpetrators, see *Re F (A Child)* [2011] EWCA Civ 258; *Re K (Care Proceedings: Fact-Finding)* [2010] EWHC 3342 (Fam); and also *Re J (Care Proceedings: Past Possible Perpetrators in a New Family Unit)* [2012] EWCA Civ 380 (which provides a useful and detailed analysis of the case-law relating to unidentified perpetrators, but which is currently pending before the Supreme Court).)

(f)   The local authority's care plan

Where an application for a care order is made in which a final care order might be made, the local authority must, within such time as the court may direct, prepare a 'care plan' for the future care of the child (s 31A(1)). The care plan will include information, for example, about the child's needs, the placement, and the management and support to be provided by the local authority. It will also provide details about contact – as before making a care order the court must consider the arrangements, or proposed arrangements, for contact (s 34(11)). In *Re J (Minors) (Care: Care Plan)* [1994] 1 FLR 253 Wall J (as he was then) said:

> 'A properly constructed care plan is not only essential to enable the court to make its decision based on all the known facts; it will or should have been compiled either in consultation with the parents and other interested parties, including where appropriate the child or children involved, or at the very least after taking their views and wishes into account. It will thus enable the other parties to focus on the relevant issues. Much court time and costs may thereby be saved.'

The court must carefully scrutinise the care plan in order to be satisfied that giving parental responsibility to the local authority will not do more harm than good for the child's welfare (*per* Hale J in *Berkshire County Council v B* [1997] 2 FLR 171). If the court considers that the care plan is not in the child's best interests, or that more information is needed, it can make an interim care order even though it is not completely happy with the plan (*Re L (Sexual Abuse: Standard of Proof)* [1996] 1 FLR 116). The court can make a final care order, even if it is not satisfied about the care plan. In *Re K (Care Proceedings: Care Plan)* [2007] EWHC 393 (Fam), [2008] 1 FLR 1 Munby J said that only in a rare case would the court's disapproval of a care plan prevent a care order being made when the threshold criteria had been satisfied and a care order was in the best interests of a child; and held that the court should have made a care order even though it was not satisfied about the contact proposed in the plan.

The duty to keep a care plan under review While the application is pending, the local authority must keep the care plan under review, and revise it or renew it if some change is required (s 31A(2)). It must also do the same once the child is in care; and must also consider whether to apply to discharge the care order (s 26(2)). A failure to keep a care plan up to date may provide grounds for an appeal as it did in *Re A (Care Plan)* [2008] EWCA Civ 650, [2008] 2 FLR 1183 where the trial judge had made a care order on the basis of an outdated care plan.

Once the child is in care, the local authority is not permitted to make significant changes to the care plan or change the child's living arrangements without properly involving the child's parents (and in some cases the child) in the decision-making process and without giving the parents a proper opportunity to make their case before a decision is made (see, for example, *Re G (Care: Challenge to Local Authority's Decision)* [2003] EWHC 551 (Fam), [2003] 2 FLR 42).

Involving parents A failure to involve a parent in the decision-making process in respect of a care plan, or a change in a care plan, can constitute a breach of a parent's human rights, and may result in a local authority having to pay damages to the wronged parent (see *Re C (Breach of Human Rights: Damages)* [2007] EWCA Civ 2, [2007] 1 FLR 1957, but where damages were not awarded in the circumstances of the case).

Challenging a care plan If the local authority fails to comply with its care plan, a parent (and/or child) can: apply to discharge the care order; make a complaint under the Complaints Procedure; bring a challenge under the Human Rights Act 1998; or bring a negligence claim (see 14.11). Independent Reviewing Officers can also provide assistance (see below). In *R (CD) v Isle of Anglesey County Council* [2004] EWHC 1635 (Admin), [2005] 1 FLR 59 a 15-year-old disabled girl successfully challenged a care plan on the ground that it had *inter alia* failed to give due consideration to her wishes in respect of the number of nights she should spend with her foster-carers.

Independent reviewing officers and care plans Before new provisions for the appointment of independent reviewing officers were introduced (see ss 24A and 24B CA 1989) there was judicial concern that, once a child was in care, a local authority could choose not to implement the proposals in its care plan to the detriment of the child and with the court having no power to intervene. The judiciary was concerned that children could drift in care with nobody, including the child, having the right to review the promises made in the care plan. Young children with parents who had no interest in them were in a particularly vulnerable position, even though local authorities were under a duty to conduct regular case reviews.

Concern about care plans was voiced by the House of Lords in *Re S (Care Order: Implementation of Care Plan); Re W (Minors) (Care Order: Adequacy of Care Plan)* [2002] UKHL 10, [2002] 1 FLR 815 where in each appeal the local authority had failed to implement the proposed arrangements in the care plan. The House of Lords allowed the appeals, and held that there was a statutory gap in the Children Act 1989, as a child whose parents were not interested in the matter might be left without an effective remedy (as required by Article 6 ECHR) to challenge a local authority's failure to implement its proposals in its care plan. The gap identified by the House of Lords was subsequently filled by new provisions requiring local authorities to appoint independent reviewing officers (IROs), who have a duty to monitor the performance of local authorities with regard to their functions in relation to looked after children (s 24B). They are responsible for participating in case reviews, for monitoring the local authority's functions in respect of case reviews, and for referring a case to a Cafcass officer where appropriate (s 25B(3)(a)). The Cafcass officer can then, if necessary, seek a court order against the local authority to put right its failings in relation to the care plan, for example by: applying to discharge the care order; applying for contact between the child and another person; or applying for a declaration under the Human Rights Act 1998 that the local authority's plans are contrary to the child's human rights. Before bringing court proceedings, the Cafcass officer will attempt to reach a negotiated settlement and will refer the case to mediation if appropriate. (See *The Cafcass Practice Note, 2011: Cafcass and the Work of Independent Reviewing Officers*, which explains the functions and duties of Cafcass in relation to cases involving IROs.)

(g) Effect of a care order – obligations of the local authority

If a care order is made, statutory responsibility for the child passes to the local authority, and the court has no power, unless expressly provided by statute, to interfere with the local authority's powers. Thus, for example, the court has no power to impose conditions on a care order in respect of the child's accommodation arrangements; or to direct how the local authority should look after the child (*Re T (A Minor) (Care Order: Conditions)* [1994] 2 FLR 423; and *Re S and D (Children: Powers of Court)* [1995] 2 FLR 456).

If a care order is made, the child is described as being 'looked after' by the local authority, whereupon the local authority has various duties and powers in respect of the child. The court no longer monitors the administrative arrangements for the child and has no say in these arrangements unless there is an application before the court. The Children's Guardian's involvement in the case also terminates.

A care order imposes a duty on the local authority to receive and keep the child in its care (s 33(1)), and the local authority has a general duty to safeguard and promote the child's welfare (s 22). A care order discharges any section 8 order, a supervision order and a school attendance order, and terminates wardship (s 91). A care order remains in force until the child reaches 18, unless brought to an end earlier (s 91(12)).

Care orders and parental responsibility A care order gives the local authority parental responsibility for the child and the power to determine the extent to which the child's parent(s) or guardian may meet their parental responsibility where it is needed to safeguard and promote the child's welfare (ss 33(3), (4)). It must exercise its parental responsibility in a way which complies with the European Convention for the Protection of Human Rights, in particular the substantive and procedural requirements of Article 8. Thus, it must inform parents of the decisions it makes, give parents opportunities to be heard and make representations, and involve them in the decision-making process.

The parental responsibility acquired by a local authority is not, however, absolute, for the child's parents do not lose parental responsibility while a care order is in force; and there is a presumption of reasonable contact between the child and his family (see 14.8). Thus, a parent remains entitled to do what is reasonable in all the circumstances for the purpose of safeguarding and promoting the child's welfare (s 33(5)), and retains any rights, duties, powers and responsibilities in relation to the child and his property under any other enactment (s 33(9)), for example, to make decisions about education and medical treatment. The local authority is not entitled to take decisions about the child without reference to, or over the heads of, the parents; and it is not entitled to make significant changes to its care plan. Neither is it entitled to make changes to the child's living arrangements without first discussing the matter with the parents, and, in some cases, the child; and it has no power to give or refuse consent to the child's adoption, or to appoint a guardian, or to change the child's religion (s 33(6)).

Restrictions imposed by care orders   While a care order is in force no person can change the child's surname or remove the child from the UK without the *written* consent of every person who has parental responsibility for the child, or leave of the court (s 33(7)). However, the local authority can allow the child to be taken out of the UK for up to one month (s 33(8)(a)) and can arrange (or assist in arranging) for the child to live outside England and Wales, subject to the court's approval (Sch 2, para. 19).

Placement of the child   The child may be placed with foster-parents, remain with existing short-term foster-carers, or be placed with members of the extended family such as a grandparent or other relative. Placing the child can be implemented under the terms of the care order, or under a residence order or under a special guardianship order. In some cases, the child may be placed for adoption (see Chapter 15). Section 22C (inserted by the Children and Young Persons Act 2008) lists a hierarchy of persons with whom a looked after child should be placed. Parents and persons with parental responsibility are at the top followed by relatives and friends and then unrelated carers. Local authorities must also comply with other requirements regarding placement, such as placing children near their homes, not disrupting their education and keeping siblings together.

(h)   Effect of a supervision order

A supervision order, unlike a care order, does not give the local authority parental responsibility but places the child under the supervision of a designated local authority officer or a probation officer (s 31(1)(b)). With a supervision order, safeguarding the child's interests remains the primary responsibility of parents. Under a supervision order the local authority merely assists and befriends the child (s 35(1)(a), (b)); and the operation of any conditions or undertakings depends on parental agreement (*Re B (Supervision Order: Parental Undertaking)* [1996] 1 FLR 676). A supervisor can, however, apply to have the supervision order varied or discharged where the order is not complied with or the supervisor considers the order is no longer necessary (s 35(1)(c)).

Parts I and II of Schedule 3 to the Children Act 1989 list specific powers in respect of supervision. For example the supervisor can give directions that the child live in a certain place, attend at a certain place and participate in certain activities. A supervision order can require a child to have a medical or psychiatric examination, but only with the child's consent if the child has sufficient understanding to make an informed decision, and only if satisfactory arrangements have been, or can be, made for the examination. A supervision order can be made in the first instance for up to one year, but the supervisor can apply to have the order extended for up to a maximum of three years (Sch 3, para 6). The court has no power to impose conditions on a supervision order (*Re S (Care or Supervision Order)* [1996] 1 FLR 753).

(i)   Interim care and supervision orders

The court has the power to make interim care and supervision orders (s 38), the purpose of which is to enable the court to maintain the status quo pending the final hearing, and for it to obtain any information it needs before making a final decision. Although an interim care order is a 'holding' order, once it is made, care of the child passes to the local authority and the manner in which the child is cared for passes out of the court's control. The power to make interim orders can be exercised only where care and supervision proceedings are to be adjourned (such as for inquiries or reports to be made), or where the court makes an order under section 37(1) directing a local authority to investigate the child's circumstances (s 38(1)). An interim order cannot be made unless there are reasonable grounds for believing that the threshold criteria for making a care or supervision order are satisfied (s 38(2)) (see p. 383).

If the court decides to make a residence order in care or supervision proceedings, an interim supervision order must also be made, unless the child's welfare is otherwise satisfactorily safeguarded (s 38(3)). There is no limit on the number of interim orders that can be made, but, as delay is detrimental to a child (s 1(2)) and it is important for a final decision to be made, interim orders are limited to a maximum of eight weeks in the first instance and four weeks subsequently (ss 38(4), (5)). However, there must be good reason for the continuation of an interim care order.

The court can include in an interim care order a requirement that an alleged abuser should leave the home, or be prevented from entering the home and/or an area round the home if it is satisfied that: there is reasonable cause to believe that by doing this the child will cease to suffer, or cease to be likely to suffer, significant harm; and there is a person living in the home who is able and willing to provide reasonable care for the child (see s 38A).

Courts must keep the European Convention for the Protection of Human Rights in mind when deciding whether or not to make an interim care order (*per* Sir Nicholas Wall P in *Re S (Care Proceedings: Human Rights* [2010] EWCA Civ 1383, [2012] 2 FLR 209). (For other cases on interim orders, see *Re B (Interim Care Order)* [2010] EWCA Civ 324, [2010] 2 FLR 283; and *Re GR (Interim Care Order)* [2010] EWCA Civ 871, [2011] 1 FLR 669.)

(j)   Directing a medical or psychiatric examination or other assessment of the child

When the court makes an interim care or supervision order it can give such directions (if any) as it considers appropriate with regard to the medical or psychiatric examination or other assessment of the child (s 38(6)). The aim of a section 38(6) direction is to ensure that all the evidence is put before the court in order to assist it in its decision-making. Thus, as Wall LJ said in *Re L and H (Residential Assessment)* [2007] EWCA Civ 213, [2007] 1 FLR 1370, before moving children permanently from their families the court must ensure that the case has been fully investigated and that all the relevant evidence necessary for the decision is in place. His Lordship said that Article 6 of the ECHR (the right to a fair hearing) required it and so did the underlying policy of the Children Act, which was that, wherever possible, children should be brought up by their parents or within their natural families. Wall LJ held that there were no general guidelines as to when the court should or should not order an assessment under section 38(6), but that the proceedings must be fair. The critical questions for the court are: does this child's welfare warrant an assessment under section 38(6); and, looking at the timetable for the child, is there evidence that the parent or other person will be able to care adequately for the child within that timetable?

A child with sufficient understanding to make an informed decision can refuse to submit to the medical or psychiatric examination or other assessment (see s 38(6)); but, as the child's welfare prevails, the court can override a child's refusal, even if the child has the required sufficiency of understanding (see *South Glamorgan County Council v W and B* [1993] 1 FLR 574, at p. 212).

Directing a residential assessment   Under section 38(6) the court may decide that a residential assessment is needed in order to assess the child and/or parents. The court can direct a residential assessment even though the local authority objects (for example because of the cost), as the purpose of section 38(6) is to enable the court to obtain the information it needs so that it can decide what sort of final order to make (see *Re C (A Minor) (Interim Care Order: Residential Assessment)* [1997] AC 489, [1997] 1 FLR 1). However, the court will take into account 'the cost of the proposed assessment and the fact that local authorities' resources are notoriously limited' (*per* Lord Browne-Wilkinson in *Re C*, above). In *Local Authority v M (Funding of Residential Assessments)* [2008] EWHC 162 (Fam), [2008] 1 FLR 1579, for example, Bodey J, having given careful consideration to the local authority's budget, made an order under section 38(6) even though the local authority, although agreeing in principle with the assessment, submitted that it could not afford to pay for it. Bodey J ordered that the local authority pay the entire cost of the residential assessment which the local authority had agreed was in the child's best interests.

A section 38(6) assessment is not restricted to residential assessments in an institutional setting. For example, in *Re A (Residential Assessment)* [2009] EWHC 865 (Fam), [2009] 2 FLR 443 Munby J held that the justices had acted within their jurisdiction by ordering an assessment to see how the child had settled with her great-grandmother and aunt. However, the House of Lords has held that a section 38(6) assessment does not include an assessment where its main focus is to consider the parents' capacity to respond to therapeutic treatment, or to secure therapy for the child or the family (see *Re G (A Child) (Interim Care Order: Residential Assessment)* [2005] UKHL 68, [2006] 1 FLR 601).

(k)   Discharge and variation of care and supervision orders

A supervision order can be varied or discharged, but a care order can only be discharged, not varied, as variation would undermine a local authority's responsibility for the child.

(i) Discharge of a care order An application to discharge a care order can be made by: a person with parental responsibility for the child; the child; or the local authority (s 39(1)). A child does not need leave of the court to apply (*Re A (Care: Discharge Application by Child)* [1995] 1 FLR 599). Persons without parental responsibility cannot apply for discharge, but can, with the permission of the court, apply for a section 8 residence order, which (if granted) will automatically discharge the care order (s 91(1)). In practice, discharge applications are made by local authorities who have an ongoing responsibility to consider whether or not to apply for discharge. As an alternative to discharge, the court can substitute the care order with a supervision order, without the need to satisfy the threshold criteria (ss 39(4), (5)).

In a discharge application the court must apply the section 1(1) welfare principle and the other section 1 provisions (see 10.3). There is no need to prove that the threshold criteria no longer apply (*Re S (Discharge of Care Order)* [1995] 2 FLR 639). A further application to discharge the care order, or to substitute it with a supervision order, cannot be made for six months after the original application, except with leave of the court (s 91(15)).

(ii) Variation or discharge of a supervision order A supervision order can be varied or discharged on the application of: a person with parental responsibility for the child; the child; or the person supervising the child (s 39(2)). An order can also be varied on the application of a person with whom the child is living, if the original order imposes a requirement which affects that person (s 39(3)). When exercising its powers, the court must apply the section 1(1) welfare principle and the other section 1 provisions (see 10.3). A further application to discharge or vary the supervision order cannot be made for six months after the original application, except with leave of the court (s 91(15)).

(l) Care and supervision orders – appeals

Any party to care or supervision proceedings can appeal against the making of, or refusal to make, a final or interim care or supervision order. The appeal court will not, however, interfere with a discretionary decision made by a lower court unless the judge has erred in law, or is under a misapprehension of fact, or the decision is outside a band of reasonable discretion within which reasonable disagreement is possible. As this is a high threshold, it is sometimes difficult for an appeal to succeed.

14.8 Contact in care

As contact between children and parents is considered to be mutually beneficial, and because children have a right to contact, cogent reasons are required for terminating contact (*per* Balcombe LJ in *Re J (A Minor) (Contact)* [1994] 1 FLR 729). The European Court of Human Rights has also recognised the importance of a child in care having contact with his or her parents and family. Thus, in *K and T v Finland* (2000) 31 EHRR 18, [2000] 2 FLR 79 it held that, while there is a wide margin of appreciation in care cases, it nevertheless remains important to scrutinise any restrictions placed by authorities on parental rights of contact. Contact is also important for children in care, because it improves their chances of being rehabilitated with their families. Article 9(3) of the UN Convention on the Rights of the Child recognises that a child who is separated from one or both parents has a right 'to maintain personal relations and direct contact with those parents on a regular basis, except if it is contrary to the child's best interests'.

Section 34 of the Children Act 1989 makes provision in respect of contact in care. It lays down a duty of contact, and gives the court power to make orders in respect of contact (see below). It also requires the court, before making a care order, to consider the arrangements the local authority has made, or proposes to make, for contact; and it must invite the parties to the proceedings to comment on those arrangements (s 34(11)).

(i) The duty to provide contact   Section 34(1) provides that a local authority must allow a child in care reasonable contact with: parents; a guardian or special guardian; a person with parental responsibility for him under section 4ZA and section 4A of the Children Act 1989; a person with a residence order in his or her favour in respect of the child; and a person who has care of the child under an order made by the High Court under its inherent jurisdiction. However, a local authority can as a matter of urgency refuse contact for up to seven days without obtaining a court order where it is necessary for the child's welfare (s 34(6)).

(ii) Section 34 orders   Under section 34 the court can make two sorts of order: an order in respect of contact; and an order authorising a local authority to refuse contact. These orders can be made on an application, or by the court of its own motion when making a care order, or in any family proceedings in connection with a child in care (s 34(5)). They can be made when a care order is made, or subsequently (s 34(10)). The court can impose conditions on an order (s 34(7)).

When exercising its powers, the court must apply the section 1(1) welfare principle and the other section 1 provisions in the Children Act 1989 (see 10.3); and it must also ensure that the order is human rights compliant (in other words that it complies, in particular, with Article 6 (the right to a fair trial) and Article 8 (the right to family life) of the ECHR.

As in private law (see 11.5) the courts are aware of the danger of authorising contact where there is a risk of the child witnessing domestic violence. In *Re G (Domestic Violence: Direct Contact)* [2000] 2 FLR 865, where the local authority was given permission to terminate direct contact, it was held that the reluctance of a child to see a parent in a case involving serious domestic violence requires careful consideration by the court.

Orders made under section 34 can be varied or discharged on the application of the local authority, the child, or any person named in the order (s 34(9)).

An order in respect of contact   Under section 34(2) the court, on the application of the local authority or the child, can make such order as it considers appropriate in respect of the contact which is to be allowed between the child in care and any named person.

Under section 34(3) the court may also make an order in respect of contact on the application of a person who has a right to reasonable contact under section 34(1) (see above), or a person who has been granted leave to apply. Although grandparents, relatives or friends of a child are not allowed contact with a child in care as of right (unless they have a residence order in their favour, or an order made under the High Court's inherent jurisdiction), they can apply for leave to apply for an order in respect of contact with a child in care (s 34(3)(b)) (see, for example, *Re M (Care: Contact: Grandmother's Application for Leave)* [1995] 2 FLR 86). Although the test which the court must apply when considering leave applications is laid down in section 10(9) (which is the same as that for section 8 orders – see pp. 273–4), the court is not restricted to considering only those matters set out in section 10(9), as it must conduct a full judicial inquiry into the application in accordance with Articles 6 and 8 ECHR (*per* Sumner J in *Re W (Care Proceedings: Leave to Apply)* [2004] EWHC 3342 (Fam), [2005] 2 FLR 468). However, a frivolous or vexatious application, or one where the prospects of success are remote, will be dismissed. An applicant for leave must prove that there is a serious issue to be tried and a good arguable case.

An order authorising a local authority to refuse contact Under section 34(4) the court can make an order (on the application of the local authority or the child) authorising the local authority to refuse to allow contact between the child and any person entitled to reasonable contact under section 34(1) (see above). An interim order can be made. If the court refuses to make a section 34(4) order, a further application cannot be made for six months except with leave of the court (s 91(17)). The court can insert conditions into an order (s 34(7)). The courts have held that contact is only to be terminated where there is no likelihood of rehabilitation and where post-adoption contact is not considered to be in the child's best interests (see, for example, *Re H (Termination of Contact)* [2005] EWCA Civ 318, [2005] 2 FLR 408).

The court may be unwilling to make an order authorising a local authority to refuse contact between a newborn baby and its mother, particularly when the threshold for a care order has not been established, unless extraordinarily compelling reasons exist. Munby J so held in *Re K (Contact)* [2008] EWHC 540, [2008] 2 FLR 581, even though, on the facts, a section 34(4) order was granted because the child's safety imperatively demanded that the court make the order. The contact between the mother and child had been poor and during a contact session the parents had been involved in a fight and the mother had thrown the baby to the contact supervisor.

14.9 Part V of the Children Act 1989 – emergency protection

Part V of the Children Act 1989 provides the legal framework for dealing with children who need protection in an emergency by making provision, *inter alia*, for child assessment orders and emergency protection orders. Part V orders are subject to certain safeguards so as to prevent unjustifiable intrusion into family life. For example, they are of short duration and are open to challenge. In some cases, emergency action will be followed by an application for a care or supervision order (see 14.7).

Under Part V a local authority also has various investigative duties when it is informed that a child who lives, or is found in its area, is the subject of an emergency protection order or is in police protection, or if the local authority has reasonable cause to suspect that such child is suffering, or is likely to suffer, significant harm (see s 47(1)). Once a local authority has obtained a Part V order, enquiries must be made to decide what action should be taken to safeguard or promote the child's welfare (s 47(2)).

As Part V proceedings are not 'family proceedings' for the purposes of the Children Act (s 8(4)), the court cannot make any section 8 order in the proceedings. When considering whether to make a Part V order the child's welfare is the court's paramount consideration (s 1(1)) and the other section 1 principles apply (see 10.3), except for the 1(3) welfare checklist, as conducting the section 1(3) exercise is lengthy and would defeat the purpose of a Part V application which is for immediate short-term emergency protection.

The following are available for emergency protection of a child under Part V: a child assessment order (s 43); an emergency protection order (s 44); and police protection (s 46). In practice, however, local authorities often prefer to make agreements with parents that a child be accommodated with the local authority instead of applying for an emergency protection order or requesting police protection (see research by Masson, 2005). In this way, they comply with one of the policy objectives of the Children Act, which is that local authorities should work in partnership with parents.

(a)   Child assessment orders

Under section 43 the court can make a child assessment order (CAO), which is an order enabling a medical or psychiatric assessment of the child to take place in order to establish whether or not the child is suffering, or is likely to suffer, significant harm. A CAO allows a local authority to intervene to protect a child where the circumstances are not sufficiently urgent or serious to justify other intervention (for example, an emergency protection order). With a CAO the child can remain at home, and so it is less severe than an emergency protection order (EPO). In practice, CAOs are not commonly made.

Grounds The court can make a CAO on the application of a local authority (or the NSPCC) if it is satisfied that (s 43(1)): the applicant has reasonable cause to suspect that the child is suffering, or is likely to suffer, significant harm; and an assessment of the state of the child's health or development, or of the way in which he has been treated, is required to enable the applicant to determine whether or not the child is suffering, or is likely to suffer, significant harm; and it is unlikely that such an assessment will be made, or be satisfactory, in the absence of an order under this section.

The court can treat the application as one for an EPO (s 43(3)). It cannot make a CAO if the grounds for an EPO exist; and it considers an EPO, rather than a CAO, ought to be made (s 43(4)). The CAO must specify when the assessment is to begin (which must not last longer than 7 days) (s 43(5)). The effect of a CAO is to order any person in a position to do so to produce the child to the person named in the order and to comply with any directions in the order (s 43(6)). The order authorises the person carrying out the assessment, or part of it, to do so in accordance with the terms of the order (s 43(7)). A child of sufficient understanding to make an informed decision may refuse to submit to a medical or psychiatric examination, or other assessment, regardless of any term in the order authorising assessment (s 43(8)), but the court can override the child's refusal if this is in his or her best interests (see *South Glamorgan County Council v W and B* at p. 212).

A child can be kept away from home for the assessment, but only if this is necessary for the purposes of the assessment, and only in accordance with directions and for the period(s) of time specified in the order (s 43(9)). The CAO must contain directions about contact (s 43(10)). Before the application is heard, the local authority must take reasonably practicable steps to ensure that notice of the application is given to: the child's parents; any person with parental responsibility; any person caring for the child; any person who has contact with the child either under a section 8 contact order or a section 34 order; and the child (s 43(11)). This notice requirement is to ensure that, where possible, the hearing takes place between the parties in order to prevent unjustifiable intervention. A CAO can be varied and/or discharged (s 43(12)). The court is required to appoint a Cafcass officer for the child unless it is satisfied that it is not necessary to do so in order to safeguard the child's interests (ss 41(1) and (2)).

(b)   Emergency protection orders

Under section 44 of the Children Act 1989 the court can make an emergency protection order (EPO), which is an order providing an immediate but temporary remedy in a genuine emergency. In an emergency, an application can be heard by a single justice and may, with leave of the clerk of the court, be made without notice (*ex parte*), although, where possible, proceedings must be heard *inter partes*.

(i) Applicants   Section 44 provides that 'any person' may apply for an EPO, but in practice it is local authority social services departments who do so.

(ii) The grounds for making an EPO   The applicant must prove that there is reasonable cause to believe that the child is likely to suffer harm if: he is not removed to accommodation provided by or on behalf of the applicant; or he does not remain in the place in which he is being accommodated (s 44(1)(a)). The court can also make an EPO on the application of a local authority if enquiries in respect of the child are being made under section 47(1)(b) and those enquiries are being frustrated by access to the child being unreasonably refused to a person authorised to seek access, and the applicant has reasonable cause to believe that access to the child is required as a matter of urgency (ss 44(1)(b) and (c)). Local authorities must keep parents informed about what is happening at the hearing, and they have a continuing duty to keep the case under review (s 44).

(iii) The approach of the courts   The courts adopt the following approach when considering whether or not to make an EPO:

▶ As an EPO is a severe and extremely harsh measure requiring exceptional justification and extraordinarily compelling reasons, the court will not make the order unless it is necessary and proportionate and no other less radical form of order will promote the child's welfare. (See *P, C and S v UK* (2002) 35 EHRR 31, [2002] 2 FLR 631, which involved the removal of a newborn baby.)
▶ Separation of the child will be contemplated only if immediate separation is essential to secure the child's safety. Imminent danger must be established. (See *Re M (Care Proceedings: Judicial Review)* [2003] EWHC 850 (Admin), [2003] 2 FLR 171.)
▶ An EPO should not be made for any longer than is absolutely necessary to protect a child.
▶ The evidence in support of an EPO must be full, detailed, precise and compelling.
▶ Save in wholly exceptional cases, parents must be given adequate prior notice of the date, time and place of the application for an EPO, and the evidence relied on.
▶ A without notice (*ex parte*) application will normally only be considered appropriate if the case involves a genuine emergency, great urgency or some other compelling reason to believe that the child's welfare will be compromised if the parents are alerted in advance (but even then some kind of informal notice to the parents may well be possible). As a result of their obligations under the Human Rights Act 1998, the courts must ensure that making an *ex parte* EPO does not breach the ECHR, for example Article 6 (the right to a fair trial) and Article 8 (the

right to family life), in particular the principle of proportionality under Article 8 (see 1.8).

▶ A Children's Guardian (a Cafcass officer – see 1.7) must be appointed immediately upon the issue of proceedings for an EPO.

The rules above were described, and applied, by Munby J in the following case, where he described an EPO summarily removing a child from his parents as a 'terrible and drastic remedy':

▶ *X Council v B (Emergency Protection Orders)* [2004] EWHC 2015 (Fam), [2005] 1 FLR 341

Three children were taken into foster-care under *ex parte* EPOs. Munby J held that, while child assessment orders, and possibly even very short-term EPOs, had been appropriate to enable medical tests and examinations to take place, it was not clear that there had been any justification for removing the children into foster-care. He said that the local authority had failed to address itself adequately to the requirements of sections 44(5) or (10) CA 1989; and it was not clear that it had exercised the exceptional diligence called for by Article 8 ECHR. The distress suffered by the children and parents due to their separation had been exacerbated by the unacceptably limited amount of contact permitted, and by the interventionist manner in which contact had been supervised. Munby J said that the Court of Appeal had repeatedly emphasised that any intervention under Parts V (and IV) of the Children Act should be proportionate to the legitimate aim of protecting the welfare and interests of the child. As Hale LJ had said in *Re O (Supervision Order)* [2001] EWCA Civ 16, [2001] 1 FLR 923, 'proportionality ... is the key'.

In *Re X (Emergency Protection Order)* [2006] EWHC 510 (Fam), [2006] 2 FLR 701 McFarlane J, approving the factors referred to by Munby J above, emphasised that EPOs should be made only in a genuine emergency and only for the purpose of providing immediate short-term protection. He said lack of information or a need for assessment could not on their own justify the making of an EPO.

(iv) Duration of an EPO   An order can be made in the first instance to last for up to eight days, but can be extended for up to a further seven days on application if the court has reasonable cause to believe that the child is likely to suffer significant harm if the order is not extended (s 45).

(v) Effect of an EPO   While an EPO is in force it operates as a direction to any person who is in a position to do so to comply with any request to produce the child to the applicant (s 44(4)(a)). It authorises the child's removal to accommodation provided by or on behalf of the applicant and the child being kept there; or it prevents the child's removal from any hospital, or other place, in which the child was being accommodated immediately before the order was made (s 44(4)(b)). It is a criminal offence intentionally to obstruct a person authorised to remove the child, or to prevent the removal of the child (s 44(15)). An EPO gives the applicant limited parental responsibility (s 44(4)(c) and s 44(5)(b)). The applicant must comply with regulations made by the Secretary of State (s 44(5)).

While an EPO is in force, the local authority cannot remove the child from his home or retain him in a place for longer than is necessary to safeguard his welfare, and must return the child or allow him to be returned when safe to do so (s 44(10)). The child can be returned to the care of the person from whom he was removed or, if that is not reasonably practicable, then to a parent, a person with parental responsibility or to such other person as the applicant with the agreement of the court considers appropriate, although while the order is in force the applicant can exercise his powers with respect to the child where it is necessary to do so (ss 44(11), (12)). Local authorities must make arrangements (subject to directions in the order as to contact and medical assessment or examination) to allow the child reasonable contact with the following persons and any person acting on his or her behalf: parents; any other person with parental responsibility; any person with whom the child was living immediately before the order was made; and any person with a right to contact under a section 8 order or under a section 34 contact order (s 44(13)).

(vi) Imposing directions on an EPO   When an EPO is made, or while it is in force, the court can give directions and impose conditions as to contact and/or may give directions with respect to the medical or psychiatric examination or other assessment of the child, which can include a condition that no examination or assessment be carried out unless the court directs (ss 44(6), (8) and (9)). Where a direction as to medical or psychiatric examination or assessment is made, a child of sufficient understanding to make an informed decision may refuse the examination or assessment (s 44(6)). Directions in an order can be varied at any time (s 44(9)(b)).

(vii) Challenging an EPO   There is no right of appeal against making, or refusing to make, an EPO. However, an application for discharge can be heard 72 hours or more after the order was made (ss 45(9), (10)) on the application of: the child; his parent; any person who has parental responsibility for the child; or any person with whom the child was living immediately before the order was made (s 45(8)). An EPO can be challenged under the Human Rights Act 1998, and judicial review proceedings may provide a useful way of challenging an order. In *X Council v B (Emergency Protection Orders)* (see above), Munby J held that, while an application for judicial review is not normally an appropriate remedy for challenging an EPO, it is not necessarily precluded in an appropriate case in order to correct an error or injustice. He said that, as the effect of an EPO was to remove a child from a parent for up to 15 days without a statutory right of appeal, judicial review might provide a mechanism for review of an unreasonable decision by the family proceedings court.

(viii) An exclusion requirement   The court can include in an EPO a requirement that an alleged abuser should leave the home or be prevented from entering the home and/or an area round the home if it is satisfied that: there is reasonable cause to believe that by doing this the child will cease to suffer, or cease to be likely to suffer, significant harm; and there is a person living in the home who is able and willing to provide reasonable care for the child (see s 44A).

(c)   Police protection

Under section 46 of the Children Act 1989 the police have various powers in emergency cases involving children. Thus, any constable who has reasonable cause to believe that a child would otherwise be likely to suffer significant harm can remove the child to suitable accommodation, or take reasonable steps to prevent the child's removal (s 46(1)). This power lasts for up to 72 hours, during which time the police must ensure that inquiries are conducted by a designated officer and that the child is accommodated by the local authority (ss 43(3)(e), (f)). The police must inform the local authority, the parents and the child of any steps it proposes to take. While the child is in police protection, the police do not have parental responsibility for the child but must do what is reasonable to safeguard or promote the child's welfare. While the child is accommodated under section 46, the parents cannot remove the child, but they are permitted to have contact.

According to research by Masson (2005) police protection is widely used, despite the lack of attention given to police protection in the child protection literature. Masson (see [2010] Fam Law 1088) is critical of the trend in practice for local authorities to seek the exercise of police powers (due in part to resource limitations) rather than to apply for an EPO, as, in her view, the police are likely to be reluctant to use their resources to support children's services which will be 'catastrophic for some children and families'.

14.10 Local authorities' duties towards 'looked after' children

Local authorities have duties under the Children Act 1989 towards children 'looked after' by them, whether accommodated under a voluntary arrangement or under a care order (s 22(1)). A local authority must safeguard and promote the child's welfare and make such use of services available for children cared for by their own parents as appears reasonable in the case of the particular child (s 22(3)). Before making a decision about a child being looked after, or proposed to be looked after, the local authority must ascertain the wishes and feelings of the child, his parents, any person with parental responsibility and any other relevant person (s 22(4)). It must also consider their wishes in respect of the child's religion, racial origin and cultural and linguistic background (s 22(5)). It must advise, assist and befriend the child with a view to promoting his welfare when he ceases to be looked after by it (s 24(1)). A local authority must encourage rehabilitation by allowing the child to live with his family, unless contrary to his welfare (s 23(6)), and ensure that the accommodation provided is near the child's home, and that brothers and sisters remain together (s 23(7)). A local authority's general duties to a child are facilitated by more specific duties, such as by the inspection of foster-parents, and children's homes. Local authorities also have a duty to promote contact (Sch 2, para 15, and see 14.8 above).

Children leaving care The Children (Leaving Care) Act 2000 inserted new sections into sections 23 and 24 of the Children Act 1989, and into Schedule 2 (see paras 19A–19C) in order to impose certain duties on local authorities with respect to children who leave care. Each local authority is required to provide a comprehensive after-care service to ease the passage of looked after children into adulthood. It has a duty to advise, assist and befriend the child with a view to promoting his welfare when it ceases to look after the child (para 19A). It must keep in touch with a care leaver and prepare 'needs assessments' and formulate 'pathway plans' in respect of education, training, careers and financial support until the person leaving care reaches the age of 21 (para 19B). It must appoint a personal adviser to keep in touch with the person leaving care (para 19C). A local authority is also required to provide financial support, including the cost of education and training up to the age of 24.

If a local authority fails to comply with these statutory requirements, a challenge can be made in judicial review proceedings (see, for example, *R (J) v Caerphilly County*

Borough Council [2005] EWHC 586 (Admin), [2005] 2 FLR 860 where Munby J held that a local authority has a duty to carry out its statutory obligations even if the person leaving care is unco-operative and unwilling to engage, or refuses to engage, with the local authority). In *R (Berhe and Others) v Hillingdon London Borough Council* [2003] EWHC 2075 (Admin), [2004] 1 FLR 439 Sullivan J held that asylum-seeking minors who had been looked after by a local authority were entitled, on reaching adulthood, to benefit from the provisions of the Children (Leaving Care) Act 2000.

In *R (G) v Nottingham City Council and Nottingham University Hospitals NHS Trust* [2008] EWHC 400 (Admin), [2008] 1 FLR 1668 a mother aged 18 successfully challenged in judicial review proceedings the pathway plan prepared for her by the local authority under sections 23A–23C and Sched. 2. Munby J held that there had been a serious failure by the local authority to comply with its statutory duties.

14.11 Challenging local authority decisions about children

Parents, relatives, children, foster-parents and others may sometimes be dissatisfied with action taken, or not taken, by a local authority. In such cases it may be possible to resolve a grievance informally, but if this is not possible, then the following procedures can be invoked.

(i) Using the Children Act 1989 One way of challenging a local authority is to appeal against an order (where this is possible) or apply to have it varied or discharged. Another option is to make a complaint to the Secretary of State, who has the power to declare a local authority to be in default, if it fails without reasonable cause to comply with a duty under the Children Act 1989, and who can require compliance within a specified period (s 84). It is not possible to apply to make a child a ward of court as a way of challenging a care order (sections 100(2)(c) and 91(4)).

(ii) The complaints procedure The Children Act 1989 requires local authorities to establish a complaints procedure (see s 26). Complaints can be made in respect of the duties and powers of local authorities under Parts III, IV and V of the Act. The following persons can make a complaint: a 'looked after' child or a child in need; a parent; a person with parental responsibility; a foster-parent; any person whom the local authority considers has sufficient interest in the child's welfare to warrant representation being considered; a young person who considers he has been given inadequate preparation for leaving care or for after-care; and a child who is the subject of a placement order for the purposes of adoption.

(iii) Advocacy services for children A child making a complaint can make use of an independent advocacy service (see s 24A). Local authorities must make arrangements to provide assistance (such as advocacy services and representation) for children and young persons who make, or intend to make, complaints under the Children Act procedures (s 26A(1)). This duty applies to the standard complaints procedure in section 26 (above) and to the procedure for young people leaving care under section 24D. The assistance which local authorities must put in place must include representation (s 26A(2)). Local authorities can choose whether to provide the assistance themselves or use the services of an advocacy service provider.

(iv) A challenge under the Human Rights Act 1998   As local authorities are public authorities for the purposes of the Human Rights Act (HRA) 1998, they must act in a way which is compatible with the European Convention for the Protection of Human Rights (s 6 HRA 1998) (see 1.8). Any person who is a victim of an unlawful act (or proposed act) of a local authority may bring an application under section 7 HRA 1998 either by way of a free-standing application against a local authority or by relying on a Convention right in any legal proceedings (s 7). Damages can be awarded for a breach of a Convention right (s 8 HRA 1998). Human rights challenges can be made in proceedings under Parts III, IV and V of the Children Act 1989 or in judicial review proceedings (see below).

Human rights claims against local authorities are usually brought on the basis of a breach of Article 6 ECHR (the right to a fair trial) and/or Article 8 (the right to family life) as the following cases show:

▶ *Re G (Care: Challenge to Local Authority's Decision)* [2003] EWHC 551 (Fam), [2003] 2 FLR 42

The parents applied for discharge of care orders and an injunction under section 7 HRA 1998 to prevent their children's removal into care, as the local authority had delayed in making a decision about the children, and had kept no minutes or written records of meetings and decisions made. Munby J held that the local authority was in breach of the right to family life under Article 8.

▶ *Re M (Care: Challenging Decisions by Local Authority)* [2001] 2 FLR 1300

The child in care's parents had a long history of alcohol and drug abuse. At a planning meeting, to which the parents and their solicitors were not invited, the local authority finally ruled out any prospect of the child living with the father. Each parent commenced separate free-standing applications under section 7 HRA 1998 arguing that they were victims of an unlawful act of the public authority, and that the placement should be set aside. Holman J held that the local authority had acted unlawfully under section 6 HRA 1998 in respect of the way in which it had conducted the planning meeting, which was contrary to the parents' right to respect for their family life under Article 8. As the local authority had failed sufficiently to involve the parents at critical moments, Holman J quashed the decision made at the planning meeting.

▶ *Re W (Removal into Care)* [2005] EWCA Civ 642, [2005] 2 FLR 1022

The parents challenged the removal of twins from their care by means of an application to discharge the care orders and by way of injunction under section 8 HRA 1998. Thorpe LJ held that an application under the HRA 1998 was the right remedy, not the application to discharge the care orders, as what they were challenging was the lawfulness of the local authority's decision to remove the twins.

▶ *Re C (Breach of Human Rights: Damages)* [2007] EWCA Civ 2, [2007] 1FLR 1957

The trial judge made a declaration under the HRA 1998 that there had been a significant breach of the mother's human rights caused by the local authority's decision to abandon the care plan without giving the mother an opportunity to participate in the decision-making process; but did not make an order for damages.

(See also *Re L (Care: Assessment: Fair Trial)* [2002] EWHC 1379 (Fam), [2002] 2 FLR 730; and *C v Bury Metropolitan Borough Council* [2002] EWHC 1438 (Fam), [2002] 2 FLR 868).

(v) Judicial review   Judicial review is an administrative law remedy which may be made against a local authority (or other public body, such as a Government department, court or health authority) by an aggrieved person, including a child. The application is made in the Administrative Court. The court can grant the following remedies: a 'mandatory order' (directing the respondent to take a particular course of action); a 'prohibitory order' (prohibiting the respondent from taking a particular course of action); or a 'quashing order' (quashing the decision of the respondent). It can order damages in conjunction with one of these orders. The Administrative Court can also issue declarations and injunctions.

Strict rules govern judicial review applications. Thus, leave must be obtained from the court for the case to proceed to a full application on its merits, which will be granted only if the court considers that there is a reasonable chance of the court deciding that the local authority's decision was so unreasonable that no reasonable authority could have come to it. Leave to apply must be sought within three months from the date on which the grounds for the application arose. Leave will not be granted unless the applicant has a sufficient interest in the matter to which the application relates. The grounds on which judicial review may be granted are: illegality; procedural impropriety (breach of the rules of natural justice); and irrationality. To succeed on the ground of irrationality, a local authority must have taken into account irrelevant matters, or failed to have taken into account relevant matters, or have come to a conclusion that was so unreasonable that no authority would have come to it. However, as judicial review is a discretionary remedy, the court may refuse a remedy even if a ground is proved.

As local authorities are public authorities for the purposes of the Human Rights Act 1998, and as judicial review is a means of challenging local authority action or inaction, challenges by way of judicial review are often based on, or supported by, human rights arguments:

> ▶ *R on the Applications of L and Others v Manchester City Council; R on the Application of R and Another v Manchester City Council* **[2001] EWHC 707 (Admin)**
>
> Children (by their litigation friend) successfully applied for judicial review of the local authority's policy whereby it paid substantially lower fostering payments to short-term foster-parents who were friends or relatives of children. Munby J held that the local authority's policy was irrational, and also breached Article 8 ECHR (right to family life), as under Article 8(2) it was neither a necessary nor proportionate response. The local authority had a positive obligation when exercising its duties under Part III of the Children Act to secure respect for family life under Article 8. The policy was also held to be discriminatory under Article 14 ECHR, as the reference in Article 14 to 'other status' included family status.

Where a local authority has wide discretion in a particular matter (as it has under the Children Act 1989) it is difficult to succeed in an action for judicial review, and, where there is another procedure for challenging a local authority, the court may not grant judicial review before that procedure has been pursued. Judicial review is therefore a remedy of last resort, and may be refused where there is another equally effective and convenient remedy (such as a bringing a complaint under the complaints procedure, see *R (On the Application of Appiatse and Another) v Enfield Borough Council* [2008] EWHC 1886 (Admin), [2008] 2 FLR 1945).

A considerable disadvantage of judicial review is that, if a 'quashing order' is granted, the local authority's obligation is merely to reconsider its original decision, and, provided that decision is not illegal, procedurally improper or irrational, then it can come to the same decision as it did the first time. The drawbacks of the court's powers in judicial review proceedings were referred to in *Re T (Judicial Review: Local Authority Decisions Concerning Child in Need)* [2003] EWHC 2515 (Admin), [2004] 1 FLR 601 where Wall J held that, while the court was in a position to direct the local authority to reconsider the question of the services it should provide under Part III of the Children Act 1989 for the child in question, it could not direct the local authority in respect of what to decide or direct that it make any special provision for the child.

There are many reported cases involving applications for judicial review in the context of local authorities' powers under the Children Act 1989, for example for: failing to allow a solicitor to attend a child protection conference and failing to supply the applicant with the minutes (*R v Cornwall County Council ex parte LH* [2000] 1 FLR 236); failing to obtain parental permission to move a child from residential care to foster-care (*R v Tameside Metropolitan Borough Council ex parte J* [2000] 1 FLR 942); and refusing to carry out assessments of children in need (*R (On the Application of S) v Wandsworth, Hammersmith and Lambeth London Borough Council* [2002] 1 FLR 469). Placing a child on the child protection register can be challenged by judicial review (see *R v Harrow London Borough Council ex parte D* [1990] Fam 133), but the courts have held that the complaints procedure (see p. 404 above), rather than judicial review proceedings, should be followed (*R v Hampshire County Council ex parte H* [1999] 2 FLR 359; and *A and S v Enfield London Borough Council* [2008] EWHC 1886 (Admin), [2008] 2 FLR 1945).

(vi) Commissioner for Local Administration   A complaint can be made to the Commissioner for Local Administration (the Local Government Ombudsman), who has a duty to investigate complaints of maladministration by local authorities. This is a lengthy and limited remedy.

(vii) An application to the Children's Commissioner   A complaint can be made to the Children's Commissioner (see p. 206).

(viii) An application to the European Court of Human Rights   A parent, child or other aggrieved party who has exhausted all the remedies available in the courts in the UK can apply to the European Court of Human Rights (ECtHR) in Strasbourg, alleging that the UK is in breach of the European Convention for the Protection of Human Rights (see, for example, *Z and Others v UK* [2001] 2 FLR 603; and *RK and AK v UK* [2009] 1 FLR 274, below).

(ix) An action in negligence   Social workers and other persons working in the child protection system are not immune from liability in negligence, although the courts are aware of the difficult task social workers have and that local authorities have limited resources. At one time claims were struck out on the ground that there was no duty of care for policy reasons, but there has been a change of attitude, due largely to the enactment of the Human Rights Act 1998 and to decisions in the European Court of Human Right. As a result, the courts in England and Wales are now much more likely to allow a case to proceed to trial. Whether a local authority has been negligent will depend on whether it has breached its duty of care and whether the damage caused was reasonably foreseeable in the circumstances, judged by an objective standard. Damages can be awarded. The following cases are examples of claims brought in negligence. The following case involved a series of related appeals involving negligence claims against local authorities in which the UK courts took a restrictive approach, but where the ECtHR subsequently allowed the victims' claims:

▶ *X (Minors) v Bedfordshire County Council and Related Appeals* [1995] 2 AC 633, [1995] 2 FLR 276

In the first appeal negligence claims were brought by five children against Bedfordshire County Council for failing to take steps to protect them from the years of neglect they had suffered, even though the defendant had been informed on several occasions that they were suffering harm. In the second appeal, the child and the mother sued the local authority (Newham London Borough Council) because the child had been mistakenly taken into care (for about one year) after a child psychologist employed by the local authority had wrongly identified the mother's cohabitant as having abused the child. The House of Lords held in respect of both appeals that the defendant local authorities owed the claimants no duty of care in negligence, and so the cases were struck out as disclosing no cause of action.

Note: Four of the children in the 'Bedfordshire case' subsequently took their case to the ECtHR in Strasbourg (see *Z and Others v UK* [2001] 2 FLR 603), which held that there had been a breach of Article 3 ECHR (as the children had suffered inhuman and degrading treatment) and Article 13 (because they had not had an effective remedy). The child and the mother in the 'Newham case' also took their case to the ECtHR (see *TP and KM v UK* [2001] 2 FLR 545), which again held that there had been breaches of Articles 3 and 13.

For a case with similar facts to that of *X v Bedfordshire* (above), but which shows how the approach to negligence claims against local authorities has changed (largely as a result of the impact of human rights), see *ABB, BBB, CBB and DBB v Milton Keynes Council* [2011] EWHC 2745 (QB) where the defendant local authority, which had failed to protect four children who had suffered appalling sexual abuse for many years at the hands of their father, was held to be vicariously liable in negligence and ordered to pay damages.

▶ *A v Essex County Council* [2003] EWCA Civ 1848, [2004] 1 FLR 749

The parents were successful in claiming damages in negligence (including damages for psychiatric injury) against the defendant local authority for failing to give them sufficient information about a boy who had been placed with them for adoption and who subsequently attacked them and their own child.

▶ *D v East Berkshire Community NHS Trust; MAK v Dewsbury Healthcare NHS Trust; RK v Oldham NHS Trust* [2005] UKHL 23, [2005] 2 FLR 284

The parents in the three appeals claimed that the medical professionals had negligently misdiagnosed child abuse of their children, when in fact the children had genuine health problems; and that this had disrupted their family life and caused them psychiatric injury. The House of Lords held by a majority (Lord Bingham dissenting) that the defendants owed no duty of care in negligence to the parents on grounds of public policy because doctors must be free to act in the best interests of children generally.

Note: The parents in the *RK* case successfully took their case to the ECtHR (see *RK and AK v UK* (2008) 48 EHRR 707, [2009] 1 FLR 274), which awarded them substantial damages as there had been a breach of Article 13 (the right to an effective remedy), as the parents had an arguable complaint concerning interference with their family life but had not had any redress for obtaining compensation for the damage they had suffered.

The father and daughter in the *MAK* case also succeeded before the ECtHR (see *MAK and RK v UK (Applications Nos 45901/05 and 40146/06)* [2009] EWCA Civ 1, [2009] 1 FLR 987) which unanimously held, awarding damages, that that there had been a violation of both applicants' rights under Article 8 and a violation of the father's rights under Article 13.

See also *OD v UK (Application No 28680/06)* [2010] ECHR 340, [2010] 2 FLR 1.

Summary

- A wide range of different personnel are involved in child protection and providing services for children in need. A multi-agency and inter-agency approach is adopted. Of particular importance are local authority social workers. Local authorities have duties and powers under the Children Act 1989 to safeguard and promote the welfare of children.

- Local authority social workers engaged in child protection have a difficult task as they must ensure that children are protected, but they must also ensure that they do not intervene too much into family life.

- The Children Act 2004, which was enacted in response to the failures of social services in the Victoria Climbié case, made structural changes to the way in which the various agencies operate to protect children. Key developments included the creation of Children's Trusts and Local Safeguarding Children's Boards.

- Local authorities are public authorities under the Human Rights Act 1998 and must therefore ensure that they exercise their powers and duties in line with the European Convention for the Protection of Human Rights. Of particular importance is the right to family life (Art 8) which requires that any intervention in family life must be lawful, necessary and proportionate. Procedural fairness is also important in order to ensure compliance with Article 6 (the right to a fair trial).

- The UN Convention on the Rights of the Child also contains various articles which are relevant to child protection, such as Article 19 which requires States Parties to take all measures to protect children from all forms of abuse while in the care of their parents, guardians and other persons.

- The Children Act 1989 is the key Act governing the duties and powers of the courts and of local authorities to take steps to protect children and to provide for children in need. Local authorities have a wide range of powers under the Children Act 1989, which include a duty to make enquiries (s 47) and to investigate a case if so ordered by the court (s 37). They have powers and duties under Part III to provide support for children in need. They can apply for care and supervision orders under Part IV; and can take emergency measures under Part V.

- Under Part III of the Children Act 1989 local authorities have a duty to provide a range of services for children in need and for disabled children, including in particular the provision of day care and accommodation. As part of the general duty to safeguard and promote the welfare of children (see s 17(1)), a local authority has a duty to provide accommodation for children in need and their families (ss 20–25). But the accommodation provisions of the Children Act 1989 cannot be used to 'by-pass' the housing and homelessness legislation (see 4.11). Local authorities also have a duty to provide accommodation for care-leavers (s 24A and B ss 24A and B of the CA 1989).

- Under Part IV of the Children Act 1989 local authorities can apply for care and supervision orders, which may be granted by the court if the 'threshold criteria' in section 31(2) are satisfied, and the court considers the child's welfare requires such an order to be made. In assessing welfare, the court must apply the welfare principle (s 1(1)), the no-delay principle (s 1(2)), the welfare checklist (s 1(3)) and the no-order presumption (s 1(5)). The standard of proof in care and supervision proceedings is the balance of probabilities. The court must ensure that it complies with the ECHR as a result of its obligations under the Human Rights Act 1998. Children can give evidence in care proceedings, but the usual way in which the voice of the child is conveyed to the court is by the Children's Guardian (an officer of Cafcass) who works in tandem with the child's solicitor. Cases where there is more than one possible perpetrator of significant harm are difficult, but the House of Lords and also the Supreme Court have held that uncertainty about the perpetrator of the alleged harm does not necessarily prevent the threshold criteria being proved.

▶ In care proceedings in which a final care order might be made the local authority must prepare a care plan about the future care of the child (s 31A(1)). The plan must be kept under review (s 31A(2)).

▶ A care order gives the local authority parental responsibility for the child, but a parent does not lose parental responsibility. A supervision order places the child under the supervision of a designated local authority officer or a probation officer.

▶ The court has the power to make interim care and supervision orders (s 38).

▶ The court can direct a medical or psychiatric examination or other assessment of the child (s 38(6)), the aim of which is to put all the evidence before the court to help it reach its decision. An assessment can include a residential assessment. A child with sufficient understanding to make an informed decision can refuse to submit to the medical or psychiatric examination or other assessment; but the court can override the refusal if it is in the child's best interests.

▶ A supervision order can be varied or discharged, but a care order can only be discharged, not varied (s 39).

▶ A local authority has a duty to allow a child in care to have reasonable contact with parents, guardians, persons with parental responsibility, a person with a residence order, and a person who has care of the child under an order made by the High Court under its inherent jurisdiction (s 34(1)), although the contact can be terminated for up to seven days as a matter of urgency (s 34(6). Under section 32 the court can make orders in respect of contact and orders authorising a local authority to refuse contact. Orders made under section 34 can include conditions (s 34(7)), and they can be varied or discharged (s 34(9)).

▶ Under Part V of the Children Act 1989 the following are available for emergency protection of a child: a child assessment order (s 43); an emergency protection order (EPO) (s 44); and police protection (s 46). The grounds for making an EPO are that there is reasonable cause to believe that the child is likely to suffer harm if: he or she is not removed to accommodation provided by or on behalf of the applicant; or he or she does not remain in the place in which he is being accommodated (s 44(1)(a)). The court can also make an EPO on the application of a local authority if enquiries in respect of the child are being made under section 47(1)(b) and those enquiries are being frustrated by access to the child being unreasonably refused to a person authorised to seek access; and the applicant has reasonable cause to believe that access to the child is required as a matter of urgency (ss 44(1)(b) and (c)). As an EPO is regarded as a severe order, an order must be lawful, necessary and proportionate. In other words, there are strict controls on it being made.

▶ Local authorities have certain duties to children 'looked after' by them whether under a voluntary arrangement or under a court order. They also have duties under the Children Act 1989 to children leaving care.

▶ There are various ways in which to bring a challenge against a local authority, namely by: applying to discharge or vary an order made under the Children Act 1989; using the statutory complaints procedure (under s 26); using the advocacy services (in the case of a child); bringing a challenge under the Human Rights Act 1998; bringing judicial review proceedings; making a complaint to the Local Ombudsman; and bringing a claim in negligence.

Further reading and references

Bailey-Harris and Harris, 'Local authorities and child protection – the mosaic of accountability' [2002] CFLQ 117.

Bainham, 'Interim care orders: is the bar set too low?' [2011] Fam Law 374.

Driscoll and Hollingsworth, 'Accommodating children in need: *R (M)* v *Hammersmith and Fulham London Borough Council*' [2008] CFLQ 522.

Hall, 'What price the logic of proof of evidence?' [2000] Fam Law 423.

Hall, 'The misfortune of being straightforward? The impact of *Re W* on children giving evidence in care proceedings' [2010] CFLQ 499.

Harwin and Owen, 'The implementation of care plans, and its relationship to children's welfare' [2003] CFLQ 71.

Hayes, 'Child protection – from principles and policies to practices' [1998] CFLQ 119.

Hayes, 'Farewell to the cogent evidence test: *Re B*' [2008] Fam Law 859.

Hayes J, Hayes M and Williams, ' "Shocking" abuse followed by a "staggering" ruling: *Re MA (Care Threshold)*' [2010] Fam Law 166.

Hemingway and Williams '*Re M and R: Re H and R*' [1997] Fam Law 740.

Howe, 'Removal of children at interim hearings: is the test now set too high?' [2009] Fam Law 320.

Keating, 'Suspicions, sitting on the fence and standards of proof' [2009] CFLQ 230.

Keating, '*Re MA:* the significance of harm' [2011] CFLQ 115.

Masson, 'Emergency protection, good practice and human rights' [2004] Fam Law 882.

Masson, 'Emergency intervention to protect children: using and avoiding legal controls' [2005] CFLQ 75.

Masson, 'Reforming care proceedings – time for a review' [2007] CFLQ 411.

Masson, 'Emergency protection: the impact of court control' [2010] Fam Law 1088.

Masson *et al.*, *Protecting Powers: Emergency Intervention for Children's Protection*, 2007, John Wiley & Sons.

Perry, '*Lancashire County Council* v *B*: section 31 – threshold or barrier?' [2000] CFLQ 301.

Ryder, The Honourable Mr Justice, 'The risk fallacy: a tale of two thresholds' [2008] Fam Law 30.

Websites

Ministry of Justice: www.justice.gov.uk

NSPCC (National Society for the Prevention of Cruelty to Children): www.nspcc.org.uk

Links to relevant websites can also be found at: www.palgrave.com/law/familylaw8e

Chapter 15

Adoption and special guardianship

This chapter deals with adoption and special guardianship. Although special guardianship is not part of the adoption legislation, it is dealt with in this chapter as it may provide a more suitable alternative to adoption in some circumstances.

15.1 Adoption – introduction

Adoption of a child is effected by an adoption order which extinguishes the parental responsibility of the child's birth parents and other persons, and vests it in the adopters. Adoption involves the complete legal transfer of parental responsibility and makes the child a full legal member of the new family.

The law of adoption is laid down in the Adoption and Children Act 2002. Adoption procedure and practice are governed by rules of courts, practice directions and various regulations. Human rights are also relevant to adoption.

(i) Adoption and human rights As adoption agencies and courts are public authorities pursuant to the Human Rights Act 1998 they must exercise their powers and duties in accordance with the European Convention for the Protection of Human Rights (ECHR) (see 1.8). Thus, they must ensure that adoption does not breach the right to family life of the child and of the child's natural parents under Article 8 ECHR. Any interference in family life must be legitimate, necessary and proportionate (Art 8(2)). Cases decided by the European Court of Human Rights (ECtHR) must be taken into account by the courts and public bodies responsible for adoption in England and Wales (see s 2(1) HRA 1998). For instance, in the following case the ECtHR emphasised the importance of children and biological parents having a right to the mutual enjoyment of each other's company:

▶ *Johansen v Norway* **(1997) 23 EHRR 33**

The child, who was in care, had been placed in a foster-home with a view to her adoption, and the mother had been deprived of contact. The ECtHR held that: 'the mutual enjoyment by parent and child of each other's company constitutes a fundamental element of family life and domestic measures hindering such enjoyment amount to an interference with the right protected by art. 8'. The ECtHR held that there had been a breach of the ECHR, as the far-reaching measures taken were inconsistent with the aim of reuniting the mother and child and should only have been taken in exceptional circumstances where they could be justified in the best interests of the child.

But each case depends on its facts. For instance, in *Söderbäck v Sweden* [1999] 1 FLR 250, on the other hand, an adoption order was held not to breach Article 8 ECHR in the circumstances of the case.

In *Keegan v Ireland* (1994) 18 EHRR 342 the ECtHR held that placing a child for adoption shortly after birth, without the natural father's knowledge or consent, may breach Article 8. However, in a similar case, *Eski v Austria (Application No. 21949/03)*

[2007] 1 FLR 1650, the father's Article 8 rights were held not to be breached, as the domestic court had carefully examined the case and given reasons; and the assessment of the interests of the child and the father's limited relationship with her lay within the 'margin of appreciation' (see p. 17) of the domestic court and justified a proportionate interference with the father's Article 8 rights.

A refusal to permit a person to adopt a child on the ground of his or her sexuality may breach the ECHR. In *EB v France (Application No. 43546/02)* [2008] 1 FLR 850, for instance, the ECtHR held that the refusal of the French authorities to allow a lesbian woman in a stable and long-term relationship to adopt a child, on the basis *inter alia* of there being no paternal role model for the child, breached Article 14 (the right not to suffer discrimination) taken in conjunction with Article 8. The ECtHR held that the case differed in a number of respects from *Fretté v France (Application No 36515/97)* [2003] 2 FLR 9 where a homosexual man was refused permission to adopt a child on the basis, *inter alia*, that there was no common ground among Contracting States as to the merits of permitting adoption by homosexuals and therefore the State had a margin of appreciation as to how it approached the issue.

The UN Convention on the Rights of the Child (see 8.2) is also relevant to the law and practice of adoption.

(ii) The role of Cafcass in adoptions   A Cafcass Reporting Officer (see 1.7) will be appointed by the court to ensure that consent to adoption has been freely given. If consent is not forthcoming, or special circumstances exist, then the court will, if needed, appoint a Children's Guardian (also an officer of Cafcass). The case will then be investigated in more depth. Under section 22 of the Adoption and Children Act 2002 a Cafcass officer is responsible for witnessing pre-court consent to adoption and reporting back to the adoption agency prior to the court application for an adoption order.

(iii) Adoption procedure   Rules of court and practice directions govern the procedure for adoption (see Part 14 of the Family Procedure Rules 2010 ('Procedure for Applications in Adoption, Placement and Related Proceedings') and its related Practice Directions). Although all three tiers of the family court have jurisdiction to hear adoptions, certain county courts are designated as adoption centres and any application for an adoption order in a county court must be commenced in such a centre.

(iv) The problem of delay   Due to concerns about delays in the adoption process, particularly with respect to children who are adopted after entering care, the Government, in March 2012, published *An Action Plan for Adoption: Tackling Delay* (Department for Education, www.education.gov.uk) setting out a range of proposals aimed *inter alia* at speeding up the adoption process for children. The action plan is the first part of a programme of reform which aims to improve the lives of children who enter local authority care. In March 2012, Ofsted announced new adoption inspection rating criteria whereby those local authorities which ensure all children identified for adoption are placed within 12 months, unless there are exceptional circumstances, are likely to achieve an 'outstanding' judgment. The Children and Families 2012–2013, which was debated in the Commons in February 2013, also includes provisions to reduce delays in adoptions and in care proceedings so that children do not face long and unnecessary delays in finding permanent, loving and stable homes; and to prevent delays in matching ethnic minority children with potential adopters as it takes much longer for black children to be adopted than other children.

(v) Agency and non-agency adoptions   Agency adoptions are adoptions involving local authority adoption services or voluntary adoption organisations (see the Consortium of Voluntary Adoption Agencies, www.cvaa.org.uk) most of which are part of local authority children's services, and which have statutory responsibilities under the Adoption and Children Act 2002 for making arrangements for adoption and placing children for adoption (ss 2–17). Local authorities are required to maintain adoption and adoption support services, which they must advertise (ss 3–5). Adoption agencies must also provide counselling, advice and information about adoption (s 2(6)).

Non-agency adoptions are adoptions which usually involve children who are not in the care of a local authority. They include children who are being adopted by a step-parent or a member, or members, of their wider family (such as a grandparent) and also children who are placed for adoption from overseas through an intercountry arrangement. Persons who wish to adopt a child who is not placed for adoption with them by an adoption agency must give notice to their local authority (see p. 420 below).

(vi) Illegal arrangements, placements and transactions   It is a criminal offence for a person or body other than an adoption agency to make arrangements for adoption and for unauthorised persons to prepare adoption reports (ss 92–94). It is also unlawful for persons to advertise for adoption (ss 123, 124). Certain payments and rewards made in connection with adoption are also prohibited (s 95), although the court may retrospectively authorise certain payments. There are also prohibitions on bringing overseas children into the UK for the purpose of adoption.

(vii) 'In family' adoptions   These involve an adoption by a relative, step-parent or civil partner. Such adoptions can have drawbacks, as they can sever the child's legal and social relationship with the other birthparent and the birth parent's family. At one time step-parents would often seek to adopt a step-child in order to acquire parental responsibility, but they had to make a joint application for an adoption order with the child's natural parent (which meant, rather bizarrely, that the natural parent was adopting his or her own child). However, the Adoption and Children Act 2002 now permits a step-parent to make a sole application for adoption. Step-parents now also have other ways of ways of obtaining parental responsibility, such as by means of a parental responsibility agreement or parental responsibility order (see 9.5), a special guardianship order (see 15.14), or a residence order (see 10.5). These alternatives are likely to be better for a child, as a step-parent adoption has the disadvantage of cutting a child off from the other half of his or her birth family and of 'skewing' family relationships.

A civil partner can also make a sole application to adopt the child of his or her civil partner (see 15.6).

(viii) Alternatives to adoption   As adoption is a radical step, in that it terminates the birth parents' parental responsibility and gives it to the adopters, it may be in the child's best interests for parental responsibility to be acquired, not by adoption, but in one of the following ways: a special guardianship order (see 15.14); a residence order (see10.5); or a parental responsibility agreement or order (see 9.3). The disadvantage of these alternatives to adoption, however, is that they lack the certainty and finality of adoption which may cause insecurity for the child and the child's carer(s).

15.2 Adoption trends and the development of the law

(a) Adoption trends

At one time adoption was much more common than it is today. For example, in 1971 there were 21,495 adoptions. However, during the 1970s the number of adoptions declined rapidly and continued to decline steadily in the decades that followed. Currently only about 4,000 children are adopted in England and Wales each year (see below).

The decline in adoptions has been due in part to fewer babies being available for adoption as a result of improved contraception, the legalisation of abortion, and the fact that single mothers are no longer stigmatised and put under pressure to give up their babies. Children who are available for adoption today are usually older children, many of whom are in local authority care.

Statistical bulletin: Adoptions in England and Wales, 2011, **published in August 2012, Office for National Statistics, www.ons.gov.uk**

Key Findings

▶ The number of adoptions in England and Wales in 2011 was 4,734, an increase of 6 per cent since 2010 when there were 4,481 adoptions.
▶ In 2011, most children adopted (62 per cent) were aged between one and four years, rising from 58 per cent in 2010.
▶ The percentage of children adopted who were born outside marriage increased slightly to 82 per cent in 2011, up from 80 per cent in 2010.

At one time many adoptions were step-parent adoptions, but this is no longer the case as alternatives to adoption are now available (see above).

(b) The development of the law

In the late 1980s and early 1990s the then Conservative Government conducted an inter-departmental review of adoption; and various research and consultation documents were published including an Adoption Bill making fundamental changes to adoption law, but this was not presented to Parliament before the Conservative Government lost the election in 1997.

When the Labour Government came into power in 1997, it announced that it was committed to improving adoption (see para 1.5, *Supporting Families*, Home Office, 1998). However, it began to realise, because of major failings in the child care system, that adoption could provide a better alternative for children in care. The 'Waterhouse Report' (*Lost in Care – Report of the Tribunal of Inquiry into the Abuse of Children in Care in the Former County Council Areas of Gwynedd and Clwyd*, 2000) identified 'drift' in care as one of the major failings of the child protection system. Tony Blair, the Prime Minister, reacted to the Waterhouse Report by announcing that he would personally lead a thorough review of adoption policy in order to ensure that the Government was making the best use of adoption as an option to meet the needs of children looked after by local authorities. The *Prime Minister's Review: Adoption* (a study of the use of adoption for children in care, by the Performance and Innovation Unit of the Cabinet Office, 2000) said that too many children were in care for too long and that they needed a family who could meet their needs on a permanent basis. It recommended that the Government should promote the increased use of adoption for children in care. The White Paper, *Adoption: A New Approach*, 2000, Cm 5017, set out the Government's plans to promote the greater use of adoption, to improve the performance of the adoption service and to put children at the centre of the adoption process. These developments led to the enactment of the Adoption and Children Act 2002, which came fully into force on 30 December 2005.

The Adoption and Children Act 2002 replaced the Adoption Act 1976 and modernised the legal framework for adoption in England and Wales. It made the following important changes to adoption law:

Changes to adoption law made by the Adoption and Children Act 2002

The Adoption and Children Act 2002:

▶ aligned adoption law with the Children Act 1989 by making the child's welfare the paramount consideration in all decisions relating to adoption;
▶ introduced a new welfare-based ground for dispensing with parental consent;
▶ abolished freeing for adoption orders and introduced new measures for placement for adoption (by parental consent or placement order);
▶ overhauled eligibility to apply for adoption by enabling single persons, married couples, civil partners, and, for the first time, unmarried couples (opposite-sex and same-sex) to apply; and introduced new provisions to enable step-parents to make sole applications for adoption;
▶ placed a duty on local authorities to maintain an Adoption Service, including new arrangements for the provision of Adoption Support Services;
▶ established an Independent Reviewing Mechanism to enable prospective adopters who had been turned down for adoption to be entitled to an independent review;
▶ established an Adoption and Children Act Register to suggest matches between children waiting to be adopted and approved prospective adopters;
▶ introduced new measures for tackling delay (courts are required to draw up timetables to prevent delay; and a 'no-delay' principle like that in the Children Act 1989 was introduced); and
▶ introduced special guardianship to provide permanence for children who could not return to their birth families, but for whom adoption was not the most suitable option.

A major aim of the Adoption and Children Act 2002 is to encourage the wider use of adoption for children in care. With a view to encouraging more adoptions of children in care, and to make them succeed, the Act places a duty on local authorities to provide comprehensive support services. To prevent delay in matching children with adoptive families, the Adoption and Children Act Register suggests matches between children waiting to be adopted and approved prospective adopters (ss 125–131).

The Government is currently engaged in reforming the law in order, in particular, to reduce the delays which are endemic in the adoption process (see p. 413 above).

15.3 The welfare principles

Section 1 of the Adoption and Children Act 2002 lays down the welfare principles which must be applied by courts and adoption agencies when coming to a decision relating to the adoption of a child (s 1(1)). They are similar to the welfare principles in the Children Act 1989 (see 10.3).

(i) The welfare principle (section 1(2)) The welfare principle is as follows:

Section 1(2) 'The paramount consideration of the court or adoption agency must be the child's welfare, throughout his life.'

Unlike the Children Act 1989 the welfare principle in adoption requires an analysis of the child's welfare through childhood into adulthood and for the rest of the child's life. It therefore emphasises that adoption is something with lifelong implications. The welfare principle also applies to the issue of dispensing with consent (see 15.9).

(ii) The no-delay principle (section 1(3)) The 'court or adoption agency must at all times bear in mind that, in general, any delay in coming to the decision is likely to prejudice the child's welfare'. Despite this provision, delays in adoption are still a matter of concern.

(iii) The welfare checklist (section 1(4)) Courts and adoption agencies, when determining the best interests of the child in any decision relating to adoption, must have regard to the following factors:

'(a) the child's ascertainable wishes and feelings regarding the decision (considered in the light of the child's age and understanding);
(b) the child's particular needs;
(c) the likely effect on the child (throughout his life) of having ceased to be a member of the original family and become an adopted person;
(d) the child's age, sex, background and any of the child's characteristics which the court or agency considers relevant;
(e) any harm (within the meaning of the Children Act 1989) which the child has suffered or is at risk of suffering;
(f) the relationship which the child has with relatives, and with any other person in relation to whom the court or agency considers the relationship to be relevant, including –
   (i) the likelihood of any such relationship continuing and the value to the child of its doing so;
   (ii) the ability and willingness of any of the child's relatives, or of any such person, to provide the child with a secure environment in which the child can develop, and otherwise to meet the child's needs;
   (iii) the wishes and feelings of any of the child's relatives, or of any such person, regarding the child.'

'Relationships' in section 1(4) are not confined to legal relationships (s 1(8)(a)), and 'relatives' includes *inter alia* the child's mother and father (s 1(8)(b)). 'Harm' in section 1(4)(e) includes seeing or hearing the ill-treatment of another (such as witnessing domestic violence). As section 1(2) and section 1(4)(c) require courts and adoption agencies to consider the child 'throughout his life', inheritance and succession interests may be relevant considerations.

(iv) The child's religious, racial, cultural and linguistic background (section 1(5))   When placing a child for adoption, 'the adoption agency must give due consideration to the child's religious persuasion, racial origin and cultural and linguistic background' (s 1(5)). However, the courts have held that, although religious beliefs must be taken into account, they are not necessarily determinative, but merely one of the factors that comprise welfare (*per* Ryder J in *Haringey London Borough Council v C, E and Another Intervening* [2006] EWHC 1620 (Fam), [2007] 1 FLR 1035). Thus, however profound the religious belief may be, the child's welfare is the paramount consideration (see also *Re S; Newcastle City Council v Z* [2005] EWHC 1490 (Fam), [2007] 1 FLR 861, where the mother wished to delay adoption for religious reasons until suitable adopters had been found).

(v) Duty to consider other powers; and the 'minimum intervention' principle (section 1(6))   Courts and adoption agencies must consider the whole range of powers available under both the 2002 Act and the Children Act 1989 (see Chapter 10); and the court must not make any order unless doing so would be better for the child than not doing so (s 1(6)). Thus, if the court were to make an adoption order when another order would be sufficient to protect the child's welfare (for example, a special guardianship order), this might be contrary to section 1(6), and possibly the principle of proportionality which is part of the right to family life under Article 8 ECHR (see 1.7).

15.4 Eligibility for Adoption

(i) Who can be adopted?   The child must be under 18 on the date of the adoption application (s 49(4)), but an adoption order can be made if the child reaches 18 before the conclusion of adoption proceedings (s 49(5)). But an adoption order cannot be made in any case if the child is aged 19 or over, or is married (ss 47(8), (9)).

(ii) Who can adopt?   Couples and single persons can apply to adopt a child (s 49), provided they satisfy certain domicile and age limit requirements (ss 50, 51):

- *Couples*   Married couples, civil partners, and cohabitants (opposite-sex and same-sex who are living as partners in an enduring family relationship) (s 144(4)) can apply. Each applicant must be at least 21 (s 50(1)), unless one of the couple is the child's mother or father, when she or he need be only 18 (s 50(2)).
- *Sole applicant*   An adoption order may be applied for by a sole applicant who is at least 21 years old and is unmarried (s 51(1)). An application may also be made by a person who has attained the age of 21 years if the court is satisfied that the person is the partner of a parent of the person to be adopted (s 51(2)) (in other words a step-parent or a civil partner of the parent of the child can apply). These requirements, other than the age requirement, can be waived if the court is satisfied that the other spouse cannot be found; or that the couple are separated permanently and are living apart; or that the other spouse is incapacitated from applying due to physical or mental ill-health (s 51(3)). The mother or father of the child to be adopted cannot apply to adopt the child unless the court is satisfied that: the other natural parent is dead or cannot be found; or by virtue of section 28 of the Human Fertilisation and Embryology Act 1990, there is no other parent, or there is some other reason justifying the child's being adopted by the applicant alone (s 51(4)).

(iii) Foster-parent applicants   A local authority foster-parent can apply to adopt a foster-child provided the child has had his or her home with the applicant at all times during the period of one year preceding the application (s 42(4)); or if the court grants leave (permission) for the application to be made (s 42(6)). The legal principles relevant to a leave application are the same as those for applications for leave to apply for revocation of a placement order under section 24(2) of the ACA 2002 (see pp. 425–6 below; and, see, for example, *Re A; Coventry County Council v CC and A* [2007] EWCA Civ 1383, [2008] 1 FLR 959, where a foster-mother was granted leave to apply for an adoption order).

(iv) Domicile requirements   At least one of the couple (or the sole applicant) must be domiciled in part of the British Islands; or both of the couple or the sole applicant must have been habitually resident in part of the British Islands for a period of not less than one year ending with the date of the application (s 49).

(v) Baby adoptions   Special provisions apply to the adoption of babies who are less than six weeks old. Thus, although such a baby may be placed for adoption without the need for formal consent under section 19 or a placement order (s 18(1)), any consent by the birthmother to placement for adoption or adoption is ineffective if given within six weeks of the child's birth (ss 52(3) and 47(4)). This time limit is to allow the mother to recover from the child's birth and to be sure that adoption is what she really wishes.

15.5 Preliminaries to making an adoption order or placement order

Before an adoption order or placement order can be made various procedures must be complied with as required by the Adoption and Children Act 2002, the Family Procedure Rules 2010 (and relevant practice directions) and the adoption regulations. These requirements are strict. Due process must be followed. Any failure to comply with the requirements may result in an order being set aside (see, for instance, *Re B (Placement Order)* [2008] EWCA Civ 835, [2008] 2 FLR 1404 where a placement order was set aside as the agency had failed to provide the Adoption Panel with the required experts' reports and had misrepresented one expert).

(i) Probationary residence requirements for adoption   In an agency case, the child must have had his home with the applicant(s) at all times for a 10-week period preceding the application (s 42(2)). In a non-agency case, the residence requirements are as follows: step-parent or civil partner of the child's parent (a continuous period of at least six months preceding the application, s 42(3)); and local authority foster-parents (a continuous period of at least one year preceding the application, s 42(4)). With other applications (such as by a relative), the child must have had his or her home with the applicant(s) for a cumulative period of at least three years (which need not be continuous) during a five-year period preceding the application, except where the court grants leave to apply (ss 42(5), (6)).

(ii) Agency adoptions – duty to provide a report (s 43)   The adoption agency must submit to the court a report dealing with the suitability of the applicants and any relevant section 1 welfare issue in respect of the child, and must assist the court in any manner the court directs. A Cafcass officer (see 1.7) is responsible for compiling the report.

(iii) Non-agency adoptions – notice of intention to adopt (section 44)　The prospective adopter(s) must give notice to the appropriate local authority of their intention to apply for an adoption order, which must be given not more than two years, or less than three months, before the date on which the application for the adoption order is made. On receipt of notification, the local authority must arrange for the matter to be investigated; and it must submit a report to the court, in particular in respect of the prospective adopters' suitability for adopting and any relevant welfare issues under section 1 of the Act.

(iv) Suitability for adopting and the Independent Reviewing Mechanism　Under the adoption regulations, an adoption agency is required to take into account various matters for determining the suitability of the prospective adopter(s), and for reporting as to their suitability. If an adoption agency decides that a person is unsuitable to become an adoptive parent, that person (or both persons in the case of a couple adoption) can challenge the refusal by applying for an independent review under the Independent Reviewing Mechanism (IRM).

In *Hofstetter and Hofstetter v Brent London Borough Council* [2009] EWHC 3282 (Admin), [2010] 2 FLR 413 Charles J emphasised that the IRM was not intended to be an appeal process, but was part of a process that provided a second opinion from an independent panel of persons with relevant skill and experience. Charles J stated that, although a decision as to the suitability of applicants as adopters is for the adoption agency, the decision of an IRM panel is an important matter; and a decision by an adoption agency to ignore it might result in a successful judicial review challenge. In *R (AT, TT and S) v Newham London Borough Council* [2008] EWHC 2640 (Admin), [2009] 1 FLR 311, for example, the parents successfully challenged the local authority's decision to overturn the unanimous decision of the IRM panel which was that they were suitable persons to adopt a child. Bennett J granted their application on the ground of procedural unfairness, quashed the local authority's decision and ordered that the matter as to their suitability be considered afresh. Bennett J also held that the welfare principle in section 1(2) ACA 2002 does not apply to cases of suitability to adopt.

(v) The 'consent condition' or 'placement condition' must be satisfied (section 47)　With respect to adoption, the court must be satisfied that: each parent or guardian consents to the making of the adoption order or has given advance consent and does not oppose the making of the adoption order; or that the consent of each parent or guardian can be dispensed with. With respect to placement for adoption (whether by the consensual route or by placement order), the court must be satisfied that the child has been placed for adoption with the prospective adopters with the consent of each parent or guardian; or has been placed under a placement order and that no parent or guardian opposes the making of the adoption order.

15.6　Applying for an adoption order

(i) The adoption order　An adoption order (see section 46) is an order giving parental responsibility for the child to the adopter(s). It extinguishes the parental responsibility of the child's mother and father, and any other person with parental responsibility; and it terminates any order made under the Children Act 1989 (s 46(2)). In the case of a step-parent adoption, however, the adoption order does not affect the parental responsibility or duties of the person who is the adopted child's natural parent (s 46(3)

(b)). An adoption order extinguishes any duty to pay child maintenance (by agreement or court order), except where the maintenance duty arises under a trust or by the terms of an agreement which expressly provides that the maintenance duty is not to be extinguished (s 46(4)). An adoption order may be made even if the child to be adopted is already an adopted child (s 46(5)).

(ii) Conditions for making an adoption order (see section 47)   An adoption order may not be made if the child has a parent or guardian unless one of the following two conditions is met (subject to the provisions on consent in section 52 – see 15.9):

1. That, in the case of each parent or guardian of the child, the court is satisfied that the parent or guardian consents to the making of the adoption order, that the parent or guardian has consented under section 20 (and has not withdrawn the consent) and does not oppose the making of the adoption order, or that the parent's or guardian's consent should be dispensed with.
2. That the child has been placed for adoption by an adoption agency with the prospective adopters in whose favour the order is proposed to be made, either with the consent of each parent or guardian and the consent of the mother was given when the child was at least six weeks old; or under a placement order, and no parent or guardian opposes the making of the adoption order.

An adoption order cannot be made in relation to a person who is or has been married (s 47(8)) or who has attained the age of 19 (s 47(9)).

(iii) How the court exercises its power   The court must take into account the welfare principle and the other principles in section 1 of the Act (see 10.3). Before making the order, the court must also consider whether there should be arrangements for allowing any person to have contact with the child (s 46(6)).

(iv) Restrictions on making a further application for an adoption order   Where a previous application for an adoption order has been refused by any court, a second application for an adoption order may not be heard unless it appears to the court that there is a change in circumstances, or other reason, which makes it proper to hear the application (s 48(1)).

(v) The status of the adopted child (section 67)   An adopted person is treated in law as if he or she was born as the child of the adopter(s). An adopted person is the legitimate child of the adopter(s), and, if the child is adopted by a couple or by one of a couple under a step-parent or civil partner adoption, the child is to be treated as the child of that relationship.

15.7   Challenging an adoption order

There are various ways in which an adoption order can be challenged.

(i) Opposing the making of an adoption order   If a parent or guardian wishes to oppose the making of an adoption order, then leave of the court is required (under section 47(3) or section 47(5)). The court cannot grant leave, however, unless it is satisfied that there has been a change in circumstances since the consent of the parent or

guardian was given or the placement order was made (s 47(7)). In other words, the circumstances must be sufficient to justify reopening the matter. However, the court has held that the right to oppose the making of an adoption order after care and placement orders is likely to be very limited, and leave will be granted only in very exceptional circumstances (see *Re P (Adoption: Leave Provisions)* [2007] EWCA Civ 616, [2007] 2 FLR 1069 as clarified in *M v Warwickshire County Council* [2007] EWCA Civ 1084, [2008] 1 FLR 1093). In *Re W (Adoption Order: Set Aside and Leave to Oppose)* [2010] EWCA Civ 1535 the Court of Appeal held that a judge must have great regard to the impact of the grant of leave on the child within the adoptive family. Here, it was held that the trial judge's approach had been too permissive: a stringent approach was necessary and the language of McFarlane J in *X and Y v A Local Authority (Adoption: Procedure)* [2009] EWHC 47 (Fam), [2009] 2 FLR 984 was to be preferred.

(ii) Appealing an adoption order An appeal against the making of an adoption order can be brought on the ground, for instance, that the trial judge was plainly wrong or that there was a procedural irregularity and/or a breach of human rights. Appeals on the basis of procedural irregularity or unfairness are sometimes brought. In *Re T (Adoption)* [2012] EWCA Civ 191 the Court of Appeal emphasised that proper legal representation and due process are fundamental where such life-changing orders are being made, and, in the circumstances of the case, it ordered a retrial.

(iii) Setting aside an adoption order Once an adoption order has been lawfully and properly made, it is only in highly exceptional circumstances that the court will permit the order to be set aside. For example, in *Webster v Norfolk County Council and the Children (By Their Children's Guardian)* [2009] EWCA Civ 59, [2009] 1 FLR 1378 the parents failed in their application to set aside adoption orders on the ground that three of their children had been taken into care and adopted on the basis of a wrong diagnosis of non-accidental injury. An application to set aside an adoption order also failed in *Re PW (Adoption)* [2011] EWHC 3793 (Fam) where an adopted woman in her sixties applied to set aside or revoke an adoption order (made 51 years earlier) on the grounds that she had not been asked about her wishes and feelings when she was adopted; and that the adoption had not been in her best interests. (See also *Re B (Adoption Order: Jurisdiction to Set Aside)* [1995] Fam 239, [1995] 2 FLR 1FLR 221.)

15.8 Placement for adoption

Sections 18–29 of the Adoption and Children Act 2002 contain provisions on placement for adoption. The aim of placement for adoption is to enable consent to adoption to be sorted out at the placement stage and for any subsequent leave (permission) for the child's natural parent(s) to oppose the adoption to be granted only if there has been a change of circumstances after the placement order was made (s 47(7)).

An adoption agency may place a child with prospective adopters or leave the child where he or she has already been placed, provided the child is at least six weeks old, and either the natural parents have consented to the child being placed (see 15.9) or a placement order (see below) has been made (s 18(1)). The adoption agency must be satisfied that the child should be placed for adoption with the prospective adopters (s 18(2)). Once a child is placed, or is authorised to be placed, for adoption by a local authority, the child is described as being 'looked after' by the local authority for the purposes of the Children Act 1989, whereupon it has certain obligations to the child (s 18(3)) (see 14.10).

(a) Placement by consent of the birthparents (section 19)

An adoption agency can place a child for adoption (except a baby aged under six weeks), provided it is satisfied that each parent or guardian has consented to the child being placed for adoption and that such consent has not been withdrawn (see s 19). 'Consent' must be given unconditionally and with full understanding of what is involved, but a person may consent to adoption without knowing the identity of the persons in whose favour the order will be made (s 52). A parent who consents to a child being placed for adoption may at the same time, or subsequently, give advance consent to the making of a future adoption order (s 20).

Consent can be withdrawn at any time (s 20(3)). The person giving consent can give notice to the adoption agency stating that he or she does not wish to be informed of any application for an adoption order, or can withdraw such statement (s 20(4)). Where consent has not been withdrawn before an adoption application has been made, but the birthparents do not wish the child to be adopted, they can defend the final adoption order but only with leave of the court (see pp. 421–2 above).

(b) Placement by placement order (section 21)

A child can be placed for adoption by way of a placement order, which is an order 'authorising a local authority to place a child for adoption with any prospective adopters who may be chosen by the authority' (s 21(1)).

(i) Preconditions A placement order can only be made if: the child is subject to a care order; or the court is satisfied that the threshold conditions for making a care order are met (see 14.7); or the child has no parent or guardian (s 21(2)). The court must be satisfied that each of the child's parents or guardian has consented to the child being placed for adoption with any prospective adopters who may be chosen by the local authority and that that consent has not been withdrawn or that their consent should be dispensed with (s 21(3) – see 15.9).

(ii) A duty or a discretion to apply A local authority has an obligation to apply for a placement order in some circumstance, and a discretion to apply in others.

A duty to apply A local authority *must* apply for a placement order if: the child has been placed for adoption by them or is being provided with accommodation by them; no adoption agency is authorised to place the child for adoption; the child has no parent or guardian; or the authority considers the threshold criteria for a care order are met (see 14.7); *and* the authority is satisfied that the child ought to be placed for adoption (s 22(1)). A local authority *must* also apply for a placement order if it is satisfied that the child ought to be placed for adoption and: an application has been made (and has not been disposed of) on which a care order might be made in respect of a child; or the child is subject to a care order and the appropriate local authority is not authorised to place the child for adoption (s 22(2)).

A discretion to apply A local authority *may* apply for a placement order if: the child is subject to a care order; and the local authority is authorised to place the child for adoption by parental consent (s 22(3)).

There is no duty or discretion to apply for a placement order if: there is notice of an intention to adopt (unless four months have passed since notification without an application having been made, or the application has been withdrawn or refused) (s 25(2)); or an application for an adoption order has been made but has not been disposed of (s 25(2)).

If a local authority is under a duty to apply for a placement order, or has made an application but it has not been disposed of, the child is described as being 'looked after by the authority' (s 22(4)).

A placement order can be varied on the joint application of two local authorities for the purpose of substituting one local authority for the other (s 23).

(iii) Making a placement order – the exercise of discretion When considering whether to make a placement order, the court must apply the welfare principle and the other principles in section 1 of the Adoption and Children Act 2002 (see 15.3). Before making the order, the court must consider what arrangements for contact the adoption agency has made, or proposes to make, for the child, and must invite the parties to comment on those arrangements (s 27(7)). The court may, in an appropriate case, make an order as to contact. The court cannot make a placement order unless an effort has been made to notify the child's parent(s) or guardian(s) with parental responsibility about the application (s 141).

As a matter of law a placement order can be made even though the prospect of placing a child may prove difficult and it is uncertain whether an adoption will actually be achievable (see *Re T (Placement Order)* [2008] EWCA Civ 542 where, on the facts, the Court of Appeal held that the two boys' best interests would be best served by long-term fostering rather than by adoption).

The court will not make a placement order merely on the basis that the long-term aim is for adoption, although the possibility of substantial difficulty and delay in finding a suitable adoptive placement, or even an ultimate failure to do so, does not prevent the court from making a placement order (see *Re S-H (A Child) (Placement Order)* [2008] EWCA Civ 493, [2008] 2 FLR 918 where Wilson LJ said that the 'necessary foundation for a placement order is that, broadly speaking, the child is presently in a condition to be adopted and is ready to be adopted').

In *Re H (Care and Placement Order: Application of Principles)* [2012] EWCA Civ 743, where the mother's appeal against both care and placement orders was allowed, the Court of Appeal held that placement orders do not follow automatically or consequentially from the making of care orders. It held that they are orders of the greatest significance and that, if they require parental consent to be overridden, albeit on welfare grounds, they must be preceded by preparations and processes that duly respect the Article 6 ECHR rights of the parents (the right to a fair hearing). Here, on the facts, it was held that there had been no opportunity for the mother to prepare and present arguments to resist the application, which was decided far too prematurely.

Directions The court can direct a medical, psychiatric or other assessment of the child where an application for a placement order is pending or no interim care order has been made – but a child of sufficient understanding to make an informed decision can refuse to submit to the examination or assessment (s 22(6)). As this power is similar to that in section 38(6) Children Act 1989 (see pp. 394–5), similar considerations are likely to apply.

(iv) Duration of the order   A placement order remains in force until revoked; or an adoption order is made; or the child marries or becomes a civil partner; or the child reaches the age of 18 (s 21(4)).

(v) Representation of the child   A child is party to placement order proceedings; and the court has a duty to appoint a Children's Guardian to safeguard the child's interests, unless it is not necessary to do so. Separate representation for the child is permitted in some circumstances.

(vi) Revocation of a placement order (section 24)   Any person (except the child and the local authority) can apply to revoke a placement order, provided leave (permission) to apply has been granted by the court and the child has not been placed for adoption by the local authority (ss 24(1), (2)). Leave can be granted only if there has been a change of circumstances since the placement order was made (s 24(3)). When considering whether to grant leave, the welfare of the child is not the court's *paramount* consideration (as section 1 of the ACA 2002 does not apply), but it is a *relevant* consideration. The court's approach to leave applications is similar to the approach to leave applications for section 8 orders under the Children Act 1989. Thus, the applicant must have a real prospect of securing revocation of the placement order; and the court must take account of the delay that granting leave might cause. In *Re A; Coventry CC v CC and A* [2007] EWCA Civ 1383, [2008] 1 FLR 959 Wilson LJ provided guidance as to the approach to an application for leave to apply for revocation of a placement order; and held that, on the establishment of a change of circumstances, a discretion to grant leave arose in which the welfare of the child and the prospect of success should both be weighed.

Even where there has been a change of circumstances, the court has a discretion as to whether to grant leave to apply for revocation. Thus, for example, in *M v Warwickshire County Council* [2007] EWCA Civ 1084, [2008] 1 FLR 1093 the mother applied for leave to apply for revocation of the placement orders (which had been made in respect of her two children) on the basis of a change of circumstances (that she had, *inter alia*, abstained from drugs, reduced her alcohol consumption and attended an HIV clinic), but her application for leave was refused by the Court of Appeal.

In *Re S-H (A Child) (Placement Order)* [2008] EWCA Civ 493, [2008] 2 FLR 918 the Court of Appeal held that it would occasionally be appropriate to grant leave even though there was no real prospect that a court would find that it would be in the child's interests to return to live with the parents. Here the Court of Appeal held that it was in the child's interests to grant leave to revoke the placement order, in order to give the court an opportunity to examine the apparent change in the child's current suitability for adoption.

In *NS-H v Kingston Upon Hull City Council and MC* [2008] EWCA Civ 493, [2008] 2 FLR 918 Ward LJ made it clear that the court must guard against opportunistic attempts to use an application for revocation for improper, collateral purposes, but the Court of Appeal granted the mother leave to apply to revoke the placement order as the child's failure to thrive in foster-care and associated developments amounted to a change in circumstances sufficient to meet the threshold for applying for revocation.

In addition to the leave requirement, revocation of a placement order is not possible if the child has already been placed for adoption (s 24(2)), which must be with a prospective, not potential, adopter (see *Re S (Placement Order: Revocation)* [2008] EWCA Civ 1333, [2009] 1 FLR 503). In *Re F (Placement Order)* [2008] EWCA Civ 439, [2008] 2 FLR 550 the Court of Appeal by a majority (Thorpe LJ dissenting) refused to grant leave (as the child had already been placed for adoption), even though the applicant for leave, who was the child's father, had not been involved in the proceedings for care and placement orders as he had been hospitalised due to a heart attack. The father's arguments based on human rights failed as the Court of Appeal held that section 24 was already human rights compliant.

(vii) Effect of a placement order A placement order gives parental responsibility to the local authority (s 25(2)) or to the prospective adopters while the child is with them (s 25(3)). During the placement the parents' parental responsibility is not extinguished until the final adoption order is made. Parental responsibility is shared with the prospective adopters and the adoption agency, with the agency determining the extent to which the parental responsibility of the child's parents or of the prospective adopters is to be restricted (s 25(4)); and with the power to remove the child from the placement. If a placement with prospective adopters breaks down, and the local authority considers adoption is still in the child's best interests, there is no need for it to apply for another placement order before it makes a new adoption placement.

Once a placement order has been made, only the local authority can remove the child. The placement order remains in force until: it is revoked (see above); or an adoption order is made; or the child marries or becomes a civil partner; or attains the age of 18.

The adoption agency can remove the child from the placement (for example, where the placement is failing), whether or not the birthparents have requested the child's return (s 30). Once placement for adoption has been authorised, contact provisions under sections 8 and 34 Children Act 1989 cease to have effect (ss 26(1), (6)), but this does not prevent an application for a contact order being made under section 26 of the 2002 Act (see 15.10).

While a placement order is in force:

▶ No-one may cause the child to be known by a new surname or remove the child from the UK (except for a period of up to one month by the person who provides the child's home), unless the court has given permission, or the child's parents or guardians have given *written* consent (ss 28(2), (3)).

▶ Any care order ceases to have effect (s 29(1)), and, on the making of the placement order, any section 8 order or supervision order under the Children Act 1989 ceases to have effect (s 29(2)). (A child subject to a placement order remains 'the subject of a care order' within section 100(2)(c) CA 1989 and, although the child cannot be made a ward of court, it remains open for a local authority to apply for leave to invoke the inherent jurisdiction in respect of the child – see *Re S-H (A Child) (Placement Order)* [2008] EWCA Civ 493, [2008] 2 FLR 918).

▶ The court has no power to make a section 8 order, a supervision order or a child assessment order under the Children Act 1989 (s 29(3)).

▶ A special guardianship order cannot be made until a final adoption order is made, but leave will be needed to apply for one. If a special guardianship order is made it does not automatically discharge the placement order. The court will have to consider whether to revoke the placement order, applying the welfare principle and the other section 1 principles.

There are also restrictions on making contact orders. Parents, guardians and other persons can, however, apply for a residence order if they have obtained the court's leave under section 47(3) or section 47(5) to oppose the making of a final adoption order.

(viii) Restrictions on removing the child pending a placement order A child who is being accommodated pending a placement order cannot be removed from that accommodation except with leave of the court or the local authority (s 30(2)). Where a placement order has been made, only the local authority can remove the child (s 34). Thus, parents have no automatic right to have their children returned to them. The only remedy they have is to apply for revocation of the placement order, which may be difficult.

(ix) Baby placements An adoption agency may place a baby who is less than six weeks old for adoption with the voluntary agreement of the parent or guardian, whereupon the baby becomes a 'looked after' child of the local authority. However, the placement provisions do not apply. Thus, the agency has no power to determine to what extent the parental responsibility of any parent, or of the prospective adopters, can be restricted under section 25(4) of the Act.

15.9 Consent to adoption and placement for adoption

Consent is relevant both to placement for adoption and to adoption. Section 52(5) of the Adoption and Children Act 2002 provides that 'consent' means 'consent given unconditionally and with full understanding of what is involved; but a person may consent to adoption without knowing the identity of the persons in whose favour the order will be made'.

(i) Whose consent is required? The consent of each parent or guardian of the child (including a special guardian) is required before an adoption agency may place a child for adoption (s 19(1)) or the court can make an adoption order (s 47(2)). As 'parent' for the purposes of consent means a parent with parental responsibility (s 52(6)), the consent of the unmarried father without parental responsibility is not required. However, where an unmarried mother consents to adoption under section 19 (placement by parental consent), a father who subsequently acquires parental responsibility is to be treated as having at that time given consent in accordance with section 52 on the same terms as the mother (ss 52(9), (10)). Where a father acquires parental responsibility after an application for an adoption order has been made, he can, with leave (permission) of the court, oppose the adoption order on the basis that there has been a change of circumstances (s 46). (For more on the rights of the unmarried father and adoption, see pp. 428–30 below.) Although the consent of the child's relatives is not needed, the court can take their wishes into account under the section 1(4) welfare checklist (see p. 417 above).

(ii) Mother's consent within six weeks of birth In respect of an adoption order, any consent given by a mother is ineffective if given less than six weeks after the child's birth (s 52(3)). The policy behind this provision is that the mother should be given time to

recover from the physical and emotional effects of birth. In respect of a placement order, however, a mother's consent may be given at any time after the child's birth.

In *A Local Authority v GC and Others* [2008] EWHC 2555 (Fam), [2009] 1 FLR 299 the parents had signed the consent to placement for adoption (under section 19) and to the making of a future adoption order (under section 20) when their child was only four weeks old, but, despite the error, Eleanor King J held that the adoption was lawful on the basis that the parents' consent could be dispensed with so that the six-week requirement did not need to be satisfied.

(iii) Formalities Consent to placement for adoption and to the making of an adoption order (including advance consent) must be given in the prescribed form (s 52(7)). Cafcass officers are responsible for advising parents on consent and for witnessing consent, and for reporting to the court on matters relating to the child (see s 102).

(iv) Withdrawal of consent Once an application for an adoption order has been made, any consent given with respect to the placement for adoption or any advance consent cannot be withdrawn (s 52(4)). Parents who wish to oppose the adoption order after the cut-off point must obtain leave to do so, and the court can grant leave only if it is satisfied that there has been a change of circumstances since the consent was given or the placement order was made (see pp. 421–2 above).

(v) Advance consent (section 20) A parent or guardian who consents to the child being placed for adoption by an adoption agency (under section 19) may at the same time, or at any subsequent time, consent to the making of a future adoption order (s 20(1)). Advance consent can be withdrawn (s 20(3)), but any withdrawal is ineffective if made after an application for an adoption order has been made (s 52(4)). A parent who gives advance consent can at the same time, or subsequently, give notice to the adoption agency stating that he does not wish to be informed of any application for an adoption order (or can withdraw such statement) (s 20(4)). If a parent gives advance consent and chooses not to be notified of the application for the adoption order, placement and adoption can proceed without that parent being involved in any way. Parents are given some protection, however, as they have a right to be notified of the date and place of the adoption application (see s 143), whereupon they can apply for leave to oppose the making of the adoption order, which the court can grant if there has been a change of circumstances since consent was given (s 47(7)). Advance consent is subject to the provisions governing dispensing with consent (see p. 430 below).

(vi) The unmarried father without parental responsibility – consent to and involvement in adoption Although there is no requirement in the Adoption and Children Act 2002 for unmarried fathers without parental responsibility to give their consent to placement for adoption or to adoption, the courts have been increasingly willing to involve them in the adoption process, particularly with the coming into force of the Human Rights Act 1998 and the risk of breaching a father's rights under Article 8 ECHR (right to family life) and Article 6 ECHR (right to a fair hearing) if he is not involved. In *Re R (Adoption: Father's Involvement)* [2001] 1 FLR 302 Thorpe LJ commented on the shift towards unmarried fathers without parental responsibility being accorded greater involvement in adoption proceedings, and held that the unmarried father might have been justified

in raising a complaint under Article 6 ECHR if he had not been given notice of the adoption proceedings.

In most cases the unmarried father will be notified about the adoption. In fact, in *Re H; Re G (Adoption: Consultation of Unmarried Fathers)* [2001] 1 FLR 646 (decided under the 'old' adoption law) Butler-Sloss P held that, as a matter of good practice, judges would be expected to give directions so that unmarried fathers were informed of adoption proceedings, unless good reasons to the contrary existed (for instance, where there was no family life between the father and the child). In *Re C (Adoption: Disclosure to Father)* [2005] EWHC 3385 (Fam), [2006] 2 FLR 589, Hedley J, referring to Butler-Sloss P in *Re H: Re G*, directed that the father without parental responsibility who was serving a prison sentence be informed about adoption proceedings despite the mother's wishes to the contrary. Hedley J said that both parents were entitled to be involved in decisions about their children, at least when the decision might have long-term implications for the child concerned. He said that, where family life was established as it has been here (they had parented other children together), then there had to be 'very compelling reasons indeed' why a parent should be shut out from notice of the existence of the child or proposals for the future of the child.

Despite the shift towards recognising the importance of unmarried fathers and their involvement in bringing up their child, and the recognition of the importance of the child having a right to know his or her identity and origins, the court may in the exercise of its discretion decide that it is not in the best interests of the child for the father to be informed about pending adoption proceedings, as the Court of Appeal did in the following case:

▶ *Re C (A Child) (Adoption: Duty of Local Authority)* [2007] Civ 1206, sub nom Re C (A Child) v XYZ County Council [2008] 1 FLR 1294

The child had been born as a result of a 'one-night stand' and the mother (aged 19) did not wish the child's father or her parents to know about the child's birth. The trial judge directed the local authority to disclose the existence and identity of the child to the extended maternal family and, if he could be identified, the putative father and any extended paternal family. The mother appealed.

The Court of Appeal allowed the appeal and gave directions pre-empting the guardian from taking further steps to identify the father. Arden LJ, applying sections 1(4)(c) and (f) of the welfare checklist, held that there is no duty of an absolute kind for inquiries to be made about the child's father when a decision needs to be made about the long-term care of a child. Such a duty only arises if it is in the child's best interests. There was no breach of the father's right to family life under Article 8 ECHR, as he had had no family life with the child. Neither was it a violation of the ECHR to deprive him of the possibility of obtaining a right to family life. The child's grandparents did have a right to family life under Article 8, but they would be able to obtain the information by making their own application under the Children Act 1989.

(For a commentary on *Re C*, see Sloan [2009] CFLQ 87, who criticises the Court of Appeal for using 'an unnecessarily narrow conception of welfare' and for giving 'undue weight to the interests of the child's mother'.)

In order to clarify the situation, it may be advisable for a local authority to obtain the authority of the court if it decides not to contact the unmarried father and/or the extended family. In *Re L (Adoption: Contacting Natural Father* [2007] EWHC 1771 (Fam),

[2008] 1 FLR 1079 the local authority under the inherent jurisdiction of the High Court (see 8.7) successfully did this.

(a) Grounds for dispensing with consent

Section 52(1) lays down two grounds on which the court can dispense with the consent of a parent or guardian to the child's adoption or placement for adoption:

▶ that a parent or guardian cannot be found or is incapable of giving consent (s 52(1) (a)); or
▶ that the welfare of the child requires the consent to be dispensed with (s 52(1)(b)).

The paramountcy of the child's welfare (s 1(2)) and the section 1(4) welfare checklist (see 15.4) apply to dispensing with consent.

Although the European Convention for the Protection of Human Rights, particularly Article 8 (the right to family life), is relevant to the question of consent, the Court of Appeal has held that the test for dispensing with consent in section 52(1)(b) does not, for this reason, demand an enhanced test beyond the welfare test set out in section 1(2); but that cogent justification must exist before consent can be dispensed with and adoption must be a proportionate and legitimate response (see *per* Wall LJ in *Re P (Placement Orders: Parental Consent)* [2008] EWCA Civ 535, [2008] 2 FLR 625). In *Re Q (Adoption)* [2011] EWCA Civ 1610, [2012] 1 FLR 1228 Munby LJ reiterated this point and also said that the word 'requires' in section 52(1)(b) above accurately captured the essence of the Strasbourg jurisprudence on necessity.

15.10 Contact

Applications for contact with respect to placement for adoption are governed by the Adoption and Children Act 2002, whereas other applications for contact are governed by the Children Act 1989. In July 2012, the Government published two discussion papers on adoption, one of which reviewed contact arrangements for children (*Contact Arrangements for Children: A Call for Views*, Department for Education, 2012). The other discussion paper looked at placing sibling groups for adoption (*Placing Children in Sibling Groups for Adoption: A Call for Views*, Department for Education, 2012.

(a) Contact and placement for adoption

Sections 26 and 27 of the Adoption and Children Act 2002 contain provisions with respect to contact in the context of placement for adoption. Once the adoption agency is authorised to place a child for adoption, it must consider what arrangements it should make for allowing any person to have contact with the child. The court will also have to consider contact between the child and his birthparents and family when it conducts the welfare exercise.

(i) Children Act 1989 contact orders not effective and applications barred Where an adoption agency is authorised to place a child for adoption (whether by consent or under a placement order), any provision for contact under section 8 or section 34 of the Children Act 1989 ceases to have effect (ss 26(1), (6)). While an adoption agency is authorised to place a child for adoption, or the child is placed for adoption, an application for contact

cannot be made under the Children Act 1989, but the court can make a contact order under section 26 ACA 2002.

(ii) A section 26 contact order Where an adoption agency is authorised to place a child for adoption (by parental consent or placement order), or the child is placed for adoption, the court can make a contact order under section 26 ACA 2002 requiring the person with whom the child lives, or is to live, to allow the child to visit or stay with the person named in the order, or for the person named in the order and the child otherwise to have contact with each other (s 26(2)). The following persons can apply for a section 26 contact order (s 26(3)): the child; the adoption agency; parents, guardians or relatives; any person with a contact order which has ceased to be effective by virtue of the child being placed for adoption; any person who had a residence order in force with respect to the child immediately before the placement; any person who has care of the child under an order made by the High Court under its inherent jurisdiction; and any other person who had obtained leave of the court. The court of its own initiative can make a section 26 contact order when making a placement order (s 26(4)).

The welfare principle and the other section 1 principles apply to the exercise of the court's discretion (see 15.3). The order may provide for contact on any conditions that the court considers appropriate (s 27(5)). The contact order is only effective while the adoption agency is authorised to place the child for adoption (or the child is less than six weeks old), but it may be varied or revoked by the court on the application of the child, the agency or the person named in the order (s 27(1)). The court may authorise the adoption agency to refuse to allow contact, if necessary to safeguard or promote the child's welfare, provided refusal is decided as a matter of urgency and does not last for more than seven days (s 27(2)).

(b)   Post-adoption contact

Once an adoption order is made, the birthparents lose their automatic right to apply for a contact order (and other orders) under section 8 of the Children Act 1989; and must obtain permission of the court to apply (see pp. 273–4), which the court may be unwilling to grant because of the possible disruption this may cause for the adopters and the child. Relatives and other persons who wish to have contact with the child also need leave to apply for a contact order under the Children Act 1989. Although post-adoption contact may help children resolve feelings of separation and loss, and give them a sense of their biological and social origins, it may deter potential adopters from coming forward to adopt children. In fact, ordering contact post-adoption is regarded by the courts as being particularly unusual if there is any disagreement or friction between the birth parents and the adopters (see further below).

Before making an adoption order, the court must consider whether any arrangements should be made for allowing any person contact with the child, and it must consider any existing or proposed arrangements and obtain the views of the parties to the proceedings (s 46(6)). Also, as the welfare checklist in section 1(4) of the 2002 Act requires the court in adoption proceedings to have regard to the whole range of powers under the Children Act 1989, the court must also consider whether to make a section 8 contact order under the Children Act 1989 of its own initiative.

The approach of the courts Although contact following adoption has become more common, the imposition on prospective adopters of orders for contact with which they are not in agreement is extremely unusual (see *per* Wall LJ in *Re R (Adoption: Contact)* [2005] EWCA Civ 1128, [2006] 1 FLR 373 where the half-sister's application for leave to apply for a section 8 contact order under section 10(9) of the Children Act 1989 was dismissed). Wall LJ's words were cited with approval by the Court of Appeal in *Oxfordshire County Council v X, Y and J* [2010] EWCA Civ 581, [2011] 1 FLR 272 where the court refused to order that the natural parents should receive an annual photograph of their former child (for a commentary on this case, see Hughes and Sloan [2011] CFLQ 393). Wall LJ's words were also referred to in *Re T (A Child)* [2010] EWCA Civ 1527, [2011] 1 FLR 1805 where a grandmother's application for a section 8 contact order (after she had been granted leave to apply) was dismissed at first instance and on appeal to the Court of Appeal because of *inter alia* the fact that the proceedings were having a highly adverse effect on the adoptive parents and therefore on the child

15.11 Adoption by step-parents, partners, relatives and foster-carers

(a) Step-parent and civil partner adoptions

A step-parent can apply to adopt a step-child and a civil partner can apply to adopt a child of a civil partner, although there are other ways of acquiring parental responsibility for the child (see p. 414). Step-parents and civil partners who wish to adopt must satisfy certain residence and notice requirements. Thus, the child must have had his or her home with the applicant at all times during the six months preceding the application (s 42(3)). Also, the step-parent or civil partner must have given notice of his or her intention to adopt to the appropriate local authority not more than two years, or less than three months, before applying for the order (ss 44(2), (3)). This enables the local authority to investigate the case and submit a report to the court in respect of the applicant's suitability for adoption and any section 1 welfare issues (ss 44(5), (6)). The consent requirement must have been satisfied.

(b) Adoption by relatives

A relative of a child can apply to adopt the child, provided the child has had his or her home with the relative for not less than three years (which need not be continuous) during the five years ending with the application (s 42(5)), or the court grants leave to apply (s 42(6)). The relative must have notified the local authority of his or her intention to apply for adoption not more than two years, or less than three months, before applying for the order (s 44(3)). The relative must be suitable for adoption (s 45), and consent to adoption must have been obtained (s 47(2)).

Although adoption by a relative may be in a child's best interests where the child's parents are dead, or where a relative has been caring for a child and the parents are no longer involved, it may be better for a relative to obtain parental responsibility by means of a special guardianship order (see 15.14) or a residence order (see 10.5) so as not to sever the child's links with the other half of his or her birth family.

(c) Adoption by local authority foster-carers

Foster-carers can adopt a foster-child in their care, but the rules differ depending on whether the case is an agency or a non-agency case. As an alternative to adoption, foster-parents can acquire parental responsibility by obtaining a residence order (see 10.5) or a special guardianship order (see 15.14).

(i) Agency cases   An agency case is one where the local authority decides to place a child with a foster-carer or to convert a foster placement into an adoption placement. A foster-carer can seek local authority approval to become a prospective adopter of a foster-child. If approval is given, the foster-child lives with the foster-carer as the prospective adopter, provided the child's parent(s) or guardian have consented to adoption under section 19, or a placement order has been made. Once the child is placed with the foster-carer(s) as prospective adopter(s), only the local authority may remove the child (ss 30, 34). Preliminary requirements must be satisfied before an adoption order can be made. Thus, the child must have had his or her home with the foster-carer(s) at all times during the 10 weeks preceding the adoption application; and investigation and reports as to their suitability must have been made and satisfied.

(ii) Non-agency cases   A non-agency case is one where the local authority has not placed the child with the foster-carer for adoption and has refused to give its approval when it was sought; but where the foster-carer wishes to apply for adoption. The child must have had his home with the foster-carer for a continuous period of not less than one year, although the court can give leave to waive this requirement (ss 42(4), (6)). The foster-carer must give notice to the local authority of his or her intention to adopt not more than two years, or less than three months, before the date on which the application is made under section 44. The consent condition in section 47(2) must also be satisfied.

15.12   Adopted persons – access to information

Adopted persons, on reaching adulthood, can investigate their origins and seek to make contact with their birth family.

(a)   Access to birth certificates

An adopted adult can obtain a copy of his or her original birth certificate, but the Registrar General has a discretion to refuse to provide a copy. Thus, in *R v Registrar-General ex parte Smith* [1991] 2 QB 393, [1991] 1 FLR 255, for instance, the Registrar General's refusal to supply a copy to an adopted person who was serving a life sentence for murder was held to be lawful. Counselling is available for adopted adults before they decide to obtain information about their birth records. Local authorities are required to provide a counselling service.

(b)   The Adopted Children Register and the Adoption Contact Register

(i) The Adopted Children Register   The Registrar General has a duty under the Adoption and Children Act 2002 to maintain this Register (s 77) and an index of the Register (s 78). The Register is not open to public inspection or search, but any person may search the index of the Register and have a certified copy of any entry in the Register (s 78(2)) and thereby trace the original birth registration of an adopted child. Where the adopted person is under 18, a person is not entitled to a certified copy of an entry in the Register unless the applicant has provided the Registrar with certain prescribed particulars.

The courts have no power to restrict the information placed in the Register, but the High Court may under its inherent jurisdiction prohibit the Registrar General from providing details of the adoption to any applicant while the child is under 18 (see, for example, *Re W (Adoption Details: Disclosure)* [1998] 2 FLR 625). The court can also authorise the Registrar General to disclose information, as it did, for example, in *Re H (Adoption: Disclosure of Information)* [1995] 1 FLR 236 where it authorised the Registrar General to provide information so that a 53-year-old adopted person with a treatable genetic disease could trace her brother so that he could be screened and treated if necessary.

(ii) The Adoption Contact Register   The Registrar General has a duty to maintain this Register (see ss 80 and 81 ACA 2002), which enables adopted persons to register their interest in contacting birth relatives (in Part I of the Register); and for relatives searching for an adopted person to register their interest in being contacted (in Part II). If there is a match, the Registrar General gives the adopted person the relative's name and address, but no information is provided to the relative. The decision to initiate contact is left to the adopted person.

The Registrar General has a duty (under section 79 ACA 2002) to make traceable the connections between the register of live births and any corresponding entry in the Adoption Contact Register, and to disclose that information, or any other information which might enable an adopted person to obtain a certified copy of his or her birth record. The Registrar General is under a duty to give the connecting birth-record information to an adoption agency in respect of a person whose birth record is kept by the Registrar General.

(c)   Disclosure of information

Sections 56–65 of the Adoption and Children Act 2002 lay down provisions governing the disclosure to adopted persons of information held by adoption agencies in connection with adoption, and for access to birth records. These provisions also cover the release of adoption agency information to birth relatives and other persons. Under these provisions, adoption agencies act as a single point of access to identifying information (including information necessary to access birth records), as they are the bodies best placed to provide support and counselling for the sensitive task of disclosure. In *FL v Registrar General* [2010] EWHC 3520 (Fam) a daughter in her late sixties applied to the court for it to authorise the Registrar General to provide her with information so that she could find out more about her father's birth family, but her application was refused as the court is only permitted to give such authority in exceptional circumstances (see s 79(4) ACA 2002).

15.13   Intercountry adoption

An intercountry adoption is an adoption of a child who is habitually resident in one country by an individual or couple who are habitually resident in another. The law, which is laid down in the Adoption and Children Act 2002 and in the Hague Convention on Protection of Children and Co-operation in Respect of Intercountry Adoption 1993, is complex. Overseas laws on adoption will also be relevant. Only an outline on intercountry adoption is given here, but further information is available, for instance, from the International Adoption Centre (IAC), www.iacentre.org.uk; and from the Department of Education (www.education.gov.uk) which has a guide and other up-to-date information available online.

A child from overseas can be adopted if: the child cannot be cared for in a safe environment in his or her own country; the adoption is in the child's best interests; and the adopter has been assessed as eligible and suitable to adopt from overseas by an adoption agency in the UK. Thus, all prospective adopters who are habitually resident in the UK and who wish to adopt a child habitually resident in another country are required to have been approved and assessed as suitable to adopt by a registered adoption agency in the UK. A person who wishes to adopt a child from overseas should therefore contact the local authority or a voluntary adoption agency that deals with overseas adoption.

(a) Taking a child out of the UK for an adoption abroad

Sections 83–91 of the Adoption and Children Act 2002 govern adoptions with a foreign element. It is unlawful to take a child out of the UK for the purposes of an adoption unless the prospective adopters have been granted parental responsibility for the child under section 84 ACA 2002, which the court has power to do if it is satisfied that: the applicant(s) intend to adopt the child under the law of the country outside the UK; they are not domiciled in England and Wales; and they have had the child living with them during the preceding 10 weeks (s 84(4)). The order confers parental responsibility on the applicant(s) and extinguishes that of any other person (for example, that of the birth parent(s) and a local authority where a care order is in force). In *Re G (Adoption: Placement Outside Jurisdiction)* [2008] EWCA Civ 105, [2008] 1 FLR 1484 Sir Mark Potter P held that section 84(4) did not, however, require the physical presence of each adopter during the 10-week period in order to satisfy the proposition that the child's home was with the adopters throughout that period. In *Re G (Surrogacy: Foreign Domicile)* [2007] EWHC 2814 (Fam), [2008] 1 FLR 1047 an order was made under section 84 to facilitate the adoption of a child in Turkey in a case involving an English surrogacy arrangement.

(b) The Hague Convention on Intercountry Adoption

Intercountry adoptions have their own set of problems, for, although adoption may give children from abroad a quality of life they did not have in their country of origin, there is a danger that such adoptions may exploit the needs of children by being too adult-centred. Intercountry adoptions may fail to take account of the importance of children remaining in touch with their own cultural roots and their birth family, and they may have been arranged privately without the checks and safeguards which exist for adoptions under domestic law.

In response to concerns about intercountry adoption, there have been an increasing numbers of safeguards put in place under international law and domestic law, including, in particular, the Hague Convention on Protection of Children and Co-operation in Respect of Intercountry Adoption 1993 to which the UK is a signatory. (The Permanent Bureau at the Hague (www.hcch.net) has information on the Convention and a list of Contracting States, and also a guide entitled *The Implementation and Operation of the 1993 Hague Intercountry Adoption Convention: A Guide to Good Practice*.)

The Hague Convention provides a framework for the regulation of intercountry adoption by setting out minimum standards for the control and regulation of the flow of children between the signatory States. The effect of the Convention is that any person in England and Wales who wishes to adopt a child from overseas must undergo the same procedures as he or she would if adopting a child under domestic law. Under these provisions there are restrictions on intercountry adoption and stringent penalties, including imprisonment, for those who fail to comply with requirements. Any person who is habitually resident in the UK who wishes to adopt a child from abroad is required to be assessed and approved to be eligible and suitable to adopt.

The number of contracting parties to the Convention has grown over the years (as at October 2012 there were 89 Contracting States). Article 1 of the Convention states that the objects of the Convention are:

'a) to establish safeguards to ensure that intercountry adoptions take place in the best interests of the child and with respect for his or her fundamental rights as recognised in international law;

b) to establish a system of co-operation amongst Contracting States to ensure that those safeguards are respected and thereby prevent the abduction, the sale of, or traffic in children;

c) to secure the recognition in Contracting States of adoptions made in accordance with the Convention.'

The underlying rationale of the Convention is for Contracting States to work together to ensure that adoption is in the best interests of the child, and only after possibilities for placement of the child within the State of origin have been given due consideration (Art 4(b)). The aim is for children to stay within their own communities where possible. Where this is not possible, the Convention makes provisions to regulate the adoption process. It does so by requiring Central Authorities to be established whose function it is to work together to protect children during the adoption process and to monitor the operation of the Convention. Central Authorities are responsible, *inter alia*, for: exchanging information about the child; ensuring that the child is adoptable; that the relevant consents have been given after appropriate counselling and that they have not been induced by payment or compensation; and that the prospective adopters are eligible and suitable to adopt the child. The Convention also provides for the automatic recognition in all Contracting States of adoptions certified by the Central Authority concerned as having been made in accordance with the Convention. Various regulations also govern intercountry adoption.

Part 2 of the Children and Adoption Act 2006 ('Adoptions with a foreign element') makes provision to suspend intercountry adoptions from countries where the Secretary of State has public policy concerns about the practices there in connection with the adoption of children (for example, child trafficking). These restrictions on adoptions from abroad came into force on 1 August 2008. The Act also amends section 83 of the ACA 2002 to make it more difficult for intercountry adopters to circumvent restrictions on bringing children into the UK.

15.14 Special guardianship

Sections 14A–14G of the Children Act 1989 (which were inserted into the Act by the Adoption and Children Act 2002) make provision in respect of special guardianship, which was introduced with the aim of giving children for whom adoption is not suitable the security and permanence of a legal family placement.

Special guardianship orders (SGOs), which give a special guardian legal responsibility for the child without taking responsibility away from the birth parents, were designed in part to provide a framework of permanency for 'children being cared for on a permanent basis by members of their wider birth family' (*Adoption: A New Approach*, Cm 5017, 2000). They are intended to fill the gap between residence orders and long-term fostering at one end of the spectrum of parental responsibility and adoption at the other. The aim is to provide a long-term care option similar to adoption but without the legal break with the birth family, and the finality associated with the making of an adoption order. Special guardianship may be appropriate, for instance, where it is not in a child's best interests to have his legal relationship with his birthparents and birth family severed by adoption, or where the child is an older child in foster-care who does not wish to be adopted, or where there are cultural and religious difficulties with adoption. However, research on special guardianship by Hall ([2008] Fam Law 148) found that, while special guardianship was being used by 'kinship carers', it was not proving to be very popular with foster-carers.

(a)   Special guardianship distinguished from adoption

The following table shows the main differences between special guardianship and adoption:

	SPECIAL GUARDIANSHIP	ADOPTION
Status of the child	The child lives with/is cared for by the special guardian but remains the child of the birthparent(s).	The child is the child of the adopter(s). The adopters are the child's parents.
Parental responsibility	Vests in the special guardian, but is retained by the birthparent(s).	Vests in the adopters.
Restrictions on the exercise of parental responsibility	Parental responsibility can be exercised by the special guardian to the exclusion of all other persons, but he/she will need the agreement of the birth parent(s) and anyone else with parental responsibility (or otherwise the court) to: take the child out of the UK for more than 3 months; change the child's surname; consent to the child's adoption; and consent to the child having serious medical treatment.	There are no restrictions on the exercise of the parental responsibility of the adopters.
Duration of the order	A SGO ceases automatically on the child reaching 18, if not revoked earlier by the court.	An adoption order is permanent.
Revocation or discharge of the order	Birthparent(s) can apply to revoke or discharge the SGO, but leave of the court is needed, which it can grant only if there has been a significant change of circumstances. The court can discharge a SGO of its own motion in any family proceedings.	An adoption order cannot be revoked (except in a wholly exceptional case, such as where there has been a serious procedural impropriety).
Maintenance of the child	Birthparent(s) continue to have a maintenance obligation to the child.	Any maintenance obligation owed by the child's birthparent is extinguished on adoption, unless there is any such obligation in a trust deed.
Death of the child	The special guardian must notify the child's parent(s) who have parental responsibility.	The adopters need not notify the birthparents of the child's death.
Intestacy (death without making a will)	The child has no right to inherit from a special guardian who dies intestate.	The child has a right to inherit from the adopters on the adopters' intestacy.

(b) Applying for a special guardianship order

(i) Applicants The following persons can apply for a special guardianship order (SGO) (s 14A(5) CA 1989):

- a guardian of the child;
- a person with a residence order in force with respect to the child;
- a person who has the consent of all those persons who have a residence order in their favour with respect to the child;
- any person with whom the child has lived for three out of the previous five years, provided he or she has the consent of any person with parental responsibility, or any person with a residence order, or the local authority (if the child is in care);
- any other person who has the consent of all persons with parental responsibility for the child;
- a local authority foster-parent with whom the child has lived for a period of at least one year immediately preceding the application.

The applicant must be at least 18 years old and must not be a parent of the child (s 14A(2)). A joint application can be made (ss 14A(1), (3)).

Other persons can apply for a SGO with leave (permission) of the court (s 14A(3)). When considering whether to grant leave, the court applies the same factors as those which apply to leave applications for section 8 orders (s 14A(12)) (see pp. 273–4). A child can apply for a SGO with leave of the court which it can grant if the child has sufficient understanding to make the proposed application (s 14A(12)).

The court can also make a SGO of its own motion in any family proceedings (see 10.9), which includes adoption proceedings (s 14A(6)).

(ii) Local authority duty to provide a report In some circumstances, written notice of an intention to apply for a SGO must be given to the relevant local authority (s 14A(7)). On receipt of this notice, the local authority has a duty to investigate the matter and prepare a report for the court about the suitability of the applicant(s) for special guardianship, and other matters (s 14A(9)). The court cannot make the SGO until it has received this report (s 14A(11)) dealing with the matters referred to in section 14A(8). The compulsory nature of these report provisions was emphasised in the following case:

> ▶ *Re S (Adoption Order or Special Guardianship Order) (No. 2)* [2007] EWCA Civ 90, [2007] 1 FLR 855
>
> The judge of her own motion made a SGO in favour of the child's foster-parent (even though the foster-parent wished to adopt the child). She did so without a local authority report being available on the basis that the child's welfare was better served by a SGO than an adoption order. The Court of Appeal held that the reporting requirement in section 14A(11) was unequivocal, and other reports containing relevant information (such as an adoption application report) could not be relied on in the absence of a section 14A(8) report. However, it held that the court should adopt a pragmatic approach, and in any case in which the court was minded to make a SGO of its own motion, then, if much of the relevant information was already before the court, the local authority should be requested to fulfil the terms of section 14A(8) by providing missing information and by cross-referencing existing reports.

(iii) Making a special guardianship order – the exercise of discretion   The rules governing the exercise of the court's discretion are laid down in section 14B(1). Thus, when considering whether or not to make a SGO, the court must apply the welfare principle and the other principles in section 1 of the Children Act (see 10.3). Also, before making an order, it must consider (see s 14B(1)): whether a contact order should be made with respect to the child; whether to vary or discharge any existing section 8 order; whether any enforcement order relating to contact should be revoked; and whether any existing contact activity direction should be discharged. On making the order, the court may also grant leave for the child to be known by a new surname and/or to leave the UK generally or for a specified purpose (s 14B(2)). To reduce delay, the court must draw up a timetable and give directions to ensure that the timetable is adhered to (s 14E).

A SGO is appropriate only if, in the particular circumstances of the case, it is best fitted to meet the needs of the child concerned (see *Re S (Adoption Order or Special Guardianship Order)* [2007] EWCA Civ 54, [2007] 1 FLR 819). Each case therefore depends on its own facts. Sometimes the court will have to decide whether it is in the child's best interests to make a SGO or an adoption order (see further below).

(iv) Effects of a special guardianship order   The effects of a SGO are as follows:

▶ **Parental responsibility**   The special guardian acquires parental responsibility for the child, which (subject to any other order in force with respect to the child) can be exercised *to the exclusion of any other person(s) with parental responsibility* (s 14C), apart from any other special guardian. This power to exercise parental responsibility to the exclusion of other persons with parental responsibility is the most significant effect of a SGO and one which distinguishes it from a residence order. However, certain restrictions apply to parental responsibility. Thus, while a SGO is in force, no-one may change the child's surname or remove the child from the UK for more than three months without the *written* consent of every person with parental responsibility for the child, or with leave of the court (ss 14C(3), (4)); but these restrictions do not apply where a placement order is in force (s 29(7)(b) ACA 2002). A special guardian must take reasonable steps to inform the birth parent(s) of the child's death, should the child die (s 14C(5)).

▶ *A right to support services*   Special guardians have a right to local authority support services, including financial support, similar to those available to adopters under the Adoption and Children Act 2002; and they have a right to make representations (including complaints) to the local authority about such support (ss 14F and 14 G). They can also bring a challenge by judicial review (see, for example, *B v Lewisham London Borough Council* [2008] EWHC 738 (Admin), [2008] 2 FLR 523 where the special guardian (a maternal grandmother) and the child were successful before Black J in having Lewisham's allowance scheme for special guardians quashed as being unlawful).

▶ *Effect on other orders*   The making of a SGO discharges any existing care order or related contact order (s 91(5A)), but it does not prevent a care order or a residence order being made while the SGO is in force (s 10(7A) CA 1989), whereupon an application will have to be made to have the SGO varied or discharged (see below).

(v) Where a placement order is in force   A SGO cannot be made while a placement for adoption order is in force (s 14A(13)), unless an application has been made for a final

adoption order, and the person applying for the SGO has obtained leave under section 29(5) ACA 2002; or is the guardian of the child under section 47(5). Written notice of an intention to apply for a SGO must be given to the local authority which is looking after the child or in whose area the applicant is ordinarily resident (s 14A(7) CA 1989, and s 29(6) ACA 2002).

(vi) Variation and discharge A SGO can be varied or discharged by the court of its own motion in any family proceedings in which a question arises with respect to the child's welfare (s 14D(2)), or on an application made by (ss 14D(1), (3)): the special guardian; a parent or guardian with leave of the court; the child with leave of the court; any person in whose favour a residence order is in force with respect to the child; and any person with leave of the court who has, or immediately before the making of the SGO had, parental responsibility for the child. The court can grant leave to applicants (other than the child) if there has been a significant change in circumstances since the order was made (s 14(D)(5)). If a care order is in force with respect to the child, leave must be obtained from the local authority.

The principles applicable to a leave application to discharge a SGO The issue of leave was considered in the following case where it was held by the Court of Appeal that a leave application to apply to discharge a SGO should be determined in the same way as a leave application to discharge a placement order under the Adoption and Children Act 2002 (see pp. 425–6).

▶ *Re G (Special Guardianship Order)* **[2010] EWCA 300, [2010] 2 FLR 696**

The mother applied for leave to apply for the discharge of a SGO (under section 14D(5)) which had been made in respect of her child (now aged 4) with the maternal grandmother as special guardian. The mother applied for discharge, as the circumstances had changed in that she was no longer causing concern for the local authority as she had successfully parented a second child on her own for more than two years. The application for leave failed at first instance as the circumstances were found not to be 'significant' for the purposes of section 14D(5); and the judge considered (applying section 10(9)(c) of the Children Act 1989) that there would be a risk of disruption to the child's life if the application were to succeed. The mother appealed.

The Court of Appeal, allowing the appeal, held *inter alia* that, until the emergence of more robust jurisprudence in relation to the proper approach to the determination of applications for leave to apply for the discharge of SGOs, the approach should be that commended in *M v Warwickshire County Council* [2007] EWCA Civ 1084, [2008] 1 FLR 1093, namely that the principles which apply to leave applications to discharge a placement order should apply to leave to apply to discharge a SGO.

(c) Special guardianship or adoption?

Whether a child's best interests are better promoted by making an adoption order or a special guardianship order (SGO) will depend on the facts of the particular case.

The following case is the leading case on the principles to be applied when the court is considering whether to make an adoption order or a SGO:

▶ *Re S (Adoption Order or Special Guardianship Order)* [2007] EWCA Civ 54, [2007] 1 FLR 819

The child (aged 6 and in care of the local authority) was placed with a foster-mother but the child's mother had regular contact, and the father had contact. The foster-mother applied to adopt the child but the judge concluded that adoption was not the best way of securing the child's welfare and made a SGO of her own motion. The foster-mother appealed to the Court of Appeal.

The Court of Appeal, dismissing her appeal, held *inter alia* that:

▶ The key question which the court must ask itself when deciding whether to make a SGO or an adoption order is which order would better serve the welfare of the child, applying the welfare checklists in the Children Act 1989 and the Adoption and Children Act 2002.

▶ Because of the importance of such cases to the parties and children concerned, judges must give full reasons and explain their decisions with care.

▶ Provided the judge has carefully examined the facts, made appropriate findings and applied the welfare checklists, it is unlikely that the court would be able to interfere with the exercise of judicial discretion, particularly in a finely balanced case.

▶ The risk of prejudice caused by delay is likely to be of less pivotal importance in this type of case; and in many cases it might be appropriate to pause and give time for reflection, particularly in cases where the order is being made of the court's own motion.

▶ The court must be satisfied that the order it decides to make is a proportionate response to the problem, having regard to the right to family life in Article 8 ECHR. Special guardianship involves a less fundamental interference with existing legal relationships than adoption, and in some cases the fact that the welfare objective could be achieved with less disruption of existing family relationships could properly be regarded as tipping the balance. However, in most cases Article 8 ECHR is unlikely to add anything to the considerations contained in the welfare checklists.

▶ Special guardianship does not provide the same permanency as adoption (as the child's parents can apply for a residence order without leave and other section 8 orders with leave, and the leave threshold is set relatively low), although a court can make a section 91(14) order under the CA 1989 to prevent further applications to the court by the child's parents. The fact that special guardianship cannot give the same permanency as adoption might tip the scales in favour of adoption.

▶ When applying its own motion powers to make a SGO the court can take into account the fact that the person concerned does not wish to be the child's special guardian. But if, applying the welfare checklist under the 1989 Act (including the potential consequences to the child of the refuser implementing the threat to refuse to be appointed a special guardian) the court came to the view that a SGO would best serve the welfare interests of the child, then that is the order the court should make.

Intra-familial cases – special guardianship or adoption? Whether special guardianship instead of adoption will be the preferred option in an intra-family adoption will depend on the facts of the case, applying the principle that the welfare of the child is the court's paramount consideration. While special guardianship may be better than adoption in an intra-familial case (for example, in the case of an applicant grandparent or relative) because it has the benefit of not skewing family relationships, adoption may be better in other situations because of the security it provides for the child. In *Re AJ (Adoption Order or Special Guardianship Order)* [2007] EWCA Civ 55, [2007] 1 FLR 507 (see below) the Court of Appeal stressed, however, that SGOs had not necessarily replaced adoption orders in cases where a child had been permanently placed within the wider family. Thus, for example, adoption may be better than special guardianship where the relationship between the applicant family member and the child's birth parent is difficult (see *Re EN (A Child) (Special Guardianship Order)* [2007] EWCA Civ 264; and *Re M-J (Adoption Order or Special Guardianship Order)* [2007] EWCA Civ 56, [2007] 1 FLR 691, below).

The following cases provide examples of cases where the court had to decide whether to make a SGO or an adoption order. They show how decisions about whether to make an adoption order or an SGO are very fact-specific.

▶ *S v B and Newport City Council; Re K* [2007] FLR 1116

Hedley J made a SGO in favour of the grandparents with whom the child (aged 6) had been living under a care order since he was 6 months old. He did so, despite the grandparents' preference for an adoption order, because adoption would skew the family relationships. Hedley J also made an order under section 91(14) CA 1989 prohibiting any further applications to the court by the child's parents and an order under section 14B(2)(a) giving leave for the child to be known by the grandparents' surname. Hedley J said that the case was 'one of those cases for which special guardianship was specifically designed' as it permitted familial carers, who were not the parents, 'to have all the practical authority and standing of parents, whilst leaving intact real and readily comprehensible relationships with the family'.

▶ *Re AJ (Adoption Order or Special Guardianship Order)* [2007] EWCA Civ55, [2007] 1 FLR 507

The Court of Appeal upheld the adoption order in favour of the child's aunt and uncle, on the basis that the child had been living with the aunt and uncle since the age of 6 months, and because adoption, unlike a SGO, provided the assurance that the security of that placement would not be disturbed. The child's father had made aggressive telephone calls to the aunt, and she was concerned that the parents were unpredictable and would litigate issues concerning the child's care. The Court of Appeal agreed with the judge that an adoption order would in the circumstances of the case not unduly distort the family dynamics.

▶ *Re M-J (Adoption Order or Special Guardianship Order)* [2007] EWCA Civ56, [2007] 1 FLR 691

The child, who was subject to a care order, had been removed from his parents and looked after by his aunt since he was 6 months old (because of the mother's alcohol and drug dependency). The aunt applied to adopt the child but this was opposed by the child's mother. The recorder considered that, although many of the child's needs could be met by a SGO combined with a section 91(14) CA 1989 order restricting the child's mother from making further applications to the court, those orders did not provide total security. He found that no lesser order than adoption would meet the child's welfare; and that an adoption order was a proportionate order to make in the circumstances. The mother's appeal, on the basis that a SGO was more appropriate in a family placement, was dismissed by the Court of Appeal, which held that there was no rule that a SGO was to be preferred to adoption in family placement unless there were cogent reasons to the contrary.

▶ *Re EN (A Child) (Special Guardianship Order)* [2007] EWCA Civ 264

The paternal grandmother, who had cared for her grandson (aged 3) for most of his life, was refused a SGO because of her fraught relationship with the child's mother. Despite the inevitable loss of the child's primary attachment to the grandmother and the potential for long-term attachment difficulties, the child psychiatrist recommended that child be removed from his grandmother because the 'deep rift' between the mother and grandmother would be a cause of ongoing emotional distress for the child. The child was placed with prospective adopters.

Summary

▶ Adoption is effected by an adoption order which severs the legal link between the birthparents and the child and creates a new legal link between the adopter(s) and the child. The law on adoption is laid down in the Adoption and Children Act (ACA) 2002. Adoption procedure and practice are governed by the Family Procedure Rules 2010 and related practice directions, and various regulations. Human rights are also relevant.

▶ Cafcass officers play an important role in the adoption process.

▶ The Government has taken steps to reduce delays in the adoption process.

▶ Agency adoptions are adoptions involving local authority adoption services or voluntary adoption organisations which have various obligations under the ACA 2002. Non-agency adoptions usually involve children who are not in care and who are being adopted, for instance, by a step-parent, relative or foster-parent. Applicants in non-agency cases must give notice to a local authority of their wish to adopt.

▶ It is a criminal offence for a person or body other than an adoption agency to, *inter alia*, advertise, make arrangements for, or provide payments or rewards in connection with adoption.

▶ As adoption is a drastic step, it may be better to consider other ways of acquiring parental responsibility for a child, namely by way of a special guardianship order, a residence order, or a parental responsibility agreement or order.

▶ The number of adoptions has declined over the years due in part to fewer babies being available for adoption.

▶ At one time step-parent adoption was common as adoption enabled a step-parent to acquire parental responsibility for a step-child, but changes to the law now enable a step-parent to acquire parental responsibility in other ways.

▶ After discussions of reform of adoption law from the late 1980s onward, by both the Conservative and Labour Governments, the Adoption and Children Act (ACA) 2002 was enacted and made radical changes to adoption law. A major aim of the ACA 2002 is to encourage the wider use of adoption for children in care. It also made other changes, in particular by introducing placement for adoption to replace freeing for adoption; and it made changes to the Children Act 1989 to create a new status of special guardianship.

▶ Section 1 of ACA 2002 lays down the welfare principles which must be applied by a court or adoption agency when a decision is being made relating to the adoption of a child. The welfare principle requires an analysis of the child's welfare through childhood into adulthood and for the rest of the child's life (s 1(2)). Courts and adoption agencies must apply the welfare checklist in section 1(4) and give due consideration to the child's religious persuasion, racial origin and cultural and linguistic background (s (1)(5)). They must also consider the range of other powers available to them under the ACA 2002 and the Children Act 1989 (s 1(6)), as well as the no-delay (s 1(3)) and the minimum intervention principles (s 1(6)).

▶ A child under the age of 18 who is not, or has not been, married can be adopted (s 49). Joint and sole applications for adoption can be made (see ss 50 and 51). Married couples can make a joint application, and so can cohabitants (opposite-sex and same-sex). A step-parent can make a sole application for adoption (which was not possible under the old law); and so can a civil partner in respect of the child of his or her civil partner. A local authority foster-parent can also apply to adopt a foster-child.

▶ Various preliminary procedures must be complied with before an adoption order or placement order can be made (such as residence requirements, reports, consent being given, etc.). These requirements are strict; and any failure to comply may result in an order being set aside.

Summary cont'd

▶ An adoption order (see s 46) transfers parental responsibility from the birthparents to the adopter(s). The welfare test, the welfare checklist and the other section 1 ACA 2002 principles must be applied by the court. An adopted child is treated in law as if he or she were born as the child of the adopter(s). One of two conditions must be satisfied (s 47): that the parents or guardians have consented to the adoption or their consent has been dispensed with; or the child has been placed for adoption.

▶ An adoption order can be challenged by: opposing the order (s 47); appealing against it; or applying to have it set aside. However, once an adoption order is made it is difficult to challenge it.

▶ Sections 18–29 of ACA 2002 govern placement for adoption. A child can be placed for adoption with the consent of the birthparents (s 19) or by way of a placement order (s 21). The court can only make a placement order if: the child is subject to a care order; or the court is satisfied that the threshold conditions for making a care order are met; or the child has no parent or guardian. When considering whether to make a placement order, the court must apply the welfare test, the welfare checklist and the other section 1 principles. The court also has a duty to consider what arrangements for contact have been, or should be, made for the child. Any person (except the child and the local authority) can apply to revoke a placement order, provided leave to apply has been granted by the court and the child has not been placed for adoption. A placement order gives parental responsibility to the local authority or the prospective adopters while the child is with them, although it does not extinguish the parents' parental responsibility. A placement order remains in force until revoked; or an adoption order is made; or the child marries or becomes a civil partner; or the child reaches the age of 18.

▶ Consent to adoption must be given, but can be dispensed with under section 52 ACA 2002 if: the parent or guardian cannot be found or is incapable of giving consent; or the welfare of the child requires consent to be dispensed with. There are restrictions about a mother giving consent where her baby is less than six weeks old. Parents and guardians can give advance consent (s 20). Although the consent of unmarried fathers (without parental responsibility) is not required to adoption or to placement for adoption, the courts have been increasingly willing to involve them in the adoption process.

▶ The ACA 2002 makes provision for contact in the context of placement for adoption. In the context of placement for adoption, a contact order can be made under section 26 ACA 2002. The welfare test, the welfare checklist and the other section 1 principles apply to the exercise of the court's discretion. If contact is sought post-adoption, an application must be made for a section 8 contact order under the Children Act 1989, but leave of the court to apply will be needed first. The courts have shown themselves to be unwilling to make contact orders post-adoption particularly where there is any friction between the adopters and the birth parents.

▶ A step-parent, civil partner, relative or foster-carer can apply for an adoption order. Certain residence and notice requirements must be complied with, and notice must be given to the local authority. There are, however, alternative ways in which such persons can acquire parental responsibility, such as by means of a parental responsibility agreement or a parental responsibility order, a residence order, or a special guardianship order.

▶ An adopted child on reaching the age of 18 can obtain a copy of his or her original birth certificate. The Registrar General has a duty to maintain the Adopted Children Register (s 77 ACA 2003), an index of the Register (s 78), and the Adoption Contact Register (ss 80 and 81). Sections 56–65 of the ACA 2002 lay down provisions governing the disclosure of information held by adoption agencies in connection with adoption and access to birth records.

▶ Various provisions are in place which govern intercountry adoption, including in particular the Hague Convention on Protection of Children and Co-operation in Respect of Intercountry Adoption 1993.

Summary cont'd

▶ The ACA 2002 inserted sections 14A–14G into the Children Act 1989 which make provision for special guardianship, which was introduced to give children for whom adoption is not suitable the security and permanence of a legal family placement. Special guardianship orders give a special guardian legal responsibility for the child without taking responsibility away from the birth parents. The governing principle is that the welfare of the child is the court's paramount consideration. If the court is considering whether to make a special guardianship order or an adoption order, it must apply the welfare checklists in both section 1 of the Children Act 1989 and section 1 of the Adoption and Children Act 2002, but each case depend on its own facts.

Further reading and references

Choudhry, 'The Adoption and Children Act 2002, the welfare principle and the Human Rights Act 1998 – a missed opportunity' [2003] CFLQ 119.

Cullen, 'Adoption – a (fairly) new approach' [2005] CFLQ 475.

Curry, '*EB* v *France*: a missed opportunity?' [2009] CFLQ 365.

Hall, 'Special guardianship and permanency planning: unforeseen consequences and missed opportunities' [2008] CFLQ 359.

Hall, 'Special guardianship: a missed opportunity: findings from research' [2008] Fam Law 148.

Hayes, 'Giving due consideration to ethnicity in adoption placements – a principled approach?' [2003] CFLQ 255.

Hitchings and Sagar, 'The Adoption and Children Act 2002: a level playing field for same-sex adopters?' [2007] CFLQ 60.

Hughes and Sloan, 'Post-adoption photographs: welfare, rights and judicial reasoning' [2011] CFLQ 393.

Quinton and Selwyn, 'Adoption: research, policy and practice' [2006] CFLQ 459.

Ray, 'Placement for adoption or legal limbo?' [2012] Fam Law 979.

Sloan, '*Re C (A Child) (Adoption: Duty of Local Authority* – welfare and the rights of the birth family in "fast track" adoption cases' [2009] CFLQ 87.

Smith and Logan, 'Adoptive parenthood as a "legal fiction" – its consequences for direct post-adoption contact' [2002] CFLQ 281.

Thoburn, 'The risks and rewards of adoption for children in the public care' [2003] CFLQ 391.

Webb, 'Leave to oppose an adoption: unhelpful legislation' [2012] Fam Law 1119.

Websites

Barnardos: www.barnardos.org.uk
British Association for Adoption and Fostering (BAAF): www.baaf.org.uk
Consortium of Voluntary Adoption Agencies: www.cvaa.org.uk
Department for Education: www.education.gov.uk
International Adoption Centre (IAC): www.iacentre.org.uk

Links to relevant websites can also be found at: www.palgrave.com/law/familylaw8e

Index

Printed and bound in Great Britain by
TJ International Ltd, Padstow, Cornwall